White Violence and Black Response

WHITE VIOLENCE AND BLACK RESPONSE

From Reconstruction to Montgomery

HERBERT SHAPIRO

The University of Massachusetts Press   Amherst, 1988

Copyright © 1988 by The University of Massachusetts Press
All rights reserved
Printed in the United States of America
LC 87–6009
ISBN 0–87023–577–x (cloth); 578–8 (paper)
Set in Linotron Sabon at Rainsford Type

Library of Congress Cataloging-in-Publication Data

Shapiro, Herbert.
White violence and Black response.
Bibliography: p.
Includes index.
1. Afro-Americans—History—1863–1877.
2. Afro-Americans—1877–1964. 3. United States—
Race relations. 4. Violence—United States—History.
5. Racism—United States—History. I. Title.
E185.2.S52 1988 973'.0496073 87–6009
ISBN 0–87023–577–x (alk. paper)
ISBN 0–87023–578–8 (pbk. : alk. paper)

British Library Cataloguing in Publication Data are available

Published with the help of the Charles Phelps Taft Memorial Fund,
University of Cincinnati.

To Judy,
my constant love
who shared every step of the way
and whose faith, strength, and wisdom
made it possible

and

to Mark and Nina,
always loyal and supportive—
fine human beings
who are the future

CONTENTS

Illustrations follow pages 144 and 304

PREFACE

THIS WORK is the product of a continuing scholarly interest in Afro-American history and culture that began when I first encountered W. E. B. DuBois's *Souls of Black Folk* on the shelves of the public library in Queens, New York. That classic work initiated my education concerning the scope and meaning of the black freedom struggle. I became aware of the central significance of the Afro-American experience in the history of the United States. Later, while a beginning graduate student at Columbia, I became especially interested in the Reconstruction era and was receptive to David Donald's suggestion that further examination of the Ku Klux Klan could contribute to our understanding of this period. That inquiry, focused upon South Carolina, uncovered ample evidence that men of property had extensively participated in the direction of organized violence against blacks. I became interested in the linkages between questions of class and race that shed light on the role of violence in perpetuating white supremacy.

My interest in the sources and consequences of racial violence ran parallel to concern with the significance of violence in other areas of American social history, but the thought remained that a broad-gauged chronicling and analysis of racist violence was needed. Such an account would provide a window through which to view the varied dimensions of Afro-American history. The concern with racial violence was reinforced when during four years of teaching at Morehouse College I saw hooded Klansmen picketing in downtown Atlanta and heard recollections of the city's 1906 riot. I also had the opportunity of participating in the Southern civil rights movement during its climactic years. Herbert Hill provided a stimulus to begin the study, when, in connection with a series he was editing, he proposed preparing a documentary history of racist violence since the Civil War and of black responses to this violence. Soon after beginning this work I decided to go beyond the publication of the documentary evidence. I preferred to draw upon the primary sources and the scholarly literature as bases for directly setting forth a comprehensive treatment of the subject. The study is divided in two parts; the first volume covers the decades from the inception of Reconstruction to the Montgomery bus boycott of the 1950s and the second, on which work is now in progress, focuses upon the civil rights struggle of the 1960s and its aftermath.

In the course of preparing this volume I have benefited greatly from the helpful suggestions and critcisms offered by Herbert Aptheker, John H. Bracey, Jr., and Louis R. Harlan. There is a debt of gratitude owed to each of these scholars.

Staff members at the Langsam Library of the University of Cincinnati have been of great assistance in making research materials available. I particularly wish to express deep appreciation to reference librarian–bibliographer Sally M. Moffitt and other members of the library's reference department. Invaluable also have been the services provided by the members of the university interlibrary loan department, Daniel Gottlieb, Carole Mosher, and Kathleen Puck. Thanks are due as well to archivists and librarians at many other institutions whose patience and cooperativeness have been unfailing.

I am indebted to Heather Hall for most ably transforming my typed pages into a word-processed manuscript.

I am obliged to Bruce Wilcox, Pam Wilkinson, and Barbara Palmer at the University of Massachusetts Press for all the encouragement and thoughtful, meticulous work of editing they have provided.

The generous assistance of the Charles Phelps Taft Memorial Fund of the University of Cincinnati in facilitating publication of this book is gratefully acknowledged.

In her sustaining love, encouragement, and insightful criticism, my wife, Judy, has been inseparable from the completion of this book.

INTRODUCTION

THE EVENTS of recent decades have made abundantly clear the falsity of the lingering myth that violence has been of only marginal significance in American society. The assassinations of the 1960s, the dozens of violent confrontations evoked by the civil rights movement, the terrible violence manifested in the Vietnam War, all have revealed to Americans the heritage of violence that exists as a major component of the American tradition. The view that orderly progress is the American characteristic, with violence merely some peculiar, temporary departure from the norm of national conduct, has been less tenable. In one of his last works, Richard Hofstadter, writing at the end of the 1960s, noted that "what is impressive to one who begins to learn about American violence is its extraordinary frequency, its sheer commonplaceness in our history, its persistence into very recent and contemporary times, and its rather abrupt contrast with our pretensions to singular national virtue." Americans, Hofstadter wrote, had become frightened by violence and "are now quite ready to see that there is far more violence in our national heritage than our proud, sometimes smug, national self-image admits of."[1] The writing of American history is beginning to recover from what the National Commission on the Causes and Prevention of Violence described as a "historical amnesia" about violence.[2]

The violence generated by white racism is one of the obvious realities of American society. Yet it is one of the ironies of contemporary experience that many Americans have been conditioned to associate violence with the behavior of black people, to concentrate their attention and their fears upon the crimes against property or persons committed by black individuals. The stereotype is perpetuated that Afro-Americans are a criminal people. The nation's political leadership, its educational institutions, and its news media do not educate us to comprehend that the committing of desperate criminal acts has its roots in oppressive social conditions. White people have also been encouraged to overlook the fact that the dominant institutions of American society have by precept and example taught the principle that violence is a justified and appropriate means of achieving desired ends.[3]

xi

The most extensive and systematic expression of that violence has been the brutal treatment of the nation's black population. White racist violence in America has always stood as overwhelming evidence that American history is deeply marked by recourse to force, to acts of intimidation and terror employed to preserve outmoded social, political, and economic institutions. White supremacy has been maintained by propaganda, political manipulation, and economic pressure but also by the ultimate weapon of violence. The American record includes the barbarous institution of lynching and urban race riots that have often taken on the character of mass assaults or "pogroms" upon the black community. Black Americans have been subjected to terror at the hands of organized groups such as the Ku Klux Klan, ad hoc bands of vigilantes, local and state police, and, on occasion, officers of the federal government.

It is the thesis of this volume that subjection to violence in various forms has been a central ingredient of the Afro-American experience, that the lives of millions of black people have been and continue to be lived in the shadow of numberless episodes of racist brutality. Violence, the actuality or the threat of death or serious injury from assault, has constituted an ever-present reality in practically every black community and for practically every black person. Modern history has witnessed brutality on a massive scale unknown to previous history. This era has known the unprecedented destructiveness of modern warfare, enormous cruelties inflicted upon civilian populations, and attempts to destroy physically entire religious, racial, and ethnic minorities. The violence of American racism has demonstrated a willingness to substitute physical extermination of supposed enemies for rational treatment of complex social problems; indeed, American racism set precedents for the terrorization and murder of innocent victims that would be emulated in other parts of the world.

Afro-Americans have directly confronted a central paradox of American society. America, it is argued, is a society based on respect for law and orderly procedures. The Constitution stands as a great safeguard of individual freedom, and the courts and the police are supposedly established to enforce the law. Controversial issues are to be resolved not in the streets but through the democratic processes of elections. But for blacks the liberal values have been turned into their opposites. The courts have most often stood silent in the face of racist violence or have turned their wrath against the victims, not the perpetrators; the police have protected the mob rather than the mobbed and have often either aided the lynchers or displayed amazing inability to identify them. Where race is concerned, legislative or judicial action to deal with controversial issues has often taken a back seat to the work of terrorists. Legitimate grievances have been allowed to fester, and when remedy has come it has come late and has been only partial in nature.

This paradox is apparently related to the fact that relations between whites and blacks in this country touch explosively upon vital interests, interests that are fundamentally threatened by change in the pattern of race relations. Certainly since the Civil War, one of the pillars of the American social order has been an arrangement in which blacks are denied economic equality and systematically discriminated against in matters of housing, education, and employment. For more than half a century this oppression was buttressed by the special institution of segregation, overtly supported by law and the disfranchisement of black voters. But the passing of most forms of legal segregation has outlined the basic conditions of discrimination and exploitation under which the great majority of black Americans live. For those committed to preserving a system of racial oppression, any basic challenge to that system is intolerable. In order to maintain the black–white caste system, racists have used force to render blacks powerless and defenseless, and when such force has failed to stifle the black demand for full citizenship and economic justice, the racists have fought with desperation, relying more openly upon the support or at least the inaction of government. As Mary Frances Berry observes, the response of government to blacks' requests for federal action to aid in improving their economic and social conditions "has always been token measures or assertions that no problem exists. If these tactics failed and black people persisted too vigorously, then force and suppression were used." In order to change the institutional response, serious dislocation of American society may be required.[4]

This study of white supremacist violence is focused in the first place on acts of direct physical coercion. In our society physical and psychological damage has also, of course, been inflicted upon blacks by indirect means, by the quiet but destructive working of established institutions, by conditions of poverty, lack of access to competent medical care, and grossly inadequate educational facilities. The damage inflicted by such means is reflected in statistics that reveal the higher rates of infant mortality for blacks and the shorter lives that blacks may expect to lead. Institutional racism has taken its toll. Blacks have suffered from living in cramped, rat-infested tenements where garbage is left uncollected and housing codes are unenforced or have known the wrenching poverty of the rural South, having grown up in shacks and cabins without running water or electricity. South and North, black Americans, in numbers disproportionate to the percentage they form of the population, have known malnutrition, lives deformed by rickets or pellagra or cut short by tuberculosis. Abundance of food is one of the splendors of the United States, but for millions of blacks it has been only a splendor enjoyed by somebody else. Lives of unusual stress, lives in which resentment and anger have often had to be suppressed and open insult or abuse by others tolerated, have given blacks a good deal more than their share of hypertension and heart disease. Physical harm has also been the result of the way in which society's research dollars have been spent. The first report of sickle-cell anemia in North America appeared in 1910, but only in the past two decades has medical research shown substantial interest in this disease that is particularly prevalent among blacks. Beyond that is the fact that preventive medicine, a field of enormous consequence especially for the deprived and impoverished, has been permitted to languish. The concept of environmental health is barely out of its infancy in terms of any serious attention devoted to it. Centers of research to investigate childhood developmental disorders are built, but the medical scientists proceed most often without acting upon the established fact that the vast majority of instances of mental retardation are related to problems of the social environment, to poor nutrition, shoddy health care, and inferior education.[5]

Then, too, we confront a recent history in which medical science has inflicted injury and ultimately death upon Afro-Americans as a consequence of flagrant abuse of any reasonable standards regarding human experimentation. Notorious, now, is the "Tuskegee Project," sponsored by the United States Public Health Service, that for decades withheld effective modalities of therapy from black victims of venereal disease. The lives of rural blacks in Alabama were sacrificed in a cause of dubious scientific validity, permeated by racist assumptions about black people.[6]

Not all blacks have grown up in all of the conditions indicated here; some blacks have lived in physical comfort, with a relative few reaching a position of affluence, have been well fed and well housed, have gone to good schools and obtained quality education in colleges and universities. Some individuals have broken out of the vicious circle of poverty, and out of the strivings of black people have come individuals who have been able to make unusual and distinguished contributions to American society and the world. Blacks have established records of achievement in every field of endeavor they have been permitted to enter. But all Afro-Americans have been affected, in one degree or another, by the psychological and cultural stresses resulting from living as black men and women in an America dominated by white racism, have had to be aware of the possibility that racial violence could be directed against them. Blacks of all classes have lived with the reality that, regardless of individual merit or accomplishment, the segregation system marked them for separation or exclusion on grounds of race. Blacks have understood that for them there was no reasonable assurance that the law-abiding citizen could expect to be treated with civility by the police.

Centering attention in this book on acts of direct violence makes it possible to focus more sharply upon those manifestations of racism that acutely and explosively express the will to damage or destroy blacks. Here the tension and hatreds of society are articulated by overt action, where the mask of pretense and hypocrisy is dropped and the act is clearly public and dramatic, reported in the newspapers or described on radio or television. Institutional racism also has its perpetrators, but most often they are hidden in the anonymity of great, impersonal bureaucracies. In the act of direct violence, the persons who actually inflict the pain or terror are usually identifiable. If we begin from that point it may be possible to shed light on the social forces that bear ultimate responsibility for the violent act.

In the face of the violence inflicted upon them, blacks have strained to the utmost to protect their lives and to assert their dignity as human beings. It is a grossly false generalization to characterize black responses to oppression and violence in terms of passivity and submissiveness, to conclude that black behavior has conformed to Stanley Elkins's "Sambo" stereotype. The generalization is of course false with regard to the period of slavery, during which slaves resisted the masters with a variety of means, ranging from organized rebellions to individual assault upon owners and overseers to such acts of sabotage as arson and the wrecking of tools and machinery and to the act of escape. Blacks defied slavery both on the level of day-to-day resistance and also in periodic encounters in which groups of slaves rose against the masters, armed with what weapons they could seize.[7]

The generalization is false also with regard to the twelve decades that have followed the Civil War. Having won the abolition of slavery and the full citizenship and voting rights guaranteed in the Fourteenth and Fifteenth amendments, blacks fought every inch of the way against those who would nullify their civil rights. They resisted the racist onslaught that would render them politically powerless, subject to the rule of terror. Every nationality and every race have had their cowards, their weaklings and opportunists, their collaborators with the oppressor, and Afro-Americans are no exception. But set against the few who would run or cringe or inform there are the many who have maintained their dignity and self-respect, who have fought back determinedly and bravely, often in the face of violence, backed by overwhelming terror, that was frenzied and sadistic. In the course of this struggle blacks have met death and defeat, but victory is also part of the record—the lynching that is prevented, the mob forced to retreat, the civil rights law that is enacted despite murderous southern sheriffs and vigilantes. Some of the victories have been moral ones, but ultimately they too have very real significance and consequence. Such victories manifest the proven strength of a people who have suffered great cruelty but who have survived and continue to press forward. They reveal the consciousness of group solidarity and pride that come from suffering and struggle. One of the ingredients of the Anglo-Saxon myth is the claim to moral superiority, but black Americans do not share the morality that is expressed in attacking school buses bringing children to a newly integrated school, in dynamiting churches and blowing to bits little black girls, in conducting medical experiments in which blacks suffering from syphilis are deliberately left untreated. Blacks have fought against those who would oppress them, but they have not organized lynch mobs and carved up the flesh of their victims as souvenirs.

Along with examining the scope and character of racist violence in the United States since the Civil War, this book will also examine the black response, the varied strategies and tactics blacks have used to protect themselves and move forward. The strategies and tactics have had to be formulated under extraordinarily difficult conditions, and blacks have had to combine courage with ability to innovate and improvise, to respond sometimes in direct confrontation and sometimes indirectly. Formulation of tactics and strategy has evoked continuing debate within the black community as blacks have not been monolithic in commitment to any one clearly defined strategy. But this debate has not been mere rhetoric; from it have come action and conclusions, wide areas of agreement on some issues, continued debate on others. To trace the evolution of this debate, on the varied levels where it has taken place, is necessary in order to gain insight into where the thinking of black Americans is today and from what sources it has come.

White Violence and Black Response

PART I

The Post-Emancipation Decades

The sooner a civilization perishes which is founded on cheating and murder the better. Better that the waters of the great river should again cover the land, which in ages it has formed, than that it should be occupied by a State which breeds her youth to fraud and assassination.

Report of United States Senate Special Committee
investigating 1883 Mississippi racial violence

We plead not for the colored people alone, but for all victims of the terrible injustice which puts men and women to death without form of law.

Ida B. Wells-Barnett, *Southern Horrors.*

John Hunter's folks told me that. They told me I was bragging and boasting that I would have the land, and the Ku-Klux were going to whip me for that.

Testimony of Lucy McMillan at hearing of U. S. Congress,
Joint Select Committee to Inquire into the Condition of
Affairs in the Late Insurrectionary States.

ONE

The Imposition of White Rule

I N THE IMMEDIATE aftermath of the Civil War thousands of Union troops were stationed in the South, and some of these troops were black. White supremacists were outraged at the sight of blacks with guns and therefore some measure of power, and they were quickly successful in having black soldiers withdrawn from the South. During Johnsonian Reconstruction the former slaves were legally free as a result of the Emancipation Proclamation and the Thirteenth Amendment, but the South's white rulers made evident their intention to reduce the freedmen to a position of powerless semislavery. Already by 1866 ex-Confederates in Pulaski, Tennessee, had formed a secret organization, the Ku Klux Klan, whose purpose it was to terrorize blacks into submission to white rule. Although the United States Freedmen's Bureau existed as some protection of black interests, the freedmen were intimidated, whipped, and beaten to compel them to agree to onerous labor contracts with landlords. The moderating influence of the Freedmen's Bureau was undermined by Andrew Johnson's commitment to white supremacy and the consequent failure to employ federal executive power effectively to protect those in the South who had supported the Union.

A summary of the violence that marked the South immediately following the Civil War is to be found in a report that Republican leader Carl Schurz provided President Johnson. "Some planters held back their former slaves on their plantations by brute force," Schurz wrote. "Armed bands of white men patrolled the country roads to drive back the Negroes wandering about. Dead bodies of murdered Negroes were found on and near the highways and by-paths. Gruesome reports came from the hospitals—reports of colored men and women whose ears had been cut off, whose skulls had been broken by blows, whose bodies had been slashed by knives or lacerated by scourges."[1] Schurz wrote not as an extremist but rather as a responsible, antislavery observer of conditions that alarmed him.

Even during this initial phase of Reconstruction, however, blacks did not respond passively. In several of the ex-Confederate states blacks held conventions to formulate programs for Reconstruction, programs that stressed protection from violence, access to education, and a chance at economic opportunity. With dignity and restraint the conventions reminded the public of the loyal support given the Union by blacks. During 1866 the desire of blacks to articulate their view of the future resulted in two major confrontations with white supremacists. In Memphis and New Orleans organized mobs of whites brutally assaulted blacks who sought to exercise the right of peaceable assembly. The New Orleans episode, particularly, focused national attention on what lay behind the ex-Confederate polite words of reconciliation. The violence, as Donald E. Reynolds writes, "was one of the principal reasons why the Radical Republicans were able to wrest control of reconstruction from President Andrew Johnson." Blacks and their white Republican allies had sought no more than to convene a state constitutional convention that would probably extend the franchise to the freedmen. Gathering in the convention hall they were attacked and slaughtered by a mob led by the city police, a force largely made up of militant Confederate veterans. A reporter for the anticonventionist *New Orleans Times* commented: "To see the Negroes mutilated and literally beaten to death as they sought to escape, was one of the most horrid pictures it has ever been our ill fortune to witness."[2] The United States Army units stationed in New Orleans failed to take any effective action to protect the convention, and the Johnson administration in Washington ignored warnings that violence was likely.[3] The New Orleans "riot" put Johnsonian Reconstruction to the test. The black and white radicals who died there succeeded in showing in microcosm what presidential Reconstruction was all about: the indifference of national authority to black lives and rights, the concentration of local power in the hands of those who only months before had fought the Union on the battlefields, the willingness of white supremacists to kill those who wanted something more than was offered in the Black Codes, all massed against proven loyalists, black and white, who wanted their legal rights. New Orleans and Memphis were significant factors leading to the overwhelming Republican victory in the 1866 congressional election that made possible the enactment of the legislative basis for Radical Reconstruction.[4]

As in New Orleans, the city police played a key role in triggering racial violence in Memphis. During several weeks prior to the riot police had been arresting black servicemen with minimum provocation and had frequently resorted to force. On April 30 the term of service of most of the blacks expired and the next day, May 1, a skirmish erupted between a number of police and a group of blacks. By nightfall the violence appeared to subside, but soon a mob invaded the black community. The local army commander was slow to act, and before martial law was imposed and some order restored, forty-six blacks and two whites had been killed. At least five black women were raped by the mobsters. Racists had been driven beyond reason by the sight of blacks in uniform and had been conditioned to employ any and all means to impose racial subordination. It is noteworthy that one Confederate veteran, after the riot had ended, was shot to death by another white man for having engaged in friendly conversation with a black acquaintance in a saloon. It will not suffice to explain this violence in the conventional terms of lower-class white resentment of black assertiveness, for a number of prominent Memphis whites led the mob, including the Tennessee attorney general, William Wallace, and the judge of the recorder's court, John C. Creighton. The federal inquiry into the riot reported that the city's mayor, John Park, took no action to suppress the riot and his influence "tended to incite it still further." It was doubtless such support in high places that had encouraged the police in initiating what James Gilbert Ryan terms "savage, almost merciless attacks" on Union army blacks. Police conduct seemed geared to inviting black retaliation, and Ryan is on target when he concludes that perhaps "the most remarkable aspect of the confrontation between the freedmen and the law men was that it did not occur earlier."[5]

The Memphis violence was set in the circumstance of demographic change and was also shaped by white-southerner resentment of the Yankee conquerors. In 1865 a city council census indicated that the city's black population had grown from 3,882 to 10,995, and in August 1865 the Freedmen's Bureau census counted 16,509 blacks out of a total population of 27,703. While blacks envisioned a new position in society for themselves, the fact of a black majority could be used to incite racial fears. Black assertiveness conflicted with the renewed aims of white supremacy. Racist violence was also a means of expressing defiance of the triumphant Union. One analyst of the Memphis riot poses the question: "Was it not safer for southerners to focus their pent-up bitterness and frustration upon the symbol of defeat—the freed slaves in South Memphis—than upon the mighty Yankee?" Attacks upon blacks compensated for inability to challenge the occupation forces frontally. In the course of the riot symbols of the Union, white and black, came under assault. White teachers, whites commanding black troops, missionaries, and even the local Freedmen's Bureau superintendent were insulted and threatened. The spirit of secessionism was at work in what took place in Memphis.[6]

From the beginning of Reconstruction blacks took great risks to come forward and testify concerning the violence directed at them by white landlords and assorted vigilante groups and gave the details of numerous acts of economic and physical intimidation. Blacks particularly came forward to testify at sessions of the Radical-controlled Joint Committee on Reconstruction, a congressional committee that sought to show the consequences of Johnson's policies. No black witness could be confident of what might await him upon return home; federal protection was an uncertain prospect, and white supremacists would surely seek revenge. Even if he were not directly assaulted, a realistic prospect was eviction or the loss of employment, quiet forms of terror that would draw little public interest. Yet repeatedly blacks came forward and told what had happened to them since Appomattox. Their testimony has the ring of authenticity and courage.

The coming of Radical Reconstruction did not put an end to racist violence in the South. Rather, it provided a new context within which the struggle as to the South's future would be fought out. Throughout Reconstruction the South was the setting for a kind of informal civil war in which those committed to a democratic, equalitarian vision of the future confronted those who would do everything in their power to establish a society rooted in hierarchical institutions of race and class. Radical rule saw the establishment of local and state governments in which blacks participated as voters and officeholders, but as the limits of Radical Reconstruction became clear the counterrevolution of white supremacy unfolded. Confining the ex-slaves to a political and consti-tutional definition of equality, national Republicans refused to back up Radical rule in the South with a program of economic reform that would include distribution of land to blacks and poor whites. Retaining their lands, the former slave owners and their banker and merchant friends in the cities were economically stronger than the local black and white Radicals. They could draw upon the militant support of thousands of Confederate army veterans. Repeatedly, acts of terror in the South chal-lenged the federal government to demonstrate its willingness to enforce constitutional rights, and the government's response was to show that it would not take the action necessary to suppress racist violence.

The Reconstruction era comes more clearly into focus if the critical role of violence in shaping the South's post–Civil War economic devel-opment is recognized. In recent years a diverse group of scholars have brought to the fore the linkage between violence and economic status. Harold Woodman notes that coercion and racial violence "were more than individual acts of cruelty; along with politics and the law they served to support and perpetuate a system of class control in the postwar South."[7] Jonathan Wiener has related the recourse to violence to the course set by the South's rulers of keeping the region on the "Prussian Road." This, writes Wiener, "increasingly required a resort to violence which is always a sign of the failure of hegemony, the inability of a dominant class to confine conflict to its own chosen political terrain."[8] Wiener traces the evolution of post–Civil War agriculture, the movement from gang labor to the sharecropping system, and points to terror as one of the methods employed by the planters to keep labor on the plantations. That the planters would use violence to control black labor was not something hidden; they openly embraced this tactic in Black Codes legislation. Wiener cites the Alabama vagrancy statute, which among other provisions allowed authorities to "cause to be inflicted on such vagrant 39 lashes upon his or her bare back." Ten thousand copies of the statute were to be printed and distributed to planters for reading to laborers.

Rejecting any supposition that the Black Belt Klan was primarily the instrument of poor whites, Wiener is critical of the approach of Reconstruction politicians and later historians that "underemphasized the role Klan terror played in creating and perpetuating the South's repressive plantation labor system." Wiener stresses the terroristic activities of "the best men" in Black-Belt Alabama. Violence was used in the effort to maintain a gang system of labor, and it became a feature of sharecropping as well. Sharecropping was, as Wiener observes, "a concession wrung out of the planters"; strictly speaking, therefore, it could be debated whether sharecropping was, as Wiener contends, "established as a repressive system of labor allocation and control," but use of terror combined with deprivation of political rights assured the repressive nature of the system.[9] A structure of informal arrangements was bound to be grossly inequitable when one side had little or no legal rights in the matter.

The economic consequences of post-Emancipation violence are carefully discussed in the work of two of the most able econometric historians, Roger Ransom and Richard Sutch. They point to the prevalence of violence aimed at disrupting black education, noting that in counties throughout the South "schools were burned and teachers threatened, whipped, beaten and in some cases murdered." There is no doubt, Ransom and Sutch find, that violence diminished opportunities to attend school as the risks involved increased. The consequence, despite persisting black interest in education, was that by 1880 only a quarter of black children had received enough education to read. Recognizing the difficulties of precisely measuring the economic impact of this situation, the econometricians note some clear economic implications: "even if illiteracy were irrelevant to the level of agricultural output, it cannot be denied that the inability to read and write would severely limit an individual's opportunities outside the agricultural sector. Quite apart from the fact that many nonagricultural jobs presupposed an ability to read and write, the illiterate farmer would be less likely to learn of job opportunities for which he did qualify. Illiteracy, if it did nothing else, helped to trap the black farmer in Southern agriculture."[10]

Ransom and Sutch further call attention to the fact that not only were blacks trapped in agriculture but that within the trap access to land ownership was rendered extraordinarily difficult. Whites who might sell land to blacks were threatened, as were prospective black purchasers. "The threat of violence," it was noted, "did not completely prevent land sales to blacks, but it did substantially escalate the costs and risks faced by both the black buyer and the white seller. These added costs and risks were so great that they virtually eliminated a market in land accessible to blacks and priced most blacks out of even the thin market that remained." The violence that blocked access to education, denied entrance to trades, or prevented land ownership undermined black efforts to realize the American Dream, for as Ransom and Sutch pointed out, these three avenues were "most commonly traveled by other Americans in their quest for self-advancement."[11] The consequence of all this was a deformed Emancipation in which blacks most often lacked economic assets of any kind and were subject to arbitrary rule by white employers.

During the peak of its activities, between 1868 and 1871, the Ku Klux Klan and similar conspiratorial groups committed literally thousands of outrages against those who desired the implementation of the Fourteenth and Fifteenth amendments. The victims included pregnant women and old people, black workers whose only offense was to be hired for a job desired by whites, blacks of all ages whose crime was to have acted "uppity," and white and black schoolteachers who attempted to bring mass education to a South in which education had been reserved for the privileged few. Black and white Radical officeholders were special targets of violence, and the Reconstruction years produced a long list of public officials who were assassinated. The list of the murdered included such capable and upright public servants as B. F. Randolph of South Carolina and Charles Caldwell of Mississippi. The Klan campaign of terror forced many thousands of blacks for months on end to sleep outdoors in order to escape a likely visit from the midnight riders.[12]

United States Army correspondence provides ample evidence of the nature of routine racial violence that characterized even the first years of Radical Reconstruction. Within a span of a few weeks between late

November 1868 and January 1, 1869, General George C. Meade, commander of the Third Military District (Georgia, Alabama, Florida), heard from field officers about serious incidents of violence in Georgia. In one report Meade was told of widespread lawlessness in Warren County, Georgia. No attempt was being made to enforce the laws; many attacks were made upon freedmen, but nobody was arrested in connection with these. People were fearful of giving testimony, as those blacks who did testify met with violence. When inquests were held the finding was uniformly that the blacks had died at the hands of "unknown parties." A second report sent to one of his subordinates informed Meade of a situation in Ogeechee, near Savannah, in which rice planters sought to arrest blacks who felt cheated with regard to labor contracts. Colonel George W. Williams wrote of the planters that "the truth is, that they desire to deprive these negroes of their just dues." A skirmish took place in which one white was killed. Williams feared that a posse organized by the planters would fire on any and all blacks it might encounter.[13]

Especially was counterrevolutionary violence effective as many Republicans, having consolidated the economic and political gains of the Civil War, lost interest in black rights as an issue. When the Klan proved an inexpedient instrument, violence and fraud were still key ingredients of the Mississippi and Georgia plans that, discarding Klan paraphernalia, worked to disrupt and eventually to destroy Reconstruction in those states.[14] In South Carolina Wade Hampton's Red Shirts waged open war against Radicals and in the 1876 Hamburg incident massacred a group of surrounded blacks.[15] The terrorists gave first priority to destroying the power of blacks to offer armed resistance. Their prime target was the black militia, companies of black guardsmen formed to protect the Radical governments. Where offered the opportunity blacks readily volunteered to join the militia and fought back when attacked by racists, but white Radical leaders in the South and federal authorities in Washington were quick to acquiesce to the demand that the black troopers be disarmed.

Urban race riots were a major feature of the counterthrust against Radical Reconstruction. Melinda Meek Hennessey cites thirty-three major riots, episodes in which more than a single life was lost, as occurring during Reconstruction. Forty-two percent of these incidents occurred in cities with populations larger than 5,000. Violent confrontations took place in some of the major cities of the South. In addition to the 1866 episodes in Memphis and New Orleans, there were also the 1868 New Orleans riot and the 1876 riot in Charleston.

A key element of the race riots of this period was that usually such incidents were linked to election campaigns. In New Orleans during the election contest of 1868, violence was initiated by whites, but blacks had anticipated the prospect of this occurring and had made some preparations. The Louisiana black leader P. B. S. Pinchback stated on September 4 that the next outrage committed by white Democrats would be "the signal for the dawn of retribution, of which they have not yet dreamed— a signal that will cause ten thousand torches to be applied to this city; for patience will then have ceased to be a virtue and this city will be reduced to ashes." The city was not reduced to ashes, but in late October four days of violence brought death to at least six whites and a minimum of fourteen blacks. Something of the tenor of racist opinion in New Orleans can be gleaned from the comment of the *New Orleans Daily Picayune* that "our Northern cousins" would care little about these events when they learned that the Radical casualties had been confined to blacks. Despite black resistance, the 1868 terror was effective in facilitating Democratic victory at the polls. The Democratic presidential ticket carried the state, and in New Orleans only 276 Republican votes were cast against a Democratic total of 23,897.

In Alabama the Eutaw riot of 1870 and the Eufaula riot of 1874 were both linked to the electoral process. The Eutaw incident was part of a widespread pattern of terrorization that included the July 1870 lynching in Calhoun County of four blacks and one white. On October 25 Democrats initiated an assault upon a rally of white and black Republicans assembled at the Greene County courthouse in Eutaw. The evidence indicates that at least two blacks and possibly as many as four were killed in this confrontation. Statewide the result of the 1870 violence was to give victory to Democrat candidate for governor Robert B. Lindsay, and Greene County, which had given President Grant a 2,000-vote majority in 1868 now gave Lindsay a forty-three-vote edge. A letter from one Eutaw white gave a candid evaluation of what had happened: "A row occasionally does no little good."

Violence that erupted in 1874 at Eufaula reflected the nature of the political struggle that gave a decisive victory to the white supremacy forces. On election day, November 3, racists attacked hundreds of blacks who had lined up to vote. State authorities estimated that thirty to forty persons had been killed, but Hennessey finds more reliable police and military estimates that seven or eight blacks were killed and between seventy and eighty men wounded, less than a dozen of them white. The outbreak of the riot prevented hundreds of blacks from casting their votes. The tragic nature of this episode is underscored by the circumstance that U.S. Army troops were within close reach of the scene but acted under orders not to interfere in matters deemed beyond the scope of federal authority. The federal government gave the black citizens of Eufaula over to the mercies of those who would murder them.

Hennessey shows that in most of the racial clashes that marked the Reconstruction era blacks were defeated, but she also stresses that blacks did not respond passively to violence. In 73 percent of the riots, Hennessey writes, "blacks fought back at least initially, and usually until they were overwhelmed by superior white numbers and firepower." And there was an exception to the usual triumph of white supremacy—the instance of Charleston where numerical advantage and political experience gave blacks the possibility of effective counter to racist assault. Despite the existence of white rifle clubs, blacks were able to hold their own in several clashes that occurred in the weeks before the November 7 election. In one collision that took place in the village of Cainhoy some twelve miles from Charleston, whites began the violence but more than met their match in the blacks on the scene. Charleston Democrats had chartered a boat to carry supporters from the city to a joint political discussion scheduled for October 16. But the discussion turned into confrontation, and blacks, angered especially by Martin Delany's role as black advocate of the Democrat position, defeated the whites who scurried back to the boat that had brought them from Charleston. In this incident five whites and one black were killed. In the 1876 election Democratic strength in the state was formidable, but racial terrorization could not then gain the upper hand in Charleston.[16]

The sociologist Allen Grimshaw has contended that in the nineteenth century southern-style race riots were caused by a perceived need to protect white women. Hennessey, through analysis of the thirty-three riots she has studied, conclusively shows that this was not the case with Reconstruction riots. Rhetoric about protecting white womanhood might be employed, especially following the violence, but the activating motivation was generally the desire to maintain political, economic, and social domination.

A phenomenon that appears repeatedly in the race riots of this era is the support given local terrorists by whites from surrounding counties and adjoining states. Based on the political experience acquired during the slave regime and the common desire to restore white rule, racists relied upon an informal network that could be quickly mobilized in a crisis.[17]

As W. McKee Evans has suggested, regarding the ineffective response of Republican leaders, it was not a question of the sufficiency of power but rather one of the will or lack of will to use available power. In the main the Republican thrust against the Klan was palsied by hesitation, short-range expediency, and the failure to understand that conditions of war still prevailed in the South. Evans sees in Republican policy the embodiment of Marx's notion of "parliamentary cretinism," the hollowness of political leaders who give only lip service to their proclaimed ideals.[18]

The evidence certainly points to excessive leniency as characterizing Radical policy. In Arkansas Radical governor Powell Clayton in late 1868 did proclaim martial law in ten terrorized communities and sent a militia led by Colonel William Monk against the Klansmen. Under the rule of this militia a number of Klansmen were convicted of murder and hung. In defense of lawfully constituted Reconstruction authority, Clayton for a time was willing to answer terror with terror. The Ku Klux Klan as an organized entity ceased to exist in Arkansas, giving the state government a lease on life that lasted until 1874 when application of the "Mississippi Plan" for overthrowing Radical power toppled the state's Radical regime.[19] But no other Radical state government matched Clayton's in stern resolution to act against the terrorists. Most importantly, the federal government did not manifest a continuing readiness to stamp out the counterrevolutionary violence practiced by the enemies of Reconstruction. Those enemies were committed to preserving a system of racial subordination and deference. The white Republican leadership was not committed to the destruction of that system. It was not that this leadership was always ineffectual. During the war when it saw fundamental questions of power at stake it acted sternly enough, finally grasping the weapon of Emancipation and waging civil war with appropriate resolution. But with Andrew Johnson's departure from the White House and growing confidence that the northern business class would continue to control national power, Republican zeal for revolutionizing the South drastically diminished, and what set in was a process leading toward appeasement of white supremacy.

At moments, as for example in 1871 when the Grant administration saw electoral prospects threatened by Klan activity, the national government took action effective enough to paralyze the infrastructure of Klan organization. This was most notably true in South Carolina where military rule was imposed upon thirteen up-country counties and hundreds of Klansmen were arrested by federal officers. But the federal government did not so act as to convey convincingly the message that it would not tolerate a renewal of terrorism. The actions of the Grant administration took on the quality of gestures, and Klanism, conspiratorial terror, and intimidation aimed at blacks and their white allies reasserted themselves, minus the robes and hoods of the organization.

The weakness of federal policy is manifested in the very limited maintenance of an army presence in the South. The historians of the long-influential Dunning school were fond of conjuring the horrors of "military occupation," but this occupation was more symbolic than substantial. During the period 1870–77, in the ten ex-Confederate states of Alabama, Arkansas, Florida, Georgia, Louisiana, Mississippi, North Carolina, South Carolina, Tennessee, and Virginia, the 1,122 troops stationed in Louisiana in 1874 made up the largest contingent assigned to any one state. The 596 soldiers assigned to Mississippi in 1875 were the largest number placed in that state, a state facing protracted and widespread violence. The maximum number to be found in South Carolina was 1,007, and that only for 1871 when martial law had been proclaimed. The federal contingent in Arkansas reached a maximum strength of 124 in 1870.

If the army presence in the South was an equivocal statement of federal commitment, so were the legal proceedings instituted against Kluxers in district courts. In South Carolina, where federal prosecution was most extensive, even in 1871 with acute concern over Klan activity prevailing, the securing of fifty-four convictions was accompanied by thirty-eight acquittals and thirty cases nol-prossed. All in all, between 1871 and 1874 convictions totaled 154, acquittals 44, and 1,119 cases were nol-prossed. There was some ability at securing convictions, but it was more than matched by willingness to drop charges against hundreds of suspected Klansmen.[20]

"The Ku Klux trials were largely a matter of sweeping the dirt under the rug," Evans writes.[21] The evidence indicates that of all those arrested for Klan involvement, no more than 10 percent were ever brought to trial.[22] Evans raises the issue of what happened to those convicted. The evidence is clear enough to conclude that remarkable leniency was shown these criminals. Within several months of the South Carolina 1871 convictions, President Grant pardoned those Klansmen serving sentences. In Mississippi only a few of those convicted of violating the Enforcement Acts, enacted by Congress to protect citizenship rights, went to prison or paid more than a small fine.[23] In Mississippi during 1872 the conviction of 262 accused Klansmen was facilitated by promising suspended sentences in exchange for guilty pleas.[24]

The federal attitude toward initiating anti-Klan prosecutions in Georgia underlines the slackness of federal authority in combating terrorism.

Evidence indicates that Klan terrorism persisted in that state well into the 1870s. This was also a state in which black legislators, under a contrived pretext, had been expelled from the state legislature. But Georgia was given a low priority for federal attention, apparently at least partly because of budgetary constraints on the Justice Department.[25] But the congressional Joint Select Committee that investigated conditions in the ex-Confederate states heard from dozens of witnesses who narrated accounts of widespread intimidation and violence in the state. Yet neither Congress nor the administration was impelled by this evidence to take action.

William Gillette, having carefully studied the general process of backing away from the commitments made to the emancipated blacks, has this to say about the government's course in upholding the freedmen's political rights: "The record of federal election enforcement was pitiable indeed. . . . Only 34 percent of the cases tried under the enforcement laws in the South between 1870 and 1877 resulted in conviction, and a mere 6 percent of them in the border states." Gillette reports that "political violence flourished unabated, and electoral fraud was commonplace, sophisticated, and highly successful . . . political violence and disturbance were so persistent, so widespread, and so formidable as to constitute civil disobedience and guerilla warfare." In assessing responsibility for the situation Gillette points to the weakness of the Grant administration, the hostility of many southern judges to suppressing racism, and the lack of wholehearted commitment to civil rights by many Republican congressmen. Most importantly, it appeared that the Republican leadership was more concerned with short-run partisan interests than with firmly setting in place a new citizenship status for blacks. Gillette concludes that the policy of enforcement "generated the highest hopes, the deepest hates, and the bitterest disappointments."[26]

The Reconstruction era also witnessed the outbreak of serious incidents of racial violence in northern cities. In Philadelphia, the City of Brotherly Love, violence during 1871 revealed persistent resistance to black exercise of constitutional rights and also vocal sentiment for the protection of black political rights. In the fall election of 1871, black voters were expected to play a decisive role in ousting the local Democratic machine and bringing the Republicans to power. And indeed the Republicans did score a sweeping victory in an election in which blacks, enfranchised by the Fifteenth Amendment, voted only for the second time in substantial numbers in a Philadelphia election. On election day, October 10, rioting broke out in several wards, and at least four blacks were killed, among them a school teacher, Octavius V. Catto.[27] Another victim was Isaac

Chase, whose head had been smashed by a white mob in the presence of his family, and there was also Jacob Gordon, shot in the back by white men as he returned home from work. Levi Bolden was shot at Seventh and Lombard streets and three weeks later died of the wound. The Philadelphia police, controlled by the Democratic party, did nothing to stop the violence. The *Philadelphia Inquirer* reported that following the outbreak of violence the black population was "frantic with terror," some individuals seeking safety in other parts of the city and many staying locked up in their homes. But there is also evidence that blacks were not passive in the face of attacks, one eyewitness recalling that "the records show 'an eye for an eye and a tooth for a tooth' in every instance."[28]

Several days following the violence the *Inquirer* placed responsibility for what had occurred on the city administration and the police. The paper observed that the police, "who were instructed that it was their duty to protect the rights of citizens in the exercises of the elective franchise, were themselves the most bold and outrageous violators of the peace. They undertook to prevent citizens from voting, and they carried on these high-handed outrages by the use of their clubs and intimidation, which resulted from the fact that they were armed with deadly weapons, which they were not slow in using." The *Inquirer* spoke bluntly: "The murders which were perpetrated on that day, in the lower part of the city, were incited by and encouraged by the city police. Catto fell a victim to the outrages which were encouraged by the Mayor's own officers." The paper declared that the police had become accessories before and after the fact. The police functioned within the context of a city in which, as noted by Roger Lane, the word *prejudice* "scarcely conveys the intensity of hatred that whites directed, often violently, against the Afro-American population." Ironically, in the aftermath of the 1871 violence the city council authorized an increase from 600 to 1,000 in the number of police.[29]

On October 13 a large public meeting was held at National Hall to condemn the lawlessness. The assemblage approved a resolution calling upon citizens to avoid the private righting of wrongs while also urging the arrest and conviction of the killers. Philadelphia black community leader Robert Purvis was among the speakers, and in his remarks Purvis declared that the turnout for the meeting "will gladden the heart of every lover of truth, humanity, justice and good government." He observed that as the blood of a black man was the first shed in the Revolution and a black was the first to die at the outset of the Civil War in Baltimore "now let us hope that the blood of our friend will be the end of resistance to the right." Another speaker, the Reverend J. Walker Jackson, paid lavish tribute to Catto's contributions, especially noting his role as educator in serving as a model to youth.[30]

Octavius V. Catto was indeed a person of considerable attainments who had contributed much to the community and who symbolized black militancy in pursuit of constitutional rights. Born in South Carolina in 1839, educated at the Quaker-founded Institute for Colored Youth in Philadelphia, Catto was appointed to the institute's teaching staff in 1859. He quickly became an outspoken leader with a widespread network of friends and supporters. In 1864 Catto gave his view of the black future in a commencement speech he delivered at the institute: "it must be the most superficial view, indeed, which concludes that any other condition than a total change in the status which the colored man has hitherto had in this country, must of necessity grow out of the conflicting theories of the parties to whose hands this question is at present committed." Change, Catto argued, would serve the interest of the entire country. In November 1864 Catto was elected corresponding secretary of the newly formed Pennsylvania Equal Rights League, which had the extension of the franchise as its central purpose. In 1866 he became involved in the fight to desegregate Philadelphia streetcars, and in 1867 he went to Harrisburg to urge legislative action on the issue. On March 22, 1867, these efforts resulted in victory as the legislature passed a bill requiring desegregation on streetcars in Pennsylvania.

At least two of the press commentaries on the murder focused on the stark contrast between Catto's standing in the community and the wanton nature of his killing. *Harper's Weekly* published a photo of Catto and noted that he was "a worthy colored citizen of Philadelphia . . . a quiet, well-educated man" whose murder was "entirely unprovoked." The *Philadelphia Public Ledger* saw Catto's character as underscoring the nature of the atrocities that the "unreasoning passion" of racism would prompt some men to commit. Catto was, the newspaper stated, "a man of gentle manners . . . a cultivated, scholarly man, engaged successfully in the highly important work of educating the people of a race who had been kept in partial or total ignorance by powerful social influences, and in some parts of our country by the operation of law." Catto was therefore "a most useful member of society, who should have commanded the respect of all, instead of the hatred of any, yet, this man, so void of offence, so useful in his vocation, so worthy of the approbation and protection of all men, falls before the weapon of the assassin, not because he, the particular victim, had given personally any offence to the murderer, but because that murderer was inflamed with furious hatred against the race of which his victim was one." Because of who Catto was and what he represented, in this incident of violence the inhuman essence of racism could plainly be seen.[31]

Thousands of Philadelphians turned out for Catto's funeral. The *Philadelphia Inquirer* reported: "White and black, side by side, participated in doing homage to the memory of the dead man." Some 5,000 persons viewed the body as it lay in state at the city armory. Those entering the building passed between black guardsmen, drawn from the Eleventh, Twelfth, and Thirteenth regiments. On the lid of the coffin was an inscription that gave Catto's name, the date he died, and his age at death. A young black woman observed, " 'Died!' It ought to have read 'Murdered October 10!' " At Mount Lebanon Cemetery one of the speakers was Henry Highland Garnet, the renowned abolitionist. Garnet read the verse, beginning:

> How short the race our friend has run,
> Cut down in all his bloom—
> The course he yesterday begun
> Now finished in the tomb.[32]

Violence and the threat of violence against individual blacks and against groups of blacks, against entire communities of black people, marked this Reconstruction era when revolution and counterrevolution were locked in direct confrontation. How did blacks respond to the violence that marked this complex struggle? Their response was shaped by several considerations: the need to maintain links to white allies both within the South and in the national government, the right of self-defense when actually confronted with violence, and the imperative that black unity and the articulation of a common program were necessary means of rallying national support. Within this general framework black Americans employed diverse tactics to gain their fundamental end of full equality. There were, of course, some individuals who reacted to racist terror by proposing abandonment of the struggle, usually resting their case on the assumption that white allies were bound to be faithless and that racist strength was overwhelming. Among them was the abolitionist proto-nationalist Martin Delany who in the 1870s urged South Carolina blacks to vote for the opponents of the Republican Radicals. Especially as state Republican parties allowed themselves to be split between warring factions, black individuals could be found who sought to make the best deal possible with the traditional Democratic politicians.

The mainstream of the black community, however, was clearly oriented toward support of the Republican party. The Republicans, of course, had led the nation in the Civil War, had supported the policy of recruiting black troops to fight in the Union army, and had enacted the Thirteenth, Fourteenth, and Fifteenth amendments. The Democratic party in the South was a bastion of secession, and in the North the party was hostile to the demand that the Civil War become a war against slavery. But support of the Republican party was also a means of access to those wielding national power. Black leaders shared with the Republicans the recollection of the common struggle to destroy slavery, could point to the fact that preserving the congressional legislation enacted during the war rested on black votes in the South that elected Republicans to Congress. These leaders believed they shared with Republicans a commitment to an America in which equal opportunity was to be open to every American, regardless of color.

At the local level, throughout this period, conventions of blacks appealed to the national government and to public opinion for action against the Klansmen and other terrorists. These assemblages recited the evidence of the suffering experienced by blacks and called for federal action to protect constitutional rights. In another form of appeal for national action, black congressmen took the floor in Congress to expose the crimes of white supremacy and to ask their white colleagues to support effective remedies. Perhaps the form of appeal for national intervention that was most impressive was the sworn testimony of hundreds of black witnesses who came forward at congressional hearings to give their accounts of the threats, whippings, lynchings, and assassinations that had become routine occurrences in the South as the racists fought to regain power. Most of the witnesses were "ordinary" people, individuals who could not expect that any substantial effort would be made to protect them against racist retaliation. Coming forward to testify took quite extraordinary courage. Racist historians later asserted that this testimony could be dismissed as self-serving political propaganda, but the judgment of such scholars had been warped by passionate hatred of Radical Reconstruction and their commitment to the heritage of questioning the truth of any statement by blacks. Read without racist blinders, the testimony constitutes an overwhelming record of the massive brutality with which Radical rule was overthrown. Much of this testimony is found in the hearings of the Joint Select Committee that was appointed by the House and Senate in 1871 to investigate the depredations of the Ku Klux Klan.[33] This committee conducted the most extensive of the congressional inquiries into violence during Reconstruction, with hearings held both in Washington and in the southern states. The testimony, the statements of black witnesses, and the evasive words of suspected terrorists and racist Democratic politicians clearly outline the agony and the heroism manifested by those who tried to make democracy work in the Reconstruction South.

Blacks sought to arouse the conscience of the nation, but they also availed themselves of the right of self-defense. They were defending not only their individual lives but the lawful state and local governments established by Reconstruction. They resisted individually and through collective effort. Black officeholders continued their work in the face of threats of assassination. The night riders who set out on a lynching expedition often found in their targeted victim a fighter who would offer the greatest possible resistance. Collectively, groups of blacks fought back against the terror and, where offered the opportunity, blacks eagerly volunteered to serve in the militias organized by the Radical state governments. The black militiamen fought bravely although often inadequately armed and only halfheartedly supported by white Republicans.

Black self-defense sometimes was transformed into retaliatory violence or at least the threat of such violence. In 1876 Charleston blacks, in response to the murder of black militiamen at Hamburg, attacked white conservatives on the streets. At a July 17 protest meeting, attended by a thousand blacks and 500 whites, a resolution was adopted that forcefully called for punishment of the terrorists at Hamburg:

> We tell you that it will not do to go too far in this thing. Remember that there are 80,000 black men in this State who can bear Winchester rifles and know how to use them, and that there are 200,000 women who can light a torch and use the knife, and that there are 100,000 boys and girls who have not known the lash of a white master, who have tasted freedom, once and forever, and that there is a deep determination never, so help them God, to submit to be shot down by lawless regulators for no crimes committed against society and law.[34]

In Macon blacks threatened to burn down the town if one black man was killed.[35] Black Republicans told a North Carolina convention that "revenge may be sweet to blacks as to whites."[36] In an atmosphere of civil war it was inevitable that violence would be resorted to by both sides in the struggle.

The effectiveness of black resistance to racist violence was related to the population statistics, the ratio in communities of black population to white. In Wilmington, North Carolina, during 1868, blacks marching with fence rails in hand were able to suppress Klan activities. In low-country South Carolina white supremacists were held in check by militant, well-organized black majorities.[37]

Response to Reconstruction violence was also expressed in the actions of many blacks who uprooted themselves and their families to seek protection from terror. At least in the case of Georgia, blacks in significant numbers moved from the countryside to the towns. In 1871 the black Georgia leader Henry M. Turner told congressional inquirers why blacks were leaving the rural areas:

> They leave the country in many instances because they are outraged, because their lives are threatened; they run to the cities as an asylum. In many instances they work by the year, and at the end of the year they receive nothing. They come to the cities and prefer knocking about and catching pennies here and there rather than to work the entire year in the country and at the end of the year be turned out of their homes, with their wives and their children, and have nothing.[38]

Even before the final defeat of Reconstruction some blacks proposed to leave the United States altogether and to emigrate to Africa. That this movement reflected protest against the violent conditions facing blacks in the Reconstruction South is clearly articulated in the testimony of the South Carolina black preacher, the Reverend Elias Hill. A resident of York county, Hill had served as the president of the local Union League and had been beaten by Klan raiders. On July 20, 1871, the *Yorkville Enquirer* reported that Hill was organizing a group of from sixty to eighty black families who planned to emigrate to Africa. The newspaper reported that the migrants were furnished transportation by the American Colonization Society and would settle in what was known as the North Carolina Colony of Liberia. Hill denied he was the leader of the movement, but he outlined the reasons that impelled himself and others to migrate: "It was because of the outrages of the Ku-Klux that I took the resolution and made and am making preparations and others are doing the like, ... we all ascribe the same cause for this movement; we do not believe it possible, from the past history and present aspect of affairs, for our people to live in this country peaceably, and educate ourselves and elevate our children to that degree which they desire." He told the Joint Select Committee that he had received material from the American Colonization Society and that he learned "that in Liberia there was greater encouragement and hope of finding peaceful living and free schools and rich land than in any place in the United States that I have read of. These things encourage us a great deal in our intention to move away to Africa. That is where my father came from." Hill affirmed that Liberia offered a refuge "for general peace, abiding peace and prosperity for me and my race, and for the elevation of our people." He added that many blacks hoped that the white terror would be suppressed so "that the times will eventually come that those who want to go away now may stay, finding that they can live in peace." But he added candidly that "certain of us" had lost hope since local whites had broken all pledges of peaceful conduct.[39] In 1872 it was reported that 165 blacks, led by Elias Hill, had emigrated to Africa.[40]

With the final defeat of Radical Reconstruction thousands of southern blacks manifested some interest in migrating from the South. A year after federal troops were withdrawn from South Carolina a party of 206 people brought together by the Liberian Exodus Joint-Stock Steamship Company left Charleston harbor on the *Azor* bound for Africa.[41] In 1879 hundreds of blacks from four states, Mississippi, Louisiana, Texas, and Tennessee, left their homes and in a sudden spasm headed for Kansas, in the wake of earlier colonization efforts led by Benjamin ("Pap") Singleton.[42] In the black consciousness Kansas symbolized cheap land and also the antislavery struggle led by John Brown. Singleton, a Nashville realtor, had campaigned for migration for at least a decade, but with the crushing of Reconstruction the move to Kansas attracted substantial support, including endorsements from such prominent black leaders as Richard T. Greener and John M. Langston. During 1879 a New Orleans black convention adopted a resolution urging Negroes to "emigrate and settle where they would be free from shot-guns." The Kansas migration movement did arouse concern among southern planters, concern reflected in a Vicksburg convention of Mississippi valley planters that pledged blacks protection "from fraud, intimidation or 'bull dozing' on the part of the whites." In Kansas, in 1879, a black newspaper explained that, when it was clear that blacks could not exist in the circumstances prevailing in the South, northern opinion would take notice.[43] But the masses of southern blacks would not and could not so readily pack up and travel to Kansas. Added to other practical obstacles, communities along the way were not overly friendly to the Kansas-bound migrants. And in Kansas itself there was little welcome for those blacks who arrived. Kansas land, though cheaper than land in the South, was still selling at higher prices than most of the migrants could afford to pay. White racism was not just a southern phenomenon, and many whites in the West believed that the lands of the Great Plains should be reserved for white people only. Their attitude was consistent with the views of those in the West who before the Civil War joined opposition to slavery with opposition to the presence of any blacks. The Kansas migration, however, did provide evidence, presented before a congressional committee, as to the violent conditions prevailing in the South.[44] The Republican party was able to show that the Kansas migration was not a Republican propaganda ploy but rather a natural response to lawless conditions in the South. The inquiry served party purposes, but it also drew national attention to the consequences of abandoning Radical Reconstruction.

The southern struggle continued in the new circumstances framed by the unwillingness of the federal government to intervene directly. During the late 1870s and 1880s some blacks continued to hold office in the South, and black suffrage remained a factor to be reckoned with, although blacks quite clearly had been thrown on the defensive politically and cut off from effective national support. But a society committed to racism could not be maintained without violence, and the evidence accumulated that violent acts against blacks were a major component of the economic and political system that now controlled the South. Blacks might be permitted to operate peaceably within well-circumscribed limits, but where black activity was seen as actually or potentially threatening, aimed at achieving genuine equality, the answer of white supremacists was forcible repression.

In Danville, Virginia, on November 3, 1883, three blacks were killed three days before a state election that was to decide the issue of funding Virginia's pre–Civil War debt.[45] The funding issue divided Virginians into two camps, a coalition of farmers, small businessmen, and blacks against large-capital bondholders and state officials. Involved in this issue was the matter of taxing the majority of citizens for the benefit of a wealthy few. For blacks and poor whites, it came down to a choice of supporting public education or paying the bondholders. In the 1883 election, issues of class and race were intertwined. Prior to 1883 the black/farmer/small-business coalition had won substantial public support and had put through several measures of direct concern to blacks. A constitutional amendment to abolish the poll tax was passed and ratified, appropriations for education were increased, and a black institution for higher education was established.

The Danville murders represented the effort of Virginia conservatives to reassert control. During the 1883 campaign conservative papers focused upon the race issue with one current cartoon picturing a black schoolmaster paddling white children. At Danville, during August, local authorities prevented a mob from lynching three blacks accused of killing a white man. Although the blacks maintained their innocence they were convicted and hanged. For racists, however, this was not enough. They utilized the episode to spread fears that blacks were getting out of hand and to call for action to subordinate blacks to white rule. White supremacists announced they would carry Danville, however it was done. When a black policeman asked how the conservatives would carry the town if they lacked the votes the answer was blunt: "We're going to carry it, votes or no votes, with double barrel shotguns, breach loading shotguns and Smith and Wesson double-action." Blacks were warned not to be on the street on election day. Racists pointed to Danville to convince white voters throughout southwestern Virginia that race really was the main issue of the election. Twenty-eight prominent white Danville businessmen issued the "Danville Circular," which purported to be a shocking exposé of black misrule. Four of the town's policemen were black, black magistrates supposedly controlled the town, and blacks were alleged to "impede the travel of ladies and gentlemen, very frequently from the sidewalk into the street." Indeed, things had come to the point where a black individual had called a white woman a liar.[46] Blacks had become so impertinent as to actually petition Washington for federal troops to be stationed in Danville on election day. There was also the practical consideration that disorder had hurt the tobacco business.

It was against this background that the November 3 killings occurred. The white supremacists were inflamed by charges that the Danville Circular was based upon falsehoods and distortions and provoked a confrontation leading to the killings. Following the November 3 incident, white vigilantes seized control of the community and prevented any further political activity by blacks and their white allies. Throughout Virginia, conservatives portrayed the Danville events as white citizens protecting their families from black crime. The bondholders' campaign was successful, intimidation substantially reduced the number of black voters, and racial solidarity had been made the leading issue among whites.

The Danville events illustrated the impact of several factors now governing the situation in the post-Reconstruction South. The white business elite used the race issue to mask their economic program, state and federal authorities would take no effective action against racist violence, and racial demagogy would blind many whites to their common interests with blacks. The 1883 episode also reveals blacks resisting within the limits of their power. In Danville few blacks were able to vote, but in Orange County blacks guarded the polls and checked off the voters as they appeared, and in Petersburg blacks held a parade and guarded the precinct polling places.

In that same year, 1883, farther to the south in Copiah County, Mississippi, another major outbreak of racial violence occurred. In this Mississippi incident, as at Danville, the critical issue was the attempt to fuse black and white voters politically against the white Bourbon Democrats. William Ivy Hair sums up the unusual features of the Copiah situation: "In Copiah, unlike anywhere else in the state, black voters were able for a time to unite politically with a large segment of the poorer white agriculturalists, and together they revived the Reconstruction experiment in a most improbable place." On October 25, shortly before the election, armed Democrats began a series of raids into the black precincts, repeatedly threatening to kill blacks known to be politically active. And it should be noted that this intimidation was not the work of poor whites. Democratic congressman Ethelbert Barksdale stated in Copiah County prior to the election: "So far as I knew, the men who composed it, were among the best in the county, a good many of them planters and men of various professions." One black farmer, Tom Wallis, was killed in the course of this preelection harassment, and Mrs. Wallis, wounded by a bullet that passed through her husband and struck her arm, later died but not before she was able to testify at a United States Senate subcommittee hearing. A common response of those threatened was to take refuge by sleeping out in the woods, and one black man later testified that some whites as well as blacks took this course. "We all had to lay out like possums when de dogs are after dem," he said. The intimidation climaxed on election day, November 6, in the murder of John Prentiss ("Print") Matthews, prominent Copiah County merchant-planter Republican. The following day the Copiah Democratic executive committee met, and among the resolves of that gathering was a statement that "from henceforth no man or set of men shall organize the negro race against the whites in this county, and if it shall be attempted in the future, we hereby give notice that it shall be at the peril of the person or persons attempting to do so."[47]

The Copiah violence was the subject of a Senate investigation with hearings held in New Orleans during early 1884.[48] Numerous blacks were among the witnesses who told the senators of the political terrorism prevailing in the county. But the federal government took no action beyond this inquiry, and the actual assassin of Matthews, one Ras Wheeler, was tried but acquitted on grounds of self-defense. Wheeler indeed was appointed city marshal of the town of Hazlehurst, thereby contributing to a Mississippi tradition of confusing law enforcement officers with killers.[49]

Four years later, in 1887, an episode in Louisiana again demonstrated the intertwining of issues of race and class and the direct role of state government as the instrument of violence against blacks. Black sugar workers in Louisiana, organized by the Knights of Labor, had struck over the refusal of employers to grant a demand for wage increases. Employers had responded by declaring that they would not recognize any labor organization, would evict strikers from their plantations, and would blacklist them. At Thibodeaux a meeting of planters resolved that "if any laborers are discharged from the plantation upon which they are now at work, or if any such discharge themselves by refusing to work, we pledge ourselves to give them no employment; that all people discharged for refusal to work be required to leave the plantation within twenty-four hours, and on refusal to obey that the powers of the law be involved to assist the owners of property in the enjoyment of their rights of property."[50] State authority, however, went further. Governor McEnery, described by the *New Orleans Times-Democrat* as someone who understood "how dangerous the negro may become when excited," sent state troops to Lafourche Parish to suppress the strike. A number of strikers were arrested, and at Pattersonville at least four laborers were murdered while under arrest. Regarding this violence one posse member stated: "Everybody thought the negroes were attacking the posse when firing was heard in front. I am informed that this firing was really done by some of the white citizens, who were presumably drunk at the time." At Thibodeaux another outbreak of violence occurred after "large crowds of white people, planters and others, from the surrounding country came into town armed, and with a determination to maintain peace and order." The result of this determination was that the armed whites marched upon the black community and that at least six and possibly thirty or more blacks were killed. Blacks, supported by the Knights of Labor, protested against the killings and demanded an investigation, but the strike of the sugar workers in southern Louisiana was broken by official violence. The *New York Age* pointed to the killings as an example of Henry Grady's "New South" and declared that "the colored people will not in the future continue to be led as lambs to the slaughter."[51] But for the time being nothing was done to punish those responsible for brutalities inflicted on the sugar strikers.[52]

The agrarian struggles that gripped the South during the 1880s and 1890s were accompanied by widespread violence. As the Farmers Alliance and Populist movements fought to check corporate and banking domination of the South, racists employed terror as a means of retaining power for the privileged few. Whereas the agrarian radicals would argue that class was the crucial dividing line of society, the racists would make white

supremacy the all-important issue. In Georgia, according to C. Vann
Woodward in his biography of the Populist leader Tom Watson, racists
resorted to election frauds, intimidation, and outright assault to maintain
Democratic control of political offices.[53]

During the years of the Populist movement the racial question was
perhaps nowhere more sharply posed than in Texas. The movement
appealed for black support, and in 1896 the *Houston Daily News* estimated that 25,000 blacks did indeed support the People's party. Blacks
participated in the activities of the movement at almost all levels. Black
delegates attended all Populist state conventions from 1891 to 1896.
Local Populist club meetings were freely attended by blacks, and a number of blacks were elected as delegates to county or district meetings. At
the state level several blacks served on the state executive committee of
the People's party. Most prominent among black activists in the movement was J. B. Rayner, born a slave in North Carolina. Rayner, who
had studied at Shaw University, came to Texas in the early 1880s, and
in 1892 turned from the Republican party to the Populists.[54]

In the Texas struggle disfranchisement and violence were closely in-
terrelated. Events in Matagorda County illustrate clearly the role of terror
in political change. In 1887 the county was represented by a black representative in the state legislature, and one county commissioner, two
justices of the peace, and one constable were black. In the summer of
1887 white supremacists moved to drive the blacks into subjection. A
white desperado murdered the black constable, Jerry Matthews, and
when seventy-five black men dared to procure guns and began searching
for the killer, the racists attacked. Some eighty-five armed whites, from
Matagorda and several adjoining counties, found several blacks barricaded in a house and killed two of the persons seeking to escape. Another
black was killed by a party of Wharton County whites, simply on the
grounds that he was carrying a gun. The historian of Matagorda County
records that this episode convinced blacks "that they were to remain in
the background, and leave the government of the county to whites. For
several years afterward the negroes would always take off their hats when
they met a white man, and keep them off until the white man had passed."
In the midst of the Populist struggle this state of affairs was formalized.
In 1894 whites circulated petitions forming the White Man's Union in
the county, and black participation in primary elections came to an end.[55]

In Grimes County the formation of a White Man's Union spearheaded
a drive to break a white–black coalition upon which Populist strength
was based. In 1899 defeated Democratic candidates and prominent white
citizens met to organize the union. The organization would nominate

candidates for county offices in elections in which only members of the White Man's Union could participate. Black disfranchisement was the organizing principle of the union, and there was a thin line between calling for disfranchisement and backing up that demand with force. By April 1900, in a mayoral election in the town of Bryan, supporters of the white candidates "reportedly made a display of force and permitted no Negroes to vote." The local white newspaper denied the claim of the Negro Baptist State Sunday School Conference that the county was unsafe for blacks. But in July a black district clerk, Jim Kennard, was assassinated, and in September another black Populist leader, Jack Haynes, was murdered. Two nights later the White Man's Union held a rally at which one of the racist candidates read some original poetry:

> Twas nature's laws that drew the lines
> Between the Anglo-Saxon and the African races,
> And we, the Anglo-Saxons of Grand Old Grimes,
> Must force the African to keep his place.[56]

The White Man's Union campaign of intimidation and murder was successful. In the November 1900 election the white supremacists took power, and active Populists were either silenced or driven from the county. Blacks quickly recognized that the political climate in this onetime stronghold of populism had changed, and many made up their minds to leave Grimes County. Those who departed were no doubt but little interested in the concern expressed by a local newspaper that the exodus was complicating the labor market.

TWO

Lynching and Black Perspectives

THE POLITICAL violence of the Reconstruction era and that of the Populist years were connected by the willingness of the white rulers of the south to employ whatever means were necessary to destroy the unity of blacks and whites. Blacks in many areas continued to vote and even to hold office, but where political activity by blacks threatened to bring to life a majority coalition that would curb the property interests of the southern elite the answer was terror.

Violent acts were not confined to the sphere of political activity, however. Although the phenomenon of lynching antedated the Civil War, in the post-Reconstruction period the killing of blacks by white mobs, either individually or in groups, became an occurrence of increasing frequency. This violence, cresting in the early 1890s, was generated, as Edward L. Ayers suggests, by a general social crisis, in which the steep economic depression of the period was a key element.[1]

The specifics of each lynching might vary, but the general pattern of this racial barbarism was clear. Whites would be roused to hysteria by accounts of some purported black offense. The hysteria could be evoked by charges that a crime had been committed, but frenzy could also be incited by simply alleging that a black man had been "uppity," had argued with a white employer, or had neglected to move out of the path of a white person. The cry of rape, appealing to the most extreme fears and hatreds, drawing upon racist myths concerning black male sexuality and a hypocritical view of white womanhood, became a summons to the mob and also was used to justify the lynching to national public opinion. The mob would then begin the search for the black or blacks reported to have offended, and if the black person identified could not be found the mob would turn its wrath upon someone else, a wife perhaps or other relative of the accused, and indeed sometimes anyone who was black would do. The point was that for the supposed crime or insult the black community as a whole was accountable, and one black victim for the lynch mob would serve as well as another. The victims of the lynch mob

30

included grown men but also teenagers, elderly women, and pregnant mothers.

The lynchers, characteristically, were not content merely to kill the victim; the act of lynching was often transformed into a public spectacle, and sometimes hundreds or thousands of whites from the surrounding countryside would come to town to observe the event. The mob inflicted death, death that was the result of extraordinary, sadistic cruelty. Before death came the victim was tortured, tormented by having limbs or sexual organs amputated, by being slowly roasted over a fire. Before or after death the body might be riddled with bullets and dragged along the ground. After death pieces of the charred remains would often be distributed as souvenirs to the mob whose members desired a keepsake as a remembrance of the notable happening. In short, the phenomenon of lynching exhibited American society in its most ferocious and inhuman manifestation.

In the face of inhumanity, public authority either was indifferent or in numerous cases cooperated with the mob. Not only did sheriffs and jailers often willingly turn black victims over to the lynchers, but officers of the law frequently joined the mob. White society refused to take any effective action to stop lynching; the members of the white community were, strangely, most often unable to identify those who participated in the violence even when photographs of the mob were available; grand juries were often unwilling to indict even when they did have the names of those responsible, and trial juries seldom brought in guilty verdicts for the crime of lynching.[2] Executing a white person for lynching was virtually out of the question. Governors only rarely were willing to use their powers to protect public order and send troops to assure the safety of a black threatened by lynching. Polite southern society was likely to pronounce lynching distasteful and to see lynching as the work of poor whites, but the leaders of society did nothing to put a stop to the practice and in actuality tended to see lynching as most regrettable but justifiable.[3] The litany of rationalization revolved around the assertion that lynching was fundamentally caused by "negro criminality." Northern opinion, in the years after Reconstruction, generally lamented lynching and found it proof of southern backwardness but largely accepted the racist argument that southern white men were motivated by the desire to protect white women against black rape.

Generally reliable statistics on lynching are available for the years following 1882. As reported to the annual *Negro Year Book,* published at Tuskegee Institute, between 1882 and 1901 the largest number lynched in any one year was 255 and the smallest 107. The total number of persons lynched in this interval was 3,130, and 1,914 of these were blacks.[4] For the period 1882–1903 the statistics show that sixty-three women were lynched, twenty-three of the victims white and forty black.[5] Lynching had become a regular, periodic occurrence in the South; word of several lynchings taking place in one week was routine news during this period. Translated from statistical abstraction, that signifies a reality that many thousands of blacks, perhaps most of the southern black population, had witnessed lynching in their own communities or knew people who had, knew the terror that struck the community when the mob was whipped to frenzy. All blacks lived with the reality that no black individual was completely safe from lynching.

Analysis of statistics concerning lynching gives the flavor of the underlying social realities. The muckraker Ray Stannard Baker reported the reasons given for lynchings in 1907 involving forty-nine black men and three black women. The figures indicate that eight of the victims allegedly were guilty of rape or attempted rape, but one black man was lynched for being the father of a boy who jostled white women, another was killed for having beaten a white in a fight, a woman was put to death as the wife of a rapist and a youth was lynched for being a rapist's son, one person was lynched for protecting a fugitive from a posse, someone was lynched for talking to white girls on the telephone, and three persons died for having expressed sympathy for the mob's victim. Among the lynch victims that year were also three persons charged with store burglary, and one individual was killed for supposedly stealing seventy-five cents.[6]

In the decades following Reconstruction white terror was with increasing frequency directed against Afro-Americans, a terror given free reign by the refusal of the federal government to enforce the guarantees of the Constitution. In this deteriorating situation Afro-Americans persisted in asserting their rights, resorted to the human right of self-defense, and sought to formulate an effective strategy that could lead to redeeming the promises of Reconstruction. The foremost leader of black America, Frederick Douglass, attempted to combine adherence to his Republican loyalties with militant calls to the American democratic conscience and uncompromisingly insisted on the full rights for which blacks had fought and sacrificed. Douglass would not agree with those he saw as proposing to abandon the southern struggle and encourage emigration to other regions. He remained the principled advocate of an effective coalition of white and black that could build a truly democratic America. Douglass's militancy and eloquence ran up against the reality that no major white force in America was now prepared to commit its strength to the cause of black rights. His posture lacked short-run effectiveness, but he held up with all that was in him the goal of full democratic rights. Not for Douglass were the tactics of expediency urged by others who would compromise with white supremacy. Douglass, until his death in 1895, stands as a link between the radicalism of the abolitionist movement and Radical Reconstruction and the twentieth-century civil rights movement.

Douglass was forthrightly critical of the policy of exodus from the South. In an 1879 speech he delivered before the American Social Science Association Douglass asked: "Is the total removal of the whole five millions of colored people from the South contemplated? Or is it proposed to remove only a part? And if only a part, why a part and not the whole? A vindication of the rights of the many cannot be less important than the same to the few." He based his position on the argument that mass migration would undermine the struggle for democracy in the South. He granted that for the moment violence denied black people their rights, but he confidently asserted that "those rights will revive, survive and flourish again." He believed that the white supremacists were confronted with the choice of allowing blacks to vote or having the South's representation in Congress reduced and that "the chosen horn of this dilemma will finally be to let the Negro vote and vote unmolested." Douglass's optimism in 1879 was grounded in his confidence that the country's Republican leadership would move toward enforcement of constitutional guarantees, and he observed that President Hayes "has bravely, firmly and ably asserted the constitutional authority, to maintain the public peace in every State in the Union, and upon every day in the year; and he has maintained this ground against all the powers of House and Senate." Douglass argued that to organize "a general stampede" of blacks from the South was to further the abandonment of the principle that citizens in every state were entitled to protection of life and property. He also offered the practical objections that exodus would diffuse black political strength in the South, sending blacks into states in which they could exert little influence, and also that black labor, the backbone of the economy, was most likely to secure its greatest return in the South.

But Douglass would not bar black migration to the northern states. The right of every individual, black or white, to move freely about the country was to be protected. "If it is attempted," he declared, "by force or fraud to compel the colored people to stay, then they should by all means go; go quickly, and die, if need be, in the attempt." Black migration from the South had served a purpose; it represented "an emphatic and stinging protest against high-handed, greedy and shameless injustice to the weak and defenseless." Although he rejected exodus as a policy Douglass pointed to the phenomenon of black migration to the North and West as evidence of prevailing injustice in the South. He characterized as "superficial, insufficient and ridiculous" the explanation of the exodus offered by racists. Blacks did not make the arduous move to Kansas because of the machinations of Republican politicians, or because of the urgings of greedy land speculators, or because of the agitational efforts of defeated southern Republicans. The actual reasons for blacks leaving their homes could be found in public testimony by blacks who told of their own experiences. Economic conditions were a major factor in the migration. Blacks were cheated by white merchants and storekeepers, and landowners conspired to prevent landowning by blacks. And added to economic oppression was violence. Douglass noted that blacks were "not only the victims of fraud and cunning, but of violence and intimidation; that from their very poverty the temples of justice were not open to them; that the jury box is virtually closed; that the murder of a black man by a white man is followed by no conviction or punishment." He told his audience that if the complaints of southern blacks were only half true they served amply to explain why some blacks had chosen to move.[7]

In 1879 Douglass was acutely aware of the oppressive conditions under which blacks of the South lived, but he also expressed the hope that the violence he pointed to signified only a passing phase in the movement from enslavement to freedom. By 1886, however, Douglass spoke more harshly, outraged by barbarous treatment of blacks in the South and the abject failure of national authorities to protect black rights. In a speech to a largely black audience Douglass gave full vent to his anger against the terrorists of the South and also to his intensely critical view of a government that did nothing while black citizens were being brutally assaulted and murdered:

I now undertake to say that neither the Constitution of 1789, nor the Constitution as amended since the war, is the law of the land. That Constitution has been slain in the house of its friends. So far as the colored people of the country are concerned, the Constitution is but a stupendous sham, a rope of sand, a Dead Sea apple, fair without and foul within, keeping the promise to the eye and breaking it to the heart. The Federal Government, so far as we are concerned, has abdicated its functions and abandoned the objects for which the Constitution was framed and adopted, and for this I arraign it at the bar of public opinion, both of our country and that of the civilized world. I am here to tell the truth, and to tell it without fear or favor, and the truth is that neither the Republican Party nor the Democratic

Party has yet complied with the solemn oath, taken by their respective representatives, to support the Constitution, and execute the
laws enacted under its provisions. They have promised us law, and
abandoned us to anarchy; they have promised protection, and given
us violence; they have promised us fish, and given us a serpent.

Douglass was now less hopeful about the performance of Republican
presidents, and he asked: "Has any one of our Republican Presidents
since Grant, earnestly endeavored to establish justice in the South?" In
the absence of such endeavor, blacks in the South were denied the rule
of law and were now subject to the lynching mob. "This mob," Douglass
declared, "takes the place of 'due process of law,' of judge, jury, witness,
and counsel. It does not come to ascertain the guilt or innocence of the
accused, but to hang, shoot, stab, burn or whip him to death. Neither
courts, jails, nor marshals are allowed to protect him. Every day brings
us tidings of these outrages. I will not stop to detail individual instances.
Their name is legion." Douglass referred to recent events at Carrollton
courthouse, Mississippi, in which armed whites, without provocation,
opened fire on a group of unarmed blacks, killing eleven instantly and
mortally wounding nine others. What particularly appalled him was that
most Americans had by now become quite indifferent to racial violence
in the South. "It is the old story verified," Douglass declared:

> Vice is a monster of such frightful mien
> That, to be hated, needs but to be seen;
> But seen too oft, familiar with its face,
> We first endure, then pity, then embrace.

In this speech Douglass addressed himself to the charge that the basic
source of southern violence was black criminality. He reminded his audience that he had earlier observed that in some cases white criminals
had disguised themseles as Negroes and that innocent blacks had been
imprisoned and murdered for these crimes. But he also insisted on the
vital relevance of social conditions to explaining criminal behavior by
individual blacks. There was a lesson the American people had to learn:
"That where justice is denied, where poverty is enforced, where ignorance
prevails, and where any one class is made to feel that society is an
organized conspiracy to oppress, rob, and degrade them, neither persons
nor property will be safe." Douglass flatly denied the allegation that
"nature" had made blacks criminals. It was slavery that had produced
the "physically and mentally maimed and mutilated men" who appeared

in the police courts. It was slavery that took the Negro slave and "twisted his limbs, deformed his body, flattened his feet, and distorted his features, and made him, though black, no longer comely." Douglass did not equivocate in the choice between an explanation of crime in terms of innate characteristics and an environmentalist view. History, the oppression and cruelty of slavery, had crippled some blacks, but Douglass took his stand with those who believed in the perfectibility of men. "Time, education and training," he declared, would restore the crippled slave "to his natural proportions, for, though bruised and blasted, he is yet a man."

In the situation that black Americans then found themselves, what was to be done? To begin with, Douglass took issue with those who argued that blacks should take up arms in order to secure the vote. He had no illusions that those who disfranchised blacks represented simply "a few midnight assassins"; blacks, he asserted, would encounter "trained armies, skilled generals of the Confederate army, and in the last resort we should have to meet the Federal army." In Douglass's view black insurrection, in such circumstances, represented only madness.

As he had done earlier Douglass rejected once again the policy of mass exodus from the South. But he now added the qualification that he favored assistance to those who desired to emigrate to other parts of the country. The policy of diffusion, a policy of encouraging the distribution of blacks throughout America, was endorsed as a constructive response to the oppression directed against blacks in the South.

Beyond urging that both blacks and whites assist those wanting to migrate, Douglass at that point could not formulate policy offering short-range hope that the position blacks found themselves in could be changed. It was useful to use appropriate public occasions as a means of keeping the grievances of blacks before the country. Blacks could not relinquish the weapon of truth. And Douglass still clung to the Republican party, believing that "if any good is to come to us politically it will be through that party," although he had no apology to make for having hoped that the Democratic administration of Grover Cleveland would curb racist brutality. Basically, what he offered was the refusal to despair of the ultimate triumph of democracy. If blacks would cultivate the work ethic, "toil and trust, throw away whiskey and tobacco, improve the opportunities that we have, put away all extravagance, learn to live within our means," they would be able to call forth effective white allies who would support the black struggle for an equal chance.[8] As was true in the years before the Civil War, Douglass was committed to an alliance of blacks and whites, but in this new period he could articulate this strategy but could not design means of bringing it to life.

In the last year of his life Douglass returned to the theme of lynching. Some of his last strength was spent in exposing the "perfect epidemic of mob law and persecution" that he saw prevailing in the South, in analyzing the pretexts employed to justify lynching, and in considering the response of the southern white elite to the situation. He demonstrated that the basic aim of the lynchers was to render blacks powerless through disfranchisement. Douglass did not argue that blacks were never guilty of criminal acts, but he rejected the charge of criminality leveled against blacks as a group. In answer to the charge that blacks collectively constituted a criminal class Douglass pleaded "not guilty." He attacked the reliability of those who argued that the white South was menaced by black rapists. First of all, the main witness against the black man was the lynch mob, and this mob, frenzied by its own fury and setting itself up as judge, jury, and executioner, was hardly a competent witness. Douglass, however, impeached the testimony of others in the South, not usually found in the lynch mobs, who justified lynching. Those who refused to obey the Constitution, who violated oaths to carry out the laws, and justified denying blacks their right to vote did not inspire belief. Douglass further answered the charge by asserting that it strained belief to hold that blacks had suddenly become a class of rapists when this was contrary to the history of blacks in America. During the Civil War, while most white southern men served with the Confederate army, the charge had never been made. It was simply impossible to believe that blacks had in a few years been transformed into a criminal people.

Basic to Douglass's argument was his analysis of the changing nature of the rationalization the racists offered. Turning back to the Reconstruction era, Douglass recalled that although the enemies of Radical Reconstruction sought every means to win sympathy for their cause they did not then raise the cry of rape. They justified violence against blacks initially on the grounds that blacks planned insurrection and that they intended to murder all white people. The propaganda of the period conjured up visions of race war, but it did not charge blacks with sexual assault upon white women. When facts showed that the black conspiracies did not exist, white supremacists shifted to the argument that violence was justified to prevent the supremacy of the Negro over the white race. Why now, then, did the white South turn to the charge of rape? Douglass's answer was that the old tales of black insurrection and black supremacy were no longer serviceable. In the 1880s and 1890s whites were no longer so likely to believe that blacks plotted insurrection against all the tremendous might of local, state, and national authority, and clearly blacks were not about to dominate politically the affairs of the

South. A new rationalization for violence was necessary, and it was found in the rape charge. The new justification not only served to excuse the barbarism of the lynch mob but also supported the campaign to deny black Americans legislatively and judicially all protection under the Constitution.

What was the perspective for black America? Douglass did not encourage excessive optimism. The immediate future appeared to him "dark and troubled," with Republicans and Democrats generating proposals for disfranchisement. Douglass, however, continued to oppose the colonization of black Americans in Africa or elsewhere. In his view the colonization movement undermined the struggle for democracy at home without offering realistic prospects of freedom and opportunity in the lands to which blacks would migrate. The race question could be solved not if it was seen as the "Negro problem" but only if it was understood as a national problem that challenged all Americans to produce a solution consistent with democratic and Christian principles. At the end Douglass appealed to white Americans to be true to the democratic heritage, to give up their racial prejudice, and to "let the organic law of the land be honestly sustained and obeyed." Douglass, after all, did not ask so very much. Whites were "only required to undo the evil they have done, in order to solve this problem." Douglass offered a powerful indictment. If blacks were treated according to fundamental standards of justice and decency America would be impregnable. "Your Republic will stand and flourish forever," he assured his fellow Americans, if they would but banish the idea of one class ruling over another and would recognize that the rights of the humblest deserved protection as well as the rights of the mighty.[9]

T. Thomas Fortune, the editor of the *New York Age* and the *New York Negro World*, was a post-Reconstruction black leader whose response to white violence differed somewhat from that of Douglass. Born a slave in 1856, as a boy in Marianna, Florida, Fortune had been lastingly affected by the Ku Klux Klan terror that prevailed during the late 1860s.[10] Writing in the 1880s, Fortune had as his starting point the recognition of the terrible violence inflicted on blacks in the South. It was Fortune's view that southern whites had been educated to regard themselves as the holders of power and to view blacks merely as subjects. That training had led to "that exhibition of barbarity on the part of the South and impotence on the part of the government which makes us go to Roumania and the Byzantine court for fit parallel." Fortune flung out the accusation of treason against the racists who engaged in violence: "If we may not call the violence, the assassinations, which have disgraced the South, *treason,* by what fitter name, pray shall we call it? If the nullification of the letters and spirit of the amendments of the Federal Constitution by the conquered South was not renewed *treason,* what was it? What is it?" Fortune further observed that the whites of the South had shown their superiority "in the superlative excellencies of murder, usurpation and robbery" and that blacks knew very well that they were disfranchised by violent means. How to react to this violence? The situation would be remedied either by violence or by recourse to reason, and Fortune declared that "no man who loves his country would sanction violence in the adjudication of rights save as a last resort." If violence was not the preferred remedy, neither was emigration to Africa. Fortune asserted:

> The colored man is in the South to stay there. He will not leave it voluntarily and he cannot be driven out. He had no voice in being carried into the South, but he will have a very loud voice in any attempt to put him out. The expatriation of 5,000,000 to 6,000,000 people to an alien country needs only to be suggested to create mirth and ridicule. The white men of the South had better make up their minds that the black man will remain in the South just as long as corn will tassel and cotton will bloom into whiteness. The talk about the black people being brought to this country to prepare themselves to evangelize Africa is so much religious nonsense boiled down to a very sycophantic platitude. . . . The black people of this country are Americans, not Africans; and any wholesale expatriation of them is altogether out of the question.

Fortune argued that self-interest required the white South to alter its racial policies. Mob violence discouraged immigrants from coming to the South and led businessmen who might otherwise invest in the area to take their money elsewhere. No Dixie politician, Fortune believed, could gain national support for high office, given the South's prevailing disorderly condition. "Thoughtful, sober people," he observed, "will not entrust power to men who sanction mob law, and who rise to high honor by conniving at or participating in assassination and murder."

The strategy Fortune urged upon blacks centered around political independence as the means by which blacks would no longer be confronted by a politically monolithic white majority. The point was that racial "clannishness" must be avoided and that Afro-Americans, like other ethnic groups, needed to embrace an "assimilation of sentiment" in which ethnic loyalty did not require adherence to one party. For blacks a monolithic political stance had the consequence of evoking a monolithic white response. Fortune was convinced that "the massing of black means the massing of white by contrast." Assimilation meant independence, an independence that would lead to Americanization. In the situation of the 1880s, where blacks could no longer expect federal protection, it was necessary that blacks maneuver between the political parties, making clear that their support was not to be taken for granted. Fortune urged that "the colored vote must be made as uncertain a quantity as the German and Irish vote." He also argued that blacks should pay more attention to their local interests and recognize that "the citizen of a State is far more sovereign than the citizen of the United States." The state was "a real, tangible reality" whereas the United States was merely an abstraction.

Though Fortune argued for political independence, it was in effect mainly an argument against commitment to the Republican party. He outlined a telling indictment of Republican betrayal. He began by noting that blacks had voted for Rutherford B. Hayes and yet Hayes and "his adversaries turned the colored voters of the South over to the bloodthirsty minority of that section." But according to Fortune, Hayes represented merely an instance of Republican infidelity:

> The Republican party has degenerated into an ignoble scramble for place and power. It has forgotten the principles for which Sumner contended, and for which Lincoln died. It betrayed the cause for which Douglass, Garrison and others labored, in the blind policy it pursued in reconstructing the rebellious states. It made slaves freemen and freemen slaves in the same breath by conferring the franchise and withholding the guarantees to insure its exercise; it betrayed its trust in permitting thousands of innocent men to be slaughtered without declaring the South in rebellion, and in pardoning murderers, whom tardy justice had consigned to a felon's dungeon. It is even now powerless to insure an honest expression of the vote of the colored citizen.

Fortune quickly added that Bourbon democracy was "a curse to our land" because it placed itself in opposition to human freedom and universal brotherhood. It was "a fundamental impossibility" for a black person to be a Bourbon, white-supremacist Democrat, but a black individual could very well become a "progressive Democrat." What Fortune was advocating was not so much that blacks form an independent bloc in politics but that black voters be found on both sides of local political contests. Blacks were obligated fully to integrate politically with the southern white population. Until this was done, he believed, "their path will lie in darkness and perhaps in blood."

Given the position he took in the 1880s, it is not strange that Fortune later allied himself with Booker T. Washington. This alliance may partly have had its roots in Washington's financial support of the newspapers Fortune edited, but it was also grounded in Fortune's view of the situation facing Afro-Americans. Already in the 1880s Fortune, though not rejecting higher academic education for black youth, maintained that "elementary and industrial" education was most needed.[11] But support for Washington also had deeper sources. Fortune favored black participation in politics and would not relinquish the claim to constitutional rights. But he proposed to operate within the constraint that racial matters were no longer viewed as a national question. Blacks had to find the ways effectively to come to terms with their white neighbors in the South. Political independence appeared a useful strategy so long as the door to political action was not completely shut. Assuming as Fortune did that there was little point in pressuring the federal government to act once the door of political action was shut, the Washington strategy of "accommodation" appeared to make sense. Blacks were to continue along the line of industrial education and to seek independence not through politics but rather through economic self-development. Fortune's thinking represented a policy in the process of transition from the militancy of Douglass to the "realism" of Washington.

Fortune proceeded from advocacy of black political independence to alignment with the leadership of Booker T. Washington. In his last years he edited the Garveyite *Negro World*. The evolution of journalist John Edward Bruce, who proceeded from championing black rights to supporting the nationalism of Marcus Garvey, was somewhat similar. But Bruce was perhaps most noteworthy in his upholding of retaliatory violence against the violence of racism. In 1889 he was especially forceful in an address he made to a Washington, D.C., audience. "The Man who will not fight for the protection of his wife and children," he declared, "is a *coward* and deserves to be ill treated. The man who takes his life in his hand and stands up for what he knows to be right will always command the respect of his enemy." Self-defense, as Bruce saw it, was proof of the falsity of racism. He stated that in the existing state of affairs "the only hope, the only salvation for the Negro, is to be found in a resort to force under wise and discreet leaders. He must sooner or later come to this in order to set at rest for all time to come the charge that he is a moral coward." Bruce explained that he hated "nambypambyism or anything that looks like temporizing" and believed that blacks should not be "rash or indiscreet," but he carefully stated what needed to be done:

> Under the Mosaic dispensation, it was the custom to require "an eye for an eye and a tooth for a tooth." Under a no less Barbarous civilization than that which existed at that period of the world's history, let the Negro require at the hands of every white murderer in the South or elsewhere a life for a life. If they burn your houses, burn theirs. If they kill your wives and children, kill theirs. Pursue them relentlessly. Meet force with force, everywhere it is offered. If they demand blood, exchange with them until they are satiated. By a vigorous adherence to this course, the shedding of human blood by white men will soon become a thing of the past. Wherever and whenever the Negro shows himself to be a man he can always command the respect even of a cutthroat.

Bruce did not merely counsel individual action but rather stressed collective action, declaring: "Organized resistance to organized resistance is the best remedy for the solution of the vexed problem of the century which to me seems practicable and feasible."

Bruce passionately indicted the system of lynching. In a piece condemning the refusal of white American Christianity to speak out against racial wrongs, Bruce wrote:

> Since the close of the late war of rebellion there has been going on in the South a systematic slaughter of innocent Negro men, women and children by white men, who control and direct the social and political affairs of that section of this country. It has been estimated that more than fifty thousand of such murders have been committed in the South within the past twenty-six years, and the cases are rare indeed where the guilty and bloody assassins have been apprehended when known, or punished for their crimes if apprehended.

In a speech he gave in 1890 to the Afro-American League he traced the features of the "modern barbarian, who is dignified by the title 'White Citizen.' " He placed this in historic perspective:

> They now roast objectionable Negroes alive in certain portions of that Christian section of our God-blessed (?) country. I have read of the deeds of cruelty committed by one religious faction against another, of how thirty thousand were burned at the stake in one

day. How men, women, and children were thrown from high em-
inences upon wagons filled with sharp pointed spikes which lacerated
their bodies and destroyed their lives; how men were hung with their
heads downward until life was extinct; of Nero the tyrant and bigot
who fiddled while the seven hilled city burned. But this modern
barbarism practiced upon the Negro in Christian America by white
men who boast of high civilization makes *me* "tremble for this
country when I remember that God is just."

In 1901 in an article entitled "The Blood Red Record" Bruce reviewed
the modern history of lynching. He itemized the twelve recorded instances
of burning at the stake, involving fourteen individuals. He outlined the
record for the year 1900, listing the names of individual victims, which
indicated that of 117 persons lynched only eighteen were even charged
with rape. He quoted an interview with the Chinese minister to the United
States, Mr. Wu Ting-fang, in which the diplomat referred to lynching as
"strictly an American institution," an institution in which peculiarly the
law officers protected the mob rather than the prisoner. And Bruce was
forthright about the role of northern indifference in perpetuating
lynching:

> The difference in the estimate of the white men of the South and the
> white men of the North, regarding the Negro, is that the former is
> frank, outspoken in the conviction that the Negro is fundamentally
> inferior to the white men, and, therefore, can never be his equal,
> while the white men of the North, who *almost* believe the same
> thing, patronize him, and in a half-hearted manner call him *brother*.
> Yet when this black *brother* is burned at the stake by his white
> Southern brother, his white Northern brother does not take on nearly
> so much, nor express himself with half the vigor, earnestness and
> bitterness that he does when Christian missionaries are massacred
> in China or when the serfs of Russia are brutally whipped with the
> knout in the salt mines of Siberia, or when the Armenian brethren
> are murdered by the hundred for *Christ's sake* by the unspeakable
> Turk.

Bruce asked why this was so, and his answer was that the Republican
party for reasons "largely commercial" had suspended the work that had
called it into being. "It is no longer the party of human rights." He asked
if expansion, ship subsidies, the building of a great navy or a standing
army were more important than protecting the rights of American citi-

zens. At least implicitly Bruce saw that the priorities of imperalism had displaced constitutional rights.

Self-defense and retaliatory violence, as Bruce saw it, were components of a broader strategy of racial unity. He explained: "The Negro must preserve his race identity, must unite his energies, talent and money, and make common cause.... Unity and harmony of sentiment and feeling, of act and deed, are the levers that must of necessity overturn American caste-prejudice." Blacks would approach a solution to racial injustice through means, he said, of cooperation, organization, and agitation. Bruce also struck a note that foreshadowed later developments in a call for internationalizing the American racial issue. He urged black leaders to "go abroad and recite the story of our wrongs at the hands of a race which murmured and fought because the heel of oppression was upon their necks." Their purpose should be to "make the name 'American' a bye word and a reproach among the Christian nations of the old world." There was in John Edward Bruce an echo of David Walker, the militant black abolitionist, who saw slavery as a fundamental feature of the American system. Bruce was plainspoken in declaring that "for more than a century *America* has lived a *lie*," and he saw abstract good intentions in the post–Civil War amendments, but he believed firmly they did not reflect any actual intent to extend the rights of citizenship to blacks.[12]

The growing white terror of the post-Reconstruction period also evoked a response that looked to long-term identification with Africa as the appropriate position of black Americans. Identification with Africa was not simply a reaction to violence. Many blacks, emerging out of the era of slavery, quite naturally viewed Africa as their ancestral homeland, the land of their origins from whence they had been kidnapped and brought to America. A special feeling for Africa was an expression of an embryonic sense of national identity and consciousness. But the interest in Africa was also shaped by the circumstances facing blacks following the crushing of Radical Reconstruction. Blacks, having been granted the forms of citizenship rights but largely denied the substance, might see Africa as a sanctuary from a violent America in which they would never truly be free. Africa could be seen as presenting an opportunity to build a new free black nation, and it was logical to believe that black nationhood in Africa would strengthen the position of those blacks remaining in the United States. In the late years of the nineteenth century, with its flowering of nationalism, blacks were among those who joined in believing that national identity and purpose were the path to power. The nationalist movement had produced a unified Germany and Italy and called forth from European Jews the Zionist striving for return to Palestine as the only possible escape from anti-Semitism. From Afro-Americans it called forth articulation of black nationalism, and that nationalism was most often in these years focused upon Africa. At the very least, a movement of identification with Africa would underscore blacks' discontent with conditions of terror in America and might lead sober white people to realize that brutal treatment of blacks could lead to loss of that work force upon which white society depended. The call to identify with Africa represented the emergence of national conscious-ness, offered hope to those who believed it futile to struggle against racism in the United States, but also served as a means of protest and pressure and was thus a part of the struggle for the full freedom of black Americans.

In this era the foremost articulator of African identification was Bishop Henry McNeal Turner of Georgia. During the war Turner had served as chaplain of the First Regiment, United States Colored Troops, coming to this post from his position as pastor of the Israel Bethel Church in Washington, D.C. He was strongly committed to a sense of racial pride, writing of blacks in August 1865: "I claim for them superior ability." He recognized the ability and at the same time was aware of the force of circumstances in denying expression to ability. Early in 1865 he wrote: "Oh, how the foul curse of slavery has blighted the natural greatness of my race. It has not only depressed and horror-streaked the should-be glowing countenance of thousands, but it has almost transformed many into inhuman appearance." A few years later Bishop Turner had expe-rienced firsthand the agony of the racist counterrevolution against Re-construction and was himself expelled from his seat in the Georgia legislature to which he had been lawfully elected. At one point Turner encountered a young black minister, Robert Alexander, who had been repeatedly beaten and stabbed by whites in Opelika, Alabama. Turner wrote that Alexander resembled "a *lump of curdled blood*" and added: "O God! where is our civilization? Is this Christendom, or is it hell? Pray for us."[13]

As radical rule was destroyed in Georgia, with the federal government refusing to intervene, Henry Turner looked to other paths along which Afro-Americans might advance, and increasingly his perspective for the future centered around Africa. At the time of his ouster from the legis-lature in 1868 Turner gave vent to his bitter resentment of white Georgia society. Cooperation of white and black no longer seemed a likely pros-pect in that state, and Turner urged a new course for blacks to follow:

The black man cannot protect a country, if the country doesn't protect him; and if, tomorrow, a war should arise, I would not raise a musket to defend a country where my manhood is denied. The fashionable way in Georgia, when hard work is to be done, is, for the white man to sit at his ease, while the black man does the work; but, sir, I will say this much to the colored men of Georgia, as, if I should be killed in this campaign, I may have no opportunity of telling them at any other time: Never lift a finger nor raise a hand in defence of Georgia, unless Georgia acknowledges that you are men, and invests you with the rights pertaining to manhood. Pay your taxes, however, obey all orders from your employers, take good counsel from friends, work faithfully, earn an honest living, and show, by your conduct, that you can be good citizens.

This was plainly not a strategy of direct confrontation. Turner added the further comment that if the black members were indeed expelled from the Georgia legislature he would call a "colored Convention" and urge his friends to "send North for carpet baggers and Yankees and...to Europe and all over the world for immigrants" and that blacks in Georgia would elect the new arrivals to office, "in preference to sending a Georgian there."[14]

Turner never proposed that blacks relinquish their claim to constitutional rights. Even during the last years of Reconstruction he maintained this position. In 1874 he expressed in poetic form his reaction to the white terror:

> The Freedman is dying 'mid carnage and gore
> God of our fathers' hast thou given us o'er
> In this bloody embrace, to these tigers a prey?
> Let vengeance be thine! thou wilt repay.
> Away with the thought!—for this is no dream;
> They war against civil rights! that is their theme.
> But soon will they cringe, as we know full well
> The crisis has come and the tolling bells tell
> We will not yield, not in fear of the grave,
> The rights that belong to the free and the brave.[15]

But some months after writing this poem Turner remarked in the journal of the American Colonization Society that once blacks had learned the doctrines of Christianity and were educated to take control of Africa they would hear the voice of "a mysterious Providence," saying to them:

"Return to the land of our fathers."[16] The following year, 1876, Turner accepted an appointment as an honorary vice-president of the Colonization Society. Turner's commitment to Africa is perhaps nowhere more clearly explained than in comments published during 1883 in the *Christian Recorder*. Turner's interest in Africa was related to the extent of racial terror aimed at black citizens in the United States, but that interest also had a broader basis. In reply to views expressed by Benjamin Tanner that colonization was a moot issue because blacks had no desire to leave the United States, Turner took issue with Tanner for covering up the brutalities inflicted upon Afro-Americans. Both the North and the South, Turner charged, connived at obscuring the extent of racial violence. He asserted that "the half has never been told" of what had been inflicted upon blacks. "There is not a night, or a day either, the year round," he declared, "that our people are not most brutally being murdered. The reign of blood and slaughter is but little less than it was ten years ago, if any." Turner was angered by the charge that his interest in Africa was motivated solely by a desire to make the continent "a city of refuge." He denied the charge, but he also asserted the right of a people, any people, to seek refuge from persecution, affirming, "Yes, I would make Africa the place of refuge, because I see no other shelter from the stormy blast, from the red tide of persecution, from the horrors of American prejudice." He searched back into history and found that "self-interest, self-preservation, and self in all its aspects" constituted the "germ thoughts" of almost all colonization and emigration movements. He attempted to put his critics on the defensive by demanding that they confront the alternatives he viewed as the only options open to blacks. Either there would be "war, efforts at extermination, anarchy, horror and a wail to heaven" or else there would be intermarriage that would eliminate racial conflict. He challenged his critics to come up with a plan that would lead to intermarriage. Otherwise, he observed, "there is no peaceable future here for the negro." It is striking that, leaving colonization aside, Turner, as did white supremacists, saw intermarriage as the crucial issue in determining the future of race relations.

Turner went on to add the broader basis upon which he would develop colonization. He began with the proposition that no race could be respected until it had demonstrated its capacity to establish a government of its own. Here was the voice of an authentic nineteenth-century nationalist. Ignoring the achievements of the great medieval African kingdoms, Turner asserted that the Negro had not yet demonstrated that capacity and that until he did so "he will be a mere scullion in the eyes of the world." The second proposition was that American slavery was a providential institution and that God intended slavery as "the primal factor" in the civilizing and Christianizing of Africa. Although he did not use the term, the implication was that slavery had created in blacks a "chosen people" who would do God's work. And, speaking in the language of moral absolutes, Turner declared that whoever opposed the return to Africa of enough blacks to begin the new mission "is fighting the God of the universe face to face."

The third principle advanced by Turner was that in an era when Western society was turning its attention to Africa it was time that the United States, too, "should awake to her share of duty in this great movement," remembering that the country owed blacks some forty billion dollars for services rendered during slavery. Finally, Turner dismissed as absurd the contention that the African climate posed an obstacle to emigration, and he made clear that he did not advocate a wholesale movement of Afro-Americans to Africa. It would be enough that five or ten thousand a year emigrate. Here he returned to the harsh realities of American racism and presented migration as the alternative to violence. It would be enough every year if merely "those who are sent to the penitentiary, hung and lynched for nothing," were taken to Africa. With such individuals alone he could "establish a government, build a country and raise a national symbol that could give character to our people everywhere." To this statement of position Turner added his urging that blacks assemble in convention, "a civil and moral convention" rather than a meeting for political purposes.[17]

In 1893 Turner was the driving force in arranging a national black convention. Meeting in Cincinnati, this assembly gathered at a time when statistics showed a steady increase in the frequency of lynchings, and the cause of citizenship rights had suffered a major setback in the defeat in Congress of the Force Bill, a measure to establish federal machinery for the enforcement of the right to vote. Turner no doubt saw the convention as an opportunity to rally support for African colonization, but clearly the central factor in bringing the delegates together was the mounting terrorization facing Afro-Americans. In the call for the convention Turner had declared: "The revolting, hideous, monstrous, unnatural, brutal and shocking crimes charged upon us daily, on the one hand, and the reign of mobs, lynchers, and fire-fiends, and midnight and mid-day assassins on the other, necessitated a national convention on our part, for the purpose of crystallizing our sentiments and unifying our endeavors for better conditions in this country, or a change of base for existence." This convention was not simply a forum for black nationalism but rather a meeting, in the tradition of black conventions, that sought to focus public attention upon racial injustice, at the same time offering an opportunity for debate about a viable strategy for the future. In his opening remarks to the delegates Turner spoke at length about lynching and about the charge of rape that was most often given by white supremacists as the justification for lynching. He began by observing that "it is known to all present that not a week, and at times scarcely a day, has passed in the last three or four years but what some colored man has been hung, shot or burned by mobs of lynchers, and justified or excused upon the plea that they had outraged some white married or single woman, or some little girl going to or from school." Turner was not concerned with showing the falsity and hypocrisy of the charge that white women were threatened by black rapists. Asserting that if the charge was true "God has no attribute that will side with us" and that the centuries-long white rape of black women was no justification, Turner proposed that an inquiry be made as to the facts. He also suggested that if the charge proved true it was the responsibility of black leadership to denounce the practice and that if that did not suffice blacks should take charge of severely punishing those guilty of rape. Granting that blacks might be guilty, Turner argued that if blacks were criminals the basic responsibility should be laid at the door of white society and that such criminal behavior was proof that being in America had corrupted blacks. He was turning the justification for lynching into support for his position favoring return to Africa. Turner pointed to Africa and insisted that "the world will have to admit that they are the purest people, outside of polygamy, in their connubial and virgin morals, upon the face of the globe." He told his audience that white women from both America and Britain had assured him that no respectable white woman would be "improperly approached" in Africa. Turner further stated that the crime of rape was also largely alien to the experience of blacks in the West Indies, informing the convention that in the islands only one charge of rape had been made against a black man since 1832.

If rape was committed by some blacks in the United States, this phenomenon was a product of the social environment. "Like begets like," declared Turner; blacks were degraded by the conditions imposed upon them in the United States, degraded at the ballot box, and, by segregation and discrimination in access to public facilities, "degraded in most of the large cities by being compelled to rent houses in alleys and the most disreputable streets." Degradation had consequences, and Turner found it possible "that in many instances we are guilty of doing a series of infamous things that we would not be guilty of, if our environments were different." He believed that change in the moral conduct of blacks required a change in their surroundings, rejecting the idea that blacks "will ever stand out in the symmetrical majesty of higher manhood, half free and half slave." Turner's analysis led him to his "African preferences," to focusing attention upon the development of a homeland "where we can cultivate the higher properties or virtues of our manhood."

Whatever his view of the allegation that blacks were guilty of sexual crimes against white women, Turner unreservedly condemned lynching as "an act of barbarism." He took his stand with the elementary legal precept that a person was innocent until "tried by an impartial process of law" and convicted. He had only contempt for the justification given for some lynchings that the victim had confessed his crime to the mob. "Confessed it to whom?" Turner asked. "Confessed it to a set of bloody-handed murderers, just as though a set of men who were cruel enough to take the life of another were too moral to tell a lie." Turner found strange the circumstances that the lynchers could never be identified but the newspapers knew every detail of a lynching, "can advance what they are going to do, how and when it was done, how the rope broke, how many balls entered the Negro's body, how loud he prayed, how piteously he begged, what he said, how long he was left hanging, how many composed the mob, the number that were masked, whether they were prominent citizens or not, how the fire was built that burnt the raper, how the Negro was tied, how he was thrown into the fire, and the whole transaction." In Turner's view lynching had two possible objectives, either to prevent blacks from speaking in their own defense or, more fundamentally, to exterminate blacks as a group.

Apart from emigration, Turner's only specific remedy for lynching was the alternative of having the rapist castrated and then turning him loose "to live and remain as a monument of his folly and madness." At least that policy would prevent the taking of lives. Mutilation, according to Turner, was the best that could be hoped for by a black accused of rape in the United States.

Beyond submitting to castration in order to escape death, Turner offered the option of moving to Africa. To remain passively in America was to grant that blacks were unfit to live as a free people. Passivity was degrading, but Turner considered physical resistance to be madness. Only an idiot would contemplate a few million ex-slaves grappling with sixty million whites, of "two hundred and sixty-five millions of dollars battling with one hundred billion of dollars."[18] What was left was colonization. Turner was not simply abandoning those blacks who remained behind in America; he was genuinely convinced that tangible links to Africa would strengthen the position of American blacks.

This 1893 convention has been judged by at least one scholar as a failure, and from the standpoint that this meeting failed to project a unified program for the future, could not resolve the debate between integrationists and emigrationists, that judgment is at least accurate in part.[19] But perhaps the most striking feature of this meeting is that a convention, convened by black America's most prominent emigrationist, served as a forum for protest against injustice and terror and set forth demands directly relevant to the racial struggle in this country. The convention adopted a resolution urging Congress to enact legislation under which federal courts would take jurisdiction of cases of mob violence "in which life is lost or property destroyed, or both, or where parties are whipped, tortured or otherwise maltreated." United States marshals would be empowered to employ detectives for the purpose of identifying the lynch mobs. The gathering also unanimously approved a resolution, offered by a South Carolina clergyman, calling upon every black man, woman, and child in the United States to set aside May 31 as a day of fasting and prayer for an end to oppression. A telegram, sent by a group of St. Louis blacks, was read to the convention, urging support for a constitutional amendment indemnifying losses of life and property to mob violence and proposing that a delegation be sent to Europe to publicize the conditions facing black Americans.[20]

At its final session the Cincinnati convention considered and adopted a resolution dealing jointly with the issues of rape and lynching. The resolution condemned assault upon "female virtue, by whomsoever perpetrated and against whomsoever directed," and pledged support for the arrest and conviction of "the foul fiend who sacrifices his manhood to the coercive lust of his passion." But condemned also was the "cowardly resort" of lynch law that had reached so low as to burn victims alive. The convention also heard a report from a special investigating committee assigned to examine the charge of rape against blacks. The committee noted that in some instances the charge was supported by evidence but contended that serious doubt of guilt existed in 20 percent of the cases and that in 10 percent the accused black was innocent. The committee took its basic stand on the concept that the dignity of law must be upheld. The committee also noted what most white Americans preferred to ignore, that in a number of instances black women were assaulted by white men and that no punishment whatever for such crimes was inflicted. A specific incident cited was that of the convicted white rapist, Tom Hill, of Spring Place, Georgia, who was set at liberty by a mob that forcibly broke into the prison where he was confined. The report of this special committee was extremely restrained and judicious and if anything tended to understatement rather than exaggeration. The tenor of this report made clear that this meeting was dominated not by radicals and agitators but by cautious and quite respectable leaders of the black community.[21]

Before adjourning, the convention also warmly received a communication from the white veteran of Radical Reconstruction, Judge Albion Tourgee. Tourgee centered his attention not so much upon the question of emigration as upon the factors that impelled some Afro-Americans to consider leaving the United States. He outlined a bill of particulars, itemizing the forms of oppression inflicted upon blacks. He bitterly condemned lynching and the failure of public authority to punish the lynchers. Tourgee observed that three alternative courses of action were urged in response to the facts, one alternative that of outright submission, the second that of direct resistance, and the third that of expatriation to Africa. Outright submission was obviously unacceptable to any self-respecting people, and confrontation would "only invite extinction at the hands of the mob, backed by the power of the States, supported ultimately by the Army and Navy of the United States." As for emigration Tourgee's view was that a white, Christian America that would not deal fairly and humanely with citizens within its boundaries was likely to be even more brutal in its treatment of aliens thousands of miles away in Africa. By implication Tourgee also counseled rejection of any notion that an alliance of blacks and poor whites was a solution to the racial issue. He emphasized that white employers and laborers had a common interest in maintaining the subjection of blacks. Tourgee's advice was to insist upon justice. Relying upon the force of public opinion was to be preferred to begging for mercy. He assured the members of the convention that the American people had learned that wrong must be righted and that though they were slow to anger they had in the Civil War, after all, sacrificed "the full measure of blood the lash had shed, in order to purchase liberty for the oppressed and put upon him the robe of citizenship, by which they meant to secure him from injustice and oppression." The delegates applauded a policy statement that largely continued the Douglass policy of demanding that American society be true to its antislavery heritage and fulfill the pledges made during the years of Civil War and Reconstruction. This convention, though offering a platform for advocates of emigration, confirmed the fact that the struggle for full equality in the United States still dominated black perspectives for the future.[22]

The Cincinnati convention did not adjourn, however, before hearing from Bishop Turner a fervent restatement of the case for emigration that stated bluntly some truths about the depths of American racism. The

Cincinnati Commercial Gazette summarized some of the points Turner made:

> He knew of at least two million of black men and women who were virtually dying to return to Africa. He could fill five hundred steamships in a month of noble-hearted colored men and women who were hungering and thirsting to return to Africa. He said this Nation had brought us here, and worked us for 250 years and turned us loose, and left us in a powerless degradation, and is now entailing upon us a proscription, and is enacting laws that make our existence worse than slavery, for in slavery times white men would protect their negroes from self-interest; now we are the prey of everybody, even foreigners, who would come here from the ends of the earth. He could prove by mathematical calculation that this nation owed the negro $49,000,000,000 for work performed and services rendered, and would have to disgorge some of that money in process of time in helping us to return to the land of our ancestors or in manufacturing missiles and engines for our extermination, unless it accorded us manhood equality, for the negro would be satisfied with nothing less than full-fledged citizenship.

Turner saw little merit in the argument that blacks should be able to migrate to any portion of the United States. The nation was contaminated by racism for, as Turner explained it,

> where he can go in this country I do not know, for the abominable and inhuman decision of the U.S. Supreme Court affects the status of the negro all over it. Men need not talk about the South any more than the North, for the North indorses everything that the South does and the South indorses everything the North does that is degrading to the negro. I live in the South, and there are thousands of good people, and many of them tell me that the first thing the negro can do is to seek more congenial quarters, for it is not their intention to accord to the negro the same as they accord to the white man, civilly or politically.

Turner fused a hatred of racism with a sense that this ideology was irrevocably linked to American society.[23]

In the last two decades of the nineteenth century concern with lynching was a consistent theme running through the public activities of practically every black leader. But to be effective concern had to be transformed into a vocal movement and public opinion aroused both at home and abroad. A prime factor in building that movement was the work of a dynamic and fearless woman, Ida B. Wells-Barnett. Her activity and leadership served to connect the struggle of the 1890s with the new civil rights movement that emerged after the turn of the century. She entered boldly into the public argument concerning lynching, providing specific evidence as to lynching's barbarous nature and tearing apart the rationalization that lynching protected white womanhood. Ida B. Wells-Barnett countered racist myth with irrefutable fact.

Already in the mid-1880s Ida B. Wells-Barnett eloquently expressed her revulsion at instances of racist violence. At the time of the 1886 Carroll County, Mississippi, lynchings she wrote in her diary: "O God, when will these massacres cease—it was only because they had attempted to assassinate a white man (and for just cause I supposed). Colored men rarely attempt to wreak vengeance on a white one unless he has provoked it unduly." Later that same year she wrote a newspaper article about an incident that occurred in Jackson, Tennessee. "A colored woman accused of poisoning a white man," she reported, "was taken from the county jail and stripped naked and hung up in the courthouse yard and her body riddled with bullets and left exposed to view! O my God! Can such things be and no justice for it?" The evidence against the woman was that rat poison had been found in her house.[24]

Wells, born in Mississippi in 1862, attended the Methodist Freedman's Aid Society's Rust College and became a teacher. Moving to Memphis she became editor of the newspaper *Free Speech*. She first drew national attention following the lynching in Memphis on March 9, 1892, of three black men, "three of the best specimens of young since-the-war Afro-American manhood," whose crime had been to operate a grocery store in competition with a white merchant. The white competitor led a raid upon the black-owned business, accompanied by police officers in civilian clothing. The blacks believed they were under assault, fired upon the whites, and three of the officers were wounded. Although the policemen recovered, the president, manager, and clerk of the store, Tom Moss, Will Stewart, and Calvin McDowell, were taken from the Memphis jail and lynched. This occurrence was one of numberless incidents refuting the contention that black achievement was the effective answer to racism. According to Wells-Barnett, although the Memphis black community seethed with rage concerning this lynching, the city's black ministers, newspaper editors, and other leaders "counselled obedience to the law which did not protect them." *Free Speech,* however, went one step further and advised blacks to leave Memphis, and as a result a number of blacks did indeed leave the city. As a newspaper that exposed the facts about lynching, the *Free Speech* irritated the city's white racist leadership, and in a few weeks the pretext was found that would result in forcing Miss Wells-Barnett also to leave Memphis. On May 21, 1892, *Free Speech* had carried an editorial noting that since the paper's last issue eight blacks had been lynched, three for killing a white man "and five on the same old racket—the new alarm about raping white women." The editorial went on to observe that nobody in the South believed "the old thread bare lie" that black men raped white women. And then came a line that infuriated the white supremacists: "If Southern men are not careful, they will overreach themselves and public sentiment will have a reaction; a conclusion will then be reached which will be very damaging to the moral reputation of their women." The racist response to this comment was to threaten violence. The *Memphis Daily Commercial* announced that "the fact that a black scoundrel is allowed to live and utter such loathsome and repulsive calumnies is a volume of evidence as to the wonderful patience of Southern whites. But we have had enough of it." The *Evening Scimitar* declared that patience was not a virtue and then exhibited something of the substance of white-supremacist "civilization": "If the negroes themselves do not apply the remedy without delay it will be the duty of those whom he has attacked to tie the wretch who utters these calumnies to a stake at the intersection of Main and Madison Sts., brand him in the forehead with a hot iron and perform upon him a surgical operation with a pair of tailor's shears." Wells-Barnett later reported that Memphis's leading businessmen met at the Cotton Exchange and threatened the owners of *Free Speech* with lynching. Her partner was forced to flee, and she herself, away on vacation in New York, was advised she could not return. Creditors seized the paper's offices and sold off the equipment.[25]

Driven out of business, Ida B. Wells-Barnett took up a new career as crusader against lynching, taking her message before any audience that would listen. She published her first pamphlet about lynching, *Southern Horrors*, in 1892. Introducing the pamphlet was a letter from Frederick Douglass, expressing both the hope and the despair that marked his last years. Douglass praised Wells-Barnett for having "dealt with the facts with cool painstaking fidelity and left those naked and uncontradicted facts to speak for themselves." He noted that, if American conscience were only half alive, "a scream of horror, shame and indignation would rise to heaven wherever your pamphlet shall be read." But he observed that even crime had the power to reproduce itself and that sometimes it appeared that blacks were deserted "by earth and Heaven." Yet there was no counsel of retreat. Douglass's conclusion was that "we must still think, speak and work, and trust in the power of a merciful God for final deliverance."[26]

Like Douglass, Ida B. Wells-Barnett sought to arouse the national conscience, but in her case the means to accomplish this was to concentrate upon the assembling and dissemination of information concerning specific instances of brutality against blacks. The muckraking movement has usually been seen as a crusade of white journalists who attempted to focus public opinion upon social problems requiring solution. Ida B. Wells-Barnett was true to the muckraking spirit, not simply denouncing injustices but carefully researching her facts and presenting them for public consideration. In *Southern Horrors* she told the story of what had happened in Memphis, quoting extensively from the white press, and added information about other lynchings that had recently occurred. This factual emphasis was also to be found in other pamphlets she was later to write. Her activity as a journalistic crusader against lynching was supplemented by many platform appearances, including talks she gave during two highly successful visits to England.[27] As earlier chattel slavery had become a matter of international concern, she used her eloquence to make lynching an international question.

In her writings and speeches Ida B. Wells-Barnett turned the charge of rape back upon the white supremacists, detailing instances of assaults upon black women. In *Southern Horrors* she contrasted two incidents that occurred in Nashville, one in which the state militia was called out to protect a white man charged with raping a black girl and another in which a black man, accused of raping white women, was brutally lynched, with the governor, the militia, and the police doing nothing to stop the violence.[28] Wells-Barnett dealt further with the question of rape against black women in an examination of lynching, *A Red Record*, published in 1895.[29]

While in England Ida B. Wells-Barnett was drawn into controversy with Frances Willard, the leader of the Women's Christian Temperance Union. Wells-Barnett drove home the point that in the interest of developing support among white southerners for the temperance crusade Frances Willard was willing to excuse acts of violence against blacks and other infringements of constitutional rights. The British public was informed of Willard's statement, during an 1890 meeting of the WCTU held in Atlanta, to the effect that it was not fair "that a plantation negro who can neither read nor write, whose ideas are bounded by the fence of his own field and the price of his own mule," should be entrusted with the ballot. Willard had further added that the white South deserved all possible sympathy because "the colored race multiplies like the locusts of Egypt" and because the safety of women and family was so menaced "that the men dare not go beyond the sight of their own roof tree." Ida B. Wells-Barnett charged Frances Willard with condoning "fraud and murder, rapine, shooting, hanging and burning; for all these things are done now by the Southern white people." The British were also informed that Frederick Douglass had denounced the statements made by Willard. When in an interview published in the *Westminster Gazette* Frances Willard attempted to refute the charge of indifference to lynching, Wells-Barnett returned to the attack, pointing to the fact that not a single black woman was admitted to the southern WCTU and that only in the *Gazette* interview was Willard moved to voice some criticism of lynching.

In *A Red Record* Wells-Barnett quoted chapter and verse from the record to document the charge that the leader of the WCTU had been silent about lynching until silence was no longer possible. Prior to the beginning of the public crusade against lynching, the WCTU "had no word, either of pity or protest; its great heart, which concerns itself about humanity the world over, was, towards our cause, pulseless as a stone." Even after public agitation against lynching had begun, she wrote, the WCTU at its 1894 convention in Cleveland had refused to adopt an antilynching resolution, and when later a statement on the issue appeared in the union's journal it was of very little use. The statement expressed the hope that the time would come "when no human being shall be condemned without due process of law" but balanced that against the hope that the time would also come "when the unspeakable outrages which have so often provoked such lawlessness shall be banished from the world, and childhood, maidenhood and womanhood shall no more be the victims of atrocities worse than death." Wells-Barnett correctly appraised this declaration as an apology for lawlessness. As Willard's most recent biographer notes, the WCTU leader "accepted the rallying cry of the lynchers who used the excuse of protecting white womanhood from assault and rape to justify their crimes."[30] In the controversy with Frances Willard, Ida B. Wells-Barnett came to grips with the phenomenon of white reform organizations that would sacrifice the fundamental interests of black people in order to obtain the support of racists.

What could be done to prevent lynching? Ida B. Wells-Barnett offered, along with the statistics and accounts of lynchings, a program for action. She called upon each reader to disseminate facts and to seek to persuade "all Christian and moral forces" to pass resolutions against lynching. Readers were also urged to bring to the attention of southerners the refusal of capital to invest in areas where mob violence ruled. Viewing the antilynching question as a moral struggle and confident in the power of truth, she urged support for a bill under consideration in Congress that would create a national commission to investigate the facts about assaults by males upon females during the past ten years and also to inquire as to the facts about "organized and unlawful violence to the person."[31] The bill was introduced by the same Senator Blair who had earlier introduced legislation to provide federal assistance to education in the South. As was the case with Blair's earlier bill, the proposal to investigate was not to be adopted. The education of blacks and poor whites in the South was not to be supported by federal funds, and the federal government would not lift a finger to protect the physical safety of blacks. With great courage and skill Ida B. Wells-Barnett used the weapon of truth in the struggle to stop lynching, but that weapon was not enough to put an end to the atrocities against blacks that continued to occur almost every week of the year. Nevertheless, the contribution she made to the movement against lynching was of fundamental importance. The struggle of ideas is inseparable from any movement for social change, and Ida B. Wells-Barnett did much to expose the lie that lynching had its justification in the need to protect outraged white womanhood.[32]

Alexander Crummell, with long experience in the United States and Liberia, was a spokesman whose thought is relevant to more fully understanding the Afro-American response to racial violence. In his later years pastor of Saint Luke's Episcopal Church in Washington and in 1897 convenor of the American Negro Academy that brought together a number of prominent black intellectuals, Crummell vigorously urged the development of black culture. W. E. B. Du Bois admiringly wrote of him: "He never faltered, he seldom complained; he simply worked, inspiring the young, rebuking the old, helping the weak, guiding the strong."[33] Firm in principle, broad in experience, committed to ideals of black progress, Crummell to some considerable extent was an earlier version of Du Bois.

During the decades of mounting violence following the Civil War Crummell was indefatigable in refusing to have the perspective for the black future defined by racism. In a paper he delivered in 1888 Crummell stated his position: "Indeed, the race-problem is a moral one. It is a question entirely of ideas. Its solution will come especially from the domain of principles. Like all the other great battles of humanity, it is to be fought out with the weapons of truth." Leaving aside the question of social relations, Crummell focused upon civic and political liberty as an idea whose time had come. The United States, he explained, "should be agitated and even convulsed till the battle of liberty is won, and every man in the land is guaranteed fully every civil and political right and prerogative.... I wish to show that the probabilities tend toward the complete and entire civil and political equality of all the peoples of this land.... it is to be observed in the history of man that, in due time, certain principles get their set in human society, and there is no such thing as successfully resisting them." The present demand of democracy, Crummell stated, was "the equality of man in the State, irrespective of race, condition, or lineage. The answer to this demand is the solution of the race-problem." The fundamental idea of American life was democracy, "and if this nation will not submit herself to the domination of this idea— if she refuses to live in the spirit of this creed—then she is already doomed, and she certainly will be doomed." There were those who desired racial oligarchy to prevail in America, but Crummell averred that "nations are no longer governed by races, but by ideas." He was confident that the spirit of democracy foretold of its own fulfillment and that disasters along the way were trivialities, "its repulses only temporary." This Crummell declared at a time when lynchings mounted in frequency and blacks were about to be almost entirely driven from participation in southern politics.

During this period when racist propaganda cried that lynching was necessary to protect white women from black sexual assault Crummell spoke of the particular oppression inflicted on black women. The voice of passion spoke in his remarks. "The lot of the black *man* on the plantation," he said, "has been sad and desolate enough; but the fate of the black woman has been awful! Her entire existence from the day she first landed, a naked victim of the slave trade, has been degradation in its extremest forms." Crummell recounted the brutal treatment of black women that characterized American slavery, but he also observed that despite the barbaric treatment "so much struggling virtue lingered among the rude cabins ... so much womanly worth and sweetness abided in their bosoms." He reminded his audience of what took place under slavery to make the point that white men had not forgotten the habits of the slave regime. Thousands of young black women served as schoolteachers, but even these women, Crummell observed, "as well as their more ignorant sisters in rude huts, are followed and tempted and insulted by the ruffianly element of Southern society, who think that black *men* have no rights which white men should regard, and black *women* no virtue which white men should respect!" Crummell spoke of the special qualities he perceived in black women, contending that "in tenderness of feeling, in genuine native modesty, in large disinterestedness, in sweetness of disposition and deep humility, in unselfish devotedness, and in warm, motherly assiduities, the Negro woman is unsurpassed by any other woman on this earth."

Crummell was anxious that an "uplifting civilization" be implanted within the race, and for this he believed the education of black women was of critical importance. Although recognizing the need for training in the fields of higher culture, he called for concentrating upon industrial and domestic education. He was particularly interested in the education of the masses, "for the raising up women meet to be the helpers of *poor* men the RANK AND FILE of black society."

Crummell advocated the involvement of southern whites in programs of black education, but he firmly insisted that whites from the North must not be excluded from such work. And he most definitely stressed that blacks must give leadership to any effort at uplifting the race. "The true leaders of a race," he said, "are men of that race; and any attempt to carry on missions opposed to this principle is sure to meet disastrous failure!" Black leaders trusted "those universal and unfailing tendencies of TRUTH, JUSTICE, and EQUITY" that marked the history of Afro-Americans.

Crummell would have black youth prepare themselves for all fields of endeavor. He proceeded from the belief that all crafts were honorable and that there was no calling in which whites were engaged for which blacks were not fit. He asked: "Is there anything *they* do, which we can't do?" Crummell celebrated work. Work was a means of climbing the ladder toward higher achievement; it represented law, system, and organization and so was a means of progress. Through work it was possible to "grasp the permanent and abiding forces of nature and society:—and through them press on to power, to majesty, to wealth, and to social and political prerogatives which ere long, will be the common inheritance of both our manhood and our intelligence!"[34]

Through all the travails that Afro-Americans endured Crummell did not relinquish his vision of the future. He believed, heart and soul, that black advancement was in harmony with the scheme of the universe, and his great sense of confidence was a source of strength to a people menaced by assault and disfranchisement. He was of that black leadership group that would not in the slightest degree trim its sails and succumb to terror.

Black leadership responded in various ways to the violence characterizing the post-Reconstruction years, but these responses, of course, were only the most visible part of the responses of Afro-Americans. Both nationally and locally the best-organized segment of the Afro-American community was the black church, and clergymen were impelled to step forward as articulators of protest, yet sometimes restrained by the need to assure the survival of the institutions they represented. The response to violence must also be looked for in the actions at the grass roots level of individuals and groups of Afro-Americans who did not publish their views or experiences but who most directly confronted white terror. It is to be found in the actions of a Reconstruction black, Zeke High, who fought with every ounce of his strength against racists who came to drag him out of his cell and lynch him.[35] It is found in the courage of a Mississippian, Charles Caldwell, who would not abandon his commitment to Radical Reconstruction and met with dignity the murderers who assassinated him.[36] It is seen in the quiet resolution of blacks who packed their belongings and began the long trek to Kansas after the crushing of Reconstruction. There was also the southern black who sought to save himself by inserting a note in the newspaper to the effect that he would have nothing further to do with politics, and there is the black clergyman of the Colored Methodist Episcopal Church in Matagorda County, Texas, who tried to smooth things over in the aftermath of violence by claiming that difficulties had resulted from "bad counsel on both sides."[37] There is the response of the Memphis blacks who did not take up arms after a lynching but who nonetheless protested by abandoning their jobs and leaving the city. Reaction to violence is also found in the memory of blacks living today who recall accounts of how parents or grandparents had been traumatically affected by word of lynchings occurring in their own or adjacent communities.

Resistance to terror is also seen in the acts of blacks who fought violence with violence, most often against overwhelming odds, and who died while fighting back but not before they took one or more of the racists with them. A case in point is the battle of Robert Charles, a New Orleans black man whose story was told by Ida B. Wells-Barnett in a pamphlet, *Mob Rule in New Orleans*.[38] Robert Charles and a black youth, Lenard Pierce, had been sitting on a doorstep on Dryades Street when three policemen approached and attempted to arrest them. One of the officers clubbed Charles, and in self-defense the black man drew a gun, shot and wounded the policeman, and in the exchange was himself wounded. That was the opening incident in what became a running battle between the New Orleans police and the wounded black fugitive.

Several hours after the incident on Dryades Street police came to Charles's home, seeking to arrest him. Charles, however, would not submit, and he shot and killed two of the officers, a patrolman and a captain. Official New Orleans now organized a massive manhunt, and the instructions were to produce Charles's body, dead or alive. Mayor Capdevielle announced that the city would pay a reward of $250 for the delivery of Charles's body, appointing himself judge and jury by describing Charles as "the Negro murderer." The *New Orleans Picayune* indicated in its news reports that Charles, if found, would be shot on sight. Hundreds of policemen patrolled the streets, and civilians were also called upon to join in the hunt. Blacks, especially when gathered in groups, were subject to indiscriminate arrest, and at least one black prisoner, in police custody, was brutally beaten by a white mob.

On the second day following the Dryades Street episode, the white mob gave full vent to its fury. Pawnshops were looted, and at least thirteen blacks were described by the *New Orleans Times-Democrat* as "severely beaten and maltreated." Inflicting injuries, however, was not enough for this mob, and it soon turned to killing. A black passenger on a streetcar was chased by a mob, kicked and beaten, and finally shot to death. Another black, seventy-five years of age, was shot and killed on his way to work at the French Market. The next day, a black woman was shot by a white mob firing through the shutters and windows of her home. Those responsible for these acts of violence were never located, and no one punished for them.

After four days the police learned of Charles's whereabouts and laid siege to his place of hiding. But Robert Charles made a notable last stand, fought a mob of 20,000, and before dying killed seven of his would-be captors, seriously wounded eight, and left twelve slightly wounded.[39] Charles was killed when the building in which he hid was set afire and he was forced to flee. The *Times-Democrat* announced that after Charles was pronounced dead his body was "shot, kicked, and beaten almost out of semblance to humanity."[40] Even while the battle with Charles was in progress another black, apparently for no other reason than that he was black, was chased by a mob in the French Quarter and shot and stabbed to death.

What happened in this episode demonstrated the reality that black individuals who would directly challenge the armed enforcers of racial oppression, who would not submit to police harassment and false arrest, had to pay the price of death. But there were such individuals as Robert Charles, and he and others like him were not lunatics. They were individuals who would rather die than submit to oppression, and if their resistance could be expressed only through individual acts, they would take that course. Such resistance did not win immediate victories—often it provided racists with pretext for further brutality against blacks—but it did serve as a warning that extreme oppression could provoke retaliation and demonstrated to those inclined to believe their own "Sambo" stereotype that blacks could fight valiantly indeed.

Who was Robert Charles? The evidence indicates that he had been interested in the emigration movement to Africa and had served as a local agent of the *Voice of Missions,* the newspaper published in Atlanta by Bishop Henry McNeal Turner. The *New Orleans Times-Democrat* noted that material found in Charles's room showed he "was desirous of improving himself intellectually in order that he might conquer the hated white race." According to several persons who knew him, Charles was a quiet, law-abiding individual. One coworker in the emigration movement wrote Ida B. Wells-Barnett that Charles was "mild but earnest" in his advocacy of emigration and that his work was "apparently prompted from his love of humanity." Robert Charles made his choice. Committed to the emigration movement and probably convinced that first-class citizenship rights could not be won by blacks, he would live peaceably and work to interest others in emigration to Africa. But he would not yield to racist brutality, and to racists that made him a desperado. Ida B. Wells-Barnett, however, had another view. She was quite certain that "to the people of his own race Robert Charles will always be regarded as the hero of New Orleans."[41] The oppressed and the oppressor can never agree as to who is a desperado and who is a hero.

Robert Charles had been in contact with the emigrationist activity of Henry McNeal Turner, and there is one common bond with another Georgia resident of that era, Professor W. E. B. Du Bois of Atlanta University. Both Robert Charles and Dr. Du Bois were deeply affected by the lynching near Newnan, Georgia, of Sam Hose. On April 23, 1899, Hose, held on suspicion of rape and murder, had been tortured and burned alive in a public spectacle facilitated by running special trains from Atlanta to witness the event. According to one of his acquaintances, Charles, upon learning of the incident, was "beside himself with fury," and he was quoted to the effect "that the time had come for every black man to prepare to defend himself." To Du Bois the Hose lynching came as a "red ray" that cut across his scholarly plans and startled him to his feet. Du Bois narrates his response: "I wrote out a careful and reasoned statement concerning the evident facts and started down to the Atlanta *Constitution,* carrying in my pocket a letter of introduction to Joel Chandler Harris. I did not get there. On the way news met me: Sam Hose had been lynched, and they said his knuckles were on exhibition at a grocery store farther down on Mitchell Street, along which I was walking. I turned back to the University. I began to turn aside from my work. I did not meet Joel Chandler Harris nor the editor of the *Constitution.*" Du Bois drew the conclusion that "one could not be a calm, cool, and detached scientist while Negroes were lynched, murdered, and starved."[42] Circumstances, temperament, and opportunity led Charles and Du Bois to differing paths of struggle, but in both men the Hose lynching stiffened a resolve to confront racial oppression directly.

THREE

In the Context of Empire

URING THE 1890s a new framework for the black struggle was emerging within American society. A central factor shaping that context was a vigorous American imperialism that looked out from the continental mainland for territories to bring under colonial rule. This colonialism, raising issues of dominating other nonwhite populations, sharpened racial antagonisms within the United States. As Confederate veterans and northern Republicans united in war against Spain, stepping forward as the champions of oppressed Cubans, the contradiction between the assumed role of upholding freedom abroad and the reality of racial oppression at home was glaringly apparent. Though most white Americans as yet closed their eyes to this contradiction, spokesmen of the black community were quick to point to the inconsistency. As the nation fought against a decayed, oppressive Spanish colonialism, violence against Afro-Americans intensified.

The fall months of 1898 clearly revealed a rising tide of violence. In Mississippi, near the town of Harpersville, a confrontation resulted from an incident in which a black man, Bill Burke, had an altercation with his white employer, Charles Freeman, in which Burke "got the best of the difficulty." A sheriff's posse was organized to seize Burke, but the whites encountered resistance from a group of blacks situated in and around Burke's home. The posse was forced to withdraw but returned the next morning, heavily reinforced, and when the shooting was over one white and at least nine blacks were dead. In Illinois, during the weeks from late September to mid-October, several blacks were killed when coal operators brought in blacks to take the places of striking white miners. On October 5, in Annapolis, Maryland, a lynching took place, the *Washington Post* reported, under "the very shadow of the State Capitol of Maryland." A black man, Wright Smith, alleged to have assaulted a white woman, was taken from the jail by a party of forty whites, most of them masked, and shot down in the street, "the base of the negro's brain entirely blown away." Although some of the lynchers were not masked, no one, reportedly, could identify any of them. In Madisonville, Ohio, near Cincinnati, police and civilians using bloodhounds searched for an unidentified black man who had allegedly assaulted a white girl, and the press report was that lynching was expected if the man was identified.[1]

At Wilmington, North Carolina, racism was expressed in a mass assault on the black community. A coalition of Populists and Republicans was crushed by the assault. For two days the white mob terrorized the black community, and at least eleven blacks were killed.[2] Thomas R. Cripps sums up the basic significance of what occurred: "the Wilmington massacre effectively announced that white violence against blacks for the next quarter of a century would be organized, collective, in strength, and in daylight, and against concentrations of blacks in their own city ghettos." White terrorism increased, and in response, Cripps writes, black awareness and group identity also increased.[3] These events did not come as a total surprise to informed northerners, for at least one major newspaper, the *Washington Post,* gave extensive coverage to the developing terror in North Carolina and indeed sought to give it some legitimacy. Two weeks before the 1898 election the *Post* gave its editorial view of the North Carolina situation: "The issue involves the preservation of enlightened institutions, of honest government, of law and order, of the integrity of the Caucasian race. . . . The negro has proved to the satisfaction of the entire country that he is incapable of conducting a civilized and wholesome government. . . . Even Gen. Grant, who had conquered the Confederate armies in the field, could not, with all the civil and military power of the country at his back, force negro rule upon the Southern whites. The thing is out of the question. It cannot be."[4] The *Post's* North Carolina correspondent, noting that Wilmington had become the storm center of the election contest, furnished an account of a Democratic party rally in eastern North Carolina in which white supremacy was plainly set out as the central political issue. At this gathering a Methodist minister, the Reverend N. M. Jurney, prayed that God would let rage and passion cease among "our people" but then went on to avow his political objectives: "Let us feel this day the vibrations of our coming redemption from all wicked rule, and the supremacy of that race destined not only to rule this country, but to carry the Gospel to all nations, and maintain civil and religious liberty throughout the world." The resolutions adopted at this meeting stated that the Democrats "contemplated no violence," but it was also declared that it was better for everybody that whites govern. The Democrats concluded: "North Carolina shall not be negroized. It is of all the States of the Union peculiarly the home of the Anglo-Saxon, and the Anglo-Saxon shall govern it."[5]

On October 30 the *Post* reported from Wilmington that Democratic strategy for the election in that city revolved around disfranchisement of blacks. The headings of the *Post* article read: "A City under Arms— Blacks to Be Prevented from Voting in Wilmington, N.C.—Prepared for a Race War—Property-holding Classes Determined Upon Ending Negro Domination." The reader was given ample notice of the prospect of violence and was told that the city was preparing for a siege rather than an election. The article declared that if blacks voted "they will do so at the peril of their lives." The *Post*'s correspondent, "H.L.W.," emphasized that the business leaders of the city played a "prominent and important" part in the white-supremacy campaign. James Sprunt, head of a major firm in the city's cotton trade, was quoted to the effect that he would not suffer another two years of black rule. T. M. Emerson, general passenger agent of the Atlantic Coast Line, bluntly set out his position: "It is the whites against the negroes, and we do not disguise the fact. . . . We are all armed and ready. I am armed and I make no concealment of the fact." H.L.W. wrote that columns could be filled with interviews expressing similar views, "for merchants, bank Presidents, clergymen, lawyers, and reputable citizens generally all talk in the same strain." The journalist predicted that despite the fact that "colored leaders, preachers, and women" urged going to the polls black voters would stay home on election day. The result would be that "the white man's ticket" would triumph, not because whites were in the majority but because only whites would be allowed to vote.[6]

On November 1, one week prior or the election, the *Post* correspondent again reported the likelihood of a Democratic victory. He left no doubt that terror was part of the formula for this victory. The racists had taken to the wearing of red shirts, reminiscent of the shirts worn by the South Carolina white supremacists who overthrew Radical Reconstruction in 1876. H.L.W. told of an incident in which a black man in a store cursed the red shirts and was promptly shot to death. The killer, the correspondent observed, would eventually be brought to trial, "but no one expects that he will be convicted." Again he declared that blacks would not be allowed to vote, "or if they appear at the polls they will do so at their own peril." A prominent Baptist clergyman in Raleigh, the Reverend J. D. Hutham, was quoted as writing to a friend, "white men and white men alone must rule in North Carolina." Democratic victory would result from white bloc voting, but where this did not suffice other means would be employed. When the future Democratic legislature met "steps will be taken to nullify the negro vote by some plan," but before that eventuality "the red shirt and the Winchester rifle will prove effective." H.L.W. added that in one county they had already proven effective, as some 100 blacks had removed their names from the registration list.[7]

The following day, November 2, the *Post* furnished a detailed report of a red-shirt rally at Laurinburg. *Post* readers learned that the town's leading citizens turned out for the event, including one Maxey L. John, "a leading lawyer and university graduate, whose gold spectacles and serious features made him appear like a divinity student." John gave his opinion that "we propose to have the white man rule, and that is what the red shirt means." Hundreds proceeded to the locale of the rally, yelling as they rode and at Stewartville precinct pausing to circle around the cabins of blacks. The *Post* reported: "There was an odd combination of modern appliances with old-time Southern ideas, for some of the red-shirters came on bicycles and the telephone was used to hasten backward delegations." At the rally itself one of the Democratic speakers declared that whites owned the state and would have it, "peaceably if we can, forcibly if we must." The same speaker added: "In our county, when a negro Constable comes to a white man with a warrant in his hands he leaves with a bullet in his brains. You want to follow in our wake and we will stand by you in anything you do." And, according to the *Post,* these remarks were "really mild" compared with other statements being made in the course of the campaign.[8]

A few days later Josephus Daniels, editor of the *Raleigh News and Observer* and later secretary of the navy in Woodrow Wilson's cabinet, told the Associated Press that North Carolina whites would use "every lawful means" to assure white supremacy. But in the *Washington Post* Daniels's statement was carried next to a report of the situation in the port city of Newbern that presented another image of the North Carolina struggle. A Democratic campaign rally had resolved that it was the duty of every white person "to do everything in his power" to defeat "negro domination" and further marked as "traitors to the white race" any white who would politically ally with blacks. The rally also resolved that employers should give preference in hiring to white labor "in all cases wherever practicable." Among the orators at this meeting was James A. Bryan, local banker and Democratic candidate for the state Senate. Bryan did not convey the restraint evident in the Daniels comment. "We will not bear the yoke of the African," Bryan proclaimed. "When the white man's civilization is at stake we are going to stand together for the white man's government and the white man's rule until the last one of us is

put in a box ten feet under ground." Bryan struck the note that white
women were endangered, and then he gave his directive for conduct of
the election: "Let the white men go to the polls next Tuesday and run
this election. You have got to run it; you have got to run it. I tell you,
you have got to win it; peaceably if you can, but if you fail that way,
win it any way you can." The *Post* reported that then "the vast audience
shouted and yelled and stamped the floor, while the ladies seated within
the bar clapped their gloved hands with vigor." The dispatch from Newbern also included news that telegraph messages had been sent from the
city seeking additional arms for use by the whites.[9]

On November 6 the *Post* published predictions of victory at the polls
made by both the Republican and Democratic state chairmen. The Democratic state chairman attempted to blunt the issue of violence, stating
he hoped the election would be peaceful and adding that North Carolina
whites had made up their minds to control the politics of the state "and
they sometimes express this resolution in very vigorous language." The
Post also tried to circumvent the issue of violence, editorializing that it
was all well and good for northerners "to hold up their hands in pious
horror at the mere mention of violence and to deplore the so-called
wickedness now rampant at the South" but such people ignored the
terrors of "negro domination." The *Post* made quite clear where its
sympathies lay in the North Carolina struggle: "It has become necessary,
after twenty years of uninterrupted peace and Christian civilization, to
teach the Southern negroes that they cannot rule over the property and
the destinies of the superior race, and that lesson will be taught on
Tuesday next, we solemnly believe."[10] Later the paper would lament the
violence that occurred in North Carolina, but prior to the election the
threat of violence seemed of little concern to the *Post* editors.

Two days before the election the *Post*'s H.L.W. gave his rationale for
standing with the white supremacists in the North Carolina election. The
heart of the matter, as he presented it, was that black officials were
"ignorant, inefficient, and much given to abusing the power placed in
their hands" and that blacks had not made a record of accomplishment.
Centering his attention on Wilmington, he wrote: "In thirty years of
freedom and fostering care, little or nothing has been accomplished by
the Wilmington negroes as a race." H.L.W. noted that in other southern
states "negro rule" had been overturned only after bloodshed, and with
regard to North Carolina whether what he termed a "revolution" would
come "through a baptism of blood" no one could say. But he did give
his prediction as to the political future of blacks in the state: "The negro

will be practically disfranchised, through constitutional amendment, and where this is not effective, the shot-gun will stand beside the ballot box."[11]

The *St. Louis Post-Dispatch* also added its voice to the call for the installation of white rule in North Carolina. On November 1 the newspaper editorially described the blacks of the state as "the serviceable ministers of a crazy political scheme." President McKinley was said to have created anarchy in North Carolina, and the *Post-Dispatch* set its position in a broad context of racism when it declared the president "would do well to settle the race question in his own country before he undertakes to deal with it among the barbarians over sea." Two days later the paper carried an article that related the experience of Phillips County, Arkansas, to the North Carolina situation. In the mid-1870s force had been used to suppress black Republicans. White "committees of persuasion" had called upon Republicans, always carrying a rope with them. "They never had to hang anybody, but they were very earnest men and they didn't intend that there should be any doubt about the result of the election." Since then white Democrats and white Republicans had gotten together amicably to divide the public offices, and this arrangement "worked admirably." "The negroes don't bother their heads about politics," it was noted. Arkansas had been able to deal with the racial situation unhampered by federal intervention. Similarly, if North Carolina whites were let alone, "they'll see that the negro gets all he is entitled to." If, on the other hand, the federal government "sticks in its oar there will be a great many colored people killed and the old trouble will spring up year after year." It was the white man who was going to rule the South, "and when he is let alone he rules much more wisely for the freedman than the negro can for himself." In the course of time race prejudice would pass away, but such prejudice could not be killed.[12]

The day after the election J. S. Carr, chairman of the Durham County Democratic party, wired President McKinley: "Men with white skins, Sons of Revolutionary ancestors, who drafted the original Magna Charta of American Independence, lovers of the Union and the Constitution . . . are leading the victorious column this morning, and will rule North Carolina ever hereafter; no need of troops now, praise God."[13] First accounts of the election at Wilmington reported a fairly calm atmosphere, but there were also warning signs of impending violence. Hardware dealers reported heavy demand for weapons, and there was also evidence that at least for some white supremacists violence was a primary objective in search of a pretext. The *Washington Post* reported: "Many of the more hot-headed white men are indignant that the day has been allowed to pass without a clash of arms between the races and contend that if the negroes pass through this election without a severe and bloody lesson the same conditions which have made this campaign so remarkably desperate will attend the city election in April, and will also have to be faced during the next general election."[14]

Within a day it became apparent that the tactic of direct confrontation urged by the extreme racists was to be adopted. The *Washington Post* portrayed the public mood: "Every street corner is crowded with men armed with Winchesters, the military is drawn up in line, and the most conservative men fear the worst." The *Post* acknowledged that the situation was a result of a rally of whites held at the courthouse. Emboldened by victory at the polls this crowd demanded that the editor of the Wilmington black newspaper, the *Record,* leave the city within twenty-four hours and that the press of his paper also be removed from Wilmington. If the editor did not leave, the rally announced it would expel him by force. The meeting adopted a resolution that stated a basic position with regard to the black role in politics: "the Constitution of the United States contemplated a government to be carried on by an enlightened people ...its framers did not anticipate the enfranchisement of an ignorant population of African origin... those men of the State of North Carolina who joined in forming the Union did not contemplate for their descendants a subjection to an inferior race." The meeting resolved that whites would not be ruled "by men of African origin" and further declared that preference in employment was to be given to whites. The tenor of this meeting was clearly one of openly advocating the political and economic subjection of blacks. And apparently this meeting was not led by riffraff, for the *Post* reported that "many leading citizens" made enthusiastic speeches to the crowd.[15]

Those attending this gathering represented a broad spectrum of the white population, but a disproportionately large percentage of the crowd came from Wilmington's business and professional classes. The occupations of 351 of the 442 signers of the November 9 resolutions have been identified, and these show that 27.4 percent held professional or managerial status whereas only 13 percent of the city's white males occupied such positions.[16]

"Race war and revolution have held high carnival," wrote the *Washington Post* of the ensuing events in Wilmington. Early on the morning of November 10 a mob of 1,000 described by the *Post* as composed of "representative white men" destroyed the office and plant of the black newspaper, and the *Post* added that the editor would have been lynched had he not already left the city. Several hours later a clash occurred between "white guards" and blacks, resulting in the deaths of six blacks with several whites wounded. In the terrorized atmosphere the officials of the existing city administration were compelled to "resign," and a slate of white supremacists was installed in office.[17]

The day following the violence the *Post* reported that blacks in Wilmington were "thoroughly terrorized" and that hundreds had fled the city. Even some white conservatives expressed concern at the expulsion from the city of the United States commissioner, R. H. Bunting, driven away because he had cooperated politically with blacks. But already it was made clear in Washington that President McKinley would not intervene in the Wilmington situation. The issue was discussed by the cabinet, and the *Post* explained that precedent for action had been set by the actions of President Cleveland during the 1894 Pullman strike, but the word was McKinley would take no action. For its part, the *Washington Post*, previously silent concerning the threat of violence, now editorially lamented its occurrence, at the same time expressing its satisfaction at the coming to power of a white-supremacist state government. The *Post*'s quarrel was with "tragic methods," not with the general drift of North Carolina politics.[18]

Estimates as to the number of blacks killed in the Wilmington violence varied. Official inquests were held with regard to the deaths of seven men, Josh Halsey, Daniel Wright, William Mouzon, James L. Gregory, John L. Townsend, Silas Branan, and Samuel McFallon. But the *Washington Post* reported that a prominent white stated that as many as twenty-five blacks had actually been killed, and the *Post* added that several blacks, "especially children," had died of exposure among the hundreds who fled to the woods in the aftermath of the bloodshed in Wilmington.[19]

Years after the event the son of the prominent black Republican John Campbell Dancy, United States collector of customs at Wilmington, recalled the fear that spread through the black community. He remembers being told that something terrible was going on and he had better stay at home. He recalled also that the main targets were men like his father, "whose crime was that they were successful and prosperous beyond the condition of the average white man." The son wrote of how he and his stepmother managed to escape from Wilmington:

How my stepmother did it, I don't know, but she managed to get a horse and buggy to take us on a wild dash for safety. There were no automobiles in town; there were no telephones in Negro homes, except for perhaps those of the doctor and the undertaker, and it was taking your life in your hands to go out of the house, but somehow she made the arrangements and the rig drew up to our house at dusk.

We were driven to the Atlantic Coastline Railrod. It was only an eight- or ten-block ride, but we were stopped several times by men who searched the buggy. We were not molested, however, and were allowed to board the train.[20]

In the immediate aftermath of the Wilmington violence several of the city's black citizens wrote President McKinley urging federal action. One woman anonymously wrote the president that Wilmington was "under the confederate laws," and Della V. Johnson wrote, "I implore you for the sake of justice to stop this outrageous sin." One letter was particularly eloquent in stating the case for federal intervention:

I a Negro woman of this city appeal to you from the depths of my heart, to do something in the Negro's behalf. The outside world only knows one side of the trouble here, there is no paper to tell the truth about the Negro here in this or any other Southern state. The Negro in this town had no arms (except pistols perhaps in some instances) with which to defend themselves from the attack of lawless whites.... I call on you the head of the American Nation to help these humble subjects.... And are we to die like rats in a trap? With no place to seek redress?.... Can we call on any other Nation for help? Why do you forsake the Negro?.... Will you for God sake in your next message to Congress give us some relief. If you send us all to Africa we will be willing or a number of us will gladly go. Is this the land of the free and the home of the brave?.... There seems to be no help for us. No paper will tell the truth about the Negro.[21]

The Wilmington violence contributed to spurring the migration of southern blacks to the North. Already in 1901 Du Bois wrote that there could be no doubt of the drift of the black South, and he added that it was said "that the Wilmington riot alone sent a thousand negroes to Philadelphia." In his view every southern failure, "every oppressive act, every unlawful excess," shifted the race problem northward. Substantiating Du Bois's report is the contemporary item appearing in the *Wilmington Messenger*, which stated that at least 300 blacks left the city by train within one month of the violence and more than 100 had purchased tickets for destinations beyond Richmond. There is also the evidence that the 1900 census noted a drop of almost 8 percent in Wilmington's black population since 1890, whereas the number of whites in the city substantially increased.[22]

There was, to be sure, some white opinion in North Carolina that took a critical position respecting the Wilmington massacre. A white Wilmingtonian, Jane Cronly, wrote that she hoped she expressed the views of many other women when she spoke up "in solemn protest" against the violence. She wrote of the November 10 violence: "It will ever be a day to be remembered in my heart with indignation and sorrow. At first indignation overwhelmed me; now sorrow has taken its place. I waited hoping a stronger voice than mine would be lifted up in defense of a helpless and much injured race, but such has not been the case." Cronly realized that the use of terror had the long-term objectives of permanent black disfranchisement. The aim was "to make Nov. 10th a day to be remembered by the whole race for all time."[23]

Another North Carolina observer was scholar John Spencer Bassett, professor at Trinity College in Durham. Writing to Herbert Baxter Adams at Johns Hopkins University, Bassett noted that the 1898 campaign ended in a riot in Wilmington, "justifiable at no point—a riot directly due to the 'white man's campaign.' " Bassett continued his account:

> After the election was carried—and the county which had a large negro majority went democratic by a large majority—the negroes were quiet. They were really cowed. The whites realized that they controlled the Legislature. They organized a mob, the leader was a lawyer, an ex-Congressman and a campaign speaker. They went down to destroy the printing office of a negro on account of an offense committed four months ago—an offense which is after all a mere statement of opinion. The press was destroyed and the office set on fire. This was the initial action of the riot. The negroes made no resistance. In a negro quarter in the suburbs some armed white men met some negroes standing on the street. There was no claim that the negroes were doing wrong. . . . They were fired into. It was claimed they fired first. I don't think many white people who understand things in the state believe the charge. After this the riot was well on. About a dozen negroes were killed—almost as many more were seriously wounded.

Bassett found richly ironic the fact that in the aftermath of the riot the prime instigator of violence, Alfred M. Waddell, became Wilmington's mayor and promptly ordered an end to disorder. If Waddell "had any sense of humor he must have split his undergarments laughing at his own joke." Bassett candidly noted that "the great majority of people" supported what had been done in Wilmington.[24]

Albion Tourgee, who had held office in North Carolina during the Reconstruction years, also responded to the Wilmington massacre. From Paris Tourgee wrote to President McKinley, expressing his "keenest apprehension" and despair at what had taken place. "If a thousand voters had been killed at Wilmington," he wrote, "I doubt if there would have been any public manifestation of any great extent, to express disapproval." He observed that the racial situation seemed to be one "of those questions which only God can handle," and he did not doubt that sometime God would take it in hand. But he also warned of the future: "it is quite possible that the American Republic may pay the price of its own injustice, by finding in the Race Problem the end of its liberties, and the destruction of its organic character. It seems to me not unlikely that the next great outbreak of barbaric slaughter, such as followed St. Bartholomew's Eve, may occur in the United States of America, and that when it has passed by, the Republic which has so long boasted of Liberty, Justice and Equality, will be only a blood-drenched theater on which inflamed factions will struggle for mastery." Tourgee had hoped that the "hideous monster" of racism would not again show its head, but it had indeed appeared.[25]

The violence of November 10 was in no way merely a spontaneous eruption. It was premeditated, occurring as the result of persistent agitation. One Democratic party leader, George Rountree, later recalled making a speech in which he started "to endeavor to inflame white men's sentiment, and discovered that they were already willing to kill all of the office holders and all the negroes." Alfred M. Waddell does not appear to have required agitation to set himself on a violent course, but in any event his cousin Rebecca Cameron added fuel to the fire in a letter she wrote him on October 26: "It has reached the point when blood letting is needed for the health of the common wealth, and when the depletion commences let it be thorough. Solomon says 'There is a time to kill.' That time seems to have come so get to work, and don't stop short of a complete clearing of the decks. If you have to start make a finish once in all. . . . You go forward to your work, bloody tho' it may be, with the heart-felt approval of any good woman in the State."[26]

On the eve of the election Alfred Waddell told Wilmington's whites, "Go to the polls tomorrow and if you find the negro out voting, tell him to leave the polls, and if he refuses kill him; shoot him down in his tracks. We shall win tomorrow if we have to do it with guns."[27]

As Hayumi Higuchi notes, the Wilmington violence was directly conditioned by the deepening American involvement in imperialism. Higuchi reports that the feeling inspired by the Spanish-American War "eventually coalesced with the Democratic 'patriotism' of white supremacy. When articles in Democratic newspapers attracted readers' interest in the war and in their regiment, they were related to white supremacy propaganda." As it was supposedly patriotic to support a war of conquest overseas it was also patriotic to save North Carolina from the supposed danger of black rule.[28]

On election day 1898, the settlement of Phoenix in Greenwood County, South Carolina, was the setting of another outbreak of racial violence, directed primarily at blacks seeking to vote.[29] A family of prominent white Republicans, the Tolberts, was also threatened by the mob. One family member, Thomas Tolbert, was fatally wounded and at least seven blacks shot down and killed, four at the Rehoboth Church near Phoenix. James A. Hoyt, who covered the story as a cub reporter, later recalled that following the Phoenix violence there were sporadic episodes of violence in Greenwood, Abbeville, and Edgefield counties. The grand jury in its presentment charged the Tolberts with having made incendiary speeches at midnight meetings, "thus inciting the Negroes to violence and lawlessness," but as Hoyt noted no mention was made of any effort to apprehend and indict the lynchers. Hoyt added: "The 'lynchers' were well known, no attempt had at any time been made to conceal their identity. What they did was done openly and boldly, with uncovered faces and in the sight of all men. Their names could have been easily secured; in fact, some of them were personally known to the reporters who were on the scene." Hoyt further recalled that the blacks, unable to secure the protection of law, did avail themselves of the one avenue of response open to them; hundreds emigrated from the area to employment in other parts of the South.[30]

The white mob responsible for the Phoenix violence was his earliest memory, writes Benjamin E. Mays in his autobiography. "I remember," he says, "a crowd of white men who rode up on horseback with rifles on their shoulders. I was with my father when they rode up, and I remember starting to cry. They cursed my father, drew their guns and made him salute, made him take off his hat and bow down to them several times. Then they rode away. I was not yet five years old, but I have never forgotten them." Mays recalls that after the Phoenix incident "never a year passed in my county that there were not several brutal incidents involving Negroes and whites."[31]

Initially it was reported that in contrast to the response to the bloodshed in Wilmington the McKinley administration would intervene in the Phoenix situation. Although R. R. Tolbert was received by President McKinley at the White House, following a conference between McKinley and Attorney General Griggs it was decided that grounds did not exist for federal action.[32] The administration simply would not move upon an issue of black rights, even when the safety of a white family, prominent in the Republican party of South Carolina, was involved.

There was widespread protest by blacks against the violence in the Carolinas. Within a few days of the November 8 election the Forum Club of St. Louis, with a membership made up of many of the city's prominent blacks, met to consider the events. Educator Peter H. Clark, now of the Sumner High School in St. Louis, formerly the principal of a black school in Cincinnati and a leader in that city's Republican and Socialist politics, introduced a resolution calling upon President McKinley to act against the race violence in the South. The resolution was adopted, and the meeting further decided to circulate the statement in the form of a petition throughout the country.[33]

An eloquent voice raised against the violence was that of the Reverend Francis J. Grimke, pastor of Washington's Fifteenth Street Presbyterian Church. Grimke declared: "After thirty-three years of freedom our civil and political rights are still denied us; the fourteenth and fifteenth amendments to the Constitution are still a dead letter." White supremacy was in the ascendancy, and those blacks who insisted on political rights were either to be driven from the South or dealt with by the "shotgun policy." What Grimke found particularly appalling was that some educated blacks seemed willing to accept political subjection. He proclaimed that such persons were traitors to the race, but he also insisted they did not speak for the majority of black people. He said of the Afro-American: "During all these terrible years of suffering and oppression, these years of blood and tears, though he has been shot at, his property destroyed, his family scattered, his home broken up; though he has been forced to fly like the fugitive for his life before the hungry bloodhounds of Southern Democracy; though everything has been done to terrorize him, to keep him from the polls, he still stands up for his rights." Grimke observed that hundreds of blacks had sacrificed their lives in defense of their rights. "And shall we be told," he asked, "and by black men, too, that the sacred cause for which they poured out their life's blood is to be relinquished; that the white ruffians who shot them down were justified; that in view of all the circumstances it was just what was to have been expected, and therefore that virtually we have no reasonable ground for complaint?" He gave a ringing answer to the question:

Away with such treasonable utterances; treason to God, treason to man, treason to free institutions, to the spirit of an enlightened and Christian sentiment. The negro is an American citizen, and he never will be eliminated as a political factor with his consent. He has been terrorized and kept from the polls by bloody ruffians, but he has never felt that it was right; he has never acquiesced in it and never will. As long as he lives, as long as there is one manly, self-respecting negro in this country, the agitation will go on, will never cease until right is triumphant.

Blacks might be forced from the polls, but they would not of their own accord abandon their rights.[34]

That Grimke did not stand alone within the Washington black community in his view of the situation was evidenced on November 21 when more than 5,000 persons attended a protest rally at the Fifth Baptist Church on Vermont Avenue. The *Washington Post* reported it was "probably the greatest outpouring of negroes ever seen in Washington." This meeting adopted resolutions condemning lynching and other forms of racist violence and calling upon the churches to speak out for racial justice. President McKinley was urged to take action in the southern states in protection of civil rights. Attorney Thomas L. Jones struck a timely note when he stated that, if the government could not protect blacks, "how could it hope to act as a protectorate over the people of distant lands?" Another speaker aroused a warm response when he spoke bluntly to the issue of self-defense. Said Colonel Perry Carson: "Prepare to protect yourselves; the virtues of your women and your property. Get your powder and your shot and your pistol." That Carson's remarks were not to be taken lightly was made evident when the *Washington Post* editorially expressed its alarm and surprise that so "sensible" a man as Carson had spoken as he did.[35]

The *Washington Post* would doubtless have found more to its taste the comments ascribed by the *New York Evening Post* to Booker T. Washington. "It must be apparent at this time," Washington was quoted as commenting, "that the effort to put the rank and file of the colored people into a position to exercise the right of franchise has not been a success in these portions of our own country where the negro is found in large numbers." He gave his explanation of the situation: "Either the negro was not prepared for any such wholesale exercise of the ballot as our recent amendments to the Constitution contemplated, or the American people were not prepared to assist and encourage him to use the ballot. In either case the result has been the same."[36]

In the black press ringing denunciations of the violence in the South were to be found. The *Washington Bee* declared that the North Carolina election "was characterized by the murdering of colored men, women and children." The *Bee* charged that the *Washington Post* approved of the butchery and that "redhanded assassins" in the South were encouraged to believe that the *Post* reflected the views of the administration. The *Bee* predicted that "in due time a wave of vengeance will sweep over the South which will demolish and destroy Calhounism, Tillmanism and Wadellism [a reference to Alfred M. Waddell, one of the Wilmington racist leaders] and upon their ruin will be erected, for the first time in the history of this Republic, the principle of justice." The *Bee* flatly rejected the contention that a "race war" existed in North Carolina, dismissing the notion that the violence was the work of "the poor vicious and irresponsible whites" and finding instead that the "best people" were engaged in the brutalities inflicted upon blacks.

The *Cleveland Gazette* gave extensive front-page coverage to the views of the Lexington, Kentucky, black editor, the Reverend C. O. Benjamin, who reacted to the actions of a Mississippi black man in resisting his white assailants. Benjamin wrote: "The Negroes should stand like men. If the whites resort to the gun and the torch, let the Negro do the same, and if blood must flow like water and bonfires be made of valuable property, so be it all around, for what is fair for the white man to teach the Negro his place, is fair for the negro to teach the white man his place. ... If the white man uses the torch and the assassin's knife, let the Negro do the same.... This question of the two races can be settled peacefully, but the whites do not appear to take this view of the matter." Commenting directly on the Wilmington massacre the *Gazette* declared that what occurred was "the indiscriminate slaughter of an innocent and inoffensive people." One paper called for the arrest of Waddell and added that for his crime of leading the mob he ought to be hung. The blacks of Wilmington had done no more than seek to exercise the franchise peacefully, but yet the Congress did nothing. In the end, the *Gazette* insisted, the sins of the nation would find it out, for "an avenging God will yet demand of the nation: 'Art thou not thy brother's keeper?' "[37] A country that tolerated anarchy and misrule could not long endure.

A powerful response to the Wilmington violence was to be found in a fictionalized account, *Hanover; or, the Persecution of the Lowly; Story of the Wilmington Massacre* (1900), written by David Bryant Fulton, using the pseudonym Jack Thorne. Fulton, who had been raised in the city, sought to portray the viciousness of the racial assault but particularly stressed the theme of black resistance. According to Fulton, Wilmington was a summer "Mecca for North Carolina's interior inhabitants," a cosmopolitan place with a population made up of diverse ethnic groups.In such a community the violence was all the more appalling, and Fulton was vitriolic in characterizing the violence. "A mob," he wrote, "headed by a minister of the gospel, and a hoary-headed deacon, after cutting off every avenue of escape and defense, and after the government had been surrendered to them as a peace offering, [that] wantonly kills and butchers their brethren, is without parallel in a Christian community."

Fulton quoted the comments of Judson Lyons, registrar of the United States Treasury and one of the nation's leading black Republicans, who said of the Wilmington mob, "They destroyed personal property, they burned houses, they wantonly took more than a dozen lives, they drove thousands to the woods where nearly a dozen infants were born and died in many instances, with their mothers the victims of exposure as the result of the cruelty of people who call themselves democrats and patriots. Weyler [Valeriano Weyler, the Spanish captain general responsible for atrocities against the Cubans] in his maddest moments was hardly more barbarous."

Fulton announced his intention to prove that the Wilmington violence had been carefully planned by "the leading wealthy citizens" of the city who hoped to make November 10, 1898, "a second Bartholomew's eve in the history of the world, by the wholesale killing of black citizens after every means of defense had been cut off." He also sought to show that "the intervention of Providence in the earnest and persistent entreaties of white citizens who were too nobly bred to stoop so low, and the strategy and cunning of the Negro himself, frustrated the carrying out to its fullest extent, one of the most infamous and cowardly deeds ever planned."

One scene of the book is that of a meeting of the Union Aid Society, an association of Wilmington black women. One of the members present states: "The buying of guns and other weapons by poor whites who are often unable to buy food, means something. It means that the rich are going to use them to perform the dirty work of intimidation and murder if necessary to carry this election." In another scene he gives us a sketch of the traitor to the race, the "Good Nigger" who is "a stubborn believer in his own inferiority and the righteousness of his enslavement." He recalls that some black individual, indeed "a prominent negro," had endorsed the deed of the lynch mob that murdered Sam Hose in Georgia. It is such a person who is willing to spy for the white supremacists in Wilmington.

A pretext for the violence was the reply of Alex Manly, the editor of a Wilmington black newspaper, to the view expressed by Rebecca Felton, prominent southern Methodist, in a speech to the state agricultural society of Georgia, that white women, especially in rural districts, needed protection from lustful black assault. Manly had suggested that sometimes white women were receptive to sexual relationships with black men. Fulton took up the issues involved, noting that Mrs. Felton "shows the narrowness of her soul when she cries aloud for the protection of white women in isolated sections of Georgia against lustful Negroes, when she knows perfectly well that Negro girls in Georgia need the protection against lustful whites." Fulton has one of the white women characters in the book comment on the significance of lynching. "The passing of laws since the war prohibiting the intermarriage of the races is proof that the men do not trust us as implicitly as they pretend. The lynchings and burnings that are daily occurring in the South are intended as warnings to white women as well as checks to black men. Men who constitute these mobs care no more for virtue than so many beasts."

One of the key scenes of the book is the encounter of the elderly black "Uncle Guy" with the new mayor of the city government brought to power by mob action. The black man indicates that above all what was remarkable was the complicity of upper-class whites, and he warns the mayor that the ghosts of those murdered would haunt the conspirators.[38]

A fictionalized account of the Wilmington events is also to be found in Charles W. Chesnutt's novel, *The Marrow of Tradition* (1901). The violent confrontation provides the setting within which the novelist portrays the interaction of various characters who act out a range of responses to racial crisis. There is the black professional who strives for success and maintains personal dignity, the white-supremacist leader who schemes to eject blacks from politics, the black militant who is ready to go down fighting, and the decent but somewhat ineffectual Quaker newspaperman who seems to know what is right but is unready to take initiative against racism.

In writing *The Marrow of Tradition* Chesnutt sought to go beyond his previous work and indeed aimed high, at the same time as he saw the limits of what he might do. When his Cleveland friend John P. Green compared some of his writing to *Uncle Tom's Cabin* Chesnutt responded that if he "could stir the waters in any appreciable degree like that famous book" he would feel his right to life vindicated "and the right of a whole race." His aspiration was "to sketch in vivid though simple lines the whole race situation," but his task was to identify the problem, not to outline a solution. He wrote Green: "If I could propose a remedy for existing evils that would cure them overnight, I would be a great man. But I am only a small social student who can simply point out the seat of the complaint."[39]

In a column he wrote for the *Cleveland World* Chesnutt sought to convey a further explanation of what he hoped to accomplish with *The Marrow of Tradition*. The question of tradition involved the presence of the heritage of slavery within the altered conditions of a modern era. Echoing somewhat the analysis of the color question W. E. B. Du Bois formulated in *The Souls of Black Folk*, Chesnutt declared: "There is no subject of more vital interest to the student of history or of life than the upward struggle of a race, as there is no issue of greater importance to the nation than a right settlement of the race problem." Chesnutt explained that the incidents of race riot described in the novel were drawn from the Wilmington experience and also that of New Orleans (probably a reference to the Robert Charles episode). He was candid about the political conclusion on which the novel rested. "The political element of the story," he wrote, "involves a fair statement, I believe, of the course and the underlying motives of the recent and temporarily successful movement for the disfranchisement of the colored race in the south, and particularly in North Carolina, where there was less excuse for it than in any other state where it has been carried through."[40]

Chesnutt placed the Wilmington drama within the broader context of America's embrace of imperialism. "The nation," he wrote, "was rushing forward with giant strides towards colossal wealth and world dominion, before the exigencies of which mere abstract ethical theories must not be permitted to stand. The same argument that justified the conquest of an inferior nation could not be denied to those who sought the suppression of an inferior race. In the South, an obscure jealousy of the negro's progress, an obscure fear of the very equality so contemptuously denied, furnished a rich soil for successful agitation." William Dean Howells found the book bitter and wished it were not so, but he added: "No one who reads the book can deny that the case is presented with great power; or fail to recognize in the writer a portent of the sort of negro equality against which no series of hanging and burnings will finally avail." Chesnutt sought to use the novel as a counter to the racist writings of Thomas Dixon, particularly to *The Leopard's Spots*, the white novelist's fictionalized vindication of North Carolina white supremacy, but *The Marrow of Tradition* failed to gain wide acceptance among white readers. The work was quite popular with black students at Tuskegee, but white people who bought books were not ready to confront the story of American dishonor to which Chesnutt would draw them.

The novel presents the contrast between the caution of the black physician Dr. William Miller and the bold defiance of the dock worker Josh Green. Dr. Miller attempts to restrain Green, warning that a quarrel with whites could lead to a lynching. He suggests an alternative course of action: "You'd better be peaceable and endure a little injustice, rather than run the risk of a sudden and violent death." But Green has a score to settle. He remembers that time years earlier when the Ku Klux Klan had killed his father. The mask on one of the killers had fallen off, and Green had recognized the man and lived for the chance to revenge his father's death. Dr. Miller cannot endorse what Green proposes and indeed attempts to dissuade him from his violent intention, but the physician, clearly speaking for Chesnutt, recognizes a significance in black rage. "Here was a negro," the novelist wrote, "who could remember an injury, who could shape his life to a definite purpose, if not a high or holy one. When his race reached the point where they would resent a wrong, there was hope that they might soon attain the stage where they would try, and if need be, die to defend a right." In *The Marrow of Tradition*, William L. Andrews writes, Green and Miller "both symbolize strategies to be followed as the black man makes his upward climb toward respect and citizenship in the South. Each man is dignified by an individual purpose in life which causes the other to respect him as well." Still, Chesnutt and Dr. Miller reflect that mere retaliation was self-defeating, that "such a revenge would do no good, would right no wrong; while every such crime, committed by a colored man, would be imputed to the race, which was already staggering under a load of obloquy because, in the eyes of a prejudiced and undiscriminating public, it must answer as a whole for the offenses of each separate individual."

When in the course of the novel the threat of a lynching appears, Chesnutt explains the general pattern of events:

> It must not be imagined that any logic was needed, or any reasoning consciously worked out. The mere suggestion that the crime had been committed by a negro was equivalent to proof against any negro that might be suspected and could not prove his innocence. A committee of white men was hastily formed.... The spontaneous activity of the whites was accompanied by a visible shrinkage of the colored population. This could not be taken as any indication of guilt, but was merely a recognition of the palpable fact that the

American habit of lynching had so whetted the thirst for black blood that a negro suspected of crime had to face at least the possibility of short shrift and a long rope, not to mention more gruesome horrors, without the intervention of judge or jury.

In this particular instance the lynching is forestalled but not before the white-supremacist Captain McBane gives his view of the matter. "Burn the nigger," he says. "We seem to have the right nigger, but whether we have or not, burn *a* nigger. It is an assault upon the white race.... It would justify the white people in burning *any* nigger. The example would be all the more powerful if we got the wrong one. It would serve notice on the niggers that we shall hold the whole race responsible for the misdeeds of each individual." Chesnutt had put his finger on the essence of the racism that animated lynching.

Through the character of a black lawyer, Mr. Watson, Chesnutt explains the futility of expecting the federal government to act against the lynchers. Dr. Miller suggests that "surely" the president of the United States would act if he knew the situation. But Watson replies that the government does not see anything that is not officially brought to its attention. "The whole negro population of the South," he declares, "might be slaughtered before the necessary red tape could be spun out to inform the President that a state of anarchy prevailed."

Chesnutt also makes clear the responsibility of respectable whites for lynching. When the white leaders of the community determine to prevent a lynching they are quite capable of taking the necessary action. Handbills revealing the innocence of the accused man were distributed, and a crack military company was assigned to guard the jail. Chesnutt notes that a change in the point of view "demonstrated the entire ability of the leading citizens to maintain the dignified and orderly processes of the law whenever they saw fit to do so."

In the midst of the riot there is a last confrontation between Josh Green and Dr. Miller. The physician argues that even temporary victory would bring only further white violence; the blacks would either die immediately or die later. Alive, Miller can be of use to the black community. He holds out hope: "Our time will come,—the time when we can command respect for our rights; but it is not yet in sight." But Green rejects this course of action, simply stating: "I'd rather be a dead nigger any day dan a live dog!" At the end Green is dead, whereas Miller remains alive and has the possibility of continuing the struggle.[41]

As in these months public debate continued as to the proper role of the United States in world affairs, black voices, drawing upon the recent events in the South, spoke to the contradiction between claims to democratic world leadership and racial brutality at home. At the end of December 1898 the Afro-American Council, involving the participation of many prominent blacks, met in Washington, and at this gathering Ida B. Wells-Barnett spoke her mind bluntly: "We are eternally opposed to expansion until this nation can govern at home. Let the negro place himself with the party that is opposed to expansion."[42] A particularly telling indictment of racist violence and hypocrisy was presented by the Reverend Charles S. Morris before the Interdenominational Association of Colored Clergymen in Boston. Morris gave a graphic account of the killings at Wilmington and spoke of the thousands of blacks forced to flee their homes. "All this happened," he noted, "not in Turkey, nor in Russia, nor in Spain, nor in the gardens of Nero, nor in the dungeons of Torquemada, but within three hundred miles of the White House, in the best State in the South, within a year of the twentieth century, while the nation was on its knees, thanking God for having enabled it to break the Spanish yoke from the neck of Cuba." Morris, referring to black women who gave birth to stillborn infants because they had been forced to seek refuge in nearby swamps, bitterly exclaimed: "This is what the nation fought for from Bull Run to Appomattox." He ridiculed the charge that the cause of violence was "negro domination." In the state of North Carolina and in the city of Wilmington, blacks held only a small minority of political offices. Morris concluded by appealing to Christian principles and pointing to the conflict between claims to democratic world leadership and the reality of racial massacres at home. In his view America could not proceed to set up republican rule in the Philippines "while the blood of citizens whose ancestors came here before the Mayflower, is crying out to God against her from the gutters of Wilmington." It is worth noting that some white people came to grips with such attacks upon racism as that delivered by Morris. At least one white writer, Charles H. Williams, in Wisconsin, asked the readers of his local newspaper the appropriate question: "When will this people, this nation take up this grave question, as they did the Spanish barbarism against the Cubans, as they do those of the Turks against the Armenians."[43]

In addition to Morris's individual statement there also came from Massachusetts an appeal to President McKinley, sent by a mass meeting of blacks assembled in Boston. The petitioners began by explaining that they were not supplicants but rather American citizens exercising their right of petition under the Constitution. The document directly criticized a Republican president for failing to act against mounting racial oppression:

We have suffered, sir—God knows how much we have suffered—
since your accession to office, at the hands of a country professing
to be Christian, but which is not Christian; from the hate and violence of a people claiming to be civilized, but who are not civilized,
and you have seen our sufferings, witnessed from your high place
our awful wrongs and miseries, and yet you have at no time and on
no occasion opened your lips on our behalf. Why? we ask. Is it
because we are blacks and weak and despised? Are you silent because
without any fault of our own we were enslaved and held for more
than two centuries in cruel bondage by your forefathers?

The appeal stressed that, if southern blacks, subject to violent reprisal,
were unable to publicly protest, the blacks of Massachusetts were free
"and must and shall raise our voice to you and through you to the
country, in solemn protest and warning against the fearful sin and peril
of such explosive social conditions." McKinley was asked "but for an
hour, in pursuit of your national policy of 'criminal aggression' abroad
to consider the 'criminal aggression' at home against humanity and American citizenship."

Referring to the recent massacres in Wilmington and Phoenix the statement noted that McKinley had toured the South, counseling "patriotism,
jingoism and imperialism" to his white audiences but "patience, industry,
moderation" to blacks. The conclusion drawn was that McKinley "in
order to win the support of the South to his policy of 'criminal aggression'
in the far East" was willing to ignore racist violence against blacks in
the South. The president had not even spoken out when during and
following a visit to Georgia several blacks had been lynched in that state,
including one whose burning had been turned into a public spectacle.
"Did you speak?" the protesters asked McKinley. The president had said
nothing, but the attorney general had observed that such events had no
federal aspect. The issue then raised is why federal power could be used
in Cuba but could not be used to suppress bloodshed and disorder at
home. In intervening in Cuba the United States government had noted
"the chronic conditions of disturbance in Cuba so injurious and menacing
to our interests and tranquility, as well as shocking to our sentiments of
humanity." The obvious question was why inaction was in order when
disturbances repeatedly occurred in the southern states. "Is it better,"
the Massachusetts group asked, "to be Cuban revolutionists fighting for
Cuban independence than American citizens striving to do their simple
duty at home?"

This open letter to McKinley closed by observing that although some

Americans had not desired intervention in Cuba those who favored action "eventually found a way to suppress a menacing danger to the country and a wrong against humanity at the same time."[44] If the president of the United States wanted to protect the rights of citizens in the South, he would be able to find a way. This pronouncement stopped short of directly challenging American imperial expansion, but it did sharply underscore the inconsistency between the avowed aims of the government in world affairs and reality at home.

The experience of black troops during the Spanish-American War highlights the contradiction between the proclaimed objectives of American foreign policy and the facts of American racism. Several detachments of black soldiers, volunteers and regular army men, were mobilized to serve in Cuba, Puerto Rico, and the Philippines, but federal service did not shield them from racism. On the one hand, a prejudiced view of black troops was given currency by Theodore Roosevelt's account, published in *Scribner's,* of how he had encountered blacks running from the field of combat in Cuba.[45] On the other hand, blacks, frequently stationed in southern encampments, were subjected to repeated humiliations and acts of terrorization but also manifested a willingness to resist such treatment.

Florida, especially the west coast area around Tampa, was the jumping-off place for Caribbean operations, and black servicemen encountered the virulent racism prevailing in that state. In Lakeland blacks reacted to threats of violence and refusal of service in stores. John E. Lewis of the Tenth Cavalry wrote of Lakeland's beauty but added: "it is a hell for the colored people who live here, and they live in dread at all times. If one colored man commits a crime, it does not make any particular difference whether they get the right party or not; all they want is a black." At a drugstore a white barber, the "main man" according to Lewis, cursed black soldiers and went for his gun, but the soldiers fired and killed him. Several weeks later Lewis wrote that in the aftermath of the shooting there had been "a marked change in the disposition of the people, and many believe that it was through the providence of God that he was killed." Apparently white merchants were now pleased to serve black customers. A black serviceman later wrote that black troopers did not find very practical advice given by white officers that they should just walk away from insult. The problem was that racist whites would often resort to violence, and the servicemen commended the example of Sergeant D. T. Brown of Atlanta, who administered a beating to a white who had struck him from behind.

Chaplain George W. Prioleau of the Ninth Cavalry went to Tuskegee, Alabama, to enlist volunteers and there encountered exclusion from a white church. Prioleau wrote that he did not fail to inform the whites that such an act was "heinous, uncivilized, un-christian...un-American." He was informed that "niggers" had been lynched in Alabama for saying less than that. The chaplain recalled his answer in this language: "We replied that only cowards and assassins would overpower a man at midnight and take him from his bed and lynch him, but the night you dirty cowards come to my quarters for that purpose there will be a hot time in Tuskegee that hour; that we are only three who would die but not alone." Prioleau and his recruiting party did not suffer violence in Tuskegee, but in South Carolina, he later reported, the recruiters were "most brutally treated, and there was no redress." He was acutely conscious of the militant racism prevailing in the state, for, as he wrote, if a black man married or even looked at a white woman of South Carolina he was promptly lynched, "swung to the limb of a tree and his body riddled with bullets."

It was not surprising that a black soldier wrote that blacks preferred going to Cuba to remaining in any part of the South. At Camp Poland, Tennessee, when black North Carolina volunteers appeared in the drill field they were fired upon by members of a white Georgia regiment. Relations were particularly tense at Camp Haskell, near Macon, Georgia. Black volunteers encountered a symbol of racism, a tree that had been used to lynch blacks. A group of black soldiers took axes and cut the tree down. Also in a local park marked by little signs saying "No Niggers and Dogs Allowed in Here" volunteers tore down the insulting notices. Blacks in uniform were discriminated against on the streetcars. "Ham," a member of the Sixth Virginia Cavalry, noted the killing of Private Elijah Turner by a streetcar conductor, an action found to be "justifiable homicide" by the jury, and put the event in context: "Hasn't a week passed since we have been in this pest hold of the South that some of Uncle Sam's black boys in blue, haven't been 'justifiably homicided,' at least this is the only word that seems to strike the minds of all juries who try cases for 'killing nigger soldiers,' and we will thank God with all our hearts when we are moved from the contaminating influences of contact with these 'Georgia crackers,' for they truly deserve the title." According to Willard Gatewood, by the time the black soldiers left Camp Haskell in early 1899 at least three black soldiers had been killed in incidents stemming from refusal to relinquish streetcar seats.

C. W. Cordin of the Seventh Infantry vividly portrayed in the *Cleveland Gazette* the racist violence that prevailed in and about Macon. He told of one of the lynchings that had occurred at the tree. The victim's name was Will Singleton, who had been caught in Alabama. "The mob took him to their tree, first cut out his———; then hung him and shot him full of holes. His———were taken to the city, put into a bottle and pickled with alcohol." He added these parts had been displayed in a local saloon until the black soldiers were about to arrive. Cordin related the economic oppression of "our country people" to violence, observing that whites would pay ten or twenty-five cents, claim the black laborer was paid in full, and "if any words are passed, a crowd comes to the poor Afro-American's cabin that night, and he is whipped and sometimes killed." Cordin further reported the cruel treatment of black women prisoners who were compelled to do gang labor on the roads and ditches and flogged as extra punishment.

As concerns the American occupation of the Philippines, Gatewood finds a broad range of opinion among black soldiers sent to the islands as participants in the war to suppress the independence movement led by Emilio Aguinaldo. This opinion was communicated to blacks back in the United States, as letters from the soldiers appeared often in the black press. At one extreme echoed the arguments of colonialism, and at the other were blacks who fully sympathized with the revolutionary cause, among whom some, most notably David Fagan of the Twenty-fourth Infantry, went over to the insurgent side. But most did what they saw as their "duty" and hoped their performance would aid the cause of full citizenship back home. But, Gatewood writes, "they never lost sight of the similarity between the predicament of the black man in America and the brown man in the Philippines." One anonymous black soldier most pointedly expressed the anguish of his position. He noted that the new white rulers "began to apply home treatment for colored peoples: curse them as damned niggers, steal from and ravish them, rob them on the street of their small change, take from the fruit vendors whatever suited their fancy, and kick the poor unfortunate if he complained, desecrate their church property, and after fighting began, looted everything in sight, burning, robbing the graves." Whites in speaking with black troops spoke of the Filipinos as "niggers," and should they be reminded of the uses back home of such language some lame excuse was made. The trooper said that if it were not for the sake of ten million blacks at home he did not know which side he would be on, but he opposed acquisition of the islands and urged election of the Democratic party pledged against this "highway robbery." The Filipino revolutionaries were particularly aware of the paradoxical position of the black troops and made efforts to reach them with placards and other means of propaganda. A black soldier, Michael H. Robinson, wrote that the placards declared that blacks in America were "being lynched and disfranchised by the same who are trying to compel us to believe that their government will deal justly and fairly by us." Most interestingly, one of the insurgent placards referred to the Sam Hose lynching in Georgia, linking Robert Charles in New Orleans, W. E. B. Du Bois in Atlanta, and the Filipino fighters for independence in recognition of what the Georgia atrocity meant.[46]

A skeptical attitude toward involvement in the Spanish-American War was widely prevalent among Afro-Americans, and outright opposition was the predominant black response to acquisition of the Philippines. The views of blacks on these issues were at least partly shaped by concern with racist violence and the failure of the national government to do anything about it. Adding to a sense that the country needed a different set of priorities than that apparently held by the McKinley administration was the killing, within two weeks of the sinking of the *Maine,* of a black postmaster and his infant son at Lake City, South Carolina. Given that the murdered man, Frazier B. Baker, was a federal officeholder, it might be expected that federal authorities would intervene, but there was no such intervention. When Ida B. Wells-Barnett was sent to Washington to urge action she found her efforts constricted by the mood of preoccupation with the likelihood of war with Spain. A black editor in Lexington, Kentucky, commented that if "Remember the *Maine*" had become the white man's slogan, blacks should make theirs the remembering of the murder of Postmaster Baker. A prominent black Ohioan, Ralph W. Tyler, wrote that he would not fight for the United States "as long as the nightmare of Lake City remains undispelled." Early in July 1898 John Mitchell of the *Richmond Planet* listed a dozen lynchings that had occurred since the declaration of war and noted that this evidence argued against the view that the war would weaken race prejudice. Bishop Henry M. Turner declared bluntly that blacks who fought in the war died for nothing, having fought for a country where enough blacks had been "lynched to death to reach a mile high if laid one upon the other."[47]

Specific instances of violence also played a role in forming black opposition to McKinley's Philippine policy. One such instance was the lynching in April 1899 of Sam Hose, and the other was the murder of a half-dozen blacks at Palmetto, Georgia, on March 15. A provocative sequel to the Palmetto lynchings was a statement by Governor Allen D. Candler that blamed the presence of black volunteers in the state for the racial tensions that had resulted in violence.[48] These killings and the continuing failure of federal authorities to take any action offered ample evidence that the United States was not fit for the work of bringing freedom to other peoples.

Willard Gatewood sums up the response of Afro-Americans to the new flowering of imperialism: "Anti-imperialism became the prevailing sentiment within the black community; increase in this sentiment coincided with the upsurge in anti-imperialist opinion among white Americans." Blacks related their view of American imperialism to what they already knew of American society as it functioned at home. As Gatewood observes: "Within the context of his own experience the black American was led to suspect that the policy of imperialism was but another manifestation of white supremacy likely to have frightful consequences for colored people abroad as well as those at home."[49] And Afro-Americans extended their hostility to imperialism to take a sympathetic view of the Filipino struggle for freedom. In voicing their opinions on the war and the American colonialism it furthered, Afro-Americans were acting on their right to speak out on matters of foreign policy, rejecting any notion that they should cut themselves off from vital issues that would shape the context in which all Americans lived. At the turn of the century black Americans set a precedent for the actions of blacks in future decades who would not be silent on the great issues of war and peace, the defining of the American relationship to the revolutionary world of the twentieth century.

PART II

From 1900 to the "Red Summer"

The tree where the lynching occurred was right under the Mayor's window. Mayor Dollins was standing in the window, not concerned about what they were doing to the boy, but that the tree would be destroyed.

"The Waco Horror," Supplement to *Crisis*, July 1916

No colored man can read an account of the recent lynching at Gainesville, Fla., without being ashamed of his people.... Without resistance they let a white mob whom they outnumbered two to one, torture, harry and murder their women, shoot down innocent men entirely unconnected with the alleged crime, and finally to cap the climax, they caught and surrendered the wretched man whose attempted arrest caused the difficulty.

No people who behave with the absolute cowardice shown by these colored people can hope to have the sympathy or help of the civilized folk.... In the last analysis lynching of Negroes is going to stop in the South when the cowardly mob is faced by effective guns in the hands of people determined to sell their souls dearly.

W. E. B. Du Bois, *Crisis*, October 1916, pp. 270–71

This boy asked to be allowed to go see his sick brother some four or five miles away, and his request was not granted. He was compelled to work by force, and had to ask for permission to leave before he could get away from the plantation. He tried to get permission several times, and it was refused. He finally one Sunday walked over to his mother's, and while there Mr. Dixon drove up with one of his men and beat the boy in the presence of his mother unmercifully with a pistol until he was bloody. Then the boy was tied around the neck, just as you tie an animal, his hands were handcuffed behind him, and the other end of the rope was placed in the hands of one of his men who was on a mule, and the boy was compelled to run afoot for six or seven miles behind this mule, while Mr. Dixon himself followed horseback whipping him whenever he would lag behind.

U.S. Attorney W. S. Reece, Jr., to Department of Justice, June 1903

Washington was saved from a dreadful disgrace when the colored men were not driven out of the city, which was the ultimate aim of the white brutes. If it were the lawless element of our race that stopped the onslaught, then the others of us should hang our heads in disgrace. We have shown how we can and will retaliate. The other race will think twice the next time before they strike a single blow. Innocent pedestrians were maltreated near the doors of the White House, while the President stood inside. Washington papers did all they could to stir up race antagonism. It was the fighting qualities of the Negro who stayed in the streets that put an end to the trouble.

William Monroe Trotter, Washington's Metropolitan
African Methodist Episcopal Church, August 1919

FOUR

The Violence of the Progressive Era

THE TWENTIETH century was heralded as the dawn of a new enlightened age of reason and peace. But in actuality mankind during the new century was to witness both revolutionary change and violence unleashed on an unprecedented scale. In the years since 1900 Afro-Americans, operating in a changed world context and expressing their demands through a more effective, organized militancy, have made progress in their struggle for freedom. But these years have also seen racial violence intensified, modernized in its methods, and extended throughout the nation.

The violence inflicted upon blacks during the early years of the twentieth century foreshadowed the genocidal treatment of racial and ethnic minorities that would become one of the hallmarks of this era. Violence against individuals or groups of individuals would become transformed into a systematic assault upon the lives and physical well-being of the entire minority group, in its most extreme form developing into an attempt to exterminate entire peoples. In the United States after 1900, lynchings continued as weekly phenomena, and mob assaults, comparable to European pogroms, against black communities became commonplace occurrences in both the North and the South. W. E. B. Du Bois was indeed prescient when he wrote that "the problem of the twentieth century is the problem of the color line." What to some appeared to be only an issue of parochial American significance Du Bois recognized as having critical meaning for the world.

An introduction to the racial brutality of the present century was provided by the 1900 "riot" occurring in the city of New York. This event was a confrontation between the black population of the nation's greatest and most cosmopolitan city on one side and the official representatives of law and order on the other. New York streets were the setting for acts of terror against blacks, and in the aftermath of mob violence the point was driven home that public authority would not discipline those responsible.

The violence was touched off by an incident on August 12. At Forty-first Street and Eighth Avenue a plainclothesman, Robert J. Thorpe, attempted to arrest the wife of Arthur Harris, a black man, for supposedly "soliciting." Harris, who later asserted he did not know the detective was a policeman, appeared on the scene and sought to rescue his wife. The policeman struck Harris with his club, and in retaliation Harris stabbed the officer with a penknife, inflicting a fatal wound.

Following the death of the policeman Thorpe, police officers and other whites were incensed, and the anger was expressed in a desire for vengeance against the black community generally. Quite clearly, whatever happened between Officer Thorpe and Mr. and Mrs. Harris, the mob responded to the incident as a racial matter. In the next few days, particularly on August 15 and 16, blacks on Manhattan's West Side were subject to repeated attacks by white toughs, with police both encouraging and participating in the violence. An attorney, Frank Moss, retained as counsel by black community leaders, summarized the role of the police:

> In many instances of brutality by the mob policemen stood by and made no effort to protect the Negroes who were assailed. They ran with the crowds in pursuit of their prey; they took defenseless men who ran to them for protection and threw them to the rioters, and in many cases they beat and clubbed men and women more brutally than the mob did. They were absolutely unrestrained by their superior officers. It was the night sticks of the police that sent a stream of bleeding colored men to the hospital, and that made the station house in West 37th Street look like a field hospital in the midst of battle. Men who were taken to the station house by officers and men in the station house were beaten by policemen without mercy, and their cries of distress made sleep impossible for those who lived in the rear of the station house.[1]

The New York police department responsible for this violence had a widely advertised record of corruption and other acts of official misconduct. During the 1890s the Lexow inquiry authorized by the state legislature had exposed a widespread system of graft that included many New York police officials. Theodore Roosevelt had been appointed as police commissioner to institute reform, and he had removed some of the better-known grafters. The system of payoffs in exchange for special favors remained, however, and it was certainly true that in 1900 the New York police department, once again under the control of a Tammany administration, did not enjoy a stainless reputation. But in the case of violence against blacks the white citizenry and responsible public officials, including the mayor, were unwilling to take any effective action to punish police wrongdoing. Exposure of graft might cause an uproar, but clubbing and beating black New Yorkers caused no scandal. The mayor, the police commissioners, and the municipal courts joined in covering up crimes by members of the police department.

If the cover-up succeeded and those responsible for violence against blacks went unpunished it was not for want of articulate, mass protest from the black community. A new organization, the Citizens Protective League, was formed for the purpose of obtaining justice in regard to the August violence and to prevent similar outbreaks in the future. Within a few weeks of formation the organization claimed to have 5,000 members. On September 12, 3,500 people assembled at Carnegie Hall to protest the brutalities. A number of blacks filed suit against the city for damage inflicted upon them by the mob. Seventy-nine individuals submitted affidavits concerning their experiences during the violence, and these affidavits were published by the Citizens Protective League as a book, *Story of the Riot,* which gave a coherent and convincing picture of the lawless acts committed by mob and police.

The response of city officials revealed how public protest could be effectively muffled by bureaucratic indifference and some skill at conducting a sham investigation. In reply to the Citizens Protective League's request for an inquiry as to the facts Mayor Robert Van Wyck stated that the matter was entirely in the hands of the police. The matter was placed in the hands of officials of a police force whose chief was charged by the league with neglect of duty. A "hearing" was held by the police board in which attorneys for black grievants and the Citizens Protective League were not permitted to question witnesses. The "hearing" closed with no action taken against any member of the police force. A grand jury "investigation" was also held, but no indictments or findings were handed down.[2] Individual citizens have frequently found difficulty obtaining remedy for injustices suffered at the hands of the police, but in this episode in New York there was abundant evidence of official misconduct and yet the city would not authorize any impartial public inquiry into the facts. The story told by black witnesses was denied by police witnesses, and in New York and the United States of 1900 that was the end of the matter.[3]

What occurred in New York was what today would most likely be termed an urban race riot, but that terminology hides more than it reveals. The riot was initiated by white aggression against the black community with police often playing a key role in either encouraging or directly participating in the aggressive acts. The aggression could be ignited when political candidates found it expedient to stir up racial hatred or because corporations hired black workers from the South to take the jobs of white workers or because a corrupt city administration decided to distract public attention by generating racial hysteria. Racial aggression was also likely to occur if blacks refused to accommodate themselves to the prevailing racial mores. Whatever the particular factor setting off violence, an ingredient present in almost every situation was connivance by public authorities and newspapers that refused to uphold law and order when the issue was the rights of black citizens. In the years before the end of World War I white aggression characteristically was met defensively by blacks, with blacks in the downtown areas seeking to escape from racist mobs and families in the black community protecting themselves as best they could. Black wage earners were often caught in a terrible quandary. If they clung to the relative safety of home they might lose their jobs or at least lose the pay required to provide necessities, but if they chose to go to work they risked death or injury from the mob. Violence and economic pressures worked together to terrorize blacks.

In the years following the 1900 events in New York, urban racial confrontation erupted in several American cities, North and South, amply demonstrating that racial conflict had become a nationwide phenomenon. The United States was rapidly becoming an urbanized nation, and as the cities grew, disparate ethnic, racial, and class groupings struggled to define their place in the urban context. The city did not dissolve existing tensions but rather provided a critically important arena within which the tensions of American society would manifest themselves. The concentration of large populations in relatively congested space made for a tendency for confrontations to be particularly explosive.

Atlanta was the city of progress in the South. Largely destroyed by Sherman's army during the Civil War, the city had been rebuilt, had become the leading business center of the Southeast, and was also a center of an emerging black middle class. In the city's western district, quite close to the downtown area, stood several institutions of higher education for blacks, including Atlanta University and Morehouse, Spelman, Clark, and Morris Brown colleges. In the early years of the twentieth century a major center of black education and culture was already growing in Atlanta. At Atlanta University W. E. B. Du Bois pursued his scholarly work as professor of sociology, producing numerous scientific studies of black life in the South. Atlanta was the city from which the white editor Henry Grady had sounded the call for a New South that would put behind it the issues of the Civil War and concentrate on material progress. And of course it was in Atlanta, in 1895 at the opening of the Cotton States Exposition, that Booker T. Washington had articulated his formula for racial accommodation under which blacks would exchange opportunity for economic advancement for a deferring of political rights and would also, at least for the time being, accept segregation.

Atlanta's self-image as a progressive city was mocked during 1906 by a mass assault unleashed by white mobs against the black community. Charles Crowe does not exaggerate in observing that although the word *genocide* did not exist in 1906, "the conditions which made general slaughter a real possibility were present before, during, and after the Atlanta riot."[4] This violence was not simply a spontaneous explosion but rather the product of political opportunism and journalistic sensationalism that exploited race hatred. The context of this eruption of violence in September 1906 was shaped by a recent bitter Democratic primary contest in which the successful gubernatorial candidate Hoke Smith had campaigned for black disfranchisement. A play glorifying the Ku Klux Klan and portraying the supposed horrors of Reconstruction, Thomas Dixon's *Clansman,* later to be made into the film *Birth of a Nation,* had lately been presented in Atlanta. Perhaps of greatest significance was a newspaper campaign, complete with lurid headlines, against crimes supposedly committed by blacks. The press of Atlanta raised the specter of outraged white womanhood before its readers, and the results were quite predictable.

Something of the tenor of Atlanta journalistic opinion was conveyed by the *Atlanta Georgian*'s editorial urging of castration for all black rapists. Several readers of the newspaper would take more drastic action. One writer declared: "Let's continue to kill all negroes who commit the unmentionable crime and make eunuchs of all new male issues before they are eight days old." Another individual, convinced that black women seduced white males in order to have mulatto children, recommended sterilization of black baby girls. These letters expressed a compound of mental derangement and racism, but as John Dittmer reports, *Georgian* editor John Temple Graves, a personal friend of Theodore Roosevelt, "printed without editorial comment these letters advocating genocide."

The *Atlanta Evening News* also contributed its ample share to the igniting of white hysteria. The *News* portrayed the situation of white women sitting next to their black chauffeurs and flavored the scene with vivid racist imagery: "To see a big black negro sitting alongside and touching the body of a white woman makes the blood in every white man's veins boil. . . . They get in these narrow seated buggies and take a big black buck up by their side, and it is utterly impossible for the woman to keep from touching the body of the negro." The paper urged the revival of the Ku Klux Klan, and for this utterance the paper's editor, Charles Daniels, was made a special deputy sheriff. In bestowing the honor Fulton County's sheriff declared: "Gentlemen, we will suppress these great indignities upon our fair wives and daughters if we have to kill every negro in a thousand miles of this place."[5]

The Atlanta confrontation was set in the context of a statewide pattern of racial violence that was most typically expressed in lynching. In the period from 1882 to 1923 Georgia led the nation in the number of lynchings. This form of atrocity, as Dittmer observes, "was tolerated and at times even encouraged by the white ruling class." Georgia law officers did practically nothing to prevent lynchings or to punish lynchers. The indifference, for example, of Judge Charles H. Brand of Lawrenceville led to three lynchings, but this official readily justified his refusal to summon troops: "I don't propose to be the engine of sacrificing any white man's life for all such Negro criminals in the country. I would not imperil the life of one white man to save the lives of a hundred such Negroes. I am opposed to lynching, but if I had called the military and some young man among the soldiers was killed or some of the citizens of Walton County were killed I would never forgive myself."

An episode that incorporated many of the characteristics of lynching as public, flaunted spectacle was the 1904 lynching in Statesboro of two illiterate turpentine workers, Paul Reed and Will Catto. The two men were charged with the murders of a white family, Henry and Claudia Hodges and their three children. Reed and Catto were convicted following perfunctory trials and sentenced to death. But lawful process was to be ignored. With a crowd of 10,000 assembled for the trial, many brought to town in extra coaches placed in service by the railroad, the lynch mob readily took command. There was a company of state militia present, but helpfully the militia troops carried unloaded weapons and in any case did nothing to interfere with the impending violence. The sheriff pointed out the convicted men, and Reed and Catto were marched to a turpentine forest. The prisoners were photographed and then burned to death in a fire of wood and oil. Following the event souvenir hunters sifted through what little remains were left. It is noteworthy that Statesboro whites who justified the lynching and did nothing to bring the lynchers to justice were at least partially joined by the *Atlanta Journal,* which asked: "Where is the man who can wholly condemn those who on yesterday avenged the cruel murder of the Hodges family?"

Blacks were not merely the passive victims of the violence inflicted by the dominant white group, sometimes reacting violently to the conditions of racial subjection. Violent acts resulted from disputes with white employers, from incidents of sexual assault upon black women, and from aggressive conduct by the police. Black resistance to the police was a particularly perilous infringement of the color line. When in 1915 Daniel Barber and his family beat up the Monticello police chief who had come to arrest Barber on a bootlegging charge, other police arrived to jail this black family. A mob of 200 dragged the Barbers from jail and hanged the family members, one by one, with the father being the last to die.[6]

The Hampton Institute periodical, the *Southern Workman*, was perfectly right in its view that anyone who followed the course of events in Georgia was not surprised by the Atlanta riot. The wonder, indeed, was that it had not come sooner. The magazine referred readers to an *Atlantic Monthly* article that cogently explained how racial rioting was a predictable result of activity by those seeking violence:

> it was certain that the full stream of oratory was again flowing. It was at first received with incredulity. The plain fact was that the Negro did not threaten the white man. Life was going on as peacefully as at any time in the history of the state.... But the cry continued that something must be done, unless Anglo-Saxon civilization was to be abandoned, and our homes ruined ... race-difference became in many minds a fierce race-hatred. There is no way to know how many crimes were provoked by this outburst of race-feeling. But every crime, little or big, that was committed was described again and again and commented on. The newspapers became unreadable by decent women. Conversation ran to criminal talk. The political orators talked crime. The redcoats of the ku-klux era reappeared. Negroes were threatened and intimidated. Even the pulpit took up the cry, "Our homes must be saved!"
>
> Of course there were protests; but they came too late. Many men who understood the insincerity of it all, and saw the harm that it was doing—for such a crusade provokes the very evils that it cries out against, and all other evils of social disorder—such men declared their objection. But they had feeble voices, because they spoke too late. The volcano was in eruption. It was too late to say there was no volcano.[7]

On the day the Atlanta riot began, September 22, the newspapers had headlined accounts of four supposed assaults by blacks upon white women. The nationally known muckraker Ray Stannard Baker, who visited Atlanta several weeks after the events and carefully assembled the facts, later reported in the *American* magazine that two of these incidents involved "nothing more than fright on the part of both the white woman and the Negro." The other two incidents, according to Baker, "may have been attempts at assaults."[8] The violence began in the downtown area with a white mob dragging out a black youth at work shining shoes and kicking and beating him to death. Another black was stabbed to death. Wherever found, blacks were assaulted, whether working in barbershops shaving customers or on the streetcars or simply walking along the street. The *Atlanta Constitution* described the scene following the murder of two black barbers in their shop. "The bodies of both barbers were first kicked and then dragged from the place. Grabbing at their clothing, this was soon torn from them, many of the crowd taking these rags of shirts and clothing home as souvenirs or waving them above their heads to invite to further riot." When the victims were dragged into the street "the faces of both barbers were terribly mutilated, while the floor of the shop was wet with puddles of blood." Finally both bodies were left, thrown together, in the alleyway leading to the new gas and electric company building. The *Constitution* reported that a third black, "caught upon the streets, was also set upon, beaten to death, and his body thrown alongside of the two already in the alleyway." All of this happened, the paper noted, "almost within the shadow of the monument of Henry W. Grady."[9] The mob armed itself with weapons taken by ransacking hardware stores. Ray Stannard Baker reported that the first response of many Atlanta blacks was to seek white protection and that indeed some prominent whites did shield a number of black people. Black Atlantans sought to make what use they could of the southern tradition of paternalism.[10]

Two days following the first outbreak, a confrontation in Brownsville, a black suburb to the southeast of downtown Atlanta, demonstrated what happened when blacks exercised the right of self-defense. As news spread of the first attacks upon blacks, residents of Brownsville determined they would defend themselves and their homes if attacked. That determination of course did not suit the racists, and police moved in to arrest black citizens for having armed themselves. By that act police clearly revealed their partisanship; whites had been allowed to seize and use arms practically at will, but when blacks, responding to news of bloodshed downtown, prepared to act in self-defense, the police took action. The police met with resistance in Brownsville, however. When police opened fire upon a group of blacks on the street the blacks responded in kind, and one officer was killed and another wounded. Several of the Brownsville residents were killed or wounded.[11]

The next day police and troops occupied the Brownsville community.Sixty blacks were arrested and charged with killing the police officer, and the Brownsville residents were all disarmed. President Bowen of Gammon Theological Seminary was beaten over the head by a policeman using a rifle butt. Four blacks were killed in Brownsville, added to six blacks and two whites killed earlier in the incidents that occurred in the center of the city. Regarding the Brownsville episode, the foreman of the jury hearing the case of arrested blacks said: "We think the Negroes were gathered just as white people were in other parts of the town, for the purpose of defending their homes. We were shocked by the conduct which some of the county police had been guilty of."[12]

Ray Stannard Baker gave his readers an account of how black Atlantans acted in response to the violence, and he also made some effort to explain how blacks felt about the events. He quoted the words of a young black man, formerly a resident of Atlanta and now studying in the North:

It is possible that you have formed at least a good idea of how we feel as the result of the horrible eruption in Georgia. I have not spoken to a Caucasian on the subject since then. But, listen: How would you feel, if with our history, there came a time when, after speeches and papers and teachings you acquired property and were educated, and were a fairly good man, it were impossible for you to walk the streets (for whose maintenance you were taxed) with your sister without being in mortal fear of death if you resented any insult offered to her? How would you feel if you saw a governor, a mayor, a sheriff, whom you could not oppose at the polls, encourage by deed or word or both, a mob of "best" and worst citizens to slaughter your people in the streets and in their homes and in their places of business? Do you think that you could resist the same wrath that caused God to slay the Philistines and the Russians to throw bombs? I can resist it, but with each new outrage, I am less able to resist it. And yet if I gave way to my feelings I should become just like other men...of the mob! But I do not...not quite, and I must hurry through the only life I shall live on earth, tortured by these experiences and these horrible impulses, with no hope of ever getting away from them. They are ever present, like the just God, the devil, and my conscience.[13]

The Atlanta events also had a traumatizing effect on another black youth, Walter White, later famous as a National Association for the Advancement of Colored People (NAACP) spokesman, who then lived with his parents in a neat little house on Houston Street, near the city's downtown section. White's father had been warned that the mob intended to march down Houston Street to "clean out the niggers," and so the lights were turned out in the house and father and son Walter, aged thirteen, took up positions, guns in hand, at the front windows. Soon the mob approached, and one of the crowd called out concerning the White home, "That's where that nigger mail carrier lives. Let's burn it down! It's too nice for a nigger to live in"—a comment in its way on Booker T. Washington's philosophy of earning white respect by economic respectability. The senior White was a man of firm sobriety and devoutly religious, but in that moment he quietly told his son, "Son, don't shoot until the first man puts his foot on the lawn and then—don't you miss!" They did not need to shoot as shots from a nearby building induced the mob to retreat, but as White recalled decades later the moment had been one of self-recognition. White wrote: "In that instant there opened up within me a great awareness; I knew who I was. I was a Negro, a human being with an invisible pigmentation which marked me as a person to be hunted, hanged, abused, discriminated against, kept in poverty and ignorance, in order that those whose skin was white would have readily at hand a proof of their superiority, a proof patent and inclusive, accessible to the moron and the idiot as well as to the wise man and the genius." White was light-skinned, with blond hair and blue eyes, and in later years while investigating lynchings in the South he was often to "pass," but now he was conscious of his true racial identity and he was glad of it. "I was sick with loathing for the hatred which had flared before me that night and came so close to making me a killer; but I was glad I was not one of those who hated: I was glad I was not one of those whose story is in the history of the world, a record of bloodshed, rapine, and pillage. I was glad my mind and spirit were part of the races that had not fully awakened, and who therefore had still before them the opportunity to write a record of virtue as a memorandum to Armageddon." Herbert Aptheker has written that a fundamental theme in Afro-American literature is "the moral superiority of the Black as compared to the white," and White's recollection of his reaction to the 1906 violence is certainly supportive of that view.[14]

If the words of White and the young man quoted by Baker expressed individual anguish at the Atlanta events, the clergyman Reverdy Ransom speaking in Boston's Faneuil Hall drew upon the incident to urge the course of migration from the South. Ransom advocated self-defense, declaring that if the black American "is doomed to forever grind the Philistines' corn and to be a victim of their cruel sports, he would prefer, like Sampson of old, to lay hold of the pillars of America's temple of

Dagon and to die with the Philistines." He contrasted the sympathy evoked by the disaster of the 1906 San Francisco earthquake with the indifferent response of much American opinion to the Atlanta violence. He said: "This Atlanta butchery is without palliation and excuse." And he also spoke plainly about the "expediency, cowardice and indifference" that advised surrendering constitutional rights "with the hope of regaining them at some distant day." Ransom rejected the argument that economic advancement was the path for southern blacks, explaining that success was counterproductive, for if the black "were too largely engaged in mercantile pursuits, having shops, stores and banks, the mob would find a ready pretext to assail him in order to plot, to plunder and to steal." Therefore, the solution was to abandon the South, and Ransom observed that if European immigrants could assist others back home to emigrate to the United States, "we can also advise, assist, and encourage millions of our people to leave the South." Ransom pointed to possibilities for settlement in New England and the states of the Midwest, and if he was overly optimistic in contending that millions could find "liberty, prosperity, and peace" in the North he was realistic in his call for a population movement that would inevitably extend the battle for racial progress beyond the southern context.[15]

Two years after the Atlanta events the phenomenon of the race riot appeared in the Midwest, in racist brutality inflicted upon the black community of Springfield, Illinois. There was irony as well as bloodshed in what happened in Springfield, for the city had been the home of Abraham Lincoln, and the desecration of the Great Emancipator's memory was obvious. And yet what particularly struck the journalist William English Walling, who described and analyzed the Springfield riot in an article, "The Race War in the North," appearing in the *Independent* magazine was the indifference of national opinion to a basic component of the riot, the deep racial hatred demonstrated by a community of northern whites. Walling observed that "we have closed our eyes to the whole awful and menacing truth—that a large part of the white population of Lincoln's home, supported largely by the farmers and miners of the neighboring towns, have initiated a permanent warfare with the negro race."[16] He found that northern opinion believed that there were "mitigating circumstances" for the racial hatred revealed at Springfield. Race prejudice was clearly a factor controlling the behavior of many whites who justified violence with the words, "Why, the niggers come to think they were as good as we are." Walling was convinced that thirty years earlier, "when the memories of Lincoln, Garrison and Wendell Phillips were still fresh," all talk of mitigating circumstances would have been set aside and the people of Springfield would have had to explain their violent conduct. But in 1908 white Springfield was not on the defensive, and indeed the local newspaper could write that "it was not the fact of the white's hatred toward the negroes, but of the negroes' own misconduct, general inferiority or unfitness for free institutions that were at fault."[17]

In mid-August 1908, Springfield reacted southern-style to inflammatory reports that a white woman had been assaulted in her home by a black man. The mob assembled for the purpose of lynching the person charged with the crime and proceeded to march upon the jail. The self-appointed executioners were unable to get their hands on their intended victim, however, and they gave vent to their frustration by lynching two other black persons. The homes of numerous black families were set afire in the course of the mob's rampage through the town. Still the racists were not satisfied with this destruction, and agitation was initiated to drive Springfield's black population out of the city. Later it was revealed that the individual charged with assault had been wrongly identified and the indictment was dismissed. But, as Ida Wells-Barnett reminded a 1909 meeting, the lynched victims were dead, "hundreds were homeless and Illinois was disgraced."[18] William English Walling used the Springfield events to arouse the national conscience: "Either the spirit of the abolitionists, of Lincoln and Lovejoy must be revived and we must come to treat the negro on a plane of absolute political and social equality, or Vardaman and Tillman will soon have transferred the race war to the North."[19]

During the Springfield violence blacks fought vigorously in self-defense. Blacks shot back when fired upon, and the first victim of the lynch mob used his shotgun in a vain attempt to protect his life and home.[20] After the violence was over, some fifty whites were among those requiring hospital treatment.

In the first two decades of the twentieth century major incidents related to the theme of racial violence occurred at least twice within the United States Army. The Brownsville episode of 1906 raised the issue of the government's reaction to charges that black soldiers had run amok in the Texas town of Brownsville. The episode was the consequence of assigning a battalion of black troops, the First Battalion of the Twenty-fifth Infantry Regiment, to Fort Brown, located near Brownsville. The obvious problem was that Brownsville was a Jim Crow town that rigidly enforced segregation etiquette and had no interest in welcoming the black troopers. One black soldier recalled years later that the town park featured a sign announcing: "No niggers and no dogs allowed." At least twice black soldiers were pushed and knocked down for supposedly behaving disrespectfully toward whites. On the night of August 13 a party of some sixteen to twenty men, never identified, shot into various buildings in the town, with the result that one police officer was wounded and a bartender was killed.[21] In the several official inquiries that followed these events the presumption was always that the black troopers must have been responsible for the violence, and pressure steadily mounted for the soldiers to admit their own guilt or, if innocent themselves, to name those among them who were guilty. The government was seeking to recruit informers and thus divert attention from the racist treatment accorded the soldiers by Brownsville whites and beyond that to evade the issue of the army's failure to protect black soldiers from such treatment.

The soldiers making up Companies B, C, and D of the First Battalion refused the request to turn informers, standing together in what one army investigator termed a "conspiracy of silence." Manifestly prejudiced in their racial views, the army officers conducting inquiries into the Brownsville affair recommended that all enlisted men of the three companies be discharged without honor and excluded from all future government service. On November 5, 1906, President Theodore Roosevelt approved this recommendation and ordered that it be carried out. One week after the November 9 congressional election the army began the discharge of 167 soldiers. They were discharged without receiving back pay and denied all allowances, pension rights, and other benefits. The discharges of the men ousted from the army in 1906 stood until September 28, 1972, when the United States Army finally ordered that the discharges be declared honorable. By that time one man, Dorsey Willis, eighty-six years of age, remained as a survivor of those belonging to the three companies.[22]

In one of his autobiographical essays W. E. B. Du Bois noted that the Brownsville soldiers "were accused of having revolted under the greatest provocation."[23] Although the identity of the persons who fired the shots was never learned, the provocation was ignored and the soldiers punished. In a matter of racial violence, the question of justice and due process would be set aside and blacks made to bear the consequences.

Roosevelt's action in this situation evoked severe criticism from Afro-American leaders. Even Booker T. Washington could not support Roosevelt on this issue and wrote Secretary of War Taft that "the race feels ...hurt and disappointed."[24] A particularly eloquent criticism of Roosevelt was voiced by the widely known black scholar, Professor Kelly

Miller of Howard University. Speaking in 1907, Miller paid tribute to
Roosevelt as a great world and national leader, but he did not mince
words in summing up the significance of Brownsville:

> This order of the President violates every principle of our jurispru-
> dence. . . . It was reserved for Senator Tillman to describe the act as
> executive lynching, a description which characterizes the deed with
> his wonted picturesque aptness of language. It possesses the essential
> characteristics of mob vengeance. It inflicts punishment on demand
> of the rabble rather than by judicial process. It furnishes victims to
> appease popular vengeance without nice regard to the identity of
> the perpetrator. The punishment of the possible innocent effectually
> destroys the evidence by which the guilty might subsequently be
> apprehended.[25]

There was indeed in Roosevelt's order of discharge something of the
flavor of the legal lynching. And there was also something of that spirit
in Roosevelt's annual message to Congress delivered in December 1906.
Miller declared concerning this message that, "however holy and righteous may have been the President's intentions, this message is calculated
to do the Negro more harm than any other state paper ever issued from
the White House."[26] Roosevelt did indeed condemn lynching, urging
whites to understand "that every lynching represents by just so much a
loosening of the bonds of civilization," but as was the case on many
questions there was ambiguity in his remarks. He legitimized the justification most often given for lynching in his comment that "the greatest
existing cause of lynching is the perpetration, especially by black men,
of the hideous crime of rape—the most abominable in all the category
of crimes, even worse than murder." Roosevelt also quoted approvingly
remarks by Governor Jelks of Alabama to the effect that such violence
as had erupted in Atlanta was provoked by the failure of the "better
elements" among black people to assist in capturing black criminals.
Roosevelt himself argued that "it should be felt as in the highest degree
an offense against the whole country, and against the colored race in
particular, for a colored man to fail to help the officers of the law in
hunting down with all possible earnestness and zeal every such infamous
offender." Roosevelt also stated in a remark he did not bother to explain
that with regard to rape cases he would urge that the punishment "may
follow immediately upon the heels of the offense."[27]

There was bitter irony in the president's words. Afro-Americans, although disfranchised and excluded from serving as police officers or

members of juries, were to assist officers of a racist South in tracking down blacks accused of rape. Such officers presumably would begin the process of seeing to it that little time was wasted between arrest, conviction, and final execution. Roosevelt was demanding that blacks give their support to a process that amounted to legal lynching.

Racism was also the key issue in the violence that broke out between police and black troops in Houston during 1917. As had happened in Brownsville, the context of the episode was determined by the army's decision to assign black soldiers to a community where they would be subject to repeated racist abuse.

Houston was a city where segregation, disfranchisement, and police brutality ruled. Regarding police treatment Robert Haynes notes that Houston blacks "were continually subjected to a double standard of justice—one for the white man and another for the colored man." Segregation extended to separate drinking fountains and to an ordinance making cohabitation between the races a crime. Beyond the city itself a pattern of terrorism prevailed in the state of Texas. The state was a leader in lynching statistics, with several of the atrocities occurring as large public spectacles. In 1893 a black victim, accused of the rape-murder of a five-year-old, was burned at the stake before some 15,000 onlookers, and there was the 1916 lynching of adolescent Jesse Washington in Waco. At least some of the black troops assigned to Houston had read accounts in the *Crisis* and in the *Chicago Defender* of the Waco incident.[28] It is a wonder that more black troopers did not conclude that the army had more urgent business in Texas than preparing for a European war.

The War Department sent the all-black Third Battalion of the Twenty-fourth Infantry to perform guard duty at Camp Logan, then under construction near Houston. Whites entering the camp repeatedly made derogatory racial remarks, referring to blacks as "niggers," and one white Houstonian stated his understanding "that in Texas it costs twenty-five dollars to kill a buzzard and five dollars to kill a nigger."[29] Blacks who demanded civility were accused of insolence. The hostility of racist Houston to the black servicemen was made clear as soon as the troops arrived in the area. White policemen assaulted and arrested black soldiers for refusing to obey Jim Crow signs. City detectives, early in August, beat two of the new arrivals on a streetcar. Despite such incidents Houston newspapers largely ignored the worsening local racial atmosphere, perhaps thinking that blacks could be kept in line by stories such as a brief account of the death of a Caldwell, Texas, black man shot for supposedly resisting arrest by a deputy sheriff.[30] With regard to local tension the press apparently carried only a report about the knifing at Camp Logan of a black civilian employee by an unidentified white man. The black man, Sam Blair, was actually the first to die in the Houston racial confrontation involving the Twenty-fourth.[31] The newspapers featured news of the progress in construction at Camp Logan, but meanwhile a deteriorating racial situation was further inflamed by an advertisement on August 20 that urged Houston residents to support Prohibition and "REMEMBER BROWNSVILLE." The ad announced that "3,000 NEGRO TROOPS" would be stationed in the city and asked: "Can the men of Harris County afford to continue the saloon in face of this?"[32]

The racial tensions between Houston police and the blacks at the army camp exploded on August 23. On that day two policemen beat a black soldier, Private Edwards, to the ground and arrested him after he had urged the officers to stop cursing and beating a black woman. Later when Corporal Charles Baltimore, a member of the provost guard, came up to the policeman and inquired about the arrest, stating it was his duty to report the matter to his superiors, he too was struck by the police, shot at when he attempted to move away, and finally arrested.

Up to this point what had occurred was a fairly standard matter of police brutality. But now there was an abrupt change in the sequence of events as the black soldiers at Camp Logan determined to seek retaliation for the insults and acts of violence inflicted upon them. The commanding officer of the Third Battalion, Major Snow, could offer no remedy when one of the enlisted men said, "We are treated like dogs here," and asked if the unit could not be moved from Houston. The soldiers had crossed the line between self-defense against immediate, direct assault and retaliatory action against those responsible for racial oppression. One of the soldiers shouted, "To hell with going to France, get to work right here." According to Robert Haynes, the leaders of the rebellion specially targeted the police who victimized the soldiers and specifically the mounted officers who patrolled the black San Felipe district.[33] Approximately 100 soldiers seized weapons and marched toward the city, soon encountering police and armed civilians. There was shooting, and when it was over twenty persons were dead, four black soldiers and sixteen whites, including four policemen.

In the aftermath of this confrontation what mattered was that blacks had taken up arms against white authority and had actually killed a number of whites. The role of racist provocation was ignored, and an attempt to settle scores with the police was transformed into a wholesale attack upon Houston. Houston clergymen joined in this process with the minister at the First Methodist Church declaring that those "who died that night to stem the black tide of death sweeping toward the homes of

Houston, they entered into the glory of God himself." One local publisher of a racist weekly asserted, "Texans expect a repitition [sic] of the Brownsville joke." It is noteworthy that the Houston Post indicated plainly that it had some understanding of what had produced the rebellion but just as plainly stated that the status quo would be preserved. "The negro soldiers," read an editorial, "resent our separate coach laws, our customs which prohibit mixed schools, mixed service at places of public enterprise, but this measure of separation is absolute and will be maintained." What maintaining the local system of racial separation entailed was made clear within a month of the August 23 incident when police shot and killed two blacks and at the nearby community of Goose Creek a mob of several hundred whites lynched a black man alleged to have raped a white woman.[34]

In response to the Houston incident the army confined 164 black soldiers to the prison stockade at Fort Bliss, near El Paso. A Texas newspaper reported on the jailed men in flagrantly racist terms. They were described by the reporter who came out to the fort as "like caged animals—silent, suspicious and thinking in a dull, unreasoning way only of their self-preservation." The reporter noted that the arrested men had not had the opportunity to talk with others, but he was also convinced they were unlikely to have anything to say. He wrote: "Only rational reasoning men who have committed felonies find the need of unburdening their minds of their crimes and reacting mentally to crush out the memories that persistently torment and often unseat the mind. But these prisoners are children psychologically, minus a child's intrinsic sense of right and wrong." But if they were children they were also blacks of "the new type" who no longer sang the old plantation songs. The new black soldier was a "colored gentleman," observed this journalist, someone "who has often associated with many whites who do not understand him or know how to treat him."

The men conducted prayer meetings, but the reporter could only comprehend that within the framework of his own racist consciousness. "It is certain," he wrote, "that the prayers represented nothing more than a response to the negro's susceptible spiritual nature, and had no element of remorse back of it. It is highly probable they would react as readily again on the impulse to slay if the same frenzied leadership had them in control." The reporter added: "It would not be fair to humanity to decide guilt by impression, but if these men were to be tried with no more evidence against them than their facial expression, their chances indeed would be small." It was further observed that, although what had happened in Houston was seemingly incredible, "yet to the mind of a South-

ern man, accustomed to the darky," it was quite understandable that
blacks could form into a mob capable of performing "almost any
atrocity."[35]

The United States Army treated with utmost severity the black soldiers
who had reacted to provocation. At a court-martial held at Fort Sam
Houston between November 1 and November 29, 1917, thirteen black
soldiers were sentenced to death, forty-two received life sentences, four
were given short prison terms, and four were acquitted.

The court-martial proceedings took place in the post chapel, a facility
earlier dedicated by President William Howard Taft, and provision was
made for segregated seating of black spectators at the extreme left of the
gallery. Many black observers stood. One of the black defendants was
threatened by an attack of appendicitis, but this soldier, W. R. Johnson,
was carried into the chapel on a stretcher.[36]

Coverage of the trial by G. Schnitzer of the *Houston Post* was blatantly
inflammatory. Early on, one of his dispatches was headlined, "Tale of
Blood Lust of Negro Soldiers," and on November 13 while the trial was
still in progress he reported that "punishment is assured." Two days later
he informed his readers that enough evidence had been entered to convict
a large number of defendants.[37] The defense had yet to open its case.

Both the findings of the court and the sentences were concealed from
the public until after the carrying out of the death sentences on December
11. The army denied the request of the black soldiers that if condemned
to execution they be shot rather than ignominiously hung.[38] There was
no review of the sentences by either the War Department or President
Wilson. Later, two additional trials of black troops were held at which
sixteen more men were sentenced to death and twelve received life terms.
As a consequence of presidential review of the trial record, ten of the
death sentences were commuted to life terms. For six of the condemned
men, however, there was no commutation and they were hanged. All in
all, nineteen black soldiers were executed as a result of the Houston
violence, and fifty were sentenced to life imprisonment.

The nation's press, South and North, largely approved of the harsh
sentences, but blacks plainly saw the extreme injustice of the treatment
accorded the soldiers at Houston. A particularly forthright statement
about the case was delivered by the the Reverend George Frazier Miller
of Saint Augustine's Episcopal Church, Brooklyn. What the military authorities in Texas had perpetrated was a legal lynching, and Miller said
so: "I here today charge that the commanding officer was guilty of a
military lynching, done for the purpose of appeasing the people of the
South, who had to be avenged." Miller stated that the federal authorities

who sent the black troops to Houston should have protected them against police brutality. Declaring that "there are thousands today whose thoughts are the same as mine," Miller added: "We should get the names of all these men. They are all heroes. They were men and only fought the wrongs of the police. We should copy their example of courage and fortitude."[39] W. E. B. Du Bois, writing in *Crisis*, granted that the soldiers of the Third Battalion had broken the law and, if the punishment was legal, declined protest, but he placed the matter in a broader context. He scored "the shameful treatment which these men, and, which we, their brothers, receive all our lives, and which our fathers received, and our children await; and above all we raised our clenched hands against the hundreds of thousands of white murderers, rapists, and scoundrels."[40]

In the years after 1900 legal lynchings were accompanied by the already established pattern of vigilante lynching. Such lynchings occurred not merely in rural, backwater areas but also in prosperous communities determined to be "modern," interested in material progress and getting ahead. One example of this phenomenon is the 1916 lynching of a black youth, Jesse Washington, in Waco, Texas. The boy, seventeen years of age, was later described as "a big, well-developed fellow, but ignorant, being unable to either read or write." He was charged with having assaulted and killed the wife of a white farmer for whom he worked. In this particular case the accused actually received something of a trial, if that is the appropriate term for a proceeding at the hands of a white judge, a white prosecutor, and a jury from which blacks had been excluded, and if a judicial atmosphere can be said to prevail in a courtroom normally holding 500 persons into which some 1,500 had been allowed to crowd. The boy was swiftly convicted and the jury urged the death penalty, but that was not enough for Waco. An election campaign was in progress, and the various candidates, the sheriff especially, could not afford to be portrayed as "soft" on black crime. In this atmosphere the way was open for the mob to take over, and they did so the moment the jury returned the verdict. The mob dragged the boy from the courtroom, put a chain around his body, and began hauling him through the streets. The *Waco Times Herald* gives an account of what followed:

> Great masses of humanity flew as swiftly as possible through the streets of the city in order to be present at the bridge when the hanging took place, but when it was learned that the Negro was being taken to the City Hall lawn, crowds of men, women and children turned and hastened to the lawn. On the way back to the scene of the burning people on every hand took a hand in showing

their feelings in the matter by striking the Negro with anything obtainable, some struck him with shovels, bricks, clubs, and others stabbed him and cut him until when he was strung up his body was a solid color of red, the blood of many wounds inflicted covered him from head to foot. Dry goods boxes and all kinds of inflammable material were gathered, and it required but an instant to convert this into searing flames. When the Negro was first hoisted into the air his tongue protruded from his mouth and his face was besmeared with blood.

Life was not extinct within the Negro's body, although nearly so, when another chain was placed around his neck and thrown over the limb of a tree on the lawn, everybody trying to get to the Negro and have some part in his death. The infuriated mob then leaned the Negro, who was half alive and half dead, against the tree, he having just strength enough within his limbs to support him. As rapidly as possible the Negro was then jerked into the air at which a shout from thousands of throats went up on the morning air and dry goods boxes, excelsior, wood and every other article that would burn was then in evidence, appearing as if by magic. A huge dry goods box was then produced and filled to the top with all of the material that had been secured. The Negro's body was swaying in the air, and all of the time a noise as of thousands was heard and the Negro's body was lowered into the box. No sooner had his body touched the box than people pressed forward, each eager to be the first to light the fire, matches were touched to the inflammable material and as smoke rapidly rose in the air, such a demonstration as of people gone mad was never heard before. Everybody pressed closer to get souvenirs of the affair. When they had finished with the Negro his body was mutilated.

Fingers, ears, pieces of clothing, toes and other parts of the Negro's body were cut off by members of the mob that had crowded to the scene as if by magic when the word that the Negro had been taken in charge by the mob was heralded over the city. As the smoke rose to the heavens, the mass of people, numbering in the neighborhood of 10,000 crowding the City Hall lawn and overflowing the square, hanging from the windows of buildings, viewing the scene from the tops of buildings and trees, set up a shout that was heard blocks away.

Onlookers were hanging from the windows of the City Hall and every other building that commanded a sight of the burning, and as the Negro's body commenced to burn, shouts of delight went up from the thousands and apparently everybody demonstrated in some way their satisfaction at the retribution that was being visited upon the perpetrator of such a horrible crime, the worst in the annals of McLennan county's history.

The body of the Negro was burned to a crisp, and was left for some time in the smoldering remains of the fire. Women and children who desired to view the scene were allowed to do so, the crowds parting to let them look on the scene. After some time the body of the Negro was jerked into the air where everybody could view the remains, and a mighty shout rose on the air. Photographer Gilder-sleeve made several pictures of the body as well as the large crowd which surrounded the scene as spectators.[41]

During the early years of the twentieth century Waco was not the only Texas city in which the lynch mob appeared. A Dallas lynch mob on March 3, 1910, seized Allen Brooks, an elderly black man charged with having assaulted a three-year-old white child, and hanged him. To carry through its purpose the mob broke into the courthouse, took hold of Brooks as his trial was about to begin, tied a rope to him, and then threw him out a second-floor window. Brooks, reportedly knocked unconscious by the fall, was dragged by the mob along the street and suspended from the spike of a telephone pole located near a city landmark, the Elks Arch. The *Dallas Times Herald* reported that a crowd of some two to three thousand "shouting men and boys" followed the mob and that five or six thousand persons were on the scene at the arch. The telephone pole from which Brooks was lynched almost fell in the street after souvenir hunters began carving bits to take home. According to the *Dallas Morning News* the only clothes remaining on the body were a flannel shirt and an undershirt. "This was in tatters, and many of the curious persons who gathered around began to pick bits of cloth from the flannel shirt."[42] The undertaker called to the scene reported that the body was a shapeless mass of flesh.

By its words and action Dallas officialdom made clear that it was unwilling to take firm action against lynching and indeed covered up for the killers. The police officers supposedly assigned to guard Brooks failed to draw their weapons in his defense. One officer was asked if any guns had been drawn during the "struggle." The officer promptly answered, "Not a gun." County attorney Dwight Lewelling termed the lynching "deplorable" but placed responsibility upon the "flimsy technicalities" used by lawyers in defense of those charged with crimes. Lynchings would not occur if the public was assured that "swift and prompt" justice would be meted out in criminal cases. In a news article the *Dallas Times Herald* ascribed the cause of the lynching to a public perception that criminals escaped punishment due to technicalities in the criminal law. Editorially, the *Times Herald* regretted that Allen Brooks was not legally tried but sympathized with the impulse that drove on the mob. "There are crimes," it noted, "which make sane and sober men mad; there are crimes which set aflame the minds of fathers and brothers and husbands and the crime of Allen Brooks was one of them. The day of reckoning had come and once within the walls of the court, Judge Lynch and his followers could not have been baffled or robbed of their prey without a fearful loss of life." As to any serious effort being made to punish the lynchers such a course was out of the question, especially as the police officers at the courthouse stated they could not identify any of the several hundred persons constituting the mob.[43]

There was not a total uniformity of white opinion in the community regarding lynching. The Socialist attorney-editor George Edwards had a record of advocating racial justice. In 1909 Edwards had written a stirring editorial in his newspaper, the *Laborer*. Itemizing such events as the lynching of two blacks in Rockwall County and the killing of a black man in Dawson because he had allegedly sent an insulting note to a white woman, Edwards went on to declare: "Every time a Negro is treated with brutal violence, the mob itself is brutalized. Every time race hatred is stirred, the Southern labor problem is made worse.... Let us not be deceived. The fruits of hatred, brutality and violence are violence, brutality and hatred." Even before being admitted to the bar Edwards was assigned to defend Allen Brooks. But instead of a trial there was a lynching, and Edwards was left to observe in his paper: "A mob of frenzied barbarians in broad day ran over forty or fifty deputies under the command of a sheriff who was thinking more about his chances for re-election than his sworn duty." Edwards reported that it appeared Brooks was "a diseased degenerate" but added that was based on rumor and hearsay "for no other sort of investigation was allowed."[44] Edwards was eloquent, and no doubt other white persons in Dallas agreed with him, but in this era of Texas politics they did not constitute a movement powerful enough to check the lynchers.

In these years of the Progressive era lynchings in the South's rural communities were a matter of steady routine. What constituted a departure from the norm was when northern opinion happened to take significant notice of a particular incident. In Mississippi during one week in February 1914 three lynchings occurred. One of the victims was Samuel Petty, a black man accused of having killed a deputy sheriff. Petty was seized in his cabin and dragged to the center of the town, where the white mob debated the question of whether to hang Petty or burn him alive. The decision was for burning, and Petty was thrust into a dry-goods box, which contained straw soaked in oil. A tub of oil was poured over Petty, and one of the mob set fire to the man. When Petty sought to escape the flames and tried to run, several hundred shots were fired and Petty fell dead. But that was not enough for the mob; they placed the corpse back in the box and incinerated the victim. The coroner's jury considered the matter and determined that Petty had died "at the hands of an outraged mob unknown to the jury." In this case, detailed word of the lynching was carried to the North, and black newspapers reported that young Afro-Americans were meeting secretly to organize vigilante groups that would put an end to lynching. Such vigilante groups did not materialize, but even the verbal interest in plans for countervigilantism signified a new militancy.[45]

As the outbreak of World War I cut off European immigration and the United States became directly involved in the war, the situation of Afro-Americans was profoundly affected by a greatly accelerated black migration into the industrial cities of the North. Events in East St. Louis, Illinois, during 1917 demonstrated that blacks might escape southern race violence only to find themselves subject to mob violence in the North on an unprecedented scale. At least forty blacks were killed in a riot having its origins in the stirring up of racial hatred in response to the employment of blacks in local industry. Contributing to the lawless atmosphere of East St. Louis was a widespread system of political and police corruption.

The East St. Louis "riot" was later described properly in a magazine article by Oscar Leonard, the superintendent of the St. Louis Jewish Educational and Charitable Association. What happened in East St. Louis was a pogrom, Leonard said. Indeed the original pogroms, the Russian massacres of Jews, paled somewhat in comparison with what Leonard observed in East St. Louis. Leonard cited the reaction of a young Russian-Jewish immigrant who accompanied him on a tour of the affected neighborhoods: "I was informed that the makers of Russian pogroms could learn a great deal from the American rioters.... He told me when he viewed the blocks of burned houses that the Russian 'Black Hundreds' could take lessons in pogrom-making from the whites of East St. Louis. The Russians at least, he said, gave the Jews a chance to run while they were trying to murder them. The whites in East St. Louis fired the homes of black folk and either did not allow them to leave the burning houses or shot them the moment they dared attempt to escape the flames."[46]

East St. Louis, a city of approximately 100 thousand, was a place where corruption and vice grew together and flourished. Saloons and gambling establishments were numerous, and they quite obviously operated with the cooperation of municipal authorities. These officials had no constructive response to offer when a local packing plant recruited black strikebreakers to take the jobs of striking white workers, and they did nothing to prevent white and black workers from being pitted against each other. Indeed, public officials participated in organized efforts to deal with existing racial tensions by inciting hatred against blacks. On May 28 the city hall was used for a mass rally of agitation against the black community. Among those attending were the mayor and members of the board of aldermen. Toward the end of the meeting a speech was made calling upon the "people" to take matters into their own hands unless the city took action to stop further black migration. Following the meeting rioting broke out, but it was brought to an end before substantial damage was done. Race agitation continued, however, and on Sunday, July 1, violence took charge of the city. Blacks, wherever found, were stoned, kicked, hanged, and stabbed. A number were burned to death in their homes. According to Oscar Leonard "a black skin was a death warrant on the streets of this Illinois city."[47]

The prelude for the July violence was the appearance in the black community of an automobile from which came repeated shots into homes. In response to that incident a number of blacks, armed with guns, gathered in the streets to meet any renewal of the shooting. They soon encountered an automobile containing several policemen and a newspaper reporter. Inclined to see the passengers in the auto as invaders of their community and likely believing the police were involved in the earlier violence, blacks shot at the car as it drove away. One policeman was killed instantly and another died subsequently. On the following day, July 2, the mob took command. As in other cities, mob violence in East St. Louis involved the participation of the police. The blacks who sought to defend themselves fought against overwhelming odds. The report of a special congressional committee that investigated the East St. Louis violence constituted a clear indictment of the city's police. To begin with, the committee found that the police force was rife with corruption, many officers having served an apprenticeship "as connivers at corrupt elections; as protectors of lawless saloons, and hotels run openly as assignation houses."[48] Proceeds from fines were divided between the police and thieving justices of the peace. The police had failed to deal with the gathering mob on May 28, and on July 2 police either went into seclusion, passively looked on as the mob attacked its victims, or actively joined in mob violence. Rioters taken to jail were promptly released with no effort made to identify them. Police fired upon a group of huddled blacks who were simply seeking safety. It was the conclusion of the special congressional committee that the East St. Louis police "became a part of the mob by countenancing the assaulting and shooting down of defenseless negroes and adding to the terrifying scenes of rapine and slaughter."[49]

Added to the conduct of the local police force was the assistance given the mob by members of the Illinois state militia. Militiamen were among those shooting at blacks, with one trooper in uniform leading a section of the mob. Three soldiers joined with the police in killing two peaceful blacks in the course of closing a black saloon. A number of the militiamen were quoted as stating that "they did not like niggers" and would not bother a white man for killing them. A *St. Louis Post-Dispatch* reporter testified that he heard a soldier tell a white man to "kill all the negroes he could, that he did not like them either." The House committee bluntly summed up the role of the state officers: "The conduct of the soldiers who were sent to East St. Louis to protect life and property puts a blot on that part of the Illinois militia that served under Colonel Tripp. They were scattered over the city, many of them being without officers to direct or control them. In only a few cases did they do their duty. They seemed moved by the same spirit of indifference or cowardice that marked the conduct of the police force. As a rule they fraternized with the mob, joked with them, and made no serious effort to restrain them."[50]

In East St. Louis a number of the factors that typified a major urban racial confrontation were evident. Involved in the episode was business-encouraged competition between white and black workers, corrupt political and law enforcement institutions and the direct participation in violence of local police and state troops.[51] Racist provocation triggered an act of violence by blacks that combined elements of self-defense and retaliation, and this act was used as the pretext for a massive assault upon the black community of East St. Louis.

Violence served to reinforce and perpetuate the economic oppression under which Afro-Americans lived. The intertwining of economic roles with acts of terror is perhaps nowhere seen more clearly than with regard to the institution of peonage. The holding of people in peonage, slavery for debt, is a crime under federal law, yet it has continued to exist as a feature of American society. The violence to which peonage gave rise is typified in a Lowndes County, Alabama, case of the early twentieth century. A black youth, Dillard Freeman, was arrested and convicted on what the United States attorney later described as "some flimsy charge." The penalty for conviction was a fine, a fine paid by the county sheriff in return for Freeman's entering into a labor contract to pay out the costs. The youth several times asked to be permitted to see his sick brother, but the request was refused. Finally Freeman left the plantation to visit his brother, only to be seized there by the sheriff and one of his men. In the presence of his mother, the son was beaten "unmercifully with a pistol until he was bloody." Then, according to the U.S. attorney, he was handcuffed, tied around the neck, the other end of the rope placed in the hands of a man riding a mule, and made to run for six or seven miles behind the mule, being whipped by the sheriff when he fell behind. When the peon was returned to the plantation he was whipped with a piece of gin belt attached to a wooden handle. The U.S. attorney noted that the severity of the whipping was evidenced by the fact that Freeman's back was "one mass of scars from his thighs to his neck." Those who profited from peonage would go far to maintain the practice and certainly to avoid punishment for the crime. When a federal grand jury heard evidence in the case of the sheriff charged with peonage, a white raiding party threatened a black grand juror and told him "he knew what to expect."[52]

FIVE

The Focusing of Debate

URING THE PERIOD from 1900 to the end of World War I, the facts show that racial violence was growing in intensity and scope. A span of seventeen years covered the violence of New York, Atlanta, Springfield, Houston, and East St. Louis, and added to these incidents was the continuation of vigilante lynching, taken together with numberless "small" acts of violence that never drew public attention. Afro-Americans had to respond to this more intensified and diversified violence in a context of rapid economic change flowing from an accelerated black migration from the rural South to the urban South and especially to the urban, industrial North. There was a range of responses, a more focused debate about alternative courses of action, and grass-roots resistance that was increasingly influenced by a civil rights movement and the black press.

On one level there was the continuation of already established forms of individual protest. The brutalities inflicted in specific incidents were brought to public attention, either by the word of the victims themselves or in accounts written by individual crusaders. Representative of auto-biographical accounts of experience with violence was an account of the life of a Georgia peon. This black man, born in Elbert County, Georgia, told how his uncle had bound him to labor for a white farmer and how when he sought to find employment for himself he was claimed by his master and given thirty lashes with a buggy whip. He had continued to work for the "Captain" until reaching twenty-one years of age and then himself made a labor contract to work on the same plantation. Later, after the owner's son inherited the place, the plantation was turned into a convict camp, and when the narrator attempted to leave the place he and others were rounded up and placed in one of the camp's stockades. For three years he was compelled to work under peonage. "Barring two or three severe and brutal whippings which I received," this man said, "I got along very well, all things considered; but the system is damnable." The narration detailed the physical punishment inflicted on the peons:

A favorite way of whipping a man was to strap him down to a log, flat on his back, and spank him fifty or sixty times on his bare feet with a shingle or a huge piece of plank. When the man would get up with sore and blistered feet and an aching body, if he could not then keep up with the other men at work he would be strapped to the log again, this time face downward, and he would be lashed with a buggy trace on his bare back. When a woman had to be whipped it was usually done in private, although they would be compelled to fall down across a barrel or something of the kind and receive the licks on their back sides.[1]

With regard to lynching, in the years following 1900 Ida B. Wells-Barnett persevered in her efforts to arouse the national conscience. In a speech delivered in 1909 she outlined three central facts: "First: lynching is color-line murder. Second: Crimes against women is the excuse, not the cause. Third: It is a national crime and requires a national remedy." She emphasized that lynching would be stopped only with federal protection of citizen rights. Noting that "several of the greatest riots and most brutal burnt offerings of the mob" had been suggested by newspapers, Wells-Barnett urged efforts to induce newspapers to refuse the role of accessories before or after the fact. She continued to believe that general agitation against lynching was helpful. But agitation and a favorable attitude by the press were not enough. "The only certain remedy is an appeal to law," she declared. "Lawbreakers must be made to know that human life is sacred and that every citizen of this country is first a citizen of the United States and secondly a citizen of the state in which he belongs."[2]

In 1909, Ida B. Wells-Barnett also connected the question of black enfranchisement to that of eliminating lynching. In a magazine article she turned back to the Reconstruction era to indicate how white supremacists had consistently resorted to violence in order to destroy the freedman's constitutional rights. Wells-Barnett reminded her readers of the Ku Kluxers "who during the first years after the Civil War murdered Negroes by wholesale, for attempting to exercise the rights given by these amendments, and for trusting the government which was powerful enough to give them the ballot, to be strong enough to protect them in its exercise." She recalled that Senator "Pitchfork Ben" Tillman of South Carolina had said that he and others in South Carolina had shot blacks to death to keep them from voting.

Then, during the decades subsequent to Reconstruction, legislative provision had been made for denying blacks the vote. The black American was deprived of his "only weapon of defense," and Wells-Barnett added, "the United States Government, a consenting Saul stands by holding the clothes of those who stone and burn him to death literally and politically." She went on to explain the deadly consequences of disfranchisement:

> With no sacredness of the ballot there can be no sacredness of human life itself. For if the strong can take the weak man's ballot, when it suits his purpose to do so, he will take his life also. Having successfully swept aside the constitutional safeguards to the ballot, it is the smallest of small matters for the South to sweep aside its own safeguards to human life. Thus "trial by jury" for the black man in that section has become a mockery, a plaything of the ruling classes and the rabble alike. The mob says: "This people has no vote with which to punish us or the consenting officers of the law, therefore we indulge our brutal instincts, give free reign to race prejudice and lynch, hang, burn them when we please." Therefore, the more complete the disfranchisement, the more frequent and horrible has been the hangings, shootings and burnings.

In this article, Ida B. Wells-Barnett also referred to recent events in Illinois in which Governor Charles S. Deneen had removed from office a sheriff, one Frank E. Davis of Alexander County, who had allowed a mob to lynch two prisoners, one black and the other white. The white man was hung in the courtyard of the jail, but the black prisoner, Will James, was hung and shot and his body burned. Following the burning the head was cut off and stuck on a fence post, and the victim's heart and other organs were cut out and distributed as souvenirs. When a new sheriff was placed in office a mob again attempted to lynch a prisoner, but this time the sheriff was ready for action. Sheriff Nellis gave the order to fire, and one mob leader was dead and several others of the mob wounded. Wells-Barnett tellingly made the point that dealing with lynch mobs was a matter of the willingness of public officials to take action.[3] And if, in Illinois, some progress was made in that regard, Wells-Barnett deserved much of the credit, for she worked energetically to have Sheriff Davis removed from office. The practice of lynching was largely ended in Illinois, although this was not the case with race riots.[4]

Another powerful individual voice raised against lynching was that of Mary Church Terrell, for several decades a leader of Washington's black community and spokesperson nationally of Afro-American women. In 1904 she wrote an article, published by the *North American Review*, that presented a broad-gauged attack on lynching and the rationalizations used to justify it. She presented evidence, as had Ida B. Wells-Barnett, showing that in the great majority of lynchings there was not even the accusation of rape. Refuting the allegation that mobs did not torture lynch victims unless they were charged with rape, she quoted a graphic description, carried in the *Vicksburg Evening Post,* of the atrocities inflicted on a black couple after the husband allegedly murdered a white planter. While preparations were made to burn the victims, their fingers and ears were hacked off and a corkscrew employed to tear away pieces of their flesh. Terrell put her finger on an essential feature of lynching when she wrote that once the members of a mob had been aroused "the first available specimen is sacrificed to their rage, no matter whether he is guilty or not." The article examined the question of the sources of lynching and found these sources within white society. What produced lynching was race hatred and lawlessness, and Terrell therefore concluded that "it is just as impossible for the negroes of this country to prevent mob violence by any attitude of mind which they may assume, or any course of conduct which they may pursue, as it is for a straw dam to stop Niagara's flow." Lynching was the aftermath of slavery, she wrote, and the view that the descendants of slaveholders rarely constituted the mobs she found dubious. The article noted that under slavery "colored women were debauched by their masters" and that since Emancipation "prepossessing young colored girls have been considered the rightful prey of white gentlemen in the South." Terrell reported recent lynchings in Springfield, Ohio, "and in other cities of the North" and concluded that race violence was rapidly spreading throughout the United States. She also saw manifestations of the concern of world opinion and particularly emphasized a November 1903 protest against lynching issued by the International Socialist Bureau at Brussels. Terrell's essay was well informed, eloquent, and convincing in making the case that lynching was an expression of racial oppression "in its ugliest and most brutal form."[5]

In this new period, however, even the individual protest against specific injustice tended to be shaped by a new context. Wells-Barnett's 1909 speech on lynching was presented to the National Negro Committee, meeting in New York, that led to the formation of the National Association for the Advancement of Colored People. Primarily the individual crusader, she now declared that "in a multitude of counsel there is wisdom," and she urged the convening of a conference to deal with lynching. The format of the autobiography of a black Georgia peon was influenced by the temper of the Progressive era. The story of this man appeared as a chapter, "The Life Story of a Negro Peon," in a collection entitled *The Life Stories of Undistinguished Americans.* The book was edited by Hamilton Holt, the editor of the *Independent,* one of the most open-minded of the magazines published during this period. The progressivism of the early twentieth century stimulated a democratic concern for the lives of ordinary people, and that led to the belief that it was proper and fitting that the hitherto voiceless be allowed to express themselves and be heard.

A new factor entering the picture after 1900 was the development within black leadership of a more systematic dialogue concerning alternative responses to racist violence, a dialogue in which the question of responding to violence was integrated with a general view of Afro-American advancement. Blacks conducted the dialogue, but in an era when problems of race relations were becoming matters of national concern, significant sections of white opinion were listening in, reading the books and articles written by various outstanding black spokesmen, and sometimes encouraging one or another viewpoint.

Serving as a prime formulator of one of the basic approaches to the position of Afro-Americans was the scholar W. E. B. Du Bois. He was a many-faceted, broadly cultured man whose thought went through a long and complex evolution, a process of growth and change affected by many factors. But there is no question that racial violence was a vital factor in shaping his thought and career. Du Bois later recalled a particular incident as having a galvanizing effect upon him. This event, the lynching of Sam Hose, revealed a savagery of racism that was not to be overcome simply by the erudition of the objective scientist.[6]

In his classic essay, *The Souls of Black Folk,* published in 1903 after the Hose lynching made its impact upon him, the question of racial violence was not the overriding theme but it was present and significantly so. The book contains passing references to the Hose lynching, and, speaking of Reconstruction, Du Bois mentioned "the terrors of the Ku Klux Klan." Speaking of the masses of Afro-Americans, he declared his insistence that "the question of the future is how best to keep these millions from brooding over the wrongs of the past and the difficulties of the present, so that all their energies may be bent toward a cheerful striving and cooperation with their white neighbors toward a larger, juster and fuller future." But in several places the angry response of blacks toward racist violence was expressed in Du Bois's prose, even if he at least once left open the issue of whether he considered such anger justified. To the oft-repeated charge that black men raped white women Du Bois threw back the accusation: "The rape which your gentlemen have done against the helpless black women in defiance of your own laws is written on the foreheads of two millions of mulattoes, and written in ineffable blood. And finally, when you fasten crime upon this race as its peculiar trait, they answer that slavery was the arch-crime, and lynching and lawlessness its twin abortion; that color and race are not crimes, and yet it is they which in this land receive most unceasing condemnation, North, East, South, and West."

Du Bois, in this book, analyzed the question of black crime in its contemporary and historical context. He asserted at the outset that "there can be no doubt" that there had been an increase in black crime during the previous thirty years. In the slums of the great cities "a distinct criminal class" had developed among blacks. Du Bois noted that two considerations were basic in explaining this criminality: first, that the increase of crime was an inevitable result of Emancipation and, second, that the southern police system was designed for the control of slaves. Emancipation had produced the onset of a process of social differentiation among slaves. With regard to people thrust into freedom, "some swim, some sink, and some hang suspended, to be forced up or down by the chance currents of a busy, hurrying world." A rising group of people, he declared, "are not elevated like an inert mass, but rather stretch upward like a living plant with its roots still clinging to the mould." Southern police were incapable of dealing effectively and impartially with crime in the postslavery era. Slavery had produced little in the way of formal penal machinery and had established a dual system of justice, "which erred on the white side by undue leniency and the practical immunity of red-handed criminals and erred on the black side by undue severity, injustice and lack of discrimination." After the war the appearance of serious black crime added to the lack of an adequate justice system led blacks to distrust southern police and courts, and for their part whites "were swept in moments of passion beyond law, reason and decency."[7] Such a situation aroused hatred and prevented attention to economic development. It is clear that Du Bois saw crime and violence very much in terms of their social role as a distraction from desirable progress.

What Du Bois wrote about black crime in *The Souls of Black Folk* was an extension of his analysis of the topic, a few years earlier, in *The Philadelphia Negro*. The Philadelphia study included a consideration of the causes of crime among blacks, and "two great causes" were among those he listed: "Slavery and emancipation with their attendant phenomena of ignorance, lack of discipline, and moral weakness; immigration with its increased competition and moral influence." But he also added a third and noted this cause might be greater than the first two, "the world of custom and thought in which he must live and work, the physical surrounding of house and home and ward, the moral encouragements and discouragements which he encounters." Du Bois observed that the environment for blacks was different from that of whites, and he explained the basis of the difference: "The real foundation of the difference is the widespread feeling all over the land, in Philadelphia as well as in Boston and New Orleans, that the Negro is something less than an American and ought not to be much more than what he is." Essentially, the social context of black crime reflected the temper of the national society and was not merely a southern peculiarity.

Du Bois noted that many unsubstantiated charges of crime were made against blacks and reported that an increase in the crime rate among blacks was accompanied by a rise in the white criminal record. He also indicated that criminals formed a distinct group within the black community, that young males were the most frequent perpetrators of the serious crimes of stealing and assault, and that "to this criminal class and not to the great mass of Negroes the bulk of the serious crime perpetrated by this race should be charged." But at the same time Du Bois wrote that there remained "a vast problem of crime" within the black community. Du Bois fully recognized the reality of the crime problem while rejecting any imputation that criminal conduct was some special racial attribute of blacks. Beginning his discussion of black crime in Philadelphia with the late seventeenth century, Du Bois in opening the subject made clear the social dimension, writing that crime "is a phenomenon of organized social life, and is the open rebellion of an individual against his social environment." He made no claim to have exhausted the study of the causes of crime, but he clearly indicated that special causes were operative with respect to crimes by blacks. The black person, in Philadelphia as elsewhere, "was the object of stinging oppression and ridicule, and paths of advancement were closed to him." The result was that the class of the "shiftless, aimless, idle discouraged and disappointed" was proportionately larger among blacks than among whites, and obviously this fact was relevant to any understanding of crime within the black population.[8]

Years later Du Bois explained something of the impulse among some Philadelphia whites that had made possible his work on *The Philadelphia Negro*. He stressed the interest of the Philadelphia Quakers in a kind of "soul-saving escapism" that enabled him to examine "what venal politics was doing by using the Negroes." Du Bois agreed with an interviewer's suggestion that his work was a preliminary to the muckraking era. And indeed Du Bois's scientific approach, his dispassionate treatment of even so emotion-laden a question as that of crime among blacks, was in keeping with the muckraker temperament.[9]

Du Bois had also turned to the theme of crime in relation to the urban

Afro-American in a series of articles about blacks in northern cities that he wrote for the *New York Times* during November and December 1901. He set the question of crime in the context of social transition: "There is without doubt a great deal of crime among Negroes. When any race passes through a vast and sudden change like that of emancipation from slavery the result is always that numbers unable to adjust themselves to the new circumstances easily sink into debauchery and crime. We should expect then to find the greatest excess of crime a generation after emancipation and then to see it gradually decrease to normal conditions." Du Bois found this pattern "partially exemplified" in Philadelphia, but he also observed that social transition was not quite normal in Philadelphia, for the city "by political protection to criminals and indiscriminate charity ... encourages the worthless and at the same time, by shutting negroes out of most avenues of honest employment, the city discourages labor and thrift."

It was extremely difficult to measure the extent of crime among blacks, Du Bois wrote. But based on available evidence for New York City he judged that "there is much serious crime among negroes," and he added, "what else should we expect?" He further asked: "What else is this but the logical result of bad homes, poor health, restricted opportunities for work, and general social oppression?" The existing situation was abnormal, and he declared, "That the negro under normal conditions is law-abiding and good-natured cannot be disputed. We have but to change conditions, then, to reduce negro crime." Du Bois linked the crime issue to the prevalence of racism. Crime by New York blacks was "not natural or normal" but rather the crime of a class of "criminals, gamblers and loafers, encouraged and protected by political corruption and race prejudice." The only sort of Philadelphia black who was encouraged was the criminal or the pauper.

In discussing remedies for the situation Du Bois defined the problem of work as central. He generalized: "There can be no reasonable doubt but that the Northern negro received less wages for his work and pays more rent for worse houses than white workmen, and that is not altogether a matter of fitness that confines his work chiefly to common labor and menial service." Du Bois advocated the opening of opportunity to blacks, that they be "given that chance to make a living and enjoy life which America offers freely to every race and people except those whom she has most cruelly wronged." But Du Bois also emphasized self-development as part of the solution, and such development included alliance with the reform movement in city government. "The police riot of New York is but one clear proof of this," he noted.[10]

In *The Souls of Black Folk* Du Bois bluntly stated his belief that "physical defence" was not an effective means of resisting racial oppression. He observed that "the death of Denmark Vesey and Nat Turner proved long since to the Negro the present hopelessness of physical defence." But he also conveyed to his readers the willingness of individual blacks to offer physical resistance to violence, even if that resistance led to death. He told of his encounter with a black man in Albany, Georgia, a man he described as "hopelessly in debt, disappointed, and embittered." The man had stopped Du Bois to ask about a black youth who had been shot and killed by a policeman in Albany for having talked loudly on the sidewalk. The man then added: "Let a white man touch me, and he dies; I don't boast this,—I don't say it around loud, or before the children— but I mean it. I've seen them whip my father and my old mother in them cotton-rows till the blood ran." Du Bois also devoted a chapter of the book, "Of the Coming of John," to the story of a black youth, John Jones, who had obtained an education and then returned to the village he came from to start a school for black children. He opens the school with the support of the white judge, who cautiously supports black education on the premise that those providing instruction "will teach the darkies to be faithful servants and laborers as your fathers were." But then the judge learns that the pupils are hearing of equality and of the French Revolution, and he wastes no time in closing the school. After all, the judge had told John Jones that if blacks wanted "to reverse nature" and even sit in his parlor, "then, By God! we'll hold them under if we have to lynch every nigger in the land." John Jones plans to leave the village, but as he goes to tell the news to his family he sees his sister "struggling in the arms of a tall and fair-haired man," the judge's son. John Jones's reaction is the logical climax of this story: "He said not a word, but, seizing a fallen limb, struck him with all the pent-up hatred of his great black arm; and the body lay white and still beneath the pines, all bathed in sunshine and in blood."[11] The predictable sequel of all this is the arrival of the lynch mob that will destroy John Jones for having protected his sister. In this chapter of *The Souls of Black Folk* there is the theme of manly, if suicidal, assertion in the face of outrage. Implicit also is the note that, with all of Du Bois's stress on education, knowledge itself is not adequate protection for the Afro-American. The larger society to which the trained black youth returns after completing school has a place available for black people only if they accept a subservient position.

In 1904 Du Bois summed up his views in a "Credo" published in the *Independent* magazine. The statement was reprinted widely in the black press. The "Credo" is an eloquent affirmation of Du Bois's belief in the

destiny of Afro-Americans to be a free people able to live with dignity
as brothers with human beings of all races. Du Bois saw no contradiction
between human brotherhood and race pride, "pride of self so deep as to
scorn injustice to other selves; in pride of lineage so great as to despise
no man's father." Along with the flat declaration that "War is Murder,"
the document also contains an oblique reference to racial violence in Du
Bois's declaration that he also believed in the devil and his minions, those
"who spit in the faces of the fallen, strike them that cannot strike again."[12]
    The spirit of the 1904 "Credo" is embodied in the 1905 Declaration
of Principles adopted by the conference of black leaders at Niagara Falls.
There is reference to the question of violence although the emphasis is
very much on a positive program for Afro-American advancement. The
declaration notes that the black race in America "needs protection and
is given mob violence," and the call for legislation enforcing the Thirteenth, Fourteenth, and Fifteenth amendments was a request for laws
that would offer substantial protection from midnight riders and
lynchers.[13]
    Subsequent to the Niagara conference, events forced Du Bois to direct
his attention explicitly to the question of racial terrorization. In *The Souls
of Black Folk* Du Bois had written that "the chance for lawless oppression
is vastly greater in the country than in the city, and nearly all the more
serious race disturbances of the last decade have arisen from disputes in
the country between master and man."[14] But as racist violence was revealed more fully in its urban and national dimensions Du Bois reacted
sharply. In the summer of 1906 the Niagara movement met at Harpers
Ferry, identifying itself with the tradition of John Brown, who had taken
the path of direct, militant action against oppression. The Harpers Ferry
address to the Niagara movement declared: "We do not believe in violence, neither in the despised violence of the raid nor the lauded violence
of the soldier, nor the barbarous violence of the mob, but we do believe
in John Brown, in that incarnate spirit of justice, that hatred of a lie,
that willingness to sacrifice money, reputation, and life itself on the altar
of right."[15] A few weeks following the Harpers Ferry meeting Du Bois
was profoundly outraged by word of the Atlanta pogrom. He was in
Lowndes County, Alabama, when the violence started, and he proceeded
home to Atlanta at once. While still on the train he wrote what was to
become a classic, "A Litany of Atlanta," expressing his passionate sense
of anger and anguish concerning the violence occurring in that city. The
"Litany" did not offer any particular program or strategy, but Du Bois
in this work, using his poetic powers, fixed the stamp of unmitigated evil
upon those who committed the violent acts and those who permitted

them to do so. The "Litany" raised the question of whether the American conscience was dead. Du Bois asked God to hear him, God who was not dead "but flown afar, up hills of endless light, through blazing corridors of suns, where worlds do swing of good and gentle men, of women strong and free—far from the cozenage, black hypocrisy, and chaste prostitution of this shameful speck of dust." Du Bois summed up what had happened in Atlanta and gave a succinct explanation for the violence: "A city lay in travail, God our Lord, and from her loins sprang twin Murder and Black Hate. Red was the midnight; clang, crack, and cry of death and fury filled the air and trembled underneath the stars where church spires pointed silently to Thee. And all this was to sate the greed of greedy men who hide behind the veil of vengeance!" He asked the curses of God upon blacks who committed violent acts, but he also asked the deeper question: "And yet, whose is the deeper guilt? Who made these devils? Who murdered them in crime and fed them on injustice? Who ravished and debauched their mothers and their grandmothers? Who bought and sold their crime and waxed fat and rich on public iniquity?" Du Bois also took the opportunity to point up the hollowness of the Booker T. Washington policy of accommodation, telling the story of the black man who followed the advice of "Work and Rise" and was law-abiding but who nonetheless "lieth maimed and murdered, his wife naked to shame, his children to poverty and evil." The "Litany" also contains the implication that the Atlanta massacre encouraged the belief that violence would have to be met with violence. "Let the cup pass from us," Du Bois wrote, "tempt us not beyond our strength, for there is that clamoring and clawing within, to whose voice we would not listen, yet shudder lest we must,—and it is red." Underscoring his meaning he added: "Vengeance is Mine; I will repay, saith the Lord!"[16]

Du Bois also responded to the Atlanta violence in an article he wrote for the *World Today* magazine. He reported that at least 100 persons had been killed or wounded and that most of these were blacks, but he also noted that "a very large proportion" of the casualties were white. As for the cause of the violence, Du Bois was unequivocal in a manner that never would have occurred to Booker T. Washington. "The real cause of the riot," he wrote, "was two years of vituperation and traduction of the Negro race by the most prominent candidates for the governorship, together with a bad police system and a system of punishing crime which is a disgrace to any civilized state." Du Bois added with regard to the police that Atlanta blacks, "even many of the best and most law-abiding, regard the Atlanta police as their oppressors." It was the South's unwritten law, he wrote, that blacks must not defend themselves from white aggression, but in Atlanta blacks did act in their own defense and so the official policy was adopted of arming whites and disarming blacks. Among the lessons taught by the riot Du Bois included the necessity for just courts and a decent, honest police force. The judicial system must work to stop crime and reform criminals rather than operating as a profit-making proposition. "The Negro must have the ballot," Du Bois declared, noting that only then could blacks peacefully defend their rights. Finally Du Bois urged that real republican rule be created in the South "by reducing the representation of disfranchising states, and by government aid to the southern public school system to reduce illiteracy and barbarism."[17]

In the aftermath of the Atlanta riot Du Bois's formulation of a southern black agenda reflected his militant equalitarianism but also his awareness of the severe racial tensions spotlighted by the Atlanta violence. On January 31, 1907, Du Bois met privately with the muckraking journalist Ray Stannard Baker and the southern moderate Episcopal clergyman, Cary Breckenridge Wilmer, both men aptly described as "benevolent racists." Du Bois explained that "as long as race antipathy is violent" he would not oppose racial separation in education in the South if accommodations were equal. His central theme, however, was the need to reject segregation as the basis for arranging southern society. A general pattern of enforced separation inflicts humiliation and insult, "makes one wish to sneak like a dog and out from the sight of men," and prevents the human contact that is necessary for mutual understanding. Du Bois told his partners in the conversation: "You have got therefore to put your face against further separation, and more than that, you have got to see if the separation has not already gone to the extent which is foolish and dangerous." He centered his criticism on those Jim Crow arrangements, particularly in public transportation, "which cannot be enforced without humiliation and injustice."[18] Highly conscious of the worsening southern racial situation, Du Bois sought to block a further hardening of segregation and thus provide an atmosphere in which the system could be dismantled. Du Bois's part of the discussion revealed a finely honed strategic sense.

Agitation, organization, and protest, the insistence on full equality, were central themes in Du Bois's response to racial oppression. He also supported the exercise when necessary of the right of self-defense. His appointment as editor of the *Crisis* magazine, established as the organ of the National Association for the Advancement of Colored People (NAACP), gave him the continuous opportunity to comment on current events in the black struggle, and incidents of violence all too frequently were among those events. He was particularly plainspoken in an editorial published in October 1916. He was appalled that in a recent lynching episode in Gainesville, Florida, blacks had not resisted the mob despite the fact that they had a great advantage in numbers. He came to the point directly: "The men and women who had nothing to do with the alleged crime should have fought in self-defense to the last ditch if they had killed every white man in the county and themselves been killed. The man who surrendered to a lynching mob the victim of the sheriff ought himself to have been locked up." Du Bois asserted flatly that lynching would stop "when the cowardly mob is faced by effective guns in the hands of the people determined to sell their souls dearly."[19]

When events of especially broad national significance occurred, Du Bois was able to use the magazine as a means of telling the full story and analyzing the meaning of what happened. A case in point was the report published in Crisis concerning the East St. Louis riot. The special report, entitled "The Massacre of East St. Louis," represented an outstanding work of investigative journalism. Du Bois was a poet, but he was also the methodical assembler of evidence. He and the writer Martha Gruening had gone to East St. Louis on assignment from the NAACP to uncover the facts. Du Bois's intense anger at what he found was evident. The United States was then at war with Germany, but it was his conclusion that the Germans had nothing on the mob in East St. Louis when it came to barbarism. Indeed, he asserted that the southern Illinois mob went the Germans one better. No one had charged the Germans with enjoying the pain and suffering they inflicted on others. But Du Bois and Gruening found that the East St. Louis mob "combined business with pleasure." The massacre had been turned into a holiday. The report amply documented this conclusion with evidence taken from the local newspapers. This report cited as evidence the statements of several dozen black witnesses and victims. There was biting sarcasm in the introduction written for that section of the report. "All our hunting-songs and descriptions," Du Bois stated, "deal with the glory of the chase as seen and felt by the hunters. No one has visualized the psychology of the quarry, the driven, hunted thing. The Negroes of East St. Louis have in their statements supplied the world with that lack." The statements told of children thrown into burning houses by the mob and of the complicity in the violence of police and soldiers. The words of those who themselves had experienced the horror of the massacre conveyed a powerful sense that, if anything, newspaper accounts minimized the violence. In this report Du Bois singled out for special emphasis the responsibility of the East St. Louis labor movement for fostering hatred of black workers. Du Bois charged that the violence, in his judgment violence that was deliberately planned and executed, grew out of the attitude expressed by a local trade unionist who referred to black migrants from the South as undesirable. At the end of the report Du Bois quoted a motto, "Labor conquers everything," and declared that indeed labor had conquered everything; "it has conquered Liberty, Justice, Mercy, Law and Democracy which is a nation's vaunt." And he asked, "what of the Federal Government?"[20] He did not answer the question, possibly because the answer might raise painful questions about his posture of support for United States partic-ipation in the war, but it was fairly obvious that the government, which had previously shown little interest in action against racial terrorism and which was now preoccupied with the war effort, was not likely to act against those who murdered blacks in the streets and alleys of East St. Louis.

Another, quite different, response to racist violence was that offered by Booker T. Washington, the prime advocate for more than a generation of black accommodation to segregation and disfranchisement. If Du Bois in dealing with white terror operated from a basic starting point of refusing to defer full citizenship rights, Washington's reaction to violence was conditioned by his assumption that racial progress depended upon partnership with moneyed whites, North and South.

At a number of points in his career Washington dealt explicitly with the theme of violence in black–white relations. His criticism of racial terrorism was usually accompanied by avowals of his continued regard for the good intentions of respectable white southerners and condem-nation of black crime. According to one of his autobiographies, *Up from Slavery,* the violence of the Reconstruction era had made a great impres-sion upon him during his early years in West Virginia, where he had witnessed the terroristic activities of the Ku Klux Klan. Recalling that period later, Washington wrote about it with considerable restraint. He described the Klan as an organization formed "for the purpose of reg-ulating the conduct of the coloured people, especially with the object of preventing the members of the race from exercising any influence in politics." He found that the Klansmen corresponded to the "patrollers" of the slavery era, and the patrollers as he remembered them "were organized largely for the purpose of regulating the conduct of slaves at night in such matters as preventing the slaves from going from one plan-tation to another without passes, and for preventing them from holding any kind of meetings without permission and without the presence at these meetings of at least one white man." In these lines about Klansmen and "patrollers" Washington simply cites facts that were common knowledge and concerning which there was little dispute. He also noted that his white patron, General Lewis Ruffner, had fought against the Klan. And he carefully made the point that he referred to the Klan in order to point out the significant changes that had occurred in the South since Reconstruction. After all, the Klan no longer existed, and he contended that the fact that such an organization ever existed was "almost" forgotten by both black and white. It was also, most importantly, Washington's judgment that there were now few places in the South "where public sentiment would permit such organizations to exist." The reference to the Ku Klux Klan was utilized to justify the policy of racial accommodation. But something of a genuine hatred of the Klan did appear through Washington's dispassionate prose. He wrote that the Klansmen were more cruel than the "patrollers," and he noted that the masked night riders sought to crush black political aspirations, "but they did not confine themselves to this, because schoolhouses as well as churches were burned by them, and many innocent persons were made to suffer. During this period not a few colored people lost their lives."[21]

In *The Souls of Black Folk* Du Bois observed that Washington "has spoken out against lynching, and in other ways has openly or silently set his influence against sinister schemes and unfortunate happenings."[22] Washington did indeed take a public position against lynching, a position especially clearly formulated in a statement he made in 1899. He delivered what he termed a "letter to the Southern people," and that letter was widely published. Washington began the letter with an explanation of why he had kept silent during a recent wave of lynchings, and the explanation was an accurate reflection of his characteristic approach to racial conflict. When the country had been shocked by the lynchings he had been tempted to speak out on the matter, he said, but he had kept silent "because I did not believe that the public mind was in a condition to listen to a discussion of the subject in the calm judicial manner that it would be later, when there should be no undue feeling or excitement." At the outset Washington made clear that his position should not be identified with any mass protest or agitation against lynching. He also expressed his view that there was no southern white man who loved the South more than he did. Most importantly, he indicated he was not in any way asking for federal intervention against lynching; he was directing his appeal not to President McKinley, "not to the people of New York nor of the New England States, but to our citizens of our Southern States, to assist in creating a public sentiment such as will make human life here just as safe and sacred as it is anywhere else in the world." Washington then got more directly to the subject. He stated that lynching had been instituted in order to punish outrages against women. He did not touch upon the question of checking outrages against black women, but he did cite the facts showing that only a small minority of lynch victims had even been charged with rape. During the previous year 118 persons had been lynched in the South, but only twenty-four of the victims had been accused of rape. During one week, Washington declared, thirteen blacks had been lynched in three southern states, but not one of the victims had been charged with sexual assault. Within a period of six years about 900 persons had been lynched in the South, and Washington reminded his readers that the total was only a few hundred less than the number of Americans killed in Cuba during the Spanish-American War. He outlined some of the "reasons" given for lynching, and they included such matters as "alleged stock poisoning," "malpractice," "race prejudice," and "mistaken identity." The incentive to stop lynching that Washington held out was cast in terms that would appeal to southern white moderates. Lynching represented disregard for law, and it distorted the southern character, plainly a reference to the white southern character. "I am not pleading for the Negro alone," Washington wrote. "Lynching injures, hardens and blunts the moral sensibilities of the young and tender manhood of the South."

To make quite clear his evenhanded approach to the question, Washington coupled his message to the white South with vehement denunciation of black crime. "Let it be understood for all time," he declared, "that no one guilty of rape can find sympathy or shelter with us, and that none will be more active in bringing to justice, through the proper authorities, those guilty of crime. Let the criminal and vicious elements of the race have at all times our most severe condemnation. Let a strict line be drawn between the virtuous and the criminal. I condemn with all the indignation of my soul the beast in human form guilty of assaulting a woman." Washington also connected crime with idleness and explained that it was for this reason that he insisted upon the industrial education of black youth.

At the conclusion of the statement Washington left no doubt that he viewed the lynching question within the framework of his continuing desire for a partnership with the white Establishment, North and South. Blacks, he asserted, had among many southern whites as good friends as they had anywhere in the world. "These friends have not forsaken us," he announced, and he was confident they would not do so. Blacks could work out their own future in the South if they would but make themselves "intelligent, industrious, economical and virtuous." The appropriate strategy for blacks was to seek "in a manly and honorable way the confidence, the cooperation, the sympathy of the best white people in the South and in our respective communities." Both races would be secure if the future found "the best white people and best black people standing together, in favor of law and order and justice."[23] Washington's statement about lynching ended as a reaffirmation of the policy of accommodation.

Washington's position in this statement was consistent with views he expressed in a brief comment made in a public speech during 1899. He indicated that the lynchers were "ignorant individuals" who had been deprived of education. The remedy for mob violence, Washington announced, was "education that shall reach the head, the hand, the heart." It was therefore appropriate, he added, to concentrate attention upon the theme of black education, because in so doing "we are considering the problem which is fundamental in the salvation of the whole South." In this speech, delivered only a few weeks following a particularly brutal lynching at Palmetto, Georgia, Washington in effect was defusing the anger felt over the recent events.[24]

The stress on education had for some years formed the core of Washington's response to lynching. In a magazine article published during 1893 he had asked what was the remedy for lynching. His answer was quite definite: "Christian education for the white man and the black man." Washington saw this education as leading to black entrepreneurship, creating a mutual economic interest of black and white that would act to prevent lynchings. With whites and blacks well educated, "the black man owning stores, operating factories, owning bank stock, lending white people money, manufacturing goods that the white man needs, interlacing his business interests with those of the white man, there will be no more lynching in the South than in the North."[25] Washington apparently did not consider the possibility that black economic achievement might be seen as threatening by those whites with a vested interest in black economic and political subjection.

The case of the lawyer Thomas A. Harris illustrated the difficulties on the level of practicality that Washington had with the question of coping with racist violence. Washington combined a refusal to come publicly to the aid of a wounded victim of a lynch mob with covert assistance to the victim. Privately he would aid the individual while not avowing his right to do so and offering no criticism of the assault itself. Harris was a black attorney who sought to establish a law practice in Tuskegee. When in June of 1895 Harris opened his home to a traveling white minister suspected of preaching doctrines of equality, the mob came to lynch the attorney, but he escaped after being wounded in the leg. Harris sought shelter at Washington's home, but the Tuskegee leader would not take him in. Instead, Washington sent Harris to a friendly black physician in Montgomery.[26] Washington's refusal to shield the wounded black man openly drew serious criticism in the black press, and at the Washington, D.C., Bethel Literary and Historical Society his conduct in the matter was termed "hypocritical and showing the natural bent of the man." Washington's biographer, Louis Harlan, has commented that the Tuskegee leader came out of the affair "with some honor," and it is true that he exhibited some degree of compassion for the wounded Harris.[27] But Washington was a national leader of Afro-Americans, and the question remains of how in this incident he fulfilled his leadership responsibilities. The prime public fact was that Booker T. Washington refused to come between the lynch mob and its victim.

Prior to the 1906 Atlanta riot Washington was aware of the racial tension prevailing in the city. At the end of August he spoke in Atlanta at a meeting of the National Negro Business League. In a letter to Oswald Garrison Villard, Washington explained the context in which he spoke:

> When I got there I found the feeling between the races intensely strong, almost to the breaking point. In addition to the bitterness stirred up by the Hoke Smith campaign, several outrages had recently been committed by colored people on white women in Atlanta and in that county which added to the bitterness. In one case an English woman who had not been in this country very long, was most brutally treated; one of her eyes was put out, her nose destroyed and several limbs broken so that she will be maimed for life. One of the afternoon papers was advocating openly the formation of a Ku Klux Klan, another had offered a thousand dollars for the lynching of a colored man guilty of one of these crimes.

While in the city Washington visited with the managing editors of four Atlanta newspapers, and he noted that "several editorials of an encouraging character" appeared in the press. He was also cautious enough to note further that "the good we did was not evidenced so much in the local newspaper reports as by the expression of individuals which we heard from many quarters." Washington reported that he received numerous letters thanking him for having come to Atlanta and "expressing the feeling of relief because of the changed situation." He was, to be sure, overly optimistic as to the change.

Washington wove several strands of thought into his speech to the National Negro Business League, but his words could be and were used to legitimize fears about black crime. He did, of course, draw a clear distinction between those blacks who committed criminal acts and the respectable classes within the black community, the businessmen such as those in his audience, the educated, and the professionals. He utilized the distinction to make once again the case for education. He also spoke out bluntly against lynching: "The crime of lynching everywhere and at all times should be condemned, and those who commit crimes of any nature should be condemned ... let us bear in mind that every man, white or black, who takes the law into his hands to lynch or burn or shoot human beings supposed to be, or guilty of crime is insulting the executive, judicial and lawmaking bodies of the state in which he resides." Washington also included a comment to the effect that without the encouragement and protection of the law "it is not possible for the negro to succeed as a laborer, or in any line of business." But what the *Atlanta Constitution* chose to feature in its account of the speech was Washington's statement about black crime. Under the caption "Law-breaking Negroes Worst Menace to Race" the paper presented as Washington's keynote the view that "the worst enemies of the negro race are those negroes who commit crimes, which are followed by lynching, and that the south is after all the best place for black men who are willing to work." And an emphasis upon black criminality was indeed present in the speech as Washington stated that "one of the elements in our present situation that gives me most concern is the large number of crimes that are being committed by members of our race. The negro is committing too much crime north and south." And again: "We cannot be too frank or too strong in discussing the harm that the committing of crime is doing to our race." There was above all in Washington's remarks no reference whatever to the possibility that the Atlanta press was manufacturing a crime wave.

Following the Atlanta violence an undertone of anger was evident in some of Washington's private correspondence. He went to Atlanta on September 28, six days after the outbreak of the violence, to observe the situation. "The treatment which some of our people received during the last few days would be hard to describe," he wrote Villard. He wrote candidly to Francis Jackson Garrison: "There were many unspeakably cruel acts perpetrated in Atlanta during the riot; on the other hand, there were some brave, fine things done by colored people and by a few of the white people in behalf of the lives of the Negro race, but so far as handling the immediate trouble is concerned, I think all agree that the police authorities were criminally negligent and, in fact, in many cases sided with the rioters." Washington was also impressed with the plainspoken

manner with which Atlanta black spokesmen communicated their grievances to white leaders in post-riot meetings. But there was another tone
to his public comments about Atlanta. In a letter to the *New York World*
he urged that "the best white people and the best colored people" should
unite in common efforts to stop the disorder, and he "especially" urged
the black community "to exercise self-control and not make the fatal
mistake of attempting to retaliate." He ended his letter, which was also
carried by the *New York Times*, with the comment that he could not
refrain "from expressing a feeling of very deep grief on account of the
death of so many innocent men of both races because of the deeds of a
few despicable criminals." Washington's meaning here was equivocal,
but he could be understood as holding that the source of the violence
was the acts of black criminals.

In dealing with the Atlanta situation an option Washington forthrightly
excluded was any recourse to the federal government. He wrote the editor
of the *Philadelphia Tribune* that "the whole continuation and genius of
our government place the states and local communities in control of local
criminal matters, and the President has no right to interfere." That, from
Washington's perspective, was the end of the legal issue. As to the wisdom
of the president's "interfering" in the situation, he believed that the
southern black future depended upon local public sentiment, and he urged
reliance upon getting "the leading classes" of southern whites to protect
blacks, rather than a policy of depending upon "some outside force."
Regarding the sentiments of President Theodore Roosevelt, Washington
was certain that "no one can question where his heart is in all such
matters." Washington's message to the *Tribune* editor drew from Roosevelt the declaration that he had "absolutely *no* authority under the
circumstances to send troops to Atlanta."

Washington also attempted to employ the Atlanta violence as an argument against emphasizing the upholding of voting rights. Charles Waddell Chesnutt, the distinguished Cleveland author, had written
Washington and stated his position that "in view of recent events" no
system excluding blacks from the use of the ballot could have any positive
effect in improving the condition of the race. Regarding Atlanta, Chesnutt
also noted that he had not failed to observe "that those best qualified to
speak, and whose utterances would carry the most weight, have not been
in a position to express themselves fully," a comment that doubtless
included Washington in its scope. Washington's response was to agree
that the ballot was valuable, but he asked Chesnutt how he accounted
for the Atlanta riot in view of the fact that Georgia was the only southern
state where blacks had not been disfranchised by constitutional enact-

ment. Chesnutt's response was to wave aside the legal formalities and to place the issue in the context of the actual dynamics of what was happening in the state. "The riot occurred in Georgia," he wrote Washington, "not because the Negroes had exercised the franchise or made any less progress or developed any less strength than elsewhere, but because of a wicked and indefensible effort to disfranchise them." Chesnutt also needled Washington with an observation that, if he wanted to answer with the *argumentum ad hominen,* he could point out that the violence took place only a short while after Washington had delivered his "splendid object lesson of the Negro's progress in business and the arts of peace." All in all, in his effort to deny the relevance of political rights in the Atlanta situation, Washington had the worst of the argument.

By December 1906 Washington's message to black Atlanta was one of urging a policy of confidence in the "prominent citizens" who were earnest and sincere in seeking "to help lift up the negro in a way that no other group of white men in any part of the country can do at the present time." Washington affirmed that blacks were entitled to and expected justice, and he also explained that black economic improvement was threatened if labor had no confidence in the justice system and if those who had accumulated property needed to feel they could be driven away by a mob. The path forward was along the line of working with the white moderates and ignoring the harmful efforts of racial agitators "who serve neither race to any good purpose." Washington did float the proposal that blacks should have some "official responsibility in the bringing of the criminal classes to justice," an idea he shortly defined in the *Outlook* magazine as involving the constituting of a force of black police "to preside in the parts of the city occupied almost entirely by colored people."[28] Washington was seeking on this issue some concession from the white Establishment, but he was very careful now not to discuss the violence that had been inflicted on the black community, much less to criticize the racial caste system that generated it.

"The Atlanta riot," Louis R. Harlan writes, "instead of shaking Washington's faith in black progress through self-help and conciliation, actually seemed to reinforce it."[29] Washington's essentially conservative response to racial terror was very plainly stated in a speech he delivered on October 11, 1906, before the Afro-American Council in New York. "In the season of disturbances and excitement," he began, it was the role of blacks to show the world that they had learned lessons of self-restraint and would not give way to passion. Victories had come to blacks, Washington asserted, through their ability to be calm and patient, "often while enduring great wrong." He went on to observe that blacks were a law-

abiding people and urged "that every iota of influence that we possess
should be used to get rid of the criminal and loafing element of our people
and to make decent, law-abiding citizens." Washington warned northern
blacks against making what he termed "rash and intemperate utterances."
Noting that "any child can cry and fret," Washington also insisted that
leaving the South was no solution to existing problems. As was often his
style, he turned an outbreak of racist violence into an occasion for com-
plimenting the white South. He would condemn "the giving of promi-
nence to the work of the mob in the South" but also would give
appropriate credit "to those of the white race who stood manfully and
courageously on the side of law and order during the recent trying ordeals
through which this section of our country has been passing." Washington
wanted to call attention to the "brave and heroic" acts of "a certain
element" of southern white people.[30] There was in this speech no specific
condemnation of those responsible for the Atlanta violence. And, perhaps
most significantly, Washington saw no necessity to reevaluate his general
position regarding an appropriate strategy for blacks. The policy of accommodation was not producing results in terms of protecting the lives
and security of blacks living in a segregated society, but Washington's
response to the facts was merely to restate the case for the policies with
which he had become identified.

Washington's leadership was compromised by his reliance on accom-
modationism and also by a related characteristic of temperament that
biographer Harlan has most clearly identified. "Washington had always
lacked the capacity for the higher registers of indignation," Harlan writes.
And this was not merely a matter of style. Washington lacked "one
essential attribute for the leader of an oppressed people—the capacity
for righteous public anger against injustice. Washington could and did
work with dogged persistence against a great variety of racial injustices
that white men perpetrated. He could chide or cajole with great skill and
subtlety. But somewhere back in his life the power to lose his temper
with a white man had been schooled out of him." Washington had himself
been injured by racism, cut off from offering bold opposition to white
supremacy.[31]

For Booker T. Washington the question of racial violence was not
always a matter of general social policy or even the issue of how Tuskegee
should relate to the racism of white Alabama. In 1911, during a trip to
New York City, he was himself a victim of assault. After checking in at
a Manhattan hotel he had entered the vestibule of an all-white apartment
building near Central Park. Washington was assaulted by a white tenant,
Henry Albert Ulrich, who contended he found the black man peering

through the keyhole of a white woman's apartment. Ulrich proceeded to throw Washington out of the building and added: "He resisted and I gave him the best beating I could. I thought I was right at the time and I think so yet." The dangerous aura of interracial sexuality was thrown over the incident when a white woman, Laura Alvarez, testified that as she passed Washington in the hall he had called out to her, "Hello sweetheart." What had taken place was inseparable from the reality of race. The attention drawn to Washington's alleged words to a white female and the physical attack itself were products of the circumstance that blacks were to be held to requirements of public conduct not imposed upon white people. Louis Harlan finds this incident to have shaped the greater willingness to speak out directly against racial injustice that marked Washington's final years. Other factors may have contributed to this willingness, but as Harlan observes, "surely the most vivid and re-current was his self-recognition as he ran bleeding through the New York streets, that in the atmosphere of American racism even Booker T. Washington was lynchable."[32] There is the painful irony that his own personal suffering furnished evidence against Washington's policy of accommodation.

Among those who saw the racism characterizing this incident was Charles Waddell Chesnutt who wrote Washington concerning the white assailant: "I can't imagine his treating a well-dressed white man in such a cavalier fashion. There are too many white men only too willing to thump a Negro with any possible excuse, and they ought to be taught that a Negro cannot be judged or treated by any different standard from that applied to other men." Washington took much comfort from expressions of sympathy coming from the white South, appreciated the sympathetic reception he received from white Tuskegeans, and indeed he exclaimed that the support he found in the South made him love it "more than ever." But there was a reminder of Dixie realities in the comment by a New Haven tailor that in the South there would not have been any opportunity to explain things in court, "the woman's word would have been taken and you would have been lynched." Perhaps, to be sure, Washington's distinguished public position might have saved him from such a fate, but the tailor's observation accurately reflected the existing racial pattern of the South. And even in the moderate southern press there were some who used the episode to reflect unfavorably on Washington. The *Atlanta Constitution,* reviewing Washington's book *My Larger Education,* contended that the Tuskegee educator scattered his efforts too much. He would do better to concentrate upon matters closer to home. Then came the jab: "If he does this he will certainly not be found in New York, in the night time, 'hunting keyholes,' and attending police courts, with himself on the criminal side of the docket."

On November 6, in a trial at the New York Court of Special Sessions, Henry Ulrich was acquitted on the charge of assault. Kelly Miller of Howard University wrote the *Washington Star* that he found the outcome of the case "the most tragic occurrence" in American history since Lincoln's assassination. And the Washington, D.C., black educator Roscoe Bruce Conkling asked some pertinent questions: "if the courts accept the testimony of a dog-fancier and wife-deserter as conclusive against that of the greatest educator and publicist of our race, of what avail is the testimony of a black mechanic or farmer however industrious and honest as against the most worthless of white men? ... if a man of Ulrich's stripe may in the North assault Booker T. Washington with impunity, pray what security of life and limb has any of us in this broad land?"[33] What happened in this affair had implications that went far beyond the injury and indignity inflicted upon Washington.

A new factor in the black response to violence was the emergence and growth of a national organization that would champion the cause of full citizenship rights, the National Association for the Advancement of Colored People. The NAACP rose from the joining together of the black militancy expressed in the Niagara movement with the new currents of racial equalitarianism found among liberal and radical whites. The association was the outgrowth of two national conferences held in New York to discuss the condition of blacks in the United States. The first meeting was held on May 31 and June 1, 1909, and the second, which actually formed the organization, met May 12–14, 1910. From the beginning of its history the NAACP spoke out forcefully against racist violence, especially concentrating its attention upon the issue of lynching. National publicity concerning the positions taken by the association was provided by the NAACP's organ, *The Crisis,* edited by W. E. B. Du Bois. At the May 2, 1911, meeting of the organization's board of directors a resolution was adopted with regard to a recent, somewhat unusual, lynching episode. At Livermore, Kentucky, a black man charged with killing a white person had been taken from the jail and placed on the stage of the town opera house. The crowd paid admission to fire shots at the victim. The NAACP resolution quoted press reports as stating: "Those who bought orchestra seats had the privilege of emptying their six shooters at the swaying form above them, but the gallery occupants were limited to one shot." The NAACP board described this lynching as a "culmination of spectacular, revolting, barbarous brutality" that disgraced the country "and impeached our civilization." The board appointed a special committee charged with urging the president of the United States to send a special message to Congress requesting appropriate action, "such action as will save this nation from this foul blot and curse on its civilization, its honor and its Christian religion."[34] President William Howard Taft did not respond to this call.

The Second Annual Report of the NAACP, issued January 1, 1912, documented the fact that much of the energies of the organization were focused upon dealing with cases of brutality against blacks. The association devoted attention to an issue that would become increasingly important in future years, the use of violence to enforce de facto housing segregation. In Kansas City blacks who purchased homes in previously white neighborhoods had been subjected to at least five incidents of dynamiting. The NAACP initiated an investigation into the violence, declaring that the notion that blacks "may be segregated by intimidation and lawlessness, ending with black-hand methods, or by city ordinances and State statutes, creating districts that recall the worst conditions of the medieval Ghetto, is an idea far too common in America today." The report pledged further efforts against such segregation.

The report also outlined what had happened during 1911 with regard to lynching. Sixty-three black persons had been lynched that year and, the NAACP emphasized, "many entirely innocent persons are among the victims." Reference was made to a lynching at Lake City, Florida, in which six blacks were strung up as targets to be riddled with shots in retaliation for the killing in self-defense of a white man, and the report further singled out Oklahoma, Georgia, and Kentucky as states in which innocent men "died deaths of torture at the hands of mobs." The report noted that women had been among the victims. As these lynchings occurred, the association had written to the various governors of the states involved demanding punishment of the guilty and had stimulated protests from individuals in many states. On November 15 the NAACP held a public meeting in the hall of the New York Ethical Culture Society. A resolution protesting lynching as "the worst indictment of American democracy that can be drawn" was sent to President Taft. Funds were collected to start an investigation of lynching, and the report announced that "the investigation is now under way." The association had also complained to the postmaster general about distribution of postal cards portraying a lynching and was successful in having the cards ruled unmailable.[35]

The NAACP operated very much within the Progressive spirit of public protest and education, based on the conviction that an aroused and informed public opinion would compel action against racial terrorism.

The association worked to disseminate the facts widely and to shame Americans into realizing the depths into which racism was leading the nation. Immediatist rather than gradualist in temper, with a number of radical Progressives and Socialists among its founders, the association did not relate its work for equal rights to any program for restructuring basic political and economic institutions. The organization in its early years was a compound of radicalism and reform.

New Orleans riot, 1866. *Harper's Weekly*
(August 1866).

New Orleans riot, 1866. *Harper's Weekly* (August 1866).

"Dam Your Soul. The Horrible *Sepulchre* and Bloody Moon has at last arrived. Some live to-day to-morrow "*Die.*" We the undersigned understand through our Grand "*Cyclops*" that you have recommended a big Black Nigger for Male agent on our nu rode; wel, sir, Jest you understand in time if he gets on the rode you can make up your mind to pull roape. If you have any thing to say in regard to the Matter, meet the Grand Cyclops and Conclave at Den No. 4 at 12 o'clock midnight, Oct. 1st, 1871.

"When you are in Calera we warn you to hold your tounge and not speak so much with your mouth or otherwise you will be taken on supprise and led out by the Klan and learnt to stretch hemp. Beware. Beware. Beware. Beware.

(Signed)
       "PHILLIP ISENBAUM,
             "*Grand Cyclops.*
       "JOHN BANKSTOWN.
       "ESAU DAVES.
       "MARCUS THOMAS.
       "BLOODY BONES.

"You know who. And all others of the Klan."

Ku Klux Klan warning against hiring black workers on North and South Alabama Railroad. *Testimony of Joint Select Committee to Inquire into the Condition of Affairs in the Late Insurrectionary States*, vol 2 (Washington, 1872).

Octavius V. Catto. RG-13, Records of the Works Progress Administration, Division of Archives and Manuscripts, Pennsylvania Historical and Museum Commission.

Frederick Douglass. Prints and Photographs Division, Library of Congress.

Ida B. Wells. From I. Garland Penn, *The Afro-American Press and Its Editors* (Springfield: Willey and Co., 1891).

Charred corpse of Jesse Washington after lynching, Waco, Texas,
May 15, 1916. Prints and Photographs Division, Library of Congress.

Courts-martial proceedings of soldiers following 1917 Houston riot.

The NAACP-sponsored Silent Protest Parade against Lynching, New York City, 1917. Archives, University Library, University of Massachusetts/Amherst

Whites chasing a black, Chicago riot, 1919. Chicago Historical Society.
Photo by Jun Fujita.

Whites stoning a black to death, Chicago riot, 1919. Chicago Historical Society. Photo by Jun Fujita.

SIX

Confrontation

THE ENTRANCE of the United States into "the war to make the world safe for democracy" did not put an end to racial violence. The violence of Houston and East St. Louis was only the most blatant manifestation of the spirit that would employ violent means to preserve racial subjection. Although much of black leadership affirmed support for the war effort, brutalities against Afro-Americans continued. Rather than the reality being that violence was receding, the fact was that the forces were set in motion leading to the mass confrontations of black and white that would explode shortly after the war's end.

The NAACP summarized the lynching statistics for the war year of 1918. The association had authenticated the lynching of sixty-three black persons as well as four whites. Confirming evidence could not be obtained with regard to an additional twelve cases believed to have occurred. The summary referred to a "lynching orgy" that had taken place in Brooks and Lowndes counties, Georgia, and the breakdown of the statistics showed that the greatest number of lynchings, nineteen, had occurred in that state, Texas coming in second with eleven. President Wilson on July 26, 1918, had issued a public statement in which he described lynching as "this disgraceful evil" and stated that lynching "cannot live where the community does not countenance it." It was Woodrow Wilson's way of both denouncing lynching and making clear he would not initiate federal action to stop it. In Georgia, the association noted, the president's words had merely the effect of keeping news of lynchings out of the press.

The NAACP analysis pointed to special features of the 1918 lynchings. Five of the victims were women. Two black men were burned at the stake before death and four after death. In Texas a mother and her five children were lynched by the mob, the mother shot as she attempted to drag the bodies of her sons from their burning cabin. The pretext for violence in this case was "alleged conspiracy to avenge" the killing of another son by officers seeking to arrest him for draft evasion. The

145

NAACP analysis also noted without comment the special circumstance in which a black victim had been handed over to the lynchers by other blacks.[1]

The NAACP was perfectly correct in its description of events transpiring in Brooks and Lowndes counties as a lynching orgy. The British writer Stephen Graham, having traveled through the South, gave his account of an episode in this area in which murder and peonage were intertwined. A white farmer had paid the fine of a black man charged with gambling, whereupon the black man was turned over to the farmer to work off the debt. But the time never came when the white man would agree that the debt was repaid, and the black peon finally went home. The farmer went to the black man's place and whipped him. But this black man had been pushed beyond limits and stopped playing by the rules of racial subordination. He paid a return call upon the white farmer and, firing through the window, killed him and wounded his wife, afterward fleeing the scene. A lynch mob was formed, and in the process of hunting for the black runaway, according to Graham, this mob lynched eleven blacks, including one woman. The mob, not knowing where to look, seized people who might have had reason for hating the dead white farmer. In one incident a man was lynched who had served a chain-gang term for having protected his wife from the farmer. The wife protested that her husband had nothing to do with the killing, and when she would not be quieted she too was lynched. Wrote Graham: "They tied her upside down by her ankles to a tree, poured petrol on her clothing, and burned her to death. White American women will perhaps take note that this coloured sister of theirs was in her eighth month with child. The mob around her was not angry or insensate, but hysterical with brutal pleasure. The clothes burned off her body. Her child, prematurely born, was kicked to and fro by the mob." Graham drew the conclusion from all this that, "from the point of view of the natural history of mankind, it put these white denizens of Georgia on a lower level than cannibals."[2] More specifically, the Georgia lynchings mocked the hopes of W. E. B. Du Bois and other black leaders that support for United States participation in the war would stimulate respect for constitutional rights.

If the war did not produce an abatement of racial violence, the months after the armistice revealed an American society in which antagonisms of race and class were sharper, more explosive, than ever. The aspirations of Afro-Americans conflicted head on with the determination of white authority to maintain existing racial mores. Black soldiers may have returned home believing that their work and sacrifice entitled them to the rights of citizenship, but for the supporters of Jim Crow the black man in uniform was rather to be feared and hated than respected. Black migrants to the urban, industrial culture of the North looked forward to a future of economic and educational opportunity, but northern society would turn the clock back, drive blacks out of jobs in industry, and maintain a racial caste system in which blacks would occupy a menial position and submit to being crowded into ghettos. The ingredients were there for violent confrontation, and all that was needed were the specific incidents of provocation that would bring conflict to the surface. What gave the racial violence of post–World War I America its special quality was the widespread, mass character of the conflict and the manifest readiness of blacks to offer determined resistance.

In the United States that now emerged as one of the victors in the war, lynching continued as a regular, routine event. In Georgia twenty-two persons were lynched, and in only two of these episodes was assault against white women charged. Blacks were lynched for a variety of alleged misdemeanors, and quite clearly returning soldiers were a high-priority target. During April one soldier was beaten to death at Blakely for wearing his uniform too long. In May Benny Richards was burned to death at Warrenton for murder. Early in August a soldier was shot for refusing to yield the road, and another was hanged for discussing the racial violence in Chicago. Another soldier was lynched at Pope City for firing a gun. At Ocmulgee whites feared that blacks planned an uprising, and as a measure of precaution one black was burned at the stake. On September 10 at Athens, seat of the University of Georgia, another black was burned to death. Americus, Lincolntown, Macon, and Buena Vista were among communities where additional lynchings took place.[3]

In May 1919 a lynching in Milan, Georgia, dramatically underscored the reality that black men would be murdered for coming to the defense of black women. Two armed white men had sought to break into the home of a widow, searching for her two daughters. Some younger children screamed for help, and a black neighbor, Berry Washington, seventy-two years of age, had come out with his shotgun in hand. The would-be rapists threatened to shoot Washington, and in an exchange of shots one of the whites was killed. In keeping with the code of racism Washington, not the surviving white assailant, was arrested. At midnight, May 25, the lynch mob took Washington from the jail and brought him to the place where the shooting had occurred. He was hanged from a post, his body riddled with bullets, and left hanging for some hours. "He was lynched," said a Milan resident who reported the incident, "because he protected his own women, in his part of the town." It should be noted that it was only because one forthright individual would not join in a conspiracy of silence that word of the Washington lynching reached the world outside of Milan. The county commissioner asked the local newspaper not to publish news of this lynching on the specious grounds that this would impede his investigation. Approximately two months following this lynching a prominent white resident of Milan wrote the *Atlanta Constitution* that "up to this time I have heard nothing from it."[4] There can be little doubt that local officials shared complicity in this lynching and also arranged to cover up the facts.

In 1919 episodes of violence also took place between blacks and white members of the armed services. A characteristic episode was the rioting that broke out in Charleston, South Carolina, during May 1919. In this incident white sailors of the United States Navy stationed at Charleston clashed with black civilians after a black man allegedly jostled a white sailor. Casualties resulting from the violence included three blacks killed and at least seventeen black men, seven sailors, and one policeman wounded. Reflecting some perception as to responsibility for the clash, Charleston's Mayor Hyde issued a public statement to the effect that "the negroes of Charleston must be protected."[5] Evidence of a new spirit was apparent in the fact that in this confrontation blacks fought back against the white servicemen and inflicted casualties as well as suffering them.

During the postwar months a serious outbreak of violence in Arkansas was a product of conflict between white plantation owners and black sharecroppers. The year 1919 saw sharp industrial conflict between labor and capital with militant strikes in such industries as meatpacking and steel. The struggle that centered in Elaine, Arkansas, revealed that class conflict also could have explosive consequences in the rural South. The root cause of the violence was that in 1919, despite the high market price of cotton, white buyers and landlords consistently dealt fraudulently with the black growers. Emerging from a war that had raised aspirations for a better life, the black farmers determined to seek redress for their grievances. They organized a Progressive Farmers and Householders Union of America and proceeded to plan a campaign of effective action. The act of organizing a union was viewed as intolerable by propertied whites, and they moved to crush the movement begun by the black cotton growers.

Tension escalated into violence when several whites clashed with blacks attending a meeting of the union at a black church at Hoop Spur in Phillips County. The whites claimed blacks had first opened fire, but the blacks stated that they had replied to shooting begun by white raiders. In any event the incident ended with one white man dead and another wounded. This violence turned Phillips County into a racial battleground with armed whites entering the county from Arkansas, Mississippi, and Tennessee. Blacks were disarmed and arrested, with hundreds confined in a stockade and unable to communicate with relatives or legal counsel. Blacks seeking to avoid arrest hid in canebrakes and were hunted down by whites. According to official figures five whites and twenty-five blacks were killed in the conflict, but an investigator for the NAACP reported that whites had informed him that as many as 100 blacks had been killed and that the total death list would never be known. Following the work of armed terror the courts were brought into play as a further instrument of suppression. In sham trials that violated basic concepts of judicial procedure, twelve black defendants were sentenced to death and eighty were given terms ranging from one to twenty years. All of these proceedings took five days to complete.[6]

Later in 1923 the Arkansas cases became the basis of the United States Supreme Court decision *Moore* v. *Dempsey* (261 U.S. 86) in which the Court overturned the convictions on the ground that the defendants had been denied a fair trial. The Supreme Court noted that the Arkansas courtroom had been "thronged with an adverse crowd that threatened the most dangerous consequences to anyone interfering with the desired result." The Court also noted allegations and affidavits that "there never was a chance for the petitioners to be acquitted; no juryman could have voted for an acquittal and continued to live in Phillips County and if any prisoner by any chance had been acquitted by a jury he could not have escaped the mob."[7] The action of the Supreme Court represented a landmark decision providing that state courts were required to provide both the form and the substance of a judicial trial. But the Supreme Court acted long after the fact, and although the lives of the convicted defendants were saved, the landlords of Arkansas succeeded in smashing a black labor movement that sought no more than elementary justice for black cotton growers.

The racial violence that marked 1919 came to be described as the "Red Summer" of 1919. The events that did most to draw the public's attention to racial confrontation were the large-scale clashes between black and white that erupted in several major American cities. Riots had previously occurred in individual cities, but 1919 represented something new in American history; within a span of weeks racial violence spread from one city to another, and every city feared its turn was next. It was clear that these confrontations could not be explained as simply a local phenomenon. As Americans learned the news of racial outbreaks in such diverse cities as Omaha, Washington, Knoxville, and Chicago, it was apparent that these explosions expressed tensions afflicting the national society. There was something new to be seen in the rapid spread of violence, and within the various incidents there was also a component of more determined and effective black resistance to assault by white racists. Resistance by one means or another has always been the core of the black response to violence, but in 1919 the resistance was more often overt and direct, defiant in its willingness to inflict as well as suffer casualties. It was a spirit that the poet Claude McKay articulated more clearly perhaps than anyone else: "If we must die, O let us nobly die, / So that our precious blood may not be shed / In vain; then even the monsters we defy / Shall be constrained to honor us though dead."[8]

In Chicago on July 27 the temperature reached ninety-six degrees, and the day was a culmination of a series of days with temperatures in the midnineties. Many people sought relief from the heat, with large crowds making use of the Lake Michigan beaches. Approximately at four o'clock a black youth, Eugene Williams, was swimming offshore at the foot of Twenty-ninth Street. What should have been only recreation soon turned into tragedy. De facto, this was a segregated beach, with a part of the frontage open to blacks while whites reserved the remaining area for themselves. That day the line was crossed, and there followed an exchange of stone throwing between groups of blacks and whites in the water. Williams had drifted into the waters controlled by whites and, possibly struck by a stone, drowned. Several black witnesses charged a white man with having stoned the youth, but the police refused to arrest him and indeed sought to arrest one of the black men present. This episode served as the provocation that brought to the surface the racial hostility existing in Chicago. The hatred stemming from a constricting job market and the efforts by blacks to secure adequate housing by moving into previously all-white neighborhoods had reached an intensity where any incident in which blacks refused to accept racial subordination could touch off a massive assault upon the black community. From the beach the violence soon spread into the adjacent community, and seemingly without effective restraint hatred could now be translated into murderous actions. For a period of seven days the South Side of Chicago was the scene of active rioting. Blacks fought back, but white rioters had superiority in numbers and firepower and the tacit sympathy of the police, and many blacks fell victims to the mob because they had to pass through white neighborhoods in order to reach their places of work. White mobs gathered at streetcar transfer points, pulled trolleys from wires, and dragged black passengers to the street where they were kicked and beaten. The casualty figures revealed both the strength of white racism and the new reality that assault upon blacks would lead to a substantial number of white casualties. Twenty-three blacks and fifteen whites died, with more than 500 injured and about a thousand persons left homeless.[9]

Bloodshed was extensive in Chicago, but from the perspective of at least one black eyewitness, there was a positive side to the events. This observer, an attorney, stressed the readiness of the black community for armed combat, claiming that blacks had 1,000 rifles "and enough ammunition to last for years if used in guerrilla warfare." He welcomed a delay in the arrival of troops, for although it cost lives "it afforded an opportunity for the Negroes to impress upon the whites their readiness, willingness, and eagerness to fight the thing through." As to the riot's future impact he was decidedly optimistic. "The riot," he said, "will make the future relations between the races decidedly better. . . . the colored man must not be kicked about like a dumb brute. Our white friends, seeing the danger that besets the nation, will become more active in our cause, and the other whites will at least have a decent respect for us based on fear."[10]

The Chicago violence was the result of a collision between racism and an enhanced black consciousness that rejected deference to white supremacy. One Chicago black man, Stanley B. Norvell, a war veteran, attempted a few weeks after the riot to explain to newspaper editor Victor F. Lawson how the war experience had altered the black perception of the world. Norvell wrote that there was now a new Negro, "a brand new Negro, if you please." Black people looked to broader horizons, had been jolted into considering world events, "treaties and boundaries and leagues of Nations and mandatories, and Balkan states, and a dismembered Poland, a ravished Belgium, a stricken France, a soviet Russia and a republic in Ireland and so on." They had come to think about the development of the political process in other nations and, most importantly, had come to understand they were a part of the American government. "It took a world war," Norvell wrote, "to get that idea into general Negro acceptance, but it is there now." An awakening had occurred "that must inevitably continue for all time." Blacks had become "new men and world men, if you please." These new men wanted what any other American citizen insisted upon, not equal rights but the same rights. The American black, Norvell explained, "must and will have industrial, commercial, civil and political equality." Norvell pointed to the international dimension of the American racial question, informing Lawson that if blacks were denied their just rights America would "stand in grave danger of losing her national integrity in the eyes of Europe and she will be forced to admit to her European adversaries that her constitution is but a scrap of paper." This black Chicagoan, who clearly was not intimidated by the recent violence, comprehended that the world was changing and the American racial pattern could not remain intact.[11]

Violence that broke out in Omaha on September 28 had its roots in an intense campaign to incite public hatred of supposed black criminality. Participating in this campaign were the city's newspapers, the chief of police, and some local labor leaders who allowed themselves to be used to further divide white and black workers. In recent strikes by meat-packers and teamsters, corporations had recruited black strikebreakers, but these leaders did not strike back at the corporations or even at the strikebreakers; succumbing to racism, they attacked the entire black community. The Omaha branch of the NAACP had sought to avert a confrontation, had urged blacks to support the labor movement, and had warned against incitement that could lead to a replica of the 1917 riot in East St. Louis—all to no avail. As in Chicago, all that was required to ignite mass violence was a specific incident that would lay bare the underlying hatred. At the end of September this was provided when a white girl was raped and said she thought the assailant was a black man.

On September 28 police arrested a black man, William Brown, and transported him to the local jail. A mob soon gathered demanding that Brown be turned over to them, and when the mayor of Omaha, Edward P. Smith, refused, the mob turned upon Smith and were about to hang him from a trolley pole when police intervened, cut the rope, and carried the badly injured mayor away. The numbers of the mob continued to swell, with thousands now demanding that the prisoner be put into their hands and many throwing stones and bricks at the courthouse where Brown was confined. Police offered only token resistance to the mob, some of the officers surrendering their clubs and guns upon the mob's demand. The mob soon enough had its way, and Brown was turned over to it. He was shot and hanged from a lamppost, and then in true Deep-South fashion his body was burned and then displayed from a trolley pole at a downtown intersection.

Further violence in Omaha was aborted only by the intervention of the United States Army. The army moved to restore order within the context of a situation in which leaders of the black community reported to city officials that blacks were well armed and prepared to act in self-defense but would not initiate violence. What can in one sense be evaluated as a move to restore law and order can also be viewed as a step to prevent the outbreak of a sharper conflict in which the white mob would not escape unscathed. In any event troops under the command of General Leonard Wood of the Central Department of the Army soon arrived in Omaha, and de facto martial law prevailed in the city. Wood took charge of the Omaha police department and announced that identified rioters would be arrested by the army but held for trial by civilian authorities. Machine guns were posted at key public buildings; troops patrolled downtown streets and challenged street gatherings of more than two persons. By October 2 fifty-nine men were under arrest for complicity in the courthouse lynching. Charges included arson, assault with intent to do great bodily injury, and murder. No doubt, moves to prosecute the lynchers were stimulated by the factor that this lynching involved a murderous assault upon a public official and a public building.[12]

Evidence of the entrenched character of racial oppression in the United States is to be found in the fact that the Omaha violence elicited a demand for more police control of existing tensions rather than any serious demand for reexamination of prevailing racist practices. Violence was not to be allowed to get out of hand, but the need for addressing the causes of racial violence was ignored. In this respect as in others the Omaha violence set a precedent that was to be followed in the urban conflicts of the 1960s. The power of the federal government was available to limit conflict and to establish a monopoly on the use of physical coercion, but that power was not to confront the social roots of violence.

That the federal government would not do anything meaningful about underlying causes of the violence of the Red Summer was to be expected in view of the government's response to the violence that erupted on its front doorstep at the beginning of the summer. Washington, D.C., was a major center of the black middle class, proud of a sophisticated cultural life and of Howard University, but it was also a city of the South, of racial exclusion and segregation. The racism prevalent in the city had been underscored by the presence of a chief executive, Woodrow Wilson, who had instituted new patterns of Jim Crowism in government departments. As much as any city in the United States, Washington was in a formal sense one city, but it was also more profoundly two conflicting communities physically joined together. Under the strains of postwar realities the fragile coexistence of black aspiration with racist segregation broke down. Racism took the initiative, seeking to reinforce and harden racial subordination.

The *Washington Post* may today be one of the nation's foremost liberal newspapers, but in 1919 the paper sensationalized a manufactured "crime wave" and concentrated its attention upon alleged assaults of blacks upon white women. On July 19 the *Post* headlined an incident in which, supposedly, two black men had jostled a secretary on her way home, attempted to seize her umbrella, and then fled. The papers headlined the affair as an "attack" and also reported that the police chief had ordered that all young men found in "suspicious" parts of the city after nightfall be held for questioning. This newspaper's reportage triggered action by 200 white sailors and marines who began a march into the black community, stopping along the way to beat up several black men and women. The government that was unable to employ its armed might to suppress the southern lynch mob could not even prevent its military personnel from constituting such a mob. In this particular instance the NAACP urged the secretary of the navy, Josephus Daniels, to restrain the involved sailors and marines, but Daniels took no action and apparently largely blamed the blacks for the violence.

From the beginning of the Washington riot, blacks moved to a posture of self-defense and retaliatory violence. On July 19 police stopping a group of blacks on the street were fired upon and one policeman was wounded. The following night blacks fought back during clashes with hundreds of white sailors and soldiers. The violence of July 20 represented an escalation of the previous day's violence, and the *Post* now added fuel to the fire by announcing on July 21 that servicemen would gather that evening for "a 'clean up' that will cause the events of the last two evenings to pale into insignificance." Government officials conferred, and there was a flurry of statements by congressmen, one urging an inquiry into police failure to apprehend black assailants of white women, another urging that the armed services prevent their personnel from joining in violence, and two others simply demanding that President Wilson declare martial law. The congressmen having done their duty by satisfying the views of their constituents, the violence, more extensive and bloodier than before, broke out again on Monday afternoon and evening. Blacks were better organized, and there was even an incident in which blacks turned the tables by boarding a streetcar and beating the white motorman and conductors. The events of Monday showed that white mob action could result in substantial white casualties. Fifteen individuals were either killed or seriously wounded, and ten of these were white. Hundreds of arrests were made. In this conflict, unlike the urban riots of the 1960s, whites, other than policemen or assigned troops, raided the black community, but blacks, riding in automobiles, also raided white residential areas. Suddenly the price of racist violence became too high, and now governmental leaders, really for the first time, made serious efforts to stop the violence. More disciplined military units were called upon, at least some government departments urged employees to remain off the streets, and contacts were initiated with black clergymen who would urge calm upon their congregations. The efforts produced success, and there was little violence on July 22. Within a few days Washington had returned to its accustomed routine. A number of white newspapers drew the conclusion from the Washington experience that the remedy for racial conflict was a stronger police force.[13]

Afro-Americans manifested a broad range of responses to the violent confrontations imposed upon them in the postwar period. At the level where feelings are translated into action, blacks individually and collectively resisted violent assault more openly and boldly, both taking measures of self-defense and passing over to the counterattack. Terror was still resorted to by white supremacists, but fear was less effective as a paralyzing means of control. Black response was shaped by experience and also by ideological debate within black leadership, operating at a higher level of sophistication that expressed the complex realities of the twentieth century.

For some black spokesmen, especially those with roots in the accommodationist section of black leadership, a prime element in their response to the violence of 1919 was appeal to the goodwill of the white power structure. Representative of this approach to the situation was the attempt of Robert Moton, Booker T. Washington's successor at Tuskegee, to elicit a condemnation of racial violence from President Wilson. In August 1919 Moton wrote Wilson that he had no desire to add to the president's burdens but he wished to call attention "to what seems to me vital not only for the interest of the twelve millions of black people, but equally as important for the welfare of the millions of whites whom they touch." Moton believed that a statement by Wilson regarding mob law would have a salutary effect, especially in countering "the apparent revolutionary attitude of many Negroes which shows itself in a desire to have justice at any cost." A statement by the president, Moton declared, "would have a tremendous stabilizing effect . . . on the members of my race."[14] Moton discussed the lynching question with Wilson, not so much in terms of lynching per se as in the context of the government's need to subdue black militancy.

The NAACP continued to rely upon public education and exposure of the truth concerning racial violence, concentrating much of its efforts upon rallying public support for an antilynching bill introduced by Congressman Dyer of Missouri. As the association's foremost publicist, W. E. B. Du Bois sought to refute press distortions concerning racial incidents and to point out the actual causes of black militancy. An example of his efforts in this direction was his answer to a *New York World* article dealing with the confrontation in Arkansas between white power and black sharecroppers. Du Bois's letter was factual and to the point in reply to the *World* article he described as "palpably unfair and misinforming." Whereas the article sought to find the source of the conflict in the work of an individual agitator, Du Bois focused upon the basic reality that "the just grievances of the negro peons in Arkansas are a disgrace to the South and a defiance of the Thirteenth Amendment." Arkansas peonage was part of a share-tenant system prevailing in the Mississippi delta, which Du Bois described as "one of the most iniquitous systems of peonage in the United States."

Du Bois affirmed the legitimacy of the movement organized by the black farmers of Arkansas, declaring that there was "not the slightest trustworthy evidence that the meetings of those negroes had any object, except to force by law prompt settlements by the landlords to better the conditions of the tenants by saving money and buying land." Du Bois also explained the process by which a pretext was contrived for mass assault upon the protesting blacks. "Somebody goes and shoots at the negroes secretly," he wrote, "and at the slightest sign of resistance the whole organization of the black belt is called into being. This organization consists of all the law officers of the county and all the white men near and in neighboring counties and states, armed to the teeth." At Hoop Spur whites fired into a meeting of blacks, and when the blacks returned the fire, killing one white man, white authority had its justification for wholesale arrests. According to Du Bois, sixty to a hundred black individuals were killed, 1,000 were arrested, and 123 were indicted, with twelve persons sentenced to death. He had only contempt for the proceeding of the Arkansas court in this matter, describing the trials of the accused blacks as an "outrageous farce." Those sentenced to death had been tried and convicted within a time span of a day and a half. Du Bois put the matter bluntly: "There is not a civilized country in the world that would for a moment allow this kind of justice to stand."[15]

This letter expressed a sharpened vehemence in Du Bois's polemic against racism. Du Bois had supported the war, but with the coming of peace he proposed a full-scale offensive against racial oppression. He recognized that in the war blacks had fought to defend varied and conflicting interests. They had fought for "bleeding France and what she means and has meant to us and humanity and against the threat of German race arrogance," and blacks had fought for the country's highest ideals but also "in bitter resignation" had defended "the dominant southern oligarchy entrenched in Washington." Fate, "the hateful upturning and mixing of things," had brought it about that blacks had protected the America "that represents and gloats in lynching, disfranchisement, caste, brutality and the devilish insult." But now the war, the war against racism that yet defended racism, was over, and Du Bois declared: "We stand again to look America squarely in the face and call a spade a spade." He observed that "this country of ours . . . is yet a shameful land," and when he listed the components of that shame he began with lynching. He described lynching as "barbarism of a degree of contemptible nastiness unparalleled in human history. Yet for fifty years we have lynched two Negroes a week, and we have kept this up right through the war." He had no apology to make for supporting participation in the war. "It was right for us to fight," he declared, adding: "The faults of *our* country are *our* faults." But now it was time to take up the battle at home. He ended an editorial in the May 1919 *Crisis* with a ringing call to action: "by the God of Heaven, we are cowards and jackasses if now that that war is over, we do not marshall every ounce of our brain and brawn to fight a sterner, longer, more unbending battle against the forces of hell in our own land. *We return. / We return from fighting. / We return fighting.* Make way for Democracy! We saved it in France, and by the Great Jehovah, we will save it in the United States of America, or know the reason why."[16] Du Bois essentially proposed a greatly intensified effort to proceed along the course charted by the NAACP, a path of public agitation and legislative action geared to securing the protection of citizenship rights. His words served as an appeal to white people who saw America disgraced by racism and also as a means to move blacks into determined action.

PART III

Peace without Justice: The 1920s

I watched an angry mob chain him to an iron stake. I watched them pile wood around his helpless body. I watched them pour gasoline on this wood. And I watched three men set this wood on fire. I stood in a crowd of 600 people as the flames gradually crept nearer and nearer to the helpless Negro. I watched the blaze climb higher and higher, encircling him without mercy. I heard his cry of agony as the flames reached him and set his clothing on fire. . . . Soon he became quiet. There was no doubt that he was dead. The flames jumped and leaped above his head. An odor of burning flesh reached my nostrils. I felt suddenly sickened. Through the leaping blaze I could see the Negro sagging and supported by the chains. . . . Then the crowd walked away. . . . "I'm hungry," someone complained. "Let's get something to eat."

Crisis, November 1925, pp. 41–42

Back of the writhing, yelling, cruel-eyed demons who break, destroy, maim and lynch and burn at the stake is a knot, large or small, of normal human beings and these human beings at heart are desperately afraid of something. Of what? Of many things but usually of losing their jobs, of being declassed, degraded or actually disgraced; of losing their hopes, their savings, their plans for their children; of the actual pangs of hunger; of dirt, of crime. And of all this, most ubiquitous in modern industrial society is that fear of unemployment.

It is this nucleus of ordinary men that continually gives the mob its initial and awful impetus. Around this nucleus, to be sure, gather snowballwise all manner of flotsam, filth and human garbage and every inhibition of alcohol and current fashion. But all this is the horrible covering of this inner nucleus of Fear.

W. E. B. Du Bois, "The Shape of Fear," *North American Review*, June 1926, pp. 291–304

I advise you to be ready to defend yourselves. I notice that the State Government has removed some of its restrictions upon owning firearms, and one form of live insurance for your wives and children might be the possession of some of these handy implements.

Hubert H. Harrison, *Baltimore Afro-American*, June 10, 1921

SEVEN

Garvey and Randolph

A S THE UNITED STATES moved into the 1920s many Afro-Americans did not find the strategy of civil rights protest an adequate perspective for the future. For a variety of reasons, gaining increasing support was the view that new conditions required a new strategy. Operating within a context of a racism more virulent than ever, some considered futile any strategy based on the assumption that white racism could be eliminated as a dominating factor in American society. Others, stirred by the anti-imperialist, anticolonial movements emerging from the war, sought a means of expressing a new consciousness of nationality, sought stronger identification particularly with the African roots of the Afro-American experience. For still others, who saw the war experience in terms of a confrontation of classes, identification with the labor movement, identification with revolutionary socialism, appeared more pertinent than affiliation with a civil rights movement influenced by middle-class intellectuals and white liberals.

Marcus Garvey was first and foremost among those who came upon the scene to generate a mass movement geared to a perspective diverging sharply from that held out by the civil rights activists. One must distinguish the popular mood that appeared to find a voice in Garvey, that propelled him forward as a mass leader, from the specific programmatic course he outlined. For those who desired to answer racism with a new pride of color, race, and heritage, for those who believed that Afro-America must develop its own independent political and economic institutions, Garvey appeared to be the right leader at the appropriate place and time. He held out the possibility that despite the formidable power of racism blacks could gain their freedom and also contribute to greater freedom for Africa. The weak link in Garvey's armor was that the success of the "Back to Africa" program was linked to reaching an accommodation with the European colonial powers and American corporations interested in Africa. Such accommodation was beyond his reach, and the final reality was that Afro-Americans could not mount an effective strug-

161

gle for African freedom that was not linked to the struggle against white supremacy in the United States.

Marcus Garvey arrived in the United States on March 24, 1916. At first he announced that his purpose in coming was to lecture on Jamaica and to seek funds for a Jamaican "Farm and Institute" which would offer the "highest educational and industrial training."[1] His first lecture in New York City, at Saint Mark's Church hall, was something of a disaster, and it was not until 1917 that Garvey began to attract public attention. That attention brought him to leadership of a mass movement of considerable proportions, a movement John Hope Franklin has characterized as "the largest Negro movement of its kind in history."[2] W. E. B. Du Bois surely underestimated Garvey when he wrote in 1923 that his influence among American blacks was "always small."[3] Whatever the precise numbers, it is established that tens of thousands of Afro-Americans supported Garvey's Universal Negro Improvement Association, along with its associated organizations and publications, and turned out for mass rallies and parades.[4] Beyond the matter of direct participation, it is also apparent that Garveyism left its imprint on the mass black consciousness, then and since. Roi Ottley, who as a youngster observed the Garveyites in Harlem, writes: "the movement set in motion what was to become the most compelling force in Negro life—race and color consciousness, which is today that ephemeral thing that inspires 'race loyalty'; the banner to which Negroes rally; the chain that binds them together."[5]

Critical in making Garvey something more than another Harlem street-corner speaker was the crisis of racial violence that erupted shortly after American entrance into World War I. Robert A. Hill finds the catalyst for the emergence of Garveyism to have been "this period of intense racial conflicts signaled by the pogromlike East St. Louis riot of July 1917." What East St. Louis initiated was invigorated by the violence of the 1919 Red Summer. Until the outbreak of war and the explosive racial violence at home the war unleashed, Garvey had largely been irrelevant to the American racial situation. But, as Hill notes, the development of mass resistance by blacks "emboldened Garvey to enlarge the range of his political discourse and action."[6] He now sought to find a place within the contending trends of resistance. Garvey became a leader, but his leadership was only created on the basis of mass initiative.

One of the earliest significant mass meetings at which Garvey spoke was a June 1917 gathering at which the Harlem radical, ex–Socialist party member Hubert H. Harrison, demanded that Congress make lynching a federal crime and take the lives of black Americans under national protection. Blacks all over the South needed to organize for the purpose of defending themselves from attack. Harrison called for the establishment of a "New Negro Movement," and Garvey spoke in support of this proposal.[7]

At a public meeting at Harlem's Lafayette Hall on July 8, 1917, Garvey gave voice to the sense of indignation gripping blacks in the aftermath of the East St. Louis violence. He termed the episode "one of the bloodiest outrages against mankind for which any class of people could be held guilty." Garvey held up to scorn the hypocrisy of an American society that claimed leadership in the international struggle for freedom but brutally treated black citizens. "This is no time for fine words," he declared, "but a time to lift one's voice against the savagery of a people who claim to be the dispensers of democracy." America condemned the atrocities committed by Germany and Turkey but at home would do nothing about the murder of men, women, and children "for no other reason than they are black people seeking an industrial chance in a country that they have laboured for three hundred years to make great." Blacks had worked to make this country what it had become, but in the eyes of whites, he said, they were still a despised people, for if they were not despised, the nation would not permit such barbarism as took place at East St. Louis.[8] The basic lesson that Garvey drew from the massacre was that whites were taking advantage of blacks because black people all over the world were disunited.

At the heart of Garvey's response to racial violence was a stress upon racial solidarity, the need for organization of the race. At a speech in Brooklyn January 9, 1919, Garvey told his audience: "Organization is the force that rules the world. All peoples have gained their freedom through organized force. All nations, all empires have grown into greatness through organized methods. These are the means by which we as a race will climb to greatness."[9] On October 1, 1919, Garvey wrote that mobs of white men would continue to inflict violence so long as blacks remained divided among themselves. "The very moment all the Negroes of this and other countries start to stand together," he wrote, "that very time will see the white man standing in fear of the Negro race even as he stands in fear of the yellow race of Japan today." Garvey stated clearly what was at the top of his agenda: "The Negro must now organize all over the world, 400,000,000 strong, to administer to our oppressors their Waterloo." Blacks must prepare themselves "to match fire with hell fire." Again in October 1919 Garvey explained the importance of organization: "The Negro cannot protect himself by living alone—he must organize. When you offend one white man in America, you offend ninety

million of white men. When you offend one Negro, the other Negroes
are unconcerned because we are not organized. Not until you can offer
protection to your race as the white man offers protection to his race,
will you be a free and independent people in the world."[10]

Again in 1920, in a Washington, D.C., speech, Garvey took up the
theme of organization in relation to violence. He asked if there was any
guarantee that next day there would not be "a terrible bloodshed" for
all blacks in the United States. Could one be certain that next day the
paper would not carry the news that 10,000 blacks had been lynched
somewhere in the South? He asserted there was no guarantee, and the
reason was lack of black organization. Blacks did not constitute an organized race, an organized people, an organized nation. A people not
organized, he stated, is a people to be abused.[11]

How was black organized strength to respond effectively to violence?
That strength, Garvey declared, must be exerted to obtain a national
home with national government. Blacks were lynched in the United States
because no government stood behind them. What was necessary was to
proclaim Africa "a vast Negro empire." The "New Negro," Garvey
proclaimed, was finished fighting for the white man and was now getting
ready for the fight for Africa. Africa had been kept by God Almighty so
that it might be redeemed by blacks, and the young men and women of
the race had pledged themselves "to plant the flag of freedom and of
Empire."[12]

Blacks were to respond to violence with an organized struggle that was
international in scope and prepared to take advantage of great power
rivalries. Reacting to the Red Summer of 1919, Garvey told an audience
at New York's Carnegie Hall that blacks in Washington, East St. Louis,
and Chicago must know they were not wanted. The same message was
given blacks in Liverpool, Cardiff, and Manchester. Blacks in the United
States, in the West Indies, in Great Britain, and in Africa had all declared
for "a free and independent race" and 400 million strong they were
coming to claim the Africa that belonged to them by divine right and
telling the white man to clear out.[13]

The struggle against lynching fit in with this concept of an international
struggle. Garvey told a July 1920 crowd at Liberty Hall that whites in
America and Europe were the same; whites in Georgia, Alabama, and
Mississippi were the same as their counterparts in England, France, or
Germany. Hence, Garvey asserted, "this lynching and burning, and dis-
respect of Negroes is not confined to any one country. It is spreading all
over the world; and it means that if we in this present age do not go out
and do something to stop lynching, every inch of ground in the world

will become unsafe for the Negro in the next twenty years."[14] The time to act was at hand, before the world was thoroughly reorganized.

Garvey appealed to the militancy of American blacks, announcing that liberty and democracy could not be obtained without bloodshed. The blood was not to be shed in America but "one day on the African battlefield" in order to repossess what properly belonged to blacks. Africa had given the world much, had indeed given civilization to mankind, had given the whites science, art, and literature. But the time had come for blacks to take back the power they had once held. "Not even the powers of hell," he stated, "will be able to stop the Negro in his onward and upward movement." Then and only then, when blacks ruled, would democracy prevail. The white man had shown he was unfit to rule, and so, according to Garvey, "he has to step off the stage of action."[15]

In terms of tactics Garvey argued that blacks held the balance of power in the world, and he noted that Africa had become a bone of contention between white Europe and Japan. A war of the races was to begin, he forecast, a war pitting Europe against Asia, and Garvey predicted that if blacks were treated fairly by the white man they would come to his aid but if not they would allow the Japanese to prevail. Garvey spoke about the possibility of helping the whites, but then he also stated that the war blacks intended to carry out was not one in Europe or America but a bloody conflict in Africa between white and black.[16]

At the 1919 Paris Peace Conference the Universal Negro Improvement Association (UNIA) was represented by Eliezer Cadet, a Haitian who had emigrated to the United States and become interested in the Garvey movement. Cadet was the only UNIA representative able to secure a passport for travel to France. Upon his arrival in Europe Cadet released messages to the people of France and to the people of England, messages probably written by Garvey. The message to the French appealed for assistance against the racial violence of the United States. "We, of North America," the message read, "beg to lay before you the awful institutions of lynching and burning at the stake of our men, women and children by the white people of that country, which institutions are in direct contravention of the established codes of civilization. We ask your help and interference in the stopping of these outrages, which cannot be regarded as national or domestic questions, but as international violations of civilized human rights, a perpetuation of which may again throw the world into war." This UNIA communication presented the peace aims that had been adopted at a New York mass meeting on November 10, 1918. Those aims included the general application of self-determination to Africa, the turning over of captured German colonies in Africa to the

Africans, and the deportation of Europeans who violated tribal customs. Beyond Africa there was also the aim of repealing "segregatory and proscriptive ordinances" against blacks in any part of the world.

The message to the British, containing a reminder of the peace aims that had already been communicated to Foreign Secretary Arthur J. Balfour, also referred to American racial violence, linking the American situation to racial oppression elsewhere. The message asked for help "to abolish the lynching institutions and burning at the stake of men, women and children of our race in the United States of America, to abolish industrial serfdom, robbery and exploitation in the West Indies and the new slavery and outrages inflicted on our race in Africa."[17] Although the central focus of the movement was upon Africa, Garvey, in the circumstances of 1919, did not and could not fail to express the protest of Afro-Americans against the specific conditions of their existence.

A high point in the history of the UNIA was its holding in 1920 of a First International Convention of Negro Peoples of the World. This convention, marked by a parade in Harlem and a crowded assemblage in Madison Square Garden, released a statement of grievances and a declaration of rights. The focus of the document, indeed, was upon Africa with endorsement of the principle of Europe for the Europeans, Asia for the Asiatics, and Africa for the Africans. The members of the convention recorded their "most solemn determination to reclaim the treasures and possessions of the vast continent of our forefathers." But the statement also in some detail expressed concern with the immediate realities of racial terror. In the list of grievances, following a general allegation of discriminatory treatment, came the charge that in certain parts of the United States blacks were denied the right of public trial "but are lynched and burned by mobs, and such brutal and inhuman treatment is even practiced upon our women." The declaration of rights was widely inclusive, but among them was the right to adopt "every means" of protection against "barbarous practices" inflicted on account of color, and the document, branding lynching as such a barbarous practice and a disgrace to civilization, declared any country guilty of this atrocity beyond the pale of civilization.[18] The convention, speaking in the name of the black people of the world, sought to establish an agenda that would guide the actions of people of African origin wherever they might live. Though geared to an African perspective it sought to relate to the needs of those facing the threat of lynching and the proscriptions of a segregated society. In sum, the UNIA program of 1920 had some connection to the militancy of the Afro-American.

Through all of the movement's history it was the target of surveillance, harassment, and provocation by British and American intelligence ser-vices and police. The point was that in the climate of the red-scare years any movement of protest against social conditions, whatever its pro-grammatic orientation, was seen as ground for the growth of bolshevism, and the UNIA was no exception. British Military Intelligence in New York in 1919 referred to the Garvey movement as representing "Pan-Negroism" and looking as a colored movement to Japan for leadership. But it was also a radical movement that followed bolshevism "and has intimate relations with various socialistic groups throughout the United States." It sympathized with all of the "alleged" oppressed nationalities. The British agent, quoting from the *Negro World*, stressed that the move-ment took inspiration from the social revolutions in Europe, including the 1918 German revolution and the already accomplished Russian Rev-olution. In October 1919 J. Edgar Hoover recorded that Garvey was particularly active "among the radical elements in New York City in agitating the negro movement" and expressed his regret that Garvey had "not yet" violated any federal law and so could not be deported as an undesirable alien. Hoover suggested, however, that it might be possible to prosecute Garvey on fraud charges.[19] Ultimately, concerned that Gar-vey's agitation might interfere with European and American interests in Africa, the federal government succeeded in convicting Garvey of mail fraud and, upon President Coolidge's commutation of the sentence in 1927, in deporting him from the United States.

During the summer of 1921, following difficulties Garvey had en-countered in obtaining reentry to the United States from a trip to the West Indies and Central America, the theme of struggle in his rhetoric was replaced by an emphasis upon race purity and coming to some accord with the oppressors of black people.[20] Earlier in 1920 Garvey gave this retort to the Ku Klux Klan: "They can pull off their hot stuff in the south, but let them come north and touch Philadelphia, New York or Chicago and there will be little left of the Ku Klux Klan. . . . Let them try and come to Harlem and they will really have some fun."[21] But in June 1922 Garvey met in Atlanta with Edward Young Clarke, acting imperial wizard of the Klan, and indeed invited Clarke to the UNIA's Liberty Hall in Harlem. Shortly after his return to New York Garvey commented on the Klan: "The attitude of the Negroes should be not to fight it, not to aggravate it, but to think of what it means and say and do nothing. It will not help us to fight it or its program." The racial problem could be solved only by creating a black government in Africa.[22]

At the 1924 UNIA convention Garvey favored and secured the adop-tion of a somewhat equivocal resolution regarding the Klan. On the one hand, the resolution stated that the "alleged" attitude of the Klan toward blacks was fairly representative of the feelings of whites toward blacks and so the only solution was establishment of a black government in Africa. On the other, the resolution affirmed it was the organization's policy to protect against atrocities committed by the Klan or any other organization.[23] In actuality, the logic of the first part of the resolution drained the second part of any real significance. If the mentality of the Klan was indeed that of the majority of Americans then there was little hope for racial justice.

Coupled with a more indifferent attitude toward the Klan was a shift away from support of the struggle for antilynching legislation. Garvey had initially given support to the Dyer bill, but by 1923 he was hostile to the campaign for its enactment, arguing it would only duplicate laws already enacted. At the 1922 UNIA convention delegates had discussed incidents of racial violence, and opinions had been voiced favoring legislation and also the right of meeting violence with violence, but Garvey cautioned against any militant resolution and there was no fruitful outcome to the discussion.[24]

Garvey embraced the position of racial purity in August 1921 when he led the second UNIA convention to adopt a resolution stating that all races should maintain "the purity of self" and opposing miscegenation that would lead to destruction of racial identity. In October 1921 President Harding, speaking in Birmingham, endorsed the notion of the "absolute divergence in things social and racial." Social equality was not to be. Garvey promptly wired Harding his congratulations for the "splendid interpretation" of the racial question Harding had provided. Garvey asserted that "all true Negroes" opposed social equality.[25]

Garvey now made clear that, as he saw things, the very presence of blacks within the United States would generate violence. In the future the white population would greatly increase in numbers; in 200 years white America would treble itself, and the result would be an overcrowded country with intense racial competition. Garvey predicted that "wholesale mob violence" would result from such a situation, particularly if in the meanwhile blacks had made political and economic gains. Given the bleak prospects he envisioned for American society, success by blacks in the struggle for equal rights could only be counterproductive. In effect, Garvey repudiated any logical basis on which a struggle could be waged for racial justice within the confines of the United States.[26]

Garvey's political decay, which eventually led him to boast that the Fascists had borrowed their ideology from him, was no wild aberration.[27] During the stormy days of the World War and the revolutionary stirrings the war generated, Garvey had captured the imagination of blacks with a grand design of international struggle for black liberation. But he never had the capacity to unify blacks everywhere behind his leadership, and at no point did he formulate a strategy and tactics oriented to the situation of blacks in the United States. Short of depending upon a universal black revolution, he formulated no conception of how victories could be wrested from American racism on its home ground. When the revolutionary tides receded in the early 1920s, when it no longer appeared that the reorganization of the entire world was immediately at hand, Garvey took up the futile task of conciliating the ruling Establishments that retained power in both America and Africa.

In the post–World War I era another viewpoint entering into the dialogue concerning black responses to racial violence was that of black Socialists who viewed the racial struggle in essentially class terms and would have Afro-Americans closely identify with the labor movement. Foremost among black Socialists during this period was A. Philip Randolph, whose career as labor leader, civil rights spokesman, and Socialist spanned much of the twentieth century. Randolph's views concerning the sources and remedies for racial violence were articulated clearly in the Socialist magazine he edited, the *Messenger*. His approach was summed up in the title of an article appearing in the March 1919 issue, "Lynching: Capitalism Its Cause, Socialism Its Cure." The article was consistent with the long-held Socialist party view of the racial struggle as purely and simply a class question. Randolph's approach was in harmony with the Socialist inclination to see the struggle for partial, democratic reforms as irrelevant to the basic objectives of working-class and black liberation. Randolph began his article by defining lynching as "punishment of offenders or supposed offenders by a summary procedure without due process of law" and went on to explain that lynching's function was "to foster and to engender race prejudice to prevent the lynchers and the lynched, the black and white workers from organizing on the industrial and voting on the political fields." The basic cause of lynching was capitalism, the economic system that employed lynching "to widen the chasm between the races." The lynching mentality was reinforced by the social institutions of the school, the church, and the press. The press, featuring sensational headlines about black rapists, was especially culpable. All three institutions produced a psychology that expressed itself through the mob. And the mob could gather at any time. "Anything," Randolph wrote, "may occasion a community to burn a Negro. It might be a well-dressed Negro; a Negro who speaks good English or a Negro who talks back to a white man."

The muckraker Lincoln Steffens visited revolutionary Russia and saw in socialism a system that removed the incentive for corruption. Randolph saw socialism as destroying the incentive for, the material basis of, lynching and other forms of racist violence. "It is now a social habit to lynch Negroes," Randolph explained. "But when the motive for promoting race prejudice is removed, viz., profits, by the social ownership, control and operation of the machinery and sources of production through the government, the government being controlled by the workers; the effects of prejudice, race riots, lynching, etc., will also be removed."

Randolph flatly declared that "lynching will not stop until Socialism comes." He did not explicitly repudiate the struggle for reform short of socialism, but he clearly downgraded the significance of political and legislative struggles to curb racial violence. "Don't be deceived," he wrote, "by any capitalist bill to abolish lynching; if it becomes a law, it would never be enforced. Have you not the Fourteenth Amendment which is supposed to protect your life, property and guarantee you the vote?"[28]

In an editorial appearing in the August issue of the *Messenger* Randolph further expounded his view of how lynching could be eliminated. He offered what he termed "an immediate program," a program made up of two elements, physical action and economic power. The element of physical action rested upon the right of self-defense, a right, Randolph declared, that is recognized in the laws of all nations. The person about to be attacked was justified in taking measures of self-defense, and such measures could include summoning others for assistance in warding off the attack. Randolph noted that his message might appear strange, coming as it did from the "pacific editors" of the *Messenger,* but the point was that they were pacific "only on matters that can be settled peacefully." Appealing to the conscience of the South was futile. The southern soul "has been petrified and permeated with wickedness, injustice and lawlessness."

In exercising the right of self-defense against the lynch mob there could be little room left for the philosophy of "turn the other cheek." Randolph presented a guide to action that was to be strictly adhered to: "Always regard your own life as more important than the life of the person about to take yours, and if a choice has to be made between the sacrifice of your life and the loss of the lyncher's life, choose to preserve your own and to destroy that of the lynching mob." Randolph did not see self-defense as an exercise in futility. Those who acted in self-defense could count upon the cowardice of the mob. It was "perfectly certain that twenty millions of people can beat down eight millions," but the cost would be too high, so great indeed that "it will deter the twenty million from its aim; and so with the mob."

Economic force was the other component of Randolph's proposed response to lynching, and the key ingredient here was the organization of black workers into unions. Union organization would enable black workers to make demands and "withhold their labor," and as a result the South "will be paralyzed industrially and in commercial consternation." Such a situation would draw the attention of the entire world, with the result that lynching would immediately become a national and an international issue.

Lynching would become a national problem because northern industry was dependent upon the products of black labor. If blacks withheld their labor the consequence would be the idling of machinery, mass unemployment, and the spread of social discontent. The government, according to Randolph, would be confronted by revolution. Action would have to be taken by both employers and workers to deal with the lynching problem, "the capitalists because their profits will be cut off, from the cessation of business, and the workers because their wages will be cut off, from the cessation of work."[29] Self-interest would lead to the elimination of lynching.

Lynching as an international question had already been discussed in the previous month's issue of the *Messenger*. The magazine ran an editorial entitled "Lynching a Domestic Question" and accused the NAACP's *Crisis* and other black publications of basing their approach to the lynching question on this "owl-like phrase." The *Messenger* cited the experience of such nationalities as the Jews and Irish in support of the view that the question of violence against oppressed minorities should be internationalized. Readers were also reminded of the efforts of the abolitionists to mobilize opinion against slavery in Europe. The *Messenger*'s position was summed up forcefully:

The beneficiary of a system or institution can never be relied upon voluntarily to overthrow that institution or system. The country which is responsible for the oppression of the Negroes, for mob violence and lynching, is not going to overthrow that wicked institution from which it benefits. No, lynching is not a domestic question, except in the rather domestic minds of Negro leaders, whose information is highly localized and highly domestic. The problems of the Negroes should be presented to every nation in the world, and this sham democracy, about which Americans prate, should be exposed for what it is—a sham, a mockery, a rape on decency and a travesty on common sense. When lynching gets to be an international question, it will be the beginning of the end. The sooner the better. On with the dance![30]

In his August discussion of lynching Randolph connected the internationalizing of the lynching issue to black economic action. During the Civil War the issue of slavery had become an international matter when the cotton output of the South amounted to only a few million bales annually. But now, Randolph asserted, each year saw the production of more than 100 million bales. To withhold that vast output from the world markets would make lynching a matter of general world concern. If blacks did not work in the fields cotton would rot, and Randolph confidently predicted "the South will get on its knees, just as it was almost on its knees over the migration during the war."

Randolph had specific advice for blacks as to what to do when talk was heard of a possible lynching. Blacks in the affected community should assemble and inform authorities that they were expected to abide by the law. The authorities should be asked to provide blacks with arms necessary to enforce order. Based on recruiting of black war veterans, "little voluntary companies" were to be organized with black officers in charge. The approach to take was to remain calm and poised, not to get excited but also to "face your work with cold resolution, determined to uphold the law and to protect the lives of your fellows at any cost." If all this were done nobody's life would need to be sacrificed, "because nobody is going to be found who will try to overcome that force."[31] The advice articulated a strategy of militant resistance, but the realism of the specifics was questionable. State or local authorities were not likely to arm blacks for the purpose of resisting the lynchers or indeed for any purpose, and whether racist authorities would remain indifferent to the existence of paramilitary black organizations was doubtful.

In September the *Messenger* outlined its reaction to the events of the year's Red Summer and presented its remedy for race riots. The remedy was not segregation, and neither was it "the meeting of white and Negro leaders in love feasts, who pretend like the African ostrich, that nothing is wrong, because their heads are buried in the sand." The *Messenger* distinguished between the remedy, a solution that was fundamental and comprehensive but might take years for attainment, and an "immediate program" calculated "to meet the demands of the transition period." The remedy was socialism. "On the economic field, industry must be socialized," the magazine stated, "and land must be nationalized, which will thereby remove the motive for creating strife between the races." In the labor movement black and white workers must unite in the same unions, demanding the same wages and working conditions. "Industrial autocracy" existed in the United States, and only the workers could be relied upon to overthrow the system. The remedy also encompassed enfranchisement for all, without regard to race, creed, sex, or color, and the revolutionizing of the school system. Segregation had to go and equal pay given to teachers "with equal equipment for school children." Furthermore, the school curriculum required change, with more teaching of the social and natural sciences and less Latin, Greek, and Bible studies. Also, as parts of the remedy, the people had to control their press, the church had to be converted into an educational forum, and the stage and screen had to be controlled by the people.

The first item on the immediate program was the use of physical force in self-defense. The use of force was to be deplored and force was to be employed only as a last resort, but "it is indispensable at times." Force might serve as a means of teaching when no other means would do; "a bullet is sometimes more convincing than a hundred prayers." Black resistance to violence had already been helpful to whites and blacks throughout the country. Such resistance had prevented riots in other cities. "Negroes have shown," the *Messenger* declared, "that riots hereafter will be costly and unprofitable, and when you make a thing unprofitable you make it impossible."

A second part of the immediate program called for adding to the number of black police. Police behavior in recent riots had justified blacks in believing that white police worked in collusion with the rioters. Having a larger black police force in black communities would help to keep down riots. The basic point was that prejudiced white officers and soldiers could not be depended upon to act impartially "when they are a part of the race doing the mobbing."

The final point of immediate action was activity by the courts to indict both whites and blacks responsible for acts of violence. The juries in such cases had to be made up of persons of both races. The editorial pointed to facts concerning the outcome of the riots in Washington and Chicago. In Chicago fifty-seven blacks and only four whites had been indicted. As for treatment of blacks in the courts of the nation's capital, the *Messenger* observed that "Negroes are justified in regarding the so-called Department of Justice as a department of injustice, where they are concerned." Two hundred blacks had been arrested in Washington and only twenty whites, and this "despite the fact that the whites in Washington, as in Chicago, are known to have begun the riots."

At the end of this statement the *Messenger* returned to the matter of a basic solution. Revolution was necessary, revolution defined as "complete change in the organization of society." Capitalism had to go, and the going would be hastened by action of the workers. Workers stood to lose from both race riots and war. Make both of these horrors unprofitable, and they would cease. This was the task for workers and "especially the white workers by virtue of their numbers, their opportunity and their intelligent class consciousness."[32]

That same issue of the *Messenger* carried an article by the Socialist W. A. Domingo entitled "Did Bolshevism Stop Race Riots in Russia?" Domingo focused upon the oppression of Jews and found the Soviet leaders able and willing to eradicate anti-Semitism. The Soviets were led by men "who had suffered the scorn of the high and the abuse of the lowly, men who could understand and appreciate the real causes of Jewish oppression." One of the first tasks undertaken by the new leaders was suppression of the pogrom makers; the Bolsheviks were willing to punish "those of the old regime who retained the old psychology of race hatred." With a few executions, Domingo wrote, Soviet Russia had become unsafe for "mobocrats" but safe for previously oppressed minorities. Domingo viewed bolshevism as not merely a phenomenon of Russian significance. He asked the question: "Will Bolshevism accomplish the full freedom of Africa, colonies in which Negroes are in the majority, and promote human tolerance and happiness in the United States by the eradication of the causes of such disgraceful occurrences as the Washington and Chicago race riots?" The answer, said Domingo, was deducible from the experience of the Soviets since taking power. Soviet Russia had become a nation "in which dozens of racial and lingual types have settled their many differences and found a common meeting ground, a country which no longer oppresses colonies, a country from which the lynch rope is banished and in which racial tolerance and peace now exist."[33] What Domingo wrote reflected the favorable view taken by most American Socialists of the Bolshevik revolution in its early years. In the midst of the terrible violence of 1919, black radicals welcomed a movement that appeared to offer prospects of overcoming racism wherever it existed.

EIGHT

Struggle on a Higher Level

THE INTENSE violence of 1919 subsided, but terror as a regular component of the black experience during the 1920s continued. Racists persisted in efforts to wipe out the gains made by blacks during the war period, and blacks met new assault, strengthened by 1919's record of resistance. Despite lynchings, bombings, police intimidation, and other forms of violence black America was not quite forced back to its prewar position. Whether during the economic decline of the first postwar years or during the prosperity period of the middle and late twenties, the struggle against white terror was played out on a higher level than before.

The pattern of racist assault and black response at the start of the decade is highlighted by consideration of events in Chicago during 1920. During 1919 and 1920 a number of homes owned by blacks were bombed. The purpose of this violence was clearly to prevent blacks from moving into previously all-white neighborhoods. The bombings occurred in the context of organized efforts by associations of white homeowners, such as the Kenwood and Hyde Park Property Owners' Association, to exclude blacks. In February 1920, however, blacks formed a public organization, the Protective Circle of Chicago, to combat the bombing campaign through lawful means "and to bring pressure to bear on city authorities to force them to apprehend those persons who have bombed the homes of twenty-one Negroes." On February 29 a mass meeting was held with some 3,000 black Chicagoans attending. The speakers representing the Protective Circle spoke in the spirit of nonviolence: "The bombers of the homes of Negroes have been allowed to get away unpunished. Judge Gary hanged numbers of anarchists in the Haymarket riot for very much less complicity in bomb outrages than these men are guilty of. Hatred can never be counteracted by hatred. We cannot put any stop to the bombings of Negro homes by going out and bombing homes of white persons." The major black organizations concentrated efforts upon educating public opinion and upon appeals for action to city authorities. During June a delegation twice attempted to see the mayor to submit its complaint but was refused an audience. The state commission investigating the 1919 violence reported that "the effect of these delegations and protests has been small."[1]

In the absence of an effective movement to stop the continued violence, conditions were ripe for a response of retaliatory violence. This was the significance of an incident on June 20, 1920, involving a black group known as the "Abyssinians." The group held a parade on that day, which ended in front of a cafe on East Thirty-fifth Street. In the course of a brief ceremony an American flag was brought forward and burned. Several policemen and a white sailor from the Great Lakes Naval Station attempted to interfere, and in the ensuing fight two white men were shot and killed. Both the *Chicago Defender* and the *Negro World* condemned the violent acts of the Abyssinians; the group itself was a small nationalist sect that looked to Abyssinia as an African homeland, a source of protection for black rights. But the incident also indicated that some Chicago blacks would not accept the exercise of police authority and would strike back at what they viewed as an illegitimate use of power. The spirit of militancy was expressed by a black veteran, quoted by state investigators. "I done my part," the ex-serviceman said, "and I'm going to fight right here till Uncle Sam does his. I can shoot as good as the next one, and nobody better start anything. I ain't looking for trouble, but if it comes my way I ain't dodging."[2] The state investigators did not relate the Abyssinian incident to the failure of city authorities to act against the bombers, but it is clear that official inaction produced a situation in which some blacks would readily strike back against the symbols of authority widely perceived by blacks as acting in collusion with terrorists.

From one incident of violence occurring during 1920 we are able to obtain a particularly acute insight into the subjective response of a black person to racist assault. The state commission conducting an investigation of the Chicago riot asked the question: "How does a Negro feel when he is being hunted or chased by the mob?" The answer it gave came from the words of a black university student who had been chased by a white gang. The youth's first reaction was fear, and he had taken flight, managing finally to outrun his pursuers and to remain hidden behind a fence until he could safely escape. But as he lay behind the fence, "anger gave place to hatred and a desire for revenge," and he thought that if ever he confronted a gang member "one of us would get a licking." But he realized that such a course would be folly "and would lead only to reprisals and some other innocent individual getting a licking on my account." Then the youth thought of his basic position as a black person in American society. "Emotions ran riot," he said. To himself he expressed the words of a bitter indictment of American racism, and it is clear that what happened to this student represented a traumatic episode that would leave some permanent mark upon him. He asked:

Had the ten months I spent in France been all in vain? Were those little white crosses over the dead bodies of those dark-skinned boys lying in Flanders for naught? Was democracy merely a hollow sentiment? What had I done to deserve such treatment? I lay there experiencing all the emotions I imagined the innocent victim of a southern mob must feel when being hunted for some supposed crime. Was this what I had given up my Canadian citizenship for, to become an American citizen and soldier? Was the risk of life in a country where such hatred existed worthwhile? Must a Negro always suffer merely because of the color of his skin? "There's a Nigger; let's get him." These words rang in my ears—I shall never forget them.

On the level of immediate practicality the student observed that the experience bred a sense of caution, not fear "but a wariness in uncertainty."[3] It was a wariness that other blacks, having experienced the postwar resurgence of racism, were to share.

Lynchings continued to occur during the early twenties with perhaps the only new ingredient being that several such incidents received fairly extensive national publicity. One such event, particularly brutal in its specifics, was the lynch murder of Henry Lowry.[4] The victim, a black Arkansas farmer, had for more than two years been held in peonage by a white planter. A few weeks before Christmas 1920 Lowry had gone to the white planter, O. T. Craig, and asked for a settlement of his account and payment of any balance owed to him. The landowner refused to settle and also struck Lowry. This black farmer, however, did not accept the situation, and on Christmas Day he returned to Craig's house. Shots were exchanged, and when all was over Craig and his daughter lay dead and two of his sons were wounded. Lowry escaped from the vicinity and got as far away as El Paso, Texas, where he was captured on January 19, after having written home to inquire about his family.

The lynching of Henry Lowry required long-distance arranging, but the matter was efficiently handled. The Arkansas governor had promised that Lowry would have a fair trial, but officers escorting Lowry back to Arkansas, instead of heading directly for Little Rock, took a wide detour that brought Lowry into the hands of the mob. The mob took Lowry from the train at Sardis, Mississippi, proceeded into Tennessee and past Memphis and then went on to Arkansas where the lynching was to take place. This was not some hole-in-the-corner group of conspirators but a public mob that appeared to have no fear of exposure or punishment. The lynching itself began with a preliminary interval of torture followed by a burning that slowly consumed the lower half of the victim's body. According to William Pickens of the NAACP Lowry never said a word until the mob brought his wife and daughter to see him roasting. Pickens reported that the mob did not quite descend to the depths; in this case, unlike others, it did not rummage in ashes for charred remains.

Publicity was given to the Lowry lynching by means of an article Pickens wrote for the *Nation* and by newspaper accounts. During the twenties several notable books dealing with race relations included graphic descriptions of the incident. Among such works was the Socialist Scott Nearing's *Black America* and Walter White's classic report about lynching, *Rope and Faggot*.[5] But greater public attention to lynching did not always reflect a greater sensitivity to the injustice involved. Publicity followed the Lowry lynching, but it also preceded it. Spokesmen for national organizations such as the NAACP and liberal or radical intellectuals might seek to rally public opinion, but the racists were bolder, publicly announcing their plans for all to know. The Memphis press had given advance word of the impending Lowry lynching, but nothing was done to frustrate the mob.[6] As Nearing pointed out in his report of the affair, this lynching required careful preparation and the involvement of hundreds of individuals in its execution.

An incident of 1923 illustrated the reality that even in modern America proximity to learning and scholarship was no guarantee against lynching. On April 29, James T. Scott, a janitor employed at the University of Missouri, Columbia, was hung by a mob for allegedly having attacked the daughter of a faculty member. While hundreds cheered and many university students looked on, a group of some twenty-five or thirty whites dragged Scott from the Columbia jail as the police did nothing, tied a rope around his neck, and pushed him over the railing of the town's Stewart Bridge. President Loeb of the University of Missouri quickly informed the press that no student had participated in the killing.

In response to this event the *New York Times* observed that a lynching in a small town of which a state university was the most prominent feature was "rather worse" than lynchings in other places. The *Times* sharply censured the sheriff and other officers who had failed to uphold the law. The newspaper also suggested that the haste in killing Scott might have resulted from fear he would be able to prove his innocence. The *Times* saw need of education in a situation where so near a university a manifestation of "vicious ignorance" still existed.

In his column in the *Crisis* W. E. B. Du Bois was rather more caustic about this lynching, pointing out the element of the macabre in what had happened:

> We are glad to note that the University of Missouri has opened a course in Applied Lynching. Many of our American Universities have long defended the institution, but they have not been frank or brave enough actually to arrange a mob murder so that the students might see it in detail. . . . We are very much in favor of this method of teaching 100 percent Americanism; as long as mob murder is an approved institution in the United States, students at the universities should have a first-hand chance to judge exactly what a lynching is.[7]

It is scarcely to be doubted that Du Bois, scholar and academic, was particularly infuriated by what took place in the shadow of a major American university.

Yet the ironic fact was that racist boldness was becoming somewhat counterproductive from the standpoint of those who would maintain lynch law. A national antilynching movement had come into existence, centering around support for the Dyer bill, and that movement, closely following the southern newspapers, told the country what southern white reporters wrote about lynching. A section of the southern white Establishment was finding itself under pressure, concerned that federal legislation dealing with lynching would be enacted and disturbed that the South was being isolated by world and national opinion that found accounts of lynchings horrifying. A case in point of such southern reaction was Governor Hugh Dorsey of Georgia. In April 1921 Dorsey convened a conference in Atlanta to deal with what he termed "mistreatment" of Georgia Negroes. Dorsey had taken a peculiar route to this meeting. Only a few years earlier he had served as the prosecutor in the Leo Frank case, the trial, held in an atmosphere of hysteria, in which a young Jewish businessman was convicted of rape-murder and ultimately lynched. Now in 1921 Dorsey acted the role of upholder of justice.

Dorsey clearly was concerned that maintenance of the lynching system and peonage would damage Georgia's standing in the nation and the world and more specifically would undermine local autonomy. He told the conference that if conditions remained unchanged "both God and man would justly condemn Georgia more severely than man and God have condemned Belgium and Leopold for the Congo atrocities." Continued toleration of racial cruelties would lead to the destruction of "our civilization." Dorsey carefully noted that the instances of brutality were confined to a small minority of counties, but he also declared that such instances "bring disgrace and obloquy upon the State as a whole, and upon the entire Southern people." He emphasized that formulation of a remedy for the situations he described should come from Georgians, not from what he termed "outsiders."

Whatever the factors that motivated Dorsey in convening the conference, the evidence he submitted for consideration added up to a formidable indictment of racist violence in Georgia. In the course of showing that southern white leadership was capable of dealing with violence, detailed evidence was placed upon the record that could be used effectively by the antilynching movement. At the very opening of his report Dorsey indicated that out of 135 cases involving mistreatment of blacks only two had any relation to the "usual crime." The 135 cases represented a wide range of brutalities, including whippings, dynamitings, police assault against black women, and five lynchings. The conference endorsed a series of proposals submitted by Dorsey of which the first was "the careful gathering and investigation by Georgians, and not by outsiders, of facts as to the treatment of the negro throughout the State and publication of those facts to the people of Georgia." The conference recommended enactment of laws that would establish a state constabulary and authorize the governor to send that force into any county where needed to quell disorder. The laws would also impose a fine upon any county in which a lynching occurred and, further, the governor would be empowered to appoint a commission to investigate any lynching and to remove from office any public official failing to uphold the law. Finally, the governor would have the power, in case of mob action, to move the place of the trial to any location in the state he deemed appropriate. In proposing this course of action the Georgia conference was plainly suggesting there was a reasonable alternative to federal legislation against lynching.[8] A public posture against lynching would also further the southern business leadership goal of slowing black migration to the North by softening the regional image of violence.[9]

"The City with a Personality" was Tulsa, Oklahoma's motto during the 1920s. Civic boosters called the place the "Magic City." Tulsa was a boomtown of the oil industry, a community with an 18,182 population in 1910 that by 1920 numbered 72,075. In 1921 the city directory listed the city's population as 98,874. Almost 11,000 blacks lived in Tulsa.[10]

In the 1950s the *Reader's Digest* described Tulsa as "America's Most Beautiful City," but there was also ugliness in the city's history. Tulsa existed in the context of Oklahoma state politics, and beginning in the 1890s a number of Jim Crow territorial and state laws were enacted, including a measure to segregate telephone booths. The "new" Ku Klux Klan, organized in 1915, was strong in Oklahoma and particularly so in Tulsa. In the last months of 1921 the city's Klan No. 2 claimed to have a membership of 3,200, and regarding local politics one historian of the KKK has written, "In Tulsa County the Klan could not lose." Klansmen were to be found among both Republican and Democratic electoral slates.[11]

Between 1917 and 1921 several incidents occurred that demonstrated the existence of official lawlessness and fears of such lawlessness. Following the bombing on October 29, 1917, of the home of oilman J. Edgar Pew a terror campaign was unleashed against the Industrial Workers of the World (IWW). The local IWW hall was raided, and twelve of the unionists were arrested on charges of vagrancy. The police captain in charge of the raid stated: "Tulsa is not big enough to hold any traitors during our government's crisis, and the sooner these fellows get out of town the better for them." The *Tulsa World* was particularly inflammatory in its incitement to violence against the radicals, suggesting the use of rope or the alternative of "a wholesale application of concentration camps." In the midst of a sham trial of the Wobblies on vagrancy charges the *World* ran an editorial, "Get Out the Hemp," which urged the citizenry: "If the I.W.W. or its twin brother, the Oil Workers Union, gets busy in your neighborhood, kindly take occasion to decrease the supply of hemp." In court the defenders were found guilty, and five defense witnesses were arrested and quickly convicted. As the prisoners were being transferred to the county jail, the "Knights of Liberty," a group of armed men wearing robes and masks, seized the prisoners and had the police drive them to a secluded ravine where they were whipped, tarred, and feathered. Scott Ellsworth, who has carefully studied this period in Tulsa's history, writes that the evidence "is conclusive that the Tulsa police worked in close concert with the 'Knights of Liberty.' "[12] Needless to say, the brutality against the prisoners went unpunished.

In March 1919 there was a shooting incident in which a white ironworker was accosted and shot on a city street, reportedly by two black men. Three blacks were arrested in connection with this affair, and when rumors spread that the prisoners might be lynched a party of armed blacks drove to the jail to investigate the situation. Some 200 black persons assembled at the jail but disbanded when assured the prisoners were safe. The episode revealed, as Ellsworth notes, that black Tulsa did not trust the authorities to protect black prisoners and was willing itself to act in defense of those menaced by lynching.[13]

In late August 1920 the city witnessed the lynching of a white man, Roy Belton, who had allegedly robbed and murdered a taxi driver. The mob seized Belton from his cell on the top floor of the courthouse and took him to the spot where the taxi driver had been attacked. While the lynching was in progress the Tulsa police reportedly directed traffic at the scene and kept onlookers at a distance. When the lynching was over the crowd rushed to snatch up bits and pieces of Belton's clothing. The city's police chief later said that this savage affair would prove "of real benefit to Tulsa and vicinity ... an object lesson to the hijackers and auto thieves, and I believe it will be taken as such." The lynching, the *Tulsa World* explained, "was citizenship, outraged by government inefficiency and a too tender regard to the professional criminal."[14] The entire episode evidenced that there did not prevail in white Tulsa a climate of opinion hostile to lynching.

During 1921 mass racial violence erupted in Tulsa. A mixture of business ruthlessness, the southern racial tradition, and political corruption came together to produce an explosive racial confrontation. Ellsworth writes of this event: "In terms of density of destruction and ratio of casualties to population, it has probably not been equaled by any riot in the United States in this century."[15] Urban race riots were not numerous during the 1920s, but Tulsa stood out as a warning that what happened in 1919 could occur again, and it also showed that urban racial conflicts were moving westward. Both racial hatred and economic affluence could thrive in the same community.

That racial violence such as occurred in Tulsa did not spread to other American cities was due perhaps, at least in part, to the fact that blacks in this city demonstrated a willingness to fight back against terror. The incident was touched off on May 30 when a white girl, Sarah Page, alleged that Dick Rowland, a nineteen-year-old black youth, had attempted to assault her in the elevator of the Drexel Building. According to Walter White of the NAACP, Sarah Page later stated that Rowland had seized her arm as he entered the elevator, and still later it was learned that he had accidentally stepped on her foot. Ultimately, Sarah Page refused to press charges, and the case against Rowland was dropped. Facts are slow to catch up with hysteria, however, and after the *Tulsa Tribune* published news of the supposed assault there was widespread talk of lynching Rowland. That evening, Tuesday, May 31, a crowd of some 400 whites gathered outside the jail at nine o'clock, and by ten-thirty the throng numbered some 1,500 to 2,000 persons. Given the situation and Tulsa's historical record it was reasonable to assume that the crowd intended to seize Rowland and lynch him. Black resistance, however, intervened. Word of the white crowd reached the black community, "Little Africa," and some seventy-five armed black men went to the jail set on assuring the prisoner's safety. The blacks were persuaded by the police to return home, but as they were about to leave a white man attempted to disarm one of the blacks, a shot was fired and then many shots, and when the clash was broken off about midnight two blacks were dead along with ten whites.

The following morning the full power of white terror descended on Little Africa. The mob now numbered some 10,000, representing all classes of the white population, machine guns were employed, and reportedly airplanes were used to observe the movements of blacks. Many homes were set afire. Walter White noted that blacks, men and women, "fought gamely in the defense of their homes but the odds were too great." The precise number of casualties from this violence was uncertain, but White estimated that approximately fifty whites had died and between 150 and 200 blacks. In the article he wrote about Tulsa for the *Nation* White threw out a challenge: "How much longer will America allow these pogroms to continue unchecked?"[16] White saw in this conflict a lesson that should be learned by every white American who believed blacks would remain meek and submissive. Rowland was only a bootblack with no standing in the community, "but when his life was threatened by a mob of whites, every one of the 15,000 Negroes of Tulsa, rich and poor, educated and illiterate, was willing to die to protect Dick Rowland." Perhaps not too many white people were moved by White's rhetoric, but the facts spoke for themselves. At Tulsa three times as many blacks as whites died, but still the cost of a pogrom against the black community came high.

Shortly before his article appeared in the *Nation* White presented the essentials of his findings in a report to the national board of the NAACP. In this report he did not dwell on the significance of black resistance, perhaps because this point was obvious to the association leadership, but he summarized the evidence as to the events themselves and their underlying causes. Both to the board and in the *Nation* article White stressed the factors of political corruption and white envy of black economic achievement, an envy he located in "the lower order of whites," people White described as "lethargic and unprogressive by nature." White omitted from his reports consideration of the role played by the Tulsa power structure, although it is distinctly improbable that the assault upon the black community could have been mounted without the approval of police and other authorities. What, after all, can be made of Mayor Evans's comment that if, as many persons contended, the "uprising" was inevitable, then it was "good generalship" to have let the destruction come to that section of Tulsa "where the trouble was hatched up, put in motion and where it had its inception."[17]

The Tulsa events were also viewed by the Socialist Chandler Owen, but in this instance the vantage point for observation was New York and Owen reported his fantasized ideas of what had occurred in Tulsa. Owen imagined he heard the words of blacks assembled to protect Rowland. The blacks were saying: "If they lynch him they've got to lynch me too"; he also heard: "I ain't got but one time to die and I expect to carry along some white man with me." Owen's emphasis was strongly upon the will to resist manifested by Tulsa blacks. His article was less a sober analysis of what took place than an exaltation of the bravery Owen saw in the blacks who fought back against lynchers, police, machine guns, and airplanes. Various types were to be seen among those who fought the racists: There was the hardened criminal who hated all whites, and there was the ordinary working black person, "the predominant type," the individual who had obtained "such education as the short-termed, poorly-equipped country school of Oklahoma afforded." But there was also the black intellectual, the representative of the group that arouses white assault because its competition is feared. The black intellectuals constituted the leadership group, Owen explained, as it is the group that "has to carry the burdens of the race on its back because it is more conscious of proscriptions, foresees more clearly the wanton narrowing of opportunity and, pricked with a thousand civilized desires, growing more intense and extensive, feels most keenly the burden of being *black things* in America." At least as expressed in this article, for the Socialist Owen leadership of the black struggle belonged not to the working class but to the educated and successful black middle class. But he also insisted that despite their diversity blacks, as he imagined them in Tulsa, were together on one thing: "All seem to have a will of iron—an invincible determination to put down the Hun in America. All seem resolved to make their dying hereafter a costly investment." All the various blacks merged into one image, and Owen asked its identity. He gave the answer: "it is 'Banquo's Ghost' to the South. It is the Nemesis of Dixie. It is the Sword of Damocles over Georgia, over Mississippi, over Texas, over Alabama, et al. It is the hand-writing on the wall for alleged white superiority in America."

Owen described the riot as beginning when a policeman sought to take the weapon of a black man; when the man resisted, the policeman shot him dead, following which firing became general. At first blacks took the offensive, but when white reinforcements appeared the blacks were forced to retreat. Retreating, they continued to fight heroically, however. "Once more," Owen wrote, "the Negroes make a stand and, like the little band of Greeks at Thermopylae, they rain death and destruction upon their opponents." As for the racists Owen was not vague in characterizing them; they were "Mad beasts, the unspeakable ghouls, the manmasked jackals, the prowling hyenas, clothed in white skins outsides, but lined with black inside . . . the white fiends . . . the gorillas of Tulsa." But despite the horror of racism Owen saw hope emerging from Tulsa as he drew the conclusion that, despite the crushing burden of injustice, "the new Negro has that perseverance and determination which will secure for him final triumph over race prejudice—even in America."[18] Taken all together, the Tulsa events gave articulate black leadership beyond the city confidence in the future. With the realization that many blacks had died and that still more would die in other confrontations there was a new sense of the unified fighting will of the black masses.

The historian John Hope Franklin, who came to Tulsa in 1925 as a ten-year-old, recalls the long-term impact of the violence upon the city's black community. According to Franklin, black Tulsans believed that many more whites had died in the riot than whites were prepared to admit. They also believed that whites had looted the homes of blacks before burning them, and it was also rumored that black women, encountering white women wearing some item of clothing they recognized, would simply claim and take the property. What black Tulsans believed, Franklin writes, had a marked effect on their self-perception and on their status in the community. "The self-confidence of Tulsa's Negroes soared, their businesses prospered, their institutions flourished, and they simply had no fear of whites," Franklin observes. "After 1921, an altercation in Tulsa between a white person and a black person was not a *racial* incident, even if there was a loss of life. It was just an incident. Such an attitude had a great deal to do with eradicating the fear that a Negro boy growing up in Tulsa might have felt in the years following the riot."[19] Franklin's view suggests that the black community's resistance to the racial onslaught of 1921 was not only a manifestation of courage but also an effective response to violence.

An episode in Detroit brought together several key features of the twenties racial pattern. The issue of housing segregation, the right of self-defense against violence, the role of the NAACP in waging a struggle in the courts, and the response of prominent white liberals, all of these questions were highlighted by the case of a Detroit physician, Dr. Ossian Sweet. Dr. Sweet had acted in the spirit of the maxim that "a man's home is his castle," but Sweet was black and so for protecting his home and family he found himself charged with murder.

Dr. Ossian Sweet had been trained at Wilberforce and Howard universities and had done postgraduate work in pediatrics and gynecology at the Universities of Vienna and Paris. Having established a practice in Detroit, Dr. Sweet in May 1925 bought a home on Garland Avenue, in the midst of a white neighborhood. The Sweet family moved into their new home on September 8, and that night a mob gathered in front of the building. The following evening a larger crowd was there, and the house was stoned; in reply, shots were fired from the house, and one member of the mob fell dead and another was wounded. The police, who previously had taken no action to disperse the mob, now entered the Sweet home and arrested Dr. and Mrs. Sweet and nine other individuals. The arrested persons were held without bail, Mrs. Sweet, ill with tuberculosis and with a fourteen-month-old baby, being released on bail after having been jailed for a month. No evidence was produced as to who had fired the fatal shots, and so the indictment was framed in terms that the defendants were charged with murder because they had entered into an agreement to kill anyone committing even the slightest trespass. The bill of particulars filed by the prosecutor expressed the concept in this language: "The theory of the people in this case is that the defendants premeditatedly and with malice aforethought, banded themselves together and armed themselves with the common understanding and agreement that one or more of them would shoot to kill, in the event, first, of threatened or actual trespass on the property wherein they were assembled, or second, of the infliction of any damage, real or threatened, however slight, to the persons or property of them or any of them."[20] The philosophy of the prosecution seems to have been that this group of blacks would use the presence of any white persons on or near their property as a pretext to kill such individuals. David E. Lilienthal, who reported on the Sweet case for the *Nation,* wrote that no effort was made to prove the existence of such agreement directly, except that the killing itself was regarded as both the crime and the proof of the joint murderous intent. Lilienthal pointed to the stake that trade unionists had in such a case. "Trade unionists," he stated, "who have suffered for generations by means of the legal sleight-of-hand known as 'conspiracy' will do well to keep their eyes upon this latest refinement upon that doctrine of oppression." Lilienthal noted that "this was no ordinary murder trial . . . hovering over and touching the whole proceeding was the somber cloud of race prejudice."[21]

Several factors had led to the mob action against the Sweets. Industrial expansion in Detroit had within a time interval of fifteen years, from 1911 to 1925, produced a tenfold increase in the city's black population, from 8,000 to 81,831. But this new population obviously could not be confined to the housing areas in which 8,000 persons had lived, and consequently there had been some penetration by blacks of previously all-white neighborhoods. Serving during the twenties to inflame the situation, working to arouse the prejudices of recent white migrants from the South and of other white Detroiters, was the Ku Klux Klan. The Klan for several years during the decade was an influential factor in Detroit politics. In 1925 a Klan-backed mayoralty candidate was defeated by a narrow margin of 30,000 votes. According to Walter White of the NAACP, in the two years prior to 1925, 90 percent of the new recruits to the Detroit police force were southern whites, susceptible to Klan propaganda. White further reported that early in 1925 the Klan had begun a series of attacks on the homes of blacks. Among the targets was the home of a physician, Dr. A. L. Turner, who was driven from his place on Spokane Avenue and forced to sell. The furniture of the Turner family was removed, and Dr. and Mrs. Turner were attacked by the mob as they drove away. The police had taken no effective action to prevent this attack.[22] Dr. Turner commented that the affair was a disgrace and added: "I don't mind their yelling and their threats, but they have no right to destroy my property." Back in April a mob of several thousand smashed windows of a house rented to a black family on Northfield Avenue. In July a black undertaker, Vollington Bristol, was threatened by a mob assembled around his house on American Avenue. A number of the whites came armed and there was shooting, but although police made some arrests charges of carrying concealed weapons were soon dropped. In any event Bristol did not leave. The day after Bristol finished moving into his house another mobbing occurred. Some 4,000 persons gathered at the home of John Fletcher on Stoepel Avenue and pelted the building with chunks of coke. Police took no action, but a shot was finally fired from the house, wounding a teenager. The occupants were arrested, but the next day the Fletcher family moved out and no indictments resulted. The *Detroit Free Press* reported that "not one window remained whole" in the Fletcher home. Within hours of the Fletchers' departure 10,000 persons attended a Klan rally on West Fourth Street and a cross was burned.[23]

The response of Detroit mayor John Smith at best represented equivocation and at worst appeasement of racism. In July Smith released a
statement opposing lawlessness. "The law recognizes no distinction in
color or race," the mayor declared. "The persons either white or colored
who attempt to urge their fellows on to disorder and crime are guilty of
the most serious offense upon the statute books.... The police are expected to inquire and prosecute any persons active in organizing such
disorder or inciting a riot." But Smith made no reference to any ethical
or moral issue involved in the question of access to housing, and following
the shooting at the Sweet home he censured the "murderous pride" of
those who moved "into districts where their presence may be resented."
In his view it "does not always do for any man to demand, to its fullest,
the right which the law gives him."[24] The alternative to Smith in the fall
mayoralty election was Klan-supported candidate Charles Bowles.

The Sweet case quickly became a national issue, arousing the fervor
of civil rights advocates. Shortly after the Sweets were arrested NAACP
assistant secretary Walter White wrote a friend that he was headed for
Detroit "where a group of five thousand Nordic gentlemen have been
demonstrating their biological and mental superiority by attacking the
home of a colored physician who was too prosperous 'for a Negro.' The
police force kept their hands off and the mob got the surprise of its life."[25]
In New York the *Amsterdam News* gave all-out support to upholding
the right of self-defense. Declaring that possibly "the most important
court case the Negro has ever figured in in all the history of the United
States" was at stake, the paper urged readers to turn the matter around
and imagine what would happen if a mob of blacks had besieged a white
family and in response the whites had shot and killed one of the blacks.
The editorial asked: "What grand jury in the United States would indict
the white family for murder in the first degree?" The Sweet family could
have sold the house and perhaps made a profit. *"But, thank God, Dr.
Sweet moved in,"* the paper exclaimed. The willingness of the Sweet
family to defend its home represented the spirit of unity, a spirit "the
Negro must more and more evidence if he is to survive." When police
and the courts fail to give protection, the Negro "faces death anyway,
and might just as well die fighting." The *Baltimore Herald* stated "that
the only way, both speedy and effective, to destroy mob law, was to fight
as the mob fights and kill, if necessary, members of the mob."[26]

Coming to the defense of the eleven blacks charged with murder was
the NAACP, which moved quickly. Within four days of the arrests,
NAACP Secretary James Weldon Johnson wired for details of the case.

Eight days following the arrests Walter White was on the scene and in contact with Johnson at the national office regarding the national significance of the events. White saw the affair "as the dramatic climax of the nationwide fight to enforce residential segregation," an analysis he later repeated in a January 1926 *Crisis* article. He reported that "people here are very much stirred," and he told how successive press reports had reduced the size of the crowd outside the Sweet home, finally reducing the number to twenty-five persons. After all, as White noted, Michigan law, 150001-Section 1, "Unlawful Assemblies, How Suppressed," required the police to disperse any group of thirty or more persons who "shall be unlawfully, riotously, or tumultuously assembled in any city, township or village." White also urged that white legal counsel be secured. On September 29 four of the defendants asked the NAACP to defend them, signing a letter that summed up the central issue. Dr. Sweet, William E. Davis, Leonard Morse, and Charles Washington contended that the case "boldly challenges the liberties, the hopes, and the aspirations of 15 million colored Americans. If the prosecution should win, in that very act, they erect over the head of every Negro . . . a very formidable threat of residential proscription whose consequences none of us can now predict." That same day Johnson sharply answered a correspondent who appeared to argue the virtues of some kind of amicable segregation. Johnson insisted that if a black person buys a home he has the right to live there, and he added: "A city street is not in any way a social rendezvous." If we were to have separate blocks, why not separate cities? On the day jury selection began, Johnson in the *New York World* described the incident as "mob segregation."[27]

The association proceeded to raise defense funds and moved to retain some of the nation's best-known liberal attorneys. Only a few months earlier Clarence Darrow and Arthur Garfield Hays had worked together in the Scopes evolution trial in Tennessee, pitting their skill and knowledge against that of the fundamentalist William Jennings Bryan. The Scopes case, the famous "monkey trial" that played out the clash of modern science with Protestant fundamentalism, had drawn wide national attention. Now Darrow and Hays, together with additional attorneys from Detroit and Chicago, took charge of the defense in the Sweet case. On October 6 White and Joel Spingarn had gone to Detroit to arrange legal counsel, and the next day Johnson wired Clarence Darrow asking him to head the defense team, asserting that the case was the "dramatic high point of the nationwide issue of segregation." W. E. B. Du Bois also communicated with Darrow, urging him to "come to the rescue of our fellow sufferers in Detroit." Du Bois had confidence in Darrow, especially on the critical point that "he was absolutely lacking in racial consciousness and because of the broad catholicity of his knowledge and tastes." Du Bois felt free to discuss "matters of race and class" with him. Darrow's credentials included the fact that as early as 1910 he was a member of the NAACP's general committee.[28]

Darrow acceded to the NAACP request and on October 16 the NAACP announced his appointment as chief defense counsel.[29] Four days later White outlined the strategy that Darrow would use in the case, a focus on black reaction to a mob: "This is the state of mind of Negroes throughout the country and doubtless played a very big part in the psychology of Dr. Sweet and the others."[30]

The trial opened on October 30, presided over by judge of the recorder's court Frank Murphy, later to serve as governor of Michigan and justice of the United States Supreme Court. The case was tried by a white judge, white prosecutors, and an all-white jury. Fortunately, the defense had in Murphy a judge set on presiding at a genuinely fair trial. According to his biographer Murphy believed that Detroit police were more likely to arrest blacks than whites and that judges and juries in the local court were unconsciously prejudiced. He regretted the fact that his judicial colleagues failed to realize it was "the opportunity of a lifetime to demonstrate sincere liberalism and judicial integrity." At the beginning of the proceedings Murphy privately expressed the spirit with which he would try the case: "Throughout it all, the question of how to secure a fair trial for the eleven colored defendants is constantly on my mind. Above all things I want them to know that they are in a court where the true ideal of justice is constantly sought. A white judge, white lawyers and twelve white jurymen are sitting in judgment on all who are colored black. This alone is enough to make us fervent in our efforts to do justice."[31] Defense counsel Arthur Garfield Hays later recorded his satisfaction with the manner in which Judge Murphy presided. "A fair and impartial judiciary," Hays wrote, "has never been better represented than by Judge Frank Murphy at this trial."[32] In its white composition the court was routine; the departure from the ordinary was the participation of Murphy and defense lawyers of the caliber of Darrow and Hays.

Perhaps most pertinent to the question of self-defense as a valid justification for the firing of shots from the house was the mindset of Dr. Sweet as he viewed the white mob in the street before his house. In his opening speech Hays announced that the defense would show "that these people had in their minds the persecution to which their people had been subject for generations. They knew of lynchings, sometimes of innocent victims in various parts of the country; of negroes taken from policemen said to be guarding them, and burned at the stake by slow fire; even of women mistreated by mobs." Hays referred to the violence of Chicago, East St. Louis, Tulsa, and Phillips County, Arkansas, to violence only two years earlier in Sweet's birthplace of Orlando, Florida, and also to the lynching of Henry Lowry by the Arkansas mob. "All these things and innumerable incidents of like kind," Hays said, "among them the fact that almost three thousand colored people have been lynched in the last generation, were in the minds of these men on that trying day and night of September 8th and during the more threatening evening of September 9th." Hays argued that self-defense was a necessary feature of an organized society, "the dearest right of a free man," and that not to "use the fullest measure of protection when home and life are threatened would be contrary to human nature."[33]

Darrow had long argued for the view that a criminal trial must become a trial of the total individual, must seek to understand the experiences and mental outlook of the defendant, and in this case that concept was implemented by calling Dr. Sweet to the stand and having Arthur Garfield Hays question him about his life. Prosecutor Robert M. Toms objected to such questioning, but Darrow countered: "This is the question of the psychology of a race—of how everything known to a race affects its actions." As whites because of their psychology would do to blacks what they would not do to other whites, Darrow argued, so must the effect of the past upon black psychology be understood. Judge Murphy allowed the questioning.[34]

Sweet explained how when he had studied in Paris he had contributed 300 francs to the American Hospital at Paris, and yet when his pregnant wife sought to have her baby delivered at the hospital she had been denied admission. In several instances referring to specific news accounts, Sweet told of his knowledge of recent racial violence, of the Tulsa riot, of the 1917 riot at East St. Louis, and of the 1919 violence in Chicago, Washington, and Phillips County, Arkansas. Sweet also told of a race riot in Orlando, where several blacks had been killed and their homes burned. When asked by Hays about his state of mind at the time of the shooting Sweet responded: "When I opened the door and saw the mob I realized that I was facing the same mob that had hounded my people throughout its entire history."[35] A crucial question in this case was what was a reasonable expectation on the part of the persons within the house. According to Walter White, Darrow used Sweet's testimony to make the case that it was not the state of mind of a white man that had to be considered "but must necessarily be that of a Negro with a white mob outside and in the Negro's brain a picture of what similar mobs have done to Negroes during the past sixty years in America."[36]

Darrow, in his closing speech, used all his consummate skill to penetrate the mindset of the jury. He focused upon the reality of race prejudice, asking the jury to stand above it. He stated bluntly: "I know that if these defendants had been a white group defending themselves from a colored mob, they never would have been arrested, or been tried. My clients are charged with murder, but they are really here because they are black." Regarding policemen who testified that no mob had assembled outside the Sweet home Darrow said: "There isn't an officer in this case who is not partly guilty of this crime and who hasn't committed perjury to protect himself... they are victims of an instinctive hatred of anything which appears as social equality of the black race." He asked the jurors to think how they would feel if they were charged with killing a black man in a black community, after a black mob had surrounded their home, and then tried before a black jury. Darrow urged the jurors to view the situation through the defendants' eyes: "You must imagine yourselves in the position of these eleven over here, with their skins, with the hatred, with the infinite wrongs they have suffered on account of their skin, with the hazards they take every day they live, with the insults that are heaped around them, with the crowd outside, with the knowledge of what that crowd meant, and then ask the question of whether they waited too long or stopped too quick." To underscore the need to comprehend the impact of race hatred upon blacks, a poem by Countee Cullen was read to the jury:

> Once riding in old Baltimore,
> Heart full, head full of glee,
> I saw a Baltimorean
> Stand gazing there at me.
>
> Now, I was eight and very small,
> And he was no whit bigger,
> And so I smiled, but he stuck out
> His tongue and called me "nigger."
>
> I saw the whole of Baltimore
> From April till December,
> Of all the things that I saw there
> That's all that I remember.

Toms gave the summary for the prosecution. He announced he would not address the race problem, except to say that perhaps it was to be dealt with on the basis of "mutual forbearance," but in any event it was not the jury's problem. Toms sought to confine the issue to that of an ordinary criminal case. But in fact he stated his view of the right involved in fair access to housing. According to Toms, "we all have many civil rights which we voluntarily waive in the name of public peace and comfort and security because we hesitate to insist on them." And he asked the jury: "Which is more important, the right to live where you please, the right to live in a certain neighborhood, or the right to live at all?"[37] The logical outcome of his position was that blacks were defenseless in situations where a mob objected to their presence.

The trial ended on November 27 when the jury after forty-six hours of deliberation reported it was unable to reach a verdict and Judge Murphy declared a mistrial. The defendants were granted bail, eight of them being released on bonds of $10,000 each. The defense successfully moved for separate trials of the defendants, and the prosecution chose to begin with Henry Sweet, Ossian Sweet's brother. This second trial held during May 1926 was again presided over by Judge Frank Murphy, and this trial too was heard by an all-white jury. As he had done in the first trial Clarence Darrow made the major closing speech, a seven-hour address, described by James Weldon Johnson of the NAACP as "the most wonderful flow of words I ever heard from a man's lips." Darrow gave a panoramic view of Afro-American history, going from the African background to the present, outlining the record of racial injustice, paying tribute to black accomplishment in the face of injustice, and indicting American society for its hypocrisy.[38]

Again in the second trial Darrow rejected the claim that this was simply a criminal case. "I insist," he told the jurors, "that there is nothing but prejudice in this case; that if it was reversed and eleven white men had shot and killed a black while protecting their home and their lives against a mob of blacks, nobody would have dreamed of having them indicted." Darrow carefully portrayed the jury as victims of prejudice. "It is forced into us," he said, "almost from our youth until somehow or other we feel we are superior to these people who have black faces." Darrow set the arrested blacks in context:

Eleven people with black skins, eleven people, gentlemen, whose ancestors did not come to America because they wanted to, but were brought here in slave ships, to toil for nothing, for the whites—whose lives have been taken in nearly every state in the Union—they have been victims of riots all over this land of the free. They have had to take what is left after everybody else has grabbed what he wanted. The only place where he has been put in front is on the battle field. When we are fighting we give him a chance to die, and the best chance. But everywhere else, he has been food for the flames, and the ropes, and the knives, and the guns and hate of the white, regardless of law and liberty, and the common sentiments of justice that should move men.

Darrow censured the police for their failure to act, and though he mentioned the violence of Chicago, East St. Louis, and Washington he concentrated on Detroit. And, as usual avoiding a tone of blame, he portrayed the racial conflict that had come to the city and explained that it was a "new idea in Detroit that a colored man's home can be torn down about his head because he is black." The choice for the city was of "law or blind force," and he asked the jurors to make the choice "with your eyes open." Toward the end of his speech Darrow returned to the theme of the distinction between the European immigrants and the blacks enslaved in Africa, "torn from their homes and their kindred; loaded into slave ships, packed like sardines in a box, half of them dying on the ocean passage." He added that whites "owe an obligation and a duty to these black men which can never be repaid."[39] Darrow told the jury he felt deeply about the subject, and his words evidenced his passionate convictions. Lamentably, this dimension of this great defender-advocate and indeed his role in the Sweet case itself have not received the attention given his other memorable cases. Henry Sweet, however, was found not guilty by the jury, and with that the prosecutor dropped the charges against the other defendants.

It is well to keep in mind what the Sweet case accomplished and what it did not accomplish. The white liberal Lilienthal was unsure that the whites had made much progress since 200 years earlier when blacks were traded for rum. "But that the black man is making headway," he wrote, "is beyond doubt." The defendants themselves were proof of progress, as was the presence of two black newspapermen at the press table. More and more blacks were being employed in factories that could be seen from the courtroom windows. And, perhaps most significant for Lilienthal, there was the fact "that Negroes can command so fair a trial in a land where most trials of Negroes have been mob-dominated travesties. For this trial was probably the fairest ever accorded a Negro in this country; had it been otherwise the defendants would now be on their way to a life in prison."[40] The acquittal was indeed a significant victory; it demonstrated that the charge of murder, at least in this instance, could not be pressed successfully against blacks who legitimately exercised the right of self-defense against impending assault. But the trial had nothing to say about what official America would do about those who mobbed blacks seeking equal access to housing and other citizenship rights. It took two trials before the charges against Dr. Sweet and the other defendants were dropped. And it also required a defense fund of thousands of dollars and the services of some of the ablest legal talent in the United States. Through a combination of circumstances resources were made available to the defendants that assured some measure of fairness in the trials. But how many blacks could be confident that that same combination of circumstances would be operative for them? Viewed in perspective it was a travesty of justice that Dr. Sweet and the others who had stood with him in defense of his home were ever brought to trial.

The Sweet case also appears in clearer perspective when seen in relation to the fact that victory for the right of self-defense in the Detroit court was soon accompanied by defeat in the Supreme Court on the question of the legality of restrictive housing covenants. In effect the Court left intact the system of housing discrimination that created the situations leading to the violence at the Sweet home. From the beginning, the NAACP's involvement in the Sweet case had been intertwined with a concern about constitutional questions directly related to fair housing. In December 1924 the association had launched a national campaign against residential segregation, announcing a mass meeting to be held at Harlem's Renaissance Casino, with speakers including Congressman Ogden Mills and the NAACP's William Pickens.[41] In his initial telegram appealing to Darrow to enter the case James Weldon Johnson referred to the NAACP's having a case on the underlying constitutional issues before the Supreme Court. While the Sweet case was in progress an internal association memo tied the case to the forthcoming Supreme Court decision. Also, in mid-November Johnson, in a letter to the *Philadelphia Ledger,* argued that with regard to the Sweet case and the matter to be decided by the Supreme Court the "fundamental question involved is the same."[42] In 1917 the Court had found unconstitutional statutes providing for residential segregation, and now the issue was to overturn the use of law to enforce private covenants. The case *Corrigan* v. *Buckley* had arisen out of restrictive covenant practices in Washington, D.C. Oral argument was heard by the Court on January 8, 1926, with the NAACP position argued by Moorfield Storey and Louis Marshall.[43]

W. E. B. Du Bois, in the midst of the Sweet case, had posed sharply the basic issue of inequitable housing practices. In the *Crisis* he wrote: "If some of the horror-struck and law-worshiping white leaders of Detroit, instead of winking at the Ku Klux Klan and admonishing the

Negroes to allow themselves to be kicked and killed with impunity—if these would finance and administer a decent scheme of housing relief for Negroes it would not be necessary for us to kill white mob leaders in order to live in peace and decency."[44] But of course there was no such scheme, and the Supreme Court, when it ruled on *Corrigan* on May 24, decided it lacked jurisdiction to act. The Court found it was "obvious" that neither the Thirteenth nor the Fourteenth Amendment prohibited private individuals "from entering into contracts regarding the control and disposition of their own property."[45] The Sweets received some degree of justice in the local court, but as far as federal law was concerned discriminatory housing practices could proceed unchecked, unless directly initiated by local statute.

The 1920s produced both victories and setbacks in the organized movement against racial violence. The Sweet case, and the Supreme Court ruling against mob justice in the 1923 *Moore v. Dempsey* decision represented significant gains on the legal front. The annual lynching rate steadily declined after 1921, but the campaign to enact federal antilynching legislation failed. Still, the field of organized protest against racial violence was dominated during the 1920s by the NAACP, with its stress on recourse to the judicial system and its orientation of working within the framework of liberal politics.

In such episodes as the fight for the Dyer antilynching bill and the Sweet case, the association was in the forefront of the struggle. *Crisis,* with its considerable readership, was an effective vehicle for regularly exposing incidents of racial violence. The victims of racial injustice were not forgotten. In 1921 NAACP secretary James Weldon Johnson led a delegation of thirty prominent black men and women to an audience with President Harding. The delegation's purpose was to present a petition, with 50,000 signatures, appealing for pardon of the soldiers still imprisoned for participating in the 1917 Houston riot. In presenting the petition Johnson stated that the delegation spoke for ten million black Americans. Johnson based the appeal on three grounds: the previous service record of the Twenty-fourth Infantry; "the provocation of local animosity" expressed in insults, threats, and acts of violence; and the severe punishment that had already been inflicted. Johnson told Harding: "This wholesale, unprecedented and almost clandestine execution shocked the entire country and appeared to the colored people to savor of vengeance rather than justice." Warren Harding, however, did not respond quickly to the petition. None of the prisoners was released during 1921, only five during the next two years, and it was not until 1938 that the last of the convicted men was released from Leavenworth.[46]

The heritage of progressivism passed on to a new liberalism, a liberalism typified by the recently formed American Civil Liberties Union, and the NAACP became a component of the liberal movement, seeking the advancement of black rights in the midst of an economic boom that seemed to make radicalism an exercise in futility. The Garvey movement never recovered from Marcus Garvey's imprisonment and 1927 deportation. As for the *Messenger*, A. Philip Randolph's periodical that served as a link to the prewar Socialist movement, it ceased publication in 1928. Although segregation continued, as did lynching, as the decade neared its end the prosperity of American capitalism appeared to some to have muted the sharpness of racial confrontation.

But it was also possible in the America in which the Ku Klux Klan was still a considerable presence, the America of the Scopes trial and the impending Sacco and Vanzetti executions, to hold that the question of racial violence was likely to assume new urgency. An interesting expression of this sense of urgency was to be found in an analysis of the racial situation formulated by the white Communist Robert Minor. A talented cartoonist who opted for the career of professional revolutionary, a Texan with a particular sensitivity to the question of racism in American society, Minor in 1926 surveyed the racial scene and saw some grim realities. He noted an episode in Carteret, New Jersey, in which armed whites drove the entire black population from the town, burned a black church, "and generally conducted an organized reign of terror of the sort which America calls a race riot and which the old Russia of the now-dead czar called a pogrom." He also noted a series of official executions of blacks in Kentucky that amounted to legal lynching, with "eighteen minute trials" mocking the legal system and state troops carrying out within a few days the purposes of the mob. Minor forecast an intensification of the black struggle as black Americans occupied a position that could not much longer be tolerated. The black masses, Minor wrote, had "a score of issues which are worth life and death to them."[47]

Reflecting a sense of urgency coupled with confidence in white liberalism was Walter White's study of lynching, *Rope and Faggot*, published in 1929. Lynching indeed remained a serious menace, but White also noted that "notable progress has been made during recent years against mob law." White granted that changes in public attitudes he pointed to represented "but a fraction of American public opinion," but he considered such changes of "immense importance" when considering that two decades earlier, according to White, there was practically no opposition to mob action. White stressed that two basic conditions produced the context for change: black migration from the South and black resistance to the lynchers. But these factors had impelled a variety of institutions and organizations to take action against lynching. First and foremost was the NAACP, and White cited the organization's antilynching work as its outstanding accomplishment. The association had carried on an effective educational campaign, both within the United States and abroad. Effective also was the Commission on Interracial Cooperation, head-quartered in Atlanta, which represented some of the best of southern liberalism. The commission particularly devoted attention to working among students and women. Other organizations credited by White with contributing to the effort were the Federal Council of Churches of Christ and the Fellowship of Reconciliation. Significant also was a more en-lightened attitude by a number of southern newspapers that sought to create a climate of opinion hostile to mob action. White was realistic about lynching's continuing menace but saw important changes taking place in the South. At the least there was the fact that an "energetic minority" was at work against mob law. It remained to be seen if that minority could overcome "the serious handicap of a century of practically unchecked mob violence."[48]

Rope and Faggot was an extension of what White had written a few years earlier in his novel *The Fire in the Flint*. In creating the tragic story of a young black physician who had come home to postwar Georgia and finally was lynched because he assisted black tenants and sharecroppers in organizing against unfair treatment by white landowners, White ef-fectively portrayed the racial atmosphere of the 1920s Deep South. Here was the identification of the Klansmen with the police, the aggressiveness of virulent racists who feared the assertiveness of blacks who emerged from the war believing a new dawn was coming, the pushing aside of older traditions of white paternalism. White drove home the point of the racist double standard regarding sexual relations and dramatized the hypocrisy of the lynchers who were confident northerners would excuse lynching if sexual assault was alleged and who coolly and cynically con-trived such charges. The novel revealed a pervasive caste system that pressed in upon all blacks, regardless of education or economic position. Indeed, black attainment was a spur to white violence. White focused somewhat inconsistently upon the dual themes of the rampant exploi-tation that underlay the southern agricultural system and the reality that merchants, bankers, and landowners profited from the labor of poor blacks, and upon the view that the source of lynching was in poor-white resentment of black progress. Against racist abuse White set the race pride of blacks who knew that access to the vote was vital and who had the courage to resist the indignities inflicted upon black women. White noted that improvement in the position of black farmers would have a favorable impact upon the welfare of the great majority of white farmers.

Walter White knew the South, and *The Fire in the Flint* has power as a work of fiction because the novel captures much of the reality of the time, the resurgence of a black will to secure better conditions through organization that was yet stifled by the entrenched power of racism. The unresolved tension of the South inexorably leads to the lynching of the physician Kenneth Harper and of his brother Bob, just before he is to go off to Harvard to study, and to the rape-assault upon their sister Mamie. But lynching is not in this era to be cost-free to the lynchers, for Bob before dying shoots and kills two of those in the mob. White does not so much urge a message upon his readers as offer a cross-section of the forces he perceives to be present in the violent culture of the South.[49]

White in *Rope and Faggot* was hopeful about prospects for eliminating lynching, but evidence he cited revealed the extent to which mob violence was still embedded in southern society. An incident illustrating this reality was the 1926 lynching of three blacks at the resort town of Aiken, South Carolina. The previous spring, the sheriff at Aiken and three of his deputies had gone to the Lowman family farm to arrest Sam Lowman on charges of selling whiskey. Lowman was gone from the place, but following an incident in which his wife Annie was shot to death and his daughter Bertha struck in the mouth, two other family members rushed to the house, further shooting ensued, and the sheriff was killed. Three of the Lowmans were arrested, charged with murder, and convicted in perfunctory trials. Two of the defendants, Demon and Clarence Lowman, were sentenced to death, and Bertha Lowman was given life imprisonment.

According to White the sheriff and his deputies were all members of the Ku Klux Klan, the allegation of whiskey selling against Sam Lowman was without foundation, and the entire incident stemmed from a desire to embarrass William Hartley, the owner of the land Sam Lowman rented. In April 1925 a mob of hooded Klansmen had come to the Lowman home, taken Demon Lowman outside, and severely whipped him, for no reason other than the feud between the Klansmen and the Lowmans' landlord. The Lowman family had good reason to fear the approach of strange whites. In any event the Supreme Court of South Carolina overturned the convictions, ordered a new trial, and at that trial the judge ordered a directed verdict of acquittal for one of the defendants.

At this point on October 8, 1926, the lynch mob entered the scene, "overpowering" the jailer and the sheriff, seizing the three blacks, and taking them to a nearby tourist camp, where a crowd of some 2,000 had assembled. The prisoners were shot to death. An NAACP inquiry revealed that the sheriff and the jailer had assisted the lynchers, as had members of the state legislature, relatives of the governor, and an assortment of farmers, lawyers, politicians, and businessmen. In short, a considerable segment of "respectable" South Carolina was involved in the lynching.

Early in 1927 the NAACP reacted sharply to what had occurred in South Carolina. The association urged President Coolidge not to appoint Thomas G. McLeod, South Carolina's governor at the time of the Aiken lynchings, to the Federal Trade Commission. During 1926, according to the NAACP, thirty-three persons were mob victims as compared to eighteen in 1925. James Weldon Johnson linked the Aiken incident and other 1926 lynchings to what had taken place in Congress regarding antilynching legislation. "While there was a threat of a federal law, with consequent jurisdiction of federal courts over this crime, the lynchers hesitated," Johnson stated. But when the Senate refused to act on the Dyer bill, "that was equivalent to serving notice on the lynchers that they could pursue their pastime virtually unmolested."[50]

An estimation of the situation with respect to racial violence during the 1920s must be set in the context of the federal government's prevailing indifference to the need for altering America's racial pattern. This indifference is clearly brought to light in viewing the response of Coolidge administration officials, most particularly Secretary of Commerce Herbert Hoover, to the racial aspects of the terrible Mississippi River flood of 1927. For hundreds of thousands in Mississippi, Arkansas, and Louisiana, black and white, the floodwaters broke up the existing routine, and thousands sought safety in refugee camps. Black tenant farmers and sharecroppers were heard to sing that the flood had washed away "the old account." They imagined a possible new reality coming out of the devastation. But in many instances they encountered not an avenue to change but refugee camps that were in fact concentration camps, places that restricted freedom of movement and made certain that those confined would have no option other than to return to labor on the plantations. National Guard troops stood outside the locked gates of the camps. In response to public criticism Secretary Hoover appointed a Colored Advisory Commission, headed by Robert R. Moton of Tuskegee. This commission took seriously Hoover's assurances that the emergency would lead to social rehabilitation, but such reform was not to be.

The enlarged federal presence was not utilized to change conditions. Moton communicated to Hoover the findings of investigators, who observed that blacks who attempted to leave and were caught "were whipped and at times threatened with death if they left the plantation again." Blacks, the investigators contended, lived in dread that if they "talked too much" they would be killed. The Colored Advisory Commission pointed to the need of addressing "one of the greatest labor questions of America, which found itself in the relation between the planter and these tenant farmers." But Hoover stepped aside from this matter, choosing instead to emphasize the general provision of relief assistance. In response to criticism by Walter White that the refugee camps were actually slave labor camps, Hoover explained that the national government had no responsibility for the economic system existing in the South.[51] Secretary Hoover had a reputation as a great humanitarian, but the 1927 flood demonstrated that his humanitarianism was coupled with a commitment to the racial status quo.

PART IV

Crisis and New Unity: The 1930s

The fact that the Negroes who so brutally murdered this girl could not be adequately punished by the law because of their ages prevents me from condemning the citizens who meted out justice to the ravishing murderers.

Comment by Colorado County, Texas, judge following November 1935 lynching of black juveniles Ernest Collins and Bennie Mitchell

At the trial they give us in Scottsboro we could hear the crowds yelling, "Lynch the Niggers." We could see them toting those big shotguns. Call 'at a fair trial?

And while we lay here in jail, the boss-man make us watch 'em burning up other Negroes in the electric chair. "This is what you'll get," they say to us.

What for? We ain't done nothing to be in here at all. All we done was to look for a job.

Appeal sent from prison by the Scottsboro Boys, April 1, 1932

NINE

Turning Left

THE ONSET of the Great Depression generally sharpened tensions in American society and brought them to the surface. Class tensions intensified as notions of mass prosperity through mass production were replaced by the realities of widespread unemployment, breadlines, and Hoovervilles. Racial tensions also came to the fore as blacks found themselves in a staggering economic disaster, and yet the customary rules of racial subordination were maintained in force. Fear of black militancy grew, especially as it was connected with anxieties that those suffering the trauma of Depression, white and black, would unite in common movements for social change. Sharpening tensions were translated into a growth of racial violence. Responses to this violence were shaped in a new context, a deep, pervasive, and seemingly endless general societal crisis, and the result was some new dimensions to those responses. In dealing with racial violence, questions of class and race were more clearly intertwined than ever before, and a segment of black America saw militant radicalism, a radicalism most clearly articulated by the Communist party, as providing a possible solution to its urgent needs.

Obvious evidence of a change in the racial situation was a marked increase in the frequency of lynchings. During 1930 twenty-one persons were lynched in the United States; one Florida victim was a foreign-born white, the others were blacks. The state having the worst record was Georgia, with six lynchings. The resurgence of mob murders led the Commission on Interracial Cooperation to undertake a study of lynching, forming the Southern Commission on the Study of Lynching for this purpose. The director of the project was Arthur F. Raper, a staff member of the Commission on Interracial Cooperation. On-the-spot investigations of each of the episodes were conducted by Walter Chivers, a soft-spoken and keenly observant professor of sociology at Morehouse College.[1]

The study that emerged from these investigations, published in 1933, revealed that southern society, except in rare instances, still refused to take effective action against lynching. The report noted "the presence of sadistic tendencies among the lynchers," and the detailed accounts of the episodes supported this conclusion. The desire merely to kill was not enough to explain the lynching of James Irwin at Ocilla, Georgia, in which the victim was jabbed in the mouth with a sharp pole, his toes and fingers removed joint by joint, and his teeth extracted by wire pullers; following these tortures and "further unmentionable atrocities" Irwin's still living body was saturated with gasoline and a match applied, whereupon hundreds of shots were fired into the body. Few of the lynchers involved in the 1930 episode had even high school educations, but the report declared erroneous any impression that all the lynchers were propertyless persons. A double lynching at Scooba, Mississippi, was reportedly organized by two men prominently identified with church, school, and other community activities. The report put forward the generalization that the more backward the community, the more likely it was that the "best people" of the community had been involved. Beyond the question of who participated in the mobs, there was also the vital issue of the wider community response to lynching. The Southern Commission on the Study of Lynching found that, with regard to the 1930 incidents, in every community where they occurred some people justified the action taken and that the apologists included people from all walks of life—judges, prosecuting attorneys, lawyers, businessmen, doctors, clergymen, and teachers as well as mechanics and day laborers. Perhaps quite as significant was the attitude of individuals, often among the "best citizens," who opposed the lynching but after an interval came to the conclusion that the sooner the matter was forgotten, the better. Similar attitudes were encountered by Gunnar Myrdal, who in his *American Dilemma* reported that though he had met few members of the middle and upper classes of the South who approved of lynching he met equally few who pretended they would take any risks to hinder a lynching, "and they made no effort to punish the lynchers." In view of such attitudes one is not surprised by the commission's finding that no communitywide effort for the conviction of the lynchers was made in any of the communities in which a lynching occurred.[2] This report supported a conclusion that, generally speaking, the balance of forces between those engaging in or apologizing for lynching and those opposed to such mob murder had not yet decisively changed in the South.

One of the aspects of the situation referred to in the report was the reality of the "legal lynching," the execution of blacks following trials held in an atmosphere of intimidation that virtually precluded impartial

court procedure.³ A legal lynching that was almost carried through to
its intended conclusion was the Scottsboro case, the famous trial of nine
black youths taken from a freight train at Scottsboro, Alabama, charged
with rape, and eight of them swiftly sentenced to death. In this case it
was the state of Alabama that would carry though the "legal" electrocution. At a specified date individuals acting on behalf of an impersonal
institution would kill the Scottsboro boys. Who was to believe seriously
that officials of the state of Alabama could be deterred from their course,
especially when the case involved the lives of black youths without connections or material resources? But new factors entered into the calcu-
lations in this case, factors that would significantly affect the future of
the black struggle. The coming into play of these factors, however, required that the Scottsboro boys themselves and their families choose the
course they would take. Would they resign themselves to what seemed
to be an inevitable fate, or would they challenge the system that condemned them? They took the path of protest, of aligning themselves with
those who would take the case out of the routine channels of Alabama
justice. Shortly after the boys were convicted in April 1931, they placed
the case in the hands of the International Labor Defense, an organization
that would combine courtroom efforts with mass agitation. The following
April the Scottsboro boys jointly signed an appeal that asserted their
innocence and asked for help. There is a moving genuineness about the
letter that illustrates how in this case the defendants themselves played
an active role on their own behalf. Those who could be moved by any
appeal against injustice were likely to respond to what the Scottsboro
boys had to say:

> We have been sentenced to die for something we ain't never done.
> Us poor boys have been sentenced to burn up on the electric chair
> for the reason that we is workers—and the color of our skin is black.
> We like any one of you workers is none of us older than 20. Two
> of us is 14 and one is 13 years old. What we guilty of? Nothing but
> being out of a job. Nothing but looking for work. Our kinfolk was
> starving for food. We wanted to help them out. So we hopped a
> freight—just like any one of you workers might a done—to go down
> to Mobile to hunt work. We was taken off the train by a mob and
> framed up on rape charges.... Working class boys, we asks you to
> save us from being burnt on the electric chair. We's only poor work-
> ing class boys whose skin is black. We shouldn't die for that....
> Help us boys. We ain't done nothing wrong.⁴

It was a letter that was relevant to the general situation of racial oppression but also specifically relevant to the desperate search by black and white youth for jobs. Thousands of American youth were riding the freight trains seeking work, any work, and the Scottsboro boys were part of that army recruited by the Depression.

An essential component of the Scottsboro case was the involvement of the Communist party and such organizations as the International Labor Defense that operated largely under Communist leadership. In appearing on the scene in the Scottsboro case the Communists did not suddenly come from nowhere. Since the party's formation in 1919 the Communist position on the black struggle had moved a considerable distance from the simplistic Socialist view that discussion of a program for Afro-Americans was finished with reference to the ultimate solution of socialism.

In April 1925 the central executive committee of the Workers (Communist) party declared that along with the forms of exploitation common to all workers "the Negroes have to endure the terrible burden of race persecution by which the capitalist class intensifies its class exploitation of the Negroes and also succeeds in dividing and weakening the exploited classes." The era of the world revolution, the Communists said, "is also the epoch of the rise of the darker races." Therefore, it was of the greatest importance that the black struggle be seen in its international context: "A movement among the Negro workers and farmers of the United States must be considered, not only in the light of the class struggle within this country, but also in connection with the anti-imperialist struggles of the millions of West Indian Negroes and the 150,000,000 natives of Africa, and the awakening of the 400,000,000 of China and the 320,000,000 of India."[5]

By the late 1920s the Communists were committed to the view that what was termed "the Negro question" constituted a "national question." According to the party the black struggle in the United States had the significance of an oppressed nation entitled to self-determination. Whatever problems and complexities were involved in this formulation, this position did raise the Afro-American struggle to an issue of world significance. Among the nations of the world seeking liberation was a black nation located within the geographic limits of the world's most powerful capitalist country.

Already in the 1920s a number of black militants had joined the Communists. One such individual emerging from A. Philip Randolph's *Messenger* group was the Harlem activist Cyril Briggs. Briggs participated in forming a black organization, the African Black Brotherhood, that expressed the Communist viewpoint. In the issues of the brotherhood's organ, the *Crusader,* Briggs called for militant, uncompromising battle against racism, describing the actions of the Ku Klux Klan as "war to the hilt against our rights and liberties, and against our very existence." Briggs argued that it was necessary that blacks make use of any and every weapon in the struggle that lay at hand. "With the murderer clutching at our throats," he wrote, "we can ill afford to choose our weapons, but must defend ourselves with what lies nearest whether that be poison, fire or what."[6]

Two Communist-oriented organizations relevant to the black struggle were formed around 1925. The International Labor Defense was formed in Chicago, and from the beginning the ILD took up cases of both white and black workers victimized by legal injustice. Also founded in Chicago was the American Negro Labor Congress (ANLC), which worked to advance the concept of working-class leadership in the black movement. According to Communist party leader William Z. Foster congress membership "was eventually confined mainly to Communists," but the organization did participate in a number of strikes and conducted classes and forums.[7] In its initial call the congress proceeded from the assumption that "the strength of the race rests in its working class," that only the black working class could eliminate racial oppression. With regard to racial oppression the congress proposed to shift emphasis from the political and legislative struggle against lynching to promotion of "interracial committees throughout the nation with the aim of bringing about a better feeling between white and black workers as a remedy against lynching." Following a record of futility in securing the enactment of a federal antilynching law, the ANLC proposed that "the seat of action be changed to the masses themselves."[8] There was something here of the disdain for political action that had previously influenced the radical labor movement, especially the IWW. By 1930 the congress was somewhat friendlier to political action and now urged enactment of a federal antilynching law that would make lynching a capital offense. Put even more sharply than in 1925, the organization's main theme continued to be the leadership role of the black working class. The congress declared that in order to resist effectively "white ruling class terrorism" in the South, the blacks in the South required the support of white and black workers. The ANLC stated that there was urgent need for the formation of "a militant mass Negro organization," but such an organization was not to be controlled by middle-class leaders who "are not concerned with the demands of the working class except insofar as the formulation of these demands can be used to force concessions for their own set or class." The congress went on to explain more fully why such leaders were not to be trusted, and there can be no doubt that the reference included the leadership of the NAACP:

> These leaders (property owners, landlords, real estate agents, preachers, prostitute college professors, editors of middle-class magazines and newspapers, heads of various "advancement" and "improvement" associations) have a stake in the system under which the masses of Negroes are oppressed and exploited. They are therefore not in favor of its abolition, but merely seek a fuller share in the exploitation of their own people and a higher social status for their own class. Moreover, they are incapable of leading the struggle because they have neither a clear understanding of the nature of the struggle (which is essentially a class struggle, and not, as they pretend, a purely racial struggle) nor the courage to prosecute it militantly enough to insure success.[9]

Following 1930 the main channel for Communist activity among blacks became a new organization, the League of Struggle for Negro Rights.[10] The league was a part of implementing a Communist party decision to pay more attention to work in the South. Within a year the Scottsboro case became a critical focus of that work.

During the several years in which the case remained a public issue innumerable demonstrations, rallies, picket lines, and other forms of vocal protest were organized. Public activity on behalf of the Scottsboro boys was extremely difficult in the South, but even in New York upon occasion violence was the result of Scottsboro demonstrations. On April 25, 1931, demonstrators, organized by the ILD, white and black, attempted to march down Harlem's Lenox Avenue, carrying banners with slogans such as "Death to Lynch Law," "Smash the Scottsboro Frame-Up," and "Down with Jim Crowism and Segregation." Between 138th Street and 139th Street the marchers were met by a contingent of police who began swinging their nightsticks. The *New York Times* reported that the police seemed to direct their blows chiefly against the banners. Four of the marchers were arrested, but others reassembled in small groups and proceeded to 110th Street and Fifth Avenue where another protest meeting was held. Mrs. Janie Patterson, mother of Scottsboro defendant Haywood Patterson, was present at the meeting.[11]

The issue of defense strategy in this case was a cause of bitter recriminations between the Communists and the National Association for the Advancement of Colored People. In an article entitled "Smash Lynching

8 Young Negroes," Communist spokesman James W. Ford declared that blacks were turning to the Communist party, turning away "from the hired and paid petty bourgeois reformist lackies who betray them into the hands of the capitalist bosses."[12] Articles in the March 1932 issue of the *Crisis* exemplify the NAACP's response to the criticism it was receiving and its resentment at failure to wrest control of the Scottsboro defense from the Communists. The association stated that it realized "that the purpose of the Communists was not only to use the Scottsboro case as a means of revolutionary propaganda, but to weaken or destroy the NAACP. The idea was to convince Negroes that they had no hope of achieving justice except through the Communist Party." Also published was a statement by Clarence Darrow. The great libertarian lawyer had been retained by the NAACP as counsel for the Scottsboro appeal in a belated effort to compensate for the association's rather slight attention to the case at the beginning. Darrow's statement expressed the spirit, quite different from that of the ILD, with which he would approach the Scottsboro defense. Whereas James Ford labeled the convictions a "frame-up," saw the case as a link "in the chain of imperialist terror against the Negro workers," and held "the steel barons and landlords of Alabama" responsible, Darrow declared that he had no interest in the religious, political, or other views of any client; the principle that animated him was the individual's entitlement to equal protection under the law. He took issue with the tactics of mass protest resorted to by the ILD. Darrow seemed to be saying that mass protests could only hurt the Scottsboro boys, referring to hundreds of letters sent to Alabama authorities "which threatened the officials and citizens of Alabama if the verdict of death should be carried out." In Darrow's view it was idle to suppose that threats would sway the Alabama officials. He would pin much of his hopes for justice in the case upon southern liberals, doubtless overestimating their strength when he referred to "a large and rapidly growing organization." This organization was made up of many of the South's "best citizens," clergymen and other professionals, and Darrow argued that these people also "deplore the threatening letters and other forms of intimidation that have been used in this case."[13]

Stepping aside from the heat of the ILD–NAACP quarrel, we can have no doubt but that the Communists waged an unprecedented publicity campaign in connection with the Scottsboro case. No single instance of racial injustice in American history had ever been the subject of a comparable worldwide campaign, one that reached millions in this country and abroad. At one point early in the developing struggle even the NAACP field secretary William Pickens wrote the *Daily Worker* that "in the present case the *Daily Worker* and the workers have moved, so far, more speedily and effectively than all other agencies put together." Pickens went on to declare that this was one occasion "for every Negro who has intelligence to read" to send aid to the *Daily Worker* and to the ILD.[14] Writing of the case in the late 1940s the NAACP leader Henry Lee Moon acknowledged the unusual character of the Scottsboro campaign. Moon, a staunch anti-Communist, nonetheless recognized that the ILD, after taking charge of the case, "conducted a vigorous, leather-lunged campaign that echoed and re-echoed throughout the world." Perhaps most significant was a point Moon made about the impact of this campaign upon black people themselves. He wrote: "the black masses seemed intrigued by this bold, forthright and dramatic defiance. Offering no quarter the Communists put the south on the defensive in the eyes of the whole world. They stirred the imagination of Negroes and inspired the hope of ultimate justice. In churches, in conventions, in union halls, in street corner meetings, Negroes were clamorous in expressing approval of this campaign."[15] Blacks saw a political party make a world issue out of death sentences meted out to black boys in Alabama, and they could not fail to note that something new was happening in American society.

The Scottsboro case remained for some years, however, as a sore point in relations between the Communists and the NAACP. Reflecting the NAACP attitude, although published six years after his resignation as *Crisis* editor, was Du Bois's discussion of the case in his autobiographical essay, *Dusk of Dawn*. Du Bois flatly asserted with regard to the Communists that, "had it not been for their senseless interference, these poor victims of Southern injustice would today be free." He was confident that if "quiet and careful methods" had been utilized the boys would have been freed "without fanfare or much publicity." Du Bois insisted that the Communists were not motivated by a concern for the Scottsboro boys' lives; in his view "the actual fate of these victims was a minor matter" for the Communists. Passing beyond criticism of the American Communists Du Bois believed that "the leaders of Russian communism thought that they saw here a chance to foment revolution in the United States." If the Russians thought that, he asserted, they revealed profound ignorance of American conditions, for white workers were not to be radicalized by centering attention on a case involving alleged sexual assault by blacks upon white females. Du Bois summed up his position with the comment that the Communists were right as to the merits of the case, but "they were tragically wrong in their methods if they were seeking to free these victims."[16] What would have happened if the ILD had not stepped into the Scottsboro case cannot be ascertained, but the fact remains that Alabama was not able to carry through the planned executions and that three of the condemned eight had been released by the time Du Bois's essay appeared; the last of the Scottsboro boys was released from prison in 1950. No one can measure the agony experienced by the Scottsboro boys as they awaited execution and, after the death sentences were set aside, as they endured the brutal punishment of long years in prison. But Alabama was forced to yield to mass pressure, and the system of "legal lynching" had been exposed for much of the world to see.

An illustration of what the Scottsboro case did to radicalize some blacks is found in the experience of Hosea Hudson, longtime Communist activist in Birmingham. Hudson recalls reading the headline accounts of the Scottsboro arrests in the *Birmingham News* and of then beginning to buy the newspapers "so my wife could read the paper and see what was going on." In the late twenties he "didn't have any mind about racial issues," although he had always hated injustice, "the way they used to treat Negroes, whip them and mob them up and run them with hounds." But with the onset of the Scottsboro case he was impressed "when these people from all over the world began to talk." Hudson summed up his new perception: "Then I could see some hope." It was no longer simply a matter of depending upon some well-meaning but futile statement of concern from the "better-class white folks."[17]

The attack by New York police on Scottsboro demonstrators was not an isolated incident. In the thirties police on numerous occasions resorted to violence as they sought to quell public protest, especially interracial protest, over acute economic issues. Two Chicago incidents offer particularly striking evidence of police brutality in suppressing demonstrations in which racial and class militancy were combined. Writing of one such episode, occurring in 1930, was Angelo Herndon, a young Communist who had come up to Chicago from Alabama to attend the National Convention of Unemployment Councils. Before the convention opened several thousand demonstrators, black and white, gathered in Union Park. At first authorities had granted permission for the assemblage but, according to Herndon, the police canceled the permit at the last minute, and the police commissioner issued orders that the crowd was to be driven from the park. The crowd was determined, however, to hold the meeting. Herndon described what happened:

A worker then mounted the ladder and began to speak. This furnished the right cue to the police. Sirens began to blow. They almost split our ears with their terrifying shrieks. The cops then formed for the attack and swooped down upon the speaker. They wielded their clubs left and right. The cries of those struck rent the air. The workers stood their ground. With their bare fists they struck back at the attacking police sluggers. Some of the policemen, inflamed by the sight of blood which they spilled, and drunk with a sort of gory pleasure looking at the smashed in skulls and prostrate forms, lost their self-control and emptied their revolvers into the crowd. By deliberate pre-arrangement, Negro cops swung their clubs at the heads of white women workers and white cops tried to bash in the skulls of Negro women. This time, strange as it may seem, when it came to the crushing of workers' skulls, no race prejudice was in evidence.[18]

As seen through Angelo Herndon's eyes, this incident quite clearly taught the conclusion that class issues were fundamental to police violence against both black and white workers.

The roots of an episode of police brutality occurring in 1931 can be found in the position of the Chicago realty interests. A spokesman for the Chicago Realty Board was quoted as stating: "The real estate men are sympathetic with the situation of the unemployed in the colored belt. We are willing to do what we can to help but it is impossible to compromise with what is strictly a business proposition." The "business proposition" referred to evictions of tenants unable to pay rent, and this in a situation where the United Charities of Chicago reported within a six-month period a 311 percent jump in the number of families applying for relief. The business attitude, backed by the position of the municipal courts that the law must be enforced and that the evicted could look only to private charity, conflicted with human need. Violence was the result when South Side blacks, mobilized by Communists, resisted the execution of eviction orders. In *Invisible Man* Ralph Ellison, writing of Harlem, presents a fictional portrayal of what it was like when the will of the police clashed with that of the crowd determined to keep a desperate family in its apartment. In Chicago on August 3, 1931, police killed three blacks in the course of a confrontation with a crowd seeking to put an evicted woman's furniture back in her apartment. The *Chicago Tribune* titled an editorial dealing with this incident "Good Police Work." The *Tribune* observed that the officers who handled the "eviction disturbance" deserved commendation, for they had "met a severe test in a way highly creditable to them and the police department and reassuring to the community."[19]

The aftermath of the Chicago deaths illustrates what was at the heart of the response of left-wingers in the thirties to racial violence. St. Clair Drake and Horace Cayton in their classic study of black Chicago write that Establishment Chicago in the thirties had a new phenomenon to contend with, the spectacle of blacks and whites, marching together, shouting such slogans as "Black and White Unite."[20] Following the police killing of three blacks, the Communist party and the International Labor Defense organized a mass funeral. A writer for the *New Masses* reported the scene: "What a sight! What a demonstration of working class solidarity; 25,000 white workers in a funeral procession joined by 35 to 40,000 Negro workers, with 50,000 more, both white and black on the line of march! Flanked by six Negro and white workers wearing belts of red cloth, and followed by thousands of others holding wreaths and flaming posters, the two vehicles bearing the coffins moved impressively to a railroad depot where the bodies were held for shipment." Something of the new fighting mood that emerged from such events is revealed in the words of one of the marchers, a black woman with a baby in her arms: "C'mon down, brudders and sisters! Yo' ain't losin' nothin'. Yo' ain't got nothin' to lose. I ain't bin able to pay m' rent. They took away ma home. C'mon down. God ain't gonna help yo'. Prayers ain't gonna do yo' no good. If yo' don't come down now, yo' is sho' comin' down later."[21]

The *Chicago Tribune*'s coverage of the August 3 killings reflected several strands of official response to what had occurred. Strident anticommunism was joined to insistence on property rights and denial that race was in any way involved. At the same time it was clear there would have to be at least a temporary suspension of housing evictions. In its first report of the violence the *Tribune* warned of the possibility of "further Red rioting" and noted five conclusions resulting from a hurriedly called meeting of city leaders. (1) There was no antagonism between the races, and the "trouble" was a product of "Red propaganda." (2) Troops were to be held in readiness at Camp Grant in Rockford, to be summoned to Chicago if needed. (3) The municipal court bailiff was to hold up all evictions "for the present." (4) Communist leaders were to be apprehended and questioned. (5) The Chicago corporation counsel was to seek the assistance of the U.S. attorney. Mayor Cermak, vacationing at Mackinac, announced that upon his return he would establish a fund to relieve the distress of the evicted. The newspaper also reported that black community leaders believed that "communist agitators, financed by Moscow, have taken advantage of the widespread unemployment among Negroes in the last few months to win thousands of colored adherents." Communists had been able to "incite" their followers to the point where in hundreds of instances they would refuse to pay rent and resist evictions or actually invite being shot.

Something of the flavor of what was happening in the black community was conveyed in comments made by the Reverend J. C. Austin, pastor of Pilgrim Baptist, reportedly the largest black congregation in the city. Austin said he was powerless to combat inroads the Communists made in his church. "The Reds," the clergyman explained, "get up on their soap boxes in Washington Park, preach all day and up to midnight, lie down and sleep in the open air, and rise up again to preach next morning. I've addressed several of the meetings myself on the subject of 'Christ and Communism,' but you can't talk religion to a man with an empty stomach." There was the implied message in Austin's remarks that Chicago's white leadership had to be more responsive to the urgent, dire need of the black community.

The next day's issue of the *Tribune* carried news that "humane consideration" would be given the homeless and that local charities had pledged assistance. Evictions were to be halted, at least until Mayor Cermak's return to the city. The *Tribune* stated that this action had forestalled further demonstrations. At the same time Judge Frank M. Padden, acting chief judge of the municipal court, announced that "the integrity of the courts must be maintained if law and order are to prevail in our community." Padden declared that anyone interfering with writs of eviction was subject to charges of contempt of court, and he also warned that such persons might be found guilty of conspiracy to obstruct justice. Judge Padden said it had always been the court's policy to delay evictions as long as possible, but defiance of court orders would not be tolerated.

On August 6 the *Tribune* ran a front-page article reporting a meeting at Saint Mark's Church of black clergy and business leaders. Cheers greeted a proposal for a rent moratorium, and one minister told the gathering: "There won't be any eviction problem after another four or five days. The communists are signing up our people by the thousands. They guarantee that, if any member of the party is evicted, the vigilance committee will replace the furniture in his home." City corporation counsel William H. Sexton and bailiff Albert J. Horan also declared that a widespread rent strike was in progress in the black community.

When Mayor Cermak returned to the city he combined condemnation of Communist agitation with expression of sympathy with the plight of the unemployed and homeless. Cermak charged the Communists with seeking to "make mischief," although they were all "well dressed, well fed fellows" who shared an aversion for honest work. But Cermak claimed he did not take this agitation too seriously, and he added: "I have no fear that the working classes of this city will succumb to their fantastic doctrines." Cermak announced he would go to the state legislature for relief, but meanwhile plans were set in motion for deportation of alien Communists. Party headquarters on West Eighteenth Street was raided, and police seized handbills announcing plans for the funeral of two of those killed in the August 3 violence.

The *Tribune* sought to minimize the significance of the funeral procession for Abe Grey and John O'Neal, but the paper acknowledged that a long queue of mourners formed to view the bodies of the slain men and that several thousand persons gathered at the funeral site, Odd Fellows Hall on State Street. The paper further reported that the marchers carried placards bearing such slogans as "Equal Rights" and "Join the Fighting Party of Your Class."[22]

The *Chicago Defender* captioned a photo of the funeral procession as "Reds in Mammoth Parade" and in a news article reported the event as a "huge demonstration" that included many white persons. Editorially, the *Defender* closely linked the events to the terrible conditions afflicting American blacks. Communism, this leading voice of black journalism declared, had no place in America, but American leaders "resist reason and dodge home questions for those far distant." The protest of the black American is spiritual, but "he employs it in communism only because he thinks he can be heard through that medium." And the *Defender* continued: "If the Negro is found where his friends think he should not be, he is there because he was driven there. The Negro is pro-American, but he can think. He was driven out of his government and exiled from his home all because he was Negro and in spite of the fact that he is American. He thinks about that. He has to think about it." The newspaper dissociated itself from the Communists but did not deny that the party had won substantial support in the black community. Above all, the *Defender* sought to utilize the situation to extract some positive response from the white Establishment.[23]

The Communist view of racial violence started from the assumption that violence against Afro-Americans was inseparable from the generally violent nature of capitalism. The analysis was well articulated in a speech made in Harlem during 1935 by the party leader James Ford. Ford, the Communist party's vice-presidential nominee in both 1932 and 1936, told his audience: "American history might easily be described as a story of capitalist violence, directed at all times particularly against the Negroes. Violence, the violent suppression of the exploited workers and poor farmers and of the Negro people, is of the very essence of capitalism." Ford declared that more than 5,000 blacks had been lynched since the Civil War and asked if this was not "the most dastardly act of violence against an oppressed people." What was the revolutionary response to such oppression? In Ford's view it was essential to develop every struggle against specific injustices and acts of oppression but also to connect these specific battles to a general struggle for the overthrow of the system. Quite alive and relevant for Ford was a tradition of black insurrection. White rulers and the black bourgeoisie taught the view that slaves would never dare act for their freedom, that freedom was something handed down from above, that blacks were servile and cowardly and accepted the rule of their masters. Ford charged "the Negro petty bourgeoisie" with consciously seeking to destroy the revolutionary heritage of blacks as part of a process of rationalization, "which quite naturally proceeds to the advocacy of a boot-licking diplomacy for the Negro people." But in actuality, Ford asserted, such "nonsensical theory" ignored the record of Nat Turner, of Gabriel Prosser, of Denmark Vesey "and scores of other Negro revolutionary leaders." It ignored the actions of the Haitians who had overthrown slavery and defended their revolution against veteran European troops.

A strategy of class solidarity was vital to the revolutionary method. The "international solidarity of the working class" was required in order to wage an effective struggle against the common enemy of capitalism. Ford implied that only the class policy advocated by the Communists was capable of overcoming racial terrorism. He argued that the ruling class used race hatred as a means of separating white workers from blacks, but now, "thanks to the leadership of the Communists," white workers were increasingly getting free of "boss-class racial prejudice." He cited as evidence the role of significant numbers of white workers in calling for the freedom of the Scottsboro boys. Class unity, the breaking of white workers with racism and black repudiation of reformist leadership that accommodated to capitalism, was in his view the requirement for a successful fight against terror and all forms of oppression.[24]

The desperately impoverished conditions of the rural South during the thirties provided a constant flow of news items concerning new manifestations of racial violence. Extreme anger and frustration were the result of crop prices that fell far below costs of production, of evictions that pushed both white and black farmers from the land, of hunger and malnutrition that brought diseases and death to many of the rural poor. At least in its early stages the economic programs of the New Deal brought benefits to the more affluent white landowner but also gave incentive for dispensing altogether with the services of tenant farmers and sharecrop-

pers. Spurred by mechanization, the concentration of landholding proceeded apace in the thirties, and with that came a sharper than ever
polarization of rich and poor. When those committed to racial subordination saw the possibility of blacks and whites coming together for
common purposes, their response most often was to reach for the gun
and the rope.

In the Scottsboro case it had been possible to prevent a "legal" lynching,
but in the first five years of the 1930s the lynchers of the South proceeded
on their way, most often still not having to heed public protest. The
resurgence of lynch law that started with 1930 continued. A report issued
by the Commission on Interracial Cooperation in Atlanta summarized
the situation with regard to the five years 1931 through 1935. The basic
point was that lynching was not going away by itself; "the optimism of
ten years ago is waning; lynchings are not fading naturally from the
American scene; the mob still rides." The commission was succinct in
itemizing the elements of a typical lynching: "The typical lynching is in
the rural South, the mob victim is a Negro, the lynchers are native-born
whites, and the courts punish no one. Though some lynchings occur
outside the South, and some victims are white, lynching is increasingly
a Southern and a racial phenomenon." There had been eighty-four lynchings during the five years, and of these seventy-two were in the South.
All but nine of the victims were blacks. The commission concluded from
the facts that a larger percentage of lynchings than ever occurred in the
South and that a larger percentage involved blacks.[25] It was clear that
among the regions of the United States the South was most obdurate in
resisting movement to eliminate lynching.

An awareness of the possibility of lynching was a part of the black
consciousness in the South. The novelist Maya Angelou left her home-
town of Stamps, Arkansas, by the time she was thirteen, but already in
her memory was the recollection of when Mr. Steward, the "used-to-be"
sheriff, rode up to warn of a possible lynch threat. "A crazy nigger messed
with a white lady today," he said. "Some of the boys'll be coming over
here later." Angelou later wrote of her feelings at the time: "Even after
the slow drag of years, I remember the sense of fear which filled my
mouth with hot, dry air, and made my body light." A part of her memory
also was what she had heard about a particular lynching: "we found out
about a man who had been killed by whitefolks and thrown into the
pond...the man's things had been cut off and put in his pocket and he
had been shot in the head, all because the whitefolks said he did 'it' to
a white woman."[26]

During the 1930s sociologist Charles S. Johnson studied the life patterns of black youth in the rural South. An eighteen-year-old black told Johnson his perception of lynching's reality: "Lynchings often happen. They are different to what they used to be, though. They used to be big mobs hunting for a nigger, but now you just hear about some nigger found hanging off a bridge." The youth recalled seeing a party of some thirty to forty white riders pass his home, armed with guns and pistols. If a black should "run up on 'em" at night he was likely to be killed, if only for "sport." The youth also told Johnson of an incident in which a three-year-old black boy had pulled up the underpants of a four-year-old white girl. A white man saw this happening "and grabbed up the little boy and castrated him." The man then, according to Johnson's informant, threw the black boy into a lake. The youth reported that generally blacks and whites "often get into it and kill each other," and it was therefore understandable that he had little to do with white people. Violence was part of a pattern of barriers that Johnson saw as having a paralyzing effect on rural black youth.[27]

Anthropologist Hortense Powdermaker in her book *After Freedom*, a study of a Mississippi community in the 1930s, portrays the impact of lynching or the threat of lynching upon blacks in the area. The black consciousness was shaped by memory but also by contemporary experience. Powdermaker generalized that by the age of puberty white people knew "that the Negro is cut out to be a victim, that the Negro cannot exact justice if he is wronged and dare not wreak revenge for himself." Blacks in the fictitious town of Cottonville (actually Indianola) told Powdermaker of an earlier incident in which the black janitor of a white school was lynched because he had reported some of the pupils to the school's principal for having thrown stones that might break windows. The principal had punished the students who in turn went home and told their parents, blaming the janitor for the principal's action. That night a mob formed and proceeded to hang the janitor. A more recent episode was one in which a black teenager had a fight with a white youth of approximately the same age, and the white boy took his revenge by spreading a rumor that the black had claimed he would have intercourse with the white boy's sister. A threatening crowd had begun to form, and violence was prevented only when the white boy's father intervened, saying he did not believe the story. There was in this event the point that the life of the guiltless black depended upon the intercession of a fair-minded white man.

There was also the occurrence of a threatened lynching while Powdermaker was at work on the study. The local paper reported an incident in which, supposedly, two blacks fatally stabbed a white man in the course of an attempted rape of a white woman. The paper's treatment of the case was hardly calculated to discourage mob action. There was the comment that the swiftest penalty that could be given the alleged rapists "will be entirely too slow for the temper of the people at present." Added to this was the observation: "We do not think the county jail has any room at present for such criminals, but we feel certain that the splendid citizens ... will properly place them should they get hold of them." The press comment was a clue to the mindset of "respectable" white opinion in the community. Powdermaker outlined the shifting moods within the white community regarding the prospect of a lynching:

> On the day after the attack, a group of these shabby men, their eyes burning, tramped up and down the road and through the woods, mingling their oaths with the barking of their dogs. The middle-class white men sitting in their offices or homes remarked that of course they did not approve of lynching, but that undoubtedly these Negroes would be lynched, and "what can you do when you have to deal with the primitive African type, the killer?" The Negroes in the neighborhood sat at home all day, afraid to go out. Those in a town thirty miles distant said that things must be getting better because a few years ago, if the mob had not found the men they wanted by this time, they would have lynched someone else.
>
> The town in which the murder had been committed was quiet. The Negroes had escaped into another state. Nobody knew where they were. At last the mob broke up; the dogs were quiet. A few of the middle-class whites murmured that perhaps the Negroes were after the man and not the girl; that maybe there was some real ground for their grudge against him. These were a few almost inaudible whispers. Most of the people said nothing. The eyes of the shabby men no longer gleamed with excitement. They had gone back to the dull routine of the sharecropper. The middle class sat back and reaffirmed that they did not believe in lynching.

Powdermaker added that a few members of the middle class openly condoned lynching.

Powdermaker offers a context within which lynching is more clearly understood, a context of black people being viewed as outside the law. She writes: "The attitude of the whites and of the courts which they control is one of complaisance toward violence among the Negroes, and even toward intra-Negro homicide." Two standards of justice existed. "When a white man kills a Negro, it is hardly considered murder,"

Powdermaker wrote. "When a Negro kills a white man, conviction is insured, provided the case is not settled immediately by lynch law." The operations of the law, she explained, encouraged blacks to violent acts against other blacks, because the black person "can hope for no justice and no defense from our legal institutions" and therefore must settle his own difficulties, "and often he knows only one way." Powdermaker viewed racial violence, including lynching, from the perspective that such brutality had systemic roots. She recognized that the poor white manifested violent expressions of race antagonism but stressed that this poor white "acts for those whites who tacitly condone and overtly deplore such behavior."

Lynching, as it functioned during the 1930s and as it always functioned, was a mechanism for the general instilling of fear within the black population. Powdermaker noted an "always latent terror of lynching" that was the basis for the often expressed fear of being mobbed, a fear that provided incentive for the controlling of temper. The terror always existed because although the actual lynchings might number, according to Powdermaker, comparatively few "the atmosphere which permits them, and to which they in turn contribute, is constant." Black women feared for their own lives, and also they feared for their men. Powdermaker summarized still existing Mississippi reality of the 1930s: "No Negro man is safe, and every Negro knows it." The black person might cope with this by trying to avoid giving offense or by trying not to think of the danger. "Most of them do both," Powdermaker commented. There was of course the third alternative of recourse to some form of self-defense, and Powdermaker did report her encounter with a young black college graduate who declared that if he had a son he would teach him to handle every sort of gun "and he himself would give him the guns. His son would know how to kill white people and to defend himself."[28]

In *Children of Bondage*, John Dollard and Allison Davis give considerable emphasis to the role of racial violence in shaping the personality development of black youth in the Deep South in the late thirties. Their study, based largely on interviews of blacks in Natchez and New Orleans, centers around the concept of caste and the downward pressure a caste society exerts upon black youth of all classes. One of the findings emerging from the study is that lower-class black youth were more likely to resist white physical aggression than was the case with youth of middle-class and upper-class position.

The threat of violence and the pressure of caste sanctions were felt particularly keenly by blacks in Natchez, a small city set in a plantation area. Dollard and Davis report the response of a black youth to the society in which he found himself: "He yields because he must; a Negro in Natchez cannot rebel against the caste restrictions without endangering his life." The thirty-eight youths interviewed in Natchez "showed a deep and immediate fear of punishment and attack by whites," and one of the interviewees told of an organized group of white men who sought to take by violence industrial jobs held by black men. Reportedly, six of the black workers were killed by a hired gang. The youth, "Martin," learned from this experience that "the subordinate position of Negroes was enforced not only by social and economic punishment, but ultimately by physical force." Martin recalled the experience: "I bet one thing, if they had been colored men killing white men, they would have found out who did it. The laws and things don't care a single bit about colored people."

Physical assault against blacks was also a feature of the social order in New Orleans. Dollard and Davis point out that a large number of such incidents are not needed in order to intimidate the population. In any event, five blacks were killed by policemen in New Orleans between 1936 and 1938, and three of those were killed while in jail awaiting trial. During October 1938 New Orleans radio stations and newspapers carried accounts of an impending lynching at the Louisiana town of Ruston. A mob of some 1,500 whites was hunting for a black who had allegedly killed a white man and assaulted a white woman. A black man, W. C. Williams, was captured and lynched by the mob, and although a grand jury heard witnesses no indictments were returned. Dollard and Davis report that the "white conservative newspaper" in New Orleans considered this lynching episode of little news value. Both at Ruston and at New Orleans the point was made that the lawless taking of black life was a matter of little consequence.[29]

Allison Davis, recalling the period from 1932 to 1935 when he interviewed both landlords and tenants in two Mississippi counties, has sharply etched for us the terror to which blacks were subjected. Davis notes that "black tenants were intimidated by the occasional whipping and shooting of their fellow blacks." Violence was meant to insure a deference to the landlord. Whippings, as Davis writes, "helped oil the system." One landlord told Davis of how he had instructed his sons to shoot or hang disrespectful black tenants. Another planter acknowledged he had beaten a tenant, not for anything specific but because he had "that insolent kind of manner about him." The wife of a planter stated that whipping was the best means of social control. A tenant was told that if he did not turn over his government subsidy check his throat would be cut. Davis adds that this system of terrorization "reached extremes of inhumanity in the whipping and beating of black women." Old women and pregnant women were among those brutalized by planters.[30]

Lynchings sometimes occurred during this period despite the efforts of such militant organizations as the International Labor Defense to prevent them. Indeed, in a number of instances the presence of the ILD intensified the fury. A case in point was the lynching during 1933 of two blacks in Tuscaloosa, Alabama. The town was the seat of the University of Alabama, but Carl Carmer, who taught at the university in the late 1920s, noted that the school's civilizing influence did not make Tuscaloosa an exception to Alabama's "general attitude." A basic reality was that differences of opinion were normally settled by physical conflict. Carmer found that Tuscaloosa culture was "generally rather a tradition than an actuality." He observed firsthand an aspect of present reality in the massing of hundreds at a Klan rally and cross burning where the speaker warned that the pope was "goin' to give Alabama over to be ruled by a nigger cardinal!"

In 1933 three black men, Dan Pippen, A. T. Harden, and Elmore Clark, had been arrested and indicted for the slaying of a white woman, Vaudine Maddox, a sharecropper's daughter. On August 1 the proceedings began, and in the courtroom were three attorneys retained by the ILD to defend the accused. Inside the courtroom the judge ruled that the lawyers lacked jurisdiction in the case, and outside the court, according to a Tuscaloosa resident, several hundred whites could be seen "to mumble to each other about those Communists from the North." The judge sent national guardsmen to escort the lawyers to the train, but as for the defendants he told newsmen: "There is no feeling against the Negroes here, and the guards were not needed to protect the defendants." The ILD attorneys reached Birmingham safely, although at Bessemer, twelve miles from Birmingham, the train was temporarily held up by a crowd of 100 whites who shouted, "Get 'em off the train." In New York the national secretary of the ILD, William Patterson, sent a telegram to the Tuscaloosa judge, Henry B. Foster, demanding that ILD counsel be permitted to defend the three blacks and expressing the intention to expose "your illegal lynch maneuvers" as counterparts of the Scottsboro case. Meanwhile, Judge Foster continued the trial to the next term of court.

The trial was never held. On August 13 Sheriff R. L. Shamblin and several deputies placed the prisoners in a car and drove away from Tuscaloosa, supposedly for the purpose of taking the three men to Birmingham, where they would be safe from lynchers. The prisoners did not reach Birmingham, however, and the facts of the situation suggest police complicity. The sheriff and two deputies rode with the prisoners in one car, followed by another car with additional deputies. The police chose to begin this journey about midnight and selected an unfrequented road as the route to Birmingham. Twenty miles from Tuscaloosa the second car turned back, and shortly thereafter two autos with armed men closed in on the sheriff's car and demanded the prisoners. The sheriff complied, and some hours later the bodies of Dan Pippen and A. T. Harden were found shot to death. Elmore Clark, left for dead, had only been wounded and, after being found and returned to jail, signed a statement that he had not seen the lynchers.

At Montgomery, Alabama governor B. M. Miller denounced the lynchings as a "heinous crime" and ordered an immediate grand jury investigation. But the grand jury, once constituted, produced no indictments, and much of the local reaction to the lynchings was cast in terms of shifting the blame to the ILD. The sheriff was quoted as declaring that the ILD was "directly responsible" for the lynching, and the *Tuscaloosa News* blamed the events on the ILD's "spreading their poisoned communistic propaganda among our contented Negro population." The *Montgomery Advertiser* explained that the two victims had been killed by "hotheads" who feared outsiders would interfere with the execution of justice. But the main responsibility for the killings lay elsewhere: "the maggoty beaks of the belled buzzards of the International Labor Defense are stained with the blood of the three Negroes." Even a liberal resident of Tuscaloosa, who clearly disapproved of lynching, expressed the opinion that the lynchings would not have taken place "had it not been for the resentment directly created by the three Communist lawyers who deliberately irritated a disturbed situation by their offensive presence." According to this observer the officials in the case would have punished the offenders if they could have obtained the necessary evidence. It was his firm opinion that Tuscaloosa's "best people" wished to uphold justice.

The presence of the International Labor Defense in Tuscaloosa doubtless aroused hatred, but the evidence does not support the conclusion that the lynching resulted from ILD efforts to participate in this case or that lynching would have been averted if the three leftist lawyers had never appeared. After all, the lynchings occurred twelve days after the defendants' families, under local pressure, had disavowed ILD involvement. Hundreds of blacks over the years had been lynched in such cases, even when radicals of any description were nowhere in sight. If anything, this Tuscaloosa incident suggests that retreating before the "red-smear" tactics of racists was counterproductive. The lynchings occurred not when the ILD lawyers were on the scene but only after they had been severed from the case and the prisoners at least temporarily cut off from a national organization interested in their defense. The lynching was fostered not by ILD militancy but by the condition of isolation in which Pippen, Harden, and Clark found themselves.

ILD officials in New York viewed this case in the context of rising class tensions. A statement released following the lynchings declared that the case was part of a "program of terror" against Tuscaloosa blacks, who had been bearing "the full weight of the losses of the cotton plow-under program" and whose resentment against landlord robbery was rising.[31] The statement made the connection between the Tuscaloosa violence and the consequences of the New Deal farm policies, which sought to restore farm prices by sharply cutting production.

The Camp Hill incident of 1931 highlights the factors operating to generate racial violence in the rural South during the thirties. What occurred was the result of efforts to form something truly revolutionary in the South, a sharecroppers' union. In 1931 Communist organizers worked to build a "Society for the Advancement of Colored People" that in fact would be a union. Much of the activity was centered in Tallapoosa County in central Alabama. Race relations in Tallapoosa may have been better than the average for Black Belt counties, as one historian has recently noted, and the economic deprivation may not have been as severe as in some other locations in rural Alabama, but such conclusions have little meaning.[32] Tallapoosa, a county in which per capita expenditure for white education came to twenty-five dollars annually and the allocation for blacks even less, shared the conditions of economic and racial oppression that marked the Black Belt.

Collective bargaining was what the Sharecroppers' Union wanted, bargaining that would enable the sharecroppers to resolve specific grievances. The issues put forward by the union expressed the sharecroppers' need for some basic economic protection and for some minimum protection of their rights. Demands included food advances by landlords until the making of crop settlements, full settlement of accounts in cash, the right to sell a crop when and to whom the croppers wanted, and the right to cultivate gardens for home use. Two dollars a day was demanded as a minimum wage.[33]

In Ned Cobb's autobiographical narrative, recorded by Theodore Rosengarten, one captures the flavor of the agitation carried on by the union organizers. To begin with, Cobb refers to the black organizer assigned to work in his district as the "teacher," and as Cobb described him the organizer did more than attend to the practical matters of organization. He had a message to communicate, that of the need for struggle to bring about a better future, and disseminating that message was central to the

organizer's work. This organizer—Cobb did not remember his name—
moved through the countryside, holding small meetings and distributing
literature about the union. In a situation in which exposure could lead
to death both for himself and for those he organized, the organizer
worked discreetly, urging secrecy on the persons he met with. According
to Cobb the meetings were held "at our houses or anywhere we could
have em where we could keep a look and a watch-out that nobody was
comin in on us." In the South of the Black Belt the very act of holding
a meeting was itself very risky, and Cobb candidly recalled: "niggers was
scared, niggers was scared, that's tellin the truth." Organization of any
kind that was separate from the church, and certainly secret organization
for purposes of protest, was anathema in the eyes of the dominant property owners. The teacher told Cobb and others attending the meetings
that if any one turned informer such person was to be done away with.

The union's message was clear, with the prime ingredient being the
right of the sharecroppers to have a union. Cobb summed up what the
union had to say:

> I heard this spoke by the officials, the people that was advertisin this
> union; they was tired of the rich man gettin richer and the poor man
> gettin poorer. They seed it was a freeze-out. . . . The first teacher
> attracted the attention of several of us by his talkin about the future
> comin. He told us, and we agreed, the future days follows the present.
> And if we didn't do something for ourselves today, tomorrow
> wouldn't be no different. . . . Well we was taught at our meetins that
> when trouble comes, stand up for one another. Whatever we was
> goin to do, whatever that was, we was goin to do it together.[34]

As Rosengarten found him, Ned Cobb was a classic storyteller but also
something more. He was an "impoverished, militant black man, im-
movable in his political conviction and confident he is transmitting history." His mind reached beyond folklore and assimilated a class
perspective shaped by experience with whites who supported the black
struggle. Rosengarten reported that Cobb furnished evidence, which
could not be located elsewhere, that "some whites aided blacks on the
run and others risked their lives to protect black neighbors from vigilantes." Rosengarten believed that as Ned Cobb recalled his life one
central theme emerged and that Cobb must have realized it: "figure out
the enemy, stand up with a clear conscience and you can win."[35]

The tension inherent in this labor struggle came to the surface near
the village of Camp Hill, Alabama, a community of 900 persons, with

three white and two black churches. Some of the white residents told a reporter that nothing much really happened there: "No, we didn't have any trouble here. Just some damn niggers got smart and we had to shoot a few to teach them their place." In reality, what happened was a confrontation between the sharecroppers and county officers bent on smashing the union. One of the town loungers interpreted the episode in terms of "damn Yankees and Communists" coming down from Chicago or New York to get money from the local blacks, but the town marshal offered the more sophisticated analysis that the Communists wanted to put their principles into practice, "to take people's property away from them and divide it up."[36]

There is little doubt but that the violence was triggered by the sheriff's provocative behavior. The reporter for the New Republic was told by several white persons that the sheriff, Kyle Young, having heard about meetings of the union, set out to break them up.[37] On July 15 the sheriff and his deputies broke up a small meeting of sharecroppers near Camp Hill. The following day the sheriff learned that a larger meeting was in progress at the Mary Church, also near Camp Hill, and accompanied by two deputies he set out to break up that meeting as well. Quite near the church they encountered a black man, Ralph Gray, carrying a bundle under one arm and a shotgun under the other. The sheriff reached back for his own gun, but Gray fired first and wounded Sheriff Young and one of the deputies, Gray also being wounded in the exchange of shots. The sheriff and the deputies hastily retreated to town where very quickly a mob formed, bent on punishing the black who had dared to resist.

The incident near the church triggered the southern phenomenon in which any individual act of black resistance to oppression and intimidation became transformed into a mass assault upon the black community as a whole. Terror broke loose in Tallapoosa County. A posse of some 500 men roamed through the area searching for Gray and others involved in the sharecroppers' union. That evening they learned that Gray had returned to his cabin, and surrounding the place members of the posse fired as many as a thousand shots into the building. It is not clear if Gray and several other persons in the cabin with him also fired although the town marshal, Wilson, was quoted by the Birmingham Age-Herald as stating that the blacks in the cabin had begun the shooting. In any event, when the shooting stopped and the posse entered the cabin they found Gray dead and the other blacks alive, perhaps because they had sought protection behind an iron stove. Only one fatality, the death of Ralph Gray, was verified, although an investigator for the Fellowship of Reconciliation reported that several other blacks had died from wounds inflicted in the shootings. Regarding several missing blacks, Marshal Wilson was quoted as having said they "had gone to cut wood, and had a lot of wood to cut."[38]

The killing of Gray and the imprisonment of others found with him did not promptly bring an end to hysteria in Tallapoosa County. Gray's body was taken to the piazza of the courthouse at the county seat, Dadeville, where many came to look. The *Birmingham Age-Herald* had headlined the episode of July 15–16 as "Race War," and hundreds of armed men continued to roam through the county. Many blacks took the precaution of staying away from their homes, and rumors abounded as to possible violence, the coming of bands of Communists from Chattanooga, or the arrival of groups of blacks from nearby Alexander City who would free the prisoners. The rumors were all false, and after a few days life returned to what could be termed normal. What was not rumor was that at least one of the sharecroppers had died and probably several more and that sixty blacks had been arrested, five charged with assault with intent to commit murder, seven with carrying concealed weapons, and twenty with conspiring to commit a felony. In the hysteria of the moment little consideration was given to the grievances at the root of the sharecroppers' militancy, to the effects of a decade-long agricultural depression climaxing in six-cent cotton.[39]

Various individuals and organizations saw the Camp Hill incident according to their own perspectives. The black Communist leader Harry Haywood wrote in 1933 of the "heroic resistance" of the Camp Hill sharecroppers, and he offered the evaluation that the union was the "first genuine revolutionary organization among the Negro poor farmers."[40] The magazine of the Urban League separated the incident from the question of communism. It acknowledged that Communists had stimulated the organization of the sharecroppers but emphasized that all the propaganda efforts "which the Communists might employ in a century of agitation" would not have amounted to anything if conditions had not impelled the Alabama blacks to act. The magazine rhetorically asked what black tenant farmers in Alabama knew of Marxian philosophy, and it gave a succinct answer: "Nothing." *Opportunity* further declared, "The threat of Communism among black tenant farmers in the South will not disappear through repression and force for on these it feeds and grows." Communist influence would diminish as "the enlightened South" made efforts to alleviate oppressive conditions. As to the police who broke up meetings of the sharecroppers' union, the magazine observed that "they were guilty of a flagrant violation of one of the basic guarantees of American Democracy." The Camp Hill episode posed an issue that went beyond class partisanship, and *Opportunity* sought to make the point in noting that the right of peaceable assembly "is so fundamental that its abrogation anywhere must be abhorrent to every right thinking individual."[41] Presenting the incident in this light would raise a meaningful issue for some of the Urban League's middle-class, liberal supporters.

The *Chicago Defender* quickly reported news of the Camp Hill violence. The newspaper gives this account of the terror that followed the incident at the church: "For three days mobs of whites patrolled the woods taking shots at every person they saw moving among the trees, and threatening to lynch any person who crossed their paths. . . . The first thing the whites did after the shooting at the church was to set fire to the structure and burn it to the ground as hundreds milled about and shouted threats at all men and women whose faces were not black." Editorially, the *Defender* took sharp issue with press accounts in the North that saw the issue of social equality as the source of the Tallapoosa violence. Ralph Gray had attempted "to organize his kinsmen on the doctrine of industrial freedom," and the *Defender* asserted that more than ever blacks in Alabama would "now meet . . . to discuss other matters than heaven." And the purpose in mind "won't be to take white women in marriage or have them out of it." As to the question of communism, the editorial was blunt: "The Negro in Alabama may turn communist. We think not, although it is in the blood of man to be something in the state. He can't be a Democrat and is afraid to be Republican and the Pops died out. . . . Whatever he is in Alabama, he has no vote and can have no voice, except in protest by motion or petition. If a Negro turn communist in Alabama, or in Massachusetts, he is driven to his new allegiance by a despair he can hardly longer control."[42]

The *Pittsburgh Courier*'s report of the Camp Hill incident outlined the demands raised by the sharecroppers and noted that the Scottsboro case and "the starvation wage and miserable working conditions" of the croppers shaped the events. The newspaper affirmed the right to organize for the improvement of conditions but also observed that whites "will interpret any organization among Negroes which implies force, even that of collective bargaining, as a threat against whites." Regarding the violence that occurred, the *Courier* stated that whites had been the aggressors. The reporter, John Henry Calhoun, writing from Montgomery, also considered the role of the Communists and concluded that "the better-class Negro" sought not to become involved, but what the mass of blacks would do was less clear. "The oppressed mass Negro," Calhoun wrote, "is anxiously wondering if there may be a chance for him in what is happening. The whites have their eyes on this mass Negro. If he turns his back on the enticing, militant Communist, all will be well. If instead, he determines to follow the Communist on a large scale, the trouble in this section has only begun. From here it may spread throughout the South." Calhoun recognized the wider implications of Camp Hill.

Editorially, the *Courier* commented that it was quite natural that southern blacks would pay attention to any group, including the Communists, that offered relief from economic distress. The basic issue was the oppression imposed on black people in America, and the editorial reflected the sense of urgency gripping blacks:

> The Negroes of the South are just like Negroes of the North, and the Negroes of the North are just like people anywhere else in the world: They do not believe that a real man, serving his country and its flag, has any business submitting forever to insults and oppression without protest.... Negroes are absolutely sick and tired of being kicked around, North and South, and if the Communists succeed in organizing Negroes into a disorderly mob, our good friends will be more responsible than the Negroes. If a meeting is orderly it is wrong to raid the meeting; and if shooting occurs that is simply another wrong.[43]

The Camp Hill incident did not destroy the Sharecroppers' Union. In 1932 organizers returned to the area in which they had worked the previous year, and again blacks, mired in the same oppressive conditions, responded favorably. Also as in 1931, the Tallapoosa County sheriff, no doubt remembering his wounds, determined that the union would be suppressed. The confrontation reached its climax at a place in the community of Reeltown. An account of this episode, with the names changed, is one of the high points of Theodore Rosengarten's *All God's Dangers*. A detailed account of the affair is also found in an article published in 1934 by scholar-organizer-poet John Beecher.[44] Up to a point the accounts largely agree. The police had been interested in discovering who was the key leader of the sharecroppers' movement, and finally they determined it was a farmer, Cliff James. In the Rosengarten account Ned Cobb states that James "was rentin his farm," whereas according to Beecher, James had indeed bought the place in 1924, but the ownership had little meaning as James still owed the entire principal plus a considerable sum advanced him for furnishings. Beecher describes James as "a tenant in all but name" but also stressed that James had paid interest on his property until Depression conditions made that impossible and that he had accumulated a substantial amount of livestock—two mules, two cows, two calves, and a heifer.

When James first came to the attention of the police his home was raided and radical literature found. Then, on December 19, 1932, Deputy Sheriff Elder came to James's farm to seize the livestock in lieu of payment on debts. Elder came accompanied by two black boys whose job it would be to ride the mules back to town. Cobb later commented about one of the boys: "That was a colored fellow had no sense; white folks could get him to do anything they wanted him to do." Beecher refers to the deputy's having reported that James told him, "You nor Sheriff Young and all his deputies is gonna get them mules." Cobb's recollection does not include these words by James but does include Cobb's saying to Elder, "Well, if you take it, I'll be damned if you don't take it over my dead body." In both the recollection of Cobb and Beecher's account Elder said that the sheriff would come and kill all of the blacks present. As Cobb remembered it the deputy had said that Sheriff Young would come down "and kill the last damn one of you."

The deputy, backed by three reinforcements, returned within a few hours. What happened next is subject to some dispute. According to Beecher, apparently depending upon articles in the Birmingham newspapers, a number of armed blacks had gathered at the James house. The officers called out James and Cobb, and almost immediately one of the white men shot Cobb in the hip. Cobb and James thereupon ran, the officer opened fire on the house, and the fire was returned by the blacks within. In the shooting every one of the officers was wounded. One black man, John McMullen, was killed in the exchange and several blacks were wounded.

As Cobb remembered it, the blacks assembled at James's house and scattered at the approach of the car with reinforced police. Cobb was left alone to meet the officers, was shot, and somehow got inside the house from which vantage point, using his Smith and Wesson revolver, he held off the whites. Finally the whites, possibly fearful that a number of armed blacks were still inside the building, retreated from the place.

There is disagreement then as to whether the whites were forced to retreat by the actions of a group shooting from within the James home or by Ned Cobb's individual stand. The accounts of events subsequent to the shoot-out pretty well coincide. A white mob quickly formed, a substantial number of whites apparently coming from other counties. The posses, numbering more than 500 men under the direction of the sheriffs from four counties, went through the area searching for people who had been involved in the sharecroppers' union. The homes of many blacks were searched and arms confiscated. Blacks took to sleeping in the woods or went to backwoods houses not likely to be reached by the mobs. Twelve blacks, including Ned Cobb, were arrested and jailed. On December 21 the posses were ordered disbanded.

Both Ned Cobb and Cliff James were arrested after they sought medical assistance at nearby Tuskegee Institute. In Cobb's case his wife and son brought him to the Tuskegee hospital where the doctors treated his wounds and asked questions as to how he had been shot. Cobb recalls giving them imprecise answers, but still they would not keep him at the hospital. As he recalls the incident: "So they treated me—they had to treat me—but they wouldn't keep me there that night, a man of their own color. Scared the white folks would come after me and fine me there and maybe tear the place up or accuse em of helpin me. It was their duty to doctor me and they did, they did, but they wouldn't keep me. They didn't tell me where to go, they didn't tell me where not to go, just leave that hospital that night. So I left. I couldn't stay there without authority." Cobb was fortunate the hospital did not call the police, but the incident of course points out the continuity between the Washington policy of accommodation and current practice at Tuskegee during the 1930s. Cobb left the hospital and was arrested sometime later.

Tuskegee took more initiative when Cliff James arrived to seek medical treatment. He had made his way seventeen miles through the countryside to the hospital where he was admitted and given first-aid treatment. Also, however, a student was dispatched to get the sheriff of Macon County. Tuskegee probably would have incurred serious risk if it sheltered James, but as Beecher observed, "it was hardly necessary for the Negro physician to curry favor by repeating damaging remarks he alleged James made to him, that 'he would have been fighting yet if his crowd hadn't run out on him' and that 'he was sorry he didn't kill any of the officers.' "

Two of the arrested blacks wounded in the affair, Cliff James and Milo Bentley, died while held in jail pending a trial. The ILD charged authorities with criminal negligence for failing to provide medical care. Bentley died two hours after being taken from his jail cell to the hospital at Kilby State Prison. Bentley is clearly the "Waldo Ramsey" of *All God's Dangers,* Ned Cobb's brother-in-law who bravely came to aid the wounded Cobb, hiding in a cabin in Macon County. The police later reported that upon their arrival at the cabin Bentley came out the back door firing as rapidly as he could reload. The two bodies were taken to Birmingham where for a week they lay in state at the Jordan Funeral Home. The ILD called upon people to view the bodies and stressed the public significance of the funeral. The community was told: "Come out in mass for the funeral. They died fighting for the rights of the poor people, and against race oppression. They were leaders of the Share Croppers and were willing to give their lives in the struggle for bread and freedom." According to Beecher a great crowd, including many whites, attended the funeral.[45]

Ned Cobb does not seem to have remembered much concerning the details of the trial of himself and other activists in the union. Other evidence, however, indicates that many sharecroppers attended the trial despite efforts by county officials to block the main roads leading to town so as to discourage black attendance. What Cobb did remember, however, points up a striking aspect of the white-supremacist response to the entire episode. When he was questioned on the stand the prosecutor was not interested in any relation between the union struggle and the shooting. Cobb put his finger on the operative mentality here in observing that "they didn't want to consider that *their* niggers would have anything to do with a union." The official view of things was that the case was just "a matter of a nigger done got into trouble trying to destroy their way of life."[46] The defendants were convicted and given jail terms ranging from five to fifteen years. Ned Cobb was given a twelve-to-fifteen-year term in the state penitentiary.

One Alabama newspaper took a somewhat objective view of what happened and at least had the minimal good sense to realize that the struggle at Reeltown was part of a national pattern of farmer discontent. Farmers in many parts of the country had resisted sheriffs and marshals who were trying to seize their land or other property in payment of debts. The *Birmingham Post*, entitling its editorial "Not a Race War," declared:

> It would be exceedingly superficial to regard the disturbance between negro farmers and sheriffs deputies at Reeltown as a "race riot." The relative small extent to which race prejudice factored in the affair is one of the things that impressed newspaper reporters most deeply. The cause of the trouble was essentially economic rather than racial. The resistance of the negroes at Reeltown against officers seeking to attach their livestock on a lien bears a close parallel to battles fought in Iowa and Wisconsin between farmers and sheriffs deputies seeking to serve eviction papers.

The *Post* also noted that "a good many farmers" sympathized with "the negroes' desperate plight" although they disapproved of resistance to law. The *Post* was not, of course, entirely accurate in separating the incident from its racial context. The brutal treatment of the black pris-

oners, the obvious lack of equal rights in the courtroom, the fact that
police did not see Alabama blacks as citizens with rights to be respected,
the general tendency of white authority to view any challenge of a white
man's word as "uppity" behavior, all supported the conclusion that what
took place at Reeltown, like what took place the year before at Camp
Hill, was a struggle against both class and racial oppression.

Other Alabama newspapers had little interest in any sober evaluation
of the events. The *Birmingham News* carried an article correctly judged
by Beecher as "verging on deliberate mob-incitation." The point of the
article was that the proper work of law enforcement officials was ham-
pered by having to adhere to constitutional scruples. The *Post* explained
that the constitutional guarantee of free speech and assembly was "the
Communist vehicle." The paper described the ideas advocated at union
meetings as including the "elimination of racial and social lines and a
banding together of the workers to take what they want." The article
also happened to mention that Communist party and ILD headquarters
in Birmingham were located in the Martin building, and that same night
"unknown persons" gagged the elevator operator at the building, ransacked the office, and carried away files.[47] No arrests were made of
anyone involved in this burglary.

John Beecher made the contemporary judgment that the Communist
organizing efforts, reflected in the Sharecroppers' Union, had disastrous
practical consequences and that the rhetoric of Communist agitation
made it very easy to cover up the organization's nonracial, economic
significance and to intensify race hatred in Alabama. But Beecher also
notes that the Alabama press possibly would have portrayed the movement in terms of race war in any case and, indeed, in the context of the
South this almost surely would have happened. The problem was that
in the prevailing conditions union organization required the involvement
of a national movement with some resources and the bringing in of
organizers from outside the local area. Such middle-class organizations
as the NAACP or the Urban League were not about to undertake the
organization of Sharecroppers into a Union. Whatever radical group did
move into the situation, whether Communist or Socialist, was bound to
be smeared, and racism would be used as a weapon against any organization that was not manifestly racist. Suffering resulted from the efforts
of the Sharecroppers' Union, but the alternative was no organization at
all. Quite apart from the circumstance that the threat of union organization may have won for some of the sharecroppers the right to cultivate
gardens and the continuation of food allocations during the slack season,
the struggle left a legacy of black resistance and militancy. Beecher put

it well; the sharecroppers' movement "indicates the presence of a will to organize and a tenacity hardly short of heroic on the part of the impoverished Negro tenants." Five years after Reeltown a writer in the *Crisis* stated that the sharecroppers' union and the battles at Camp Hill and Reeltown "will never be forgotten." In the writer's view the sharecroppers' union was part of a continuum, including the Socialist-sponsored Southern Tenant Farmers' Union and the Farmers' Union that had organized tens of thousands of tenants and sharecroppers across the South.[48]

The Sharecroppers' Union may have brought death and jail terms, but some black sharecroppers, even after Camp Hill and Reeltown, persisted in supporting the union. Writing in 1934 John Beecher noted that the union had not died out. In the fall of 1933, according to the Communist newspaper *Southern Worker,* membership in the union had increased to some 5,500. As late as 1935 organizers of the union continued activity in the Black Belt areas of Alabama.[49]

Something of the continuing militancy that marked the Sharecroppers' Union is reflected in a public appeal by union secretary Albert Jackson. *New Masses* readers were told of the murder of union activist Joe Spinner Johnson, who had been seized by a landlord vigilante gang and taken to the Dallas County jail at Selma. A few days later Johnson's body was found in a field near Greensboro. Jackson declared: "In spite of the murder and terror raging in Alabama the Share Croppers Union is forging ahead faster than ever." Outlining a series of demands that included the arrest of local officials implicated in Johnson's murder, the placing of white and black sharecroppers on the jury, and federal intervention against the lynchers, Jackson sought to arouse public pressure: "Every person who opposes the Hitler Terror in Germany, who stands for human rights, who believes human beings have the right to eat, and live, must join in the struggle to force the prosecution of the lynchers, must put in his protest to stop the terror drive of the landlords and their lynch gangs with tacit agreement of state officials."[50]

The Camp Hill and Reeltown events affected the Birmingham black community, and Hosea Hudson's autobiographies shed light on that impact. Hudson links Camp Hill to Scottsboro as factors radicalizing himself. Birmingham had a direct link to Camp Hill in the presence of Mack Coad, a black Communist steelworker who worked to organize the sharecroppers, later a volunteer with the Abraham Lincoln Brigade in Spain. Another Birmingham steelworker and Communist, Al Murphy, also was involved, as organizer of a three-county rural area that included Camp Hill and Reeltown. But Hudson notes that the "better class of

Negroes" also sympathized with the plight of the sharecroppers. Hudson offers an inside view as to how in the conditions of Alabama even holding a funeral for Cliff James and Milo Bentley involved struggle. A first problem was to find an undertaker who could not be intimidated, and finally mortician Hickman Jordan stepped forward, telling funeral organizers: "You all take care of the living, I'll take care of the dead." During visitation time at the funeral home a few white women activists paid respects and ignored policemen who entered, announcing: "You all come out, you can't sit up there among niggers." Hudson fleshed out John Beecher's statement that there was "a great crowd" at the funeral: "All the police in town was at the funeral. Everybody was saying anybody could have went on downtown, take everything they wanted, because seems like all the police in town was out there in North Birmingham.... It was quite a line-up.... That was one time one Negro funeral was recognized in Birmingham."[51] What becomes clear in all this is that the community response to the James and Bentley deaths was strong enough to bend the caste rules of Birmingham.

In an NBC radio network speech broadcast on April 3, 1935, Socialist party leader Norman Thomas declared: "There is a reign of terror in the cotton country of eastern Arkansas. It will end either in the establishment of complete and slavish submission to vilest exploitation in America or in bloodshed, or in both. The alternative is effective compulsion on the planters to observe the ordinary civil rights of workers, white and colored, and to stop wholesale evictions. For the sake of peace, liberty and common human decency I appeal to you who listen to my voice to bring immediate pressure upon the federal government to act."[52] Thomas did not exaggerate in his reference to terror, for in the cotton counties of Arkansas there was indeed extensive violence inflicted on tenant farmers and sharecroppers who would no longer meekly submit to the arbitrary rule of landowners. This terror was permeated with racism, as well as class arrogance.

The wrath of the propertied in Arkansas had been aroused by the birth of a new organization, the Southern Tenant Farmers' Union (STFU), that sought to voice the demands and express the aspirations of the rural poor, black and white. Whereas the Sharecroppers' Union came into being while the Hoover administration still clung to office, the STFU functioned within the framework of the agricultural policies laid down by the New Deal.

The STFU began with a small meeting convened in early July 1934 in a schoolhouse just south of Tyronza in Poinsett County. According to H. L. Mitchell, who became the secretary of the new organization, eighteen people attended that first meeting, eleven of them white and seven black.[53] One of the blacks present was Isaac Shaw, who had participated in the post–World War I organizing effort in Phillips County that culminated in the Elaine massacre. Howard Kester reports one of the blacks at the meeting, probably Shaw, as declaring:

> We colored people can't organize without you and you white folks can't organize without us. Aren't we all brothers and ain't God the Father of us all? We live under the same sun, eat the same food, wear the same kind of clothing, work on the same land, raise the same crop for the same landlord who oppresses and cheats us both. For a long time now the white folks and the colored folks have been fighting each other and both of us has been getting whipped all the time. We don't have nothing against one another but we got plenty against the landlord. The same chain that holds my people holds your people too. If we're chained together on the outside we ought to stay chained together in the union. It won't do no good for us to divide because there's where the trouble had been all the time. The landlord is always betwixt us, beatin' us and starvin' us and makin' us fight each other. There ain't but one way for us to get him where he can't help himself and that's for us to get together and stay together.[54]

The decision was made to proceed on an interracial basis, and on July 26, 1934, the STFU was incorporated under the laws of the state of Arkansas. By the end of 1934 the union had about 2,000 members.

The STFU soon proceeded to draft a constitution and bylaws, and these documents expressed the spirit animating the new organization. Recognition of the existence of class conflict was a point of departure. The STFU stated that those involved in agriculture "from a production standpoint" were divided into two classes and that the interests of these classes "are opposite or antagonistic." On the one hand there was a small owning class "who depend upon exploiting the working class," and on the other there were "the actual tillers of the soil who have been ground down to dire poverty and robbed of all their rights and privileges." The point was further made that all productive laborers had been exploited, as had the landless "tillers of the soil," and both groups now found it necessary to join forces. Based on these assumptions, the union declared three basic principles: (1) The landless, the small-farmer class, and the laborers in other productive fields must organize into their own union "and must oppose the powers of the landlords and the owners of the machinery of production." (2) There was the need to affiliate with any and all other farmer and labor unions whose aims accorded with their own, and "the solidarity of all the workers regardless of trade, race or nationality" must be proclaimed. (3) "Since all imperialistic wars are fought by the workers in the interests of the owning class, we hereby declare against such wars." This organization was to have little in common with routine business unionism, choosing rather to ground itself in belief as to the class nature of society. The second article of the STFU's constitution laid out the movement's aim. That aim was to be the mutual benefit of members "who join together to secure and protect our rights and interest as individuals by collective action." Then followed language that brought together commitment to function responsibly within the framework of the existing society with articulation of a broader social vision: "We seek by orderly procedure to establish a cooperative order of society. Since the earth is the common heritage of all, we maintain that the use and occupancy of the land should be sole title. We stand ready at all times to defend the rights of our fellow workers and at the same time promise to fulfill to the limit of our ability all labor contracts and pledges in regard to farming and other agreements we may enter into." Membership was to be limited to men, aged eighteen or over, "without discrimination as to race, color, religious or political beliefs," who were either sharecroppers, tenants, or small-farm owners whose lands were worked by themselves or by members of their immediate families. Laborers, ministers, and teachers were also eligible to belong.[55]

From its inception the organization followed a nonviolent course of action, but, as Howard Kester explains, rallying support for this policy took considerable effort. Soon after the union came into existence rumors spread that planters were buying machine guns. According to Kester the sharecroppers decided to prepare themselves for a possible massacre. They got out their old shotguns, oiled and cleaned them. But when they went to buy cartridges for these weapons the store managers said they had been ordered not to sell firearms or ammunition to tenants or sharecroppers. "It was, nevertheless," Kester writes, "a common sight during the latter part of the summer of 1934 to see a sharecropper walking down along a dusty plantation road or a national thoroughfare with a shotgun slung in a businesslike fashion under his arm." When the sharecroppers arrived at a meeting place they would stack their guns in a corner within near reach in the event the planters attacked. Kester credits this posture of being prepared for self-defense for the union's survival during the first crucial months. He writes: "Thus it was that the sharecroppers sprang to the defense of the *one* thing that offered them hope and freedom and thus it was that the union survived the first onslaught of the enraged plantation aristocracy. Had they not responded as they did, it is altogether likely that the union would have been completely crushed during those first few summer months." But there was also the danger that the use of arms, even in self-defense, would give the planters the pretext they desired to engage in massive repression. Kester notes that the union leaders recognized the danger and so requested that those coming to meetings leave their guns behind. Meetings were held in the open to minimize the possibility of surprise attack, and leaders, according to Kester, stressed the necessity of proceeding "legally, peaceably and democratically." H. L. Mitchell, in his autobiography, recalls that at the STFU's second convention a resolution, worded by Howard Kester, was adopted making explicit the union's policy of nonviolence. Regarding the union's commitment to interracialism and nonviolence Mitchell contends that "it was probably the first such organization in the rural South."[56]

Whatever role Socialist party activists played in the organizing process that created the STFU, the root of the organization was in the grinding poverty, the miserable living and working conditions inflicted on the South's rural poor. Such poverty and misery were particularly flagrant in the cotton counties of eastern Arkansas where the movement came into existence. The British writer Naomi Mitchison visited this area in 1934 and reported her impressions in the *New Statesman and Nation*. Referring generally to the conditions experienced by the sharecroppers working on the South's cotton plantations, Mitchison summed up the situation, "It is a nightmare." But she found conditions in Arkansas particularly appalling. She described the shacks, usually two rooms of unplastered wood, as worse than any rural housing she had seen in Europe, "except some pre-revolutionary peasant huts near Leningrad which were about to be pulled down in 1932." After outlining the system of shares, in which the cropper, after repaying the advances furnished him before the harvesting of the crop, was left with little or no cash income, Mitchison went on to say of the sharecropper: "He is 'free'— to starve or do anything else open to men without money in the present state of society." Even more graphic in its description of the conditions Mitchison observed was an account she furnished Howard Kester of her visit to Arkansas:

I have traveled over most of Europe and part of Africa but I have never seen such terrible sights as I saw yesterday among the share-croppers of Arkansas. Here are people of good stock, potential members of a great community, and they are being treated worse than animals, worse than farming implements and stock.... They are dressed in rags, they have barely enough food to keep them alive; their children get no education; they are a prey to diseases which the scientific resources of modern civilization could easily eliminate. I saw houses, if one can call them that, in which whole families lived in conditions of indescribable misery. Here was a log cabin half sunk in flood water and in it eight people, one of them a mother yellow and boney with malaria with a newborn child in her arms. The only furniture in the house was a table, a bench and stove and two beds for everyone. In another home a bed this time out of old bits of rusty iron, patched with rags. The youngest child was two years old but his mother was still nursing him; she could at least be sure he got some milk that way. She herself was gray haired with a face of such misery that it seemed scarcely possible she could go on living.[57]

The journalist Josephine Johnson also was struck with the awfulness of the living conditions evident among Arkansas's rural poor. She wrote in the *New Masses:* "There is one truth, however, that cannot be hidden nor in any way whitewashed. It is the simple fact of the sharecroppers' living conditions. No juggling of figures or flat denial can conceal the thousands of shacks that are visible for miles along the highway. They cannot be dismissed as a mirage or a 'nigger tale.' Two-room or one-room houses like wooden crates perched up on stilts. No screen. Weeds and earth seen through wide cracks in the floor. The walls stuffed with cotton to keep wind out in winter." Johnson outlined the features of the exploitative "furnish" system and contrasted the reality with the rhetoric of the planter who said of relations with the sharecroppers, "We give them everything in the world." Johnson acidly commented: "if the planter gives his tenant 'everything in the world' he is pursuing a wise policy indeed, because in most cases he gets it all back in the end, and with the assistance of the commissary store, his bread upon the waters returns to him as cake, with a few extra raisins thrown in." She noted the crucial point that the system left the sharecropper at the mercy of the individual planter.

With the coming of the New Deal the basic oppressiveness of the sharecropper system was compounded by the farm policies the Roosevelt administration put in place. As actually implemented, the crop reduction plan established under the Agricultural Adjustment Act (AAA) gave the planters incentive to dispense with the services of tenant farmers and sharecroppers. The planters "neglected" to share allocation payments with those who worked their land and increasingly found it expedient to shift to a system of hiring day laborers. The actions of the planters were reinforced by a mindset that facilitated rationalization. Josephine Johnson explained: "Unfortunately the planter's psychology is such that to him honesty involves more than what appears to be the simple truth. He justifies himself in various ways and in most cases is wholly sincere in his belief that his action is for the best."[58] The basic consideration was that the planters viewed the land and profits produced by working or not working the land as belonging rightly to them and that they were not truly obligated to share equitably with those who were propertyless.

W. J. Cash laid bare the grasping nature of absentee landlords as they squeezed gain from the workings of the AAA:

> Chiseling on the tenants and sharecroppers attached to such baronies was not always the work of the owners but often of the managers and other understrappers, to whom the system gave a perfect opportunity. But by one or the other or both, the practice was, as I say, very usual from the first. And despite frequent changes in the law, no few of them have known how to go seizing the great part of the subsidies intended for their dependents; sometimes by reducing them to the status, real or nominal, of mere wage-hands; sometimes by threats of dismissal and black listing; and sometimes by threat of violence or the police, who, in areas in the Deep South at least, are often pretty completely under the control of local representatives of the absentees.

Cash adds that local landlords "were often only a little less adept in chiseling and in adjusting themselves to the fluctuating law than the absentees, many times no less." Cash also explained why landlords felt no qualms about such practices: "under the tradition of the South the seizing of benefits intended for the tenants was frequently, in all sorts of landlords, both absentee and resident, not felt as constituting dishonesty at all, but as being simply a part of the natural right of the man of property to claim all revenues over and above what was required to feed and clothe the workmen after the established standard."[59]

The pressure of world market competition and the process of mechanization were transforming American cotton agriculture, but the AAA policies insured that this transformation would be undergone with little concern for those at the lower end of the rural social scale. Whatever may have been the good intentions of New Deal officials—and such intentions must be set alongside of the expediency involved in satisfying the demands of the southern Democratic planter constituency—a de-humanized mechanization had come to the South.

It is understandable that the rural poor in Arkansas, facing such prospects, were drawn to the Southern Tenant Farmers' Union. The union grew with loosely affiliated supporters considerably outnumbering members. H. L. Mitchell wrote that the truth was that "the STFU never had many dues paying members, but there were perhaps a hundred involved for every ten that got their names enrolled." Mitchell explained that if one member of a family joined he counted three more as members also.[60] But apart from formal membership figures, the holding of large, widely reported public meetings and the conducting of significant strikes by cotton sharecroppers during 1935 and again in 1936—these events amply documented in the extensive collection of STFU papers—leave no doubt that the union had the support of thousands. For what these estimates are worth, David Eugene Conrad, author of *The Forgotten Farmers*, accepts 30,000 as having been the membership figure by the end of 1935. By 1939 the union claimed a membership of 35,000 ranging over five states. H. L. Mitchell does not give any specific figure for formal membership but writes he is certain that at least 200 thousand people "came into the union" during the years 1936 to 1938.[61]

Much of the support, probably most of the support, for the union came from blacks. Donald H. Grubbs, author of the most extensively researched study of the STFU, *Cry from the Cotton*, states that the union was from half to two-thirds black. In the Missouri sharecropper roadside demonstration of 1939, the STFU activity judged by H. L. Mitchell to have been the "most spectacular event to occur in the sharecropper movement," government investigators on the scene reported that 90 to 95 percent of those protesting were blacks. Jonathan Daniels, the North Carolina editor, helps us to understand that in key areas organizing that excluded blacks would have been simply absurd. In Crittenden and Mississippi counties of eastern Arkansas, centers of STFU activity, black tenant farmers numbered 10,000 out of a total tenant population of 15,638.[62]

The union did consistently pursue a policy of organizing both blacks and whites, and the union's executive board was fairly evenly divided between both groups. Donald Grubbs emphasizes that STFU leaders worked to draw blacks and whites together, that the STFU "was cognizant of race only to the extent necessary to create a movement in which race would become unimportant." Howard Kester considered the interracial character of the union to be a prime source of strength, undermining any attempt by planters to pit black and white workers against each other. Kester added that if the union had organized blacks and whites into separate locals, breaking the union "would have been infinitely less difficult than to crush them when they were united within the same organization." Naomi Mitchison declared to Kester: "For the first time in the history of the United States, perhaps in the history of the world, white and colored people are working together in a common cause with complete trust and friendship." In her *New Statesman* piece Mitchison again reported that the STFU was a completely integrated organization, stating that within this union "there is absolutely no distinction between white and coloured men and women."[63] In 1935 Secretary Mitchell expressed his views with regard to organizing both blacks and whites. "For many years," he wrote, "the Boss Class has succeeded in keeping the two races divided, and at the same time robbed both the Negroe [*sic*] and the White equally.... There are no 'niggers' and no 'poor white trash' in the Union. These two kinds of people are all lined up with the Planters. We have only Union men in our organization, and whether they are white or black makes no difference."[64]

Yet we must not suppose that the STFU was a fully integrated organization. This was not the case. Jerold Auerbach has pointed out that on the local level the union was not integrated, with a large majority of members belonging to locals containing members of one race only. Louis Cantor explained how the union leadership dealt with this matter: "Officially stated STFU policy was biracial. Realistically, however, the union frequently left the decision of whether to have mixed or segregated to the individual local." A letter by STFU staffer Evelyn Smith outlined the leadership's somewhat laissez-faire position on this issue: "The decision as to whether or not your local shall have both races represented in it rests entirely with your members. Many locals are mixed. Some are not. The national office leaves that matter entirely up to the locals. Certainly, it is all right to mix the races in your locals." Donald Grubbs has written that the union "solved the prejudice problem" and stresses that important decisions were taken at integrated mass meetings but acknowledges that many locals were either all-white or all-black. Grubbs does not cite evidence that this tendency toward separate organization diminished as the union developed. He exaggerates somewhat when he writes that it could be argued that within the STFU "America's greatest problem, that of race relations, was solved as well as any realistic observer could expect."[65]

The planter opposition to the STFU heavily relied upon racism as its prime ideological weapon. Repeatedly, antiunionism was expressed in the rhetoric of racist demagogy. When Norman Thomas attempted to address a union meeting at Birdsong, Arkansas, he was told by gunmen who surrounded the platform: "We don't need no Gawd-damn Yankee Bastard to tell us what to do with our niggers and we want you to know that this is the best Gawd-damn county on earth." At the town of Marked Tree one of the vocal antiunionists in that place was the Reverend Abner Sage, who told Raymond Daniell of the *New York Times,* "We have had a pretty serious situation here, what with the mistering of the niggers and stirring them up to think the Government was going to give them forty acres." In 1936 Josephine Johnson had gone to Arkansas to observe the sharecropping situation and after being detained by the police was released with the warning: "Go where you want to. See what you want to. You're welcome. *But don't talk to niggers.*" Johnson was arrested when she sat down to discuss local conditions with a black man.[66] When union activist Ward Rodgers was arrested on charges of anarchy, attempting to overthrow and usurp the government of Arkansas, and "blasphemy," the prosecutor in Rodgers's trial stressed the defendant was teaching "niggers" to read and write and that he called black men "mister."[67] At one point in 1935 two white volunteers from Commonwealth College went to the town of Gilmore to attend a meeting of black sharecroppers. Shortly after the meeting began with the singing of the union song, "We Shall Not Be Moved," armed white men entered and broke up the meeting, shouting at the blacks, according to H. L. Mitchell, "that the next time they were caught at a union meeting, they were going to be lynched." The two white volunteers, Lucien Koch and Robert Reed, were seized by the armed whites and taken before a local judge. Reed reported this encounter with Arkansas justice:

He was a kindly faced old gentleman, and as much of a racist as anyone I ever saw. They wanted to know our background, where we came from, and why we were in their county, and what were white men doing involved in dealing with blacks, though they didn't call them that—they called them "niggers" but that's a word I find difficult to use. The old judge questioned us. He told us about how they had a lot of black politicians in Arkansas up until the turn of the century, and hundreds had been driven into the Mississippi River, and that a lot of lives were lost then, and the whole thing was likely to occur over again if we persisted in the sort of activities we were in.[68]

The planters, seeing their domination of society threatened by this new agrarian unionism, did not confine their response to racist rhetoric but proceeded to make use of acts of terror.[69] Many white persons became the victims of violence, but brutal acts against black sharecroppers and tenant farmers were particularly numerous.[70] The entire wave of violence was set in the context of a regional society that had legitimized the use of force to keep blacks in a subject status. As W. J. Cash tells us the post-Reconstruction South had begun to generate "a type of deliberate nigger-hazers and nigger killers, men who not only capitalized on every shadow of excuse to kick and cuff him, to murder him, but also with malice aforethought baited him into a show of resentment in order so to serve him."[71] Racism had produced a vicious segment of society, and it was readily available to serve the purposes of the planters.

The organization of the union, as Donald Grubbs points out, did not result in a massacre, partly because of behind-the-scenes efforts by President Roosevelt to prevent violence and partly, no doubt, because of realization that mass killing would stimulate support for antilynching legislation.[72] But Norman Thomas spoke accurately when he described the situation as a "reign of terror." The evidence is extensive. Many of the incidents of violence were summarized in a 1935 document the STFU issued, *Acts of Tyranny and Terror*, which served as the basis for a listing of terroristic acts Howard Kester included in *Revolt among the Sharecroppers*. The introduction to the document is a sweeping indictment of the prevailing violence: "Since the Southern Tenant Farmers' Union was organized in July of 1934 its members, officials and friends have been subjected to the most vicious and brutal attacks ever used in the stormy annals of the American Farm and Labor movement.... Members and leaders of the Union have been mobbed, beaten, illegally arrested, jailed and shot. Meetings have been broken up and homes have been riddled with bullets. Every vestige of Democratic Government has utterly disappeared. Northeastern Arkansas is as truly Fascist as Hitler's Germany." Among the specific acts reported was the beating of the Reverend C. H. Smith, an STFU organizer, in Crittenden County during August 1934. The beating left Smith injured for life. Violence directed against black STFU leaders A. B. Brookins and E. B. McKinney was also reported. On November 20, 1934, the Reverend A. B. Brookins was kicked and beaten while working to organize a black local in Cross County. Then, on March 21, 1935, Brookins's family was the target of violence while at home. A mob riddled the house with bullets, and the report continued: "Brookins fled in his night clothes and his wife and child escaped the rain of bullets by hiding under the bed." On April 2, 1935, the home of STFU vice-president E. B. McKinney was attacked and many bullets fired with the result that two men were injured, and the household was warned that unless they left Marked Tree within twenty-four hours they would all be killed. The STFU further reported that on March 29 black organizer John Allen had narrowly escaped death at the hands of planters and law officers. Allen escaped to Memphis, but while officers searched the homes of union members a riding boss struck a black woman with a gun, severing her ear from her head.[73]

There were other incidents of violence against blacks besides those mentioned in *Acts of Tyranny and Terror*. On January 16, 1936, deputies broke up a union meeting held at Saint Peter's Methodist Church near Earle, Arkansas. One of those present, James Ball, reacted by grabbing his gun but was quickly beaten senseless by the officers and taken to jail. The officers later returned to the church and wounded two fleeing blacks. It happened that one black man, Willie Hurst, had witnessed the events, and a few days after the incident at the church, two masked men came to Hurst's home and murdered him. Also in 1936, Sam Bennett stayed away from work during an STFU-conducted strike and found himself threatened by planter J. H. Shaffer, who stood in the doorway of Bennett's home carrying a shotgun. Bennett fled and finally escaped to Chicago, but a mob, hunting him, blocked the streets of the black community, beat a boy to get information, and broke into the home of Bennett's brother, beating him until convinced the man, a minister, did not know where his brother had gone. Another incident that year was the assault on Frank Weems, a black man involved in holding a picket march of sharecropper strikers. Grubbs notes that white strikers "were seldom molested as they marched, but whenever a predominantly Negro group attempted the tactic its members ran great risks." A group of white men drove up and smashed Weems with baseball bats, and for a time it was thought Weems had been killed. A fatal injury was indeed inflicted upon Mrs. Eliza Nolden who died in a Memphis hospital from the beating she received.[74] In 1935 there had also been the mobbing of a group of black families returning from church near Marked Tree and the burning of a black church at Holly Grove, apparently because the church was used as an STFU meeting place.[75]

The terror did not succeed in preventing blacks from voicing their protests against the workings of the sharecropping system. The presence of Arkansas blacks at the 1935 conference held at Howard University on the theme, "Position of the Negro in the Present Economic Crisis," was striking. One of those who spoke was a sixty-seven-year-old black man who told of his house having been shot up by night riders. He had hidden in the cornfield during the attack while his wife had hidden under the bed. A child had been grazed by a bullet. Told that the mob was after him the man had fled the area and within a few days had suffered a paralytic stroke, but still he stood on the platform at the Washington meeting to tell of his experience.[76] The man was probably A. B. Brookins, who also declared at the STFU's 1937 convention: "They shot up my house with machine-guns, and they made me run away from where I lived at, but they couldn't make me run away from my Union. . . . I am not afraid to go on being a union man." McKinney was another black leader of the union who would not be intimidated. Following the violence directed at himself and his family, he continued in a leadership role and held to his belief in the need for an interracial movement.[77]

Violence ran like a thread through all of the planters' opposition to the union. As it was evident at the beginning in 1934 the question of violence appeared toward the end of the union's history in the Missouri roadside demonstration of 1939.[78] The demonstration was the result of the eviction of some hundreds of sharecropper families from the land they had been working. The key leader of the protest was Owen Whitfield, who worked with the STFU and also with the United Cannery, Agricultural, Packing, and Allied Workers of the Congress of Industrial Organizations (CIO). He estimated that about 900 families in Missouri's Bootheel counties were scheduled for eviction, set to take place on January 10, 1939. But something more than the planters expected took place that day. The croppers would make themselves visible to the outside world by taking to the public highway and staging what amounted to a rural sit-down. As Louis Cantor described what happened, "Early on the morning of January 10, therefore, motorists passing along U.S. Highways 60 and 61 were shocked to see the roadsides strewn with broken-down autos, old wagons, trucks piled with bedding, pots and pans, wire chicken coops, and of course, poorly clad croppers."[79] The planters and their governmental representatives found the situation intolerable, and they took action to remove the protesters. Violence as well as the threat of violence were parts of the process.

Violence was a part of local tradition. In the early twentieth century the coming of cotton to the Bootheel area had been accompanied by terrorism directed at blacks. Poor whites and blacks were pitted against each other in economic competition. In October 1911 at Caruthersville a black boardinghouse had been burned by a white mob. In the town of Parma several of the blacks who had been recruited for the local work force were assaulted. In New Madrid County, during September 1911, blacks hired to harvest cotton were victimized by roaming white terrorists with four blacks suffering gunshot wounds and hundreds fleeing the area. A few weeks later black cotton pickers in Pemiscot County on at least two occasions came under assault by white mobs. Also in 1911, Pemiscot

County was the scene of a lynching. A black man, A. B. Richardson, had been arrested on a charge of stealing some merchandise and was seized and murdered by a mob whose original target of wrath was another black who had been arrested for supposedly following a white woman. Richardson's body was found in the Mississippi River. Local authorities did nothing about this murder, and Irvin Wyllie's account of early twentieth-century Bootheel racial violence does not report any effective action by the legal system in the area against such violence. Wyllie adds the telling comment that from 1912 on "race crises recurred almost as regularly as the local floods, and like the floods came to be accepted as part of a way of life." This was the background against which the 1939 events took place.[80]

The labor reporter Carl Hirsch, covering the 1939 Bootheel events, was greatly struck with the atmosphere of violence he encountered. "I've never lived for so long a time in the center of so much concentrated hostility," he wrote. "I've never heard such a continuous use of words of violence ... words that are brutal in themselves, that are knife thrusts into my insides. All day long I hear the talk of planters and of their stooges, deputies, state troopers, bureaucratic small-time officials. And when they say nigger and nigger-lover and lynch and agitator and communist ... they mean violence. And all of it is directed against a few hundred mild and wonderful people, simple, quiet, intelligent, honest, loving people who are starving in a swamp." Hirsch went out to the "dismal bog" where the protesters had camped. He sat in one of "those excuses for a tent" and talked with the people he met. What he was told offered a deep glimpse into the underside of American rural life:

> I heard stories today that would make your blood freeze. And through it all ran the same savage depravity. About a planter who whipped a sharecropper's hog to death because it was on his land ... about a sharecropper who was tied to a post and flogged to death ... about a little Negro boy who was starving and stole some beans and was beaten and forced to work in the field for a week to pay the damage.... The planter autocracy is something awe-ful and sickening. Frankly these people frighten me. There's a crazy leer that they have that I've only seen on the faces of some cops in the North.[81]

Something of the flavor of the strike is also conveyed in the diary entries recorded by Charles M. Barnes, local cotton farmer, gasoline station operator, and one-term mayor of Marston, Missouri. On January 10 Barnes noted: "The Croppers Protest Movement is in evidence today as hundreds of families who are being evicted or dispossessed are piling their household goods and camping their families along Highways No. 60 and No. 61." On January 11 Barnes detailed the location of the strikers and observed: "It is a protest against the present custom of changing croppers annually." The following day brought rain and snow, and Barnes noted that "the campers along the roads must be in deplorable condition unless they have been removed or their conditions alleviated by providing shelter for them." On January 13 the diary read that landlords had met at New Madrid and declared that the strike was no fault of theirs, but Barnes saw things differently: "it is evident," he wrote, "that they held their 'notices to move' or vacate and they had no place to go.—It's only the sore spot of S.E.Mo. farm social economics coming to a head,—like the social 'boil' that it is. . . . Most of these people are the down and outs, largely as a result of their own lack of thrift and stability, but some just never had a chance and cannot get a break in their favor. They are poor—poorly fed, worse housed, and clothed, sickly, ignorant and are wafted from place to place by the winds of circumstance. Social unfortunates." On January 15 Barnes recorded that the health department was taking a hand in moving the sharecroppers off the highway.[82]

The state police, assisted by local sheriffs and deputized individuals, removed the demonstrators from along the highways. Some of the sharecroppers had among their belongings guns used for hunting game to be used as food. The police forcibly disarmed the sharecroppers, and in the course of this encounter one black was assaulted with pistol and cane. An investigation conducted by the Federal Bureau of Investigation found that the only recourse to violence during the demonstration was on the part of law enforcement officials.[83] The following year Whitfield asserted that he had been instrumental in dissuading the evicted farmers from using force.

Although acts of violence occurred in the course of the protest, ironically the STFU had chosen the Bootheel for the demonstration because the union believed a relative absence of violence would prevail in Missouri. On the first anniversary of the roadside action the union explained in handbills it distributed that it acted "not because cotton labor is treated less fairly in Missouri than elsewhere. We know that is not true. We staged it in Missouri because we had less fear of bloody violence in Missouri." This was perhaps not so much a comment on the peaceableness of Missouri as a reflection of the murderous racial atmosphere of the Deep South.[84]

By the early 1940s the STFU was a fading organization, and if in 1946

Mitchell received an American Federation of Labor (AFL) charter for a new organization named the National Farm Labor Union, this was an entity, unlike the STFU, that did not focus on the unionization of the sharecroppers and tenant farmers of the South's plantations. The STFU was limited in its effectiveness by several factors, including divisiveness over the issue of working with Communists and, probably most importantly, the failure to obtain collective bargaining rights under federal law. The union did not receive the umbrella of protection and legitimacy that in the 1930s had greatly contributed to union growth. The failure to win that protection and legitimacy was connected to the political conservatism that dominated the South. That conservatism was kept in place by a system of illegality and terror that deprived poor people in the South of their constitutional rights.

The STFU did register some important accomplishments. It gave, of course, a legacy to the future, a heritage of experience, of courage and resourcefulness, of recognizing the need to mobilize national public opinion, that would be drawn upon by later farm worker movements. In its own day it was instrumental in President Roosevelt's decision to constitute a special Committee on Farm Tenancy, and the work of that committee spurred the establishment of the Farm Security Administration that represented some commitment by the Roosevelt administration to assist the rural poor. Also to be remembered is that the lawlessness directed at the South's sharecroppers and tenant farmers played a key role in the process that created the investigation undertaken in the Senate by the La Follette Civil Liberties Committee.[85] This committee conducted a sweeping inquiry into corporate lawlessness and violence directed against the rights of workers. The sufferings of the poor in the southern cotton fields led to exposing the arbitrary, antilabor practices engaged in by much of American business, but La Follette's committee did not directly touch upon the conditions faced by the sharecroppers. The American labor movement benefited from the La Follette committee inquiry, and that benefit was secured in large measure because of the sacrifices made by the cotton farm workers who did not directly share in the gains. The rising of the sharecroppers did not solve the problems of southern agriculture, but it did advance the interests of labor throughout the nation. That rising is part of American labor history, but it is also inseparable from the black struggle for freedom.

One of the manifestations of racial brutality that made its way into the national consciousness during the thirties was the experience of the chain gang. In 1932 the Hollywood film, *I Am a Fugitive from a Chain Gang*, drew attention to this feature of the southern penal system, centering upon the experience of a white prisoner but also portraying a black convict as the instrument of a jailbreak.[86]

An account written by an escaped black chain-gang prisoner, Jesse Crawford, conveys a vivid portrait of the brutality involved in this penal system. Crawford, born in Atlanta, was arrested and convicted in 1931 on a charge of possession of a stolen automobile. Sentenced to serve twelve months on a chain gang Crawford was assigned to a camp in Atlanta. He served for two months before joining other prisoners in breaking out of the camp. The essence of the chain-gang system was compulsory, backbreaking labor, and violence was depended upon to assure that such labor was performed. Crawford later wrote of the guards who would stroll up and down the chain-gang line and every so often strike the prisoners across the back with a hickory stick. Prisoners were struck for a variety of reasons, including the offense of picking the worms out of the soup served them. The inevitable result of such treatment was rebellion, and one day the convicts refused to respond to the call to begin work and instead sat on their bunks "and gave vent to hatred loudly and long." The authorities' answer to protest was merely to intensify the level of brutality inflicted upon the prisoners. When the men refused to heed the pleas of the warden to be "sensible" the police filled the prisoners' dormitory with tear gas. According to Crawford the rioters "fought back like cornered wild cats," but the authorities had overwhelming power and the revolt was crushed. Crawford told what happened next: "When most of the rioters had been beaten to a mushy pulp, they threw us in dump trucks and carried us to the quarry. There, we were forced to work in the scorching sun which was so hot that it blisters our bodies raw. When some of the boys refused to work because they were utterly disabled after the merciless beating, the guards sent for the warden and started to flogging the helpless creatures all over again."

Crawford escaped from Georgia and, assuming a new name, sought to begin a new life in Detroit. Eight months following his escape Crawford was arrested and detained as a fugitive. But this was now the 1930s, and northern public authorities could no longer always routinely return escapees to the brutal conditions of the southern convict system. In the Crawford case, attorneys for the NAACP and the ILD cooperated, and following a hearing in Lansing, Frank Murphy, now governor of Michigan, refused to extradite Crawford to Georgia.[87]

A major role in exposing chain-gang conditions was played by the left-wing investigative reporter John L. Spivak. Spivak's forte was on-the-scene reporting, and to gather the material for his study of the chain-gang system he managed to visit the camps in Georgia and to obtain

revealing photographs. Calling upon the state prison commissioner, Spivak secured access to the file entitled *Official Punishment Reports from
Georgia Penitentiary* and was horrified by the routine accounts of barbarous treatment of prisoners. He read of prisoners being placed in stocks
for refusing to work and of a convict who was stuffed into a barrel for
talking back to a guard. He also came across notations of deaths that
occurred in the camps, and yet no official inquiry had been made by
anyone as to the circumstances. In his autobiography Spivak recalled the
feeling of rage that came over him: "To think that such things were done
in the United States in the year 1930." At the time he asked himself why
he had never heard of such conditions, and in the autobiography he
observed that those who ignored this "negative" side of the American
experience preferred to hear about things "that contribute to the American image as one of universal kindness, compassion and Christian
charity."[88]

Convinced he had to see the camps for himself, Spivak persuaded the
commissioner to give him a general letter of introduction and set out on
a tour of inspection. He observed and photographed the methods of
punishment employed by wardens and camp guards, the use of stocks
and the process of "stretching." The stocks were a sadistic refinement of
a colonial method of punishment, the refinement consisting of locking
in the convict's arms and legs and then pulling the board upon which
the prisoner sat, leaving him hanging. In "stretching," the prisoner was
tied to a concrete post, a rope was tied to the handcuffs binding the
prisoner's hands, and the rope was then pulled around a second post
placed several feet away from the prisoner. The result was that the prisoner's arms were almost torn from their sockets. The person left in that
position, especially under the hot Georgia sun, would most often lose
consciousness within an hour.

One of the most moving parts of Spivak's reporting on the chain-gang
experience was his telling of appeals scrawled by desperate prisoners,
appeals, most often ignored, sent to responsible officials in Atlanta. These
letters, despite poor spelling and grammar, were eloquent in stating how
camp conditions broke the prisoners' health and led them to beg for some
act of mercy that would relieve the cruelty.[89]

Violence against black labor was at the heart of the racial caste system.
The targets of terror included homeless and jobless black youth, the black
poor, rural and urban, and also skilled black workers. An instance of
singling out skilled workers for murderous attention was to be seen during
1932–33 in the killing of seven black firemen working on the Mississippi
division of the Illinois Central Railroad. Six of the seven, Frank Kincaid,

Ed Cole, Aaron Williams, Wilburn Anderson, Frank Johnson, and Will Harvey were cut down by shotgun blasts. Anderson's head, reportedly, was almost entirely blasted away from his body. In the *Nation* Hilton Butler wrote regarding these killings: "Mississippi, in its own primitive way, had begun to deal with the unemployment problem. Dust had been blown from the shotgun, the whip, and the noose, and Ku Klux practices were being resumed in the certainty that dead men not only tell no tales but create vacancies."[90]

Ira De A. Reid and T. Arnold Hill, representing the Urban League, both fixed responsibility for this brutality upon the railroad brotherhoods. Reid pointedly wrote that liberals had laughed in 1926 when the president of the Brotherhood of Locomotive Firemen had told the Detroit convention that he hoped to report at the union's next convention that not one black remained on the left side of a locomotive cab. Reid explained that, as the pay and status of the fireman's job rose and as white workers were affected by the dire employment situation created by the Depression, white firemen demanded the places previously held by blacks. Hill wrote in the Urban League magazine, *Opportunity,* that for "more than twenty years there have been numerous efforts to check and curtail the employment of Negroes on railroads. The chief proponents of this policy are the four major railroad transportation brotherhoods, whose unions are open to 'white men over twenty-one years of age.' "[91]

Certainly, the racist brotherhoods were not without responsibility, although the role of the Ku Klux Klan as a likely participant in this savage business should not be ignored. But there is also the fact that neither public officials nor railroad executives took any effective action to curb the violence. The number of black firemen continued to dwindle as official indifference allowed the killers to go unpunished.

TEN

In the Midst of the New Deal

I N DEALING with the reality of racist violence the 1930s saw the continuing dialogue between the legalistic strategies advocated by the NAACP and the mass action, mass publicity techniques of left-wing radicals. But in the formation of the National Negro Congress (NNC) a new factor entered the situation, the coming into being of a movement that worked to unify various black protest movements. This was a serious and purposeful attempt to give organizational structure to race unity, quite different from the fiasco back in 1924 when Kelly Miller had assembled an All-Race Negro Assembly or Sanhedrin of black notables in Chicago that produced little more than a set of platitudes.[1] The congress was an outgrowth of the Joint Committee on National Recovery, a coordinating council of black organizations whose establishment in 1933 had been encouraged by the Roosevelt administration. In May 1935 the joint committee, in cooperation with the Division of Social Sciences of Howard University, held a conference at Howard to discuss a program for action by black Americans. This meeting produced the call for the National Negro Congress, and the first national meeting of the new organization was held in Chicago, February 14–16, 1936. Sixty-eight men and women served on the original executive council, including Ralph Bunche, Lester Granger, Henry Lee Moon, Benjamin J. Davis, Jr., and Max Yergan. John P. Davis, the secretary of the congress, described the new movement as "a federation of organizations formed for the purpose of pooling the strength of the various constituent groups in the attack upon the evils retarding the securing by the Negro of his manhood rights."[2]

Richard Wright described the atmosphere of excitement and tension prevailing as delegates and observers assembled at the Eighth Regiment armory in Chicago. "All the talk takes the form of questions," he wrote, " 'What do you think we can do?' 'Will things be different?' These are the words of sharecroppers who hitchhiked through the cold to come to the National Negro Congress. These are the words of industrial workers, doctors, shop girls, politicians, teachers, social workers, labor leaders, preachers, as they stand or sit, waiting."[3] The keynote speech was written by A. Philip Randolph, who could not make the trip to Chicago due to illness. The speech was read to the delegates by Dr. Charles Wesley Burton, regional vice-president for Illinois and Indiana. As regards motive for Randolph's involvement George S. Schuyler stressed resentment at exclusion by "NAACP brahmins," and Randolph's biographer writes: "It may or may not have been true that he felt insufficiently recognized by the NAACP elite."[4]

Whatever role such resentment may have played, Randolph's commitment to the National Negro Congress clearly was related to the opportunity he recognized to further his long-held view that the future of blacks and the future of the labor movement were intertwined. After reviewing the world scene and noting the menace of fascism both abroad and within the United States Randolph summarized the relationship of racial to class oppression: "Our contemporary history is a witness to the stark fact that black America is a victim of both class and race prejudice and oppression. Because Negroes are black they are hated, maligned and spat upon; lynched, mobbed, and murdered. Because Negroes are workers, they are browbeaten, bullied, intimidated, robbed, exploited, jailed and shot down." Randolph informed the delegates that in order to further black interests new instrumentalities would have to be created, and the most important of these were the industrial union and an independent working-class political party. Randolph saw the possibilities of a black–labor alliance unfolding in the context of the united front strategy. The concept of the united front, a concept advanced by Communists and others on the left as a response to the world menace of fascism, offered a realistic basis for partnership with white labor and other groups of democratic-minded Americans. Randolph declared that the task of overcoming the enemies of democracy was too big for any one organization. What was required was the integration of various black organizations, "church, fraternal, civil, trade union, farmer, professional, college and what not" into a united front with white workers and "those whose liberties are similarly menaced for a common attack upon the forces of reaction." He also addressed himself to the issue of tactics to be utilized by the united front. Legal action as well as parades, picketing, boycotting, mass protest, and distribution of literature were all to be employed. In speaking of the united front Randolph made clear his position that blacks would not approach united action with whites as supplicants but would insist on terms of equality and the right of the black movement's independence. In what may be interpreted as a foreshadowing of a later rupture with the Communists but which could also be understood as a slap at the NAACP, Randolph declared that "the Negro peoples should not place their problems for solution down at the feet of their white sympathetic allies which has been and is the common fashion of the old school Negro leadership, for, in the final analysis, the salvation of the Negro, like the workers, must come from within."

The National Negro Congress, as Randolph envisioned it in this speech, would be a component of the general struggle for democracy in America. He rejected an approach of narrow parochialism, and when he spoke of the task of the Negro people, a task confronting blacks "at a time when new atrocities and nameless terrorism" are directed against black Americans, that task included taking up a wide range of issues. The denial of access to hotels and restaurants and to transportation facilities were clearly issues, but so were matters such as cuts in relief allocations, denial of free assembly, freedom of the press, the forcing of teachers to take loyalty oaths, the activities of William Randolph Hearst and the Ku Klux Klan, and what Randolph described as "the goose-stepping of students in the school system through the R.O.T.C." The speech, though it concentrated on issues of immediate concern, was also set in the framework of anticapitalism. What had brought blacks to their present situation was inseparable from capitalist exploitation, "the profit system which provides and permits the enrichment of the few at the expense of the many," a capitalism that "makes for the robbery and oppression of the darker and weaker colonial peoples of the world."[5]

Richard Wright eagerly welcomed Randolph's speech, finding that each sentence was "a blow of logic breaking a new path." The speech, Wright believed, opened two perspectives before blacks; one, that of "a national solidified movement among Negroes of all classes and occupations"; and second, that of an alliance of blacks with "progressive and class-conscious elements" in America and the world. He described the congress as a whole in terms that stressed both its radicalism and its inclusive breadth.[6]

One of those attending the congress was Roy Wilkins, then NAACP assistant secretary. On assignment from the NAACP board of directors, Wilkins observed the proceedings and submitted a report favorable to association endorsement of this new movement. There were rumors that the congress had been financed by the Communists, the Republican party, or the big-business Liberty League then gearing up for its effort to prevent Roosevelt's reelection, but Wilkins dismissed such tales as "wholly without foundation," noting that funds trickled in and came from widely diverse sources. The NAACP board was informed that a number of prominent NAACP members supported the congress, including Marion

Cuthbery, herself a board member, and William H. Hastie and Louis L. Redding of the National Legal Committee. "The Congress was unusually democratic in setting up its machinery and in proceedings," Wilkins reported. And apparently he found a prevailing spirit of democracy that was more than a matter of formal structure. Wilkins was quite struck with the youth of a great many of the delegates and with the fact that the delegates "came at great personal sacrifice and...owed their allegiance only to organizations committed to a militant fight for the Negro. It was not a congress of school teachers, college presidents and others, whose first allegiance was to forces who might be sympathetic with their aims, but who were not in a position to aid them in fighting for their aims." Beyond question, Wilkins declared, the congress expressed "the willingness of masses of the people to sacrifice and fight." Wilkins appears to have been moved by the genuineness and promise of the congress, and he agreed with William Hastie that the new organization was consistent with NAACP objectives and offered an opportunity to reach people in a broader arena. Roy Wilkins also greatly respected John P. Davis, the prime mover in organizing the congress. Davis, he reported, had "an excellent mind, a capacity for hard work, and a grasp of the economic and civic plight of the Negro second to none of his contemporaries," an evaluation that might be taken as a slight to NAACP secretary Walter White.[7] The NAACP did not join the congress, but Roy Wilkins's response evidences that association leaders varied in their appraisals of the organization's significance.

At the second meeting of the National Negro Congress, held in Philadelphia during 1937, A. Philip Randolph restated his view of the united front character of the movement. He declared that the NNC represented all sections of black opinion, at the same time making clear that it did not seek to supersede existing organizations. According to Randolph the congress did not "seek to impose any issue of philosophy upon any organization or group, but rather to unite varying and various organizations, with various and varying philosophies, left, center, and right among the Negro people upon a simple, minimum program so as to mobilize and rally power and mass support behind vital issues affecting the life and destiny of the race." Manifesting a more overtly friendly attitude toward the NAACP Randolph expressed support for the association's efforts on behalf of a federal antilynching bill. Articulating the united front concept of building upon the American democratic tradition, Randolph wanted it known "that the Congress does not seek to change the American form of government, but rather to complement it with new and rugged morals and spiritual sinews to make its democratic traditions, forms and ideals more permanent and a living force."

In this speech, as throughout his earlier career, Randolph held firmly to his advocacy of black people's identification with the labor movement. Without directly mentioning the alternative of nationalism, Randolph powerfully stated the case for a policy of alliance. He started from a simply stated premise from which his conclusions logically flowed: "The Negro people are an integral part of the American commonwealth." Blacks like whites died in war and suffered from the effects of the Depression. The task of blacks then was that of "consolidating their interests with the interest of the progressive forces of the nation." Collective bargaining brought power to the black worker as well as to the white, and the abolition of the company union allowed black and white workers a voice in determining wages and working conditions. The strengthening of the labor movement, Randolph insisted, "the improvement of labor standards, brings comfort, health and decency to blacks as well as to white workers."

Blacks, of course, had other concerns apart from the strictly economic struggle, and Randolph referred to the struggle, especially in the South, for elementary democratic rights. Jim Crowism, disfranchisement, and Ku Klux Klan terror were all evidence of the special discriminations imposed upon blacks. Randolph placed particular stress upon the battle against peonage. In this system of debt slavery, physical brutality, denial of civil rights, and economic oppression were most plainly interconnected. What could be done about this? The answer was a united front of all black organizations and unity "with the progressive and liberal agencies of the nation whose interests are common with Black America." With the united front, according to Randolph, the Scottsboro boys still in prison could be released, peonage could be wiped out, and "the horror of lynching in America may be eliminated and mob terror relegated to oblivion."

The struggle for democratic rights, Randolph made plain, rested on the firm grounds of the United States Constitution as amended after the Civil War. Nineteen thirty-seven was 150 years since the drafting of the Constitution, and Randolph hailed the birthday, speaking in the city where the document had been drafted. Blacks still were not assured the rights promised them, but "the Constitution, at least, vouchsafes complete citizenship rights and provides the grounds of principle and promises to secure it." Those rights, however, could be guaranteed only by the efforts of black people themselves. "Freedom is never given," Randolph declared, "it is won." The Reconstruction era had failed to secure black rights because the Constitution, "without the force of enlightened public opinion back of it," could not accomplish what the revolution of the Civil War did not accomplish. Noting the breakdown of "the great and inspiring experiment of Reconstruction," Randolph explained that the end of this experiment in democracy left the former slave owners "free to use the shotgun, the tissue ballot and the Ku Klux Klan terror, to drive the negro back into a semi-caste status."

In the closing section of his keynote address Randolph summed up the contributions made by the congress during the first year of its existence. "It has kept the faith," he announced, and he cited the evidence. The congress had worked effectively and bravely to bring black workers into the new industrial unions of the CIO. "Our men," he stated "did not fail or faint before blood or bullets—in the South, Chicago, Detroit, Michigan, Ohio and Pennsylvania." The congress had also encouraged black youth to participate in the organizing of tobacco workers in Virginia and had carried the message of labor organization to laundry workers in Washington. The congress had also entered the legislative field in joining with the NAACP in support of a federal antilynching bill, and it had brought a fighting spirit to the efforts to free the Scottsboro boys and Angelo Herndon, the Young Communist League organizer imprisoned in Georgia on charges of seeking the state's overthrow. But the National Negro Congress had not only fought the fight at home; it had enlisted in the world struggle against Fascist violence, and Randolph proudly referred to the NNC's efforts in supporting the Spanish Republic, the independence of China, and the restoration of an independent Ethiopia. Randolph ended in an exultant mood: "Long live the spirit of world democracy! Long live the memory and love of the Black Revolutionists of the 19th Century, led by Denmark Vesey, Nat Turner, Gabriel Prosser, Harriet Tubman, Sojourner Truth and Frederick Douglass!" Clearly standing out in this speech was the affirmation that black Americans in meeting the threat of racism were not and would not be isolated but rather formed a vital component of the worldwide battle for democracy. Randolph closed with words that pointed to a goal and also outlined the means: "Forward with the torch of Education, the instrument of agitation, the weapon of organization to a day of peace on earth and toward men, good will!"[8]

Gunnar Myrdal, in *An American Dilemma*, wrote that "as late as 1939 and 1940, when the present writer traveled around in this country, the local councils of the National Negro Congress were the most important negro organizations in some Western cities."[9] Activities on the local level engaged in by the congress included vigorous campaigns of resistance to racial terror. The Washington affiliate, for example, centered its work on the issue of police brutality. During 1938 the council sponsored a meeting on police brutality that involved representatives of more than fifty organizations. This meeting was followed up with radio broadcasts and mass rallies giving publicity to the issue, and within several months 24,000 signatures were secured on petitions protesting brutal police treatment of innocent blacks. The campaign was able to record a victory, the establishment of a civilian trial board and punishment of two officers who had killed blacks without cause. On the national level the question of violence was most significantly responded to in the form of coordinated activity on behalf of federal antilynching legislation. In 1938 the congress's national office organized numerous demonstrations in support of the Wagner–Van Nuys antilynching bill, sponsored a meeting in Washington of more than a hundred organizations on the bill's behalf, and brought delegations to the Capitol to lobby with members of Congress.[10]

The National Negro Congress represented a new sophistication and breadth of scope of the black movement. It attempted to deal with the complex issues of creating racial unity and solidarity within the context of an overall policy of forging alliances among democratically minded segments of the white population. It dealt with individual instances of racial injustice, but the congress also sought to pass over to the offensive, to institutionalize political, legislative, and economic advances and thus raise the level of the struggle for freedom. Problems the congress encountered in its later history do not diminish the contributions made by this movement in seeking to bring to life the forces required to uproot the sources of racial oppression in American society.

The militant moods of struggle engendered by the thirties, added to the desperate situation confronting the black masses in the midst of the Depression, combined to produce an explosion of anger within the black community of New York. Since Tulsa in 1921 there had been no large-scale racial confrontations in the cities, but in 1935 thousands of Harlem residents rebelled against the oppressive conditions imposed upon them. Gunnar Myrdal summed up the sources of the Harlem "riot" in his comment that such events as this episode "will be due to continuing discrimination from the whites and to growing realization by Negroes that peaceful requests for their rights are not getting them anywhere."[11] The outbreak was touched off on March 19, 1935, by the arrest of a boy, Lino Rivera, accused of shoplifting from a Kress's five-and-ten-cent store at 125th Street and Lenox Avenue. Rumors spread that the boy had been killed, and the consequence was widespread attacks on stores and defiance of police authority. The incident at the store itself symbolized two elements of the explosive situation, the white-owned retail establishment that was located in the black community and yet refused to hire black clerks, and the police who often enough had given evidence that they were quite capable of excess use of force in arresting a fourteen-year-old accused of taking a ten-cent knife. For two days the rioting continued until efforts by Harlem community organizations and the liberal mayor Fiorello La Guardia restored some degree of "normalcy." The 1935 episode presented a new dimension to the racial "riot," a new level of militancy revealed in a lashing out at the visible symbols of oppression. This was not a clash between white and black communities but rather fundamentally an attack upon property, not perhaps the property of the great corporations headquartered downtown but the commercial establishments that cheated the Harlem consumer and would not even give the Harlemite a chance to work. To those able to look at events in some perspective, this rebellion, especially coming as it did in the midst of the Depression, was a foreshadowing of other possible explosions, and it was therefore appropriate to study what had occurred and to formulate programs of action to deal with legitimate grievances.

The official reaction was to be found in the work of a mayor's commission, which filed a report in March 1936.[12] Few things have been as unwelcome in American history as the reports of riot commissions, and this report was no exception. The document was not made public until on July 18, 1936, the New York *Amsterdam News* reprinted the material in full. The report was the work of a commission made up of prominent leaders of the black community and several well-known white liberals. Chief author was the distinguished sociologist E. Franklin Frazier, and among black commission members were Hubert T. Delany, tax commissioner and later judge; poet Countee Cullen; and A. Philip Randolph. The whites included Oswald Garrison Villard, for many years editor of the *Nation* and also an officer of the NAACP; William J. Schieffelin, financier and Tuskegee trustee; and two American Civil Liberties Union attorneys, Morris Ernst and Arthur Garfield Hays.

The report both analyzed the sources of the riot and made recommendations for future policy. Recommendations were offered that sought to eliminate discrimination against blacks in employment. Proposals were also made for improvements in administration of relief and for construction of new schools and expansion of recreational facilities. In the area of health care, recommendations were made for improving the quality of services at Harlem Hospital and for the admission of black physicians to the staffs of all city hospitals. The commission also called for a citizens' committee to hear complaints against the police. This recommendation was grounded in the considerable evidence presented to the commission concerning police mistreatment of Harlem residents. The report noted that "nothing revealed more strikingly the deep-seated resentments of the citizens of Harlem against exploitation and racial discrimination than their attitude toward the police when the latter were called to testify before the commission." Observing that the resentment was not due solely to killings "that had dramatized the brutal behavior of the police," the commission found that the community feeling had its basis in ordinary police routine. The report quoted a letter sent by a Harlemite to Mayor La Guardia in which it was stated that on April 16, 1935, several weeks after the March riot, police, acting without search warrant, had entered his apartment, had failed to identify themselves, and without explanation had proceeded to search through the individual's belongings. The commission declared that one might believe that this letter exaggerated the facts "had not policemen themselves testified at the hearings that they entered the homes of Negro citizens without a warrant and searched them at will." Arbitrary action taken by police also included interference with association between white and black persons. Although the police were most likely to interfere if the situation involved a black man and a white woman, in one case, according to a witness, a light-complexioned man seen walking with a black woman was held at the police station until he could convince the officer he was not white.[13]

Arbitrariness was also expressed in acts of direct violence, and the commission recounted in some detail the experience of a black man, Thomas Aikens, who on March 13, 1935, was standing in the breadline at the 369th Infantry armory building. In this incident racism and the victimization of the hungry were seen operating together. Aikens had gotten in line at about ten-thirty in the morning and found some 150 others ahead of him. Approximately at one-thirty, when he had reached the point where he would shortly receive food, he was shoved out of position by other men. Two police officers came up and, instead of restoring Aiken to his place in line, abusively told him to go to the end of the line, now numbering some 500 men. Aikens at that point protested, and with that the officers called him a "smart nigger" and assaulted him. He was struck with a blunt instrument and shortly fell unconscious to the armory floor. The policemen called for the patrol wagon, but someone else had summoned an ambulance, which arrived before the patrol wagon. Aikens was taken to Harlem Hospital where it was found that he had suffered a rupture of the left eyeball. The police, learning of the seriousness of the injury, countered by charging Aikens with "willfully and wrongfully" striking an officer. Aikens was later taken to the prison ward of Bellevue Hospital where finally it proved necessary to remove the eye. Even after this the police and the Manhattan district attorney's office continued efforts to press the case against Aikens. The commission reported these facts and also noted that, ignoring the fact that Harlem Hospital records failed to show any evidence of the police officer's being treated at the hospital, the hospital superintendent had provided a statement that Patrolman Egan had indeed been treated. The commission angrily stated: "Thus it is apparent that an official in one of the most important institutions in Harlem is willing to assist policemen in their efforts to justify their brutality towards Negroes."[14]

The report also noted an instance in which plainly a police officer, Patrolman Labutinski, had used excessive force in dealing with a disorderly individual. About four o'clock on the morning of March 25, 1935, Labutinski had been called by the manager of a Lenox Avenue restaurant to arrest Edward Laurie, who had been drinking. Laurie struck the officer a slight blow whereupon Labutinski knocked Laurie to the sidewalk with such force as to fracture his skull. Fifty minutes later Laurie died in the hospital. The commission offered the opinion that the officer could have dealt less violently with Laurie and that such action "would have prevented a killing and thereby not offered further confirmation of the belief of the majority of the Negro citizens of Harlem that the life of a Negro is cheap in the estimation of the police."[15]

The commission report was forthright in ascribing responsibility for such individual acts of brutality not merely to the offending officers involved but to the New York police department as a whole. The report noted that, of course, "there are many conscientious and humane policemen," but the basic point was that "inasmuch as the Police Department makes no effort to discipline policemen guilty of these offenses, but either hides behind such subterfuge as the exoneration given by grand juries or actually justifies the infringement of the rights of Harlem's citizens, then the Police Department as a whole must accept the onus of these charges."

The commissioners' findings reflected a consciousness that police brutality against Harlemites was linked to both racial and class oppression. The report observed that citizens of the Harlem community understood that disregard of their rights "is due not only to the fact that they are Negroes, but also to the fact that they are poor and propertyless and therefore defenseless." Noted was the testimony of one police officer who had been asked if he would behave toward persons on Fifth Avenue and Park Avenue as he acted toward Harlem citizens. The policeman "hesitated, stammered, and finally gave no answer." The commission put forward a warning from the evidence it assembled, a statement that probably explains, at least in part, why public release of the report had been delayed. "In spite of the helplessness which their poverty imposed upon them," the commission declared, "the citizens of Harlem are realizing more and more the power of their organized number. The outbreak of March 19, though spontaneous and without leadership, is strengthening the belief that the solution of their problems lies in mass action. Police aggression and brutalities more than any other factor weld the people together for mass action against those responsible for their ills." A dangerous situation was thereby created, the commission stated, a situation in which another police act of brutality could trigger an explosion with more dangerous consequences than the March events. The police were charged with the responsibility of acting in such a way "as to win the confidence of the citizens of Harlem and to prove themselves the guardians of the rights and safety of the community rather than its enemies and oppressors."[16] This was rather blunt language, coming as it did from an official body established by the city of New York, and certainly it did not conform to the police department's image of itself as the unquestioned guardian of law and order.

The basic framework within which this commission operated was a refusal to see the March events in isolation. The issue was that black acts of violence were a response to police brutality and to the institutionalized violence of oppressive living conditions. On March 19, 1935, Harlemites, said the report, "after five years of the depression which had made them feel more keenly than ever the injustices of discrimination in employment, the aggressions of the police, and the racial segregation, rioted against these intolerable conditions. This spontaneous outbreak, the immediate cause of which was a mere rumor concerning the mistreatment of a Negro boy, was symptomatic of pent-up feelings of resentment and insecurity." The report went so far as to protest against the apparent response of city authorities to the outbreak. What Harlemites saw were extra policemen on the corners and mounted patrolmen riding through the streets. The commission explained the impact of this: "To Harlem this show of force simply signifies that property will be protected at any cost; but it offers no assurance that the legitimate demands of the citizens of the community for work and decent living conditions will be heeded."[17]

The report presented quite specific recommendations dealing with the legitimate demands of Harlemites, at the same time noting that the community's economic and social problems, "which are deeply rooted in the very nature of our economic and social system, cannot be cured by any administration under our present political and civic institutions." But the report also affirmed that the city's existing administrative machinery could act to prevent discrimination in municipal institutions and could take some action against private concerns and individuals practicing discrimination and that then "the people of Harlem would at least not feel that their economic and social ills were forms of racial persecution." Among the various recommendations were several that directly applied to the police. First of all, the police were to be instructed that they were not to interfere with association of whites and blacks, and disciplinary measures were to be taken against officers violating this instruction. Second, the police were to close up "dives and pleasure dens" that catered to the appetites of white patrons. The police were to close any place of entertainment that refused to admit blacks. Further, the police commissioner was urged to appoint a biracial committee of Harlem citizens to whom individuals could bring complaints of police misconduct. The committee would also serve as an advisory committee to the police department with regard to relations with the black community. To give some assurance of the committee's independence, the group was to include one or more persons "who are dissenters from established institutions and also men who are likely to have contact with victims of injustice." Also recommended was a policy that officers who break the law should be subject not only to police discipline but also to prosecution by the district attorney. The report got to the nub of the matter in asserting that it was too readily assumed that an officer who kills or injures a citizen is acting in the line of duty and that failure to uphold the officer would weaken police authority. Every instance of a shooting by the police should receive careful investigation by one of the department's highest officers, and the result of such inquiry should be communicated to the entire force.[18]

The 1935 riot spurred the city to create a commission capable of producing a call for meaningful action to deal with the grievances of the Harlem community. At the same time the failure of the La Guardia administration officially to release the report, much less to commit itself to the specific recommendations as a comprehensive program, expressed the continuing powerful pressure exerted by racism in the decision-making process of New York City.

In actuality, the conflict between a tendency to see the March events in terms of conspiracy and a willingness to look for deeper causes had been articulated in the immediate aftermath of the riot. A number of Harlem community leaders had gathered on March 20 at the home of the Reverend Adam Clayton Powell, Jr., on Saint Nicholas Avenue and had later released a statement arguing that the incident's basic cause was "economic maladjustment; segregating and discrimination against Negroes in the matter of employment." The *New York Times* reported that "many representative Negro leaders" in Harlem had stated that the real cause of the trouble was the question of employment in Harlem stores. The *Times* further quoted Adam Clayton Powell, Jr., who linked the issue of jobs in local stores to resentments stemming from the Scottsboro case and the Italian invasion of Ethiopia. Powell stated: "Continued exploitation of the Negro is at the bottom of all this trouble, exploitation as regards wages, jobs, working conditions. Think of all the milk used in Harlem, yet not one bottle of it is delivered by Negroes. We see our boys and girls come out of college, well-trained, compelled to go on relief or work as red caps."[19] A statement as to the sources of the riot was also made by William Jay Schieffelin, chairman of the good-government Citizens Union. Speaking over radio station WMCA, Schieffelin stated that the roots of the riot were to be found in "injustice, exploitation and prejudice." Another civic leader who spoke out against explaining the events in terms of scapegoats was Dr. Robert W. Searle, general secretary of the Greater New York Federation of Churches. Searle believed that Communists had sought to utilize discontent for their own ends but insisted that "we cannot make the Communists the scapegoat for a basic condition which made possible such a hysteric outburst." Searle recognized that the basic condition was economic insecurity.[20]

The notion that what had occurred in Harlem could be accurately ascribed to a malicious few was given some support on Wednesday, March 20, when Mayor La Guardia issued a proclamation addressed to the people of New York. La Guardia declared that the "unfortunate occurrence" of Tuesday and Wednesday was "instigated and artificially stimulated by a few irresponsible individuals." He did not relate the violence to social conditions, going no further than to state that every city agency stood ready to scrutinize any charge of racial discrimination.[21] More inclined to use the riot as the basis for a campaign of witch hunting was the New York County district attorney, William C. Dodge. Announcing that the grand jury would investigate the riot, Dodge told reporters: "My purpose is to let the Communists know that they cannot come into this country and upset our laws. From my information Communists distributed literature and took an active part in the riot." The following day Dodge had further comments for the press on responsibility for the situation. "The Reds," said the district attorney, "have been boring into our institutions for a long time but when they begin to incite riots it is time to stop them" He also urged that persons found guilty of participating in the riot who were on the relief rolls should be promptly removed. Dodge announced that he intended to ask the United States commissioner of immigration to deport any alien found guilty of taking part in the riot and then moved afield to state that "half the trouble in the labor unions here is being caused by the Reds." The radicals had been safe "because we are sticklers for free speech," but when free speech caused riots "action" had to be taken. The view that agitators were the cause of the violence found further support in a statement issued by the merchants' association of Harlem. The retailers who had consistently failed to hire black clerks, much less supervisory personnel, now called upon Governor Herbert Lehman to send troops to Harlem. The merchants complained that local authorities had done nothing "to cure the irresponsible racial and religious agitation carried on by well-known leaders of outlaws and hoodlums." With their racism in rather plain view the merchants asserted that "last night beastly instincts of mob violence broke loose beyond control," with the result that more than a thousand business establishments "suffered the worst ruin in the annals of our glorious State."[22]

Two representatives of influential trends of thought within the black community who publicly discussed the 1935 riot at some length were the Communist spokesman James W. Ford and the scholar Alain Locke. Ford's position on the situation was consistent with his party's stress on avoiding provocations while at the same time calling for radical steps to deal with the causes of the riot. Already on March 20 the Communist-sponsored League of Struggle for Negro Rights had denounced the spreading of rumors that police had substituted Puerto Rican Lino Rivera for a black youth killed in the rioting. The *Times* reported that the New York District of the Communist party and the Young Communist League called upon black and white workers not to be stampeded into race riots. Copies of the *Daily Worker* conveying the Communist position attracted many buyers, with headlines presenting the themes of protest against police brutality and warning against provocative action.[23] Ford spelled out his position on the riot in a statement presented to the mayor's commission during April 1935. At the very outset of his presentation Ford graphically described conditions in Harlem: "The masses live on the brink of starvation. Disease and pestilence stalk the community. Police brutality drives the people to the point of desperation." The March 19 outbreak, Ford declared, had brought these conditions to the attention of the entire country. Ford also wasted no time in associating Mayor La Guardia with the corporate interests who exploited the black community. It was his view that the bankers and merchants and the mayor were "most concerned with making profits out of the blood of the Negro masses." The immediate cause of a high death rate and other deplorable conditions was "capitalist barbarism." Ford charged that it was to the advantage of the mayor "and his capitalist friends" to conceal the fact that the capitalists were responsible for the misery of the black masses and that the city government was a tool for the maintenance of the oppression of blacks.

Ford was not content with the liberal rhetoric that spoke in general terms of Harlem "conditions" but asserted that he would prove that "capitalist exploitation and national oppression" were responsible for the state of affairs in Harlem. The key issue he focused on was police brutality, and Ford outlined specific instances of police conduct, which he believed formed a pattern that showed the police "to be definitely arrayed against the masses of the people." The train of events he narrated began with a police attack during March 1934 on a public gathering assembled to hear Mrs. Ada Wright, mother of one of the Scottsboro boys. After outlining various instances of brutality Ford restated his conclusions at greater length and came down quite hard on La Guardia. "The above facts," Ford asserted, "show that the Negro people are treated like dogs in New York City, shot down and beaten up by the police at the least provocation. . . . The police department of New York City is an instrument of ruling class oppression, just like the sheriffs and lynch gangs in the South." As for La Guardia, Ford argued that events had proved the correctness of the Communist evaluation of him during his election campaign. La Guardia, "several times decorated by Mussolini for his faithful services to the fascist butchers of the Italian workers," was one of the most dangerous agents of big capital. La Guardia was a former everything, a man, the Communist implied, of no principles, "a former Republican, a former Socialist, a former Progressive, and a former highly paid consulting counsel for a Tammany administration." La Guardia lived up to his record by using the police to assault the citizens of Harlem. Turning from the mayor, Ford demanded that citizens' rights be adhered to. Specifically, he demanded protection of the right to assembly and organization, including the right to demonstrate, the right to picket without police interference, no police harassment of association between whites and blacks, a stop to beatings of arrested persons in police stations, and an end to the entering of homes or other establishments without proper authorization. Ford summed it all up in a general demand: "A stop to all forms of terror and intimidation by the police in Harlem." In another section of his statement Ford referred to a particularly galling grievance, brutal police treatment of individuals seeking assistance at the home relief bureaus in Harlem. In putting forward a program of demands Ford briefly noted how these demands could be realized. The remedy for such conditions, he told the mayor's commission, "can only be achieved by organized, ceaseless and relentless struggle of the masses."[24]

Alain Locke's discussion of the riot started from recognition that the rosy optimism of the period of the Harlem Renaissance had been succeeded by something else, "the prosy ordeal of the reformation with its stubborn tasks of economic reconstruction and social and civic reform." There were various analyses of the March 1935 riot, but whichever alternative one selected it was apparent that the riot, "like a revealing flash of lightning...etched on the public mind another Harlem than the bright surface Harlem of the night clubs, cabaret tours and arty magazines, a Harlem that the social worker knew all along but had not been able to dramatize, a Harlem, too, that the radical press and street-corner orator had been pointing out but in all too incredible exaggerations and none too convincing shouts." In the perspective of time it would be realized that the riot had exposed "the actual predicament of the mass life in Harlem" and demolished an attitude of Pollyanna complacency. The Harlem Renaissance could not exist in isolation from the real situation of the community. Locke, one of the prime spokesmen of the cultural flowering that was the product of the Harlem Renaissance, now clearly expressed the relation of the intellectual's life to that of the mass: "no cultural advance is safe without some sound economic underpinning, the foundation of a decent and reasonably secure average standard of living; and no emerging elite—artistic, professional or mercantile—can suspend itself in thin air over the abyss of a mass of unemployed stranded in an over-expensive, disease- and crime-ridden slum." It was easier to absorb oneself in "black Bohemia" than to contemplate the unpleasant social realities of Harlem, but those realities could not be ignored. There was, Locke asserted, "no cure or saving magic in poetry and art" for the atrocious conditions prevailing in the black community, "for capitalistic exploitation on the one hand and radical exploitation on the other."

Locke placed his remarks within the framework of a clearly positive evaluation of the La Guardia administration. He declared that the findings of the mayor's commission would shock the public, but he also quickly added that the reported deplorable conditions were a legacy of long years of Tammany neglect. Now, however, socially minded city and national governments were in office, and "the prospects of Negro Harlem—and for that matter all handicapped sections—are infinitely brighter." Already there was evidence that public authorities were moving to improve things, and Locke referred to such specifics as steps to recondition Harlem Hospital, appropriations for two new schools, and the dedication of the new Harlem River housing project. "Harlemites," Locke said, "may not be disposed to look gift horses in the mouth, though a few professional agitators may." It was his conclusion that the La Guardia administration had become aware of the community's legitimate needs "and is taking steps to meet some of them." Locke quoted approvingly from a recent La Guardia speech in which the mayor explained that the mistakes of the past fifty years could not be corrected in a day, "but we are going places and carrying out a definite program." Locke went on to stress the vital importance of having blacks in administrative positions, able to play an executive role in agencies having an impact upon the black community. He noted that blacks were often accused of "race chauvinism" for their insistence on representation on policy councils, but he insisted that "the principle of this vital safeguard is of manifest importance." In situations of accumulated resentment, even practical expediency called for the "public assurance and reassurance" of such black participation.

Locke concurred fully with the commission findings that the root cause of the disorders was in the social conditions prevailing in Harlem. He noted, however, that there were those "even in official circles" who placed responsibility for the situation upon radical propaganda. "To do so," Locke argued, "seriously misconstrues the situation by inverting the real order of cause and effect." The result of ignoring the causes would be the spreading of radicalism. Locke quoted an article he had written a decade earlier for the *Survey Graphic* in which he had said that the Negro was as yet only a "forced radical, a social protestant rather than a genuine radical." But he had also predicted that under the pressure of continuing injustice "iconoclastic thought and motives will inevitably increase." Now in 1936 he underscored that earlier statement and called for prompt remedial action. In an emergency a "special—perhaps even heroic—remedy becomes necessary where preventive long-term treatment should and could have been the scientific course." Locke fully endorsed the recommendations put forward by the mayor's commission.

Locke portrayed Harlem as representing a test, both of the pressures exerted by the Depression and of the general position of the black community. Economically, the situation of the Harlemite was of crucial significance because "as the man farthest down, he tests the pressure and explores the depths of the social and economic problem." The black resident of Harlem was more than the man who should not be forgotten; "he was the man who cannot safely be ignored." But Harlem was also the natural locale for race leadership. As the community had led the

Renaissance it would have to lead the "economic reconstruction and social reformation" he outlined. Locke held out two alternatives for the future: One was for a Harlem that was "community conscious and progressively cooperative," and the other was for a community "racially belligerent and distempered." Locke ended by drawing the contrast between a recent Works Progress Administration art festival featuring varied cultural activities, a Harlem "gaily and hopefully celebrating," and that other Harlem, the Harlem of the recent violence, "a bedlam of missiles, shattered plate glass, whacking night-sticks, mounted patrols, police sirens, and police bullets." It was to be hoped that constructive leadership would turn Harlem away from the dismal second alternative of violence.[25]

Locke's article must be read in the light of a recent finding that the piece constituted "a politically biased (and censored) analysis written on behalf of the La Guardia administration." The article, apparently, had been written with the explicit cooperation of the mayor. Locke was given access to confidential materials, but in exchange for that privilege the story was submitted to the mayor's office prior to publication and several deletions and additions were subsequently made.[26] The article did not fully articulate Locke's views, as indicated by the fact that in a confidential memo he criticized the administration for not having made the report public. Locke was especially critical of the fact that the city departments that most actively took issue with commission findings were the agencies, according to the commission, that refused cooperation with the investigation.

The Harlem 1935 riot vividly demonstrated that violent acts by public institutions produce a violent reaction. Long-prevalent police brutality had prepared Harlemites to believe the rumors about the killing of the boy in the Kress store. The result was a mass explosion of anger, directed in the first place against property and secondarily at the police. By the time the spasm of violent anger had subsided three persons had been shot to death. In the aftermath of these events economic conditions in Harlem were somewhat alleviated by a variety of New Deal welfare measures, but basic change in institutional policy did not occur; the police did not abandon reliance upon arbitrary force as the prime mechanism for control of the black community.

ELEVEN

The NAACP and Radical Voices

THE 1930s put every organized segment of the black community to the test of adapting itself to the urgent situation produced by the Great Depression; to stand still was to risk irrelevance. The NAACP, with middle-class roots and a mass following that extended beyond that class, was particularly sensitive to the changed conditions and, although not without some difficulty, it managed to retain a leadership position among Afro-Americans. As the center of gravity of black opinion drifted leftward toward support of industrial unionism and embraced the New Deal, and as blacks often saw a new legitimacy in the views of the Communist party, the association also drifted to the Left but at the same time retained its place as a voice of moderation. It continued its championing of civil rights, took a friendlier view of labor unionism, but also maintained its emphasis on working through the courts and avoided any formal involvement with Communists in united front activity, especially on the national level. The opinions of white liberals were still a significant factor in shaping the organization's direction. Reacting to the enhanced position of leftists within the black community, the association accelerated its antilynching activities, thereby providing a focus for broader unity while seeking to strengthen its ability to compete with the radicals for the allegiance of the masses. It should be noted that for much of this period the NAACP was in the position of responding to pressures coming from the Left.

A shift in the association's position was a process, and a significant episode in that process was the divergence between W. E. B. Du Bois, editor of the *Crisis,* and the main group of the organization's officers. The question of racist violence and of black response to that violence was one of the issues addressed in that debate. There were, to be sure, personal elements in the rupture. Du Bois did not believe that Walter White was the proper person to lead the NAACP, and there was also Du Bois's perception that the organization was in a state of general crisis. In mid-1934 he wrote that the association's leaders were called upon "to formulate a positive program of construction and inspiration" and added his comment: "We have been thus far unable to comply." He believed that the NAACP was "the greatest organization for the emancipation of Negroes" that the nation had ever had, but currently he found that it was "in a time of crisis and change, without a program, without effective organization, without executive officers who have either the ability or disposition to guide the National Association for the Advancement of Colored People in the right direction." He stated that a dispute about policy dealing with segregation was an occasion, "and an important occasion," for the division, but it was not the underlying cause. The dispute, however, illuminates diverging mindsets that would end Du Bois's editorship of the *Crisis,* and the issues raised merit further consideration.[1]

The development of Du Bois's position that culminated in his departure from the NAACP can be traced in articles he published in the *Crisis* during 1933–34. The thrust of Du Bois's thought was toward economic radicalism but, at least for the time being, a radicalism enclosed in the shell of nationalism. Unprepared to base strategy upon the possibility of alliance with white workers, he returned to an earlier theme in his intellectual evolution, serious critique of capitalism and respectful consideration of Marxism. The May 1933 issue of the *Crisis* carried his essay, "Marxism and the Negro Problem." Du Bois observed that until the Russian Revolution Marx "was treated condescendingly in the universities, and regarded even by the intelligent public as a radical agitator whose curious and inconvenient theories it was easy to refute." But events had changed things, and Du Bois noted in a comment that might be made on his own career, "we see in Karl Marx a colossal genius of infinite sacrifice and monumental industry, and with a mind of extraordinary logical keenness and grasp." In light of the Russian experience and the reality of the Great Depression, thoughtful persons, Du Bois wrote, were beginning to admit that recurring industrial crises and wars were "forcing the world to contemplate the possibilities of fundamental change in our economic methods; and that means thorough-going change, whether it be violent, as in France or Russia, or peaceful, as just seems possible, and just as true to the Marxian formula, if it is fundamental change; in any case, Revolution seems bound to come." Du Bois saw this direction of events reflected in "our re-examination of the whole concept of Property," a reexamination that he apparently saw in some of the early New Deal measures, "our banking moratorium; the extraordinary new agriculture bill; the plans to attack unemployment."

Du Bois then asked the question: "What now has all this to do with the Negro problem?" He placed the mass of American blacks as belonging to the "working proletariat," and he recognized that white and black workers had similar complaints against capitalists, "save that the grievances of the Negro worker are more fundamental." But though Du Bois viewed the working of capitalism as generally responsible for the exploitation of blacks it was the white workers to whom he ascribed direct responsibility for the most bitter oppression of blacks. Regarding the condition of black labor, he wrote: "the lowest and most fatal degree of its suffering comes not from the capitalists but from fellow white laborers. It is white labor that deprives the Negro of his right to vote, denies him education, denies him affiliation with trade unions, expels him from decent houses and neighborhoods, and heaps upon him the public insults of open color discrimination." He emphasized that it would not suffice to say that capital encourages this oppression of blacks. That may have excused, he explained, "the ignorant and superstitious Russian peasants in the past" and some of the poor southern whites. But as for the bulk of American white labor, that was another story: "It knows exactly what it is doing and it means to do it. William Green and Matthew Woll of the A. F. of L. have no excuse of illiteracy or religion to veil their deliberate determination to keep Negroes and Mexicans and other elements of common labor, in a lower proletariat as subservient to their interests as theirs are to the interests of capital." Here Du Bois blurred any distinction between the rank and file of American labor and the retrogressive influence of the representatives of an entrenched craft-union bureaucracy. He also may have underestimated the power of the opinion-shaping mechanisms of American society that worked to manipulate the American mass mind.

Within the white population Du Bois saw a stratum of engineers and better-paid workers whose interests were bound up with those of capital. The ordinary worker, on the other hand, rather than "being motivated by any vision of revolt against capitalism, has been blinded by the American vision of the possibility of layer after layer of the workers escaping into the wealthy class and becoming managers and employers of labor." The result was a frantic scramble to advance economically on the backs of black labor and foreign immigrants. Adding to the influence of this scramble was the impact of colonialism that in Europe and America bribed white workers with opportunities to exploit colored labor.

"How now," Du Bois asked, "does the philosophy of Karl Marx apply today to colored labor?" He was unequivocal in the first part of his response: "colored labor has no common ground with white labor. No soviet of technocrats would do more than exploit colored labor in order to raise the status of whites." He proceeded to the conclusion that Marxism was a valid diagnosis of the situation in nineteenth-century Europe but that it must be modified in the United States and especially as concerned blacks. Blacks were exploited in the United States, but that exploitation came from white capitalists "and equally from the white proletariat." Communists, he wrote, sought to break down racial barriers, but their "shrill cry" was not listened to. For the black American, then, the appropriate response—Du Bois's adaptation at this point of Marxism to American reality—was such "internal organization" as would offer protection against both white capital and white labor "and such practical economic insight as will prevent inside the race group any large development of capitalistic exploitation." He ended this essay with the comment: "In the hearts of black laborers alone, therefore, lie those ideals of democracy in politics and industry which may in time make the workers of the world effective dictators of civilization." In this piece the elements of both anticapitalism and nationalism were readily apparent.[2]

During June 1933 Du Bois was commencement speaker at Fisk University, and part of his address appeared in the August issue of the *Crisis.* Du Bois's topic was "The Negro College," but in reality his words were a general commentary on the position of blacks in American society. He began from the premise that the university for black students must be a black university. He asserted that "there can be no college for Negroes which is not a Negro college and that while an American Negro university, just like a German or a Swiss university may rightly aspire to a universal culture unhampered by limitations of race and culture, yet it must start on the earth where we sit and not in the skies whither we aspire." To start on the earth was to proceed from the existing situation, and Du Bois bluntly outlined the realities as blacks confronted them in 1933: "We are politically hamstrung. We have the greatest difficulty in getting suitable and remunerative work...or suffer social ostracism which is so deadening and discouraging that we are compelled either to lie about it or to turn our faces to the red flag of revolution. It consists of studied and repeated public insult of the sort which during all the long history of the world has led men to kill or be killed." In this context it was absurd to expect that the institution for blacks, functioning within American conditions, could simply transmit some universal world culture without being specifically shaped by the life experience and heritage of Afro-Americans. Du Bois was most certainly not advocating a narrow parochial education for black youth, as he made clear when he defined what he envisioned as the appropriate role for the black university: "Starting with present conditions and using the facts and the knowledge of the present situation of American Negroes, the Negro university expands toward the possession and the conquest of all knowledge. It seeks from a beginning of the history of the Negro in America and Negro tribes and kingdoms in Africa, to interpret and understand the social development of all mankind in all ages. It seeks to reach modern science of matter and life from the surroundings and habits and aptitudes of American Negroes and thus lead up to understanding of life and matter in the universe." In short, the educational life of black people must be based on the roots of the black experience.

Following up this thought, Du Bois posed the question of why the "renaissance of literature" of the 1920s had not taken root among blacks. His answer constituted a severe judgment of that cultural phenomenon: "It was because it was a transplanted and exotic thing. It was a literature written for the benefit of white people and at the behest of white readers, and starting out privately from the white point of view. It never had a real Negro constituency and it did not grow out of the inmost heart and frank experience of Negroes; on such an artificial basis no real literature can grow."

Du Bois in this speech was reflecting the realities of the Depression decade, although when he referred to "sinister signs about us" he said they were unconnected to the Great Depression. He described conditions that antedated 1929: "The organized might of industry north and south is relegating the Negro to the edge of survival and using him as a labor reservoir on starvation wage. No secure professional class, no science, literature, nor art can live on such a sub-soil. It is an insistent, deep-throated cry for rescue, guidance and organized advance that greets the black leader today, and the college, that trains him has got to let him know at least as much about the great black miners' strike in Alabama as about the age of Pericles." To be sure, the realities Du Bois pointed to had a long history, but it was also true that they had been underscored by the events of the economic crisis. So too was he striking a theme given particular point by the Depression when he observed that the role of the black university as "a center of applied knowledge" had become all the more necessary "since we easily see that planned action especially in economic life, is going to be the watchword of civilization." Du Bois was here reflecting the general process of radicalization that was underway in American thought.

In his remarks Du Bois took occasion to make clear that his advocacy of leadership by a talented elite was not to be a program for leadership by the children of the economically advantaged. To choose students on the basis of their parents' money, he said, was to imitate the white world, and that basis of selection "is going to give us an extraordinary aggregation." The talented and the gifted, he declared, were to be chosen quite without regard to economic or social standing. "There is no other way," he added.

Toward the end of his speech Du Bois struck a note of economic radicalism when he held out to the graduates a vision "of a world without wealth, of capital without profit, of income based on work alone." But he also faced the question of whether his speech represented a program of segregation. He gave his answer: "It is and it is not by choice but by force; you do not get humanity by wishing it nor do you become American citizens simply because you want to." The truth was that American blacks were segregated, "apart, hammered into a separate entity by spiritual intolerance and legal sanction backed by mob law...no character, address, culture or desert is going to change it in our day or for centuries to come."

As to some ultimate direction of history, Du Bois stated that it was not then known. It might be "a great physical segregation" of the world along the color line; it might be an economic rebirth that insured integrity among diversity; it could be "utter annihilation of class and race and color barriers" in one mankind, but whatever the outcome he believed it was a matter of centuries, not years. Whatever the future, it was "thought, plan, knowledge and organization" that would lead to it. He was insistent that the way forward was not one of violence, for "the alternative of not dying like hogs is not that of dying or killing like snarling dogs." Here, as always in his thought, was the emphasis upon reason. The viable alternative was one of conquering the world "by thought and brain and plan; by expression and organized cultural ideals."[3]

In Du Bois's "Postscript" column in the May 1934 issue of the *Crisis*, he again returned to the issue of segregation. It seems a girl "with brown and serious face" had come up to him following a lecture and commented: "It seems to me that you used to fight Segregation, and that now you are ready to compromise." Du Bois wrote that he gave the reply that he had fought segregation with facts, reason, and agitation and that he continued so to fight it and to say that segregation was wrong. But, he added, he would fight segregation with segregation. He gave as an illustration of his policy the instance of government support for replacing slum housing with "beautiful, simple, clean homes, for poor colored people, with all modern conveniences." He would support that replacement because the alternative was either that segregated housing or none at all. He was not bothered by talk that he was compromising. Something else, however, did much bother him. "Negro poverty and idleness and distress," he wrote, "they bother me and always will."

In this column Du Bois turned to the issue of violence..He wrote that some young blacks, "inspired by white Radicals," were looking toward violence as a means of resolving grievances. He rejected this course. Asked what the difference was between the situation of the plight of blacks in the United States and that of the Haitian slaves, Du Bois recalled the circumstances of Haiti in which blacks greatly outnumbered whites. He noted that in the contemporary United States twelve million blacks were "totally surrounded" by 110 million whites. "Under such circumstances," he declared, "to talk about force, is little less than idiotic." He further explained that recourse to violence or even thoughts of violence would solidify white opposition. That opposition, using the tactics Hitler was then employing in Germany, "would seek to annihilate, and spiritually, even physically, re-enslave the black folk of America." As Du Bois viewed the situation, use of violence by the racially oppressed would produce an escalation of violence that would gravely threaten the oppressed themselves. It should be noted that Du Bois's rejection of violence was not absolute, for he added a last comment that it was "our clear policy not to appeal to force until clearly and evidently there is no other way." In this discussion of violence Du Bois made clear that his emerging orientation toward economic radicalism and nationalism did not imply rejection of nonviolent methods of social change.[4]

In the summer of 1934 Dr. Du Bois and the NAACP officers came to a parting of the ways, and on July 1 his resignation as editor of the Crisis took effect. During March Du Bois had submitted a resolution for consideration by the board that embodied his current emphasis upon independent development while again stating basic opposition to segregation. His proposal indicates he was still committed to working within the framework of long-term association policy:

The segregation of human beings purely on a basis of race and color is not only stupid and unjust, but positively dangerous, since it is a path that leads straight to national jealousies, racial antagonisms, and war. The NAACP, therefore, has always opposed the underlying principle of racial segregation, and will oppose it. On the other hand, it has with equal clearness, recognized that when a group like the American Negroes suffers conscious and systematic segregation against which argument and appeal are either useless or very slow in effecting changes, such a group must make up its mind to associate and cooperate for its own uplift and in defense of its self-respect.

The NAACP, therefore, has always recognized and encouraged the Negro church, the Negro college, the Negro public school, and Negro business and industrial enterprises, and believes they should be made the very best and most efficient institutions of their kind judged by any standard; not with the idea of perpetuating artificial separation of mankind, but rather with the distinct object of proving Negro efficiency, showing Negro ability and discipline, and demonstrating how useless and wasteful race segregation is.

President Joel Spingarn met this resolution with a counterproposal that was essentially no more than a slightly softened statement of the Du Bois text, but NAACP secretary Walter White insisted upon pushing through the board his own resolution that eschewed any attempt to accommodate Du Bois's position. Following White's lead, the NAACP board stated that the association was "opposed to the principle and the practice of enforced segregation of human beings on the basis of race and color. Enforced segregation by its very existence carries with it the implication of a superior and inferior group and invariably results in the imposition of a lower status on the group deemed inferior. *Thus both principle and practice necessitate unyielding opposition to any and every form of enforced segregation.*" When Dr. Du Bois, to the surprise of nobody, continued to advance his views in the pages of the *Crisis,* the board at its May meeting adopted a resolution stating that the *Crisis* was the organ of the NAACP and no salaried officer of the association shall criticize the organization's policies in the magazine. Du Bois was now forced either to allow himself to be silenced or to resign, and anyone with any knowledge of Du Bois could predict the outcome. He resigned, and although there was some attempt made at reconciliation, after a brief interval he insisted that his resignation as editor of the *Crisis* and his departure from the NAACP stood.[5]

In the wake of his departure from the NAACP Du Bois followed his own light, and the association maintained its commitment to working within the premises of corporate capitalism. But the organization could not simply continue unchanged in its previous course and recognized that fact by developing a campaign against lynching that could be embraced by both reformists and radicals. In launching this effort the NAACP was able to draw upon an established record of working against mob violence. Though the immediate issues of racial violence were indeed of grave consequence, strategically speaking, the association's leaders opted for an end run around troublesome long-term questions.

The antilynching campaign was accompanied by a new emphasis on the economic underpinnings of racism, but this emphasis was more a matter of rhetoric than of substance. After Du Bois's departure from the organization a number of militants, especially oriented toward involvement in economic issues, continued to function in and around the NAACP. One of these was Ralph Bunche, who criticized excessive leadership concern with the views of prominent white sponsors, persons Bunche characterized as, "in the main, either cautious liberals or mawkish, missionary-minded sentimentalists on the race question." He wrote that concern with the opinions of these whites "has been a powerful factor in keeping the Association thoroughly 'respectable,' and has certainly been an influence in the very evident desire of the Association to keep its skirts free of the grimy bitterness and strife encountered in the economic area." Board member Abram Harris was particularly active in seeking to move the NAACP upon a new course of stress on economic demands. At the 1935 annual conference Harris declared that current problems were "fundamentally economic" and urged going to both white and black workers with a program that would underscore their common interests.[6] In July 1934, on the heels of Du Bois's resignation, the NAACP board of directors appointed a special committee, the Committee on the Future Plan and Program of the NAACP, to consider the organization's future direction. Harris chaired the committee, was able to rely on support from committee members Rachel Davis Du Bois and Sterling Brown, and managed to organize the work so as to involve several individuals, among them Benjamin Stolberg, William Hastie, E. Franklin Frazier, and Ralph Bunche, who recognized the need for a relevant economic program. The committee's report called for a main emphasis on the building "of a labor movement, industrial in character, which will unite all labor, white and black, skilled and unskilled, agricultural and industrial." The report further recommended a program of workers' education and the preparation of literature relevant to workers' needs. In terms of structure the committee urged the creation of a five-member advisory Committee on Economic Activities, which would implement the proposals made in the report.

The NAACP board gave its approval to much of what the committee proposed, although substantially modifying the organizational structure. But as Raymond Wolters has observed, this approval did not reflect the central direction along which the association's leaders wished to move. The preference of the leadership was for activities in the legal area, for education and lobbying, and conflicting priorities were dealt with "by announcing one program and pursuing another." Endorsement of the economic program was grudging in any event, and as association leaders lacked both will and ability to take up the economic challenge, "the rhetoric of the association moved to the Left, but the program continued in the traditional civil-libertarian framework." Perhaps the rhetoric eased some of the apprehensions raised by Du Bois's resignation, but it did not express an actual commitment to focus upon the economic roots of racial oppression. In a sense the outcome was inevitable, given the circumstance that most NAACP board members continued to believe, as Wolters notes, that "ignorance was the root cause of exploitation and that meaningful progress would be achieved once men of good will became aware of desperate conditions." The rhetorical concern with economics was by no means meaningless; it helped to legitimize black support of unionization efforts and was part of the process that placed blacks in the New Deal political coalition and laid a basis for future collaboration with the labor movement. But it did not impel the core of the NAACP program toward mass-action tactics, and it permitted the organization to give first priority to legal-legislative lobbying work.[7]

In 1933 Walter White began to point the association toward concentration on the issue of lynching. The issue itself gripped White, as it consistently gripped black Americans generally, and he brought to it his own youthful experience with the 1906 Atlanta violence and his record as investigator of lynchings in the South. It was a subject upon which he could speak with extensive firsthand knowledge and authority. Robert Zangrando has written that anxiety about growing radical and particularly Communist influence on black opinion was a factor animating White, and doubtless White felt impelled to project a militancy that could yet retain connections with respectable whites. The time was right. White and other NAACP officials needed a counter to the challenge from the Left. White liberals, morally revulsed by the barbarism of lynching, could probably be won to support a drive against lynching, and the early 1930s had produced a renewed surge of lynchings that decent opinion could not ignore. The coming to power of the New Deal raised hope that action against lynching could be placed on the national reform agenda. Prominent NAACP figure Charles Houston wrote White in 1935 that "lots of us feel that a fight for anti-lynching legislation without just as vigorous a battle for economic independence is to fight the manifestation of the evil and ignore its cause," but his advice in this matter was to go unheeded.[8]

The NAACP, under White's direction, began a major publicity and lobbying effort in support of antilynching bills under consideration in Congress. The campaign centered upon the Costigan–Wagner bill of 1934 and the Wagner–Van Nuys–Gavagan bill introduced in 1937. The measures focused upon federal penalties to be imposed on local or state officers who failed to protect citizens from lynch mobs or to arrest and prosecute the perpetrators of mob violence. Heightened national interest in federal action was spurred by the October 1934 lynching of Claude Neal at the northern Florida town of Marianna, an atrocity in which the victim was burned with irons, his penis cut off, and his body stretched from the limbs of a tree. A crowd of thousands gathered, hoping to get a glimpse of the torture. This event received extensive coverage by news media throughout the nation.[9] Initially there were grounds for hope that the Roosevelt administration would make enactment of antilynching legislation a priority item. The drift of public opinion was clearly toward support of an antilynching measure, as revealed in a 1937 Gallup poll that showed large affirmative majorities in every region of the nation, but at no point would Franklin Roosevelt commit himself and the administration on this question.[10] Support of an antilynching measure would have risked conflict with the congressional southern Democrats, and Roosevelt could and did cling to the rationale that the general program of New Deal reforms took precedence over movement on antilynching legislation.

Doubtless encouraged by the administration's failure to take up the cause, the opponents of federal action were unyielding in blocking enactment of an antilynching bill. That opposition was led by strident bigots whose racism was blatant, but some of the moderate and liberal voices of the white South also opposed dealing with the issue on the national level. In the Senate, James Byrnes of South Carolina sought to raise the specter of endless black demands by appealing to fears that Walter White would proceed to seek legislation protecting the right to stop at hotels and also providing for federal supervision of elections. Mississippi senator Theodore Bilbo expressed his unvarnished, primitive racism when he told the Senate he wished to inquire what senator would not understand "that the underlying motive of the Ethiopian who has inspired this proposed legislation, the antilynching bill, and desires its enactment into law with a zeal and frenzy equal if not paramount to the lust and lasciviousness of the rape fiend in this diabolical effort to despoil the womanhood of the Caucasian race, is to realize the consummation of his dream and ever-abiding hope and most fervent prayer to become socially and politically equal to the white man."[11]

Opposition or equivocation from southern white liberals was not so predictable, but it was manifested and helped to give some thin veneer of legitimacy to congressional foes of antilynching legislation. It could now be said that even those with long records of hostility to lynching did not support enactment of a federal statute. The Commission on Interracial Cooperation, led by the well-known liberal Will Alexander, in 1935 endorsed in general terms passage of a federal bill but did not support any particular bill and did not throw its energies into campaigning for congressional action.[12] Lining up in direct opposition was Jessie Daniel Ames of the Association of Southern Women for Prevention of Lynching. Ames had given much of her life to work in the South against mob violence. In 1934 she had moved quickly to call for federal intervention in the impending Claude Neal lynching, urging the attorney general to launch a federal investigation under the kidnapping statute and take steps to punish those responsible for the "abduction." Ames realized that lynching, particularly the ability of the mob to act with impunity, was related to black disfranchisement and general political powerlessness, that southern sheriffs were unlikely to act effectively against lynching so long as they did not need to relate to blacks as voters.[13] But when the NAACP undertook its campaign she withheld her support. In 1938 she went so far as to write Senator Tom Connally concerning the fate of the Wagner–Van Nuys–Gavagan bill: "It will be a great relief to the public to have that measure laid on the shelf in order that the Senate may go about important and far-reaching legislation." After public release of her letter W. E. B. Du Bois wrote Mrs. Ames in candid criticism of her position:

> Instead now of your following up the excellent work which has been done by Southern people and upheld by leading Southern periodicals, utterly to stamp out lynching, you begin by congratulating a Senator because he is about to win the fight to defeat the Anti-Lynching Bill, and you assume there is important far-reaching legislation which outweighs the effort to stop lynching. I am sorry and distressed that a person in your position should think or seem to think this and under any circumstances it is a singular anticlimax to have you actually say that the South will be somewhat on the spot when the first lynching takes place after the Anti-Lynching Bill is laid aside.[14]

Ames, however, did not alter her stance, a stance that compromised her record as an articulate and energetic crusader against lynching.

Ames, to be sure, desired that the South itself deal with lynching. But beyond that consideration she expressed a southern liberalism that opposed lynching but also was hostile to mass pressure tactics, particularly when those tactics were employed by blacks. J. Wayne Dudley, in his study of the Association of Southern Women for Prevention of Lynching, has written that the organization represented a conservative force in the antilynching movement. Dudley writes of some of the ASWPL members:

> They resented the efforts of so-called "outside groups," such as the NAACP, and rejected their efforts towards a congressional guarantee which would extend federal protection to all citizens including Southern blacks. In the late 1930s, they demonstrated an inordinate fear that passage of a federal bill would enhance the status of the NAACP and the black voters at the expense of the Southerners and the South within the Democratic Party and the nation. They also believed that passage of the bill would trigger a more aggressive push by blacks for more "radical" changes which the women perceived as dangerous.[15]

Jacquelyn Hall finds a source for Ames's rejection of federal legislation in her paternalistic attitudes. Hall explains how Ames's work against lynching coexisted with her position on the congressional bills:

> Ames seldom saw blacks as equals even in the struggle against their own oppression. She devoted her life to the protection of those too weak to protect themselves, even while rejecting and fearing such guardianship for herself. Uneasy among her equals, fearful of her own vulnerability, and unwilling to accept the claims of intimacy, she found confirmation of her own strength in promoting the welfare of men and women who were comfortably unequal and safely separate. Without a second thought, she had eliminated blacks from the women's anti-lynching movement; when a question of strategy arose she felt no obligation to be responsive to black agendas for reform.

Hall, too, finds conservative implications, a "double-edged" analysis, in some ASWPL material. The organization worked to uphold law and order as against the lawlessness of the lynch mob, but as Hall writes, usually implicitly "but sometimes openly, the demand for law and order promised that blacks could be kept in their place more efficiently, more permanently, and with less social disorganization by a legal system firmly under the control of whites than by extralegal lynchings." Ames and the ASWPL did not speak for all southern white women on the matter of federal action. In 1934 the Southern Methodist Women's Missionary Council, representing 250 thousand members, unanimously voted support of federal legislation, and a number of individuals working with the ASWPL also favored such action.[16] But the fact that the southern white women's organization that had most often spoken out against lynching was absent from the antilynching bill coalition and that the Commission on Interracial Cooperation gave only nominal support surely worked to undermine the NAACP's efforts. Southern white liberals could be valuable allies in the struggle for black rights, but often they would not, then or later, be easily moved to follow black initiative and leadership.

Robert Zangrando emphasizes the positive side of the NAACP antilynching campaign of the 1930s. The effort, he writes, "had forced the American people to confront the most brutal aspects of racism. The lesson, however painful to acknowledge and absorb, helped in significant ways to prepare the national conscience for reforms that would follow in the next quarter century."[17] Raymond Wolters, however, while granting some truth to Zangrando's evaluation, contends that for the association to remain at the cutting edge of reform it might better have given its energies to basic economic analysis of the conditions facing black people.[18] But the fights against lynching and economic analysis were not mutually exclusive as approaches to the black struggle; lynching, after all, had its roots in the economic oppression of blacks and poor whites. Educational and propaganda work against lynching was still a necessity— Wolters is overly optimistic in contending that the association had already accomplished its task of changing the American mindset regarding race— but more might have been achieved if the organization had been less concerned with narrow bureaucratic interests, if its lobbying work had been combined with mass demonstrative protest and a more vigorous program of support for the growing labor movement.

The militant moods of the 1930s affected every segment of the black protest movement, and the National Association for the Advancement of Colored People was no exception. Gunnar Myrdal refers to serious criticism of the association voiced by radicals, criticism that revolved around the organization's failure to come forward with a program for basic economic change. Myrdal sided with the NAACP against its critics, generally evaluating its strategy and tactics as realistic and constructive, although he did note that in the course of its work the association "often accepted segregation, and in fact, has sometimes had to promote further segregation, while it has been pressing for increased opportunity and equality within the segregated system."[19] But, quite apart from an evaluation of long-term trends in NAACP strategy, it should be noted that increasingly in the mid- and late 1930s the association expressed a more militant response to racial brutality. Loren Miller of the New Masses, covering the association's 1935 conference held at St. Louis, perceptively reported the ambiguities he observed in the organization. On the one hand he wrote that the NAACP was "still a very vital factor in Negro life and to that extent in the life of the nation," and on the other he indicated that many branches were inactive and association income had dropped sharply. The central theme of his report was the considerable distance between the militant tenor expressed by delegates and the resolutions adopted at the meeting and the conservative, bureaucratic spirit manifested by the self-perpetuating leadership. But still the leadership could not quite contain the militancy, however much it may have wanted to.[20]

Militant stirrings and some receptivity to united action with radicals became evident at the level of branch activity and in the pages of the *Crisis*. In 1935 in Cincinnati representatives of the NAACP, the International Labor Defense, and the American Civil Liberties Union joined forces in efforts to save the life of John Montjoy, a black youth sentenced to death in nearby Covington on an alleged charge of rape. The three organizations jointly appealed to interested persons to write the Kentucky Court of Appeals, urging a new trial.[21]

In the *Crisis* there were now to be found articles reflecting a fiercely anti-Fascist spirit. The NAACP organ at least gave some space to writers who were ahead of those Americans who still saw no danger in the policies of the Fascist states. The *Crisis* published Langston Hughes's speech to the Second International Writers Congress, held in Paris during July 1937, in which the writer generally excoriated fascism and, referring to Franco and his allies, stated that "to them now the murder of women and children is nothing." The slogans of racism had long been used in the United States to divide and conquer, and now "the Fascists of the world use it as a bugaboo and a terror to keep the working masses from getting together." Hughes at the end of his speech related his antifascism to a radical perspective, declaring that "the Fascists know that when there is no more race, there will be no more capitalism, and no more war, and no more money for the munition makers, because the workers of the world will have triumphed."[22] Antifascism was also expressed by William Pickens, for many years one of the association's national spokesmen. Pickens had visited Spain during the Civil War, and there he encountered some of the black volunteers who came to Spain to fight with the Loyalists. "All honor to those boys!" Pickens exclaimed. With regard to the issues of the war Pickens's sympathies were clear. The Spanish people, he wrote, "are fighting on the front for popular government,—for self government. It is our fight."[23]

In November 1934 the editors of the magazine published a piece,

"Southern Terror" by Louise Thompson, described as "the leading colored woman in the Communist movement in this country." The article was an account of brutal treatment she received at the hands of police in Birmingham, but it was also a succinct statement of the Communist position on the black struggle. Thompson wrote: "Being a Communist in the South is synonymous with being a fighter for the rights of the Negro people, of being a 'nigger lover,' of trying to bring white and Negro workers and poor farmers together—of fighting against lynching, of challenging the southern ruling class traditional manner of treating Negroes." Thompson told of the White Legion, the racist terror organization operating in Birmingham, and went on to explain that it was not coincidence that the legion always linked communism with the black question. It was the Communist party, she wrote, "which has analyzed the Negro question as that of an oppressed nation of people, defined the alignment of class forces for and against the Negro people's struggle for liberation, and begun the organization of white and Negro working masses together." Some organizations within the black community, Thompson observed, were as vehement in criticism of militancy and a radical program as the White Legion, and she added: "Such organizations accept the present system of capitalism and are willing to be satisfied with what hollow reforms may come without fundamental change." But, Thompson argued, it was impossible to take a step for black rights that was not revolutionary. Capitalism in the United States developed on the basis of the superexploitation of blacks and the division between black and white labor. To challenge that division was to challenge American capitalism. The southern ruling class would not yield, and beyond that class was the massive power of American finance capital. Any groups, she wrote, that did not point out these class relationships "become the voice of reaction in the midst of a people struggling for freedom." There was need for a new black leadership, for the emergence of working-class leaders, "the Angelo Herndons, who will not be stopped by jail, by a desire to cling on to jobs, by death itself in leading the Negro people through the final conflict to complete emancipation."[24] Publication of this article certainly did not signify that the NAACP was about to endorse communism or that it favored united front action with Communists, but it did represent acknowledgment that the Communist viewpoint was entitled to a hearing within the black community.

A renewed militancy was also expressed in *Crisis* articles dealing with specific instances of racial violence in the United States. A May 1936 article by Roy Wilkins told the story of the lynching at Gordonsville, Virginia, of a black man, William Wales, and his sister Cora. Wilkins described this incident as one of "cruel, bestial, atavistic degeneracy by some white people." The brother and sister had for years resisted efforts to induce them to sell their property, land desired by the town for expansion of a cemetery. To pressure Wales the charge was made that he had threatened a white woman, and this provided the basis for the sheriff to seek to arrest the black man. But Wales was set upon resistance, and when the sheriff came to serve the warrant Wales shot and killed him. As Wilkins explained it, what happened next was that "the lid was off." Against this black man who had dared to fight the white police anything could be done. And indeed there was to be no limit to the racist response to Wales's act of rebellion. A crowd of some 5,000 surrounded the house of these two elderly blacks, held off for a time by shotgun and rifle fire. To destroy the two persons defying the crowd a request was sent off for the assistance of United States Marines stationed at nearby Quantico. The marines were not made available, and the mob had to wait for nightfall. Then a torch was thrown, igniting the house, and as each of the blacks was silhouetted against the flames they were shot down. But that was not all. When the embers of the house had sufficiently cooled the murderers entered the building and hacked the bodies into small pieces to be taken away as souvenirs. According to Wilkins even pieces of bone were carried off. The usually restrained Wilkins commented angrily: "If the tradition of American lynchers was faithfully followed, there reposes now on the mantelpieces of many a Virginia home a bit of flesh or a bone preserved in a jar of alcohol to remind children and grandchildren of the indomitable courage of a brother, father or son of the family who battled to the death to prevent two Negroes from overcoming 5,000 white Virginians."

Wilkins in this article sought to reconcile the NAACP's traditional reliance upon legal processes with the right of self-defense. Rhetorically, he asked the question: "Does *The Crisis* mean to imply by this article that its policy is to defend colored people who kill sheriffs?" His answer was that blacks had to be for law and order, even though the law gave blacks little protection. But Wilkins could understand the factors that drove Wales to a desperate act. Everywhere he looked he was confronted with racial oppression. Among other things, "he saw his people hanged, roasted and mutilated by mobs while legislators called points of order and an aspirant to the Presidency fiddled with clauses, periods and commas in the so-called Bill of Rights." Wilkins's conclusion was that the "system" killed the sheriff. Wales was merely the agent. Those in the mob who tormented the two blacks "already are half-dead." "*The Crisis* defends William and Cora Wales," Wilkins stated. As for the charge that they were crazy, Wilkins's answer was that the sane people were inside the house. The 5,000 in the mob were indeed mad. What Wilkins did in this article was to seek to vindicate the two murdered blacks without abandoning the association's emphasis upon legal action. But it is significant that Wilkins did put a stamp of legitimacy upon the action of blacks who took up arms against their oppressors.[25]

In the 1930s racial oppression continued as always to rely heavily upon the sanction of violence. Parallel to a decrease in the recorded frequency of mob lynchings from the midthirties onward was a greater prevalence of the "legal" lynching, the victimization of blacks clothed with the appearance of legality. What most stood out in this era was a new sophistication in strategies for basic change in the American racial system. Fascism threatened all democratic forces with violence, and it was clear that the struggle against racial brutality in the United States was increasingly merging with a worldwide struggle.

A new sophistication and ideological maturity were to be found in an analysis, published in 1935, by Ralph Bunche. In time Bunche moved into the American foreign policy Establishment, and later he served as a distinguished official of the United Nations. But in the thirties his thought reflected the radical currents of the time. Bunche carefully dissected the various alternative strategies available to blacks. He did not see need for serious consideration of violent tactics. Blacks constituted a minority of the population and were scattered about the country, and these factors precluded the possibility of black revolution. Blacks were also unlikely to affiliate in the short run with nonblack revolutionary movements. As Ralph Bunche saw them, Afro-Americans retained the American dream and were basically conservative and imbued with a peasant psychology. Bunche, however, did envision a meaningful role for the radical movements. Their job was that of developing radical class consciousness among both whites and blacks, looking forward to a future of black and white cooperation in a militant labor movement. This radical perspective was clearly for the future; in the here and now blacks were not ready for violent revolution under any sponsorship.

While downgrading the possibility of violent black revolution Bunche also found fault with various nonviolent tactics that did not encompass basing the black struggle on identification with the working class. He gave short shrift to racial separatism, noting that Garveyism offered blacks an emotional escape but was essentially impractical. Fundamental was the greed of the imperialist nations and the fact that Garveyism could offer only Liberia to American blacks. Next to receive Bunche's scrutiny was the strategy of economic passive resistance. Bunche noted that supporters of this approach looked to Gandhi for guidance. Those taking this line believed that justice could be wrung from the ruling economic interest group "by striking at its most sensitive spot, its markets, and by shaming its Christian conscience." But, Bunche observed, the passive resistance movement had not succeeded in India, and its chances for victory in a highly industrialized country were much less. A version of this strategy was embodied in the "don't buy where you can't work" movement, but Bunche was convinced that such a slogan could not bring meaningful relief to the black masses. The outlook of such a movement was too narrowly racial and failed to formulate a program for the creation of new jobs. Although blacks might displace some white workers holding jobs in the black community, the pressure would mount for replacing black with white workers in the white community. Such a strategy, Bunche concluded, "could create only a vicious cycle of job displacement." It would widen the gulf between white and black workers and, if carried to its logical conclusion, the slogan would lead to advocacy of organizing black workers as strikebreakers. Bunche at least engaged in serious consideration of economic passive resistance; the policy of economic separatism, in later years restyled as "black capitalism," he evaluated as a "virulent creed" and quickly dismissed it.

Bunche was also quite critical of strategies that depended upon such remedies as electoral action and reliance upon the courts. The basic flaw in such approaches was that they failed to take into account the role of the state as reflection of the dominant economic and social interests prevailing in society. Politics and law could not be divorced from their economic underpinning. Urging that black leadership "should recognize the limitations of opportunistic and socially blind policies," Bunche called for formulation of a program "in terms of the broad social forces which determine its condition." The condition of the masses of any minority group could be improved only with the betterment of the situation of the masses of the dominant group.[26] In this statement of his position Bunche articulated an outlook, much influenced by the Marxian focus upon class, that was widely influential among thoughtful black leadership in the 1930s.

The audience for Bunche's analysis was largely confined to academics and professional observers of the racial scene. On a much broader level, a mass readership was brought to confront the black response to racism and particularly to racist violence through exposure to the writings of Richard Wright. Allison Davis has perceptively pointed to some of the elements of paradox in Wright's response to racism. On the one hand Wright's works, according to Davis, "stand as the most effective literary attacks against the system by which American whites have subordinated blacks." His decisive contribution was perhaps unique: "He freed educated Negroes from the fear of expressing anger at their persecution, segregation, and exploitation." At the same time Richard Wright manifested a hatred of both the black working class and the black bourgeoisie that was linked to self-hatred.[27] After all, Wright speaks to us quite directly in these lines from *Black Boy:* "After I had outlived the shock of childhood, after the habit of reflection had been born in me, I used to mull over the strange absence of real kindness in Negroes, how unstable was our tenderness, how lacking in genuine passion we were in those intangible sentiments that bind man to man, and how shallow was even our despair."[28] But whatever the contradictions in Wright's response to racism, there is consistency in his continuing emphasis upon the question of violence. His life's experiences prepared him for what he was to write, and the consciousness of the 1930s enabled his thought to take powerful literary expression.

Wright's *Black Boy,* his autobiographical account of growing to young manhood in the South, draws a portrait of a life shaped in the context of racial terror. It is not merely racism in general that he describes but a race hatred that destroys and threatens the right to life.

When he was almost nine years old he had experienced the killing of his Uncle Hoskins by whites who coveted the black man's liquor business. Wright's aunt was unable to claim her husband's body or any of his property. Wright recalled: "Uncle Hoskins had simply been plucked from our midst and we, figuratively, had fallen on our faces to avoid looking into that white-hot face of terror that we knew loomed somewhere above us." It was as close as white terror had ever touched him, he wrote, and his mind reeled. He also asked his mother why they had not fought back, and for asking the question his mother slapped him.

The racial violence triggered by World War I deeply imprinted itself upon Wright's consciousness. He described what happened to him:

A dread of white people now came to live permanently in my feelings and imagination. As the war drew to a close, racial conflict flared over the entire South, and though I did not witness any of it, I could not have been more thoroughly affected by it if I had participated in every clash. The war itself had been unreal to me, but I had grown able to respond emotionally to every hint, whisper, word, inflection, news, gossip, and rumor regarding conflicts between the races. Nothing challenged the totality of my personality so much as this pressure of hate and threat that stemmed from the invisible whites.

Wright became tense at the very mention of whites. He was reacting to what appeared as an unpredictable natural force. "I had never in my life been abused by whites," he wrote, "but I had already become as conditioned to their existence as though I had been the victim of a thousand lynchings." Wright's recollection reveals the role of racial terror as a means of utilizing the sufferings of the immediate victims of violence to enforce racial subjection.

After he graduated from school and went to work at a series of jobs Wright had his own brushes with racial violence. He was struck by white men because he had neglected to say "sir" when replying to a question. He was stopped and searched by police because while making deliveries he was in a white neighborhood late at night. He was forced to leave a job for fear that the two white craftsmen in the shop would assault him. And Wright also experienced the provocative, dehumanizing behavior of whites who sought to instigate a fight between himself and another black worker. The whites apparently drew perverse pleasure from the prospect of two black men being made to turn upon each other. Something of the sense of extreme caution that was impressed upon southern blacks is reflected in Wright's comment that "the safety of my life in the South depended upon how well I concealed from all whites what I felt."

Very clearly Wright saw terror as a dominant feature of the South he was to leave. The consequences of overt rebellion impelled him to head for the North, for he believed that such rebellion could never win. If he fought openly, he wrote, he would die, and he did not want to die. "News of lynchings were frequent."[29] While still in the South he was coming in touch with the world of formal culture, but he knew his self-development could not continue if he remained within the violent society in which he had grown up.

Wright's first major literary success, *Uncle Tom's Children,* published in 1938, conveyed vividly the experience of southern racist violence.[30] There was the experience of Big Boy in "Big Boy Leaves Home," who managed to escape the lynch mob but who from his hiding place could hear and see the savagery of the lynchers as they burned to death his friend Bobo after carving souvenirs from his body. This is a story of cruelty and escape and of the unpredictability of either experience. In "Down by the Riverside," evocative of the 1927 black experience of the Mississippi flood, we are shown how the natural disaster becomes in this society of terror a calamity of racial violence. The central figure, Brother Mann, attempts to take his wife to the hospital in a boat his brother has stolen from a white man. While searching his way in the darkness he encounters the owner and in self-defense kills the white, but that same night he takes part in rescuing the family of the man he has killed. But no explanation of the circumstances will save him, and in the end he is shot down by the soldiers. The twisting of life, the distortion of human values produced by racism, is dramatically etched in this story.

The story "Long Black Song" centers around the black couple Silas and Sarah and the consequences of a white salesman's sexual aggression directed at Sarah. The husband Silas learns of what has happened in his absence, and the tensions within him generated by racism suddenly explode. He has had hope that things will be better; he has bought some additional land and expects to produce more cotton next year. But now he puts caution and calculation aside and shoots the white man when he returns to complete a sale. Silas rages at the trap of racism; he curses the white men who take the land, deprive blacks of freedom, and also take the black man's woman. "Yuh die ef yuh fight! Yuh die ef yuh don' fight!" There is death either way, but Silas chooses to go down fighting, and when the lynch mob comes he resists, bringing down at least two of the whites, until burned to death in the shack.

"Fire and Cloud" is a story of the triumph of collective action that refuses to be diverted by terror. In a black community beset by hunger the Reverend Daniel Taylor is uncertain as to a course of action but finally gives his support to a protest demonstration. His faith in the people becomes even clearer after he is seized by racists and beaten. What is decisive is not to allow anything to separate the individual from the people. In this story the power of violence is more than matched by the strength that comes from unity. In fictional form Wright sets out here a strategic response to the violence of American racism.

"Bright and Morning Star" is a story of terror, of the cruelties inflicted by racist police and the white mob, but above all the theme is the heroism of the black mother. The setting is that of an organizing effort, spurred by Communists, and the violence triggered by this campaign. The situation that is the focus of the story is the need to alert those coming to a meeting that the police have the location spotted. Johnny Boy, the son of Aunt Sue, goes to spread the warning but is captured, and Aunt Sue, knowing the importance of the mission but unable to go herself, slips and reveals the names to Booker, a white man she does not quite trust. The mother learns that Booker is an informer and, determined to frustrate his betrayal, she conceals a gun in a burial sheet and goes to the place where her son is being tortured and will be lynched. She knows that Booker will come there, looking for the police, and when he does arrive, eager to pass on the names he has learned, she fires and kills him.[31] The police kill her and Johnny Boy, but Aunt Sue, dying, still realizes that she has denied the police what they wanted. At the very end of the story Wright gives us the opposites of "the doomed living and the dead that never dies."

In each of these stories we are shown the viciousness and bestiality of racism, but at the center of this collection is the theme of resistance. The resistance is born of hope, fury, the willingness to sacrifice, the need for retaliation, and the imperatives of safeguarding others. The forms of resistance vary. But there is little of passivity; the full humanity of blacks emerges as they strive to fight back against the awfulness of racial terror.

The question of racial violence is at the center of Wright's classic *Native Son*, a book published in 1940 that is set in the context of black life in Chicago during the 1930s. In writing the novel Wright used material drawn from the Chicago case of a black, Robert Nixon, who had been charged with rape by the police. Under police coercion, Nixon confessed to additional crimes.[32] On one obvious level Wright shows us the violence inherent in Bigger Thomas's accidental killing of Mary, the leftist daughter of his employer. Bigger compounds his deed by dismembering Mary and stuffing her body into the furnace. As frenzied as he is with fear, Bigger is conscious from the beginning of the meaning white society would find in his act. Wright tells us: "The reality of the room fell from him; the vast city of white people that sprawled outside took its place. She was dead and he had killed her. He was a murderer, a Negro murderer, a black murderer. He had killed a white woman." But Bigger Thomas, as Richard Wright conceived him, was not governed by guilt or remorse for having killed Mary or his girlfriend Bessie. From his acts of violence, from becoming the initiator rather than the passive object of society, Bigger Thomas had achieved a kind of identity. The author writes of Thomas: "out of it all, over and above all that had happened, impalpable but real, there remained to him a queer sense of power. *He* had done this. He had brought all this about. In all of his life these two murders were the most meaningful things that had ever happened to him. He was living, truly and deeply, no matter what others might think, looking at him with their blind eyes." It was a commentary on American society, on the stultifying force of racism, that this ghetto youth could come alive only through having taken life.

In conceptualizing Bigger Thomas as he did, Wright sought to remove sentimentality, moralizing, from consideration of the American racial scene. In his essay, "How 'Bigger' Was Born," he explained that the direction the book took was partly influenced by the popular response to *Uncle Tom's Children*. "When the reviews of that book began to appear," he wrote, "I realized that I had made an awfully naive mistake.

I found that I had written a book which even bankers' daughters could read and weep over and feel good about. I swore to myself that if I ever wrote another book, no one would weep over it; that it would be so hard and deep that they would have to face it without the consolation of tears."[33] Wright decided to focus not upon a noble black hero but rather upon a character whom the white world would see as the incarnation of the racist stereotype. He would show that the figure was generated by American racism, a racism that expressed the essence of American society and that if not eradicated could lead only to catastrophe. He would reveal that the real menace was not Bigger Thomas but the impersonal arrangements of society that made him possible. Taking the American mass audience as Wright believed it existed, he provided instruction as to the enormous cost of racism.

Wright gave added power to the character of Bigger Thomas by presenting him as representative of black people as a group. He has Max, the Communist defense lawyer who represents Thomas at the trial, tell the jury in summation, "Multiply Bigger Thomas twelve million times, allowing for environmental and temperamental variations, and for those Negroes who are completely under the influence of the church, and you have the psychology of the Negro people." Wright was quite prepared to have the broadest consideration of the American racial situation flow from knowledge of Bigger Thomas.

To make his point about the horror of racism Wright goes beyond merely making us generally aware of the ghetto conditions of joblessness, inadequate housing, and crass exploitation that provide the background for Thomas's actions. The incident itself becomes a force that brings to the surface the varied manifestation of racist violence contained within Chicago society. There is the counterpoint between Thomas's individual acts and the massive violence of society that is now given full reign as officials and the press create a mood of hysteria. There is gripping power in Wright's portrayal of a city gone mad with racism, ready to take on the quality of a lynch mob. Wright shows us that American racism, North and South, is marked by demonic fury and hatred that in their cruelty know no limits. What emerges, although this is not explicitly stated, is that the Richard Wright who in coming to Chicago had left behind the viciousness of southern racism had not really escaped.

Repeatedly Wright calls our attention to the larger violence triggered by the case of Bigger Thomas. The press assumes that the killing of Mary Dalton was a sex crime, that Thomas was a murderer and a rapist. In the course of the hunt for Bigger Thomas the black community becomes an open hunting ground for the police. The homes of hundreds of blacks are searched, and numerous incidents of racial harassment occur. There are calls for lynching, and indeed the mob outside the court calls for blood as the trial is in progress. At one point Bigger sees the burning cross of the Ku Klux Klan. What is one to expect of the larger society when the prosecutor in his summary refers to the prospect of fear "that at this very moment some half-human black ape may be climbing through the windows of our homes to rape, murder and burn our daughters"?[34]

Along with widespread recognition of the artistry and great power of *Native Son*, there was also extensive critical discussion of the novel. Among Wright's associates in the Communist party there was a range of responses. Reviews written by Samuel Sillen and Mike Gold were quite favorable, but Benjamin J. Davis, Jr., prominent black Communist leader, had some serious reservations. Davis did write that the novelist had done "a brilliant and courageous job, with bold initiative," and he observes that the book "is a document of positive social significance." Wright had taken a jobless black youth through the crimes "into which he is forced and entrapped by his white capitalist oppressors, and shows to this youth and to the world that the Communist Party is the only organization profoundly interested in relieving the terrible plight of the Negro people." All this Davis welcomed as positive, but he was also much concerned that the Communists presented in the book in their patronizing attitudes were not typical and that the social reality of blacks uniting in the course of struggle for change was omitted. Davis fully understood what Wright was seeking to accomplish by focusing upon Bigger Thomas, but he was unwilling to have this character appear as representative of all black people. Above all, Davis would prefer that the counter to racism in this book be found not merely in verbal argument, even the eloquent closing words of defense lawyer Max, but in the activities of Communists as engaged in the issues of the day.[35]

In his view that *Native Son* excessively generalized from the instance of Bigger and had not given us other, more positive responses to oppression Davis had a point. But what Wright did accomplish was extraordinary. He gave us an awesome account of the racist terror inflicted upon black people everywhere in the United States, and he also showed us the possibilities that might exist for other jobless, victimized black youth to make the transition from blind rage to social awareness. His novel shaped by both Marxism and nationalism became an enduring part of the American cultural heritage.

PART V

World War II and the First Postwar Years: The Racial Struggle at Home

Here in Detroit, many patriotic and forward-looking citizens are asking, "why not start practicing the Four Freedoms in our own back yard?" They are right.
Vice-President Henry A. Wallace, Detroit speech, July 1943

Ellenville, Georgia: A Negro farm mother and two of her youthful sons are awaiting death by electrocution at Reidsville State Prison as a result of their conviction last week for the November, 1947, slaying of a white farmer.

The slain man is accused of attacking Mrs. Rosa Lee Ingram, the doomed woman, with rifle in hand, when she sought to stop him from shooting her farm animals. Judge W. M. Harper sentenced 45 year old Mrs. Ingram and her two sons, Wallace, 17 and Sammy, 14, to death in the electric chair on February 27 in the slaying of John Ed Stratford, a white farmer.... The all-white jury disregarded the testimony of the Ingrams that Stratford advanced on the mother with a rifle, and engaged in a tussle with her, whereupon the sons intervened and death blows resulted in their self-defense.
Atlanta Daily World, February 3, 1948

We Americans must recognize that the seeds of fascism have taken root on our native soil and race riots make the field fertile for their future growth. Until we recognize the implications of the current wave of violence against the Negro minority, we Americans will have gained nothing from the experiences of the conquered peoples of Europe. Those who profess a love for a better world, a world of plenty and of peace, can start building that better world now by digging up in our own backyard those wild weeds of fascism and racial hate.
Michigan Chronicle, July 31, 1943

The President did not hesitate to call out the Army and Navy during the railroad strike when he considered a national emergency existed. Well, he'd better do something now. This is a national emergency. The temper of the Negro people is changing. If they are continued to be shot down and lynched, there are going to be several national emergencies.

Paul Robeson, statement to American Crusade to

End Lynching, September 1946

TWELVE

Wartime Violence

THE 1940s dramatically changed the context within which the struggle against white racist violence was fought out. A basic factor was war and its effect upon the internal dynamics of American society. First, the conditioning factor of war operated as World War II brought the United States into armed conflict with Fascist nations avowing theories of racial superiority and domination over so-called inferior races. Then, following 1945, American society was shaped by the context of the cold war, the years-long era of tension and conflict that saw the United States project itself as the champion of democracy against the assumed absolute evil of communism. The war society produced a rapid acceleration in the urban migration of blacks from the South's rural areas into the cities of the South, the North, and the Far West. Afro-Americans approached the point at which they would be the most urbanized of any ethnic group in American society. The world influence now exerted by the United States internationalized in a qualitatively new way the situation of American blacks. Out of the war would emerge the United Nations, and that international organization would provide a forum from which American racism could be indicted. The experience of fascism had convincingly demonstrated that there was not an absolute line between a nation's foreign policy and the structure of its society, and many would believe there was something profoundly wrong with a leader of world democracy that tolerated brutal treatment of minority people.

The war experience, in both its hot and cold versions, accustomed American society to greater reliance on force. A society now possessing incalculable means of destruction could convince itself that force was the efficacious method for resolving difficult issues. These years also institutionalized policies of repression on a scale and with consequences that we have only recently begun to comprehend with recourse to disclosures authorized by the Freedom of Information Act and the publication of congressional findings concerning governmental abuse of power.

A significant feature of the 1940s was the effective use of anticommunism as a means of disorienting and dividing black protest. In the forties, with the exception of the World War II years, the tactic of united front was undermined by the launching of sharp attacks against Communists and left-wingers generally as representatives of a foreign interest not genuinely concerned with the welfare of Afro-Americans. Prominent black radicals were hauled before congressional committees of inquisition, and the world-famous black artist Paul Robeson was threatened with physical assault for voicing unpopular views. In years when a given of the situation was that national security was imperiled by the Communist world menace, the pressure was on to view public activity about racial conditions in the United States as unpatriotic aid and comfort to the enemy. What is remarkable about this period is that in spite of pressures for conformity acts of racial violence were still met by vocal, militant, and sometimes effective opposition. In this era of sweeping world changes, despite the tendency to orthodoxy within the United States, racism could not escape challenge and indeed would have to yield some of its positions. The 1940s were years of formative change, changes in the makeup of Afro-American society, and basic changes in the world framework. This period of transition would lay the basis for new and more powerful movements of black activism in the fifties and sixties.

At the beginning of the 1940s the world crisis impinged on the black movement as A. Philip Randolph, president of the National Negro Congress, attacked policies supported by most of the delegates to the organization's 1940 convention. The convention met some eight months after the Soviet-German pact and the outbreak of World War II, and understandably it was influenced by the situation in which Communists rejected involvement in what was termed an "imperialist" war while the Roosevelt administration gave increasing support to the powers at war with Nazi Germany. The war and the question of response to the Roosevelt administration, now largely immersed in the problems of the war, became a pervasive issue in American society, and it made its impact upon the National Negro Congress. John L. Lewis of the CIO came to the meeting to call for support of Labor's Non-Partisan League in a move away from Roosevelt. Opposition to Roosevelt's foreign policy was doubtless a significant factor in evoking a friendly response to Lewis. The congress did go on record as holding that "the Negro people have everything to lose and nothing to gain by American involvement in the imperialist war." It condemned the administration "for the steps it has taken towards involvement and the partiality it has shown."[1] But domestic issues also played a part in stimulating disenchantment with the administration. The fact was that by 1940 the dynamism of the New Deal reform program had largely become stagnation, and certainly the administration did not propose to take the initiative on issues specifically concerning blacks. During the presidential election campaign President Roosevelt met with three black leaders, Walter White of the NAACP, A. Philip Randolph of the Brotherhood of Sleeping Car Porters, and T. Arnold Hill of the Urban League. From this meeting, however, came a White House statement reaffirming the policy of segregation in the armed services. Max Yergan of the National Negro Congress responded sharply to the announced White House position: "Once more, a President is not chief executive for all the people." But White, Randolph, and Hill also sharply objected in a telegram to the White House: "We are inexpressibly shocked that a President of the United States at a time of national peril should surrender so completely to enemies of democracy who would destroy national unity by advocating segregation. Official approval by the Commander-in-Chief of the Army and Navy of such discrimination and segregation is a stab in the back of democracy."[2] Also in 1940 the president did nothing to prevent the killing of an antilynching bill in the Senate. In its election issue *Crisis* ran on the magazine's cover a poem that juxtaposed the words of the Pledge of Allegiance to the details of the hanging, burning, and dismemberment of a black youth accused of assaulting a white woman.[3] Given the situation prevailing in 1940, it was understandable that the congress, quite apart from any issue of communism, had cordially received Lewis's call for a political alternative other than Roosevelt.

A. Philip Randolph sought to turn the Congress in another direction and toward that end made communism the central issue. He had been willing to represent a pressure force that worked within the New Deal coalition, but he would not go along with a policy that closed off access to the administration. He presented a statement to the congress in which he grouped the Soviet Union with other imperialist powers of the world and declared that what served the national interest of the Soviet Union was not necessarily in the interest of world peace and democracy. Randolph went on to attack the Communist party. He scorned the idea that the Communist party could constructively pursue the interests of Afro-Americans. He told the congress: "The Communist Party is not primarily, or fundamentally, concerned about the Negro or labor in America, but with fulfilling and carrying out the needs and demands of the consolidation of the foreign position of the Soviet Union in world politics." Randolph referred to what he described as "ridiculous shifts" in Communist positions on a variety of questions, ranging from issues of peace and war to the question of self-determination and the desirability of a

Roosevelt third term. Declaring that Negroes could not afford to add the stigma of being "red" to the handicap of being black, Randolph now described the Communist party as the tool of a foreign power: "The Negroes do not reject the Communist Party because it is revolutionary or radical, or because of its alleged extremism. They reject it because it is controlled and dominated by a foreign state, whose policy may or may not be in the interests of the United States or the Negro people."[4] Randolph also spoke in opposition to endorsement of Labor's Non-Partisan League, employing the argument that such support would undercut the nonpartisan nature of the congress.[5]

Shortly after the Congress adjourned Randolph issued a public statement repeating the positions he took at the meeting but articulating his basic anticommunism in even more vehement terms. He now made it clear that his polemic against the congress's direction was based, at least partly, upon his evaluation of the nature of Soviet society. His reference now was quite different from earlier favorable comments about the "Soviets of the workers." Randolph explained: "I quit the Congress because I was opposed to it or its officials expressing sympathy for the Soviet Union, which is the death prison where democracy and liberty have walked their 'last mile,' and where shocking 'blood purges' wipe out any and all persons who express any dissenting opinions from Dictator Stalin."[6] A. Philip Randolph was no longer agreeable to participating in a united front movement that included Communists.

In the months following his break with the congress, Randolph emerged as the foremost leader of the March on Washington movement that by late June 1941 could take credit for Franklin Roosevelt's Executive Order 8802 establishing the Fair Employment Practices Committee (FEPC). Always a leader of formidable talents, Randolph was quite successful in retaining a leadership position within the black movement. But the divisive issue of communism had been injected as a critical line of differentiation within the organization, which had shown the potential of serving as a militant spearhead of black protest. That injection weakened this movement and foreshadowed what could occur in a national context even more firmly gripped by anticommunism. The decline of the congress, culminating in the disbandment of the organization in 1948, represented a retreat from that goal of a black–labor–Left alliance to which Randolph earlier had been committed.[7] Randolph had laid a basis for association between labor and black organizational leadership in which anticommunism would be a cardinal principle.

During the year following establishment of the FEPC, the March on Washington movement carried through several significant activities. At

THE SHAME OF AMERICA

Do you know that the United States is the Only Land on Earth where human beings are BURNED AT THE STAKE?

In Four Years, 1918-1921, Twenty-Eight People Were Publicly BURNED BY AMERICAN MOBS

3436 People Lynched 1889 to 1922

For What Crimes Have Mobs Nullified Government and Inflicted the Death Penalty?

The Alleged Crimes	The Victims	Why Some Mob Victims Died:
Murder	1288	Not turning out of road for white boy in auto
Rape	571	Being a relative of a person who was lynched
Crimes against the Person	615	Jumping a labor contract
Crimes against Property	335	Being a member of the Non-Partisan League
Miscellaneous Crimes	453	"Talking back" to a white man
Absence of Crime	176	"Insulting" white man.
	3436	

Is Rape the "Cause" of Lynching?

Of 3,436 people murdered by mobs in our country, only 571, or less than 17 per cent., were even *accused* of the crime of rape.

83 WOMEN HAVE BEEN LYNCHED IN THE UNITED STATES
Do lynchers maintain that they were lynched for "the usual crime"?

AND THE LYNCHERS GO UNPUNISHED

THE REMEDY

The Dyer Anti-Lynching Bill Is Now Before the United States Senate

The Dyer Anti-Lynching Bill was passed on January 26, 1922, by a vote of 230 to 119 in the House of Representatives

The Dyer Anti-Lynching Bill Provides:
That culpable State officers and mobbists shall be tried in Federal Courts on failure of State courts to act, and that a county in which a lynching occurs shall be fined $10,000, recoverable in a Federal Court.

The Principal Question Raised Against the Bill is upon the Ground of Constitutionality.

The *Constitutionality* of the Dyer Bill Has Been Affirmed by—
The Judiciary Committee of the House of Representatives
The Judiciary Committee of the Senate
The United States Attorney General, legal adviser of Congress
Judge Guy D. Goff, of the Department of Justice

The Senate has been petitioned to pass the Dyer Bill by
29 Lawyers and Jurists, including two former Attorneys General of the United States
19 State Supreme Court Justices
24 State Governors
3 Archbishops, 85 bishops and prominent churchmen
29 Mayors of large cities, north and south.

The American Bar Association at its meeting in San Francisco, August 9, 1922, adopted a resolution asking for further legislation by Congress to punish and prevent lynching and mob violence.

Fifteen State Conventions of 1922 (3 of them Democratic) have inserted in their party platforms a demand for national action to stamp out lynchings.

The Dyer Anti-Lynching Bill is not intended to protect the guilty, but to assure to every person accused of crime trial by due process of law.

THE DYER ANTI-LYNCHING BILL IS NOW BEFORE THE SENATE
TELEGRAPH YOUR SENATORS TODAY YOU WANT IT ENACTED

If you want to help the organization which has brought to light the facts about lynching, the organization which is fighting for 100 per cent. Americanism, not for some of the people some of the time, but for all of the people, white or black, all of the time

Send your check to J. E. SPINGARN, Treasurer of the

NATIONAL ASSOCIATION FOR THE ADVANCEMENT OF COLORED PEOPLE
70 FIFTH AVENUE, NEW YORK CITY

THIS ADVERTISEMENT IS PAID FOR IN PART BY THE ANTI-LYNCHING CRUSADERS.

W. E. B. Du Bois at his office in *The Crisis*. Schomburg Center for Research in Black Culture, The New York Public Library, Astor, Lenox and Tilden Foundations.

State highway officials dispersing sharecroppers, New Madrid County, Missouri, 1939. Library of Congress. Photo by A. Rothstein.

Crowd formed to prevent blacks from moving into Sojourner Truth Projects, Detroit, 1942. Archives of Labor and Urban Affairs, Wayne State University.

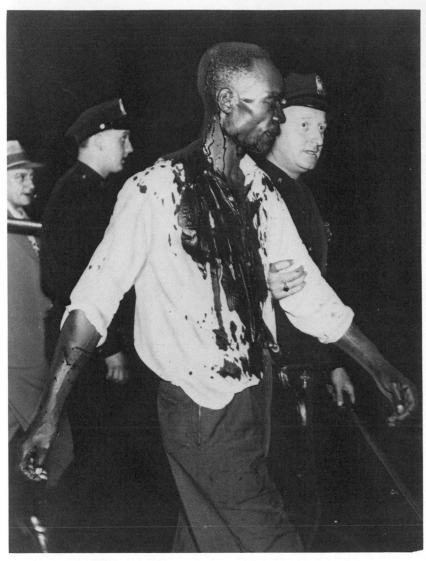

Harlem racial violence, 1943. Wide-World Photos.

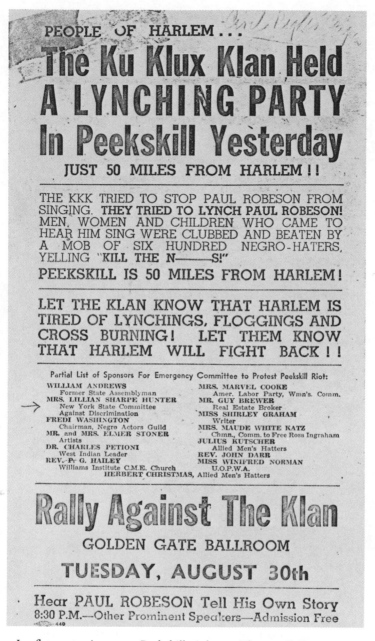

PEOPLE OF HARLEM...

The Ku Klux Klan Held
A LYNCHING PARTY
In Peekskill Yesterday

JUST 50 MILES FROM HARLEM!!

THE KKK TRIED TO STOP PAUL ROBESON FROM SINGING. **THEY TRIED TO LYNCH PAUL ROBESON!** MEN, WOMEN AND CHILDREN WHO CAME TO HEAR HIM SING WERE CLUBBED AND BEATEN BY A MOB OF SIX HUNDRED NEGRO-HATERS, YELLING "KILL THE N——S!"

PEEKSKILL IS 50 MILES FROM HARLEM!

LET THE KLAN KNOW THAT HARLEM IS TIRED OF LYNCHINGS, FLOGGINGS AND CROSS BURNING! LET THEM KNOW THAT HARLEM WILL FIGHT BACK!!

Partial List of Sponsors For Emergency Committee to Protest Peekskill Riot:

WILLIAM ANDREWS
Former State Assemblyman
MRS. LILLIAN SHARPE HUNTER
New York State Committee
Against Discrimination
FREDI WASHINGTON
Chairman, Negro Actors Guild
MR. and MRS. ELMER STONER
Artists
DR. CHARLES PETIONI
West Indian Leader
REV. P. G. HAILEY
Williams Institute C.M.E. Church

MRS. MARVEL COOKE
Amer. Labor Party, Wmn's. Comm.
MR. GUY BREWER
Real Estate Broker
MISS SHIRLEY GRAHAM
Writer
MRS. MAUDE WHITE KATZ
Chmn., Comm. to Free Rosa Ingraham
JULIUS KUTSCHER
Allied Men's Hatters
REV. JOHN DARR
MISS WINIFRED NORMAN
U.O.P.W.A.

HERBERT CHRISTMAS, Allied Men's Hatters

Rally Against The Klan

GOLDEN GATE BALLROOM

TUESDAY, AUGUST 30th

Hear PAUL ROBESON Tell His Own Story
8:30 P.M.—Other Prominent Speakers—Admission Free

440

Leaflet protesting 1949 Peekskill violence. Thomas E. Dewey Papers, Department of Rare Books and Special Collections, Rush Rhees Library, University of Rochester.

Paul Robeson, Peekskill concert, September 4, 1949.
Wide-World Photos.

Montgomery deputy sheriff fingerprints Mrs. Rosa Parks.
Wide-World Photos.

Martin Luther King, Jr., flanked by Montgomery city officials, appeals for
calm from porch of bombed King home, 1956.
UPI/Bettman Newsphotos.

St. Louis and Chicago marches protesting discriminatory practices were held. On July 25, 1942, several hundred blacks marched silently in New York responding to the execution of Odell Waller, a Virginia sharecropper condemned for supposedly killing his landlord in a quarrel over shares. But in the wartime context Randolph's movement was unable to sustain its momentum as a campaign geared to mass demonstrative protest. On the one hand, Randolph was criticized by members of the movement's youth contingent for having called off the original March on Washington, criticism that Randolph identified as the "outcome of manipulation by an artful and aggressive fraction that religiously follow the Communist Party line."[8] On the other hand, Randolph later was able to gain little support for a program of civil disobedience. The *Pittsburgh Courier* judged Randolph to be guilty of demagoguery, and said, furthermore, that he did not succeed in making the case that during the war such a strategy would be effective. The threat of a march on Washington did lead President Roosevelt to create the FEPC, and that was a notable victory, although Richard Dalfiume notes that Roosevelt thereby undermined opposition to his racial policies, a process that often is a by-product of reform.[9] But as a force unifying black leaders and organizations the March on Washington movement was unable to maintain itself.[10] Randolph's anticommunism and exclusion of whites from the March on Washington movement did not produce a greater measure of organizational viability than that experienced by the National Negro Congress, and in fact its life span was considerably shorter.

In the midst of World War II violence against blacks remained a prominent feature of American society. In addition to the usual accounts of lynchings and police brutality there were numerous violent clashes between whites and blacks at United States Army camps. Selective service had been instituted even before formal American entrance into the war, and this brought thousands of black and white conscripts together, but on the stigmatizing terms of segregation. Many of the camps were located in the South, placed near Jim Crow communities in which blacks would not receive civil treatment. During the summer of 1941 forty-three blacks serving in the Ninety-fourth Engineers Battalion, stationed at Camp Custer in Arkansas, abandoned maneuvers. The soldiers had run off after having been threatened by a party of armed white men. One of the soldiers gave this account:

> As we were walking along the highway we saw a gang of white men with guns and sticks, and white state troopers were with them. They told us to get the hell off the road and walk in the mud at the side

of the highway. One of our white lieutenants walked up to a state trooper and said something, I don't know what. Anyway, the trooper told him to get them blacks off the highway "before I leave 'em laying there." Then out of a clear blue sky the state trooper slapped the white lieutenant. . . . Some of our men began to talk about returning to Camp Custer for protection. That night they left by bus, train, and walking. Three of us hopped freight trains after walking forty-two miles to avoid white people, who we felt would attack us because of our uniforms.[11]

At Fort Bragg, North Carolina, violence was the product of the clash between racists and blacks who insisted they be treated with dignity. A soldier, Ned Thurman, had objected to an attack on a fellow black soldier, and as a consequence he was clubbed by two white military policemen. In wrestling to protect himself the black man managed to seize the gun of one of his assailants. Stepping back, he cried: "I'm gonna break up you M.P.'s beating us colored soldiers!" He fired a shot, killing one of the policemen, and was in turn shot to death by the remaining MP. Following this incident a number of black companies at Fort Bragg, not involved in the shooting, were made to stand all night with hands above their heads while military policemen patrolled the camp.[12]

Racial tensions at military installations persisted and may indeed have intensified after entrance into the war. A suggestion made by the NAACP that military instruction courses include material on the war's racial implications was rejected. The urgent need for such instruction was highlighted by an incident at Fort Dix, New Jersey, in which three soldiers were killed and five wounded. According to the army, the violence was touched off by a scuffle among soldiers lined up outside a telephone booth. When a military policeman fired a warning shot at a black soldier who had attempted to seize his pistol a number of shots were fired from the barracks across the road. A fifteen-minute battle ensued involving white and black soldiers and several military police who had been called out. Newspaper inquiries shed some light on the factors underlying this incident. The precipitating factor was an influx of a detachment of southern military police who tried to enforce the racial norms with which they had been inculcated. A black officer told a New York newspaper reporter that the new policemen "immediately started kicking the Negro troops around." On buses going to and from the camp the policemen would order seated black soldiers to stand and give their places to whites. The military policemen, however, were not the only aggravating factor. The white commander of the black regiment to which the involved black soldiers belonged had posted a particularly offensive notice at temporary headquarters at Marcus Hook, Pennsylvania: "Any cases between white and colored males and females, whether voluntary or not, is considered rape and during time of war the penalty is death." After protests by black organizations the notice was withdrawn, but the atmosphere apparently did not appreciably improve. The black officer told the reporter for the New York daily *PM:* "I've been at Fort Bragg, where things were bad enough. But this is worse. Hell may break loose unless something's done quick." He suggested removing the southern policemen, but in fact little or nothing was done to alleviate the underlying tensions, and a few months after this first episode another shooting took place in which a black soldier was killed.[13]

There were many other episodes of brutality involving black servicemen. During 1944 the liberal *Christian Century* carried a brief report sent in by an editor of a black Memphis newspaper. Nat D. Williams wrote: "I saw a Negro soldier beaten half to death in the Grand Central Station at Memphis last Tuesday night. I did not have a chance to find out his name. The shore patrol police were beating him too fast."[14] The black soldier had been standing in line when military police came up and questioned him. Not liking his answer, they began hitting him.

A chronicle of racial violence in the armed forces, covering the last two years of the war, is found in Florence Murray's *Negro Handbook, 1946–1947.* The incidents illustrated the variety of situations that could give rise to racial confrontation. In one incident at Brookley Field, Alabama, black soldiers drove out MPs and a white civilian who started to search the black soldiers' quarters for a soldier who had allegedly robbed the civilian. The blacks believed that the police would turn over to Alabama civilian authorities whomever the white man identified. After the white intruder was driven out the soldiers and military police exchanged shots. As many as a thousand shots were fired and a black sergeant, not involved in the affair, was seriously wounded. Typifying its usual response to such encounters, the army subsequently court-martialed nine black privates on charges of mutiny and failure to suppress mutiny and rioting. All were convicted, with three receiving sentences of twenty-five years and others sentences ranging from sixteen to twenty-two years. In another incident at Camp Claiborne, Louisiana, black soldiers seized weapons and began firing after a rumor spread that police had shot and killed a black soldier who supposedly looked like a man believed to have raped a white woman. Three persons were wounded during the course of the affair following which courts-martial were held for fourteen of the blacks. Thirteen were convicted on charges that included mutiny, disobedience, attempts to seize arms, and holding two officers prisoner. In both the Brookley Field and the Camp Claiborne incidents a critical factor was the question of relations with the racist communities adjacent to the camps.

An incident in which blacks initiated violence in reprisal for various discriminatory acts was the assault on Italian prisoners of war by black soldiers at Fort Lawton, Washington. On August 14, 1944, the prisoners in their barracks were attacked, and thirty of them were seriously injured. Following its usual way of dealing with racial conflict, the army put forty-three black soldiers on trial, and twenty-eight were convicted in a trial that ran until mid-December. The convicted men were sentenced to prison terms, which were later reduced. The basic cause of the outburst appears to have been favored treatment of the Italians in comparison with blacks.

Florence Murray also listed three incidents of violence against individual black servicemen. On July 8, 1944, a white bus driver in Durham, North Carolina, shot and killed Booker T. Spicely, a black army private. Spicely only reluctantly moved toward the back of the bus as white soldiers got on and when leaving the bus was shot by the angered driver. The driver was indicted on charges of second-degree murder but acquitted by the jury after it heard the argument that the driver had shot in self-defense when Spicely advanced toward him with his hand in his pocket.

At the bus station in Elizabethtown, Kentucky, on July 9, 1945, three black women, members of the Women's Army Corps, were beaten by civilian policemen because they did not move rapidly enough from the "white" waiting room to the overcrowded "colored" room. A policeman had raised his club after declaring: "Down here, when we tell niggers to move, they move." Upon their return to Fort Knox, from which post they had been on leave, the women were charged by the army with disorderly conduct but acquitted after a hearing. The army made no complaint with regard to the conduct of the Elizabethtown police.

Also involving police action was the killing of a black soldier, Willie L. Davis, by the police chief of the town of Summit, Georgia. On July 3, 1943, the chief had been called to a roadhouse to restore order, and after order had been restored Davis was killed. The Justice Department filed an information against the chief in United States District Court at Dublin, Georgia, charging violation of a citizen's civil rights, but the case was later dropped for lack of evidence.[15]

A month prior to the Summit incident the NAACP at its Emergency War Conference in Detroit spoke out bitingly against brutal treatment of black servicemen. The conference adopted a "Statement to the Nation," which noted that blacks experienced "a constant recurrence of brutalities and murders by civilian and military police," that such incidents reached into the "homes and hearts" of blacks and furnished material for Axis propaganda. The declaration further stated: "The continued ill treatment of Negroes in uniform, both on military reservations and in many civilian communities is disgraceful. Negroes in the uniform of the nation have been beaten, mobbed, killed and lynched." The NAACP hailed the Four Freedoms, the proclaimed war aims, but declared that colored people the world over would regard such declarations as hypocritical until President Roosevelt acted to end discrimination against blacks in the armed services. The statement was read at a June 6 mass meeting by NAACP assistant secretary Roy Wilkins.[16]

The issue of treatment of black servicemen was raised with President Franklin D. Roosevelt in a press conference with black newspaper publishers held in February 1944. The conference was a useful step in efforts to solidify black support, looking ahead to Roosevelt's bid for a fourth presidential term. Ira Lewis of the *Pittsburgh Courier* spoke to Roosevelt about the "grievous and vexing" issue of mistreatment of the servicemen. Lewis posed the issue and assigned ultimate responsibility:

It has to do with the treatment of our boys in the armed services. They haven't been treated right by civilian police, and by the MP's. We know of instances where soldiers on furlough have come home and taken off their uniforms, on account of intimidation. And they think, Mr. President, that that is your responsibility. They think that you alone can correct that. I think you can put your hand right on the question, which will do more towards strengthening morale and making more for unity and making the Negro citizen believe that he is a part of this great commonweal. Just one word from you, we all feel, would do that.

Roosevelt's reply was friendly, but its main thrust was to place responsibility somewhere else. The president said he was glad Lewis had brought the matter up, and he noted, "it is perfectly true, there is definite discrimination in the actual treatment of the colored engineer troops, and others." But the problem was with "the attitude of certain white people—officers down the line who haven't got very much more education, many of them, than the colored troops and the Seabees and the engineers, for example." In Roosevelt's opinion it was not a question of orders; "it's a question of the personality of the individual." On the one hand, Roosevelt declared that "we are up against it, absolutely up against it"; on the other hand, he believed "that it probably is improving." He liked to think that "mere association" was helpful.

After making this somewhat equivocal statement the president went on to a comment that he himself may not have taken quite seriously but that foreshadowed the postwar international dimensions of the American racial question. Roosevelt explained that he had discussed with Churchill the possibility of the United Nations having an inspection committee that would probe conditions in the British colonies. Churchill apparently had replied that in that case the United Nations ought to send an inspection committee to the American South. Roosevelt told the editors that he had informed Churchill that the idea was agreeable to him, and he explained further: "It would be a grand thing. I wouldn't mind if we had a committee of the United Nations come here and make a report on us. Why not? We have got some things to be ashamed of, and other things that are not as bad as they are painted. It wouldn't hurt at all—bring it all out."[17] After the war, indeed, United Nations concern with American racial oppression would be seriously proposed.

In civilian society, there took place during the war several major outbreaks of racial violence. The incident that attracted most attention and aroused most concern, involving large numbers of blacks and whites, was the racial clash in Detroit that broke out on June 20, 1943. According to Walter White of the NAACP the Office of War Information had warned a year earlier that "all hell will break loose in Detroit" unless positive action was taken by public officials.[18] *Life* magazine during August 1942 had published an illustrated warning, "Detroit Is Dynamite"; and in its June 1943 issue the *Wage Earner*, the Detroit newspaper of the Association of Catholic Trade Unionists, had said: "To tell the truth, there is a growing subterranean race war going on in the city of Detroit which can have no other ultimate result than an explosion of violence, unless something is done to stop it."

On March 27 the *Michigan Chronicle*, a Detroit black newspaper, entitled its editorial "Growing Strife" and warned its readers of what was to come. "Racial strife in Detroit," the paper stated, "is rapidly approaching a critical stage which not only threatens the peace of the community but menaces war production itself." Positive action was needed "to avert a riot and forestall violence in our community." Various forms of low morale could "be traced to the operation of these insidious elements who are working for a fascist America." The *Chronicle* called for a federal probe of the Klan and urged city leaders to take their heads out of the sand and face reality.[19]

Within two days prior to the outbreak in Detroit the White House received two appeals for urgent action to avert racial conflict. One came from Philip Murray, president of the CIO, who related the issue to the war effort. Murray informed President Roosevelt that the situation was "more than a problem either of mob prejudice or juvenile delinquency" but was indeed "a grave question of our relations with our allies and test of our ability to present a truly united front to the Axis." The CIO head recommended the undertaking of an educational campaign by the armed services and also called for the Department of Justice to investigate the situation. Roosevelt also heard from New York congressman Vito Marcantonio, who pressed very hard for action. Citing a number of incidents that had already occurred, Marcantonio declared: "There is a peculiar Hitler-like pattern running through all these occurrences which in my opinion is more than accidental." It was especially noteworthy that incidents clustered around centers of war production. The congressman called upon the president to provide leadership on this matter, urging that he devote one of his fireside chats to the racial situation. "I urge you," Marcantonio wrote, "to place your high office back of guarantees that Negro people and other minority groups will be freed from every hindrance which prevents their full participation in our war effort."[20] There is no indication that these letters excited any special interest at the White House.

In June 1943 thirty-four lives were lost in the Detroit racial confrontation. Hundreds were injured before order was restored. A writer for the *Detroit Free Press*, Malcolm Bingay, compared the violence to an incident he had seen earlier in Atlanta: "I thought that I had witnessed an experience peculiar to the Deep South. On the streets of Detroit I saw again the same horrible exhibition of uninhibited hate as they fought and killed one another—white against black—in a frenzy of homicidal mania, without rhyme or reason."[21]

Whatever journalists wrote or local officials believed, the federal government had indeed been adequately warned as to the potential for serious violence in Detroit. In early March 1942 an Office of Facts and Figures report candidly outlined the housing situation in the city as it affected blacks. Those who read the report learned that in Detroit "there is a legal bar against negroes living in many sections" and that the problem was small compared to what it would become. The dimensions of the crisis were not underestimated. "It now appears," wrote staff member Nelson Foote, "that only the direct intervention of the President can prevent not only a violent race riot in Detroit but a steadily widening fissure that will create havoc in the working force of every Northern industrial city." A slogan frequently heard among blacks was, "If you've got to die for democracy, let's die for it at home." Foote related his findings to reports trickling in of rising tensions in other cities and gave a sober judgment: "It is not melodrama when city officials here say this conflict is the most serious the city has faced since way back beyond the time of the big strikes. They didn't go far enough in what they say. It would be nearer realism to say that, if not today, tomorrow, this country, or let us say the war effort, will face its biggest crisis all over the North." Polarization in the city was fed by an apparent police policy of suppressing blacks and by the newspapers, almost uniformly hostile to black demands.

It should be noted that this report was a call for federal intervention to deal with what was presented as a black versus immigrant conflict, not a blanket endorsement of a fight against racism. Although the presence of the Klan as a factor in Detroit was mentioned, criticism of the Communist role was explicit, and indirectly this was also in some degree a criticism of the black community. The Communists were charged with using the "ugly tactics" of puffing up the whole affair as a Fascist plot that had been concocted to hinder the war effort. Foote indicated that the Citizens Committee, the most outspoken leadership group in the black community, gave credence to this position. "The Communists are giving every effort and every dollar to aiding the Negroes in direct friendly ways," Foote wrote, and he warned that unless the controversy was ended "the Communist element among Negroes will expand." A more compelling reason, according to Foote, was the judgment that the blacks of Detroit would not submit, due to the northern setting of the conflict and the clear need for their services in the war effort.

Already evident in Foote's report was the weakness of the city administration. In the midst of a 1942 housing crisis the mayor held a council session to discuss a city horticultural project, and Foote reported that "the large Negro audience gradually melted away in enraged confusion and despair." The city government's intentions were found to be concealed. The equivocation of the government was accompanied by misleading information furnished the public by the Detroit newspapers. Foote reported that the press seemed "to be following a line of much bias against the Negroes." The people of Detroit, therefore, were not being made aware of the gravity of the situation.[22]

Ample warning was also furnished federal officials in an Office of War Information (OWI) report prepared in December 1942. This report, based partly on 300 interviews with Detroiters and candidly described as experimental in its impressionistic portrayal of a city, was prepared for any federal administrator dealing with Detroit. The city was judged necessary to the winning of the war, and therefore the existence of "constant turbulence" among groups in Detroit was "cause for concern and an attempt at diagnosis." The report cited the self-fulfilling prophecy offered by a local AFL leader who anticipated racial conflict and feared that nothing could be done to ease rising tension. "In the main," the report observed, "AFL feels the Negro problem is insoluble because it regards race prejudice as an inherent human trait." As for the general climate of white opinion, there still apparently prevailed a mindset that would consign blacks to a second-class position: "The respondents often say that the Detroit Negroes should be segregated 'like in Chicago,' that the Negro preferred it that way and the whites certainly would. They might grudgingly grant the Negro a chance at better jobs, but they do not want him to have social and political equality." A factor in the situation was the extension of overt southern racism to the Detroit scene. White southerners and blacks competed for the same jobs, and the southerner "proceeds to enforce his own Jim Crow rules against the Negroes he comes in contact with, and incidents from road gangs and from elevators are common." The report observed that the white southerners frequently succeeded in disseminating the "Southern view" on Negroes. This OWI presentation was clear-sighted in its view that the turn of events depended upon white willingness to understand that the era of a new relationship to the darker-skinned peoples of the world was at hand:

The Negroes are united in their determination to win democracy for themselves. They want to do so by peaceful means, and even the militant younger members are still willing to listen to older leaders who advocate a strong, systematic but determined advance toward equality in Detroit. Bitterness and resentment toward inequality and the half-hearted policy of the government occasionally flares up, especially among the teenagers, and when this feeling clashes with the anti-Negro sentiments of various white groups, trouble results. Whether or not there will be racial violence in Detroit depends upon the success of the United Nations concept among whites in Detroit.

Federal officials, however, did not notably strain themselves to win white Detroit to a more equalitarian view of the future and thus avert a racial clash.[23]

A factor that no doubt worked to prevent recognition that serious racial issues had arisen in Detroit was the raising of the red bogey by area congressman Rudolph Tenerowicz. When in January 1942 a number of Detroit civic leaders protested plans for exclusion of blacks from the Sojourner Truth housing project, Tenerowicz took the list of signers to the House Un-American Activities Committee, and according to the congressman, committee files revealed references to sixteen of those signing. Tenerowicz announced the hardly startling news that Pat Toohey, state secretary of the Michigan Communist party, had an extensive record of Communist party activity and connected Toohey to the Detroit racial situation by noting that a member of the committee to contest black exclusion from the Sojourner Truth project was scheduled to speak at a party meeting at which Toohey also spoke. Speaking to the house on February 27, Tenerowicz quoted at length from a report, source unrevealed, that alleged the controversy regarding the housing project resulted from an intense campaign of Communist agitation. One of the tidbits in the report was the item that Coleman Young, then executive secretary of the local National Negro Congress, in remarks to the annual Lenin memorial meeting had charged that the Sojourner Truth project had been stolen from blacks and also had branded Tenerowicz as a fifth columnist. After reading this anonymous report Tenerowicz concluded that this "evidence" clearly showed "to what length certain Negro leaders and the communistic element will go in their attempt to achieve local and national disunity." Tenerowicz's remedy for the situation was to turn the matter over to the House Un-American Activities Committee, and he informed the House that Congressman Dies had assured him the HUAC would investigate the matter. From this perspective the issue of communism, not the menace of racism, was the critical problem facing Detroit.[24]

Tenerowicz returned to the red-baiting theme in remarks to the House on April 21, 1942. Responding to criticism from the NAACP, the congressman announced he had found the names of some Communists among the officials of the association. He alleged there was something sinister about the so-called black cabinet that advised President Roosevelt on racial matters. And Tenerowicz inserted in his comments a letter from white residents stating, without apology, that the Conley-Seven-Mile Neighbors Club was "composed entirely of white residents, and furthermore is restricted to all but members of the Caucasian race." Supposedly, this letter was evidence of the legitimate nature of white concern with the siting of the Sojourner Truth project.[25]

Black leadership did speak out vigorously against Tenerowicz's redsmear tactics. In March 1942 the Citizens Committee for the Defense of the Sojourner Truth Homes charged that the congressman deliberately sought to divide the American people and that he had acted "in a manner becoming an agent of the enemy." The committee urged Tenerowicz's ouster from Congress and urged the Department of Justice to investigate links between Tenerowicz and fifth-column activity. The following month Dr. James J. McClendon, president of the Detroit branch of the NAACP, called for a federal grand jury inquiry into Tenerowicz's efforts to foment racial conflict, and on April 23 Walter White wrote to the congressman urging him to resign. Regarding Tenerowicz's allegations of Communist involvement in black protest activities White countered: "If organizations which have Communist or Republican or Democratic affiliations or inclinations choose to take a position which is clearly in accordance with right and justice and which is the same as that of the NAACP, then that is their concern and responsibility and not ours." White declared that the congressman should resign and frankly ally himself with "the mobbists, Ku Kluxers, Nazi and Fascist forces in Detroit who seek to undermine government and to violate the Federal Constitution." Black leaders were alert to the menace posed by smear tactics, but most white political leaders were unwilling to take up the challenge Tenerowicz presented.[26]

The 1943 Detroit violence can be viewed from several different perspectives, which lead to directly conflicting conclusions. One view is that offered by a committee appointed by Michigan governor Harry Kelly. This official inquiry contended that the violence had been provoked by irresponsible black leadership and absolved the police of any improper conduct. The report told of racial scuffles that occurred at Detroit's main recreation area, Belle Isle Park, on June 20. Although several persons were injured there were no serious casualties, and the commission concluded that "had the disturbance ended with the incidents at Belle Isle and the bridge approach, none of the deaths occurring in the riot would have resulted." More serious violence occurred as a result of the spreading of a false rumor at a dance hall, the Forest Club, located some five miles from Belle Isle. The rumor was that whites had killed a black mother and her child at the park. Hundreds of blacks had milled about the intersection of East Forest and Hastings streets and had begun attacking automobiles driven by whites. Within a brief interval the crowd had begun stoning white-owned businesses. The report noted that violence was also initiated by some whites, stating that a group of whites began stoning black-operated automobiles at Charlotte and Woodward shortly after 4:00 A.M., June 21, and generalizing that thereafter "numerous acts of violence were perpetrated by whites, until approximately eleven o'clock the following night." The report also observed, however, somewhat contradictorily, that "the only serious threat of whites toward any portion of the colored section" existed between 6:00 and 9:00 P.M., June 21, when a crowd of whites assembled to enter the black community.

This solitary threat had been thwarted by effective police action. In its conclusion the committee found that the riot resulted from smoldering racial tension inflamed by several incidents at Belle Isle, "provoked by a group of Negroes," and that the looting and other violence were the result of the spreading of a false rumor by a black employee of the Forest Club.

The flagrant bias animating this committee came through most plainly in the second section of the report. In this section, adding insult to injury, the committee set its findings about the riot in the context of a racist analysis of the Detroit situation. Declaring *ex cathedra* that "characteristics of color, stature, and speech have always marked off and distinguished one people from another," the committee explained that concepts of racial superiority could be overcome "only by education." The committee had no criticism of race leaders who sought to remove racial barriers by lawful means but censured "those irresponsible leaders, who by their words and conduct, actively inspire among their followers a disregard for law, order, and judicial process, in seeking the racial equality to which they are entitled." The committee spoke in general terms of both whites and blacks being responsible for violent acts, but clearly the main thrust of its attack was directed at black militancy. According to Governor Kelly's appointees these were the pertinent questions to be asked: "Where have these young hoodlums been told they have a license to lawlessness in their struggle to secure racial equality? Who has told them it is proper themselves to redress actual and presumed grievances? Who has exhorted violently to overthrow established social order to obtain racial equality?" The committee's sensitivity was obvious when it asked: "Who charges by their news stories and their editorials that all law enforcement agencies are anti-Negro, brutal, and vicious in the handling of Negroes, and bent upon their persecution?"

What the committee basically found objectionable was any attempt to wage a struggle for democracy at home as a counterpart to the war effort against the Axis. The committee observed that black newspapers "loudly proclaim" that a victory over the Axis would be meaningless unless the forces "which these papers charge prevent true racial equality" were also overthrown. The report contended that to repeat the statement, "This nation cannot exist half free and half slave," was intended "to arouse a belligerent reaction." Issue was also taken with a statement ascribed to A. Philip Randolph. Randolph had reportedly said: "Justice is never granted, it is exacted. It is written in the stars that the darker races will never be free until they make themselves free. This is the task of the coming year." The Michigan governor's committee concluded that this

statement "clearly constitutes an appeal to extract 'justice' by violence."
If this report found fault with supposedly militant leadership it also
criticized "responsible Negro leaders" who had to share the blame "for
the unfortunate attitude of certain Negro elements." Such responsible
persons had demonstrated "an anti-social and factional outlook," which
could account for the militant attitude of others. All in all, the 1943
governor's committee report gives some insight into the climate of opinion
prevailing among those making public policy in Michigan. Those who
wrote this report were not part of the solution to racism; they were very
much a part of the problem.[27]

Speaking sharply against the findings of the governor's committee was
the *Michigan Chronicle*. If one used the methods employed by the committee, the newspaper observed editorially, "passages could be taken out
of the Holy Bible which would make the Scriptures equally inflammatory.
As a matter of fact if the committee had read the Bible, their report would
have repudiated the principle of the brotherhood of man as an incitement
for oppressed Negroes to riot." Continuing, the *Chronicle* quoted the
"all men are created equal" precept of the Declaration of Independence
and then noted that the report would gain immortality not for what it
said but for what was left unsaid. What was omitted was any reference
to the climate of racial hatred that prevailed in Michigan.

The fact that five officials of the state of Michigan [the *Chronicle*
declared] should investigate the riot of June 20 and brush aside the
hate strikes, the slums, jim-crow practices, police brutality, the infringement of our civil liberties, and the countless attacks upon our
citizenship is beyond belief. The fact that the Klan, the Black Legion
and front organizations which have been active for years in the
business by systematically robbing the Negro of his birthright, have
all been dismissed as of no consequence in racial tensions in this
area clearly demonstrates that these officials are either stupid or
dishonest.

The newspaper stated that blacks "who are moving up the broad stream
of democracy" knew full well that with regard to the source of violence
those who wrote the report "have put the shoe on the wrong foot."[28]

In New York a sharp rejoinder to the report of the Michigan fact-
finding committee came from Adam Clayton Powell, Jr. The publisher
of the *People's Voice* criticized the substance of the report, its method
of presentation, and the makeup of the committee. Those who produced
the report "were the very people who must share not only a large part

of the blame for the Detroit riot but the major share of the blame for the needless killing of a score of Negroes." Powell declared: "The New Negro does not condone violence." But, he added, "the New Negro is not going to retreat one inch from his position for a full democracy now for all peoples." Blacks knew that the greatest stumbling block to winning the peace was the "Empire philosophy" of Winston Churchill and that the racial question was essentially the issue of democracy against fascism.[29]

An analysis of what happened in Detroit different from that generated by Governor Kelly's fact finders is found in the report released by the National Association for the Advancement of Colored People. First, as to the facts, in the section of the report written by Walter White, "What Caused the Detroit Riots?," reference was made to the negligence or worse of the police in not preventing assault by whites upon blacks along Woodward Avenue. In one incident four blacks, promised protection by the police, were turned over to the mob by these same police and then severely beaten. Revealing also was a photograph taken by the *Detroit Free Press* showing an elderly black man whose arms are pinioned by two officers while a white rioter strikes him in the face. There was no evidence that the police made any effort to protect this individual, much less to arrest the assailant. White drew the general conclusion that "the willful inefficiency of the Detroit police in its handling of the riot is one of the most disgraceful episodes in American history." Twenty-nine of the dead in this incident were black, and White saw the violence as stemming basically from white aggression against blacks. An aspect of the situation that particularly disturbed him was the youth of many of the white rioters. White noted a statement by John Bugas, head of the Detroit office of the FBI, to the effect that 75 percent of the rioters were between the ages of sixteen and twenty-five.[30]

A section of the NAACP report written by Thurgood Marshall, then special counsel to the association, amplified White's observations about the riot. Marshall stated that more than adequate evidence existed to justify the convening of a grand jury to investigate "the nonfeasance and malfeasance of the police as a contributing factor in the Detroit riots." Marshall referred to the 1942 incidents at the Sojourner Truth housing project in which police sided with the white mob seeking to prevent black tenants from moving into their apartments. Whereas blacks approaching the project were stopped and searched, whites were passed through unmolested. Marshall's judgment was that "white hoodlums were justified in their belief that the Detroit police would act the same way in any future disturbances."

According to Marshall the Detroit police in 1943 were true to form.

He was convinced the violence reached the proportions it did "because the police of Detroit once again enforced the law under an unequal hand." Marshall sharply denounced the police argument that their recourse to violence against blacks was justified by criminal acts committed by blacks in the course of the rioting. Marshall granted that some blacks had been involved in looting, but it was also true that whites had turned over autos belonging to blacks and had beaten blacks with pipes and clubs; yet, the fact remained that all of the seventeen persons killed by the police were black. Marshall detailed the racist conduct of the police along Woodward Avenue. Although groups of whites roamed the street shooting at cars with blacks in them and yanking blacks from streetcars, the police in dealing with the white mob refused to use force and at most attempted to "reason" with the rioters. In Marshall's opinion even the use of night-sticks or the drawing of revolvers or turning on of fire hoses would have saved the lives of a number of blacks. "None of these things were done," Marshall wrote, "and the disorder took on the proportions of a major riot. The responsibility of this rests with the Detroit police."

The brutality of the Detroit police was typified by their conduct on June 21 at the Vernor Apartments on East Vernor Highway. Nearby, a policeman had been shot, and in turn the assailant was killed by another officer. The police thereupon attacked the apartment building, throwing searchlights on the structure and firing indiscriminately into all apartments facing the outside. Tear gas was fired, and all tenants were forced into the street. The apartments were ransacked, and residents reported that money and other items of personal property were missing when they returned to the apartments. Marshall visited the Vernor Apartments shortly after the riot and reported that "they resembled a part of a battlefield."

The allegations as to police brutality were confidentially supported by General William Gunther, the army commander sent to Detroit. Reporting to his army superior, Gunther noted regarding the Detroit police: "They've been very handy with their guns and clubs and have been very harsh and brutal.... They have treated the Negroes terribly up here and I think they have gone altogether too far. That kind of treatment of course will keep this thing going longer than if they get back to normal." In the aftermath of the violence there was also the reference by fourteen leaders of national organizations such as the Urban League, the YMCA, the YWCA, the Federal Council of Churches of Christ in America, and the Catholic Interracial Council to eyewitness accounts that "Negroes have been victimized by police in the name of law and order as well as by lawless mobs."[31]

In a memorandum addressed to President Roosevelt, Walter White outlined the key factors operating to cause the Detroit violence. White referred to the extensive migration to Detroit of southern whites who resented blacks working at the same jobs and wages in the shops and also resented blacks voting in elections. A second factor was the presence of various right-wing extremist organizations such as the Ku Klux Klan and the Black Legion, which "though numerically small, are active and effective in rousing anti-Negro, anti-Semitic, and other prejudices." Further causes were found in the "timorousness and inefficiency" of the police and city leaders along with the demagogic role of nationally known racist leaders such as Congressman John Rankin of Mississippi. Finally, White pointed to the conservative coalition dominating Congress, a combination of southern Democrats and conservative northern Republicans he described as "anti-Roosevelt, anti-labor, anti-Semitic, anti-Negro, and anti-liberal generally."

The memorandum included recommendations for action by Roosevelt to deal with the situation. The recommendations were framed in terms of the Detroit situation, but it was noted that most of them were nationally applicable. Heading the list of recommendations was a proposed fireside speech by Roosevelt calling upon Americans to refrain from violence and racial hatred. The NAACP would have the president stress the global nature of the problem and point out that Axis propagandists capitalized on the American racial situation. To assure the rioting did not resume in Detroit, Roosevelt was urged to keep federal troops in the city. Walter White stated that in his opinion "only the presence of federal troops for some time can avert further trouble, deaths and bloodshed." Three of the proposals referred to federal grand jury investigations, one of the Detroit city police, one for "possible misfeasance, nonfeasance, or malfeasance in protection of federal rights" committed by Detroit mayor Edward Jeffries and other city officials, and a third of the conduct of the Michigan state police. The only proposal with regard to legislation was a recommendation for enactment of a statute making violence against members of the armed forces and violence to prevent minority group members from performing war work a federal offense. A group of proposals dealt with the basic issues of housing and jobs involved in causing the riot. The association urged that the federal government release building materials that could be used in providing adequate housing for the many thousands of Detroit residents lacking such housing. As it was vital to build camps for soldiers it was also imperative that housing be available for the workers making war goods. Roosevelt was also asked to compel the National Housing Administration and the Federal Public Housing Authority to cease discriminating on account of race, creed, color, or national origin. The Housing Administration was held partly to blame for both the 1943 violence and the Sojourner Truth episode of 1942. As concerned jobs the memorandum called for an end to vacillation on the part of the Fair Employment Practices Committee in carrying out its obligation to insist on equal opportunity in hiring.[32]

In his response to the Detroit violence White carefully noted the positive role played by the local labor movement. White described as "one of the most extraordinary phenomena" of the riot the fact that there was neither a physical nor a verbal clash between white and black workers within the plants. This fact was attributed at least partly to a firm stand against racial discrimination and segregation taken by the United Auto Workers– CIO. The union stood firm despite racist haranguing of workers that went on outside some of the plant gates. During the period of violence in the city R. J. Thomas, UAW president, had issued an eight-point program, widely publicized, which called for a grand jury investigation of the violence and for steps to meet the housing and recreational needs of Detroit citizens. Thomas had also proposed formation of a biracial committee, which would make further recommendations for the elimination of racial friction. White wished to preserve the cooperative relationship that had been built up in recent years between black organizations and the labor movement.[33]

Part of the problem underlying the Detroit violence was that the Roosevelt administration did not seriously confront the sources of racial tension. There was little response to the *Pittsburgh Courier*'s "Double-V" campaign for victory in the struggles against the Axis and against American racism. Pointing up the deficiencies in the administration's approach was a proposal, quoted by the journalist Earl Brown in an account of the Detroit violence, made by Attorney General Francis Biddle. During March a Detroit newspaperman had written to Biddle expressing concern at the critical state of affairs in the city, only to be met with the reply: "Your letter has received careful consideration, although it does not appear that there is sufficient evidence of violation of any federal statute to warrant action by this department at this time." But following the violence Biddle wrote to President Roosevelt on July 15, proposing "that careful consideration be given to limiting, and in some instances putting an end to Negro migrations into communities which cannot absorb them, either on account of physical limitations or cultural background. This needs immediate and careful consideration.... It would seem pretty clear that no more Negroes should move to Detroit." Biddle also predicted that in the postwar era the situation would become far more acute. Biddle informed Roosevelt of his belief that the Detroit violence was not an isolated case but was typical of what could occur in other cities.[34] By 1943 the federal government, which had arbitrarily relocated thousands of Japanese-Americans during 1942, also contemplated curbing the free movement of Afro-Americans.

Two professors at Wayne University, Alfred McClung Lee and Norman D. Humphrey, conducted a study of the Detroit riot, which confirmed the findings published by the NAACP. They presented a detailed chronicle of events during and subsequent to the violence. The study referred to the international impact of the racial clash, mentioning that the Nazi-controlled Vichy radio described the situation as a reflection of "the moral and social crisis in the United States." Vichy commented that on the basis of the Detroit experience the French people "realize the dangers for European civilization inherent in the American aims of world domination." Yet, despite the apparent broader implications of what had taken place, authorities in Detroit failed to take up the struggle against racism and indeed heaped abuse upon black leadership. The post-riot role of public officials can only be termed provocative and irresponsible. The mayor, police officials, and city councilmen all joined in rejecting the calls for a grand jury inquiry. Mayor Jeffries took the lead in attacking black leadership as he publicly declared that he was rapidly losing patience "with those Negro leaders who insisted that their people do not and will not trust policemen and the Police Department." Jeffries found black leaders more articulate in criticism of the police "than they are in educating their own people to their responsibilities as citizens." Lee and Humphrey reported that on the same day that Jeffries spoke out the mayor's words were supplemented by the comment of Councilman Comstock to the effect that "the racial conflict has been going on in this country ever since our ancestors made the first mistake of bringing the Negroes to this country."[35]

This study made clear that Detroit officials had learned little indeed from the terrible experience the city had gone through. When the president of the NAACP replied to criticism of black leadership the reply was brushed aside and the campaign of intimidation continued. On July 1 Dr. James J. McClendon of the association issued a statement observing the disparity between the deaths of many blacks and the lack of a "shoot-to-kill" policy with regard to white rioters. McClendon was forthright: "Killings, vile name-calling, wanton, unnecessary arrests of colored citizens, inspired no regard for a Police Department which spoke of some of our citizens as 'niggers.' " But on July 26 the Wayne County prosecutor William E. Dowling and the Detroit police commissioner both issued statements placing blame for the bloodshed on the black community and especially the black press. Dowling asserted that several editors of black newspapers had caused dissension within the community and specifically charged Louis E. Martin of the *Michigan Chronicle* with being "the principal instigator of dissension in this area." Accusing both the NAACP and black newspapers of troublemaking, Dowling stated: "They have been fomenting trouble with their crusades in the Negro neighborhoods from the start. If you want to do something constructive in this situation you might try to control the Negro press." According to an affidavit sworn by a Detroit minister, Dowling privately stated with regard to the NAACP: "They were the biggest instigators of the recent race riot. If a Grand Jury were called, they would be the first indicted." Dowling later denied having made the statement but apparently only after learning the association would sue for libel. Police commissioner John H. Witherspoon publicly stated his opinion that NAACP complaints against police brutality "had a tendency to encourage rather than discourage improper conduct on the part of Negroes." While city officials concentrated upon criticism of blacks, Gerald L. K. Smith continued to disseminate his propaganda of race hatred. In a piece published in the July issue of his organ, the *Cross and Flag*, Smith announced that most white people would not agree to racial intermarriage or the mixing of races in hotels, restaurants, or residential districts. Whites, according to Smith, would not agree to "intimate relationships" between blacks and whites in the schools or to what he termed "promiscuous mixture" of blacks and whites in streetcars and trains, especially where black males were permitted to sit close to white women. The city's public leaders did little to counter this campaign of incitement.[36]

If the NAACP would have American society commit itself to the drive for racial equality, William J. Norton in the *Survey Graphic* symbolized those white moderates who would restore goodwill while deferring any substantial change in the American racial system. The violence of Detroit did not lead him to reexamine his approach to the racial question. His was a voice of moderation that would only frustrate the black demand for equality. Norton understood that the war stimulated the demand for black rights, and he would have American cities "stop, look and listen," but after the pause he would have "able Negro leaders and their idealistic white friends," of whom he counted himself one, urge "piping down on stentorian drives for equality." It would take only a bit more inflammatory oratory and writing to precipitate riots all over America. As Norton saw things, whites simply were not prepared to extend total equality to blacks. The struggle for equality, even for equality among whites, was generations old, "and it will go on for a long, long time."

The black quest for full equality should live "forever," as should Norton's commitment to the cause. But "saner and different" means should be employed, and right now the job was to reconstitute goodwill between the races. The Norton piece sheds light on the critical state of affairs in Detroit. In Norton's hands had been placed the leadership of Mayor Jeffries's "Inter-racial Committee," and clearly with such a director the committee was not likely to attempt any real change in the city's racial pattern. The views of such "moderates" as Norton helped create the political climate in which the Roosevelt administration would continue its indifferent policy with regard to racism at home.[37]

On the radical left the Communists energetically sought to make the question of eliminating the sources of racial violence a matter of wartime patriotism. In its analysis of the Detroit events the Communist-oriented *New Masses* stressed the damage inflicted on the war effort. The magazine called for a cleaning out of the fifth column, "from top to bottom." The paid agents of Hitler operating in the situation could not be named, although it was hoped that the FBI had their names and would act accordingly, but the names of those benefiting Hitler could be listed. First on the roll was William Randolph Hearst, followed by such southern congressional Bourbons as Congressmen Starnes and Rankin. There was also Joseph Pew of Sun Oil, an industrialist identified as part of the "Lamont du Pont crowd," who would like to negotiate with Hitler. Detroit, the magazine declared, represented insurrection, an "anti-administration, anti-war insurrection raging in the land today." Action was called for by the administration and also most urgently from the labor movement, for it was within the power of the unions to break the insurrection. Responding to the 1943 racial crisis Communists continued to rely upon the common action of the black movement with organized labor.[38]

The *New Masses* first considered the Detroit violence in its issue of June 29. The following week the magazine reported on the situation in greater detail. The point was pounded hard that the outbreak of race violence served the interests of the Axis powers. A report on Detroit was introduced by Joseph North, who noted that the Allies had won a great battle in Tunisia but had lost a great battle in Michigan. Other such battles could also be lost unless effective action were taken. North quoted the Detroit official of the War Production Board who had said that Hitler bragged his agents would bring about a racial situation of the kind that had erupted in the vital war production center of Detroit. At a time when the war was going well for the Allies, the Nazis resorted to splitting tactics, and the Detroit assault upon blacks was one of those tactics.

North stressed the progress that had been made recently in race relations, progress in terms of greater opportunities for upgrading in industry and progress toward enactment of an anti-poll-tax bill in Congress. It was in the midst of this progress that the Detroit insurrection had taken place. North found dangerously naive the view stated by John Bugas that race violence in the city had been simply a spontaneous eruption. The FBI, North wrote, by this time should know how Axis agents operate.[39]

A recent study of interracial violence during World War II has shown that the violence of 1943 led many white liberals and some black leaders away from serious struggles for equality at home and toward mouthing empty generalizations about "good" race relations.[40] North and the Communists generally proposed to respond to the demand for equality that was articulated in the willingness of blacks to fight back against racist aggression. North, for example, called for unity, urging the mass of whites who stood on the sidelines to end their passivity and take a stand for democracy. And while urging fraternization between the races North went on to urge programs of action to deal with the social and economic needs of black communities. Action to deal with the urgent need for housing and action to enforce FEPC guidelines were stressed. In formulating such programs labor had to provide leadership. Consistent with a strategy of mass action, North proposed the holding of mass meetings and a "Niagara of resolutions" to make tangible the popular will. Delegations should call upon federal, state, and local authorities. Pressure was to be exerted upon the government, although North carefully stopped short of urging more demonstrative forms of activity that might be viewed as interfering with the war effort.[41]

The emphasis on linking the Detroit violence to the war effort represented an attempt to make action for equality a matter of war necessity that could be justified as being in the nation's highest and most urgent interest. It is a measure of the federal government's lack of understanding of the situation, of Roosevelt's failure to break with the racial attitudes of paternalism, that this strategy produced few results. Undoubtedly compounding the problem was the fact that Roosevelt, in wartime, largely followed the advice given him with regard to racial matters by southern members of his staff who had little sympathy for the thrust toward equality.[42]

A contrast to the passivity of the Roosevelt administration on the racial question was the effort by prominent figures in the entertainment industry to recognize the significance of what had taken place in Detroit. In New York an Emergency Committee of the Entertainment Industry was formed with the participation of such personages as Tallulah Bankhead,

John Garfield, Lillian Hellman, Groucho Marx, Paul Robeson, Orson Welles, and Edward G. Robinson. The committee succeeded in arranging a coast-to-coast radio broadcast expressing opposition to race riots, and the program was carried by the Columbia Broadcasting System on July 10. Some of the scenes of the Detroit violence were reenacted, and Wendell Willkie, 1940 Republican presidential candidate, spoke. Walter White recalls that the overwhelming majority of comments received after the broadcast were favorable, and the program was given the Peabody Award by the University of Georgia. But the Emergency Committee was soon forced to disband for lack of staff and funds, not, however, before drafting a code regarding treatment of minorities in the entertainment industry that White believed "materially affected" the media.[43]

Some of the most pointed responses to the Detroit violence were voiced by leading figures of the black press. In an analysis of Detroit he wrote for the liberal magazine *Common Ground*, Louis E. Martin of the *Michigan Chronicle* noted that journalists, government investigators, and thousands of the city's residents had been convinced racial clashes were inevitable. Martin saw housing pressures as a major factor in the situation. As both whites and blacks poured into the area to work in the war industries, the prevailing racial housing pattern was kept in place by restrictive covenants on the one hand and mob violence on the other. Blacks, however, sought to challenge the racial lines and found themselves rebuffed by Mayor Jeffries, who on April 29, 1943, seven weeks prior to the riot, announced that the "racial characteristics of Detroit neighborhoods" must not be infringed upon. Added to a crisis about housing was conflict concerning the desire of black workers for access to job upgrading. In this field racist "hate strikes" were the choice tactic for preserving the color line. A third ingredient of crisis was discriminatory treatment at public facilities of black servicemen and the composition of a police department that had less than forty active black officers on a force of 3,600.

Although a number of cities faced the general configuration of racial issues present in Detroit, Martin believed that the city was special in that it "may also be the capital of American fascism." Detroit was the headquarters of Gerald L. K. Smith, and an adjoining community, Royal Oak, had served as the center of Father Coughlin's pro-Fascist Social Justice movement. Martin observed that a network of right-wing organizations served as a screen "for activities which can in practice fulfill all of the purposes of Dr. Goebbels."

Martin stressed some of the long-term implications of what had happened. "The integration of the Negro into the industrial fabric of America," he wrote, "into many sacred precincts during this emergency, has alarmed whites. The Negro is fighting for his economic security, prodded in this struggle by the knowledge that he is the marginal man of industry." What accentuated the fears in Detroit was realization that the city was a place "of big booms and bigger depressions." Martin also recognized the profound consequences that stemmed from the nature of the war. The souls of black folk had to be seared, he wrote, by the paradox "of the American people fighting racist tyranny abroad while the majority sanction the doctrine of white supremacy and racial discrimination at home."[44]

The syndicated columnist Elmer A. Carter eloquently addressed the international implications of Detroit. "We who are American citizens of African descent," Carter wrote,

> we didn't lose at Detroit as much as America lost. It is true that the number of our dead and dying is greater by far than that of our attackers who were evidently aided and abetted by officers of the law sworn to protect the lives and property of the citizens no matter what their race or color. But we lost no prestige; we lost no respect; we lost no honor. But America lost and the measure of her loss is incalculable. For to the ends of the earth wherever there are men and women who are oppressed and who yearn for freedom, wherever there are those who possess skins that are dark, and they are numbered in countless millions, the luster of America's name will be tarnished and faith in the American democracy will begin to ebb.

P. L. Prattis of the *Pittsburgh Courier* asked some very direct questions concerning the performance of the Detroit police, and he gave equally direct answers: "What were the police doing when Negroes were being beaten in the Negro district? Arresting Negroes. What were the police doing when streetcars were stopped by the mob and Negroes mobbed and beaten? They were arresting Negroes. What were the police doing when automobiles bearing Negroes were stopped, turned over and demolished and their occupants beaten? They were arresting Negroes. It is crystal clear that in no American community is the police power going to be used against the majority from which the mob comes to protect the minority from which the victims come."[45] Prattis voiced black America's profoundly skeptical view of the police.

Forty days after the Detroit violence liberal journalist James Wechsler furnished a discouraging report as to the situation he observed in the city. Wechsler noted that the Detroit public library had issued a four-

page leaflet quoting prominent Americans concerning the perils of intolerance, and he believed that Mayor Jeffries "wants to get a better
break for minorities." But in terms of what steps were being taken to
avert future violence he found a lack of significant progress. "Only the
first faltering moves have been made to avert another flare-up," he wrote.
"The prevailing mood is a mixture of fatalism and wishful thinking."
Wechsler recognized that housing and police brutality were critical issues
affecting the black community, but the prospect for serious measures to
deal with these problems appeared remote. A major obstacle was that a
number of city officials, previously regarded as responsive to the black
community, had not risen to the occasion. Wechsler found that they had
become "embittered, defensive, belligerent." They resented black criticism of their compromises. The mayor's Interracial Committee was going
through its motions in an atmosphere of unreality, lacking direction from
City Hall. Wechsler summed it all up: "Detroit, 40 days after, still is
trying to muddle through."[46]

Among the interracial organizations that responded to the Detroit
violence the National Lawyers Guild was particularly outspoken in its
characterization of the events and its analysis of what needed to be done.
The guild's reaction to the Detroit events was set in the context of the
organization's vigorous condemnation of wartime violence against
blacks. Already in November 1942 the national executive board of the
guild had endorsed a report prepared by William H. Hastie, dean of
Howard University's Law School, and Thurgood Marshall, NAACP
counsel, that warned a crisis regarding racial relations was in the making.
"A show down is inevitable," the guild said, between the majority of
Americans and those who would lose the war if that was necessary to
preserve white supremacy. The report noted that six lynchings had taken
place in 1942 and added that constitutional guarantees were "worthless
scraps of paper to the people who are prevented from exercising these
rights by the constant threat of mob violence." Only federal action could
free blacks from lynching and the threat of lynching.[47]

In the immediate aftermath of the June 20–22 violence the city's guild
chapter on the practical level stepped forward to urge the recorder's court
to institute a "cooling-off" period with regard to holding trials of the
hundreds of persons, overwhelmingly black, who had been arrested. The
guild also urged reasonable bond provisions and the providing of defendants with full opportunity to secure competent legal representation.
The organization volunteered to the courts the services of a number of
its members who would be available to serve as counsel in cases where
arrested persons could not otherwise secure legal defense.[48]

Regarding the violence itself the chapter on June 26 issued a statement outlining its view of what had taken place. The statement proceeded from the premise "that we can, we must and we will achieve a civilized, decent community relationship between white and negro citizens. That relationship can rest securely only on a basis of actual, real equality of right and opportunity for the negro citizen." As to the immediate precipitating causes of the violence, the guild lamented the unwillingness of governmental agencies to consider the possibility that "enemy action or treasonable conspiracy" was involved. But the guild also pointed to an underlying cause, and that was "the persistent, irrational prejudice of the white against the negro." The organization made clear its view of the extent of racism within white society: "the sadistic cruelty of white mobs that dragged unoffending negroes from streetcars and automobiles and beat them to unconsciousness is merely the expression on the level of their own warped characters and personalities of the same contemptuous prejudice that inspires more respectable whites to speak habitually of 'niggers.' " Every black person was aware of this racism, and this consciousness was "the basic condition of the ultimately violent reaction of so many negroes to the first evidence of actual, threatened, or imagined white violence."

Although noting that individual policemen acted with restraint, the guild statement questioned why so many more blacks than whites had been killed and also observed that the disproportion between the number of whites and blacks arrested was "difficult to square with the known facts of the rioting." The guild asked for an "immediate and searching" investigation of the police department's conduct and of the adequacy of police training and equipment. Such inquiry was to focus particularly upon the police commissioner's understanding of the city's social tensions, his fitness to give leadership in assuring the security of those living in Detroit. The city council was proposed as the proper agency to conduct such inquiry, and it was further recommended that the council be assisted by special counsel, both white and black. Beyond the holding of an inquiry concerning police conduct, the guild also proposed the establishment of a commission to further interracial accord. The commission was to have broad investigatory powers and was also to develop a comprehensive educational program concerning racial relations.[49]

On September 9 the Detroit guild released an analysis of the report drawn up by the governor's fact-finding committee. The guild bluntly charged the framers of the report with racism and declared that they were unfit to hold public office. At the beginning of its analysis the guild stated the conclusions it drew from the evidence: "we believe that the report clearly reflects a malignant prejudice against the Negro; that it willfully obscures the issues; that it is, in its total effect, a reckless and defamatory attack on the entire Negro community." The committee found that the killing of eighteen of the twenty-five blacks who died in the violence was "justifiable," but the report did not refer to any coroner's inquests or to grand jury hearings, and apparently the word of the police was relied upon in determining the justifiable nature of the killings.

Insofar as the governor's committee placed responsibility for the violence upon the city's black organizations and press for having protested against various manifestations of racism, equating lawful protest with incitement to violence, the guild found there was no room for doubt "as to the prejudice which animated the Committee." The nub of the guild's evaluation was summarized in the comment: "The document reeks of an implied assumption of 'white supremacy' and arrogant resentment at Negroes presuming to complain of anything whatever."

The guild concluded its analysis with an expression of optimism. The organization spoke with eloquence: "We believe that the spirit of the last station on the underground railway inspires us yet. There is a will in Detroit, shared by Negro and white alike, to achieve a community life of equal right and opportunity for all men. Hatred of or contempt for the Negroes is as alien to the sentiments of the great mass of Detroiters as is the hysterical nonsense and prejudice of the Governor's Fact Finding Committee. We know from experience in Detroit that Negro and white can, in the absence of deliberate provocation, work, play and live in harmony."[50] The conscience of liberal, progressive Detroit was awakened, but very much remained to be done if democracy was to become a living reality in that great city of American labor and industry.

The urban violence of the summer of 1943 was not confined to Detroit. In Detroit the pattern was that of a clash between white and black persons with the police abetting white violence and striking hard at any black resistance. In New York the igniting act of aggression came when a policeman, James Collins, shot army private Robert Bandy in the course of an altercation at the Hotel Braddock. The hotel was under police surveillance as a "raided premise," and Collins had placed a black woman, Marjorie Polite, under arrest after she had argued with hotel employees about inadequate accommodations. Bandy apparently protested the officer's action, and a scuffle began that ended with the wounding of Bandy. This incident triggered an explosion of anger on the streets of the community. "Georgia had come to New York" was the feeling of most Harlemites, according to one clergyman in the community. Retaliating against the shooting of Bandy, blacks attacked property, the prop-

erty of white-owned businesses.[51] Claude Brown recalls his child's
perception of what was happening. Lying in bed, he heard loud noises
that made him think the Germans or the Japanese were bombing New
York. The next morning he stepped into the street, although not sure
that this was really his street. "None of the stores had any windows, and
glass was everywhere. It seemed that all the cops in the world were on
145th Street and Eighth Avenue that day. The cops were telling everybody
to move on, and everybody was talking about the riot." Later he went
to look at a nearby pawnshop and went through the ruins of the burned-
out store. "Everything," he wrote, "I picked up was broken or burned
or both. My feet kept sinking into the wet furs that had been burned
and drenched. The whole place smelled of smoke and was as dirty as a
Harlem gutter on a rainy day."[52] Sidney Poitier also recalled his experience of the riot: "In a restaurant downtown where I was working I
heard that there was trouble in Harlem. After work I took a train uptown,
came up out of the subway, and there was chaos everywhere—cops, guns,
and people running and looting, with shots going off everywhere and
debris and broken glass all over the street. Many stores had been set on
fire, and the commercial district on 125th Street looked as if it had been
bombed." Poitier joined in the looting of a store and as he ran from the
building toward home was shot in the foot.[53]

In the aftermath of the riot author Richard Wright went up to Harlem
and later shared with the newspaper *PM* his observations of the scene:

> The streets were littered with debris and broken glass. I spoke to
> several Negroes. They had not slept all night and seemed apprehen-
> sive, as if a little slip or an accident could make things worse.
>
> I had the feeling that more Negro policemen could have given the
> crowds the confidence they needed. During my walk up to 120th
> St. I didn't see a single one.
>
> I don't think it's a race riot—though it has possibilities of turning
> into one. I had the feeling it was a spontaneous outburst of anger,
> stemming mainly from the economic pinch. The shooting of the
> soldier was indeed the spark that set it off.

Wright's view was that the violence was not the work of organized mobs,
and he stressed that people in the street seemed very watchful. Asked
what remedies for the situation he would suggest he gave first place to
alleviating the plight of blacks in the armed services.[54]

There was some physical hostility directed at white persons who happened to be in Harlem. Walter White recalls: "We saw Negroes attempt-

ing to get at white people in automobiles who, unaware of the riot, had driven into the heart of it."[55] But the focus of the 1943 violence was upon white property, and in that the incident was similar to the 1935 Harlem riot and also resembled the pattern of the urban racial violence of the 1960s. What was somewhat out of the ordinary was that in the 1943 situation the city administration, under Mayor Fiorello La Guardia, curbed police excesses and, relatively speaking, behaved with restraint. As Dominic Capeci notes, La Guardia in the midst of the crisis "was at his best, displaying the composure, resourcefulness and circumspection that he always seemed to muster in times of crisis." The mayor did not cower downtown but rather toured the riot area, accompanied by three community leaders closely aligned with the Communist party, Ferdinand Smith of the National Maritime Union, Max Yergan of the National Negro Congress, and attorney Hope Stevens. He also toured Harlem with Walter White of the NAACP, and at one point, hearing the crash of a brick against a storefront, La Guardia had the car stopped, jumped out, and screamed at the crowd, whereupon the crowd dispersed. Unlike his counterpart in Detroit, Mayor Jeffries, La Guardia acknowledged that the black community had legitimate grievances and pledged steps to remedy them. But still the 1943 violence was costly: Six persons were killed, more than 550 individuals were arrested, and some 1,450 stores were damaged or destroyed.[56]

Although La Guardia acted with restraint and some sense of responsibility once the violence had begun, we must also note that acts of omission and commission by the city administration contributed to setting the stage for the explosion of anger. One index to the prevailing racial situation in New York was that in 1942 there was not one black among the permanent faculty members at the city's four municipal colleges. When in 1942 city councilman Adam Clayton Powell, Jr., challenged this de facto policy of racial exclusion, his allegations were overwhelmingly rejected in the council, with Powell joined only by the Communist member Peter V. Cacchione.[57] The city administration did not admit, publicly at least, that a real issue existed. Regarding this situation the excuse might be offered that it was of long standing, but then only weeks before the Harlem outbreak the administration directly affronted the black community in what Capeci characterizes as "one of the gravest errors of his [La Guardia's] career in the field of civil rights."[58] Accepting plans negotiated by parks commissioner Robert Moses, La Guardia authorized a contract with the Metropolitan Life Insurance Company to build Stuyvesant Town, a quasi-public housing development for lower Manhattan. From the start, given Metropolitan's reputation for discriminatory employment practices and statements by company officials, it was clear that Stuyvesant Town was to be lily-white. One analyst of La Guardia's mayoralty contends that the mayor was in part influenced by his belief "that since he had the Negroes in his camp anyway he could get away with it."[59] Whether this was the case or whether La Guardia rationalized that providing housing was more urgent than establishing a nondiscriminatory occupancy policy, the fact remains that his action affronted a black population whose need for improved housing was most obvious. The decision alienated black opinion and laid the basis for an acrimonious dispute that continued through the balance of the decade.

Beyond these specific actions of city government, a number of factors came together in 1943 to produce the incendiary mixture that led to the violence. There was resentment at continuing discrimination in employment and at repeated manifestations of police brutality. Harlemites were also painfully aware that, although they were asked to support the war against Hitler, people of color in the South lived under a racist system more appropriate to a Fascist state than to a democracy. The community was particularly provoked by reports of brutal treatment inflicted on black servicemen. In the fall of 1942 a Harlem reporter commented, "I haven't found a single [black] soldier who is convinced that he's fighting for democracy." Capeci sums up the situation: "From the time that blacks were admitted into the war effort as soldiers, they encountered resentment and reprisals from white citizens, officials and soldiers. It was common for a black soldier to experience verbal harassment and physical abuse, which sometimes resulted in death. Afro-American servicemen had undergone similar treatment in the Great War, but twenty-five years later the race was less tolerant and the times less receptive to such injustices."[60]

An official of the Brooklyn Urban League called attention to this aspect of the violence in referring to "the obvious connection between a Negro soldier being shot in Harlem and the numerous reports of unjust attacks on Negro soldiers in the South." Lorenzo F. Davis asked: "Could it be this unbearable correlation which made the flame of anger so hot among Harlem's citizens to start them on the road to blind madness and retribution? It is possible." Davis asked for protection of black soldiers in the South.[61]

The 1943 incident was touched off when at the Hotel Braddock two critical manifestations of racism appeared linked together, police brutality and unjust treatment of black servicemen. Given the prevailing conditions of the time, it is probable that some incident would have released the pent-up anger existing in the Harlem community. Walter White wrote that "the Bigger Thomases of New York passed like a cloud of locusts over the stores of Harlem," and this situation was the product not of some natural criminal bent but rather of the frustrations intensified by the war.[62]

An analysis of the Harlem events that shed light on the basic realities of racism and upon the responsibility of the La Guardia administration for what had happened was provided New York newspaper readers by Albert Deutsch, investigative reporter for *PM*. Deutsch asserted that the violence climaxed "the mounting tensions within the Harlem community itself, the piled-up resentments against segregation and discrimination, against the pushing around the Negro has been getting in civil and military life." He considered the sources of the riot, and he also urged that the solution be found "in reason, not force, in justice, not repression; in understanding, not blind hate and/or fear."

Deutsch gave his readers generalizations, but he also vividly sketched Harlem as he saw it in the immediate aftermath of the violence. "Harlem yesterday morning," he wrote, "resembled a bombed-out city wherein destruction miraculously stopped at the first story. Virtually every show window along the main shopping districts was shattered, their contents cleaned out or in disorder. Plate glass littered the sidewalks and gutters; trampled clothes, canned goods, bric-a-brac and every conceivable item of goods were strewn about the area."

Mayor La Guardia had acted with restraint in the crisis and, according to Deutsch, deserved high commendation "for putting the police under wraps, and for his prompt and efficient handling of the situation in other respects." But what took place in 1943 could not be separated from the violence of 1935 and from the recommendations for remedial action that had then been urged upon La Guardia. La Guardia had chosen not to act on those recommendations, indeed had not released the 1935 report, and La Guardia's reasoned response to the 1943 events could not absolve him of responsibility for not having taken the steps earlier that might have averted the violence. Deutsch noted that La Guardia had an "almost unbroken record of inaction in the face of repeated appeals by responsible civic groups during the years that followed the suppressed report of his own Commission." The 1935 commission had furnished a "masterly" report, but the mayor had failed to act. Deutsch did not blame La Guardia for the national dimensions of the situation, for the economic discrimination and insecurity that plagued all of America's ghettos. But La Guardia had not taken the steps that were specifically within his power. "No essential reforms," Deutsch wrote, "have been introduced to alleviate Harlem conditions." La Guardia, "by acts of commission and omission," had helped aggravate the Harlem situation. He was particularly at fault for having permitted the city to become a party "to the obnoxious Stuyvesant Town project"; had he not linked the city to this discriminatory housing plan, his stand would have been worth more than all his positive measures taken after the outbreak of violence. La Guardia had manifested a friendly attitude toward blacks, had appointed a number of blacks to office, but he had not developed a program to deal with the fundamental needs of the black community.

In a second installment of his analysis Deutsch sought to educate his readers to understand the tensions generated by American racism in 1943. He linked the Harlem violence to occurrences in other places and found a common pattern. It was a pattern in which blacks, buttressed by the FEPC, had gained access to some new job opportunities but "still meet with overt and concealed economic discrimination at every hand." Upgrading was difficult in some plants, impossible in others. And discrimination was not merely a private matter. Blacks were segregated in the armed services and most commonly assigned to labor battalions. Of critical importance were the indignities heaped upon blacks in the service and upon family members who wished to visit a black soldier stationed in the Jim Crow South. In addition to war-related manifestations of racism there were all the standard forms of discrimination, segregation, and ghettoization, still in place. Deutsch affirmed that blacks sought the defeat of the Fascist enemy, but their desire encountered frustration. "You are blocked at nearly every turn. To cap it all, you are accused of lacking patriotism by the very elements who put obstacles in the way of your displaying it." Deutsch asked his white readers to imagine themselves in the position of blacks and to ask if they then could maintain indefinitely an attitude of sweet reasonableness. Deutsch placed the racial crisis at the top of the nation's domestic agenda: "The extension of full liberty and justice, with full rights of citizenship, to the one-tenth of the Nation now denied these benefits is...the most important home-front task of this war. Sincere believers in American democracy can no longer afford to avoid that task lest they become hypocrites and betrayers of the credo. That task cannot be postponed as a postwar project. It is a vital war aim." Deutsch articulated a militant liberalism that related the war to a vision of a more democratic, humanistic America. But during the war years those moved by that vision lacked the strength to secure basic alterations in the institutional arrangements of American racism.[63]

Within the black community the *People's Voice* was a forceful journalistic voice for a constructive response to the Harlem explosion. From the beginning insisting that what happened in Harlem was not a race riot, the newspaper sought to provide reliable information and to rally the community. The newspaper dispelled rumors that Private Bandy had been killed by providing an interview with the soldier. The *Voice* described the violence as one "of the worst pieces of wanton vandalism any city has ever suffered," but readers were also informed the police bent backward to prevent the riot. An appeal issued by Adam Clayton Powell, Jr., Congressman Vito Marcantonio, police official Samuel Battle, and judges Hubert T. Delany and Steven Jackson, stressing the paramount importance of restoring order, was prominently featured. Individually, Powell called upon the residents of Harlem to return to work immediately, keep children indoors, especially at night, stay off the streets except for necessary business, cooperate with police, and not believe rumors.

The newspaper looked backward to the 1935 Harlem violence and forward to measures that would alleviate tensions in the community. Reporter Marvel Cooke noted that some of those engaged in the 1935 episode were like Bigger Thomas of *Native Son:* "they resented deeply— sorely—the way they had been kicked around." What happened was dreadful, but in the aftermath of 1935 some progress had been made. Now was the time for further progress. Cooke wrote: "Harlem must rise again, bigger and better and finer than ever." Community leaders had formulated some of the immediate measures needed, including the institution of rent control, the breaking down of Jim Crowism in the armed forces, and the expansion of the wartime price control program. These steps were necessary so that the fifth columnists would not have their way. The *Voice* also gave two pages to an appeal for support issued by the interracial City-Wide Citizens Committee on Harlem, cochaired by clergymen Adam Clayton Powell, Sr., and Algernon D. Black. The appeal stressed the importance of enforcing price ceilings.

In its August 14 issue the *People's Voice* listed on its front page the key demands called for in the situation. They were: the elimination of Jim Crowism in the armed forces, an end to second-class citizenship, equal job opportunities, no more riots, enforcement of price control, and unity for victory at home and abroad. Harlem, the paper said, "looks to the future for these and other citizenship rights." There was also an editorial, which warned against complacency and urged unified action by both blacks and whites to eliminate grievances. "There was no RACE riot in Harlem," the *Voice* stated, and there would be none if local and federal authorities took appropriate action.[64]

In what manner did the Roosevelt administration respond to the events in New York? The president rejected one specific proposal set before him that might have led to formulating a program to remedy black grievances.

The proposal had emerged from consultations between presidential adviser Jonathan Daniels and Howard Odum of the University of North Carolina's Institute for Research in Social Science. Under the terms of the plan a committee of prominent Americans would be assembled in a conference that would recommend Roosevelt's appointment of a President's Committee on Race and Minority Groups. The committee would study the situation and make public its findings. Daniels submitted the proposal to Roosevelt, but the answer was no.[65] At least in terms of a public response, the New York situation as well as the earlier violence in Detroit were to be treated basically as local matters. To a large extent the sources of the violence were national in scope, but the national government did little to meet its responsibilities, and in New York even the relatively enlightened La Guardia administration did not commit itself to a program that would democratize New York's hiring, housing, and educational practices.

Two years after the 1943 violence Adam Clayton Powell, Jr., looked back at what had happened. He insisted that one thing above all needed to be understood: *"The Harlem Outbreak Was Not a Race Riot."* What it was amounted to "the last open revolt of the black common man against a bastard democracy." Powell stressed as causative agent "the whole sorrowful, disgraceful bloody record of America's treatment of one million blacks in uniform." The violence had accomplished nothing, but it taught the black community a lesson. Nonviolence was the only way, and that meant electoral action. That recognition of the superiority of nonviolence, Powell explained, led to the election of Communist Benjamin Davis, Jr., to the New York City Council and to his own election to Congress.[66]

All in all, during 1943, according to the Social Science Institute at Fisk University, 242 racial battles took place in forty-seven cities.[67] Detroit and New York were clearly not isolated phenomena. Axis agents may have played some role in all this, but fundamentally these events resulted from a conflict between the insistence by blacks that a war for democracy produce some democracy at home and the determination of white authority to preserve existing racial patterns, at whatever cost.

The *Crisis* was on target when it editorialized that the 1943 violence stemmed from the whole structure of racism, from newspapers that headlined accounts of "black brutes," from racist textbooks that portrayed blacks as contributing nothing to America, from industrial and banking magnates who frustrated aspirations for job advancement, from Hollywood films with their racist caricatures, and from government that tolerated the doings of such politicians as Senator Bilbo and Congressman

John Rankin. There were also the scholars and publicists "with their shoddy statistics, their pseudo-science, their learned lectures, and their published papers." The editorial expressed anger but also the accurate perception that powerful segments of the American public still wanted the racial status quo. The result was that when blacks asserted themselves the consequences were riots "or, better, pogroms."[68]

The racial violence of 1943 was not confined to outbreaks on city streets. In Mobile the focus of confrontation was the shipyards of the Alabama Dry Dock and Shipbuilding Company. The company, producing ships vitally needed for the war effort, employed thousands of workers in both skilled and unskilled positions. Yet the company was one of many southern employers resisting fair hiring and upgrading practices. As explained in a recent study of FEPC activities with regard to southern shipyards:

> Employers believed that the social structure would not countenance intermingling of the races on skilled jobs and reacted accordingly. When questioned about their attitude toward Negro labor, most employers mentioned prevailing myths and half-truths, involving high illiteracy rates, instability on the job, and inability to adjust to the confinement of industrial work. Others mentioned social diseases and Negroes' poor health, a belief that was hardly consistent with the fact that most jobs available to blacks involved heavy manual labor. In Mobile, employers said that Negroes were both uninterested and incapable of acquiring education and skills. Blacks in Mobile also allegedly feared heights and elevated work places.

One Mobile shipbuilder commented that it was not traditional to hire blacks and also asserted that upgrading black workers was "impractical and utopian."

The FEPC moved into this situation, holding hearings in Birmingham during June 1942 that revealed to the public the discriminatory pattern prevailing in the southern shipbuilding industry. On the basis of these hearings Alabama Dry Dock in November 1942 was ordered by the FEPC to cease and desist from discriminatory practices. By that time over 4,000 blacks were already employed on the production line in riveting and spray painting. The company, however, dragged its feet on upgrading blacks, although leaders of the CIO International Union of Marine and Shipbuilding Workers of America supported the proposal. When the War Manpower Commission urged that the company begin upgrading black and white workers, while avoiding race conflict by maintaining segregated shipways, Alabama Dry Dock responded with a provocative action probably calculated to produce trouble. Without informing the workers or the union beforehand or undertaking any educational program, the company announced it would integrate black and white welders on the shipways. The anticipated trouble broke out. On May 25 a crowd of whites attacked black workers with pipes and clubs. Blacks were told, "Get going, Nigger. This is our shipyard." At least two black workers were thrown into the river; several hundred blacks left the yard. Another outbreak took place at the shipyard the following day.

After the violence the company, responding to the insistence of the FEPC, the Maritime Commission, and the navy, announced a plan to use skilled black workers on four of the shipways. The plan gave some opportunities to black craftsmen while not directly offending the structure of segregation. The upgrading plan provided no opportunities for black machinists, pipefitters, and electricians, and black workers on the job were subjected to repeated insult. Apart from the shipyards, Mobile's pattern of Jim Crowism continued in full force. Blacks had been able to make some headway by making clear that they would not work under conditions of violence, but they were unable, even under the duress of war, to break through the wall of segregation.[69]

Even in cities that did not experience major incidents of racial violence there was ample evidence about the prevalence of bitterness among blacks, especially in relation to the violence often directed against them. A study, conducted during June 1942, of how blacks in Baltimore and Cincinnati regarded the war gives a vivid picture of the feelings of many in the black communities of those two cities. There were these comments by a young unemployed black domestic worker: "One thing they could stop—the white cops from arresting colored people and beating them with their guns. You could just turn around and chop their heads off... the other day they run a black boy in here—they knew they had him. After they had him they took their guns and beat him with their guns, and that happened right down in this yard. If I'd had a bomb I would have tried my best to blow them to hell." Many blacks believed that racial treatment in the army was poor. Said a mill worker in Cincinnati: "you would think that when you get in the Army and show that you want to help fight this war they would treat you all right, but they don't. The officers will call you nigger and treat you any kind of way and in some of these southern towns the white people will beat you up." The study noted that in Baltimore police brutality was very much on the minds of blacks and that there had been retaliatory measures with instances occurring of blacks disarming police officers and beating them with their own sticks. An NAACP worker gave warning: "White people are sitting on a powder keg... blind to what is developing. I expect to see race riots flare up all over the country unless something is done to give the Negro a real opportunity in this war effort." A young black man told an interviewer of a recent incident in Baltimore in which a soldier was shot in the back by a policeman. In Cincinnati a black woman expressed hope the United States would win the war but also desired that "colored people get a fair chance to make a living and equal rights as the white man." She favored equal rights legislation, not only for Cincinnati "but all over the U.S.—even down in the deep south where they're treated like dogs."[70]

Langston Hughes supported the war effort, exulted in the Soviet triumph at Stalingrad, but also poignantly expressed his bitterness at being confronted with the twin evils of fascism abroad and racism at home:

> Looky here, America
> What you done done—
> Let things drift
> Until the riots come
>
> Now your policemen
> Let the mobs run free.
> I reckon you don't care
> Nothing about me.
>
> You tell me that hitler
> Is a mighty bad man.
> I guess he took lessons
> From the ku klux klan.
>
> You tell me mussolini's
> Got an evil heart.
> Well, it mus-a been in Beaumont
> That he had his start—
>
> Cause everything that hitler
> And mussolini do
> Negroes get the same
> Treatment from you

You jim crowed me
Before hitler rose to power—
And you're still jim crowing me
Right now, this very hour.

Yet you say we're fightin
For democracy.
Then why don't democracy
Include me?

I ask you this question
Cause I want to know
How long I got to fight
BOTH HITLER—AND JIM CROW.[71]

Racist violence within the armed services and violence involving civilians mocked the call for an all-encompassing national unity in the
common struggle against fascism. Blacks responded to such provocation
within the context of the need to protect their rights and lives while at
the same time recognizing the legitimacy of the war effort. One such
response was found in the reaction of the black Communist leader William L. Patterson to a lynching that occurred shortly after United States
entrance into the war. In late January 1942 a black man, Cleo Wright,
was lynched in the town of Sikeston, Missouri. Wright, a cotton mill
worker, allegedly had attacked a white woman and while held in jail was
seized by a mob of more than 300, stuffed into the trunk of an auto,
and taken to the town's black district. There he was dragged behind the
auto, and later his body was set afire. The *New York Times* pointed out
that a dozen armed men out of Sikeston's 8,000 population could have
stopped the mob.[72]

Patterson spoke about this murder in a speech he delivered at a St.
Louis Washington–Lincoln–Douglass meeting. Patterson's speech was
entitled "Sikeston; Hitlerite Crime against America," and the main theme
was that racist violence within American society represented the domestic
counterpart of fascism. To the indictment of lynching as racist murder
Patterson added the ingredient that in the context of the war it represented
sabotage of the war effort. Patterson placed the Sikeston lynching alongside the burning of the liner *Normandie* in New York harbor and "with
the sabotaging of the production of equipment and munitions of war
without which the task of defeating fascism becomes infinitely more
difficult." He stated that the South had become the nation's leading

economic problem in part "because of the license extended to the bestial enemies of the Negro people." In ordinary times, he said, there was only verbal protest against lynching. But 1942 was not an ordinary time, and Patterson insisted that protest must take a more effective form. "Death to lynchers, the destroyers of American democracy," he argued, "is the slogan of victory."

Patterson saw a new urgency in efforts to enact a federal antilynching law. That section of white America that refused to pass such an act had not only been guilty of complicity in murder but was now guilty of treason. Patterson flatly denied that lynching could not be eliminated in the midst of the war. He posed the question: "Is lynching a condition necessary for victory over fascism?" Answering that it was not, Patterson set forth the thesis that blacks and their white allies had to press the fight on two fronts, "always understanding that Hitler is the main danger." The "cesspools of cannibalism," Patterson declared, had to be cleaned up.[73]

Patterson's speech suggests that the notion that the American Communists abandoned the fight for black rights during World War II is a considerable oversimplification. The Communists did place winning the war against fascism as the paramount objective, but the fight against racism at home was seen as consistent with that aim. Perceptive on this point are Drake and Cayton, who in their classic study of Chicago, *Black Metropolis,* wrote that many blacks became dissatisfied with the failure of Communists to organize mass demonstrations for equal rights during the war but that many blacks in the labor movement "saw that while 'the Reds' played down mass action they continued to fight for Negro rights *within* the labor unions, and tried to inject the issue of Negro rights into the political coalitions they formed with liberals and the Democratic machine."[74]

A view of the black ideological response to racial oppression was set forth with considerable sophistication by Horace Cayton in 1943. Cayton's essential argument was that the war had produced a new spirit of internationalism among Afro-Americans. He saw the black American as having broken out of the mindset of caste and as now viewing his social position "as identified with that of the darker races of the world." Blacks no longer confined their demands to their own rights; now, Cayton asserted, "they are for democratic rights for all peoples throughout the world." Blacks had shifted from a position of some indifference to the war effort to one of demand for participation in every aspect of the war so as to be in a position to help shape the peace. What Cayton recognized was that blacks were moving from a posture of seeking concessions to one of a demand for full equality. He put his finger on a basic mood that laid the basis for future action.

Cayton saw that the first response of many whites to the new black mood was one of fear or hate. There were liberals who reacted with some understanding, but the stronger thrust of white response was expressed by "moderates" who urged caution upon blacks and by a lumpenproletariat that "whips itself up into a lynch mood." What most well-meaning whites failed to comprehend was that gradualism was obsolete. "With a world revolution in progress," Cayton wrote, "one group of people cannot be held apart from the stream of thought and told to have faith in education and good-will. To ask the American Negro to go slowly is to attempt either to slacken the international pace of social change or to isolate the Negro from the world forces in which he is engulfed." If an explosion resulted from the situation, the violence would represent not the desires of blacks but the militancy of racist resistance to change. Cayton felt that the possibility of nonviolent change was enhanced by the context of the war, a war with proclaimed objectives of guaranteeing democratic rights to all peoples. He saw no sense to the argument that blacks should relinquish their claim to democratic rights in the midst of a war "fought for the right of peoples everywhere to be free." Cayton was cautious in terms of advocating a specific strategy for securing black rights; there was no set solution to be offered. But "perhaps" the first step toward a solution was the realization that the racial question in the United States was a world problem, "that it is part of the problem of all the common people of the world." If this were seen it might be possible to understand that the war was part of a larger struggle to attain a new moral order. Cayton equated in importance the fight for black rights at home with the battle for military victory.[75]

Cayton was by no means a solitary voice in advancing his call for a changed American future on the basis of realizing the broader implications of the war. Such an analysis was also to be found, for example, in Detroit's *Michigan Chronicle*. Shortly after the racial explosion of June 1943, the paper declared: "we must take note of the tremendous implications of this great war and how they affect the status quo of race relations. The very character of this war—a war for freedom, for democracy, for liberation—has of necessity produced profound changes in our own thinking and has accelerated the hopes of all of us for a new America and even a new world." Democracy in this war was encountering the forces of reaction, and the *Chronicle* explained that this "is what is meant when we refer to the World War as a world revolution." If blacks were isolated in American society the time would not be far off "when tyranny shall prevail and this noble experiment called democracy which was conceived by our forefathers will end in abject failure." The enemies of democracy had to be eliminated, and it was the beauty of the American form of government "that we can do this job without resorting to violence and bloodshed."[76]

If the Communists viewed the issue of equal rights in relation to the overwhelming need for the defeat of fascism and Horace Cayton saw a war for democratic goals as creating a favorable climate for progress, the Congress of Racial Equality (CORE) focused singlemindedly on the struggle for black rights. The organization came into being in Chicago during 1942, initiated by a group of active members of the long-established pacifist organization, the Fellowship of Reconciliation. CORE offered a definite alternative, an alternative to violent retaliatory action, to the gradualism of the traditional civil rights organization, and also to the Marxian concept of identification with the working class. CORE offered a strategy of nonviolent direct action. Where the Marxists had focused on the context of the black struggle and related tactics to the larger situation, CORE concentrated on method. A prime articulator of the CORE ideology in its early period was the former member of the Young Communist League, Bayard Rustin, youth secretary for the Fellowship of Reconciliation. In an article published in October 1942 he spelled out the basis for the CORE approach. Rustin, the pacifist, saw war as the generator of hatreds that would become more intense within American society, and he outlined a rising trend of organized violence. He referred to a number of arrests and beatings of blacks who had insisted on access to transportation overcrowded by war conditions. Several unprovoked shootings of blacks, by both police and civilians, were itemized, and mention was made of a Georgia incident in which the world-famous singer, Roland Hayes, was beaten and arrested because his wife had insisted on normal service in a shoe store. Rustin noted that such episodes had a marked effect on the mass of blacks and stirred unprecedented moods of militancy. Rustin was not unqualifiedly pleased with this militancy, especially insofar as it expressed a belief that large-scale violence impended in America. According to Rustin the majority of blacks could not conceive of a solution "by reconciliation and non-violence." Whereas Horace Cayton had doubts as to the strategy to be employed in responding to oppression Rustin had no such hesitation. The Afro-American, Rustin argued, could attain progress "only" if he used the method of nonviolent direct action. Although he referred only in passing to "our war resistance," clearly for Rustin there was no problem of relating the struggle for black rights to the need for military victory over fascism. He wrote in terms of relating to immediate racial conflicts, but the tenor of his comments indicated that he was thinking of the postwar future as well as the situation at hand. The most vital thing a believer in the nonviolent method could do was to be in a position, "by becoming a real part of the Negro community," to offer leadership "when troubles come." Rustin was convinced that the American black possesses the qualities required for nonviolent direct action, the qualities of enduring suffering and of being able to "admit his own share of guilt." The world context was not altogether treated as irrelevant, but in the midst of the struggle against the racism and militarism of fascism Rustin singled out for special reference only the Gandhian movement in India. Rustin was setting forth a view that would aim at the compartmentalization of the racial struggle for justice, apart from the general mainstream of world democratic currents.[77]

The ideological assumptions of CORE differed from more influential, radical trends of the 1930s not only in its downgrading of the anti-Fascist cause but also in its challenge to the concept, rooted in Marxian ideology, that racial oppression and violence were based on a clash of interests between Afro-Americans and their exploiters. During the first decade of CORE's history its most influential leader was the pacifist George Houser. Houser strongly emphasized the impact of the nonviolent effort upon the consciousness of the persons engaged in racist practices. It was his opinion that "a non-violent campaign cannot be considered a total success unless attitudes are changed in the process of changing policies."[78] Houser took along with him into CORE the stress on reconciliation that was central to the program of the Fellowship of Reconciliation.

In its early years especially, CORE exhibited a distinct strain of elitism. CORE activists tended to be a close-knit group who spent much time together developing a common philosophy and program of action. August Meier and Elliot Rudwick, who have most carefully examined the history of the organization, note the contradiction that "CORE's founders saw themselves as a well-disciplined, elite group with rigid membership requirements, while also dreaming of becoming a large-scale, broad based movement." Houser expressed the early animating spirit of CORE in his comment at one point that there was a "unique place for CORE... a place in organizing a small disciplined activity on the race relations front."[79]

In its official statements CORE quite clearly outlined the special nature of its view of the black struggle. The organization avowed one purpose, the elimination of racial discrimination, and but one method, "inter-racial, non-violent direct action." The individual member was asked to abide "by all democratic group decisions" and to accept the organiza-tion's discipline in all projects in which he participated. In a statement of its "Action Discipline," CORE made clear its basic belief that a world without violence could be brought into being only on the basis of non-violent methods. Conflict would not be resolved by violence but only aggravated by it. There was also the expedient consideration that it was suicidal for a minority group to use violence because it would result in complete subjugation at the hands of the majority. A result of CORE's tendency to isolate the racial struggle was the posing of the fight for equality as the concern of a minority, implicitly rejecting the point of view that black liberation was bound up with the self-interest of the great majority of Americans.

The "Action Discipline" spelled out the individual's guarantees to the group and the group's guarantees to the individual, and it is noteworthy that the former made up a much longer list than the latter. The individual was assured that CORE policy would be arrived at only through dem-ocratic group discussion, that the member had the right to dissent from a group decision, and finally that if trouble resulted from carrying out the organization's work the member would receive uncompromising sup-port, "financially and otherwise." The activist undertook many com-mitments, including a commitment to careful investigation of the facts before determining that racial injustice exists and a commitment to un-derstanding the attitude of the person engaged in discriminatory action. The CORE member would also never engage in any action in the or-ganization's name except when authorized and would when engaged in an action project cheerfully obey orders from the leader of the project. No personal or family consideration was to be permitted to divert a member from the group discipline once he or she agreed to a particular project. The "Action Discipline" was a list of requirements perhaps ap-propriate to a committed set of cadres; the maintenance of such require-ments in a mass movement would be more difficult.[80]

In its initial stages CORE's activities were concentrated on local issues, with specific gains won almost exclusively in campaigns to desegregate places of public accommodation. It was not until after the war in 1947 that the movement was able to carry through its first national project. This project, termed a Journey of Reconciliation, involved sixteen per-sons, eight white and eight black, who left Washington on April 9, 1947. The aim was to ride on an integrated basis on buses traveling along interstate routes in the South. The participants in the project would put into effect a 1946 Supreme Court ruling in the Irene Morgan case that found unconstitutional Virginia legislation requiring segregation in interstate carriers.[81] Believing that an attempt to integrate bus routes in the Deep South would evoke an extremely violent reaction, CORE decided to confine the trip to the upper South.

Before leaving Washington the travelers took part in a two-day training program in techniques of nonviolence. The sessions set a pattern that would be applied, during the 1960s civil rights movement, in many training programs for nonviolent activists. General principles were discussed as well as what was to be done in specific situations that could arise aboard the buses. What was to be the response to insult or to actual assault? Members of the group staged mock encounters in which they would simulate the act of confrontation, taking turns playing the roles of bus driver, police, hostile segregationists, and themselves. The response to provocation and violence was to be a combination of nonviolence and firmness. The riders would not leave their seats unless directly arrested by the police.

During the journey the sixteen were most often split in two groups, one riding the Greyhound line, the other Trailways. Twelve arrests resulted from challenging Jim Crow seating arrangements. One incident of violence occurred during the trip. Near the North Carolina university town of Chapel Hill a group of taxi drivers, milling around the bus station, assaulted James Peck, who had left the Trailways bus to make bond for four of the riders who had been arrested. Peck later recalled that the assault culminated a period of racial tension in Chapel Hill. "The explosion might have occurred," Peck wrote, "when Eleanor Roosevelt, refusing to eat at a segregated function of the university, dined on Coca-Cola and sandwiches on its steps. It might have occurred when Dorothy Maynor, noted Negro singer, gave a concert on the campus at which seating was unsegregated. It might have occurred when Reverend Charles Jones, courageous white minister who housed our group, permitted an interracial CIO union meeting in his church some weeks before our meeting." Peck responded nonviolently to the attack, but the white taxi drivers continued to harass the riders even after they had been released on bail. Shortly after Peck, together with Bayard Rustin, Igal Roodenko, Joe Felmet, and Andrew Johnson, arrived at Jones's home someone called to threaten, "Get the niggers out of town by nightfall or we'll burn down your house." In any event the riders were due at a meeting in Greensboro and soon left Chapel Hill in cars driven by three university students.

The 1947 journey showed that nonviolent activists could apply their principles in confrontation with southern racists. It was also a foreshadowing of future, larger-scale challenges to the segregation system. The trip also, according to Peck, showed that bus drivers and passengers were ready to accept desegregation. Although occasional arrests occurred, in many instances nobody did anything about the fact that the CORE travelers defied the segregation norms. But in the short run the journey did not give life to the Supreme Court decision. For some years segregation would continue, even in interstate transportation.[82]

THIRTEEN

Victory without Peace

I F THE ONSET of American participation in World War II set a context for a new, nonviolent civil rights movement, victory over the Axis stimulated longer-established centers of the black movement to connect their activities with an appeal to world opinion. The establishment of the United Nations in 1945 provided a forum through which such an appeal could be directed. The defeat of fascism was a defeat for policies of racism and colonialism, and in this setting it was apparent that the position of Afro-Americans had international implications. Although the National Negro Congress and the National Association for the Advancement of Colored People were in sharp disagreement with regard to basic views of the black struggle, in the aftermath of the war both groups saw the usefulness of recourse to the United Nations. Whereas appeals against racist violence had often in the past been directed to officers of national government, now the issue was to be laid before a world authority.

The National Negro Congress presented its document, *A Petition on Behalf of 13 Million Oppressed Negro Citizens of the United States of America,* to the United Nations at Hunter College in New York on June 6, 1946. The appeal drew upon the contribution of blacks to the American democratic heritage. Max Yergan of the NNC declared: "We have fought to preserve the unity of our country within, and to defend it from enemies without. And when the fascist enemies of all mankind recently threatened to overrun the whole world, we joined hands with our country men and with freedom-loving peoples of other lands to crush the fascist monster and to lay the basis for a genuine 'Parliament of Man,' the United Nations." The petition was sharply critical of the Truman administration. Yergan wrote that "it is with genuine anger and disgust that the Negro people like all other friends of freedom, view the hypocrisy of our Government's professions to leadership in the promotion of 'freedom and democracy' throughout the world." Yergan asserted that Secretary of State James F. Byrnes subscribed to the same racist policies as did Adolph

Hitler. In its published form the appeal to the UN was accompanied by a letter from Yergan and Executive Secretary Revels Cayton to President Truman in which Truman was told of the petition and also bluntly informed that his administration had "reversed the democratic program of the Roosevelt government, both internally and in relation to foreign policy."

In presenting the petition the NNC referred to basic UN documents to support its contention that racial oppression in the United States should be an appropriate concern of this international body. The language of the United Nations Charter was quoted, language in which it was stated that the UN's purposes included "promoting and encouraging respect for human rights and for fundamental freedoms for all without distinction as to race, sex, language, or religion." The charter was also cited with regard to the authority of the UN's Economic and Social Council to make recommendations with respect to human rights. The council exercised this function through the Commission on Human Rights. The commission "would encourage the acceptance of higher standards in this field and help to check and eliminate discrimination and other abuses." The congress made three requests of the UN: (1) that the world organization study conditions in the United States regarding "political, economic and social discrimination against Negroes because of their race and color"; (2) that appropriate recommendations be made to the end of eliminating racial discrimination; and (3) that such further steps be taken "as may seem just and proper to the end that the oppression of the American Negro be brought to an end."

To support the petition the congress provided a factual outline, written by historian Herbert Aptheker. Peonage and violence were among topics highlighted in this factual section. Aptheker did not quantify these phenomena, noting that neither was as yet subject to exact statistical formulation, but he also observed that it was unquestionable that both were widespread and that "each deserves full, thorough investigation by groups independent of the dominant Southern cliques." He began from the premise that violence aimed at blacks was so common, especially in the South, as to be institutionalized. Lynching was most publicized, and though organized protest reduced its frequency it still occurred and the threat of its use was still quite real. Of greater importance currently, however, was the "dry lynching," the destruction of a black by a small group of persons, often police officers. The United Nations was told that "this is certainly a type of barbarism that should be thoroughly investigated and absolutely extirpated."[1]

The National Negro Congress petition was an outline of the dimensions of racial oppression in the United States. Aptheker has since recalled that the petition was deliberately kept brief so that it could receive widespread distribution, and indeed, he notes, 100 thousand copies were distributed.[2] A more detailed and formidable presentation was made by the National Association for the Advancement of Colored People. The NAACP statement, entitled *An Appeal to the World: A Statement on the Denial of Human Rights to Minorities in the Case of Citizens of Negro Descent in the United States of America, and an Appeal to the United Nations for Redress,* was prepared under the supervision of W. E. B. Du Bois. Among the authors of various sections of the document were Du Bois, Cornell professor Milton Konvitz, Chicago black community leader Earl B. Dickerson, and the historian Rayford Logan. In the introductory section, Du Bois detailed the credentials of the NAACP as spokesman for black Americans. What Dr. Du Bois termed "a small body of interested persons" had become by the end of 1946 an organization with a membership of 452,289 in 1,417 branches. The NAACP was described as "the oldest and largest organization among American Negroes designed to fight for their political, civil and social rights."

Du Bois provided a brief outline of the history of racial oppression in the United States. He focused especially upon the consequences of political disfranchisement, rejecting the notion that only blacks suffered the results of being excluded from the polls. It was Du Bois's view that "the disfranchisement of the American Negro makes the functioning of all democracy in the nation difficult; and as democracy fails to function in the leading democracy in the world, it fails in the world." Du Bois contended that the restriction of the franchise made it easier for concentrated wealth to control the politics of the southern states and thus to control national affairs. For the majority of southerners the result was economic deprivation based on a cheap labor system. Political disfranchisement, according to Du Bois, laid the basis for a reactionary stance of American government in world affairs. He declared that the federal government had "continually cast its influence with imperial aggression throughout the world and withdrawn its sympathy from the colored peoples and from the small nations. It has become through private investment a part of the imperialistic bloc which is controlling the colonies of the world." Du Bois further observed, quite contrary to the thought of those who would center national attention on conflict with the Soviet Union, that the main source of danger to American interests was to be found at home. He asked the question: "When will nations learn that their enemies are quite as often within their own country as without?" His answer was that it was not Russia that threatened the United States so much as Mississippi. The real problems were not Stalin and Molotov but Bilbo and Rankin; "internal injustice done to one's brothers is far more dangerous than the aggression of strangers from abroad."

Du Bois dealt at some length with the issue of the appropriateness of directing the appeal to the United Nations. He noted that "many persons" contended that the subject matter of the appeal represented a purely domestic question and that therefore the document should be addressed to the American people and government. Du Bois disagreed. He explained that "from the very beginning of this nation," and even before in the colonial era, blacks had sought redress of their grievances and had offered evidence in support of their claims. He also stated that "this continuous hammering upon the gates of opportunity in the United States" had had effect. But this hammering was not enough. He argued that "no large group of a nation can lag behind the average culture of that nation, as the American Negro still does, without suffering not only itself but becoming a menace to the nation." He went on to assert that the United States owed something to the world and to the United Nations. He considered as very relevant the headquartering of the United Nations in New York. The United States was obligated not only to protect its own people but also "to guard and respect the various peoples of the world who are its guests and allies." But the mores of American racism posed a threat to all nonwhite persons. Du Bois wrote: "Because of caste custom and legislation along color lines, the United States is today in danger of encroaching upon the rights and privileges of its fellow nations. Most people of the world are more or less colored in skin; their presence at the meetings of the United Nations as participants and as visitors, renders them always liable to insult and to discrimination; because they may be mistaken for Americans of Negro descent." The American racial situation was "primarily" an internal question, it was true, but inevitably became an international question also "and will in the future become more and more international, as the nations draw together."

Finally, in justifying the NAACP's petition to the UN, Du Bois made the point that blacks in the United States constituted "one of the considerable nations of the world." By numbers alone the American black community had a right to be heard, and though the standing of smaller independent nations in the United Nations was a cause for rejoicing "we maintain equally that our voice should not be suppressed or ignored." The people of this nation were not to be regarded as completely ignorant, poverty-stricken, or diseased. Du Bois noted that black literacy was higher than in most of the countries of Asia and South America and many of the countries of Europe. Blacks were propertyholders in many instances, and substantial numbers of them had acquired some formal education.

The question of violence was discussed by Earl Dickerson in an essay tracing the denial of legal rights of Afro-Americans from 1787 to 1914. Mob violence was one of four principal methods employed to deny blacks their constitutional rights. Dickerson appended to his article an outline of thirty-two decisions by the United States Supreme Court between 1875 and 1915 dealing with the legal rights of Negroes. A number of the decisions involved the issue of violence, most often in the form of trial verdicts in which blacks were to be punished for, supposedly, having murdered white persons. The first of the thirty-two cases, *U.S.* v. *Cruikshank* (92 U.S. 542), posed the issue of applying the Enforcement Act of May 30, 1870, to several white men charged with violently breaking up a black political meeting in Louisiana. The Court in this case had ruled that the Fourteenth Amendment did not provide that persons could look for federal protection against invasion of rights by the private acts of others. As early as 1879, in *Virginia* v. *Rives* (100 U.S. 313), a case involving two blacks charged with killing a white man, the Court decided that all-white juries did not violate the Constitution unless it could be shown that blacks were excluded from the jury solely on grounds of race or color. In additional cases the Court refused to overturn local legal processes that would lead to the infliction of officially sanctioned violence upon accused blacks. In one case, *Pace* v. *Alabama* (106 U.S. 583), the Court found that an Alabama law providing for more severe punishment in the case of fornication between blacks and whites than between members of the same race was not deemed to contravene the equal rights guarantees of the Fourteenth Amendment. The refusal in the *Cruikshank* case to extend federal protection against "private acts" was confirmed further in the 1906 ruling in *Hodges* v. *United States* (203 U.S. 81) that a case involving alleged intimidation of black laborers by several white men did not fall within the jurisdiction of the federal court. In this appendix Dickerson furnished convincing evidence of the failure of the federal legal system to protect the citizenship rights of blacks from violence at the hands of white individuals or white-dominated courts.

The question of legal recourse against racial violence was also dealt with by Milton Konvitz in his discussion of the legal status of blacks since World War I. Konvitz quoted a statement by United States attorney general Tom Clark to the effect that federal action in cases of mob action against blacks hung upon "a very thin thread of law." Both Clark and Theron Caudle, head of the Justice Department's Criminal Division, rec-

ommended further legislation to provide for federal protection of constitutional rights. Konvitz considered the federal government legally
impotent in the area of protecting civil rights, and he supported this
conclusion by outlining the status of the only two significant pieces of
civil rights legislation still on the books. One of the statutes was Section
51 of the Criminal Code, which declared that if several persons conspire
to injure or threaten a citizen in the exercise of any rights conferred by
the Constitution or federal law they shall be guilty of a crime. Rulings
by the courts sharply limited the area in which the law was viewed as
prohibiting action by private persons. The law gave no protection against
lynch mobs but was held to apply to protection in the execution of federal
court decisions, protection as a witness in federal court, access to federal
courts, the right to vote for federal officials, and the right to run for
federal office. The other statute that might offer some protection was
section 52 of the Criminal Code, which provided that whoever, under
cover of state law, should willfully deprive any citizen of federally conferred rights shall be guilty of a crime. This law applied only to local
and state officers acting in an official capacity, and until 1940, according
to Konvitz, it had been used in only two reported cases. The statute was
further weakened by the 1945 ruling of the Supreme Court in the *Screws*
case, which held that the deprivation of rights must be willful. Konvitz
quoted Caudle as to the Justice Department position that the *Screws*
decision made federal prosecution most difficult, "no matter how heinous
is the offensive conduct charged, for the very reason that the government
must carry the burden of proving that the act was committed solely for
the purpose of denying the victim of a federal right." In any event, section
52 did not cover mob violence, unless a state officer was a part of the
mob and he acted willfully to deprive a person of a federally secured
right. Konvitz did not particularly assess blame for the situation but rather
stressed the inadequacy of existing statutes and the need for new
legislation.

The question of racial terrorization was further considered in the section of the petition written by William R. Ming, Jr. Ming noted a number
of court decisions favorable to black rights but stressed that despite such
rulings shocking abuse of blacks by law officers continued. Ming referred
to evidence found in *Chambers* v. *Florida* that law officers had boasted
in court of tying down black suspects and flogging them with chains until
obtaining "confessions." Ming summed up the situation: "The spectacle
of the unwillingness of law enforcement officers to seek out, much less
prosecute or punish, members of lynch mobs is a ghastly, but familiar,
demonstration of the failure of the law to protect Negroes. Of equal

significance is the apparent inability, or worse, of some officers to hold their Negro prisoners against bloodthirsty lynch mobs. And, on occasion, this sanction of violence as a means of 'keeping Negroes in their place' results in tolerance of murder in its most aggravated form." Ming noted a 1941 Texas case in which a black man had been charged with rape of a white woman. The defendant, Bob White, had twice been found guilty, but the convictions had been set aside for insufficiency of evidence. On the opening day of the third trial the deputies guarding White withdrew as court adjourned for lunch. The husband of the woman who was allegedly raped then shot and killed the defendant in full view of judge, jury, and spectators. The husband was immediately arraigned and charged with murder. The trial was held next day, the husband was acquitted, and the prosecutor extended his congratulations. Ming also observed that court decisions were not an adequate index to the extent of racial violence. Newspaper files told more of the story, but no source told it all. Even black newspapers, Ming explained, would report beatings of blacks but could not be expected to find much news value in repeated accounts of governmental nonaction. It was simply not news. Complicity in acts of violence against blacks was compounded by the failure of both the legislative and the executive arms of the government to do anything about lynching. Since 1920 a fight had been waged to secure enactment of an antilynching bill, but tolerance of the southern filibuster in the Senate, the refusal to invoke cloture and thus force a vote, had blocked passage.[3]

In the years immediately following the close of World War II one of the manifestations of racism that drew increasing attention was police brutality. Hundreds of thousands of blacks had served in the armed forces or had worked in the war industries that produced the means of victory, but on the streets of black communities in both the North and the South blacks were repeatedly harassed, beaten, and sometimes murdered by officers of the law. An episode that evoked strong public protest was the killing by a police officer of two black men at the Freeport, New York, bus terminal. A hub of suburban Nassau County, adjoining New York City, Freeport like other Long Island towns was an outpost of segregation and racial exclusion. A reporter for the newspaper *PM* noted that the town was pleasant, not too hot in the summer and brisk in the winter, but also observed that Freeport blacks "have an elementary school in their own neighborhood, sit on the right-hand side in movie houses, and are confined to menial work." One out of every eleven persons in the community was black, living in the slum-ridden neighborhood of Bennington Park.

On February 5, 1946, Charles Ferguson, an Army Air Force service-man, and his brother Alfonzo, a discharged war veteran, were shot to death at the Freeport terminal by patrolman Joseph Romeika. Four Ferguson brothers had been denied service by the manager of the terminal restaurant, who also summoned the policeman. Although the brothers had left the eating place Romeika lined them up and proceeded to open fire. Romeika justified his actions by claiming that Charles Ferguson had pretended to be armed although in fact the brothers were unarmed.

The killings at the terminal evoked widespread protest, both in Nassau County and in nearby New York City. News of the incident itself and of hearings held to inquire into what happened was extensively reported by *PM* and the *Daily Worker*. The political organizations of the Left, the Communist party and the American Labor party of New York, took up the case, with the Communist party declaring: "The spirit of Hitler is alive in Freeport." But concern with the killing of the Fergusons ranged beyond the organized Left as many community organizations and individuals spoke out. At the 1946 dinner of the Nassau County committee of the National Conference of Christians and Jews, Rabbi Roland B. Gittelson of Rockville Center declared: "I am positive that if the four brothers had been white men, they'd be alive today." The Jamaica, New York, chapter of the NAACP held a protest meeting, with speakers including a Veterans of Foreign Wars post commander, the president of the NAACP chapter, the pastor of Jamaica's Amity Baptist Church, as well as Harry Raymond of the *Daily Worker*. In Freeport itself, hundreds of black and white citizens assembled at Pythian Hall on February 17 to demand the immediate suspension of Patrolman Romeika. At this meeting state assemblyman Hulan Jack declared: "I shall not rest until the Grand Jury has indicted Romeika for a crime, and if justice is thwarted, I shall take the case to the State Legislature." A few days later Congressman Adam Clayton Powell, New York City Councilman Michael J. Quill, and Assemblyman Jack gave their support to a citywide emergency conference protesting the Freeport killings.

Joining in the criticism of the Freeport violence was the *Crisis* of the NAACP. The magazine ran a brief editorial, which observed, "it is difficult to classify this double killing as anything but murder." The offense of the Fergusons was to have argued with a policeman and, according to the *Crisis,* this was the type of police action "which creates the tensions that lead to riots."

Several well-known New York liberals were among those who voiced concern with the case. While other calls for investigation were sent to Governor Thomas Dewey a telegram was sent to U.S. Attorney General

Tom Clark urging an immediate federal probe. Among the signers were Arthur Garfield Hays of the American Civil Liberties Union, Will Maslow of the American Jewish Congress, Attorney Paul O'Dwyer, prominent civil libertarian Osmond K. Fraenkel, and Thurgood Marshall of the NAACP.

The Freeport incident also brought forth an artistic response from folk artist Woody Guthrie. Written to be sung to the tune of "Streets of Laredo," Guthrie penned these lyrics:

> The town that we ride through is not Rankin Mississippi
> Nor Bilbo's Jimcrow burgh of Washington, D.C.,
> But it's Great New York, our most fair-minded city
> In all of our big land and streets of the brave.
> Who'll tell these three sons that their daddy is gone
> After whipping the Fascists and the Nazis to death?
> Who'll tell these three sons that Jimcrow coffee
> Has killed several thousand the same as their dad?[4]

Despite the protests, no action was taken to punish Patrolman Romeika. The episode served to alert public opinion as to the continued menace of police brutality, showing once again that such brutality extended beyond the South. But Freeport also demonstrated that responsible public officials would not readily be moved to act to restrain racist police officers.

In the South numerous acts of racial terrorism occurred during the late 1940s. Violence took both legal and extralegal forms, and several instances of terrorism attracted national attention. A case that dramatized the continued menace of lynching was the Willie Earle incident in South Carolina. Willie Earle, a resident of the community of Liberty near Greenville, was an epileptic, currently working on a construction job. On the morning of February 16, 1947, Earle was arrested at his home on a charge of having robbed and stabbed a white taxi driver, T. W. Brown. Earle was held in the jail at Pickens, South Carolina, but early next morning a group of fifty whites arrived at the jail demanding that Earle be handed over to them. The mob was asked not to use profanity, as the jail was the residence of the jailer and his wife, but the group was led to Earle's cell and the prisoner was handed over. At 6:45 AM Earle's body was found on Old Easley Bridge Road about five miles from the jailhouse. The body was marked by knife wounds, and half of Earle's head had been blown away by a shotgun blast. In the days following this murder it became clear that local authorities could not without further ado sweep the matter under the rug. National condemnation of this lynching was intense, pressure grew for action, and the federal government could not remain completely passive. The Earle lynching was the first reported in South Carolina since February 1941. The case, which made it clear that post–World War II America still had not eliminated lynching, might be used to push for federal antilynching legislation, and within hours after the lynching South Carolina representatives of the NAACP were on the scene. Shortly, the national organization and various branches appealed for action by the governor, Strom Thurmond, and also wired President Truman and Attorney General Tom Clark. With the cold war already providing a basic context within which all issues would be considered, the association both referred to the injustice of lynching and noted that Communists abroad would give full coverage to the Earle incident. The NAACP publicized the fact that South Carolina had an antilynching statute requiring indictment by a grand jury.

The Earle lynching evoked response by both state authorities and the federal government. Governor Thurmond in Columbia declared: "I do not favor lynching and I shall exert every resource at my command to apprehend all persons who may be involved in such a flagrant violation of the law." Agents of the FBI, apparently on the orders of Attorney General Clark, were assigned to collect evidence, take statements, and generally investigate as to whether Earle's civil rights had been violated. Initiative as to prosecution of those responsible for the lynching, however, was left to state authority. On March 12, thirty-one white persons were indicted by the grand jury, thirty charged with conspiracy to commit murder and one white man, Roosevelt Charles Hurd, charged with two counts of murder, having been identified as the "trigger man" in the killing.

South Carolina held a trial of those indicted, but the outcome of the case demonstrated that hope of dealing with lynching through local courts was illusory. Federal agents had investigated, but action to bring the defendants to trial in federal court, where convictions might more readily have been obtained, was not forthcoming. The case was heard by an all-white jury in a segregated courtroom where blacks were confined to the balcony. The defense relied on white prejudice, calling upon the jury to repel northern meddling and to furnish a verdict that would not encourage the crimes allegedly committed by Earle. One defense counsel told the jury, "Willie Earle is dead and I wish more like him were dead. ... If a mad dog were loose in the community I would shoot the dog and let them prosecute me." The jury, after five and a half hours' deliberation brought back the expected verdict, not guilty on all counts.

There was some variation in the response of black spokesmen to the verdicts. Blacks in Greenville expressed sentiment for a boycott of white taxis, but the feeling was not organized into effective action. From the Communist party rose a demand, voiced by the party's organizational secretary Henry Winston, for imposition of martial law, and the Communist members of the New York City Council urged a boycott of all goods produced in the South. In Harlem Congressman Adam Clayton Powell organized a "Death to Lynchers" rally to protest the verdict, and the rally voted to send a delegation to Washington to urge passage of a federal antilynching law. The Harlem newspaper, the *People's Voice*, condemned the trial as a farce and urged readers to protest and "raise all manner of hell." But the response of other black newspapers revealed a tendency to accept the playacting at law enforcement as the real thing. In opposition to the views of radicals who saw no alternative to mass action, such newspapers as the *Chicago Defender* and the *Pittsburgh Courier* were more prone to find evidence of progress in the South Carolina trial. Although the papers continued to call for antilynching legislation they also found in the trial evidence that murder of Negroes was to be taken more seriously; the very fact of a trial having been held was a sign of progress. The variation in response exemplifies the late 1940s division between those who would wage uncompromising struggle against racial oppression and those black leaders, unwilling to break with the Truman administration, who found justification for a policy of gradualism. Those who chose the latter course tended to exaggerate the progress to be found in trials producing no convictions and in FBI investigations that never led to direct federal intervention in matters involving violation of civil rights.[5]

In South Carolina during the later 1940s, there also appeared a harbinger of the violence that would mark the struggle for the desegregation of public schools. The center of conflict was Clarendon County, where in 1948 a black man sued white officials for having denied him and his children the equal protection of laws guaranteed by the Constitution. As noted by the author of a recent history of the school integration struggle, "No such thing had happened before in the memory of living men in Clarendon County, South Carolina." Clarendon County was cotton country and an example of a southern community that knew the superficial peace born of long-established racial subordination. Although there were some 4,000 farms in the county, less than a quarter of them were owned by the farmers working them. In 1950 the average annual income for two-thirds of the county's 4,950 black households was less than $1,000. A survey taken in the late 1930s showed that 35 percent of all blacks in the county over the age of ten were illiterate. And, with this illiteracy, the records showed that in the school year 1949–50, $179 was spent for each white child whereas for each black child the expenditure was forty-three dollars. Clarendon County operated on the maxim that the public school system was designed essentially to serve the white taxpayer.[6]

Joseph Albert DeLaine was a Methodist minister and schoolteacher in Clarendon County, and this black man served to gather the support needed to bring suit in the United States District Court charging that school officials unlawfully discriminated against black children by denying them free bus service while providing it for white children. Later on, during 1949, DeLaine was the focus of activity that organized a group of plaintiffs who would seek remedy for the generally discriminatory conditions prevailing in Clarendon's public school system. Those who challenged the dominant racial mores had to be prepared to pay a price, and DeLaine was singled out as the target of persecution. The church where DeLaine pastored was stoned, and shotguns were fired at him. In 1951 his home and church were burned to the ground, and the state made its contribution by charging him with felonious assault for having shot back the night he had been fired upon.[7]

In Georgia a case that raised before the country the right of blacks, particularly of black women, to defend themselves against threats and violence was that of Mrs. Rosa Lee Ingram and her sons. In February 1948 Mrs. Ingram and her two sons, Wallace, seventeen, and Sammy, fourteen, awaited electrocution at Georgia's Reidsville Prison. The condemned prisoners had been convicted of having killed a white farmer, John Ed Stratford. The Ingrams were arrested by the Schley County sheriff on November 4, 1947. Indicted by the county grand jury, the Ingrams on February 3, 1948, were given a one-day trial by an all-white jury and convicted. According to Rosa Lee Ingram the incident revolved around Stratford's sexually aggressive behavior. She testified on the witness stand: "Me and this man had some words. It was about giving him a date. I told him that I was not that kind of a woman. He told me that I would not live hard any more if I would do like he said, but I did not do what he wanted me to do. Me and my children were getting along all right until he started at me. He could not make me go his way, and he was mad. And that is just what it is about me not having him." Mrs. Ingram stated that Stratford had drawn a gun on her and had hit her with it. Shortly afterward her two sons came rushing up, and one of them, Wallace, struck Stratford, who did not move again. Mrs. Ingram stated further: "If it had not been for my sons this man would have killed me. My son begged him to let me alone, and the boy picked up the man's gun and hit him. When my son hit him, the man was still holding on to me. He wouldn't turn me loose until my son hit him again . . . and then he fell down across the road."

The Ingram case, highlighting the issue of a black woman's right to protection from assault and the flagrant unjust legal processes of the southern court, aroused interest from a broad range of organizations, providing an issue upon which black radicals and moderates, the NAACP and the Communist party, and many church and women's groups could agree. On March 25, 1948, an NAACP attorney, A. T. Walden of Atlanta, argued a motion for a new trial. There would be no new trial, but on April 6 Judge William M. Harper, Schley County Superior Court judge, reduced the sentences to life imprisonment. Following the denial of a new trial, NAACP counsel Thurgood Marshall convened a legal strategy meeting at Howard University. Although the fourteen attorneys present announced agreement on further legal moves in the Ingram case, the association did not actively pursue further court action. The NAACP, however, did continue to publicize the case and at annual meetings adopted resolutions calling for the Ingrams' release.

Parallel to the NAACP, black and white leftists undertook widespread activity concerning the Ingram case. Largely as a result of these efforts thousands of appeals from hundreds of organizations around the world were sent to the Georgia authorities and to the federal government. During 1949 W. E. B. Du Bois drafted an appeal of the case which was submitted to the governments belonging to the United Nations. Du Bois's brief was presented to the United Nations on September 21, 1949, by Mary Church Terrell, distinguished leader of the Washington black community. During the 1948 presidential election Progressive party candidate Henry Wallace wired Georgia governor Melvin E. Thompson demanding a new trial and charging that the Ingrams had been sentenced "under circumstances which would clearly indicate a gross miscarriage of justice." Giving extensive coverage to the case were such papers of the Left as the *Daily Worker* and the *National Guardian*. From China came an appeal from the All-China Federation of Labor. The appeal stated that the Ingrams "have been illegally kept in prison for more than four years and are suffering from cruel torture, on account of the fact that they defended their honor and stood against racial discrimination." The Chinese appeal, sent during the midst of Chinese involvement in the Korean War, viewed the Ingram case in the context of what was seen as the basically reactionary nature of American society. Declaring that American imperialists' "brutal treatment toward negroes is no different from that of the fascists toward the Jews," the Chinese demanded the unconditional and immediate release of the Ingrams.

A number of women's organizations were particularly outspoken on this case. From abroad women's organizations in England and Australia cabled appeals, and at home the National Association of Colored Women's Clubs and the Georgia Federation of Colored Women's Clubs urged the Georgia governor to permit Mrs. Ingram to return home and resume the rearing of children she had left behind.

The Ingram case provided a clear illustration of how in the post–World War II situation a matter of a black citizen's right to defend herself could become an international issue. Although the Ingrams remained in prison until granted parole in 1959, the pressure was enough to prevent execution. Clearly, the execution of a black mother and her two teenage sons, in circumstances where there was strong reason to believe the prisoners had acted in self-defense, would have damaged the American world image. The Ingrams were to live, and five years after their release the Georgia pardon and parole board restored their civil and political rights.[8]

An ingredient of racial violence that increasingly stood out during the later 1940s was a resurgence of police and National Guard wholesale terrorism against black communities. This was to be seen most clearly in a Columbia, Tennessee, incident in late February 1946. Five hundred national guardsmen had mounted an assault against Columbia's black community, Mink Slide. Officers had fired machine guns on blacks barricaded in their homes, and numerous business establishments in the community were wrecked. Triggering the violence was a dispute between a black woman, Mrs. Gladys Stephenson, and William Fleming, a white radio repairman. James Stephenson had come to his mother's aid after the repairman had kicked and slapped her. The police arrived, arrested James Stephenson, and beat him. A lynch mob that formed in Court Square was frustrated in its design as Mrs. Stephenson and her son were taken out of the state. Fearing attack, members of the black community had prepared to defend themselves, and it was at this point that police and guardsmen struck. In the course of the attack, 101 blacks were arrested, and on February 28, two of the prisoners, William Gordon and James W. Johnson, were killed by police while held in the jail. After being shot, Gordon and Johnson were denied treatment at the local "whites only" hospital and instead were driven forty-three miles to Nashville where they died. At the end of March thirty-one blacks were indicted on a variety of charges, including attempt to commit murder. The violence of the Columbia incident was a product of the black community's demonstrated willingness to defend itself from racist insult and attack. Two black persons resisted abuse, and then the black community showed its readiness to fight back. In response, white power revealed it would employ overwhelming might to crush any resistance. It was as though by sheer force of arms the clock could be turned back to an earlier era of unchallenged white supremacy.[9]

The more militant voices within the black community spoke out forcefully against the Columbia violence. In New York, Adam Clayton Powell's *People's Voice* declared: "The lynch terror being directed against the Negro citizens of Columbia, Tennessee, should cause deep shame to every decent American. More than this, it should galvanize us all into action to uproot this fascist-like jimcrow power which threatens otherwise to destroy the democratic liberties of us all." The newspaper went on to say that what took place in Columbia "could easily have happened in Hitler's Germany" and noted that the basic purpose of the violence was to assure the superexploitation of black workers. Warning that Columbia represented the attempt to build a Fascist America, *People's Voice* urged its readers to demand federal intervention and called for mass protest meetings throughout America. A guest editorialist, Seton Eversley, also related the Columbia situation to the experience of Hitler's Germany and called for action to guarantee that blacks killed and maimed in the war had not died in vain. Black America, he stated, "must make it clear that we intend to fight with every means at our command the sort of thing that happened in 'Mink Slide,' U.S.A., because we will be damned if we fought fascism abroad, only to have it go serenely on its way here."

But the relatively moderate *Crisis* magazine of the NAACP was only slightly less vehement than the *People's Voice* in its denunciation of the Tennessee terror. An editorial in the magazine's April issue announced that Columbia "fulfilled predictions of many persons that mob violence would be used after the war to force the Negro back into his 'place.' " Evaluating the incident as "terror, pure and simple," *Crisis* saw what happened as evidence "that Negroes, even in small communities like Columbia where they were outnumbered almost three to one, do not intend to sit quietly and let a mob form, threaten, and raid their neighborhood." Calling for "swift, impartial steps to keep order," the NAACP organ pointed to the danger black America faced: "Once the idea gets abroad that whites are free to do as they please, that Negroes are fair game for police, and that Negroes may not depend upon any authority, local, state or federal, for equal protection under the law, then we will have terror, riots, bloodshed, and death—and Storm Trooper Fascism in the flesh."[10]

The NAACP devoted considerable energy to the Columbia situation, seeking to protect the rights of those arrested and urging intervention by the Truman administration. The federal authorities, however, exhibited only a token interest. President Truman refused an association request for an appointment to discuss the matter, and a federal grand jury called to investigate the situation produced no indictments of local or state officials involved in the violence. Thurgood Marshall, one of the NAACP attorneys assigned to the case, had a narrow escape from death after being arrested by four white men on trumped-up charges of drunk driving. Marshall's life was most likely saved only due to the fact that his colleagues closely followed the arrest vehicle as it maneuvered along country roads.

Reporter Harry Raymond, who was riding in the car with Marshall, was certain that plans to go ahead with a lynching were afoot. He wrote: "Thurgood Marshall was the intended victim...the lynchers failed to carry out their plan because they are cowardly men and they knew we had the entire Columbia Negro community mobilized behind us." Raymond and NAACP defense attorneys Z. Alexander Looby and Maurice Weaver, following the police car carrying Marshall away, were able to alert the black community to the impending danger.

The NAACP was successful in securing the freedom of those arrested in Columbia, and it was also effective in mobilizing the concern of various prominent personalities. A National Committee for Justice in Columbia, Tennessee, was organized with Eleanor Roosevelt and Dr. Channing Tobias as cochairmen, joined by such participants as Roger Baldwin, Helen Gahagan and Melvyn Douglas, Frank P. Graham, Joe Louis, and Lillian Smith. In early August, again under the NAACP's impetus, the National Emergency Committee against Mob Violence came into being, bringing together a number of organizations to speak out against racial terrorism.[11]

The Columbia situation helped shape the atmosphere of the NAACP's thirty-seventh national convention, which assembled at the end of June in Cincinnati. Among the first to arrive from Columbia were Harry Raymond, *Daily Worker* reporter, and NAACP counsel Thurgood Marshall. Raymond wrote that crowds at Cincinnati's Union Terminal overwhelmed Marshall and himself with questions "about the brave Negroes battling valiantly for freedom in the terror-ridden Maury County courthouse." At a convention marked by local reminders of racism as Thurgood Marshall and several other blacks were denied service at the Frontier Coffee Shop of Cincinnati's Netherland Plaza Hotel, Gladys Stephenson spoke, expressing appreciation for NAACP support.

At a closing session held at Nippert Stadium on the University of

Cincinnati campus a resolution was adopted stating that the federal government was responsible for "affirmative action to bring about prosecution of guilty state officials" in the Columbia case. The resolution, forwarded to President Truman and Attorney General Tom Clark, continued: "we urge you to take all necessary steps to insure prosecution of guilty parties in the Columbia incident and to protect Negroes throughout the South as well as the right to vote and other civil rights guaranteed by the United States Constitution." Marshall, honored at this convention with the Spingarn medal, set forth the goal of complete equality, stressing that the baby of a Mississippi black sharecropper at birth was endowed with the same rights as any other American. Linking the present racial situation to the war, Marshall declared that the war had as yet done nothing "to break down the vicious system of second class citizenship in our own country," and he also noted increased activity by "homegrown fascists."

Marshall referred to the Columbia events in the context of electoral activity by blacks. He noted that Tennessee governor James McCord, placed in office by the corrupt Crump–McKeller machine, had commended the mob action at Columbia. McCord was running for reelection, and Marshall asked: "How many Negro votes is he going to get?" Marshall also connected the Tennessee machine to the federal grand jury proceeding that had only praise for the police officials in Columbia. The grand jury, he declared, had embarked on a witch hunt aimed at blaming organizations such as the NAACP and the Southern Conference for Human Welfare for what happened in Columbia. The grand jury report was an indication of what might be expected by white mobs in the South, "who are even now contemplating open violence to prevent returning Negro veterans from exercising their rights and from preventing all Negroes from exercising any of their civil rights."[12]

A picture of the prevailing pattern of racist violence during the late forties is found in the report *To Secure These Rights,* issued in 1947 by the President's Committee on Civil Rights.[13] The committee had been appointed by President Truman on December 5, 1946, charged with formulating recommendations "with respect to the adoption or establishment by legislation or otherwise of more adequate and effective means and procedures for the protection of the civil rights of the people of the United States." Truman asserted that "Freedom from Fear is more fully realized in our country than in any other on the face of the earth," but he also declared that not all segments of the American population were equally free from fear. Freedom had been gravely threatened in the aftermath of the First World War, and it was also true that currently democratic institutions were again under attack. "In some places," Truman stated, "from time to time, the local enforcement of law and order has broken down, and individuals—sometimes ex-servicemen, even women— have been killed, maimed, intimidated." The establishment of the committee may well have been dictated by Truman's concern with 1948 reelection prospects, especially in view of the considerable uneasiness felt by many liberals at the recent ouster from the cabinet of commerce secretary Henry Wallace, but the work of the committee shed much light on the existing state of race relations. The report of this committee could not be dismissed as the statements of radicals because the committee members were plainly persons of national visibility, distinction, and respectability. Among those serving were Charles E. Wilson, president of General Electric, and Charles Luckman, president of Lever Brothers; Attorney Francis P. Matthews, former supreme knight of the Knights of Columbus; the Reverend Henry Knox Sherill, presiding bishop of the Protestant Episcopal Church; John S. Dickey, president of Dartmouth College; and Frank P. Graham, president of the University of North Carolina. Lending a distinguished family name was Franklin D. Roosevelt, Jr., while the labor movement was represented by James Carey of the CIO and Boris Shishkin, American Federation of Labor economist. The two blacks appointed to the committee were Sadie T. Alexander, assistant city solicitor of Philadelphia, and Channing Tobias of the Phelps Stokes Fund, nationally known as a black leader of moderate and cautious views.

Early in the pages of its final report the committee highlighted various items pointing to progress in race relations, but the committee also exposed the limitations of that progress. In 1946 at least six persons in the United States were lynched by mobs, it was reported, and three of those persons had not been charged with any offense by anyone. Of the three persons charged, one allegedly had stolen a saddle, a charge disproven by the arrest of the real thieves after the lynching. A second person was supposed to have broken into a house, and a third was said to have stabbed a man. All of those lynched were black. The committee briefly stated the facts concerning two of the 1946 lynching incidents. In one episode Roger Malcolm, a young black man, had been arrested following a fight with his white employer in which the latter had been stabbed. On July 20, 1946, a white farmer had posted bond for Malcolm's release from the Monroe, Georgia, jail. The farmer, Loy Harrison, started to drive Malcolm, Malcolm's wife Dorothy, and a black veteran, George Dorsey, and his wife Mary out of Monroe. The committee told what then happened:

At a bridge along the way a large group of unmasked white men, armed with pistols and shotguns was waiting. They stopped Harrison's car and removed Malcolm and Dorsey. As they were leading the two away, Harrison later stated, one of the women called out the name of a member of the mob. Thereupon the lynchers returned and removed the two women from the car. Three volleys of shots were fired as if by a squad of professional executioners. The coroner's report said that at least sixty bullets were found in the scarcely recognizable bodies. Harrison consistently denied that he could identify any of the unmasked murderers. State and federal grand juries reviewed the evidence in the case, but no person has yet been indicted for the crime.[14]

The second lynching discussed took place at Minden, Louisiana. John Jones, a black youth, had been arrested on suspicion of housebreaking. Another black youth, Albert Harris, was also arrested in an attempt to implicate Jones. On August 6, before any trial had been held, Jones and Harris were released from jail only to find a group of white men waiting for them in the jail yard. With the assistance of a deputy the two released prisoners were placed in a car and driven into the country. Jones was beaten to death, but Harris, thought to be dead, revived and escaped. A federal trial of five persons, including two deputy sheriffs, brought verdicts of acquittal. The president's committee reported that these were two of the less brutal lynchings of recent years. At least the victims had not been mutilated or burned.

The committee stated that the record for 1947 was incomplete but evaluated as an "impressive instance of state prosecution" the holding of a trial in the Willie Earle case. Also seen as encouraging were efforts reportedly made by the governor of North Carolina to bring to justice those involved in the attempted but frustrated lynching of Godwin Bush, arrested on a charge of approaching a white woman. But again balanced against the notation of progress was the declaration that lynching still remained "one of the most serious threats to the civil rights of Americans." The fact was that in certain areas of the country a mob could abduct and murder a person with almost certain assurance of escaping punishment. At least forty-three lynchings had taken place between 1936 and 1946. No person was given the death penalty for any of these crimes, and in the great majority of cases there had been no prosecutions. Lynching, the committee went on to explain, was not only a matter of private action. The role of local officials was outlined: "Punishment of lynchers is not accepted as the responsibility of state or local governments in these communities. Frequently, state officials participate in the crime, actively or passively. Federal efforts to punish the crime are resisted. Condonation of lynching is indicated by the failure of some local law enforcement officials to make adequate efforts to break up the mob. It is further shown by failure in most cases to make any real effort to apprehend or try those guilty. If the federal government enters a case, local officials sometimes actively resist the federal investigation."

The emphasis upon both negative and positive elements continued as the report went on to deal with attempted lynchings. Most of those saved from lynch mobs, apparently, had been rescued by local officials. The committee saw "heartening evidence" that an increasing number of officers had the courage to defend their prisoners from the lynchers. But sometimes the actions of these officers were not motivated by a humane concern for prisoners. The committee reported that in some instances lynchers were dissuaded by assurances that the ends desired by the lynchers would be accomplished "legally." It was also noted that sometimes legal institutions were responsive to the arranged bargain. In short, although the term was not directly used, law officers participated in processes that constituted "legal lynching." Furthermore, in a number of communities the protection of the rights of innocent individuals was subordinated to a concern that the community reputation might be injured.

The president's committee well understood the significance of lynching. This form of violence had consequences not shown simply by counting the number of victims. Lynching was a basic weapon of racial subordination, and the report succinctly summed up how this weapon was used:

When a person is lynched and the lynchers go unpunished, thousands wonder where the evil will appear again and what mischance may produce another victim. And every time lynchers go unpunished, Negroes have learned to expect other forms of violence at the hands of private citizens or public officials. . . . Moreover, lynching is the ultimate threat by which his inferior status is driven home to the Negro. As a terrorist device, it reinforces all the other disabilities placed upon him. The threat of lynching always hangs over the head of the southern Negro; the knowledge that a misinterpreted word or action can lead to his death is a dreadful burden.

What is glaringly absent from the committee's discussion of lynching is the responsibility of the federal government. The means by which southern Democrats and northern Republicans had collaborated to frustrate enactment of antilynching legislation were ignored as was the Justice Department's record of inaction in using what legislation already existed to suppress lynch mobs. Indeed, the committee seemed to accept at face value explanations offered by FBI director J. Edgar Hoover for "thwarted efforts of the Justice Department to identify those responsible for one lynching." In no way, at least in its public report, did the committee explore the question of the federal government's lack of commitment to eradicating lynching.

The effort to present a balanced picture of the situation continued as the committee discussed the question of police brutality. Probably more significant than the specifics of what was said was the fact that a report prepared by a committee appointed by the president of the United States recognized that police brutality really was a problem. It was noted that such brutality was not universal and that many law enforcement agencies had made progress in stamping out such abuses. But still, even in the careful language of the report, it was apparent that police brutality, especially toward blacks as well as other minority groups, constituted a widespread abuse of power. Drawing upon evidence in Justice Department files, the committee told of instances in which blacks were beaten and whipped in order to extort confessions and of jails in which black inmates were routinely pistol-whipped and beaten with a rubber hose. There was the phenomenon of trigger-happy officers who had shot blacks, "supposedly in self-defense, under circumstances indicating, at best, unsatisfactory police work in the handling of criminals, and, at worst, a callous willingness to kill." The report tended to view this question as of concern mainly in the South and failed to consider the racist practices engaged in by police in northern communities, but at least with regard to the South it was apparent that local efforts had not sufficed to bring the police under the restraints of law.

The committee pointed to a "particularly shocking" instance of police brutality that both shed light on the seriousness of the problem and showed the federal government as responsive. The incident was the killing on July 11, 1947, of eight black prisoners at the state highway prison camp in Glynn County, Georgia. The prisoners had been killed by white guards, supposedly as they attempted to escape. Actually, the men were among a group of twenty-seven who had refused to work in a snake-infested swamp without boots. The county grand jury exonerated the camp warden and the guards of all charges. Later a witness testified as to the guards' action: "There was no justification for the killing. I saw the Negroes where they fell. Two were killed where they crawled under the bunkhouse and two others as they ran under their cells. The only thing they were trying to escape was death. Only one tried to get over the fence." A federal grand jury, the committee reported, indicted the warden and four guards on October 1, 1947.

The committee refused to accept at face value police claims in such cases of having acted in self-defense. Even if the police shot to prevent escape, the very need to have recourse to such violent means reflected upon police conduct. "Other officers in other places," the committee explained, "seem able to enforce the law and to guard prisoners without resort to violent means."

The section dealing with police brutality ended on a note of balance. Americans everywhere deplored such violence, and the committee further recognized that many law enforcement officers in both the North and the South did not commit violent acts against blacks and other "culprits." But still the fact remained "that the incidence of police brutality against Negroes is disturbingly high."

The report raised questions about the FBI's role in the area of civil rights, questions whose full implications were not to be recognized publicly until the mid-1970s. But even in 1947 the findings noted about the bureau should have served as a warning of some basic problems with regard to that agency's views of minority issues. That this did not happen undoubtedly was due to the carefully tended image of the FBI as an efficient, impartial, and thoroughly dependable guardian of law. Even the president's committee noted that "it is unnecessary to comment on the remarkably successful record of the FBI in the general field of law enforcement." But somehow it appeared that in some instances FBI activities in the civil rights field did not measure up to the bureau's high standards. Evidence indicated that the bureau found it "burdensome and difficult" to undertake as many investigations of civil rights violations as were requested. Furthermore, investigations, when undertaken, were not as thorough as the circumstances demanded. Finally, it was reported that the tendency of FBI agents to work in close cooperation with local officials sometimes impeded investigations. It was difficult for FBI agents to work independently of or in conflict with local police. Although the committee report did not seek to explain these deficiencies, the findings themselves underscored the need for further inquiry.

To Secure These Rights included an appraisal of the civil rights section of the Justice Department's Criminal Division. The report indicated that blacks desiring protection of civil rights had a slender reed to lean upon in this unit. When taken together, the section's defects were formidable: "Its relative lack of prestige in the Department of Justice, the legal and constitutional difficulties which confront it, the problems caused by its administrative relation to the FBI, the hostility of some United States Attorneys, the force of local prejudice, and the size of its staff all combine to make the Section less effective and less self-assured than the challenge of its assignment demands." And this agency constituted the heart of what efforts the federal government was willing to make to protect blacks from racial violence. No doubt without intending to, the report of the President's Committee on Civil Rights furnished evidence about the federal government's complicity in subjecting blacks to the continued threat of lynching, police brutality, and other forms of violence.

Among the recommendations formulated by the committee were several directly relevant to racial violence. In citing reasons for action, the committee referred to moral and economic imperatives, but it also stressed the international context. The committee accepted the ambitious goals of American foreign policy as stated by the Truman administration. "Our foreign policy," it was said, "is designed to make the United States an enormous, positive influence for peace and progress throughout the world." The United States had "perhaps the greatest responsibility ever placed upon a people" to keep alive the promise of democracy. But the American civil rights record had become an issue in world politics, and Secretary of State Dean Acheson was quoted as declaring that American spokesmen had problems explaining the gap between American principles "and the facts of a particular situation." Only still greater achievements would keep alive the promise of democracy. Certainly Americans might very well find ludicrous the belief that the United States was an oppressor of underprivileged peoples, but for others the matter was not so clear, and the essential point was that "the final triumph of the democratic ideal is not so inevitable that we can ignore what the world thinks of us or our record." The committee told President Truman that it had reviewed the American heritage and had found in it again "the great goals of human freedom and equality under just laws." But the government had to assume greater leadership, and toward that end several items of legislation were recommended, including an antilynching act and an act directed specifically toward the problem of police brutality. The antilynching law would be broadly inclusive and would cover participation by public officials in lynching or the failure of officers to protect accused persons from mob violence. A law dealing with police brutality would explicitly define rights that could not be lawfully infringed upon by police officers. By specifying protected rights it was hoped that the law would help meet the problem presented by the Supreme Court decision in *Screws* v. *United States,* which had held that prosecutors must prove that police had willfully deprived persons of a specific constitutional right. These proposals for legislation were elements of a broad-gauged program that would attack from many angles the corroding influences of segregation, discrimination, and overt violence upon American society. The program, implementation of which would have transformed this nation, largely remained on paper, and this was especially true of items, such as the antilynching and police brutality bills, that would require congressional action. The Congress of the period was not prepared to take action to protect blacks from mob violence and the lawless acts of racist police officers.

To Secure These Rights had greatest significance as a means of public education. As Donald R. McCoy and Richard T. Ruetten observe, "a great educational campaign" was set in motion by the report.[15] The document was reprinted in a variety of formats with circulation of many thousands, several national radio broadcasts were devoted to it, and a number of social action organizations helped disseminate the findings. It is fair to say that the report gave a new respectability to the cause of civil rights. Although the favorable response of most liberal newspapers was accompanied by the critical reaction of some conservative papers, the report was securely established as a resource that for years would be drawn upon by civil rights advocates.

Whatever its merits, *To Secure These Rights* functioned for President Truman above all as a political device that could paper over his problems in relating to black leadership. Truman for some months had difficulty in relating seriously to so prominent a black spokesman as the NAACP's Walter White, noting on a memo White sent him regarding discriminatory practices at Fort Benning in Georgia: "I don't care for this white negro and I am always doubtful of anything he says." In January 1947 Truman, Mrs. Truman, and daughter Margaret crossed a picket line protesting segregated seating practices at Washington's National Theater. *Blossom Time* was the play the Trumans went to see, and the Washington NAACP branch wired that those "who are laboring for the 'Blossom Time' of mutual respect, brotherhood and understanding, for all people in the capitol of the nation are urging immediate explanation and clarification of your position." Perhaps because Truman several weeks earlier had appointed the Committee on Civil Rights, the NAACP stopped short of condemning him for his action. A facet of the role the committee could play was clearly illuminated by the comment of White House staffer David K. Niles that Truman "may be interested to see how his Civil Rights Committee is taking him off the hot seat." In the Willie Earle case, Chairman Charles E. Wilson sought to divert pressure from Truman by urging Walter White to send additional information about the incident to the president's committee. For Niles, Wilson's action served as a substitute for direct presidential involvement.[16]

Confronted in the aftermath of the war with a wave of racial violence, Truman found it imperative at least to appear to take action. In 1946 events led blacks and their white allies in the liberal and labor movements to prod the administration. Along with the Columbia incident there was the blinding of Isaac Woodward, a discharged veteran still in uniform, by a South Carolina police chief. Among those moved to act by this cruelty was R. R. Wright, black banker, educator, and Spanish-American War veteran, who wrote Truman: "Now, Mr. President, I think that it is a terrible disgrace to our beloved South and to the United States, that a returned veteran who had risked his life for the purpose of maintaining freedom of our country, is not permitted to travel in his own native country, subject to decent treatment by the officers of the land, without being beaten unmercifully and deprived of his eyes."[17] Major Wright requested Justice Department action, and prosecution of the policeman was undertaken, but the South Carolina jury found valid the defendant's plea of self-defense. In Georgia Macio Snipes, who had dared to vote, was shot down in his front yard by four white men. And on July 25 at Monroe, Georgia, there occurred the murder of four blacks that was to be chronicled in some detail in *To Secure These Rights*. Following these killings there was an uproar of protest, with large demonstrations in New York and at the Lincoln Memorial in Washington. The *Amsterdam News* declared that "the struggle against Talmadge-Bilboism lynch terror calls for all-out effort. All forces that want Americanism must join together to demand: 'BRING THE GEORGIA LYNCHERS TO JUSTICE!' "[18]

It was in this charged atmosphere that Truman on September 19 raised with a delegation from the National Emergency Committee against Mob Violence the proposal to appoint an investigatory committee dealing with civil rights. It is yet noteworthy that as Truman announced his intention to the delegation he presented himself as helpless on civil rights matters unless backed by public opinion. As William Berman observes, Truman's course "was an ingenious solution that would serve Truman's political need by allowing him through symbolic action to improve his standing among Northern liberals while, conversely, avoiding the alienation of the South."[19] At the core of Truman's civil rights policy was a reluctance to take a broader view of federal power and so take prompt steps to counter racist violence in the South. Truman's words about a civil rights inquiry were paralleled four days later by his meeting with representatives of the National Conference on Lynching led by Paul Robeson and Mrs. Harper Sibley, a session in which Truman was unresponsive to a call for a public statement attacking lynching and commitment to a definite program to stop violence.[20] If Truman did anything with regard to civil rights it was, as Berman points out, a response both to domestic pressures and to the gathering cold war, which transformed American racial matters into a world question.[21] There was in the final analysis an element of demagogy in Truman's approach to the black demand for change in the nation's racial pattern.

In 1946 there also appeared the threat posed by a new racist organization that was overtly Fascist in rhetoric and symbolism. This was the group known as the Columbians, whose activities were centered in Atlanta. In their application for a state charter, founders spoke of aiming for a "national moral reawakening" and of seeking to build a "progressive white community," but what lay behind the verbiage was soon made clear. The key leader of the Columbians was Homer M. Loomis, Jr., who had made contact with Fascists in various parts of the country. Loomis was quoted as stating that the group would initiate a campaign against blacks and on that basis move to elect some Columbian mayor of Atlanta. The next step would be to drive blacks out of Atlanta. Jews were also to be expelled from the city.

According to a membership list obtained by investigators, 178 individuals belonged to the organization. Prospective joiners were asked the questions "Do you hate Negroes?" and "Do you hate Jews?" and whether they could pay a three-dollar membership fee. Only two or three women enrolled in the group. Wearing khaki shirts and black ties Columbians patrolled the streets, questioning blacks who appeared in white neighborhoods. Information obtained from two defectors from the Columbians indicated the leaders plotted to dynamite and burn black homes and to flog Ralph McGill, liberal editor of the *Atlanta Constitution*. The president of the Columbians, Emory Burke, reportedly told an audience that blacks were the shock troops of a future Jewish-Communist revolution. Loomis announced that any move to integrate schools would lead to the end of the white race. Only a year after the defeat of the Nazis these Atlanta haters affirmed that they would exterminate Jews and bury blacks in the sand.

The Columbians did not confine themselves to threatening rhetoric. On October 28, 1946, a black man, Clifford Hines, was beaten by three Columbians on the street. The group honored one of the attackers with a medal of honor. There ensued several incidents of shooting and stoning of homes occupied by blacks. On October 31 the home of a black family was bombed by persons in a passing car. The violence was centered in a district of southwest Atlanta in which racial boundary lines were in flux. The Columbians exploited the tensions of the situation.

There was also some evidence that the Columbians were encouraged by some of the city's business interests. During 1946 the operators of the Exposition Cotton Mill were engaged in a campaign to defeat organizing efforts by the CIO Textile Workers Union. Charles Gilman, chairman of the Georgia State CIO Industrial Union Council, declared: "It is our understanding that Exposition Cotton Mills was helping to organize the Columbians. I know the Columbians met there and were formed during the strike. I think Loomis and Burke are fronts. Several influential people here and in Decatur were among those who were supervising and financing the Columbians." Dan Duke, an assistant attorney general of Georgia who directed legal proceedings against the organization, stated that Loomis and Burke appealed to the mill owners for funds. "The Ku Klux Klan," he said, "has a history of always starting drives for memberships when big labor organizations come in to organize the South. So it was in 1933 and so it is today."

The Columbians represented a clear menace to society, but in this instance the community, white and black, rallied to defeat the threat. Various veterans organizations spoke out as did many other civic and religious groups. The two white-owned newspapers of Atlanta, the *Constitution* and the *Journal*, repeatedly attacked the Columbians, and Ralph McGill reminded his readers that Nazis were all alike. The city's black newspaper, the *Atlanta Daily World*, also condemned the organization, adding to a plea for uprooting the Columbians the observation: "The marvel is that such programs have been permitted to run so long unchecked." *The Southern Israelite* of Atlanta, the paper of the Jewish community, saw the organization as a threat to the security of the city and noted the resemblance to the activities of Hitler's Brownshirts. What emerged in Atlanta was a broad consensus of opinion that was determined the city would provide no haven for this criminal organization of rabid hate. It was all a little too close in time to the experience of World War II for an avowedly Fascist organization to gain public acceptance in a major American city, even a city of the Deep South. In 1947 the state charter earlier granted the Columbians was revoked, and as a coherent entity the group soon disintegrated.[22]

The violence in Atlanta was dangerous, but its scale was slight compared to the major incidents occurring in Chicago. It has been held conventionally that in contrast to the post–World War I years relatively little racial violence erupted in American cities following World War II.

Arnold Hirsch in his study *Making the Second Ghetto* has shown that this generalization certainly does not take account of the Chicago experience, and the racial history of most other American cities after the war is yet to be written. To be sure, there was no single spasm of violence such as took place in the Chicago of 1919; rather, a "persistent undercurrent of violence lurked beneath the headlines, just beyond the recall of popular memory." This violence occurred in the course of a process in which the ghetto "was continually being renewed, reinforced, and reshaped." In what Hirsch evaluates as "chronic urban guerrilla warfare" hundreds and sometimes thousands of whites rioted against black entry into previously all-white housing areas. Between 1945 and 1950, of 485 racial incidents reported to the Chicago Commission on Human Relations, 357 related to housing.

In late 1946 rioting broke out at Airport Homes on the Southwest Side in an attempt to prevent black occupancy of temporary housing for veterans. A mob estimated as numbering between 1,500 and 3,000 persons battled police and destroyed property.

Violence also took place in mid-August 1947 at Fernwood Park Homes. Rioting continued over three successive nights, and during the first two nights crowds ranged in size from 1,500 to 5,000 persons. Unable to break through police lines, mobs assaulted cars carrying blacks. Gangs roamed beyond the immediate vicinity seeking black victims, and blacks were taken from streetcars and beaten. At least thirty-five black individuals were known to have been injured. An eyewitness to the Fernwood violence described the situation: "One of the agitators in the mob yelled that if they could stop traffic, the cops would have to straighten it out, at which time the crowd could break through the weak police lines and rush the project. So the traffic was impeded. Then a boy shouted 'Nigger, Nigger.' A stone flew, a safety-glass window crunched. And there started a bloody game of 'bash their dirty brains in' which continued unchecked for almost 20 minutes. Every Negro driver was attacked."

In November 1949 the Englewood neighborhood was the setting for rioting in response to the sale of a home to a black family. Fueled by rumors of a Jewish-Communist plot to destroy the area, crowds grew from several hundred to a maximum of some 10,000. Denied access to the house by police, the mob vented its fury upon "strangers" defined as passersby, Jews, Communists, and persons affiliated with the University of Chicago. As one contemporary observed, rioting was aimed at "everybody and everything." Hirsch observes: "That a false rumor that blacks were about to move into the area was enough to trigger the riot also indicated the depth of the tension current in many white areas bordering the Black Belt."

We are helped in understanding the Englewood situation if reference is made to the workings of the Chicago courts in relation to the violence. Judge Joseph H. McGarry freed the rioters brought before him and stated that, in his opinion, "the original incident in front of the Bindman home ...as well as all the incidents which followed on the four succeeding days, was the result of a miserable conspiracy, hatched and put into effect by a small but highly organized and highly vocal band of subversive agents, professional agitators and saboteurs bent upon creating and furthering racial and religious incidents in this neighborhood for the purpose of discrediting the City government, the Police Department and the Court and the people who reside in this district." McGarry, to be sure, was not talking about those in the mob.

Violence in the Park Manor neighborhood was an intermittent reality for several years, beginning in 1945. A major mob incident took place on July 1–2, 1946, as several thousand persons protested the arrival of a black physician in his newly acquired home. The garage was set afire, and the mob bombarded the house with rocks, breaking windows. The physician left his home and did not return. Then, again, on July 25, 1949, a mob of some 2,000 attacked the home purchased by Roscoe Johnson. Police prevented the crowd from entering the building but, like the Detroit police more than two decades earlier, failed to disperse those assembled, and this mob threw gasoline-soaked rags and flares into the building. Before the incident was over considerable damage had been done to the Johnson property.

In Chicago racial violence played a role in preserving the essentials of a segregated, if somewhat modernized, housing pattern. Police ineptness, based on the racism of individual officers, gave sanction to violence, and as Hirsch notes, a few hours of instruction in human relations were not likely to change long-standing attitudes; in any event, most officers did not take such instruction. At the end of the decade red-smear tactics were used to undermine the effectiveness of some of the more committed advocates of housing integration. The public agencies responsible for giving leadership on housing issues and such a powerful private institution as the University of Chicago threw their weight on the side of racial restrictiveness. And all during this period news coverage of the racial violence was substantially suppressed. Whatever the subjective motivation of those authorities who implemented this policy, the effect was to isolate the racial situation in Chicago housing from national opinion and even from much of the public in Chicago.[23]

FOURTEEN

Peekskill

THE LATE 1940s called forth commitments by white liberals to civil rights for blacks, but this was also a period in which the intermingling of cold war anticommunism with racial hatred produced a major episode of mob violence aimed at one of the nation's most widely known cultural figures, singer and actor Paul Robeson. The setting for the violence was Peekskill, New York, a Hudson River valley community in upper Westchester County. In and around this town, during late August and early September 1949, occurred what novelist Howard Fast described as "the first great open manifestation of American fascism."[1] Paul Robeson was scheduled to give a concert on August 27, 1949, at Lakeland Acres picnic grounds, a few miles north of Peekskill. The concert was to be the fourth in an annual series of concerts given by Robeson at various places in the vicinity. The *Peekskill Evening Star*, intensely hostile to Robeson, had reported that the artist had sung at Peekskill Stadium in 1947 and had also performed in 1948 at a place on Crompond Road under auspices of the Committee for the Protection of Negro Rights.[2]

On August 27, 1949, however, there was no concert. Instead, about 120 persons, most of them women and children, who had gathered early for the concert, were assaulted by several hundred vigilantes, using billy clubs, brass knuckles, and rocks as weapons. The vigilantes blocked the path to the picnic grounds, preventing both exit and entrance to the area. Their mood is suggested in a comment made by one of the party: "Give us five minutes and we'll murder the n—— bastards." Forty-two men and boys held off the several attacks launched by the mob. One episode is described by Fast:

This was, in a way, the worst attack of that night. For one thing, it was still daylight; later, when night fell, our own sense of organization helped us much more, but this was daylight and they poured down the road and into us, swinging broken fence posts, billies, bottles, and wielding knives. Their leaders had been drinking from pocket flasks and bottles right up to the moment of attack, and now as they beat and clawed at our lines, they poured out a torrent of obscene words and slogans. They were conscious of Adolph Hitler. He was a god in their ranks and they screamed over and over, "We're Hitler's boys—Hitler's boys!" "We'll finish his job!" "God bless Hitler and —— you n—— bastards and Jew bastards!" "Lynch Robeson! Give us Robeson!" "We'll string that big n—— up!" "Give him to us, you bastards!" I remember hoping and praying that Paul Robeson was nowhere near—that he was far away, not on the road, not anywhere near.

Later the mob burned a cross, and those under attack could see that "the symbol of all that is rotten and mean and evil in our land had blessed us." A display of books and pamphlets was also set afire. All this happened without action by law enforcement authorities to stop the violence. The report of the Westchester Committee for a Fair Inquiry into the Peekskill Violence reported on the role of the police: "On at least three separate occasions, from 7:30 until the police arrived at 10 p.m., men from the group defending the road and bandstand made their way out of the ambush to telephone the local police, the state police, the State Attorney General's office and Governor Dewey—all without result. The three sheriffs and three FBI men, who had been on the scene from the beginning, made no arrests and held no one for questioning, though fourteen cars were overturned and at least thirteen people were hurt seriously enough to require medical attention."[3] Finally, however, the police did intervene, and those who had sought to attend the Robeson concert were able to go home peacefully. No lives had been lost, but the right to assemble lawfully had been blatantly and violently abridged.

The state police reported that eight persons had been injured, four of them blacks. Howard Fast's reference to a cross burning is substantiated by a New York state police investigator assigned to the scene. The cross was located some thousand feet northeast of the concert area. The police evaluation was that this was a prank, ignoring the racial symbolism of the act regardless of its subjective motivation. A black resident of the area wrote to Governor Dewey, explaining that after reading the local papers he "quickly realized it would not be an anti-Communist protest but would be mob violence with racial hatred being the central issue." This observer described the would-be concertgoers returning from the scene, "the men with black eyes and bruises and the women with dirt, bruises and torn clothes," noting he felt that if he were darker he would be in the hospital.[4]

Following the Lakeland Acres violence, the American Civil Liberties Union quickly intervened. John Haynes Holmes, Arthur Garfield Hays, and Roger Baldwin jointly communicated with Governor Dewey and U.S. attorney general J. Howard McGrath. The ACLU spokesman informed Dewey that, as the incident "has taken on worldwide significance, we feel that you will agree with us that it is desirable to have the federal, as well as the state government act promptly in this matter." McGrath was informed that the ACLU was "unalterably opposed to communism" but federal intervention was urged, based on the Supreme Court *Screws* decision and the conclusion that in Peekskill officials had not acted to stop violence.[5]

A large public meeting held at Harlem's Golden Gate Ballroom showed that many in the New York black community were deeply angered by the incident at Lakeland Acres. Leaflets urging attendance at the rally were headed "The Ku Klux Klan Held a LYNCHING PARTY in Peekskill Yesterday," and Harlemites were informed that those who came to hear Robeson "were clubbed and beaten by a mob of six hundred Negro haters, yelling 'kill the N——s.' " The community was urged to "let them know that Harlem will fight back!"[6] Some 5,000 persons filled the hall, with several thousand others, unable to gain admission, assembled outside. It was clear that what particularly angered the crowd was the realization that the mob intended to harm Paul Robeson physically. A friend said to Fast, "They don't like to think that Paul Robeson could have died up there. This is the way they feel about that." To the overflow crowd outside the Golden Gate, Communist leader Benjamin J. Davis, Jr., declared, "Let them touch a hair of Paul Robeson's head and they'll pay a price they never calculated." Fast observed concerning the audience that "for these people the vileness—that specific and stinking vileness which has sent the stench of American lynching into every corner of the earth—was directed against the one great man who had broken through their bonds and bondage, who would not be jimcrowed, who would not hang his head, who would not crawl and who would not be bought off, not with dollars and not with cheap handouts from a cheapened and bloodstained government." Fast remembered Robeson as saying: "Yes, I will sing wherever the people want to hear me. I sing of peace and freedom and of life!" Following the meeting the audience swept into the streets, and several thousand persons paraded along Lenox Avenue. The mounted police appeared, but they did not interfere with the march.[7]

The day following the Lakeland Acres violence it was decided at a meeting of some 1,600 held on the lawn of a Mount Kisco home to renew the invitation to Paul Robeson to sing at Peekskill. The second Robeson concert took place on Sunday, September 4, in a picnic grounds area that once had been the Hollow Brook Country Club. The place was located a half-mile farther from Peekskill than Lakeland Acres, and it was also approached by a private road leading from the highway.

Upward of 20,000 persons attended the September 4 concert, but that did not prevent violence from occurring. Hundreds of trade unionists formed a defense perimeter within the grounds, and the vigilantes were unable to break through. But up on the state road, beyond the defense perimeter, the work of violence began. Clearly, what made this violent activity possible was the sympathy of the police for the vigilantes. Police took no action as the marchers hurled rocks at those protecting the concert area. Blocking off the entrance to the Hollow Brook grounds shortly after the concert began, the police themselves beat and clubbed several blacks who had arrived late for the concert and insisted upon entrance. A state trooper responded to Pete Seeger's question as to whether there would be trouble: "I don't know. But someone told me the whole road was lined with rocks. I hope it's the vets who picked them up."[8]

The concert proceeded as planned, despite reports that some of the guards had found two individuals, equipped with high-powered rifles and telescopic sights, up in the hills overlooking the concert grounds. As a measure of protection, fifteen persons, white and black, formed a wall around Robeson when he stood up to sing. The crowd was greatly stirred as it heard "Old Man River," especially as Robeson sang the words, "I must keep fightin / Until I'm dyin." Pete Seeger also sang briefly, including in his program the song "If I Had a Hammer" with its themes of danger, warning, justice, and love.[9]

The concert concluded, but the departure of the thousands present became the signal for assault on a widespread scale. There were approximately a thousand police on the scene, local officers and state troopers, but their roles were those of encouraging attack upon the concertgoers or of direct participation in the violence. Fast gave an account of the setting at the entrance to the grounds:

A small cluster of hell was at work at the entrance; cops, in a craze of hate, were beating cars, not people, with their long clubs, smashing fenders, lashing out against windshields, doing a dance of frenzy as the autos rolled out of the place. Even through our closed windows we could hear the flood of insanely vile language from the police, the unprintable oaths, the race words, the slime and filth of America's underworld of race hatred compressed into these "guardians" of the law, and released now. There were about thirty of them grouped there at the entrance, and they flogged the cars as if the automobiles were living objects of their resentment.[10]

For several miles along the roads leading from the concert site rock throwers were emplaced, some stationed individually and others assembled in groups. At many points police were close by, and almost everywhere the police did nothing, beyond laughing at the damage inflicted upon the passing cars and their passengers.

Mario Cassetta, one of those attending the concert, recalls the experience of going through the gauntlet set up along the road: "The veterans stood on an embankment and heaved a boulder from up there. It hit the windshield like a cannonball. The highway was strewn with these rocks; steering through them was like crossing a minefield. We could feel the buffeting and the rocking and the terrible noise of these huge stones ringing against the car." And at the end of the gauntlet the agony was not quite over. Cassetta again recalls: "We got to the end of the run and there was a clearing. We stopped. Some people were sitting and we asked, 'Do you know the nearest hospital?' And they all started laughing and cackling. *Cackling.* I remember one woman rocking back and forth slapping her knees, like she's heard a good joke. It was unbelievable, like I imagine Nazis would have been in those early street gang days in Berlin. All the way into the Bronx—more than twenty miles—you could see the injured, a long bloody alley."[11]

The free-speech issues raised by the Peekskill events were clear, and the American Civil Liberties Union was quick to respond to them. On September 8 the ACLU announced the offer of a cash reward for information leading to the arrest and conviction of private persons or police officials who incited or participated in the mob action. The organization also informed Governor Dewey it was forming, along with other groups, a Westchester County committee of citizens to assist in placing responsibility for the outbreak. Individuals having pertinent information were asked to communicate with ACLU general counsel Arthur Garfield Hays.[12]

Investigation by the ACLU clearly placed responsibility for the violence upon the police and civilian vigilantes. The union found that local newspapers were mainly responsible for creating a hate-filled atmosphere, that "terrorism was general against all who advocated freedom of speech, freedom of assembly and preservation of constitutional rights," that effective police protection had been denied at the first concert, and that police preparations to enforce the law at the second concert were a sham, at least with regard to the Westchester County police. In the aftermath of the September 1949 concert the ACLU expressed concern that legal authorities in the area "are moving toward restriction of freedom of speech and assembly, presumably in violation of the Constitution."

Introducing the ACLU report was a foreword signed by several prominent liberals, including the ACLU's Roger Baldwin, Rabbi Irving Miller of the American Jewish Congress, Michael Straight of the American Veterans Committee, and Roy Wilkins of the NAACP. These individuals made very clear their own anticommunism, stressing they were "wholly opposed" to Communist political purposes and setting their concern with Peekskill within an anti-Communist context. The point was that condoning the violence aided Communist propaganda and lowered American democratic standards "to the level of the Communist police-state which denies all civil liberties to opponents." But they saw Peekskill as involving more than the issue of communism, noting that "behind the anti-Communist sentiment . . . lay prejudice against Negroes and Jews" and declaring that the outbreak represented "the combined expression of the most explosive prejudices in American life—against Communists, Negroes and Jews." Effective protection of the right of peaceful assembly was urged.

The authors of the ACLU report rejected any contention that the Peekskill violence resulted from Communist provocation. Provocation, it was explained, required threats of violence and unlawful incitement, and it was not found in a determination to hold a peaceful meeting on private property. The report noted that many Peekskill residents even saw provocation in black men and white women riding the same autos into the concert area.[13]

The American Civil Liberties Union was not alone in condemning the violence inflicted upon those desiring to attend the Robeson concerts. The *Nation* magazine spoke up sharply to criticize the role of public authorities, which made the violence possible. In its first comment upon the affair the *Nation* quoted words uttered by Governor Dewey during 1948 to the effect that it was folly "to beat down ideas with a club" and called upon the New York governor to now act upon that sentiment. The magazine referred to Robeson's having "warped political views," but it also declared that those views "have nothing to do with his right to speak, much less with his right to sing." The police, the magazine noted with regard to the first concert, whether through design or negligence, had failed to protect the gathering or to take minimum precautions.

The *Nation* observed that the incident ended in a free-for-all, "in which cars were wrecked, scores were injured, racial tensions flared up, and the lynch spirit arrived in Westchester, complete down to the burning of crosses." If the initial violence was disturbing, the violence of September 4 horrified the *Nation*. The magazine totaled results of what it called the "Battle of Peekskill": at least 140 persons injured and innumerable cars wrecked, and an atmosphere created in which radio commentators upon the scene asked whether this could be the United States of 1949. The *Nation* declared that in a very real sense Governor Dewey was now on trial to determine if he would authorize an impartial and thorough inquiry into the violence. But more important than the question of official responsibility was the question of the "sinister layer of hate and hysteria" that the anti-Communist demonstration had brought to light. The *Nation* did indeed rebuke Robeson for recent statements it described as "stupid and uncalled for," but the journal recognized that anticommunism was not all that was involved at Peekskill. The violence was "anti-Negro and anti-Semitic and charged with indiscriminate hatred."[14] In an editorial a week later, the magazine, disappointed that Dewey did not promptly authorize an appropriate investigation, wrote a brief scenario of what Dewey could do as a minimally decent step. He could, it was imagined, "come to Peekskill himself, mount the platform from which Paul Robeson sang, and tell the people of that hysterical community, calmly and reasonably, the simple truths about Americanism, which their veterans presumably fought for though they do not appear to know it."[15] Dewey, of course, did not make the gesture. Rather, during the next few days he announced his judgment that "the Communist groups obviously did provoke this incident" and that local and state police had used every reasonable means to preserve order and to protect freedom of speech and assembly. Dewey's findings appeared to have relied mainly upon the conclusions drawn by the Westchester district attorney, who was responsible for law enforcement in the area, and the governor certainly gave no hearing to the victims of the violence. Earlier the *Nation* hoped that Dewey would speak out, but now the magazine stated that "we regretfully conclude that he would have done better to remain silent." A group of local clergymen had urged the community to show shame and contrition, and to this the *Nation* said "amen" and urged that Dewey be among the contrite.[16] In sum, the *Nation* made clear its critical view of Robeson, but it expressed a quite genuine repugnance at the violence that had occurred and at the indifference or worse manifested by public officials.

The influential *Pittsburgh Courier* exemplifies the ambivalent response to the Peekskill incident manifested by much of the established black leadership. On the one hand the paper reflected the sense of outrage felt by blacks concerning the mob violence directed at Robeson and those who would listen to him, and on the other hand the paper's response was conditioned by the prevailing anticommunism of the time. The *Courier* first dealt with the violence in a front-page account of the first concert. The paper declared that the incident "left the nation aghast this week." The story noted that a cross was burned on a nearby hill, and it was reported that many of the so-called veterans who staged the demonstration were actually imposters "who were definitely 'anti-Robeson' and disguised themselves as 'veterans' to help precipitate the affair."[17] Following the September 4 violence, the *Courier* gave major attention to the Peekskill incident, devoting numerous articles to the affair and in news articles conveying a dramatic and accurate sense of the scope of the mob violence. The *Courier* reporter Billy Rowe made no effort to mask his subjective reaction to the events. He was there, and he was clearly moved by what he observed. His news report, again on the *Courier*'s front page, began: "For five hate-filled hours Sunday, wild-eyed 'defenders of law and order,' with teeth bared and wearing the uniforms of New York State Troopers and special deputies, joined the vicious mob of hoodlums disguised as 'World War II veterans' in putting on one of the blackest and most shameful spectacles in American history." Rowe reported that some 1,200 officers had been assigned to the concert but that police nightsticks wrought as much mayhem as the stones, clubs, and bottles hurled by the "veterans." Rowe declared that "the officers openly and brazenly broke the very laws they had sworn to uphold." Rowe clearly respected Robeson's courage, writing: "Yes, Paul Robeson—American—came back to Peekskill Sunday afternoon . . . just as he had promised . . . and Paul Robeson sang just as he had promised, in spite of the mobsters! He came back in spite of the threats that had been made against his life!" For the perpetrators of violence Rowe had only loathing. He identified them: "These young hoodlums—men, women and children—were in every respect, Nazi storm-troopers, exact reproductions of Mussolini's Fascist, Dixie's infamous Ku Klux Klan and a mixture of Captain Kidd's murderous pirates! They were Georgia lynchers, Mississippi mobsters, Chicago Capone-era gangsters and thugs . . . and their ranks were more sharply emphasized by the 'defenders of law and order,' who Sunday trampled law and order—and the U.S. Constitution—in the dust."

Rowe respected Robeson's courage, and he also emphasized Robeson's long-standing role as a champion of black rights. He viewed the violence as a "plain, cold demonstration of violent hatred of a man who has consistently demanded that the rights of 15,000,000 American Negroes be respected in accordance with the Constitution of the United States." The day was one of challenge to freedom of assembly and freedom of speech—and song. Rowe suggested that perhaps it was Robeson's insistence upon equal rights that offended those who would stop the concert.

The *Courier's* news report outlined various details of the day's events. Rowe reported that among the songs Robeson presented were "Old Man River," "Go Down Moses," and "Warsaw Ghetto." Also noted was the presence among the 1,200 police officers of four black officers, two from New Rochelle and one each from Yonkers and Westchester County. Even among the local police black representation was minuscule, and Rowe did not report seeing any blacks among the state police present. He reported that police clubs never landed on the bodies of persons other than those who attended the concert. The reporter concluded that state troopers were just as vicious as the "veterans" in attacking the concert-goers. Rowe emphasized the racist nature of the conflict, pointing out that in this "barbaric display" innocent and guilty were victimized alike and that two busloads of blacks returning from a visit to the Franklin D. Roosevelt Library at Hyde Park were also stoned. The reporter observed: "Everybody who seemed to be a Negro was automatically taken as a Robesonite and received the full weight of the joint attack of the police and the 'veterans.' " The article left little doubt that this affair was not merely a matter of pro- or anticommunism.

The *Courier* also reported that the Civil Rights Congress would seek to institute civil and criminal proceedings against those responsible for the violence. It was also reported that the NAACP had voiced a demand for an inquiry by the New York State attorney general. Roy Wilkins wired Governor Dewey: "It is our opinion that the county and local officers cannot conduct an impartial investigation to determine all the facts." The *Courier* noted that an NAACP member who had complained to a local newspaper about inflammatory editorials had been threatened.[18]

The issues brought to the surface by Peekskill were further discussed by Horace R. Cayton, the *Courier's* editorial columnist. Cayton was appalled by the violence of Peekskill, but he also stated his critical view of Robeson's statement, delivered in Paris, that American blacks would not participate in a war against the Soviet Union. According to Cayton, Robeson was acting hysterically; in his judgment Robeson's statements "certainly created fear and hatred in the minds of thousands of whites and many Negroes have fear of retaliation." Robeson's statements, however, Cayton insisted, were not a racial matter. Whatever Robeson had said it was a "question of America's attitude towards the Communist Party and the Soviet Union."

If Robeson's views were not a racial matter the reaction of many whites was something else again. Robeson, Cayton said, had made a foolish comment, but he wondered what might be the reaction if a member of a white ethnic group had made a similar statement. Cayton asked if that position, taken by a white man, would have caused such consternation. Clearly, Cayton felt the answer was no, observing that when a black singer, "not a political or a race leader, claims affection for Russia, automatically doubts are cast on the loyalty of all American Negroes according to many of our papers." That whites cast such doubts was plainly a racial matter. The point, Cayton argued, was that whites knew blacks were "treated unfairly" and that they also knew that if they were so treated they would resent it and want to strike back.

Cayton briefly affirmed his support for Robeson's rights. His comment, "He has the right to sing no matter who sponsors him," summed up the heart of the issue, and Cayton also took his stand with Voltaire. "Like Voltaire," he wrote, "I may not like what he says, but would fight for his rights to say it." But Cayton would also make capital out of the Robeson issue. What was appropriate was not to apologize for Robeson but to point out "that Negroes are suffering from great injustices and that they are deeply resentful." The way to fight communism effectively was to assure that blacks received their rights of citizenship. When all was said and done, the Robeson controversy was useful. "After all," Cayton explained, "the Negro can stand anything but being ignored."[19]

The news coverage given by the *Courier* to the Peekskill incident reflected the anger of the paper's reporter, who saw at first hand the assault mounted against a world-famous black artist. Editorially, however, the newspaper took a quite different position, concentrating on assuring *Courier* readers that racism was not involved in the incident. To begin with, the *Courier* sought to "cool" the emotions aroused by the violence, informing readers that "there has been so much contradictory testimony on both sides and so many angles to the case that have not as yet been cleared up, that we feel judgments should be suspended until such time as all the facts are in." The paper further observed that "there is no certainty that the Ku Klux Klan had any part in the disturbance, that the outbreak was anti-Negro or that the war veterans were solely responsible for it." The conclusion was reached that "the outrage was anti-Robeson and anti-Communist rather than anti-Negro." The *Courier* did call for an impartial inquiry into the violence and for punishment of those who failed to provide adequate police protection for a lawful gathering, but the editorial's main tenor was one of isolating Robeson, of making the point that the violence directed at him was not a race matter of special concern to blacks. The *Courier* walked the thin line between seeming indifference to the Peekskill violence and any appearance of sympathy for Robeson's current political position as a radical critic of American foreign policy.[20]

Peekskill was a traumatic experience for those present at the event. Memory carries forward the recollection of what happened and in the case of Pete Seeger a physical reminder has been built into his life. At Seeger's home in the Hudson valley one of the stones thrown at Peekskill has been cemented into the chimney. "I glued the rock up there so I'd never forget," Seeger told his biographer, David King Dunaway. There is still emotional force in Seeger's recollection: "People threw stones at women and children, with intent to kill. At my own family. I had two little babies in the car."[21]

In terms of the response of black leadership to the struggle against racial violence during the late 1940s the critical dividing issue was the extent of independence from the Truman administration and the prevailing national atmosphere of anticommunism. On one side were blacks who supported the Progressive party slate of Henry Wallace and Glen Taylor, such nationally prominent figures as Du Bois and Robeson, and black radicals who either belonged to or worked in cooperation with the Communist party and various left-wing groups friendly to the party. Taking the contrary view was much of the established leadership of such organizations as the Urban League and the NAACP and most of those blacks active in the Democratic party. The division within black leadership is probably most clearly seen in the position taken by W. E. B. Du Bois in 1948 and the response of the NAACP to that position. In the aftermath of World War II Du Bois laid out a perspective of militant protest against racial oppression. In 1946 he had spoken at the convention of the radical Southern Negro Youth Congress and had pointed out a path of the southern struggle. Du Bois called upon the black youth of the South to remain in the region of their birth and carry on the struggle for democracy. His words made clear his love of the South and his sense of the crucial international importance of the southern struggle. "The future of American Negroes is in the South," he said. "Here three hundred and twenty-seven years ago, they began to enter what is now the United States of America; here they have made their greatest contribution to American culture; and here they have suffered the damnation of slavery, the frustration of reconstruction and the lynching of emancipation." But along with oppression the South offered a challenge, an opportunity; it had a magnificent climate and "the fruitful earth under the beauty of the Southern sun." In the South, "if anywhere on earth, is the need of the thinker, the worker and the dreamer." This was the place of decisive confrontation, "the firing line not simply for the emancipation of the American Negro, but for the emancipation of the African Negro and the Negroes of the West Indies; for the emancipation of the colored races; and for the emancipation of the white slaves of modern capitalistic monopoly."

Du Bois based his perspective on the view that blacks in their struggle did not stand alone. Du Bois recognized the hold of racism upon many whites, but he stressed the possibility of alliance with sections of the white population. Among potential allies "first and greatest" were the South's white working classes. White workers had to be made to comprehend their common interests with blacks even though in the past they had been led to see blacks as their enemy. Du Bois also listed as allies the white youth of the region, who could not realize their ideals without taking up the racial question. A source of strength also was the intellectual elite, despite the fact that, as Du Bois noted, "they have always lacked, and some still lack, the courage to stand up for what they know is right." In the long run the South's men and women of culture could be depended upon "to follow their own clear thinking and their own decent choice." After dealing with the question of allies and indicating that the emergence of a majority coalition for democracy was a realistic perspective, Du Bois turned to the question of how the battle should be carried on, of what tactics were necessary and appropriate in the struggle. He bluntly acknowledged that sometimes it was necessary to die, stating that he was the last to insist "that the uplift of mankind never calls for force and death." But after the experience of the world wars, he observed, "we ought to be the last to believe that force is ever the final word." Reason was the final salvation of mankind, and reason, Du Bois believed, would prevail, but only with publicity that brought the truth to the world's attention. To make people aware of the truth would demand sacrifice, but that made no difference; it was the duty of the black youth to remain in the South and to expose the prevailing racial oppression.[22]

Du Bois's increasingly radical position was expressed in his support of the 1948 Progressive party candidacy of Henry Wallace. He could not go along with the many spokesmen of the black bourgeoisie who endorsed Harry Truman. Describing Truman as a "border state politician of apparent good will but narrow training and small vision," Du Bois asserted that probably in the next presidential election the majority of blacks would vote either for Wallace or for a Republican, a political forecast not borne out by events. Du Bois made it clear that his support of Wallace was based on more than the Progressive party's position on civil rights, although no doubt he must have been struck by Wallace's courage in attempting during 1947 an integrated speaking tour of the South in which he spoke out against racial injustice. In declaring for Wallace, Du Bois stressed the candidate's position on peace and particularly his friendly attitude toward the Soviet Union. "I cannot escape the feeling," Du Bois wrote, "that the attempt of Russia to change the economic foundation of modern life is an even greater phenomenon than the French Revolution."[23] At the 1947 NAACP convention Du Bois, long influenced by Socialist ideas, directly linked the black struggle to the general conflict between capitalism and socialism. "Socialism is an attack on poverty," he stated, adding that the United Nations "is the greatest hope of abolishing colonialism and thus abolishing poverty in all the world."[24] In a situation where those who shaped the NAACP's policies had charted a course of alliance with the liberal anticommunism symbolized by Truman it was inevitable that an open break would occur between Du Bois and the association. Du Bois was removed from his position as the NAACP's director of research shortly after he argued, in a memorandum to the association's board, that Walter White's acceptance of a post as consultant to the United States delegation to the United Nations would bind the organization to "the reactionary war-mongering colonial imperialism of the present administration."[25] In late 1948 the *New York Times Magazine* had published an article by Du Bois, but within a year such left-wing publications as *Masses and Mainstream* and the *National Guardian* became the outlets for his writings. By 1950 his main concern with violence was with the violence of war. Du Bois told a New York election rally that, "as war has become universal and so horrible and destructive that everybody recognizes it as murder, crippling, insanity and stark death of human culture, we realize that there is scarce a victory formerly claimed by war, which mankind might not have gained more cheaply and more decently and even more completely by methods of peace." Without reservation he placed the responsibility for existing international tension upon the United States, declaring that "of all nations of earth today the United States alone wants War, prepares for war, forces other nations to fight and asks you and me to impoverish ourselves, give up health and schools, sacrifice our sons and daughters to a Jim-crow army and commit suicide for a world war that nobody wants but the rich Americans who profit by it." He explained that it was his concern with the question of peace and war that had led to his candidacy for the United States Senate.

Du Bois called upon Harlem to vote for peace and civil rights, viewing those issues as intertwined. "I ask Harlem," Du Bois said, "to vote overwhelmingly for Peace and Civil Rights against Dewey and Lynch."[26] Du Bois charted a course for the connecting of the domestic racial struggle with world issues, a course most elements of black leadership were not then prepared to follow.

PART VI

The 1950s: From Willie McGee to the Montgomery Struggle

Come gather around
And listen to me,
I'll tell you the story
Of Willie McGee!

It's away down South
The land of cotton—
Where a rich man's sins
Are soon forgotten!

But a black man's ways
Never are quite free,
And that was the case
With Willie McGee.

Don West, "The Ballad of Willie McGee," in West, *A Time for Anger*

Laurel:
Name sweet like the breath of peace

Blood and blood
Hatred there
White robes and
Black robes
And a burning
Burning cross

        cross in Laurel
        cross in Jackson
        cross in Chicago

And a
Cross in front of the
City Hall
In:
New York City

Lord
Burning cross
Lord
Burning man
Lord
Murder cross

Laurel
Name bitter like the rhyme of a
lynchsong

I can hear Rosalee
See the eyes of Willie McGee
My mother told me about
Lynchings
My mother told me about
The dark nights
And dirt roads
And torch lights
And lynch robes

        sorrow night
        and a sorrow night

The
Faces of men
Laughing white
Faces of men
Dead in the night

        sorrow night
        and a
        sorrow night

Lorraine Hansberry, "Lynchsong," *Masses and Mainstream,* July 1951, pp. 19, 20

Although law is an important factor in bringing about social change, there are certain conditions in which the very effort to adhere to new legal decisions creates tension and provokes violence. We had hoped to see demonstrated a method that would enable us to continue our struggle while coping with the violence it aroused. Now we see the answer: face violence if necessary, but refuse to return violence. If we respect those who oppose us, they may achieve a new understanding of the human relations involved.

    Martin Luther King, Jr., *Our Struggle: The Story of Montgomery*

FIFTEEN

Executions, Little Rock, Genocide

URING THE EARLY 1950s racist violence persisted as a component of American life at the same time as international pressures mounted upon official society to modify oppressive racial practices. Repeatedly, segregation and discrimination were buttressed by official violence as in such cases as those of Willie McGee and the Martinsville Seven. The racist stereotype of the black rapist served to justify execution of black defendants who had been convicted in trials that mocked proper judicial procedures. On February 2, 1951, the seven blacks known as the Martinsville Seven—Joe Henry Hampton, Howard Hairston, Booker Millner, Frank Hairston, John Taylor, James Hairston, and Francis Grayson—were executed at Richmond, Virginia, for allegedly having raped a white woman. On May 8 of the same year McGee was executed by the state of Mississippi. McGee had been convicted of raping a white woman, Mrs. Willamette Hawkins, but evidence indicated that Hawkins had forced McGee into a relationship he later tried to sever. Once the charge of rape had been raised, Mississippi was incapable of legitimizing the concept that a white woman had sought a sexual relationship with a black male. Along with these instances of official violence, 1951 was also marked by the murders of two NAACP activists, Harriet and Harry T. Moore. The Moores, involved in voter registration efforts in Florida, were killed Christmas night by a bomb placed beneath their home.

The mindset operative in the McGee execution was made clear when Harvey McGehee, chief justice of the state Supreme Court, was confronted with a suggestion that there was something hidden in the case. "If you believe, or are implying," he asserted, "that any white woman in the South, who was not completely down and out, degenerate, degraded and corrupted, could have anything to do with a Negro man, you not only do not know what you are talking about, but you are insulting us, the whole South. You do not know the South, and do not realize that

395

we could not entertain such a proposition; that we could not even consider it in court."[1]

The Mississippi legal proceedings against McGee were indeed perfunctory. His first trial lasted one day, motions for a continuance and a change of venue were denied, and the main evidence against the defendant was a signed confession obtained fourteen days after his arrest and a deputy's testimony that McGee had verbally confessed. In finding McGee guilty the jury took all of two and one-half minutes. This conviction was overturned on appeal to the state Supreme Court, as was a second conviction. The court successively found that denying change of venue and exclusion of blacks from the jury panel invalidated the convictions. At the third trial a young white attorney, John R. Poole, defended McGee, and near the close of the trial, before the summations, Poole was warned of a threat to "get" him. In this situation both defense counsel and prosecutor waived rights of summation, and Poole made his exit from the court and fled town.[2] This time the jury took less than an hour to find McGee guilty, and the judge, F. Burkitt Collins, again sentenced McGee to death.

The decisions of the Mississippi appeals court reflected race prejudice and seemed less concerned with the defendant's rights as an individual than with polishing the image of the Mississippi legal system. The 1948 Mississippi Supreme Court ruling overturning McGee's second conviction on the grounds that blacks had been excluded from the grand jury and the trial jury was accompanied by Judge McGehee's dissent, which took judicial notice that black registration in the state had been increased by "northern agitators who want to win the favor of the Negro vote in the national election and in the local elections in the northern states." McGehee, joined in dissent by Judge Roberds, appeared to see as irrelevant to judicial due process that in the county only ninety blacks were among the eight to ten thousand persons registered to vote. There was vehemence in the dissent, whereas the finding reversing the conviction was constructed as narrowly as possible to meet federal requirements. Reading the majority opinion, one gets the impression the main purpose was to obviate the possibility of federal intervention.

In April 1949 the Mississippi Supreme Court upheld McGee's third conviction. Three blacks had served on the grand jury that indicted McGee, and one black had actually been called to the trial jury, although he was excused as a physician. Noting these facts, the Supreme Court had little patience with any further objections to McGee's conviction. The minimum federal test appeared to have been passed, and that was quite enough. The court found no problem with the fact there was only a two-week interval between McGee's third indictment and his trial, with the necessity of new defense counsel taking charge of the case, and that this counsel was denied a continuance to prepare more adequately. Another court might have seen here a "rush to judgment" but not the Mississippi Supreme Court. One of the grounds of the defense appeal had been that the prosecution had failed to prove absence of consent on the part of the alleged victim. The judges' emotions were clearly engaged when they termed this charge itself a "revolting insinuation." Something of the sensibility that informed this court is to be seen in its statement that for "nearly a century and a half, the decisions of this Court have developed a high tradition of impartiality in its adjudications, always on the search for truth and justice, regardless of the condition or station of litigants, whether rich or poor, high or low, significant or unimportant, and whether white or black." That was the record, whether with regard to the slavery era or later, as seen by the Mississippi Supreme Court, in a state where only blacks were executed for the crime of rape and the Fourteenth and Fifteenth amendments were routinely ignored.[3]

The most the defense could get out of the federal courts were stays of execution by Justice Burton and Justice Black. No federal court would overturn the conviction or the penalty or would consider the argument that in Mississippi execution for rape was reserved for blacks only. U.S. District Court judge Sydney Mize, later to earn repute as a fervent judicial opponent of civil rights, was particularly staunch in rebuffing efforts to seek a federal remedy. At a hearing in Vicksburg, Civil Rights Congress attorneys Bella Abzug and John Coe were told by Mize: "I have read the record twice and his guilt is plain."[4] A few hours before McGee's scheduled execution Mize, sitting in Jackson, rejected efforts of Attorneys Abzug and Ernest Goodman to postpone the execution, asserting that no defendant had had more exhaustive hearings than McGee and adding: "The time has arrived when courts ought to rise up and defend themselves."[5]

Rebuffed in federal court, the two attorneys made one last desperate plea, proceeding to the executive mansion in Jackson to ask the intervention of Governor Wright. Abzug and Goodman found the governor and the attorney general and their wives engaged in a bridge game, and after brief discussion the request for delaying the execution was denied. The officials noted that there had been ample appeals in this case. After leaving the mansion, with its setting of beautiful flowers and magnolia trees, Goodman placed a call to a newsman at the execution scene at the Laurel courthouse and over the phone heard the "rebel" yell of the gathered mob. The next day the attorneys went home.[6]

The actual issues of the McGee case were covered over by the bogus issue of communism. As journalist John Herbers, who covered the final hearing in Judge Mize's court, later observed: "The feelings against McGee and his defenders were highly emotional—it was Mississippi against the Communists . . . justice, whatever it was, could not well prevail in that climate."[7] Anticommunism was the refuge of white supremacists in Mississippi committed to the precept that a black could not be innocent if a white woman alleged he had assaulted her and also of northern opinion makers who found a ready excuse for inaction. In Mississippi a columnist for the *Jackson Daily News* referred to Bella Abzug as the "Communist-paid white woman lawyer," and in a summary of the case the paper described former congressman Vito Marcantonio as a "New York Communist Party leader." Civil Rights Congress attorney Emanuel Bloch was identified as "a long-time organizer for the Communist Party," and readers were further informed that the Justice Department had listed the congress as "subversive."[8] A few days later the *News* returned to the Communist issue, now declaring: "The recent Willie McGee case was a striking illustration of the desperate tactics Communists use to gain ground for their cause. They spent at least $100,000 in defense of Willie McGee, a proven rapist, not because they cared anything whatever about the defendant, but they were boldly and impudently seeking to create disrespect for law and order among Negroes throughout the nation, and especially in the Southern states."[9]

Up North, *Time* stressed that Communists used the case as "surefire propaganda" and dismissed Mrs. McGee as a "captive" of the Communists.[10] *Life* contended that the death sentence might not have been carried out because, after all, no white man had ever been executed for rape in Mississippi. But unfortunately, according to *Life,* the case had been taken over by Communists, and such organizations as the NAACP consequently drew back. Along the way the magazine backhandedly admitted that the case had been reopened due to funds raised by the Communists.[11] Liberal commentators took up the refrain without either seriously challenging the failure of moderates to speak up or determining that Mississippi authorities would have responded to appeals purged of all Communist taint. That Mississippi itself would move was most dubious, given the virulent racism of the state's politics and the explosive linkage of sex and race conjured up in the case. Such pressure was unlikely to appear so long as avoiding the "red" taint was the paramount consideration. But liberals such as Max Lerner in the *New York Post* and Mary Mostert in the *Nation* did not focus upon racism as the central factor in the outcome of the case and would not come to grips with why moderates had largely ignored the case when earlier there was no issue of Communist involvement.[12]

During the period of McCarthyism, involvement in the effort to save Willie McGee's life became one of the items that might be cited as evidence of susceptibility to "red" influence. In 1953 actress Kim Hunter, in the course of an affidavit she furnished AWARE, the blacklisting organization operating in the television and radio industry, was induced to mention her having signed a clemency petition for McGee as one of the instances in which she had not realized the sinister nature of Communist activity. If the actress was to work at her profession she had to recant an honorable act protected by the Constitution.[13]

There was significant protest in the Willie McGee case. Albert Einstein's name appeared in public statements opposing this injustice, and in Mississippi, rising above the local climate of opinion, William Faulkner commented that the case was an outrage and that Mississippi was adhering to a fetish of long standing, although privately he told Jessica Mitford that McGee and the woman he was accused of raping should both be destroyed.[14] Brave, almost beyond measure, were the protesters, blacks and whites, especially white women, who came to Mississippi to witness their opposition to the McGee execution. The threat of violence facing such persons was very real. Months before the climax of the case Californian Aubrey Grossman of the Civil Rights Congress was assaulted at his hotel, and the response of the *Jackson Daily News* was to suggest with regard to the assailants that "if we could locate those chaps we surely would punish them severely for not doing better jobs."[15] But these threats did not stop the protests. The climax came on May 5, 1951, when hundreds of blacks assembled in Jackson in preparation for a "Sunrise Prayer Meeting" on the Capitol lawn. The purpose was to pray that the Lord might inspire Governor Fielding Wright to do justice in the McGee case. The blacks were to be joined by twenty-four white women who had journeyed to Jackson from New York, Chicago, California, and Virginia. But the police prevented the holding of the prayer session by arresting those who approached the Capitol. Forty-three individuals were seized and released only upon agreement to leave the state. Although the plan for mass prayer at the Capitol could not be implemented, it was remarkable, in view of the general political atmosphere, that hundreds of southern blacks were prepared to risk brutal treatment at the hands of Mississippi police in order to appeal publicly for justice in a case that aroused the deepest racist hatreds.[16]

James Baldwin described a lynching in his story "Going to Meet the Man." The lynching is recalled by a white man who had seen the event as something "like a Fourth of July picnic." The lynching was indeed an occasion for socializing, for renewing acquaintances, a time of peculiar pleasure for the whites witnessing it. "Those in front," Baldwin wrote, "expressed their delight at what they saw, and this delight rolled backward, wave upon wave, across the clearing, more acrid than the smoke." For the white boy through whose eyes the lynching was seen, the event was a rite of initiation into a community of shared racial values.[17] Jessica Mitford saw the mood Baldwin described reflected in the atmosphere surrounding the Willie McGee execution, a mood "compounded of bloodlust and jollity."[18] The *Jackson Daily News* account of the execution supports Mitford's analogy. On its front page the *News* ran a photo of the scene as the hearse drove away with McGee's body. Over the photo a caption read, "A Yell Went Up As They Drove Away with Willie's Body." Under the photo there was a description of the crowd's temper: "There was mumbling and laughter throughout the night as a crowd gathered in Laurel to await the death of Willie McGee." According to the *News*, when McGee was brought to the Jones County jail two hours before the execution a crowd of some 300 had assembled, and this audience grew to 500 by the time of the execution. The *News* described the crowd: "They were orderly, some talking in low tones, teen-age boys did some laughing and there were a few girls and women in the throng." As the crowd waited a highway patrolman shouted, "Let's everybody be nice," and he added, "You have been patient a long time." One C. D. Hill, a Laurel plumber, climbed a cedar tree on the courthouse lawn so as to have a clear view of the courtroom, which served as the execution chamber. Even after the electrocution, as the undertakers carried the body out, one man asked, "How do you know this isn't a dummy?" If the hundreds gathered at Laurel enjoyed the execution, so too did Frederick Sullen, the *Jackson Daily News* front-page columnist, take his satisfaction in McGee's death. "Willie has gone to a place," he wrote, "where civil liberties and Communism are never subjects of discussion. Whatever complaint Willie may have from now on will be concerning the prevailing temperature." The *News* reporter, Jimmy Ward, wrote of Willie McGee's "disgraceful death," and there was indeed disgrace in the case, that of the judicial and executive authorities who committed a legal murder.[19]

Willie McGee did not flinch before his executioners and recognized that his death was part of the oppression of blacks in America. Before going to his execution he wrote his wife: "tell the people the real reason they are going to take my life is to keep the Negro down in the South. They can't do this if you and the children keep on fighting. Never forget to tell them why they killed their daddy."[20] At the Hinds County jail, where he was held before being taken to Laurel, McGee sang a hymn during his last hours: "Only the Father, He'll understand. / The Father alone, he knows why / When I see Jesus, he'll know the reason / Only the Father, he'll understand."[21] It was quite clear that in racist Mississippi he would not find understanding. What the state authorities understood was that the system had been challenged and, as John Herbers has written, those who made the challenge "had to be defeated at all costs whatever the guilt or innocence of McGee in the same way the white community in Philadelphia, Miss., in 1964 came to the defense of the defendants in the slaying of three civil rights workers."[22]

An interesting view of the McGee case is that offered by journalist Carl Rowan. While the McGee appeals were still pending in the courts Rowan visited Laurel and talked with various persons in the black community. Rowan did indeed see ambiguities in the defense version of the facts and felt the defense effort was "wishy-washy." But he also reported the palpable fear that gripped Laurel blacks and prevented any of them from coming forward with what they believed or knew to be true about the relationship between McGee and Mrs. Hawkins. And because of that fear he recognized that "it meant absolutely nothing" that blacks had been placed on the jury panel in the third trial.[23] No black juror who lived in that community would dare hold out against a white majority that voted for conviction. Rowan's portrayal of the racism of Laurel gives credibility to the view that McGee would have realistic fears about the consequences of breaking with Hawkins and that the mores of white society would make almost impossible any admission by a white woman that she had voluntarily entered into a sexual relationship with a black man.

A case that reached its climax early in 1954 outlined how the American armed services could play the role of perpetrator of violence against black individuals. On January 27, 1954, two black men, Herman P. Dennis, Jr., and Robert W. Burns, were put to death by hanging at the Northwest Military Air Field located on Guam. Five years earlier the men had been condemned to death for the rape-murder of Ruth Farnsworth, a clerk in a Guam curio shop. Dennis and Burns were executed despite considerable evidence of torture employed in their "questioning" and a public campaign spearheaded by the *Pittsburgh Courier* to stop the executions. In the days before the scheduled hangings the *Courier* urged readers to wire President Eisenhower asking for a delay of execution.[24] Supporting the paper's efforts was an account of the case written by Sergeant Burns. The articles by Burns present his view of the facts and also his response to the years of living death through which he had passed since his arrest.

It is very difficult to believe that the man who wrote these articles was a rapist-murderer. What comes across is the horror of the death sentence inflicted upon a black man because it was expedient to do so. Burns summed up what his confinement, awaiting execution, had done to him: "My mind, body and my soul are dead, dead is the very center of my being." All that was left to him, Burns wrote, was a small spark of sanity that he had tried to keep aglow "by forcing into limbo black memories of the past fifty-six months, that would otherwise rob me of my wit and leave me stark, raving mad."[25]

In the *Courier* William G. Nunn, the newspaper's managing editor, told of the efforts being made to save Burns and Dennis. Readers were informed that thousands of telegrams and letters had reached the White House concerning the case. Nunn began his story with the words, "Tonight the lights in the White House are burning brilliantly" and indicated his belief that President Eisenhower was considering the matter. Although barely any time remained, Nunn saw a ray of hope, noting that "we have knowledge that there is deep and vital concern in the quarters where it counts most. . . . We know that men who make final judgments in cases of this kind, have not closed the door in our faces." In the article Nunn carefully restated the reasons for the *Courier's* concern with the case. Though referring to a statement by Thurgood Marshall to the effect that the men were "not guilty," the *Courier* based its interest mainly upon the view that the rights of Burns and Dennis to due process had been violated. Adding to the concern was the fact that blacks had played no part in the investigative processes where the lives of black persons were involved. Nunn asked the question of whether the condemned men were guilty and answered: "Only these men . . . and their Maker . . . know!" But nothing was more important than human life, and taking into account the strong doubts in the case the *Courier* asked President Eisenhower to delay the execution.[26]

The president, however, took no action to delay the executions, and in its February 6 issue the *Courier* reported the hangings of Burns and Dennis. Now that the men were dead Nunn focused upon the future and expressed the hope that the executions would result in a review "of the manner in which Negro men, accused and convicted of a crime against a white person, are handled." Nunn called for a "thorough airing" of courts-martial proceedings and for acceptance of the *Courier's* request "that competent and qualified Negroes be called when the lives of Negroes are at stake." Next to the paper's masthead the *Courier* quoted the final words of the executed men. Burns had said: "You are just complying with an order, sir. You have not solved the crime." Dennis also avowed his innocence: "They are making a big mistake and they are not accomplishing anything by executing me. Even after my execution, if they find the guilty parties I do not hold in my heart anything against them. But I pray forgiveness for them and I pray for those who are making this mistake." Their final words certainly gave no assistance to the effort to portray them as vicious killers. Following the execution NAACP attorneys Robert Carter and Thurgood Marshall were quoted as believing that the men were innocent.[27]

Even after the executions the *Courier* continued to run the series of articles by Burns. In the February 6 installment Burns told of receiving a truth serum test and then of awakening to find himself locked in a barrel cage. Burns described the situation: "It was made obvious by the dried excretion on the floor, that the cage had some time ago been used to house a kind of animal. This cage was situated not more than eight feet from the main road of Agana where an enraged crowd shouted curses and threats in vile profanity." Only after three days was Burns moved back to the jail compound. Burns also wrote in some detail about the "trial" he received. The proceeding, convened May 29, 1949, was held at the Cross Roads Service Club. According to Burns, the setting was more appropriate to a carnival, "more like a country clam bake," unsuitable to a military tribunal. An audience of approximately 800 men, women, and children attended the trial. At the end of the first day's proceedings one of the prosecutors came to ask Burns once more if he would cooperate, an offer Burns refused. When asked if he would take the stand Burns recalled replying:

Yes, Sir, I surely am. I'm going to tell the world what a dirty rotten mess this whole command is. I am going to reveal the names in the ammunition black market, from the highest to the lowest. I will expose the activities of the signal corps photographic laboratory, and mammoth shipments of tires and machinery to Manila and Singapore, disguised as salvage, where it is sold on black markets. I'll ask to introduce witnesses to prove the Jade Shop was a headquarters for shipping narcotics to Hawaii. I'll show the court how prostitution is promoted by American men and women within military installations.

Burns did not testify during the second and last day of his trial. He told his defense counsel the proceeding was a farce, pointing to vendors walking about the audience selling Coca-Cola, hot dogs, and ice cream, and yet asked to be put on the stand. But according to Burns his counsel ordered him not to testify. The trial quickly came to an end with the trial board returning a verdict of guilty and sentencing Burns to hang. Later, placed in an Agana cell, Burns met Herman Dennis and learned that Dennis also had been found guilty and condemned. The following day, May 31, 1949, Burns and Dennis were flown to Tokyo where they were to remain until shortly before the execution.[28]

Quite apart from a judgment as to the guilt or innocence of the executed men—and Herbert Aptheker has persuasively argued the view that the men were framed—what is striking in this affair is the contrast between the concern expressed by black newspapers and public figures and the indifference of the white media.[29] For the *Pittsburgh Courier* the case was of major significance, raising the whole question of unfair judicial treatment afforded blacks in the armed services, but for the white commercial media the case was of no consequence at all. Significant segments of the black community and some white radicals might protest the execution, but as far as the consciousness of the overwhelming majority of white Americans was concerned the case was barely noticed. The white press and other suppliers of information, faced with the conflict between the verdict of a court-martial and protestations of innocence by blacks, were prone to believe there simply was no issue. A case in which at the very least there is strong reason to believe that guarantees of due process, even by court-martial standards, were violated was transformed into a nonevent. But Herman Dennis and Robert Burns on January 27, 1954, were indeed hanged until dead. The names of these two men belong on the list of victims of legal injustice in the United States.

To better understand the Burns–Dennis case the history of racism in the military administration of Guam should be kept in mind. Walter White had visited the island base at the end of 1944 and observed the state of racial relations. Shortly after his arrival White was told by an army public relations officer: "The black sons-of-bitches are getting out of hand and we are going to teach 'em a lesson." White spent several weeks at Guam and later wrote that what he had seen and heard was "so tragically typical of the racial practices our country transported overseas during World War Two." Forty-four blacks had been arrested at Agana, charged with offenses such as unlawful assemblage, rioting, theft of government property, and attempted murder. White explained that the "very efficiency and progress of the transformation of Guam into a highly organized military and naval base increased the opportunity of some of the Negro-phobes to translate their prejudices into action." A camp for black servicemen was sited adjacent to a new six-lane highway connecting one end of Guam to the other. A series of assaults upon the servicemen had provoked some blacks to set off on trucks for Agana, presumably seeking revenge, and only with this action did authorities intervene, arresting the blacks. White wrote that earlier blacks had complained about attacks upon them but the commanding officers "sought to cover up the attacks or to justify them." The forty-four black prisoners were brought before courts-martial, and all were convicted and received prison terms, the convictions being overturned only after appeals to the secretary of the navy and the White House.[30]

Fresh examination of the documentary record leaves little doubt that racism is what produced the injustice in the Burns–Dennis case. According to Attorney General Herbert Brownell, Burns "was convicted principally upon the testimony of one Calvin Dennis." Dennis had also been charged with complicity in the Farnsworth murder. Following the trial Calvin Dennis in several affidavits repudiated his testimony, stating his confession was coerced. Brownell waved this circumstance aside, apparently without critically evaluating the preference of the appeals tribunal for the original Calvin Dennis confession. Brownell coolly remarked there was no assurance of reward in exchange for the confession but also notes without comment that Eisenhower had commuted Calvin Dennis's death sentence to life imprisonment, thereby outlining a situation in which to accept Dennis's recantation might cast doubt on the integrity of the clemency process. Neither Brownell nor the board of review was swayed by evidence that one of the key interrogators had stated in response to a question as to how confessions had been obtained: "We kind of give them the business or rough them up." The board was satisfied by testimony that this statement "could have been" said in a joking manner. In the opinion he furnished Eisenhower, the attorney general simply ignored this matter. Entered into the trial record and accepted as pertinent evidence by the board of review was testimony that was blatantly racist in character, that in itself contaminated the case by drawing upon acute racial and sexual fears. It was deemed relevant that Herman Dennis supposedly had said to a white woman that he did not believe in racial segregation, that it was "too hard for a man to be away from a woman so long," and that he asked the woman's permission to take her photo in a bathing suit. Doubtless those of a white-supremacist mindset would find this relevant evidence in a case of rape-murder. Surely, if race was not a factor in the case it is difficult to believe the prosecution would waste time with evidence that the defendant might have been seeking to initiate a social relationship with some woman. That Mr. Brownell saw no reason even to refer to such a line of questioning is a comment on the racial turn of mind of the Eisenhower administration.[31]

June 15, 1953, was a day on which the United States Supreme Court twice refused to examine critically the fairness of judicial proceedings that resulted in death sentences. By a vote of five to four, with Justices Douglas, Black, Jackson, and Frankfurter in the minority, the Court refused to stay the impending execution of Julius and Ethel Rosenberg. The Court also on that day refused to overturn the courts-martial convictions of Burns and Dennis, with Justices Douglas and Black dissenting and Justice Frankfurter arguing that the case should be set down for further argument. The core of the majority position was that the claims of the convicted men had received fair consideration by the military appeals courts. Indeed, the majority noted that the court of appeals "may have erred" in considering the evidence in the trial record, although it is to be wondered that a judgment can be made as to the fairness of an appeals proceeding without considering if the appellate decision is reasonably supported by the trial record. Justice Minton even took the further position that the review power of the Court extended only to the question of jurisdiction. In his view military personnel properly brought before a military tribunal had no recourse to the federal courts.

In the majority decision there was the implicit theme that the appellate procedure had been fair because those hearing the appeal said they considered the claims of Burns and Dennis. Officers and gentlemen apparently were to be taken at their word. Set next to this finding the dissent of Douglas and Black introduced a note of reality. To begin with, they insisted that some of the basic guarantees of the Fifth Amendment, including the guarantee that one may not be compelled to be a witness against oneself, applied to military personnel as well as civilians. The logic of their position was powerful. Why in the language of the amendment was the protection of only one segment explicitly denied to servicemen if the amendment as a whole was inapplicable to the military? The dissenters then outlined a situation in which the federal courts should act: "If a prisoner is coerced by torture or other methods to give the evidence against him, if he is beaten or slowly 'broken' by third-degree methods, then the trial before the military tribunal becomes an empty ritual. The real trial takes place in secret where the accused without benefit of counsel succumbs to physical or psychological pressures. A soldier or sailor convicted in that manner . . . should have relief by way of habeas corpus." With regard to the specific issue at hand Douglas and Black noted: "The *undisputed* facts in this case make a prima facie case that our rule on coerced confessions . . . was violated here. No court has considered the question whether repetitious questioning over a period of five days while the accused was held incommunicado without benefit of counsel violated the Fifth Amendment." The Air Force judge advocate general had merely stated that the voluntary nature of the confessions was a matter for the triers of the facts and that the court's decision as to voluntariness was "presumptively correct and will not be disturbed unless manifestly erroneous." Douglas and Black argued that before the men were executed it was appropriate to consider the facts surrounding the confession in the light of the Fifth Amendment protections. It might be added, apart from the view advanced by the dissenting justices, that the racial history of the American armed services and the racist mystique surrounding the charge of rape leveled against black males constituted further reasons, in social reality if not in law, to question the voluntary nature of the confessions. Although the dissent breathed a spirit of regard for individual rights, neither the majority nor the minority allowed the subject of race to appear openly on the record, in a situation where it would have been almost miraculous if it had not played some role.

Although Justice Frankfurter did not join the dissent his opinion lifted a corner on another aspect of reality concerning the case. Frankfurter revealed that, due to concern with enabling indigent defendants to have the Supreme Court review the case, the justices had required that only one copy of the relevant materials be provided them. According to Frankfurter, in the time available not every member of the Court had the time to review the record. He knew for a fact that with respect to one justice, himself, there had not been time. By implication, at least, Frankfurter was suggesting that the Court was acting in haste in a matter where human lives were at stake. In his legalistic manner, though not willing to make a decision on the merits of the appeal, Frankfurter made a damning comment on the treatment accorded this case.[32]

As there was a sharp difference of opinion among the Supreme Court justices in this case, so there had also been a clear difference earlier in the judgments rendered in the Circuit Court of Appeals. The majority, Judges Prettyman and Proctor, in upholding the convictions, essentially argued that allegations as to denial of due process had been considered at the original trial and in subsequent military appeals. Regarding the charge that the Herman Dennis confession was obtained under duress while the prisoner was held incommunicado, Prettyman and Proctor observed only that "military procedure does not provide for arraignment until the court-martial is convened." In his dissent Judge David Bazelon approached the issues differently. He would look at the totality of the allegations and attempt to determine, if supported by evidence, their general significance. "The fairness of a trial," he wrote, "must be determined by appraisal of the whole rather than by picking and choosing among its component parts. A total configuration of the allegations in these cases discloses something which the separate parts do not. The totality, if proved, would constitute the antithesis of fairness." Bazelon's opinion was especially telling in its criticism of the detention of Dennis and Burns for a number of days without access to counsel. He declared that what was required by military or Guam law was "of small moment." The issue was one of fundamental constitutional rights. Some feeling comes through as Bazelon continues:

> We are concerned here with "fundamental principles of liberty and justice." Although the exact point at which appellants were free to consult with counsel is not clear from the record, it appears that they did not receive assistance until after a long period of incommunicado detention with repeated questioning, and until after Dennis had confessed. In my view, this suggests "all the evil implications of secret interrogation of persons accused of crime." I put aside all arguments based on the emergencies of the battlefield and the impracticability of reasonable promptness in furnishing defense counsel under such circumstances. Whatever validity these arguments have where the detention occurs in a combat zone, they have no application to the Island of Guam—which was under a civil administration—in the relatively peaceful year of 1949.

Regarding the contention by Calvin Dennis, the third defendant in the case, that his confession had been coerced, Prettyman and Proctor related this to their finding as concerned suppressed evidence that the federal court had discretion in determining if the case at hand was one of those exceptional instances that required the court to inquire into the proper administration of justice in lower courts. Apparently, Prettyman and Proctor did not view Calvin Dennis's repudiation of his trial testimony as an exceptional matter. Bazelon was of another mind. Whereas the majority turned quickly from the issue of the Dennis confession to emphasize that the accused had been vigorously defended, Bazelon concluded that the repudiation was "clearly new evidence of a vital nature which calls for a reappraisal of the voluntariness of his confession." Whereas the majority of the Circuit Court of Appeals appeared to focus on whether the proceedings were proper in form, Bazelon seemed more interested in determining if the spirit of lawful process had been adhered to. For Bazelon the gravity of the allegations was significant for, as he noted, if proved they would "paint a portrait of inquisitorial zeal rather than of a fair trial in the Anglo-American sense."[33]

The Burns–Dennis execution introduced an interesting, if brief, interval of candor into relations between the *Courier* and the White House. On January 10, 1954, Mrs. Robert L. Vann, the *Courier* publisher, had written to President Eisenhower asking for a stay of execution until further investigation was made to determine if the condemned men had received justice. She declared that "there is serious reason to doubt their guilt and to question the methods used to implicate them in the crime and to find them guilty." Nine days after writing to Eisenhower, Vann wrote to *Courier* readers urging them to contact the president promptly, and the following day *Courier* columnist George Schuyler addressed an appeal to his friends for similar action. The administration response was for White House special counsel Bernard Shanley to receive Vann and managing editor William Nunn, and Shanley also wrote to Mrs. Nunn informing her that Eisenhower's decision against delaying the executions remained unchanged. Following the executions Nunn wrote Shanley, and his letter was a reminder of the *Courier*'s support for the administration and also a complaint that Eisenhower had not replied directly to Vann. Nunn went further and referred to the general context of racism in which the case had been decided: "I say to you, Mr. Shanley, that having been a Negro for some fifty odd years, I know the thinking and the feeling of Negroes. They just don't take without question the opinions of white men in cases where whites and Negroes are involved. This is a lesson you must learn. Practically every other minority group in America with the exception of Negroes, have personal representation in government at policy-making levels. We don't ... and it was with this knowledge that we wrote asking that a court of last resort be established with a Negro as a member to go into the case." Within a few days Shanley replied, expressing resentment at what he saw as the implication that Eisenhower had not been fully informed about the case. Nunn again wrote Shanley, assuring the president's counsel of regard for his integrity and stating his feeling that "whatever action you took was taken only after a full and deliberate search of the record and the facts as they were presented." Still, Nunn asked if Eisenhower had received Mrs. Vann's appeal and whether he felt it was not necessary to reply personally. Shanley did not answer the first question, and his reply to the second was that after Shanley had met with Vann and Nunn the president had seen no need for further reply. On this basis, with mixed notes of cordiality and resentment, the record of the Burns–Dennis case was closed as a matter of controversy between the *Courier* and the White House.[34]

As violence has always been the response of those frightened by any movement toward racial equality, the mid-1950s produced a violent counteroffensive launched to negate the May 17, 1954, Supreme Court decision in the *Brown* case. The Court had overthrown the "separate but equal" doctrine and had laid out a cautious path toward school integration with its "all deliberate speed" strategy, but white supremacists would employ whatever means were necessary to stop integration regardless of the speed with which it was to be accomplished. Open resistance to school integration was urged by the Ku Klux Klan and by the newly organized White Citizens Councils. In Congress 101 members put their names to a Southern Manifesto that declared the *Brown* decision to be a "clear abuse of judicial power" that gave the force of law to the personal political and social views of the justices. The signers of this declaration pledged "to use all lawful means to bring about a reversal of this decision which is contrary to the Constitution."[35] The ambiguous response of the executive branch of government to the integration ruling was symbolized by President Eisenhower's refusal to support the rightness of the *Brown* decision. In 1956 Eisenhower observed: "I think it makes no difference whether or not I endorse it," and indeed the most the president would say was that we must all "help to bring about a change in spirit so that extremists on both sides do not defeat what we know is a reasonable, logical conclusion to this whole affair, which is recognition of equality of men."[36] Eisenhower legitimized the concept that those who insisted upon implementation of the integration decision were extremists. Clearly, what he said and what he failed to say helped create a national atmosphere in which segregationists could calculate that disorder would encourage delay in enforcing integration.

Following the *Brown* decision violence was sometimes utilized in relation to specific issues involving integration, but there was also recourse to indiscriminate terror, expressing a sense of rage that the racial status quo was breaking down. One such incident was the 1957 castration of a black man, Edward Aaron. This deed was the work of a group of Klansmen active in the East Lake section of Birmingham. The members of the group also belonged to the White Citizens Councils. All of these individuals had some high school education, and two were high school graduates. The leader, Jesse Mabry, had once been mentioned in the newspapers in connection with a Klan assault upon singer Nat ("King") Cole. Cole, while singing at the Birmingham Municipal Auditorium, had been attacked by several persons, including Mabry, and only police intervention had saved the singer from serious injury. Mabry paid a fine for disorderly conduct.

On September 2, 1957, Mabry and five other Klansmen set forth on a venture designed to prove the qualifications of one of the group for

Klan leadership. The test was to be willingness to engage in "cutting a nigger." Edward Aaron was the black man they seized. Aaron, thirty-four years old, had served with the army during World War II. Aaron's captors interrogated their intended victim before castrating him. The words convey some sense of their mentality: "Look here, nigger! You ever heard of a nigger-loving Communist named Earl Warren?.... You think nigger kids should go to school with my white kids? You think you got right to vote? Or eat where I eat? Or use the same toilet I use?" This questioning was followed by the act of castration. After they had finished with Aaron the six Klansmen threw him from their car onto the side of a road. Later, Aaron was found by the police and taken to the Veterans' Administration Hospital in Birmingham.[37]

In 1955 the NAACP saw murder as a central feature of the system of racial subordination that characterized the state of Mississippi. The association stressed that such violence was encouraged by a climate of opinion that defied the rule of law. What was to be made of the executive secretary of the Mississippi Citizens Councils who told Homer Bigart of the *New York Herald Tribune:* "Sir, this is not the United States. This is Sunflower County, Mississippi"? In a pamphlet *M Is for Mississippi and Murder,* the organization reported three racial murders as occurring between May 7 and August 28, 1955. On May 7 the Reverend George W. Lee of Belzoni was killed by shotgun blasts from a passing car. Lee was the first black to register to vote in Humphreys County, and he had urged others also to register. No charges were brought in this case, and the sheriff reportedly stated that lead pellets in Lee's jaw and neck could have come from fillings in his teeth. On August 13 Lamar Smith was shot dead in front of the Brookhaven courthouse. Three suspects were arrested, but a grand jury failed to indict. On August 28 Emmett Louis Till, fourteen, was kidnapped, beaten, shot, and thrown into the Talla-hatchie River. Till was alleged to have "wolf-whistled" at a white woman. Two white men charged with Till's murder, J. W. Milam and Roy Bryant, were acquitted by an all-white jury. The sheriff of Tallahatchie County announced that the body taken from the river was not that of Till but represented an NAACP plot. In a postscript added to the second printing of the pamphlet, the NAACP reported the November 25, 1955, shooting of Gus Courts, Belzoni NAACP branch president, and the murder on December 3 of Clinton Melton by a white customer of the gasoline station where Melton worked. The Melton killing occurred in Glendora, eight miles from the site of the Till trial.[38]

The 1950s episode of racial violence that probably drew more national and world attention than any other occurred in Little Rock, Arkansas.

The context for the violence was the decision of Arkansas governor Orval Faubus to place National Guard troops around Central High School in order to prevent compliance with desegregation orders. On September 4, 1957, armed troops and a howling mob were pitted against a few black schoolchildren who sought to enter the high school.

A key figure in the Little Rock situation was Daisy Bates, elected in 1952 as president of the State Conference of NAACP branches. By the 1950s Bates already had a proven record of activity for black rights. As publisher with her husband of the *State Press,* a black weekly newspaper, Bates during World War II had spoken out against police brutality. Police had responded with increasing brutality to the presence of black soldiers assigned to nearby Camp Robinson. When on March 2, 1942, Little Rock police cold-bloodedly shot a black soldier, the *State Press* described the incident as "one of the most bestial murders in the annals of Little Rock." Later on, in 1946, Mrs. Bates was also outspoken in criticizing a judge who sentenced three pickets to a year's imprisonment for, supposedly, violating an Arkansas "right to work" law. Bates had the background to give leadership to Arkansas blacks in seeking to effect desegregation.

Orval Faubus directly contributed to creating a public atmosphere of mass hysteria by employing the guardsmen to block court-ordered desegregation and by his comments in a radio speech that "blood would run in the streets of Little Rock" if blacks sought to enter Central High School. On September 3 the black students were unable to attend the high school, but that same day federal judge Ronald N. Davies ordered the Little Rock school board to put its desegregation plan into immediate operation. The students would seek admission to Central High School the following day. One of the parents, facing this situation, recalled an earlier Little Rock, the city of 1927. Birdie Eckford told Daisy Bates:

> I am frightened. Not for myself but for the children. When I was a little girl, my mother and I saw a lynch mob dragging the body of a Negro man through the streets of Little Rock. We were told to get off the streets. We ran. And by cutting through side streets and alleys, we managed to make it to the home of a friend. But we were close enough to hear the screams of the mob, close enough to smell the sickening odor of burning flesh. And, Mrs. Bates, they took the pews from Bethel Church to make the fire. They burned the body of this Negro man right at the edge of the Negro business section.

Bates tried to be reassuring. She believed it was inconceivable that troops would let a mob attack children. But she was wrong. The mob would be allowed to terrorize blacks who attempted to enter Central High School.

Eight of the children approached Central High School escorted by four clergymen, two of them white and two black. As they drew near the school, the children were pushed and shoved. A National Guard captain informed the group that on orders of Governor Faubus he could not allow them through the guard line. Following this confrontation, Mrs. Bates and the students proceeded to the offices of the United States attorney and the FBI, where they reported what had occurred. In her account of the Little Rock episode, published in 1962, Bates wrote: "I might add here that during the school year the FBI interviewed hundreds of persons. Many of those who had participated in the mob could easily have been identified from photographs taken in front of the school. Yet no action was taken against anyone by the office of the United States Attorney, Osro Cobb, or the Department of Justice."[39] In view of what has since come to light concerning the view of the civil rights movement taken by the FBI, this inaction is not difficult to explain.

One of the nine children, Elizabeth Eckford, had not been informed of where and when the group seeking entrance to Central High School would assemble. She had proceeded to the school unescorted. What happened there was told to Mrs. Bates by Benjamin Fine, education reporter for the *New York Times*. It was a classic manifestation of the frenzied racial hatred that is a component of American society.

I was standing [wrote Fine] in front of the school that day. Suddenly there was a shout—"They're here! The niggers are coming!" I saw a sweet little girl who looked about fifteen, walking alone. She tried several times to pass through the guards. The last time she tried, they put their bayonets in front of her. When they did this she became panicky. For a moment she just stood there trembling. Then she seemed to calm down and started walking toward the bus stop with the mob baying at her heels like a pack of hounds. The women were shouting, "Get her! Lynch her!" The men were yelling, "Go home you bastard of a black bitch!" She finally made it to the bus stop and sat down on the bench. I sat down beside her and said, "I'm a reporter from the *New York Times*, may I have your name?" She just sat there, her head down. Tears were streaming down her cheeks from under her sunglasses.... There must have been five hundred around us by this time. I vaguely remember someone hollering, "Get a rope and drag her over to this tree." Suddenly I saw a white-haired, kind-faced woman fighting her way through the mob. She looked at Elizabeth, and then screamed at the mob, "Leave this child alone! Why are you tormenting her? Six months from now you will hang your heads in shame." The mob shouted, "Another nigger-lover. Get out of here!" The woman, who I found out later was Mrs. Grace Lorch, professor at Philander Smith College, turned to me and said, "We have to do something. Let's try to get a cab." We took Elizabeth across the street to the drugstore. I remained on the sidewalk with Elizabeth while Mrs. Lorch tried to enter the drugstore to call a cab. But the hoodlums slammed the door in her face and wouldn't let her in. She pleaded with them to call a cab for the child. They closed in on her saying, "Get out of here, you bitch!" Just then the city bus came. Mrs. Lorch and Elizabeth got on. Elizabeth must have been in a state of shock. She never uttered a word. When the bus pulled away, the mob closed in around me. "We saw you put your arm around that little bitch. Now it's your turn." A drab, middle-aged woman said viciously, "Grab him and kick him in the balls!" A girl I had seen hustling in one of the local bars screamed, "A dirty New York Jew! Get him!" A man asked me, "Are you a Jew?" I said, "Yes." He then said to the mob, "Let him be! We'll take care of him later."[40]

Elizabeth Eckford, too, remembered the details of that encounter. She recalled the guardsmen looking meanly at her and being frightened and not knowing what to do and seeing the mob move toward her. She told Mrs. Bates: "I tried to see a friendly face somewhere in the mob— someone who maybe would help. I looked into the face of an old woman and it seemed a kind face, but when I looked at her again, she spat on me. They came close, shouting, 'No nigger bitch is going to get in our school. Get out of here.' " Elizabeth Eckford made her way to a bench at the bus stop where Benjamin Fine and Grace Lorch came over to assist her.[41]

Following this day's events Judge Davies ordered that Faubus cease interfering with the desegregation of Central High School. On September 23, with Little Rock police assigned to control the mob, the nine students entered the school. The mob had been drawn away from the entrance used by the students. Several black newspaper reporters and photographers approached the grounds, and the mob, eager for any black victims, turned to assault the representatives of the press. White journalists also came under attack, with every *Life* staff member present being beaten. The underlying attitudes of the police were conveyed when the three men from *Life* were arrested for inciting a riot. At approximately eleven-thirty the police also decided that they could not hold back the mob and ordered that the black students be removed from the school. Mrs. Bates announced that the students would remain away from Central High until President Eisenhower guaranteed them protection.[42]

The violence at Central High spread to various parts of the city, and residents of Little Rock witnessed what Bates described as "a savage rebirth of passion and racial hatred that had lain dormant since the Reconstruction days." Two black women were pulled from their car and beaten as were two black men driving in a truck near the high school. Harry Ashmore, editor of the *Arkansas Gazette,* summed up the situation when contacted by the Justice Department: "I'll give it to you in one sentence. The police have been routed, the mob is in the streets and we're close to a reign of terror."[43]

The next day President Eisenhower finally did move, taking action to federalize the Arkansas National Guard and directing the secretary of defense to send in additional regular troops as necessary.

Only a few days earlier Roy Wilkins had privately expressed his sharp dissatisfaction with Eisenhower's equivocal role in the crisis. He wrote to Congressman Adam Clayton Powell: "I have great difficulty in speaking calmly about the role of President Eisenhower in this whole mess. He has been absolutely and thoroughly disappointing and disillusioning from beginning to end.... The situation has hardened not because the NAACP is insisting on obedience to the Supreme Court, but because the White House has abandoned its own Supreme Court and has abdicated leadership in a great moral crisis."[44] But Eisenhower, faced with the prospect of surrender to Faubus and the mob, finally acted to enforce the court-ordered desegregation.

It should be pointed out that a basic factor in the situation was the determination and militancy of a black community that would not be intimidated by the hoodlums gathered in front of Central High. What one black man said to Mrs. Bates when informed of Eisenhower's proclamation authorizing use of federal troops expresses the mood: "Proclamation be damned! We've had the Constitution since 1789 and I doubt whether those goons who took over our town yesterday can read. Last night they came into our neighborhood and rocked our houses, breaking windows and all that. We've taken a lot because we didn't want to hurt the chances of Negro kids, but I doubt whether the Negroes are going to take much more without fighting back. I think I'll take the rest of the day off and check my shotgun and make sure it's in working condition."[45] It was such determination, the fact that the black community rejected any policy of appeasing the mob, that led to federal intervention.

The Eisenhower administration sent troops in 1957, but President Eisenhower continued his silence on the question of the rightness of desegregation, and administration officials, following the September events, took only such action as was clearly politically necessary. In July 1959 Bates informed the United States attorney of several episodes of fire bombing, rock throwing, and cross burning involving the Bates home, further noting that local law enforcement officials had apprehended none of the perpetrators of these acts and asking for federal protection "in Little Rock, United States of America." Two days later Bates was informed by Assistant Attorney General W. Wilson White that there was no basis for federal jurisdiction concerning the criminal acts Bates described. During August 1959 state police undertook harassment of the guards protecting the Bates home, and Mrs. Bates wired President Eisenhower, appealing for "the basic protection that will give us the freedom from fear to which citizens of our free American society are entitled." Four days later Mrs. Bates was informed by Eisenhower's deputy assistant, Gerald D. Morgan, that although the matter seemed to be within local jurisdiction Mrs. Bates's complaint would receive "prompt and appropriate consideration" from the Justice Department. Bates later reported: "No action was forthcoming from Washington."[46]

A critical dimension of the Little Rock struggle was its international scope, its impact upon millions in other nations who could not fail to observe the contradiction between vast American world power and the refusal to uphold elementary democratic rights at home. A clear sense of the world impact registered by the Arkansas desegregation battle was conveyed to the historian John Hope Franklin as he participated, during August and September 1958, in the Seminar in American Studies at Salzburg. The European members of the seminar, coming from fifteen countries, did not articulate the views of the more severe critics of American policies; Franklin noted that "there was no acrimonious or bitter condemnation of American practices." But still, in the aftermath of Little Rock, the questions and comments during the seminar on "Races and Minorities in American Life" were rather pointed. A French participant demolished the argument that American federalism was a substantial impediment blocking national action for civil rights. "You have," he said, "big government in Washington that is growing more powerful all the time. Your government builds houses, finances highway construction, produces and sells electricity. It is difficult for me to accept any argument based on federalism and states' rights. It appears to the outsider that federalism stands in the way of nothing that the national government actually wants to do; but it is always used as an excuse for the national government's not protecting the rights of Negroes." Quite succinctly, this gentleman had summed up the hypocrisy at the core of the official American attitude toward civil rights. To Franklin's observation that in Little Rock troops had been called out when law and order broke down, the members of the seminar responded that this had happened only after the black children had been barred from the high school and only after federal authority had been openly flouted. Then a Yugoslav member of the seminar noted another critical inconsistency in the American posture. "It is all very strange to me," he observed:

The leader of the free world can dispatch at a moment's notice thousands of troops to Lebanon to prevent the overthrow of the government there. Yet, it has great difficulty in protecting the constitutional rights of eight or nine Negro children who seek an education. When troops were reluctantly and finally dispatched to Little Rock, the howls of objection and resentment could be heard around the world. Why this willingness, even anxiety, of Americans to send troops to protect the rights of peoples in remote places and, at the same time, this loathing to use force to protect the rights of its own citizens?

In 1958 Franklin told the Catholic Interracial Council of New York that "there was no ready answer" to the question posed by the Yugoslav.[47]

The international context of the Little Rock confrontation was also plainly referred to by President Eisenhower in his address explaining his executive order with regard to the use of federal troops. He did not refer to the harm inflicted upon the Little Rock schoolchildren, but he was much concerned with the harm to American world power and prestige. He declared: "At a time when we face grave situations abroad because of the hatred that communism bears toward a system of government based on human rights, it would be difficult to exaggerate the harm that is being done the prestige and the influence, and indeed to the safety, of our nation and the world. Our enemies are gloating over this incident and using it everywhere to misrepresent our whole nation. We are portrayed as a violator of those standards of conduct which the peoples of the world united to proclaim in the Charter of the United Nations." At the conclusion of his speech he expressed the hope that resistance to the federal court orders would cease and that the image of the United States as the land of justice and liberty would be restored.[48]

In the early 1950s the international context of the American racial question was the basis of an appeal to the United Nations. The appeal, bearing the explosive title *We Charge Genocide,* constituted a searing, documented indictment of racial oppression.[49] Edited by William L. Patterson of the Communist-oriented Civil Rights Congress, *We Charge Genocide* articulated the views of those who would indeed seize upon United States claims to world moral leadership as an opportunity to expose before an attentive world audience the full dimensions of racial oppression in the United States.[50] The kernel of the indictment was stated in the subtitle, *The Historical Petition to the United Nations for Relief from a Crime of the United States Government against the Negro People.* The charge was presented to the United Nations and released to the public media in 1951, at a time when rampant McCarthyism was already seriously hampering the capacity of the American Left to participate in the political process. But it was not possible to altogether stifle the voice of the Left, although efforts were made to block presentation of the appeal to the United Nations. Handed over simultaneously by Patterson, to the fifth session of the General Assembly meeting at the Palais Chaillot in Paris, and by a delegation led by Paul Robeson to the office of the secretary general in New York, the *Charge* was part of the process that increasingly focused world opinion on the facts of American racial violence.[51] It also represents a benchmark, a summing up of the extent and intensity of racism as it existed in this country from the mid-1940s onward. In the fierce anti-Communist atmosphere of the times the auspices of *We Charge Genocide* might be questioned, but the facts itemized here were stubborn realities that could not be wished away by smear rhetoric.

The events of 1951 underscored the new significance that now adhered to racial violence in American society and supported the allegation that more was involved here than individual acts of wrongdoing. Along with the murder of the Moores and the executions of Willie McGee and the Martinsville Seven, 1951 was also marked by appalling incidents of violence against blacks in a Florida jail and in the Chicago suburb of Cicero. In Florida, in what became known as the Groveland case two black prisoners, charged with raping a white girl, were shot by Lake County sheriff Willis McCall when he transported the handcuffed men back to the town of Tavares for a new trial. One prisoner, Samuel Shepherd, was killed, and another, Walter Irvin, was critically wounded. Two years earlier, in 1949, the Florida NAACP had urged the governor not to place the prisoners in the custody of Lake County officers but rather to place them under special guard, a recommendation ignored by the authorities. In response to this shooting, circuit court judge Truman Futch found that the sheriff had acted "in line of duty," and so the case was closed. It quickly became apparent, however, that this case had an international aspect. The representative of the Commission of the Churches on International Affairs, O. Frederick Nolde, cabled the Florida governor that the episode "has serious adverse impact on public opinion reflected at the Paris session of the United Nations Assembly." Walter White of the NAACP stressed the world implications of the matter when early in December he spoke to a large NAACP public meeting in West Palm Beach. White joined comments about the fundamental integrity of American society, a reference to our having laid "the bricks of our structure of democracy," to mention of "flaws" that must be removed to make the house indestructible. But he drew a stark picture of what the flaws could lead to. White declared: "You wipe out the values of all the money we are sending to foreign lands to prove to the world that we have democracy, when we have Groveland cases at home." He explained that distrust of the United States abroad was fostered by apprehensions about American racial conditions, and he pointedly remarked: "Unless the patterns of racial and religious discrimination and segregation existing in the U.S. are replaced by 'democratic fellowship' the U.S. and the Western World stand the risk of losing all Asia and Africa to the USSR."[52]

The Cicero events were a clear demonstration that the continuing problem of race violence was not merely southern in locale. In Cicero the animus of thousands of whites would be mobilized against one black family, that of war veteran Harvey E. Clark, and the local authorities were part of the problem, not its solution. One black family had rented a Cicero apartment, and a mob estimated at 6,000 persons gathered to wreck the building in which the Clarks planned to live. Five companies of Illinois national guardsmen were assigned to restore order but arrived after the riot had taken place. One eyewitness reported: "Women with babes in arms were in the crowd which was a duplicate of the familiar Southern mob scene. Teenagers made up the most aggressive vandals, forcing their way into the building where they wrecked apartments and furniture with abandon amid cheering yells from their admirers on the outside."

Cook County prosecutor John S. Boyle took the case before a grand jury, and five persons were indicted for conspiracy to incite to riot. The Cicero police chief was one of those indicted, but the others included one distributor of "Communist" literature, the NAACP attorney representing the Clark family, another attorney who represented the owner of the building, and a real estate broker involved in the rental. The rioters were to go unpunished whereas those supporting the right of equal access to housing were charged as criminals. The Chicago Council against Racial and Religious Discrimination spoke up: "The grand jury ignored the actual rioting and destruction of property. It disregarded the legal rights of people to live where they choose. It discounted the duty of public officials to maintain law and order and to protect the Constitutional rights of all persons."[53] Beyond the immediate significance of the Cicero events, what stands out is that here was a warning as to the potential that existed for large-scale urban racial violence and yet precious little was done to learn from what had happened or to deal with its sources. More might well have been done if in 1951 American public opinion had given greater consideration to the portrait of American racism outlined in *We Charge Genocide*.

The appeal was signed by ninety-four individual petitioners. Among the signers were a number of individuals prominent as officials of the Communist party, including Isadore Begun, Benjamin J. Davis, Jr., Claudia Jones, James Ford, Maude White Katz, and Pettis Perry. But the list also included persons with established records as leaders of Afro-America. Former New York City councilman Benjamin Davis was a member of the party's national board but he was also a well-known Harlem public figure. And joining Davis as signers were the Los Angeles publisher Charlotta Bass; Detroit attorney and later judge George Crockett, Jr., in 1980 elected to the United States Congress; W. E. B. Du Bois; Eslanda and Paul Robeson; the venerable leader of black women and of the Washington black community, Mary Church Terrell; and the editor of the *Cincinnati Union* and historian of the city's black community, Wendell Phillips Dabney. To be sure, spokesmen for the major national black organizations and editors of the most prominent black newspapers and magazines were not among the signers, but it is fair to say that those who petitioned the United Nations in 1951 were legitimate representatives of the more militant sections of black leadership, especially of that leadership which would not trim its sails to weather the prevailing storm of red baiting.

Some of the established black leadership, however, became particularly vocal at about this time in rejecting any allegation that racial oppression was deliberate American policy. Speaking at the 1951 UN General Assembly session, Soviet foreign minister Andrei Vishinsky had referred to the shooting of the Groveland prisoners. U.S. alternate delegate Channing H. Tobias responded that in the United States such incidents were not covered up and occurred "in defiance of the law not by order of the law." Tobias added: "We prefer not to be reminded of such offenses by a country such as Mr. Vishinsky's, which practices slave labor, deportations and political executions." Ralph Bunche was keenly aware that international concern with the American racial situation was a serious matter, noting in a talk at the American Club of Paris that racial incidents "shock and raise doubts about us among our friends and our potential friends." But, though Bunche urged that such incidents should not be explained away, he also stressed that "these undemocratic prejudices took place within an essentially democratic society where the struggle against such abuses gradually is being won." The *Pittsburgh Courier* bluntly indicated it saw nothing constructive in the petition to the UN. The paper declared that the sole reason for the petition was "to spread disunity and to foster acrimony and mutual hatred and fear." The *Courier* stressed the progress made by Afro-Americans and exclaimed: "If this is 'extermination,' then let us have more genocide; and the rest of the world will demand it, too." The newspaper's parting shot was a comment that blacks "do not intend to be catspaws for the Soviet Fifth Column."[54]

The legal basis for *We Charge Genocide* was the Genocide Convention adopted by the UN General Assembly on December 9, 1948, with the United States one of the nations voting in favor. No doubt the signatories of the appeal were not alone in seeing some relation between the convention and American racial practices, for otherwise it is impossible to explain the continued refusal of Congress to ratify the convention. There has even been the spectacle of a well-known white supremacist, Leander Perez, then director of the National States Rights Committee, testifying that the convention would create the "over-hanging threat" that American citizens might have to face an international tribunal. Taking a similar position was Alfred J. Schweppe, speaking for the Committee on Peace and Law through the United Nations of the American Bar Association, who acknowledged that acts of violence such as lynchings and race riots might be construed as genocide. The ABA committee, in opposing ratification, did not challenge the applicability of the convention to American racial practices but instead took issue with the United Nations definition of genocide. The committee report warned that "subversive elements" would encourage minorities to address their grievances to an international body. The report urged "that no part [of] the Genocide Convention shall become domestic law of the United States or of states of the United States ... which shall change in any way the division of power of Federal and State governments, shall enlarge the present constitutional jurisdiction of Congress or detract from the powers of the states of the United States." At its 1949 meeting, the ABA House of Delegates opposed ratification of the convention.[55]

In testimony before the Senate Foreign Relations Committee during early 1950 supporters of the Genocide Convention sought to calm anxieties that the UN concept of genocide could be viewed as applicable to the American racial scene. The solicitor general of the United States, Philip B. Perlman, told the committee that the American form of government was guarantee against genocide. In response to questioning from Senator Hickenlooper, Perlman stated: "We are not going to have genocide. We are not going to be condemned by other nations. We are entering into this thing, if we do, in cooperation with other nations to stamp out something that may occur abroad, but which has never occurred here and never will occur here so long as we have our form of government." Toward the end of his testimony Perlman assured the senators: "Genocide has never existed in this country." Concurring in this opinion was Deputy Undersecretary of State Dean Rusk, who informed the senators that "genocide, as defined in this convention, has never occurred in the United States and is not likely to occur here in the future." Rusk also set the Genocide Convention within the framework of the developing cold war, announcing that the document was a major element in the struggle to mobilize spiritual and moral resources on the side of the forces of the free world. As for the applicability of the convention to specific racial crimes within the United States, Perlman testified that the convention was not to be understood as relating to racial riots or lynching.[56]

The question opened up by Dean Rusk, the role of the Genocide Convention in the cold war, was pursued by others in the course of the 1950 hearings. The document was discussed on its merits but also in the expedient terms of what ratification or nonratification would do to the United States position in the world struggle. In an exchange with Frank Goldman of the B'nai B'rith, Senator Lodge suggested that failure to ratify would seriously damage the American cold war stance, an opinion Goldman agreed with. In his appearance before the committee, Stanley Ruttenberg, director of the CIO's Educational Department, emphasized that the definition of genocide could now be applied to the Soviet prison camp system. Ratification was also endorsed by a spokesman for the American Committee for the Investigation of the Katyn Massacre, who believed the convention would assist efforts to prove that the Soviets had murdered Polish officers.[57] Clearly, as to ratification two considerations were weighed against each other: the possible utility of the genocide concept as a means of putting the Soviet Union on the defensive against the chance that sections of the world community would accuse the United States of genocide.

The American Bar Association sought to convince the senators, apparently successfully, that the Genocide Convention was of doubtful use as a weapon in the cold war. George Finch, of the ABA's Special Committee on Peace and Law through United Nations, informed the subcommittee of the nonapplicability of the convention's provisions to acts committed by "totalitarian governments behind the iron curtain." The catch was that the convention's definition of genocide embraced only acts against national, ethnic, racial, or religious groups. The concept of genocide could not be applied to political crimes. Finch went on to point out that it was already granted that genocide had never occurred in the United States "and it is hoped never will be." Since it was true that the convention could not be applied to the internal practices of Communist regimes, Finch concluded, "no reason remains why the Senate should run the risk of having the convention interpreted, if not by us then by one or more of the other contracting powers, as being applicable to domestic questions in the United States." Finch made clear which domestic questions he had in mind when he asked pointedly: "Can it be successfully denied that segregation laws are susceptible of being denounced as causing mental harm to all members of the group against which such laws discriminate?.... Can there be any reasonable doubt that if Congress fails to enact the civil rights laws now being urged upon it and if this convention is ratified as submitted, members of the affected groups will be in a position to seek legal relief on the ground that this so-called Genocide Convention has superseded all obnoxious State legislation?" It is noteworthy that when a leader of the ABA referred to civil rights legislation it was not to urge its passage but to offer the very existence of the issue as a reason for blocking the convention.[58]

Perhaps because the relevance of the Genocide Convention to the American racial situation had already become a sensitive issue, black support for ratification was expressed without linking the convention to racial matters. The senators were informed of a resolution, adopted in early 1948, by the board of directors of the NAACP, which had urged the UN "to immediately adopt a genocide treaty to outlaw mass destruction of national, racial and religious groups." A resolution of support was also submitted by the National Association of Negro Business and Professional Women's Clubs.[59] The sole black witness to appear at the hearings was Eunice Carter, representing the National Council of Negro Women. Mrs. Carter's testimony is interesting in that she first separated the American racial situation from the Genocide Convention and then made some connection. At the very beginning of her testimony, Carter declared: "The situation of the Negro people in this country is in no way involved. The lynching of an individual or of several individuals has no relation to the extinction of masses of peoples because of race, religion, or political belief." But then Carter reminded the senators that blacks were members of a minority. "The victims of genocide," she stated, "are minorities. There is no safety for any minority anywhere so long as their extinction goes unchecked and unpunished."[60] Although not explicitly expressed, the suggestion was present that although current American practices did not fall within the meaning of genocide, black Americans in the future might find protection by recourse to the Genocide Convention.

Against this background of congressional debate in which racial anxieties were mingled with considerations of foreign policy expediency, the Civil Rights Congress in 1951 asserted the relevance of the convention to existing American practices regarding blacks. During January 1951 the convention had entered into force, twenty member nations of the UN having ratified this document in accord with Article XII. The We Charge Genocide petition therefore appeared within a context in which the Genocide Convention had become a valid component of international law, despite the American failure to ratify. The petition charged the United States government with violation of practically every provision of the convention. A basic component of the crime as viewed by the petitioners was the failure to enforce basic constitutional guarantees. This failure, it was contended, "has become a legal authorization of genocide. It is the enabling act for genocide." The lack of enforcement served notice that blacks had no rights that would be protected by the United States government. The argument that the federal government could not be held accountable for crimes committed within political subdivisions was flatly rejected. "A sovereign state," We Charge Genocide asserted, "must accept responsibility for international crimes committed within its confines. Genocide is such a crime."[61]

In enumerating the articles of the Genocide Convention violated by the American government, the petitioners focused upon Articles II through IX. Article II was the kernel of the convention, containing the definition of genocide, which made clear that a central issue was that of intent and that genocide was not limited to the extermination of an entire national, ethnic, racial, or religious group. The article read: "In the present convention, genocide means any of the following acts committed with intent to destroy, in whole or in part, a national, ethnic, racial or religious group, as such: (a) Killing members of the group; (b) Causing serious bodily or mental harm to members of the group; (c) Deliberately inflicting on the group conditions of life calculated to bring about its physical destruction in whole or in part; (d) Imposing measures intended to prevent births within the group; (e) Forcibly transferring children of the group to another group." The petitioners contended that the United States government, through actions "both by individuals and state and federal officials," had violated clauses *a, b,* and *c* of Article II. The signers of the appeal further charged that government officials in all three branches, executive, judicial, and legislative, were guilty of committing the crimes defined by Article III, the crimes of genocide, conspiracy to commit genocide, direct and public incitement to commit genocide, attempt to commit genocide, and complicity in genocide. After noting Article IV, which provides that persons committing the acts specified in Article III shall be punished, whether they are private citizens or public officials, *We Charge Genocide* declared that the United States government was guilty of violating Article V, which specified that the signatories of the convention would enact appropriate legislation giving effect to the Genocide Convention's provisions and establishing effective penalties. Significant was the contention that the government was pledged to enact such legislation, regardless of whether or not the document was ratified. But the government had not sought the enactment of legislation implementing the provisions of the convention, and the petitioners saw the failure to seek the legislation as double-dealing. "Failure," it was alleged, "could only be interpreted as a desire for the credit of signing the Convention without the obligation of observing it or the onus of opposing it."[62] If there were any such desire, *We Charge Genocide* was clearly designed as a means of highlighting the contradiction inherent in the American position: signing the convention but failing to ratify or to seek laws implementing its provisions. It was further alleged that the United States government had not only failed to enact appropriate new legislation but had also not enforced the civil rights guarantees provided by the Fourteenth and Fifteenth amendments. "The Supreme Court of the United States," *We Charge Genocide* observed, "has in fact denied the language, purpose and intent of these Amendments by tortuous constructions holding that the authority of the Federal Government cannot protect the rights of the Negro people if those rights are violated by individuals and not by the actions of one of the several states."[63]

The evidence contained in the petition was arranged chronologically, under the various components of genocide as defined in the convention. This was indeed a chilling record and, especially taken all together, the itemization refuted claims that racial violence was something other than an institutionalized practice of American society. The document covered incidents between 1945 and 1951, when *We Charge Genocide* was presented to the United Nations. The listing of racial murders, extraordinary by itself, was accompanied by the reminder that historically many episodes of violence against blacks have gone unrecorded. The killings occurred in a variety of circumstances, many of them resulting from encounters between victim and police officers. Several of those murdered were war veterans. Many of the deaths resulted from violence directed against individuals, but others occurred in the context of assault upon groups of blacks; a highlight of 1946 was the attack by hundreds of national guardsmen and local police upon the black community of Columbia, Tennessee, followed by the killing of two blacks while in police custody. In almost all the episodes cited, the perpetrators of violence had gone unpunished, as authorities refused to investigate, grand juries refused to indict, or juries acquitted those charged with killing blacks. Of course, in those incidents in which blacks were executed on dubious charges, the state itself was the killer.[64]

That a serious group of American citizens was prepared to charge its own government with the offense of genocide was indeed a remarkable development. That this had happened was a fact not to be forgotten, either by militant partisans of black rights or by those who feared the convention could be used as a weapon against American racist practices.[65] When a subcommittee of the Senate Foreign Relations Committee, in 1971, again held hearings on the still unratified convention the senators were reminded of *We Charge Genocide*. The reminder was provided by Eberhard Deutsch, representing the American Bar Association. Deutsch informed the senators that reservations proposed for inclusion with ratification would not prevent action against American institutions for the genocidal crimes itemized in *We Charge Genocide*. One of the proposed reservations would construe the words "mental harm" to mean permanent impairment of faculties, but Deutsch informed the committee that in *Brown* v. *Board of Education* the Supreme Court had ruled that racial segregation of black pupils fostered feelings of inferiority as to community status "that may affect their hearts and minds in a way unlikely ever to be undone." Because one of the charges leveled by *We Charge Genocide* was that racial oppression inflicted "extreme mental harm" upon blacks, it was doubtful, viewing the matter in the context of the *Brown* case, that the reservation had much meaning.[66] Reference to *We Charge Genocide* was also made by another representative of the American Bar Association, Alfred J. Schweppe, who was one of those who had opposed ratification in 1950. Schweppe focused on the fact that nobody had raised the charge of genocide against the Soviet Union but that the United States had indeed been so charged. Schweppe observed: "Here is a book which charged the United States with genocide against the Negro people, and they take it seriously, if you take the opportunity to read this book. They claim that all of the things that the United States has done to the Negro people in one form or another are genocide within the meaning of this convention, and it is on file in the United Nations." Schweppe did not know what the UN would do with the petition, but it was clear that "we are going to be charged with all kinds of genocide but the Communist countries are not."[67]

We Charge Genocide spotlighted a dilemma in which the United States government found itself. Ratification of the Genocide Convention might legitimize international scrutiny of American racism, but failure to ratify still did not prevent the raising of the genocide issue, and the very failure to ratify could be viewed as giving credence to the allegation. Until February 1986, when the convention finally was ratified, the dilemma would be dealt with by three administrations, those of Truman, Nixon, and Carter, who went on record for ratification while Congress refused to act.[68] The federal government would strike an ambiguous posture on this matter, and in the absence of ratification only the petitioners of We Charge Genocide would formally arraign the United States before the United Nations. The UN was not about to act on a complaint made against one of the great world powers when that power had yet to ratify the convention upon which the complaint was based. Probably such a nongovernmental charge had little chance ever of being taken up by the United Nations.

SIXTEEN

The Emergence of Dr. King

W*e Charge Genocide* was presented to the United Nations at a time when in the United States, traumatized by McCarthyism and cold war fears, the fight for black freedom was thrown on the defensive, gradualism seemingly being the strategy espoused by key segments of black leadership. But in the aftermath of *Brown v. Board of Education* the freedom struggle was to take on the character of an offensive. The question of violence presented itself no longer merely as the issue of crimes against an oppressed, long-suffering people but now as the issue of the means employed by racists to frustrate blacks as they moved en masse through constitutional, peaceful means to secure their rights. The overwhelming contrast would be drawn between the sadism of southern police with their cattle prods, clubs, and fire hoses and the determination of blacks who were willing to endure enormous sacrifices in order to attain their rights. Whatever ultimate judgment is made of the nonviolent strategy of the 1950s and 1960s civil rights movement, it would be a gross error to underestimate the power of that contrast to mobilize national and world public opinion. *We Charge Genocide* presented the facts of racial violence, but it could not effectively focus world pressure; the visible, massive challenge to segregation initiated in the midfifties, on the other hand, compelled millions throughout the world to drop the posture of indifference and to choose sides between the oppressors and those struggling to be rid of segregation and discrimination. It was now to be made clear, through a movement of remarkable scope and militancy, that the racial status quo could no longer continue in the United States.

The prime articulator of this nonviolent movement was, of course, Martin Luther King, Jr. Much has been written about King's career and thought, but it is still true that his life and his place in history have as yet been inadequately studied. There are only two full-length scholarly biographies, and collections of his speeches or letters are yet to appear. The other side of the coin has been the fashionable tendency to denigrate

428

King as too conservative, too conciliatory to the Kennedy and Johnson administrations, too inclined to seek the plaudits of the respectable, too comfortable with the black bourgeoisie, and as fundamentally unwilling to lead a genuinely militant mass struggle against racism. To a considerable extent, King's ideological position within the civil rights movement was to be most seriously threatened from the "left," by those in the Student Nonviolent Coordinating Committee who mocked him as "de Lawd," by Stokely Carmichael who in 1966 sought to raise "Black Power" as the counter to King's nonviolent direct action, by those who saw him as a representative of a basically conservative black middle class that desired no more than access to all of the trappings of bourgeois society. It is now close to twenty years since the assassination of Martin Luther King, and the reality of large-scale demonstrative activity for black rights is now seldom encountered, at least on the national level. The mass movement of the 1960s has passed into history, and black leadership is suspended between the slogans of the past and whatever slogans will in the future stir the black masses in response to worsening economic crisis, the decay of urban services, continuing school segregation, and the calculated meanness of the Reagan legislative program. From this vantage point it is in order to take another view of King's leadership, to evaluate its sources and impact, taking into account the obstacles it had to reckon with, the realities of the mid-1950s out of which it came.

Experience with the culture of racial violence had deep roots in the history of the King family. Martin Luther King, Sr., "Daddy" King as he was later to be known, recalled the days of his Stockbridge, Georgia, boyhood when, if a dispute between a white and a black occurred, "a man's color was the deciding factor, and a Negro who argued too much or too often was leaning toward his own death." He recalled also witnessing the lynching of a black man by a group of whites infuriated at the sight of the black man counting his pay. King recalls candidly what the event had led him to understand, "that I'd carry a hatred in me for white people until the day I died. I would hate every one of them and fight them day and night, trying my best to destroy any of them I had a chance to." His reaction was reinforced by an experience with a local millowner who beat him when he refused an order to fetch a bucket of water. Martin Luther King, Jr.'s maternal grandfather, the Reverend A. D. Williams, had lived through the violence of the 1906 Atlanta riot.[1]

In the midst of an America that was still emerging from the period of McCarthyism, Martin Luther King, Jr., was able to establish a basis upon which a mass movement against segregation could be built. On the one hand, in the America of 1955 such a movement could not affirm that it drew its perspective from Marxian ideology; on the other, the method of Gandhian civil disobedience, as embodied in the Congress of Racial Equality (CORE), seemed appropriate only for an activist elite. It is claimed often enough that King was not an original thinker, but the fact remains that it was King who breathed life into the nonviolent strategy as a concept that became the focus of mass action. Fusing Gandhian civil disobedience and the American democratic tradition, King found firm ground from which to project the view that the civil rights struggle rested upon the most basic ideas of humanism. From the beginning King's leadership was radical in that it called for an interracial mass movement, recognizing the need for a coalition with other movements for social change. It is pointless to argue that the forms of activity urged by King may not have always been models of tactical perfection, false to claim that his leadership essentially represented a brake upon black militancy. Effective mass movements in history do not simply generate themselves; the role of the individual in history is to crystallize the tendencies inherent in an era, to understand the unspoken desires of people, and to articulate them in a context where rhetoric leads to action. More than any other leader of Afro-Americans in modern history, Martin Luther King, Jr., was the mass leader who succeeded in moving people from inactivity and quiet rage to overt action against the system of segregation. Out of incoherent anger at the evils of racism he was able to generate motion geared to realizing specific objectives. As Herbert Aptheker has observed, "as Du Bois picked up the torch from the hands of Douglass, so it seems likely that future historians will conclude that King has carried forward the torch from Du Bois."[2]

David Lewis is probably correct when he writes that King was not an original philosopher, but he is mistaken in the contention that his intelligence was "essentially derivative."[3] Of course, in a sense all knowledge is derivative in that it builds upon what has already been learned, but it is also true that King, as a public leader, as philosopher-activist, was something more than a communicator of concepts formulated by others. Lewis writes that King was "capable of occasional insights bordering upon genius," but Lerone Bennett, this author believes, has more accurately described King's role. " 'Tracked down' and 'chosen' by the times," Bennett writes, "King transcended the occasion, changing the times and transforming a diffuse uprising into a mass movement with passion and purpose. As a catalytic agent, he created a revolutionary point of departure, a new tissue of aspirations and demands. As a magnet and exemplar-myth, as an invitation to a new way of life, King attracted and released the energies of men and women of varying viewpoints." Among other contributions, King solved what Bennett describes as a "technical problem," in actuality a basic problem of tactics. Blacks could not stage an open revolt, for to do so in the face of entrenched racism would be suicidal. King found the means to solve the problem by "clothing a national resistance movement in the disarmingly appealing garb of love, forgiveness, and *passive* resistance."[4]

The editors of a documentary history of black protest thought note that King's outlook "was closely akin to, and largely derived from, that of the founders of CORE."[5] Clearly, the intellectual linkage between the Gandhian, civil disobedient tradition of CORE and King's nonviolence is there, but if read in the context of events there is also a departure from what had come before. King was the charismatic leader with a direct relationship to a communitywide mass movement, which is something different from being a participant in a movement whose effort centers around its trained cadres. That distinction is apparent in a piece King wrote for a CORE publication in 1956. The piece is an account of a movement in which thousands are participating rather than an affirmation of personal witness or an analysis of the problems faced by leadership. Without dwelling on his leadership role, King slips into a new position, that of leader of mass nonviolent protest. Writing at one point of "we Southern Negroes," he makes it clear that for him there is to be a fusing of the leader with the people for whom he speaks.

Martin Luther King's ability to communicate to the white community has often been noted, but this 1956 article helps to explain what is frequently underestimated, his impact upon blacks. In one brief written statement King outlined many of the themes that gripped black Americans. To begin with, he stressed the question of self-respect and dignity. Whites had come to believe that the black person "was incapable of advancing beyond a fixed position and would therefore be happier if encouraged not to attempt the impossible." Under the pressure of white supremacy, "through forced separation from our African culture, through slavery, poverty, and deprivation," many blacks had indeed lost self-respect. But that loss was not absolute, and King asserted that the black masses of the South had begun to reevaluate themselves and had discovered "that we had never really smothered our self-respect and that we could not be at one with ourselves without asserting it." He pointed to a new reality, "the Negro's new and courageous thinking and his ever-increasing readiness to organize and to act," as the basis of a sense of dignity that replaced self-pity. King was fully conscious of the crucial significance of dignity for blacks. That dignity was to be based on action, on clear evidence that existing racial stereotypes about blacks were false.

Blacks had come to share the image of themselves in which they were seen as incapable of consistently joining together for common purposes. But the growing nonviolent movement was shattering that stereotype. The Montgomery bus boycott, lasting 382 days, had demonstrated that blacks could assert their dignity and hold to the assertion. "Montgomery has broken the spell," he wrote.

An oppressed people requires a sense that it can effectively struggle against oppression and that it can win. King now presented these propositions as fact. He recalled that only a few years earlier young blacks had commonly said, "I'd rather be a lamp post in Harlem than Governor of Alabama." Now, according to King, in churches, schools, pool rooms, restaurants, and homes, the word was, "Brother, stay here and fight nonviolently. Cause if you don't let them make you mad, you can win." Experience had now shown that blacks could stick together, that black leaders did not have to sell out, and that "threats and violence do not necessarily intimidate those who are sufficiently aroused and nonviolent."

Outlining a chronicle of the Montgomery bus boycott, King drew the conclusion that the Montgomery authorities, failing to realize the new determination of blacks, served as unwitting agents for social change in that "every move they have made has inadvertently increased the protest and united the black community." And not only did segregationist brutality serve to unite the black community, it also "brought a sympathy for our cause from men of good will all over the world." He noted that world interest in this antisegregation struggle appeared to rest upon the fact that "we in Montgomery have adopted the method of non-violence." King believed he had found a means for maintaining the momentum of the movement for civil rights, declaring that nonviolent resistance "permits a struggle to go on with dignity and without the need to retreat. It is a method that can absorb the violence that is inevitable in social change whenever deep-seated prejudices are challenged."

Even in his early writings about the nonviolent movement King did not view nonviolence as simply an expedient approach to social issues, noting that for him it was a question of moral principle. The principle was not an abstraction, as King explained that violence was immoral because "to seek to retaliate with violence does nothing but intensify the existence of evil and hate in the universe." There was in life a chain of hate and evil, and someone had to cut that chain. The way to do that was through love, love as a transforming power "that can lift a whole community to new horizons of fair play, good will and justice."

Already by 1956 King has set the civil rights movement in the broadest of contexts. [The crucial issue was not buses but the basis of injustice, "man's inhumanity to man." Fundamentally, King defined the struggle in moral terms, a definition that enabled him to stand on high ground, although not in itself providing an analysis of the sources of racial oppression.] As he viewed the racial problem it was clear that "the real tension is not between the Negro citizens and the white citizens of Montgomery, but it is a conflict between justice and injustice, between the forces of light and the forces of darkness." Victory in the conflict would be "a victory for goodness in its long struggle with the forces of evil." And for King the moral nature of the struggle was found not only in its objectives but also in the circumstances that in a world in which men sought to defend their values by using weapons of destruction it was "morally refreshing" to hear Montgomery blacks shout "Amen" to exhortations to pray for those opposing them.

The moral definition of the struggle sustained a willingness to sacrifice and perhaps die in pursuit of human rights. As King analyzed the southern scene in 1956 there was strong likelihood of violent response to black insistence upon rights. Violence might be expected from the traditional white supremacists "who honestly believe with one side of their minds that Negroes are depraved and disease-ridden." Such persons, King explained, feared race "mongrelization" and were convinced that racial equality was a Communist idea. The caste system, they believed, was the greatest attainment of human organization. But what had also to be taken into account was the immobilization of the southern moderates. The moderates, never fully reliable as a barrier to racial violence, now recognized that even the slow approach of gradualism had revolutionary implications. "Placing straws on a camel's back, no matter how slowly, is dangerous," King wrote. The realization of that truth had immobilized the white liberals of the South. King took issue with the argument advanced by novelist William Faulkner that "for a moment" the NAACP should stop its campaign for civil rights. Faulkner was claiming the privilege, often desired by the white moderate, of setting the timetable for the attainment of rights. King tartly noted: "It is hardly a moral act to encourage others patiently to accept injustice which he himself does not endure." Aware that in a period of change a strategy of delay "is tantamount to retreat," King made clear his rejection of the "go slow" advice: "We Southern Negroes believe that it is essential to defend the right of equality now. From this position we will not and cannot retreat."[6]

A Mississippi woman once said to the writer Louis Lomax: "Lord, Child, we colored people ain't nothing but a bundle of resentments and sufferings going somewheres to explode."[7] An explosion of those resentments took place in Montgomery, Alabama, on December 1, 1955, when Rosa Parks, riding in a bus, refused to give up her seat to a white man. Asked to explain Mrs. Parks's action, King wrote, "She had been tracked down by the *Zeitgeist*—the spirit of the times." The point is that King, as well as Rosa Parks, was moved to action by the context of events. Lerone Bennett summed up the situation: ["On May 31, 1955, the Supreme Court ordered school desegregation with 'all deliberate speed.' In the wake of this event, White Citizens Councils sprang up over the South and the atmosphere turned sultry, darkening with thunderheads of unrest. There then followed an atrocity that cauterized almost all Negroes and prepared them for more radical departures. On August 28, Emmett Till, a fourteen-year-old Chicago boy who was vacationing with relatives near Money, Mississippi, was kidnapped and lynched. The effect of all this on King, as on so many other Negroes, was explosive."[8]

[Exerting influence in propelling King forward as leader was E. D. Nixon, longtime local NAACP activist and active member of the Brotherhood of Sleeping Car Porters. It was Nixon, along with white attorney Clifford Durr, who arranged bail for Mrs. Parks, and it was Nixon who initiated action to organize a bus boycott. He also set the first meeting of what became the Montgomery Improvement Association at King's Dexter Avenue Baptist Church. Roy Wilkins writes that Nixon "was the true godfather of the boycott; through him all the years of fighting and organizing done by the Brotherhood of Sleeping Car Porters and the NAACP came to fruition in Montgomery."/ Along with the years of experience in struggle that he brought to the movement, Nixon was flexible enough to circumvent bureaucratic obstacles. When informed that the local NAACP chapter could not assume direction of the movement without authorization from the New York office, Nixon, realizing the danger of delay, turned to Montgomery's black clergymen.[9]

In many ways King had been prepared for the assumption of leadership. He had certified credentials of respectability and competence. His father, pastor of Atlanta's Ebenezer Baptist Church and active in the Baptist State Convention, was solidly rooted in the community's black middle class. The younger King had attended Morehouse College, a liberal arts institution oriented to the intellectual and professional training of upwardly aspiring black youth, and he had gone on to graduate study at Crozer Seminary and at Boston University, where in 1955 he was awarded the doctorate. Not exceptional as a student at Morehouse, he yet went on to demonstrate that he could meet the standards of "white" academia. He was unusually well equipped to carry out at a quite sophisticated level the role of the black clergyman as communications link to the white world, while maintaining his basic roots within the black church and the professional class of his native Atlanta. Following his assumption in September 1954 of the pastorate at Montgomery's Dexter Avenue Church, King demonstrated his capacity for skillful church leadership and for oratory. In King's record, prior to the Montgomery boycott, there is the potential for leadership, and it is reasonable to infer that a young, educated Baptist preacher would naturally emerge as a community spokesman. There was in King's leadership, however, a special quality of genius that enabled him to become the herald of a new period in the black struggle. He set the local features of the Montgomery boycott within a broad ideological context that was obviously relevant to the general situation of blacks in the United States. At the mass meeting held at the beginning of the Montgomery struggle, he drew upon the words of Jesus and Booker T. Washington to support the case for relying upon nonviolent methods. He gave his audience a sense of the historical import of what they were doing and appealed to the deep wellspring of a people's pride.

King's speech to the crowd in the Holt Street Baptist Church was an eloquent affirmation of the spirit he would have guide the movement. Those assembled in the church, he said, were there in pursuit of a general purpose, because they were determined to acquire their American citizenship "to the fullness of its meaning." They were there, too, because of deep belief "that democracy transformed from thin paper to thick action is the greatest form of government on earth." But there was also the specific purpose of the bus situation and the need to correct that wrong. He articulated the unwillingness of the black community to put up any longer with dehumanizing treatment on the buses, and what he said had implications that ranged beyond that particular humiliation. He declared: "We are here this evening to say to those who have mistreated us so long that we are tired—tired of being segregated and humiliated; tired of being kicked about by the brutal feet of oppression."

The unity of the movement was essential, and that unity would be based on the justice of the cause. "If we are wrong," he explained, "the Supreme Court of this nation is wrong. If we are wrong, the Constitution of the United States is wrong. If we are wrong, God Almighty is wrong." This was a movement on behalf of law and order that would exclude the methods of violence. And, in closing, he held out a place in history for those who would hold to the strategy of militant nonviolence: "If we protest courageously, and yet with dignity and Christian love, when the history books are written in the future, somebody will have to say, 'There lived a race of people, of black people, of people who had the moral courage to stand up for their rights. And thereby they injected a new meaning into the veins of history and civilization.' " His speech was related to the needs of the moment, but it also expressed a philosophy of the civil rights struggle in America.[10]

Vincent Harding has noted the messianic theme in black religion, and in this speech there is indeed something of that messianic quality. King's message was a part of the "only consistent tradition of prophetic ministry in America," which James Melvin Washington evaluates as the special contribution of the black preacher.[11] King also gave evidence of the strength of his commitment to nonviolence in his response to the bombing of his home. In this episode the question of violence or nonviolence suddenly arose as a quite concrete matter. During the evening of January 30, 1956, a bomb split the porch of the King home and blew the shattered windows into the living room. A crowd of angry blacks had quickly gathered, confronting city police, Montgomery's Mayor Gayle, and Police Commissioner Sellers. The crowd swelled in numbers, and Coretta King later recalled that white reporters were afraid to leave to file stories. The principal of Montgomery's Booker T. Washington High School accused the mayor of responsibility for having created the atmosphere in which violence occurred. King spoke to that crowd, meeting what Mrs. King considered "the first deep test of his Christian principles and his theories of non-violence." King calmly said: "I want you to go home and put down your weapons. We cannot solve this problem through retaliatory violence. We must meet violence with non-violence. . . . We must meet hate with love." Then, fully conscious of the implications of the bombing, he added: "Remember, if I am stopped, this Movement will not stop, because God is with this Movement. Go home with this glowing faith and this radiant assurance."[12]

King's action that night of holding to his nonviolent strategy in the face of urgent personal danger revealed that he had laid out a course from which he would not swerve. By example, King had put forth a guideline that could be considered applicable to other situations of violent assault upon blacks. Even as the Montgomery movement got underway King was aware that what was happening transcended a local situation. He later wrote that early in the struggle he conceived of the movement "as an act of massive noncooperation." He rarely, he noted, from that time on used the word *boycott*.[13] As early as mid-January 1956 King told a local reporter that he sought more than some improvements in the way bus segregation in Montgomery worked. "Frankly," he explained, "I am for immediate integration. Segregation is evil, and I cannot, as a minister, condone evil." King also articulated a "social gospel" view of the ministry, stating his belief that a clergyman "should attempt to improve social conditions of men at every point where they are not proper—educational, cultural and economic." The minister, he believed, "must not only change a man's soul but a man's environment, too." King saw the Montgomery struggle in a world context. "It is part of a worldwide movement," he was quoted as saying. "Look at just about any place in the world and the exploited people are rising against their exploiters. This seems to be the outstanding characteristic of our generation."[14]

It is futile to look for any one philosophical view that represented *the* formative influence in shaping King's thought. He was influenced by Gandhian notions of passive resistance, although locally any relation between Gandhianism and the boycott went without public comment until a white librarian, Juliette Morgan, compared them in a letter to the *Montgomery Advertiser.*[15] During his stay at Crozer Seminary King had heard the president of Howard University, the distinguished minister Mordecai Johnson, expound upon Gandhian principles and had read several studies of Gandhi to prepare for writing a paper about the Indian leader. Also incorporated in King's thought was the dialectical philosophy of Hegel. King rejected Hegel's veneration of the state but was impressed by the Hegelian stress on contradiction, on the struggle of opposites and the resolution of thesis and antithesis in synthesis. Marx, too, made his impact upon Martin Luther King's thought. King was moved by the Marxian critique of capitalism and was probably led by his study of Marx to an economic philosophy that was largely socialist in spirit while avoiding the American stigma of the label. Able to draw guidance and inspiration from Gandhi, Marx, and Hegel, he also was responsive to the contemporary "Christian realism" advocated by Reinhold Niebuhr. Niebuhr's recognition of the reality of evil in the world, his pragmatic pacifism that did not preclude the use of force under all conditions, was congenial to King. Niebuhr was helpful to King in making clear the inadequacy of liberal ideology that was superficial in its optimism about progress, progress divorced from serious conflict. What Niebuhr in 1932 wrote about the American racial scene is reflected in King's activity as mass leader. Niebuhr, the theologian, was quite prophetic:

It is hopeless for the Negro to expect complete emancipation from the menial social and economic position into which the white man has forced him, merely by trusting in the moral sense of the white race. It is equally hopeless to attempt emancipation through violent rebellion. . . . However large the number of individual white men who do and who will identify themselves completely with the Negro cause, the white race in American will not admit the Negro to equal rights if it is not forced to do so. Upon that point one may speak with a dogmatism which all history justifies. On the other hand, any effort at violent revolution on the part of the Negro will accentuate the animosities and prejudices of his oppressors. Since they outnumber him hopelessly, any appeal to arms must inevitably result in a terrible social catastrophe. Social ignorance and economic interest are arrayed against him. . . . The technique of non-violence will not eliminate all these perils. But it will reduce them. It will, if persisted in with the same patience and discipline attained by Mr. Gandhi and his followers, achieve a degree of justice which neither pure moral suasion nor violence could gain.[16]

Niebuhr's words offered a means of infusing the black movement with a militant spirit while at the same time accepting certain constraints upon that militancy. King's admiration of Niebuhr was apparently reciprocated by the theologian. In 1969 Niebuhr wrote: "my enthusiasm for Dr. King's nonviolence despite my anti-pacifism was due to my distinction between a pacifism designed to prove our purity and a pacifism designed to establish justice. I thought that Dr. King leading a ten percent Negro minority was a good combination of idealism and pragmatic realism."[17] If we take account, however, of all of the various ideological trends that shaped Martin Luther King's thought, the point remains that he was not exclusively defined by any one of them and that what he was about was the placing of the movement for equal rights in the mainstream of world, democratic thought. Furthermore, to the black citizens of Montgomery who sustained the boycott, the ideology that seemed most directly relevant to the nonviolent character of their struggle was the Christianity that preached human brotherhood and compassion. King wrote in *Stride toward Freedom:* "From the beginning a basic philosophy guided the movement. This guiding principle has since been referred to variously as nonviolent resistance, noncooperation, and passive resistance. But in the first days of the protest none of these expressions was mentioned; the phrase most often heard was 'Christian love.' It was the Sermon on the Mount, rather than a doctrine of passive resistance, that initially inspired the Negroes of Montgomery to dignified social action. It was Jesus of Nazareth that stirred the Negroes to protest with the creative weapon of love."[18] The blacks of Montgomery verbalized their protest in terms of a philosophy that had long been a part of their historical experience.

King was a leader of unusual breadth and vision. But what was most fundamental in the Montgomery struggle was the mass commitment of the city's black community to a confrontation with segregation. Blacks in the city showed that they could overcome division and act together, that they were willing to sacrifice and to take the step of public protest against the status quo, and that they were capable of dealing with provocation meant to terrorize them. Appropriate as it is that we study the emergence of King's leadership in Montgomery, it is also vitally necessary to understand the spirit of a people whose willingness to open an offensive against segregation was of paramount importance. As in all mass movements the individual leader and his following interacted upon each other, and in the process both were transformed. Writing retrospectively of the Montgomery movement, Lerone Bennett captured the essence of the chain reaction that had begun: "The Negro people had grown, tremendously; and so had Martin Luther King, Jr. In the days ahead King and the Negro people would grow together, reciprocally influencing each other, King contributing to the radicalization of the Negro people and the growing radicalization of the Negro people pushing King to new postures, the whole process pushing upward and outward in an ascending curve of resistance." It should be stressed, however, that King did not create a spirit of militancy among Montgomery blacks; in December 1955 the willingness of the black population to move against segregation was a "given" factor in the situation. Bennett offers the insightful comment that basic to understanding Montgomery is an understanding of the fact that "Negroes had already changed."[19] King and the Montgomery Improvement Association devised a specific set of tactics, a program of demands, and stamped a rhetoric upon the movement, but the receptivity to the call for action was not something to be predetermined by any leadership. At that level the leader in Montgomery who was closest to the mood of the community was Rosa Parks, who explained her refusal to give up a seat on the bus: "I don't really know why I wouldn't move. There was no plan at all. I was just tired from shopping. My feet hurt." Even King, who quickly assumed leadership of the movement, at the beginning underestimated the support that would be given the boycott. King later wrote that on the eve of the boycott he "still wondered whether the people had enough courage to follow through." He had seen many ventures fail, after all. That evening and upon awakening December 5 he was still speaking in terms of 60 percent cooperation as evidence of success. Mrs. King writes that before the boycott got underway its success seemed only a "slender hope." Bennett states that King and other leaders believed they would be lucky to achieve the 60 percent.[20] In fact, the boycott was almost 100 percent effective. King was to call December 5 "That Day of Days," and he outlined the phenomenon that he witnessed as he toured the city:

> A miracle had taken place. The once dormant and quiescent Negro community was now fully awake. All day long it continued. At the afternoon peak the buses were still as empty of Negro passengers as they had been in the morning. Students of Alabama State College, who usually kept the South Jackson bus crowded, were cheerfully walking or thumbing rides. Job holders had found other means of transportation or made their way on foot. While some rode in cabs or private cars, others used less conventional means. Men were seen riding mules to work, and more than one horse-drawn buggy drove the streets of Montgomery that day. During the rush hours the sidewalks were crowded with laborers and domestic workers, many of them well past middle age, trudging patiently to their jobs and home again, sometimes as much as twelve miles. They knew why they walked and the knowledge was evident in the way they carried themselves.[21]

Martin Luther King, Sr., although directly connecting his comment to a later Atlanta struggle, pointedly summed up the basic significance of carrying through a successful mass boycott. It represented a break with the pattern of merely treating segregation as a matter for endless discussion. King wrote: "Southern white folks are among the greatest talkers and story-tellers in the world. They can go on for hours, for days and weeks, just running their mouths without ever getting tired. Without a tactic to break that flow of talk, nothing would ever have been solved for the Negro in the South during the middle of this century. A boycott brought all the chatter to a halt. White business men feared boycotts more than they feared the flood."[22]

Mass support, critical in determining the success of the boycott on December 5, was also decisive in making the boycott more than a one-day protest. At the first meeting of the Montgomery Improvement Association one participant articulated the conventional wisdom that it was important the boycott not fizzle out; perhaps after having made a point the campaign should be suspended. The speaker had a seemingly logical argument: "We have already proved our united strength to the white community. If we stop now we can get anything we want from the bus company, simply because they will have the feeling that we can do it again. But if we continue, and most of the people return to the buses tomorrow or the next day, the white people will laugh at us, and we will end up getting nothing." At bottom, the argument, which depended on the belief that blacks would not be able to endure the sacrifices required for a protracted boycott, represented an underestimation of the community's determination to change conditions, but King wrote that those attending the meeting found this view so convincing "that we almost resolved to end the protest." The leaders, however, were in doubt, and so it was determined that the question of continuing the boycott would hinge on the support expressed at a mass meeting scheduled that evening at Holt Street Baptist Church. The size of the crowd at the church and its manifest enthusiasm were a clear call for continuation of the boycott. A capacity crowd had filled the church some two hours before the meeting, and several thousand people stood outside listening to the proceedings on loudspeakers. Even before he spoke King's doubts were dispelled. He wrote: "The question of calling off the protest was now academic. The enthusiasm of these thousands of people swept everything along like an onrushing tidal wave." The thousands attending that meeting unanimously adopted resolutions calling for courteous treatment of passengers, a policy of first-come, first-seated with blacks seated from the back while whites were seated from the front, and the hiring of black drivers on predominantly black routes. A great public meeting generates its own atmosphere; it can generate a sense of strength and commitment not even anticipated by those who arranged it. At Holt Street Church it became clear that Montgomery blacks could and would sustain a struggle for more than a few days. King himself apparently felt lifted by the event for he was to write: "The unity of purpose and esprit de corps of these people had been indescribably moving. No historian would ever be able fully to describe this meeting and no sociologist would ever be able to interpret it adequately." The meeting itself provided King with evidence of victory, a victory already won in that "thousands of black people stood revealed with a new sense of dignity and destiny."[23]

In the days and weeks after December 5 the momentum of the movement was carried forward by regular mass meetings, attended by thousands. Here was a mechanism through which leadership and following could interact with each other, the audience finding its feelings and desires reflected in speeches from the pulpit and King and other leaders able to gauge continually the mood of the community. The institution in which this mechanism was centered was the church, providing a traditionalist context for a new departure in social action. In Montgomery, especially, the church was an indispensable channel of communication because the city had neither a black radio station nor a widely read black newspaper. Beginning with a twice-weekly schedule, later reduced to weekly, the meetings, according to Mrs. King, attracted thousands. In *Stride toward Freedom* King noted that the crowds cut across class lines, physicians, teachers, and lawyers being among those present, but he also stressed that "the vast majority present were working people."[24] It was of course true that the boycott's success depended upon the active support of the working people. They were the section of the community who regularly used the buses in order to get to and from work and to shop. Their determination to remain off the buses and to rely upon improvised means of transportation was the bedrock of the boycott, to which was added the involvement of the middle class, of blacks who suffered generally from the indignities of segregation but who did not themselves ride the buses. In this respect King was tied to the middle class, but he also sought to transcend any class boundary. *Jet* quoted King as saying, "I am not a bus rider, but when my brothers and sisters were hurt, I felt just as they felt."[25] Exemplifying the spirit that moved the mass of boycotters were comments by two persons, one a laborer who by February 1956 was judged to have walked 335 miles to and from work and the other a domestic worker. The laborer told a reporter: "I'll keep on footing it. Walking is awfully hard on shoes [he had worn out two pairs], but riding them buses would be harder on my conscience." The domestic worker commented, "I told my boss lady not to come pick me up because this is the colored folks fight. And this thing's a blessing for me. I was suffering from arthritis and neuritis when I was riding them buses. Now that I'm walking all them things vanished."[26]

The meetings served to solidify a collective will to maintain the struggle. At one of the meetings, according to *Jet*, "a greying Negro, his voice trembling with emotion," shouted, "These white folks are pushing us too far now and I'm going to stand up to them." The response was thundered by the crowd: "You won't stand alone. We'll stand with you."[27] The meetings usually followed a standard format, highlighted by a "pep talk" given, according to King, by a different minister at each meeting. King in his weekly speeches would stress the themes of nonviolence and Christian love. Occasionally a speaker would give vent to hatred but King observed that "instances of offensive language were surprisingly few."[28]

The courage of the black community was manifested in a variety of ways. Striking was the willingness of twenty-eight individuals to come forward in a Montgomery trial of Martin Luther King and testify for the defense. More than a hundred individuals had been indicted on charges of violating a state law prohibiting conspiracy to prevent the operation of a lawful business. King's trial was held on March 19, 1956. Stella Brooks told how her husband had entered a bus, paid fare, and was ordered to get off and reboard through the back door. Seeing there was no room in the bus, Brooks told the driver he would leave and walk if the driver returned his dime. An argument followed, police were called, Brooks was shot by an officer, and he later died of the wounds. Martha Walker testified to an incident involving her blind husband who was seeking to exit from a bus. The driver slammed the door, and Walker's leg was caught. Although Mrs. Walker called out, the driver failed to stop and her husband was dragged some distance before freeing himself. Sadie Brooks testified to seeing a black passenger threatened by a driver for lacking the correct change. Another witness, Della Perkins, told the court of being called an "ugly black ape" by a driver. King later wrote of his special delight in the evidence given by Georgia Gilmore, who told of having paid the fare, of then being ordered by the driver to reboard by the back door, and of then seeing the bus go off leaving Gilmore behind. Mrs. Gilmore verbalized an essential component of the injustice involved in segregation when she turned to the judge and stated: "When they count the money, they do not know Negro money from white money."[29] In Montgomery, Alabama, in 1956, as was true generally in the South, for black persons to testify against white authority required bravery, for there was always present the possibility of economic retaliation and physical assault.

In Montgomery the commitment to nonviolence held firm, despite considerable provocation. Perhaps crucial here was the factor that the posture of nonviolence offered promise of victory, that national and international attention was being drawn to the struggle. Acts of violence were therefore plainly steps of desperation aimed at intimidating the boycott's leadership in the early stage of the movement and later at robbing the black community of the fruits of victory. The community was not deterred from nonviolence by the January 30 bombing of the King home. This incident was a response to the failure of the Montgomery power structure to induce the movement leadership to abandon the boycott. A Ku Klux Klan motorcade of November 14 was a reaction to the news that the United States Supreme Court had found unconstitutional Alabama state and local laws requiring segregation in buses. Blacks treated this provocation with contempt, keeping porch lights on and doors open and continuing to walk the streets as the Klansmen rode by. A number of incidents of violence erupted on December 28, 1956, a week after the desegregation of the city's bus system went into effect. Several buses were fired upon, a teenaged girl was beaten as she stepped from a bus, and a pregnant black woman was shot in the leg. On January 10, 1957, a wave of bombings occurred. Targets included Ralph Abernathy's home and his First Baptist Church; the home of the Reverend Robert Graetz, white minister of a black Lutheran church and board member of the Montgomery Improvement Association; and three other churches, Bell Street, Hutchinson Street, and Mount Olive. There was a further spasm of violence on January 28, with bombings of a service station and the home of a hospital worker, Allen Robertson. On the same day a crudely made bomb was found smoldering on the porch of the King home.[30] Blacks did not react violently to any of these serious provocations. Concerning the January 10 bombing, King wrote that at each site a number of angry people assembled, "but with a restraint that I never ceased to wonder at, they held themselves under control."[31] The point was that the violence did not change the facts; desegregation of the buses had come to Montgomery and would remain. Unable to split the black community and confronted with the clear-cut antisegregation ruling of the Supreme Court, the Montgomery business leadership came to recognize the counterproductivity of further violence. The *Montgomery Advertiser* spoke out against violence as did a business leadership group, Men of Montgomery.[32] On January 31, 1957, seven white men were arrested in connection with the bombings, and although a Montgomery jury would not convict those accused, the arrests themselves evidenced a desire by the city's leadership to erase the image of Montgomery as a community that encouraged violence.

The King strategy of nonviolence must be evaluated in terms of the concrete conditions in which it was applied. King personally had an absolute commitment to nonviolence, but what gave the nonviolent approach its strength was its effectiveness as a means of dealing with violence triggered by a mass defiance of segregation. It was a strategy relevant to a movement taking the offensive against racist practices in conflict with the Constitution, relevant to a situation in which the contrast between racist violence and peaceful insistence upon constitutional rights would exert powerful pressure upon federal authorities. King, for all his commitment to nonviolence, was quite aware of the expedient element involved in his approach. In *Stride toward Freedom* he put it succinctly: "When ... the mass movement repudiates violence while moving resolutely towards its goal, its opponents are revealed as the instigators and practitioners of violence if it occurs. Then public support is magnetically attracted to the advocates of non-violence, while those who employ violence are literally disarmed by overwhelming sentiment against their stand."[33] The King strategy linked nonviolence to mass activity, and thereby public attention was compelled to focus upon a struggle in which there could be no mistaking which side was true to the American democratic tradition and which not. In the specific context of the South, with its police and other officials upholding segregationist laws and regulations, the strategy was to prove a powerful force for social change. As long as the struggle against segregation remained the central concern of the black movement, nonviolence would tend to dominate black strategic thinking.

There was clearly a radical component of the Montgomery struggle. The crux of the matter was not the moderate nature of the movement's demands but the fact that it made demands at all and would support them with mass action. Montgomery in that very basic sense represented a quite serious challenge, the most serious challenge, certainly, since World War II, to the mores of racial subordination. Blacks might supplicate, might politely request, but the racial structure of the South dictated they were not to demand anything. The attorney for the Montgomery City Lines, Jack Crenshaw, understood the nature of the basic issues at stake in the bus struggle. At a negotiating session Crenshaw told his white associates: "If we granted the Negroes these demands they would go about boasting of a victory they had won over white people; and this we will not stand for."[34] The issue was power, the capacity to impose change, any change, upon the customary practices of the city. Creating a situation in which the mass of the black community might feel that through its strength a change in conditions could be won was a radical step, for if blacks gained confidence in their power who was to determine what further changes would be demanded? The Montgomery boycott opened a door on possibilities that segregationists were determined to slam shut.

After Montgomery, King turned his attention to formulating a program for struggle that would have national impact. During May 1957 he joined with Roy Wilkins and A. Philip Randolph in sponsoring a Prayer Pilgrimage to Washington. On January 9 King had participated in an Atlanta meeting that formed a temporary organization, the Southern Conference on Transportation and Nonviolent Integration. From this meeting had gone a telegram to President Eisenhower asking him to "come south immediately, to make a major speech in a major Southern city urging all Southerners to accept and abide by the Supreme Court's decisions as to the law of the land." This message received no reply, and so at the organization's second meeting, held in New Orleans on February 14, at which the permanent name of Southern Christian Leadership Conference was adopted, Eisenhower was asked to convene a White House conference on civil rights and was further informed that, "if some effective remedial steps are not taken, we will be compelled to initiate a mighty Prayer Pilgrimage to Washington."[35] This communication also received no response, so planning for the pilgrimage went forward, with the Reverend Thomas Kilgore as national director, the Reverend Ralph Abernathy as associate director for the South, and veteran civil rights activists Bayard Rustin and Ella Baker as special organizers.

At first there was some doubt that King would participate personally in the Prayer Pilgrimage, but the Reverend A. L. Davis of New Orleans, one of the signers of the February 14 appeal to Eisenhower, quickly announced that Dr. King definitely could lead the march. Ralph Abernathy declared: "If the President doesn't act favorably on our request we are going to get a half million Negroes and all the whites who will join us and march on Washington." Abernathy told a New York City gathering organized by Local 1199 of the Retail Drug Employees Union that unless Eisenhower spoke out against racial violence in the South "we shall lead hundreds of thousands of Negro and white Americans to the White House steps in a mass pilgrimage of prayer." At a talk he gave at a dinner sponsored by the Brooklyn branch of the Urban League Abernathy spoke with great pride of the Montgomery struggle and predicted a million Americans, black and white, would go to Washington.

On April 6 James L. Hicks of the *New York Amsterdam News* reported that the date of May 18 had been set for the march (Hicks was off by one day) and that Dr. King believed half a million blacks could be mobilized to participate. A week prior to the May 17 event King went to New York to rally support. He told an assemblage of some 3,000 in front of the Hotel Theresa: "The motor is cranked up, and we're moving up the highway of freedom toward the city of equality. We can't afford to slow up, because our nation has a date with destiny, and we can't be late." While in New York King also spoke at the Stephen Wise Synagogue and at Harlem's Abyssinian Baptist Church, where he stated: "This is no time for rabble rousers or money hungry leaders. . . . Let it be known that this struggle is bigger than any denomination or one individual."[36]

The Prayer Pilgrimage assembled at the Lincoln Memorial on May 17, 1957, the third anniversary of the Supreme Court school desegregation decision. The crowd, variously estimated at from 15,000 to 37,000 persons, included a number of prominent personalities, including Jackie Robinson, novelist John Killens, and actress Ruby Dee. Mahalia Jackson sang, and among the speakers were Randolph, the Reverend Fred Shuttlesworth, Mordecai Johnson, Roy Wilkins, Adam Clayton Powell, Charges Diggs, and media celebrities Harry Belafonte, Sammy Davis, Jr., and Sidney Poitier. Martin Luther King, introduced by Randolph, received an enthusiastic reception from the audience before beginning what was his first national address. In his speech King broadened his focus from bus segregation to the question of the vote, affirming that access to the ballot would give blacks a potent weapon against violence and other forms of racial injustice. Using the rhetoric of repetition that became a feature of his oratory, he declared:

> Give us the ballot and we will no longer have to worry the federal government about our basic rights. Give us the ballot and we will no longer plead to the federal government for passage of an anti-lynching law; we will by the power of our vote write the law on the statute books of the Southern states and bring an end to the dastardly acts of the hooded perpetrators of violence. Give us the ballot and we will transform the salient misdeeds of bloodthirsty mobs into the calculated good deeds of orderly citizens. . . . Give us the ballot and we will quietly and nonviolently, without rancor or bitterness, implement the Supreme Court's decision of May 17, 1954.

Although King's leadership was later to be counterposed to the slogan of "Black Power," the key importance of black political power stood out plainly in this speech. King, however, coupled his insistence on power with rejection of any notion that could be interpreted as "black supremacy." He explained: "Our aim must never be to defeat or humiliate the white man, but to win his friendship and understanding, and thereby create a society in which all men will be able to live together as brothers." King was sharply critical of inaction on the part of the executive and legislative branches of the federal government. Arguing that the executive branch was "all too silent and apathetic" and that the legislative was "all too stagnant and hypocritical," King also stated that the lack of leadership with regard to black rights was not confined to one political party. "Both parties have betrayed the cause of justice," he declared. Democrats had capitulated to the prejudices of Dixiecrats, and Republicans had capitulated "to the blatant hypocrisy of right-wing, reactionary Northerners." In words that lent themselves to being remembered, he added, "these men so often have a high blood pressure of words and an anemia of deeds."

King cast his appeal very widely, calling upon the federal government to provide "a strong, moral and courageous leadership" and even explaining to the enthusiasts of the cold war that civil rights is "an eternal moral issue which may well determine the destiny of our nation in the ideological struggle with Communism." He also called for a positive response from southern moderates and northern liberals. King was restrained in criticism of the moderates, confining himself to expressing the hope "that the white moderates of the South will rise up courageously, without fear, and take up the leadership in this tense period of transition." He also called for a northern liberalism, "which will be thoroughly committed to the ideal of racial justice," but he was more forthrightly critical of what he termed "quasi liberalism which is based on the principle of looking sympathetically at all sides." He called that "a liberalism which is neither hot nor cold, but lukewarm." There was also in King's remarks a certain ambiguity in his references to the legal victories won by the NAACP. On the one hand, he observed that "every person of good will is profoundly indebted to the NAACP for its noble work" and warned against taking on the psychology of victors. But his speech could also be understood as urging movement beyond the NAACP's achievements. "We must not," he said, "remain satisfied with a court 'victory' over our white brothers." And he indicated that integration meant establishing a relationship between equals. Just before concluding his speech King declared: "We must act in such a way as to make possible a coming together of white people and colored people on the basis of a real harmony of interest and understanding. We must seek an integration based on mutual respect."[37] All in all, the King speech at the Prayer Pilgrimage clearly represented progress in his advancement to leadership of the civil rights movement on the national level. Journalist Hicks minced no words in his evaluation: "Dr. Martin Luther King, the 28-year-old minister from Montgomery, has emerged from the Prayer Pilgrimage to Washington as the number one leader of sixteen million Negroes in the United States."[38]

A perceptive appraisal of the pilgrimage was made by W. E. B. Du Bois. As seen by Du Bois, the demonstration was a very meaningful event. The meeting avoided the extremes of hysteria and a moderation devoid of content, which he contended "the paid Red-baiters tried to ensure." He found that "tremendous self-repression pulsed in the air" although a crowd had assembled "which could have sung like the thunder of cataracts and groaned with memories that few peoples could match." Du Bois considered this restraint, but he also noted that it passed understanding that President Eisenhower "could sit silent through this meeting and 'never say a mumblin' word.' " Du Bois believed that this pilgrimage betokened something new, a sense of political independence from the existing major parties. The throng was thinking of Montgomery and of the reprisals inflicted upon blacks for supporting the boycott and of the innumerable communities in the South "where local government has sunk to bribery, cheating, mob violence and anarchy under local dictators like 'Senator' Eastland, Chairman of the Senate Committee on the 'Judiciary.' " Democracy would revolutionize the government of the South, and Du Bois went further to say that if people took back control of local government "freedom and democracy will rule the nation as they once did until the Slave Power seized control of the Federal Government." Du Bois stressed the right to vote but also connected that to a constellation of rights that would make democracy a reality. The voters would need to be informed; public schools run by each community and a free local press would have to exist, and in general the voters "must have the whole undergrowth of rank weeds and noisome swamp cleaned from the local governments of the southern South." Du Bois had one caution, that the "white South and its new industry will never allow eligible Negroes this right to vote, if they can help it."[39] Du Bois, no doubt, was aware that a serious effort to gain the vote—and the pilgrimage seemed to mean business—would require mass pressure and movement. Du Bois's words indicated basic approval of the course projected by King.

A month earlier than the above remarks, Du Bois in an interview indicated his belief that basic social change could be achieved nonviolently. Though his comments were specifically in response to a question as to how socialism would come to the United States, Du Bois's answer had broader implications. "There was a time," he said, "when I thought that the only way in which progress could be made in the world was by violence. I thought that the only way that the darker people were going to get recognition was by killing a large number of white people. But I think that most of us are beginning to realize that it is not true, that the violence that accompanies revolution is not the revolution. The revolution is the reform, is the change in thought, is the change of attitude on the people who are affected by it."[40] It clearly would distort the facts to contend that Du Bois's views were in opposition to the strategic thinking of a resurgent civil rights movement seeking to realize the goals of racial equality he had set forth decades earlier. Du Bois was responsive to the need for a less doctrinaire model of socialism and also to the new reality of mass civil rights activism.

In 1957 Du Bois, writing in an Indian journal, viewed the Montgomery boycott as confirming the truth of the Gandhian philosophy. In 1929 Gandhi had sent a message to the *Crisis* in which he stated: "Let us realize that the future is with those who would be pure, truthful and loving. . . . Truth ever is, untruth never was." And now, eighteen years later, the boycott underscored the power of truth. Du Bois wrote:

> The black workers led by young, educated ministers began a strike which stopped the discrimination, aroused the state and the nation and presented an unbending front of non-violence to the murderous mob which hitherto has ruled the South. The occurrence was extraordinary. It was not based on any first-hand knowledge of Gandhi and his work. Their leaders like Martin Luther King knew of non-resistance in India; many of the educated teachers, business and professional men had heard of Gandhi. But the rise and spread of this movement was due to the truth of its underlying principles and not to direct teaching or propaganda. In this aspect it is a most interesting proof of the truth of the Gandhian philosophy.

Gandhianism was upheld, even if there was no direct connection between the strategy advocated by the Indian leader and the activity of blacks in Montgomery. Du Bois went on to note that blacks in America were not yet free, but he expressed the thought that the gaining of human equality and brotherhood might well come "only under the leadership of another Gandhi."[41]

Later, in 1959, Du Bois did express some reservations concerning the direction in which he saw King heading. Du Bois wrote that he was left "a little in doubt" regarding King's application of the Gandhian strategy. He was sorry to see King lauded for his opposition to Robert F. Williams, the North Carolina activist who advocated armed resistance to racial terror. In Montgomery King "suffered and stood firm without surrender," but according to Du Bois, "it is a very grave question as to whether or not the slavery and degradation of Negroes in America has not been unnecessarily prolonged by the submission to evil." Gandhi had submitted, but he also followed a positive program to offset the refusal to employ violence. He had organized protest in South Africa, and he had an economic program to resist the oppression of Indian labor. In Montgomery blacks had suffered, and many had lost their jobs. Du Bois asked: "What program have King and his followers to offset this?" Such a program was not yet evident although Du Bois noted that King was perhaps thinking along these lines.[42]

During the following year King's rhetoric became more forceful in its attack upon racism, although he retained a nonviolent commitment. A speech delivered by King on Lincoln's birthday, February 12, 1958, outlines the two themes to which he would return in the future, the inter-relationship between the racial crisis and the American world position and the class question, the impact of racism upon poor people, both white and black. The spirit of the radical activist is evident in this speech:

America must begin the struggle for democracy *at home*. The advocacy of free elections in Europe by American officials is hypocrisy when free elections are not held in great sections of America. To Negro Americans it is ironic to be governed, to be taxed, to be given orders, but to have no representation in a nation that would defend the right to vote abroad.... Let us make our intentions crystal clear. We must and we will be free. We want freedom now. We want the right to vote now. We do not want freedom fed to us in teaspoons over another 150 years.... There is blood on the hands of those who halt the progress of our nation and frustrate the advancement of its people by coercion and violence. But despite this, it is our duty to pray for those who mistreat us.... The ghastly results have not been borne alone by the Negro. Poor white men, women and children, bearing the scars of ignorance, deprivation, and poverty, are evidence of the fact that harm to one is injury to all.... Today, because the Negro cannot vote, Congress is dominated by Southern Senators and representatives who are not elected in a fair or legal manner.... We southerners, Negro and white, must no longer permit our heritage to be dishonored before the world.... We have the duty to remove from political domination a small minority that cripples the economic and social institutions of our country and thereby degrades and impoverishes everyone.[43]

King had found the way to combine militant polemic against oppression with nonviolence.

During 1958 King initiated the tactic of accepting imprisonment as a means of underlining the principled nature of the movement. The willingness to be jailed would be turned into a weapon against the segregationists. Influenced in this matter by deeper study of nonviolence and by the advice of Bayard Rustin, King decided he would no longer be processed through the legal sham involving trials that always ended in conviction and release secured through payment of a fine. On September 3, 1958, King was denied entrance to a court hearing involving Ralph Abernathy, and when, as Mrs. King recalls, "Martin stood his ground" two officers seized him and, twisting his arm, hauled him to the police station. As King was pushed into a cell he was kicked several times. He was tried and convicted on September 5 on charges of refusing to obey an officer. The fine was ten dollars, but King told the judge: "I could not in good conscience pay a fine for an act that I did not commit and above all for brutal treatment that I did not deserve." He told the court of how police had seized him and then twisted his arms, choked him, and kicked him. King stated that the police were the victims of their environment, and he added that he had "compassion for them as brothers, and as fellow human beings made in the image of God." But he also declared: "The Negro can no longer silently endure conditions of police brutality and mob violence."[44] King would no longer by his cooperation legitimize the actions of a racist police and judicial system. His fine was paid by city police commissioner Clyde Sellers, but King had established a policy for himself. He told a meeting at Dexter Avenue Baptist Church: "We have a mandate from God to resist evil.... We must go out of this meeting with the determination to take a firm and courageous stand against police brutality. We must go out and no longer be afraid to go to jail. This has taught us one thing—we no longer have to fear going to jail."[45] If that willingness to go to jail were indeed to become the stance of substantial numbers of blacks, the civil rights movement now had a further potent weapon at its disposal.

Capping the broadening scope of the nonviolent movement during the 1950s was King's interest in extending the nonviolent philosophy to the international arena. Those who later viewed his opposition to the Vietnam War as an unprecedented departure from his course were ignorant of the record. During his 1959 visit to India, King addressed himself to the challenge of violence on a world scale. On the eve of departing from India, in the course of a news conference held on March 9, King stated his position on the peace question:

The peace-loving peoples of the world have not succeeded in persuading my own country, America, and Soviet Russia, to eliminate fears and disarm themselves. Unfortunately, as yet America and the Soviet Union have not shown the faith and moral courage to do this. ... India may have to take the lead and call for universal disarmament, and if no other nation will join her immediately, India should declare itself for disarmament unilaterally. Such an act of courage would be a great demonstration of the spirit of the Mahatma and would be the greatest stimulus to the rest of the world to do likewise. Moreover, any nation that would take such a step would automatically draw to itself the multitudes of the earth that any would-be aggressor would be discouraged from risking the wrath of mankind.[46]

Noteworthy in this statement were King's evenhanded criticism of the United States and the Soviet Union and above all the indication, in his comment on a vitally important international question, that he would freely express his views on world matters when he deemed that appropriate.

Stride toward Freedom, King's account of the Montgomery struggle, was published on September 17, 1958. The book was generally reviewed quite favorably.[47] Many thousands throughout the country, black and white, read with great interest this book that was at once an account of the bus boycott and also a personal narration of the making of a mass leader. If we take into account the techniques of red baiting that were to be applied to King, it is interesting that a careful review, balancing praise with criticism, appeared in the journal of the Communist party, Political Affairs. The reviewer, James E. Jackson, noted that Montgomery was a milestone in the black people's struggle while also observing that "each concession gained can only mark the point of departure for still another phase of the struggle." The essence of the book, Jackson wrote, was the narration of the Montgomery struggle, and in his focus upon this theme "Dr. King is a rewarding writer and an inspiring challenge to his readers." Jackson also found interesting King's revelations concerning the "inner conflicts and reactions he experienced in confronting the exacting claims on personal courage and self-sacrificing denial demanded of those leaders who would make their identity with the cause of the poor, of the oppressed, and the humiliated masses of the Southern Negro." Jackson saw King's "historical merit" in his standing as a symbol of leadership that served as a catalytic agent of mass struggle. Further, it was Jackson's view that King's role as leader was "far more profound and important to the cause of Negro freedom and social progress than are the philosophical elements of the 'King Doctrine' of neo-Gandhianism garnished as it is with divisive prejudices of anti-Communism." But Jackson, at some length, subjected King's philosophical views to sharp criticism. Accusing King of "name-dropping," Jackson wrote that "when Rev. King enters upon lengthy side trips into the bogs of idealist philosophy and theological mysticism . . . one must take leave of him." Jackson added that "King can only echo the stalest canards of bourgeois prejudice when he treats of Karl Marx, V. I. Lenin, and Communism." It was Jackson's view that King was a victim of interpretive works on the writings of Marx and Lenin and that Stride toward Freedom "reflects the fact that he is a theological idealist in need of a much greater knowledge of, and deeper moorings in, the political, social, and historical developments of our country and our world." Jackson also found contradictory King's endorsement of appeals against nuclear weapons testing and his statement: "War, horrible as it is, might be preferable to surrender to a totalitarian system—Nazi, Fascist, or Communist."[48] If others might praise King for this echoing of the Niebuhrean position on war, not so Jackson. Omitted from the review was any specific consideration of the effectiveness of the King nonviolent strategy. All in all, this was a friendly estimation of the civil rights leader but one that stressed the contrast between successful activity and perceived ideological shortcomings.

A critic of the Left who very clearly saw King as still in process of development was Louis E. Burnham, staff writer for the *National Guardian* and leader of the earlier Southern Negro Youth Congress. Burnham noted that the success of the Montgomery movement "provided a precedent which inspired other Negro communities and enraged white supremacists everywhere." There was a lesson of great importance in how unity had been forged in the Montgomery black community. Burnham noted that King was an eclectic, a philosophical idealist who yet borrowed from materialist political and social science. King argued that the racial question was basically a moral issue, a conclusion that Burnham found doubtful. But Burnham stressed that the book revealed King as a man at the start of his service and "with a considerable capacity for candor and for growth."[49]

SEVENTEEN

Robert F. Williams and the Black Muslims

A MONG THOSE directly involved in Montgomery, disagreement about the question of nonviolence could be noticed. King referred to this in *Stride toward Freedom:* "Occasionally members of the executive board would say to me in private that we needed a more militant approach. They looked upon nonviolence as weak and compromising. Others felt that at least a modicum of violence would convince the white people that the Negroes meant business and were not afraid." A member of his church apparently came to King and suggested the advantage of killing some white people. Such action would be meant to prove that blacks were no longer governed by fear. The killings, King was told, would call forth federal intervention. Other individuals argued the case for self-defense or retaliatory violence, telling King they would not initiate violence but would hit back if attacked.[1]

Even among some black activists who would not directly challenge the strategy of nonviolence, criticism of the Montgomery strategy could be heard. The nub of this criticism was that King and his associates were not aggressive enough in their tactics, within the framework of nonviolence. James Forman, later executive secretary of the Student Nonviolent Coordinating Committee, was to write that at the time he disagreed with the approach of maintaining the boycott while seeking a favorable decision in the courts. According to Forman, he had felt "this was a very negative attitude and that King should call for a creative confrontation with the racist bus companies." Forman judged that "the boycott had become a passive kind of protest and should be turned into a more positive, aggressive action similar to what Gandhi did at the salt mines." At the same time Forman stressed the powerful impact of Montgomery as showing the practical possibility of black unity. Forman admits that judging the Montgomery situation from the distance of Chicago was "a very dangerous thing to do," but beyond that it is very questionable whether the more "militant" tactics he advocated would have strengthened black unity or undermined it.[2] Militancy, after all, is not an abstraction; rather, it is linked to the power of a program or tactic to encourage and give direction to mass movement.

Criticism of the King movement within the framework of nonviolence was one thing, but soon the nonviolent movement itself came under serious ideological attack. One such attack emerged from the intense, bitter struggle that for several years of the late fifties and early sixties gripped the North Carolina town of Monroe. The setting was a community located fourteen miles from the South Carolina line, in which blacks composed a fourth of the population. Monroe, the seat of Union County, is located some twenty-five miles from Charlotte, the largest city in North Carolina. Julian Mayfield has written: "Some Southern towns are lovely, with great old houses that slumber on broad streets beneath spreading, ancient trees." But Monroe, he added, was not such a town. "It is ugly," he explained. "There is little distinction in the architecture of its finest houses; and although it is built on hills, there is a dreary flatness about it. Worse, it is a composite town. Unpainted one-room shacks, which rent for an inflated ten dollars a month, sit within a stone's throw of the tiny, neat, unimaginative bungalows of the white middle class."[3] In the mid-1950s unionism was nonexistent in the town, but there did exist a small if not very active chapter of the NAACP. Shortly after the election in 1956 of a returned marine veteran, Robert F. Williams, to the presidency of the NAACP, the organization assumed a more activist course.[4] Closely associated with Williams was a physician, Dr. Albert Perry. Early in 1957 Perry became president of the newly formed Union County Council on Human Relations. There was nothing inflammatory in the program put forth by the council. Urging the citizens of Union County to "have the courage to face up to problems that must be faced by responsible leadership in a changing world," the council indicated that one of its purposes was the furthering of equal opportunity "for all citizens in employment, education, recreation and all other phases of community life." Perry was quoted as hoping that Brotherhood Week 1957 would strengthen a resolve to build a community "in which people are united in mutual love and respect, without regard to race or creed and where everyone lives with benefit of unlimited opportunities." At first the Monroe movement was able to make some gains without arousing substantial opposition. In 1957 the public library was integrated "without any friction at all," according to Williams.[5]

That same year, however, serious conflict resulted from the effort to obtain adequate swimming facilities for blacks. City officials were totally unresponsive to this request, refusing even to consider the alternative of granting blacks access to the municipal pool on a once-weekly basis. At this point Williams moved toward demonstrative activity, escorting groups of black youth to the pool where they would be denied entrance. The Monroe movement also made plans for legal action against this denial of public facilities. At least with regard to recreational facilities, Monroe was unwilling to provide "separate but equal facilities." One did not have to judge the equality of the facilities; the city of Monroe provided no public swimming facility for blacks. Stepping into this situation was the Ku Klux Klan. The Klansmen started circulation of a petition calling for the ouster of Perry and Williams from the community.[6] The Klan held a series of rallies, drawing at times an attendance of several thousand persons. Threatening phone calls started coming, and in response the first steps of self-defense were taken. A guard was established at Perry's house. He later told James Forman that "some fifty fellows would stay at the house all night, leave the house and go to their jobs, and another shift would come in the next night." The self-defense effort was not haphazard; Robert Williams secured a charter for a gun club from the National Rifle Association.[7] In a 1970 interview Williams described the self-defense effort: "we spent the summer in foxholes behind sandbags. We had steel helmets. We had obtained gas masks. And we had a better communication system than they have now."[8] It is possible that Williams had more than self-defense in mind, but in any event continued Klan activity provided occasion for the exercise of this legitimate right. The robed racists organized motorcades that rode through the black community, blowing their horns and firing guns. The police did nothing. Finally, on October 5, 1957, a confrontation occurred. Julian Mayfield described the event:

It was just another good time Klan night, the high point of which would come when they dragged Dr. Perry over the state line if they did not hang him or burn him first. But near Dr. Perry's home their revelry was suddenly shattered by the sustained fire of scores of men who had been instructed not to kill anyone if it were not necessary. The firing was blistering, disciplined and frightening. The motorcade of about eighty cars, which had begun in a spirit of good fellowship, disintegrated into chaos, with panicky, robed men fleeing in every direction. Some abandoned their automobiles and had to continue on foot.[9]

The Klan ceased its motorcades, but Perry was accused of having performed a criminal abortion on a white woman. It was apparently in reference to this episode that Martin Luther King paid tribute to the effective use of nonviolence in Monroe. "Indeed, in Mr. Williams' own community of Monroe, North Carolina," King wrote, "a striking example of collective community action won a significant victory without use of arms or the acts of violence. When the police incarcerated a Negro doctor unjustly, the aroused people of Monroe marched to the police station, crowded into its halls and corridors, and refused to leave until their colleague was released. Unable to arrest everyone, the authorities released the doctor and neither side attempted to unleash violence."[10] Dr. Perry was convicted, however, and, denied a hearing by the United States Supreme Court, was imprisoned until July 7, 1960.

A foreshadowing of later public conflict between Robert Williams and the national NAACP was seen in the "kissing case" of 1958–59. On October 28, 1958, James Hanover Thompson and David ("Fuzz") Simpson, seven and nine years old respectively, were arrested for having kissed a white playmate in the course of playing house. Juvenile court judge J. Hampton Price sentenced the boys to an indefinite term in reform school, after a "hearing" in which the boys were unrepresented by counsel. Williams requested intervention by President Eisenhower, but it appears that the North Carolina NAACP and the national office in New York would not enter the case.[11] The association intervened only on December 31, 1958, after Williams had called the New York attorney Conrad Lynn into the case, after the *New York Post* on November 10 carried a story on the case by Ted Poston, and after the *London News Chronicle* on December 16 published a photograph of the boys being visited by their mothers at the reformatory. Unquestionably, the association had moved slowly, too slowly, in this case, although it is also likely that Roy Wilkins's announcement of NAACP involvement in the matter facilitated the release of these two children. On February 13, 1959, the boys were unconditionally released. Several factors worked together to produce this victory: Robert Williams's initiative in bringing Lynn into the case, the sensitivity of governmental authorities to the national and especially the international attention given this flagrant instance of racial injustice, and the eventual support of the NAACP. But it appears that in this venture Williams and the NAACP leadership saw each other as opponents rather than as collaborators in a common cause.[12]

During that spring of 1959 the conflict broke into the open. The occasion was the trial of Louis Medlin, a white man charged with entering the home of a pregnant young black woman, seeking to rape her. According to Julian Mayfield, several of Robert Williams's group favored seizing Medlin and lynching him, as Mack Charles Parker on April 25 had been lynched in Poplarville, Mississippi. Whatever the practicality of this proposal in a situation where racists controlled the police power, Williams convinced his followers to wait for the outcome of the trial. As was to be expected, given the double racial standard applied to assaults upon women, Medlin was acquitted. In response to this acquittal Williams made a statement that was to be widely quoted. On the courthouse steps he declared:

> We cannot take these people who do us injustice to the court and it becomes necessary to punish them ourselves. In the future we are going to have to try and convict them on the spot. We cannot rely on the law. We can get no justice under the present system. If we feel that injustice is done, we must right then and there, on the spot, be prepared to inflict punishment on these people. Since the federal government will not bring a halt to lynching in the South, and since the so-called courts lynch our people legally, if it's necessary to stop lynching with lynching, then we must be willing to resort to that method. We must meet violence with violence.

Williams's statement, as Julian Mayfield observed, "was a final chucking off of optimism about a nation that had no place for him at its inception," but it also articulated a specific tactical policy.[13] It expressed the frustration and anger of blacks at the failure of the legal system to protect black women from criminal assault, and it also amounted to a renunciation of the political and legal struggle for justice. Confusing the tactics that could be employed by racists, who had the passive or active support of the police and the courts, with tactics appropriate for the struggle of the oppressed, Williams's statement could be interpreted as legitimizing lynching. Although Williams apparently later added the qualifier that he did not mean "that Negroes should go out and attempt to get revenge for mistreatments or injustices," his original statement could be read as implying the contrary.[14] It was to be expected that disagreement with Williams's position would be expressed by much of the established black leadership.

On May 6 Roy Wilkins, NAACP executive director, issued a statement suspending Williams, but he also noted "that the mood of Negro citizens from one end of the nation to the other is one of bitterness and anger over the lynching [of Mack Charles Parker] in Poplarville, Mississippi, April 25 and over numerous instances of injustice meted out to Negroes by the courts in certain sections of the South."[15] Wilkins insisted that blacks were no longer willing to accept a double standard of justice, but he also would not tolerate identification of the NAACP with an ambiguously stated strategy of violence. Williams's suspension was referred to the association's Committee on Branches, which held a hearing in New York on June 3. Williams's counsel informed the committee that Williams "believes the message of armed self-reliance should be spread among Negroes of the South."[16] This was not merely advocacy of the right of self-defense but a political strategy. Reliance was not really being placed on "self-reliance"; rather, this slogan was to be used to induce federal action on behalf of civil rights. In the statement submitted to the Committee on Branches the point was made that Williams was convinced "that a somnolent national government will only take action when it is made aware that individual Negroes are no longer facing the mobs in isolation but are acquiring the habit of coming to the aid of their menaced brothers." Julian Mayfield, Williams's close friend, later affirmed that the Monroe leader was convinced "that the federal government offers the only real hope the Negro has of winning any large measure of his civil rights."[17] The precise meaning of "armed self-reliance" was not defined, but the language in the original Williams statement about stopping lynching with lynching was clear, and it was also clear that this was not a strategy likely to produce unity among all sections of the black population, much less an interracial mass movement. That such a policy was capable of inducing the desired federal action, that it represented more than a formula for the isolation of black militants, is highly dubious. In any event the Committee on Branches upheld Williams's suspension.

The year 1959 was the fiftieth anniversary of the founding of the NAACP, and the organization chose to hold its annual convention in New York, where the association had first met. Williams chose to appeal his suspension to the convention, and in reply the national office released to the delegates a pamphlet summarizing its position. The national position was upheld overwhelmingly; at the same time, the convention resolved that "we do not deny but reaffirm the right of an individual and collective self-defense against unlawful assaults."[18]

Martin Luther King, Jr., also took issue with Williams's position. King essentially viewed the matter in the context of the frustration experienced by black people as they saw policies of tokenism and gradualism appear to gain the upper hand. There were two kinds of reaction to frustration, King observed. One was a stress on the building of "a wholesome social organization" as a means of rebuffing the opponents of progress. The other, which King identified with Williams, was "a confused, anger-motivated drive to strike back violently, to inflict damage." King evaluated this second response as "punitive—not radical or constructive." King went on to outline three varying positions on the question of violence. The first was that of pure nonviolence, "which cannot readily or easily attract large masses, for it requires extraordinary discipline and courage." The second was violence "exercised in self-defense," and King added that all societies, from the most primitive to the most sophisticated, accept self-defense "as moral and legal." King also noted that not even Gandhi had condemned this principle. The third view was "the advocacy of violence as a tool of advancement, organized as in warfare, deliberately and consciously." King found "incalculable perils" in this approach. The greatest danger was that this line would fail to attract blacks to collective struggle and would confuse the uncommitted who had not yet taken sides in the civil rights struggle. King cited Williams as holding that there was no practical alternative to this third course, as holding that blacks "must be cringing and submissive or take up arms." King believed that this was to distort the true situation, and, he insisted, "there are other meaningful alternatives." The alternative he urged was nonviolent mass action. He outlined a variety of forms of struggle appropriate to this strategy: the mass boycott, sit-down protests and strikes, sit-ins, mass marches, and mass meetings. After his death some commentators sought to separate nonviolence from mass action, but in his 1959 comment on Williams the emphasis upon the mass character of the civil rights movement was clear. He believed in nonviolence on philosophical grounds, but he was also convinced that only on a nonviolent basis could a unified, powerful movement be developed. "There is more power," he wrote, "in socially organized masses on the march than there is in guns in the hands of a few desperate men. Our enemies would prefer to deal with a small armed group rather than with a huge, unarmed but resolute mass of people." King called for an end to internal squabbling and for turning to the enemy, "using every form of mass action yet known" and creating new forms.[19]

Robert Williams was to claim that he was not opposed to the nonviolent methods advocated by Martin Luther King. His difference with King, he asserted, was over the universal applicability of nonviolence. Williams stated: "My only difference with Dr. King is that I believe in flexibility in the freedom struggle. This means that I believe in non-violent tactics where possible.... Massive civil disobedience is a powerful weapon under civilized conditions, where the law safeguards the citizen's right of peaceful demonstrations." But the point is that Williams considered nonviolence as irrelevant to the entire southern movement. At the time he made the statement that brought his suspension by Roy Wilkins, he also told his followers that "the South is not a civilized society; the South is a social jungle, so in cases like that we had to revert to the law of the jungle."[20] Williams was doing more than arguing for tactical flexibility; he was urging the setting aside of nonviolence as a guide to action in the South.

Despite rejection at the hands of the national NAACP and the criticism advanced by King, Robert Williams's views continued to have some appeal. Williams and his followers had broken up Klan motorcades. The Monroe movement had taken up such obviously valid issues as access to swimming pools and the protection of black women and children from assault and unjust treatment in court. Williams verbalized the intense anger felt by blacks at the violence inflicted upon them with impunity. It was quite understandable that in the South, a South that seemed to live by the code of violence, some blacks would draw the conclusion that violent means would be required to settle the issue of civil rights. Williams gave a truthful account of the black experience in a South permeated by the reality of the threat of violence. He wrote: "The majority of the white people in the United States have literally no idea of the violence with which Negroes in the South are treated daily—nay, hourly. This violence is deliberate, conscious, condoned by the authorities. It has gone on for centuries and is going on today, every day, unceasing and unremitting. It is our way of life. Negro existence in the South has been one long travail, steeped in terror and blood—our blood."[21] Whatever judgment is made as to the strategic wisdom of Williams's policy of "armed self-reliance," it cannot be forgotten that racists had made violence a central component of the American experience long before Robert Williams was ever upon the scene.

During July 1959 the general American public, watching a CBS television documentary entitled "The Hate that Hate Produced," first became aware of the Nation of Islam, the Black Muslims of the United States. The Muslims, however, had already established a significant position in the black community. In 1956 the *Pittsburgh Courier* reported on the growth of the Muslim movement in the Chicago area, and the following year Elijah Muhammed was awarded a plaque by the *Courier* "in recognition of outstanding achievement as messenger and spiritual leader of Muhammed's Temples of Islam." In November 1958 an informed source, close to Muhammed, stated that there were 3,000 registered Muslims, over 15,000 believers, and nearly 50,000 sympathizers. Muhammed had demonstrated the capability of drawing audiences of thousands in a number of cities, including New York, Washington, Detroit, Pittsburgh, Chicago, and Los Angeles.[22] With a base mainly in the larger cities of the North the Muslims offered an alternative to the strategies advocated by the civil rights organizations.

Though Elijah Muhammed was the recognized national leader of the Black Muslims, Malcolm X, born Malcolm Little, was to emerge as the movement's most charismatic spokesman. Malcolm, described by C. Eric Lincoln as "the ubiquitous Malcolm X, whose adroitness and cunning, displayed during many of his numerous radio interviews, led a Boston critic to name him 'the Harlem Asp,' " was unusually able at presenting a biting, forceful indictment of racism.[23] Alex Haley called Malcolm X "whip-smart," and doubtless his eloquence complemented Muhammed's organizational leadership of the Nation.[24] Beginning in 1952 Malcolm served as minister of New York Temple No. 7 in Harlem. Malcolm's leadership in New York first drew widespread attention following an incident that occurred on April 26, 1957. Two Muslims had witnessed an altercation between the police and a man the police charged with beating an unidentified woman. Seeing the police working over the man, one of the Muslims, Hinton Johnson, reportedly called out, "You're not in Alabama, this is New York." Ordered by the police to move on, Johnson apparently did not move rapidly enough to suit the officers and was placed under arrest. Before Johnson was taken to the Twenty-eighth Precinct station one of the policemen, Patrolman Mike Dolan, hit him with his nightstick. Once inside the station Johnson was clubbed again, this time by the lieutenant in charge. Meanwhile, a crowd had gathered outside, and Malcolm X was finally permitted to see Johnson. Malcolm later described the scene: "When I saw our brother Hinton, it was all I could do to contain myself. He was only semi-conscious. Blood had bathed his head and face and shoulders." Malcolm succeeded in having Johnson taken to Harlem Hospital for examination although he was shortly returned to the station to await arraignment. Impressive that night was the discipline of the crowd, which amazed the police, and the crowd's demonstrated willingness to follow Malcolm's instructions.

Later, after Johnson's release on bail, physicians at Sydenham Hospital discovered he had a clot on the brain. Muslims demonstrated quietly in front of the hospital, but when word spread that Johnson might die, reports spread through Harlem of a possible riot. The police arranged a meeting with Malcolm X, and according to the *Amsterdam News* the Muslim leader told them: "We do not look for trouble. In fact we are taught to steer clear of trouble. We do not carry knives or guns. But we are also taught that when one finds something that is worthwhile getting into trouble about, he should be ready to die, then and there, for that particular thing." Johnson, however, survived, although a metal plate had to be implanted in his skull, and eventually he was awarded $70,000 by the jury in a police brutality suit. The *Amsterdam News* reported this entire episode as front-page news, and as Malcolm later recalled, "for the first time the black man, woman, and child in the streets was discussing 'those Muslims.' "[25]

The Black Muslims did not advocate violence but did indeed believe in the right of self-defense. It is true that Muhammed appeared to urge a policy of retaliatory violence. "We must take things into our own hands," he was quoted as saying in early 1960. "We must return to the Mosaic law of an eye for an eye, and a tooth for a tooth. What does it matter if ten million of us die? There will be seven million of us left, and they will enjoy justice and freedom."[26] But it is also true that such advocacy appeared to have an eschatological character, put forward as an ultimate recourse rather than as a short-term guide to action. C. Eric Lincoln and E. U. Essien-Udom, careful students of the Black Muslims, agree that the Nation stressed nonviolence in its teachings, although Lincoln added that the Muslims "display a kind of contained aggressiveness, which may occasionally provoke violence without actually initiating it." The violence would have to be started by others, however. Fundamentally, it is clear that the Muslims sought to avoid being provoked themselves into acts of violence. Lincoln concluded that Muhammed preferred "to disassociate his Movement from violent activity of any kind" and noted that members were forbidden to carry weapons and cautioned not to carry any instrument that might conceivably be considered a weapon.[27] Essien-Udom reported a discussion with Elijah Muhammed in which the Muslim leader explained his position with regard to violence. Asked what would happen if a black person attacked a Muslim at a meeting, Muhammed answered that the idea of hitting back was unthinkable "because all of them are taught to refrain from doing any kind of violence, including hitting a brother or a wife." Such violence would be a violation of the law of Islam and punishable. Muhammed further explained that he was issuing a directive to his ministers "to drum it into their ears that they must never be aggressive nor resort to violence except in defense of their own lives when such is clearly in danger." The Muslims were especially concerned with the internalization of violence among blacks, the turning of anger against fellow blacks, but Wallace Muhammed, Elijah Muhammed's son, flatly denied that "Muslims preach, think, or act violence." The Muslim view of violence must be seen within the context of the basic ideological position taken by the Nation. The point was that the Black Muslim leadership did not seek any direct confrontation, violent or nonviolent, with racist institutions. Essien-Udom put his finger on the matter when he evaluated the Nation of Islam as representing a policy of accommodation to the existing realities of American society. Explaining that most Muslims admired white southerners for the definiteness of their views, Essien-Udom wrote that "membership in the Nation assists the Negro in adjusting to the present pattern of race relations in both the North and South and in rationalizing his own subordination and humiliation." He believed that many Muslims, by separating themselves from ordinary blacks, were seeking to appease white hostility. Analyzing the movement in terms that could be applied generally to conservative black nationalism, Essien-Udom found that Muslim ideology was nonrevolutionary and indeed apolitical. The alternatives propounded by Muhammed "appear just as impracticable as the prophetic expectation of the Kingdom of Righteousness." With regard to the movement's political ideology, Essien-Udom observed that it constituted "no more than a rationalization of the existing distribution of political power between blacks and whites in the United States."[28] It provided a means of affirming dignity and self-respect while continuing to experience oppression. This ideology provided hope without requiring struggle. At some unspecified point in history white society would destroy itself or racial oppression would be destroyed by the intervention of Allah.

The basic issue separating the Muslims from most black organizations was not the question of violence. More fundamental was the Muslim rejection of the integration struggle, of any struggle that involved alliance with whites. It was inevitable, given the separatist course advocated by the Nation of Islam, that it would come into conflict with the major civil rights organizations. In an interview in April 1959 Muhammed praised the NAACP for doing a good job "within its limitations" but also advanced the concept of a "Black Council" that would design a strategy looking forward to independence from all contact with whites. For its part, the association by July 1959 took an openly critical view of the Muslims. Roy Wilkins, asked in a television interview for his appraisal, commented that "for years the NAACP has been opposed to white extremists preaching hatred of Negro people, and we are equally opposed to Negro extremists preaching against white people simply for the sake of whiteness." By August the NAACP felt constrained to issue a more formal, direct criticism. As usual the association sought to turn its criticism into a means of pressure on politicians who were dragging their feet on civil rights measures. The NAACP stated: "The NAACP opposes and regards as dangerous any group, white or black, political or religious, that preaches hatred among men. Hatred destroys men—the haters and the hated. The so-called Muslims who teach black supremacy and hatred of all white people have gained a following only because America has been so slow in granting equal opportunities and has permitted the abuse and persecution of Negro citizens. At this very moment the Congress is shadowboxing with a milk-and-water civil rights bill. All this furnishes ammunition for the use of opportunistic leaders." Particularly emphatic in denunciation of the Muslims was Thurgood Marshall, then chief legal counsel for the association. In an address at Princeton University, Marshall evaluated the Muslims as a group "run by a bunch of thugs organized from prisons and jails, and financed, I am sure, by Nasser or some Arab group." Martin Luther King also criticized the Muslims, although in language more restrained than that of Marshall. In a speech before the National Bar Association, the professional organization of black attorneys, King referred to the Muslims as "one of the hate groups arising in our midst which would preach a doctrine of black supremacy."[29]

The Muslims were vitriolic in their response to these criticisms. Malcolm X described Marshall as a "twentieth century Uncle Tom" and stated that Muhammed was "too busy to worry about the envious yapping of every jealous dog that is paid to bark at him." The basic problem with the NAACP, according to the Nation's unofficial organ, the *Los Angeles Herald-Dispatch*, was that it was subordinated to Jewish influences. The newspaper declared that Marshall's speech was "Zionist ideology at its ugliest," and beyond that the argument was advanced that Jews sought to promote integration as a diversion while seeking to exploit the black community economically. Jews, it was contended, had managed to entrench themselves in the black community. In the early thirties, Jews, operating businesses in the black areas, "had an excellent opportunity to study the habits and weaknesses of the Negro." Then, during the Depression years, "through the activities of the Communist Party" Jews had further entrenched themselves, "to the extent that by 1940 the Negro was almost entirely dependent upon the Jews and had accepted the thinking and ideology of the Jewish people." Subsequently, the Jews had gained control of the NAACP. The main task of 1960, it was said, was to rid blacks of "this phony Jewish leadership." Muslims participated in booing L. Joseph Overton, president of the New York branch of the association, at a reception given in Harlem for President and Mrs. Sekou Toure of Guinea.

The Black Muslims repeatedly attacked Martin Luther King, questioning his personal integrity. They would of course find repugnant King's concept of loving those who harm black people, even loving in the form of *agape* that was universal and impersonal in character. More than that, however, was involved. There was no common ground on which Muslim separatism and visions of white doom could stand with King's concept of community, of a society in which genuine interracial fraternity would exist. King was committed to the forging of a national coalition that would put an end to discrimination and segregation; the Muslims believed such a strategy to be futile and destructive of black integrity. They censured King for having "turned many potential freedom-fighting Negroes into contented, docile slaves" and particularly denounced the southern leader for his decision, announced in Montgomery November 19, 1959, to move to Atlanta, the headquarters of the Southern Christian Leadership Conference. The *Herald-Dispatch* accused King of cowardice: "In February, this same Reverend Martin Luther King, the Darling of the South, Honey Boy of the North, is now moving his headquarters from the increasingly hostile atmosphere of Alabama to the more lucrative haven of Atlanta. Is this a retreat from the bloody racial struggle soon to erupt in Alabama? Has his philosophy developed from 'turn the other cheek' to 'turn and run away'? If all of us are going to die and go to heaven as the Negro Christian ministers have been preaching, why must Reverend King flee the 'portals of death' in Alabama, conveniently seeking safer refuge among the wealthier Negroes of Atlanta?" The Muslims ignored the mass nature of the developing southern movement and instead insisted King tell blacks they would progress only when "they are ready and willing to shed blood or die fighting for it."[30]

Quite apart from the specific content of the Muslim program, the Nation of Islam gained support among blacks because its spokesmen articulated central aspects of their experience, boldly exposed and excoriated white racism, and would substitute racial pride for self-effacement. In a nation where some commitment to the Judeo-Christian heritage seems to be a requisite for any respectability, the Muslims were not afraid to repudiate this heritage, to break unreservedly with the Christian tradition. Charles Silberman correctly perceived that the Muslims spoke to some basic forces in black life, that they gained a wide audience "by articulating feelings which most Negroes share but fear to voice in public." As Silberman observed, even a great many blacks committed to integration responded to Muslim exposures of white duplicity. James Baldwin explained why this was the case: "The brutality with which Negroes are treated in this country simply cannot be overstated, however unwilling white men may be to hear it. In the beginning— and neither can this be overstated—a Negro just cannot *believe* that white people are treating him as they do; he does not know what he has done to merit it. And when he realizes that the treatment accorded him has nothing to do with anything he has done, that the attempt of white people to destroy him—for that is what it is—is utterly gratuitous, it is not hard for him to think of white people as devils." Relevant also is Baldwin's explanation that although most blacks did not allow such feelings to dominate their thought and action there was, he believed, "no Negro living in America who has not felt, briefly or for long periods, with anguish sharp or dull, in varying degrees and to varying effect, simple, naked and unanswerable hatred; who has not wanted to smash any white face he may encounter in a day, to violate, out of motives of the cruelest vengeance, their women, to break the bodies of all white people and bring them low, as low as that dust into which he himself has been and is being trampled."[31] The Muslims effectively appealed to such feelings, giving voice to hatred of whites while stressing the need for blacks to assert a more positive self-image of themselves. The fact was that in the United States white racism would continually generate new evidence, new instances of brutality and dehumanization, that the Muslims could cite in support of their position.

From a variety of perspectives E. U. Essien-Udom, C. Eric Lincoln, James Baldwin, and Charles Silberman offered thoughtful, serious appraisals of the Muslims. The television presentation, "The Hate that Hate Produced," was something else again, and its version of what the Nation of Islam represented was seen by an audience of millions. As seen in retrospect, what marked this documentary was a tendency to caricature, to equate racist violence with the temper of the Muslims, to urge a narrow American provincialism upon blacks, and to set forth gradualism as *the* path for black advancement. In effect, whatever the intention of the producers, the impact was to divert attention from the reality of American racist violence.

To begin with, there was the opinion voiced by the narrator Mike Wallace that the Muslims preached "a gospel of hate that would set off a Federal investigation if it were preached by Southern whites." The fact, however, was that southern bigots were avid purveyors of hate propaganda, that this bigotry found expression in the activity of such organizations as the Klan and the White Citizens Councils, and that local government officials and members of Congress joined in the preaching of racial hatred. The federal government did practically nothing about such agitation. Wallace asserted that the Muslims were "fighting back with the same weapons that were used to subjugate them." To justify this conclusion reference was made to the Muslim morality play, *The Trial,* in which the white man was put on trial for his crimes against blacks, convicted, and sentenced to death. And the broadcast presented Elijah Muhammed as stating that in a coming war between God and the devil there would occur the destruction of the white man and a "resurrection" of blacks. But there was of course no specific Muslim plan for violence against whites, and such violence was almost totally lacking from the contemporary or future record of the Muslims. The television narration confused condemnatory rhetoric with actual commitment to violence against whites. With regard to white-supremacist rhetoric about violence there was a history of translating racial animus into action. The difference was more than a matter of degree.

An extensive segment of "The Hate that Hate Produced" was devoted to presenting the views of two black nationalists, John Davis and James R. Lawson, both of the United African Nationalist Movement. The only specific link to the Muslims was mention that Lawson had brought greetings to Elijah Muhammed on the occasion of a Muslim celebration in Chicago. The reason for the attention to this group may have been to draw out the information that Lawson had given greetings from President Nasser of Egypt (as well as President Tubman of Liberia), a reference that in 1959 was quite likely to stir a hostile reaction from many white liberals. By indirection the Muslims could be portrayed as having dangerous international involvements.

Among those interviewed was also Anna Hedgeman, formerly administrative aide to New York mayor Robert Wagner. Dr. Hedgeman stated that American society had never fully permitted blacks to identify with that society and added that of course the American black was "part African...he's some of everything." When Hedgeman noted that the "largest portion" of the American black was African, Mike Wallace interjected: "And there you have it. Tragic and irrefutable evidence that a small, but growing segment of the American Negro population is giving ear to a flagrant doctrine of Black supremacy." A search for identification that is perceived as normal on the part of almost every other ethnic group in this case was twisted into a desire for supremacy.

At the end of the telecast Wallace called for help to race leaders engaged in "counseling patience and the relatively slow operation of legal measures." Coupled with this was rhetoric about the need to make the United States truly a nation "indivisible, with freedom and justice for all." But there was no indication that Wallace was proposing to accelerate the pace of change in the American racial pattern, and so the program was at bottom irrelevant to any attempt to deal seriously with the dynamics that generated support for the Nation of Islam. The message was still one of gradualism, a posture that contributed to the mood of anger and resentment that sought outlet beyond the confines of the established protest organizations. Television had helped make the Muslims a part of the American mass consciousness but in a distorted form that neatly balanced white and black extremism.[32]

The 1950s, with their protests against genocide and lynching, their struggle over school desegregation, their bus boycott, were a prelude to the great struggles of the sixties. Many of the issues were defined: the elimination of segregation, the protection of blacks from legal and extralegal violence, and the guarantee of political rights to vote and hold office. The concepts of nonviolence, self-defense, and retaliatory violence, strategies of alliance with whites as against separatism, were advanced and debated. A number of individual leaders emerged from whom more was to be heard: Martin Luther King, Jr., Robert Williams, and Malcolm X. A new civil rights organization, focused upon the South, with its base in the black church, the Southern Christian Leadership Conference, had come into being. At the decade's end, however, the struggle against racism in the United States seemed to be at a stalemate. Terror and intimidation had compelled retreat from the effort of a black student, Autherine Lucy, to gain admission to the University of Alabama. "All deliberate speed" appeared to mean no speed at all, and white authority seemed to believe that tokenism offered a way of avoiding major shifts in policy. The federal government was headed, in the person of Dwight Eisenhower, by a president who would not endorse the *Brown* decision and connected in his mind resistance to school integration with a legitimate need to protect little white girls. The breaking of the stalemate would require a scale of mass movement that would make the maintenance of segregation too costly for American society to bear.

In the 1960s the inherent tendencies, the possibilities created by the changed context of post–World War II American society, would have to be played out fully in the course of mass confrontation with racism. The warning was already plain—blacks were no longer prepared to put up with the old order—but racists would not yield to law and reason. If serious progress toward racial justice and equality were to be made it would come only as a result of a social convulsion unprecedented since the Civil War era. In such a situation the question of racial violence would appear in new dimensions that nobody could ignore.

NOTES

Introduction

1. See Richard Hofstadter, "Reflections on Violence in the United States," in Richard Hofstadter and Michael Wallace, eds., *American Violence* (New York: Vintage Books, 1971), pp. 5, 7. There was some ambiguity in Hofstadter's emphasis upon the American tradition of violence. He wrote that what must be observed "is the circumscribed character and the small scale of the typical violent incident." Setting aside the unique instance of the Civil War, Hofstadter wrote of the United States that "its riots and massacres and other spontaneous outbursts of savagery do not otherwise loom inordinately large when projected against the backdrop of history." But he also reported the findings of the experts of the National Commission on the Causes and Prevention of Violence, which "confirm our sense that the United States is far from being the most peaceful among the Western or other industrial nations with which comparison seems most appropriate."

2. The National Commission on the Causes and Prevention of Violence states that probably "all nations are given to a kind of historical amnesia or selective recollection that masks unpleasant traumas of the past. Certainly, Americans since the Puritans have historically regarded themselves as a latter-day 'Chosen People' sent on a holy errand to the wilderness, there to create a New Jerusalem. One beneficent side effect of our current turmoil may be to force a harder and more candid look at our past." See *To Establish Justice, to Insure Domestic Tranquillity: Final Report of the National Commission on the Causes and Prevention of Violence* (Washington, D.C.: Government Printing Office, 1969), p. 16.

3. See Hofstadter, "Reflections on Violence," p. 30. Hofstadter writes here: "And even in our day, I think it should be emphasized, the growing acceptance of violence has been unwittingly fostered from the top of society. The model for violence, which has rapidly eroded the effectiveness of appeals to non-violent procedures, has been the hideous and gratuitous official violence in Vietnam."

4. Mary Frances Berry, *Black Resistance/White Law: A History of Constitutional Racism in America* (New York: Appleton-Century-Crofts, 1971), p. 238.

5. Regarding the significance of environment in mental retardation, see Roger L. Hurley, *Poverty and Mental Retardation* (Trenton: New Jersey Department of Institutions and Agencies, 1968).

6. See James H. Jones, *Bad Blood* (New York: Free Press, 1981).

7. See Herbert Aptheker, *American Negro Slave Revolts* (New York: Columbia University Press, 1943); Raymond A. Bauer and Alice H. Bauer, "Day to Day Resistance to Slavery," *Journal of Negro History*, October 1942, pp.: 388–419. A somewhat different perspective is found in Eugene D. Genovese, *From Rebellion to Revolution: Afro-American Slave Revolts in the Making of the Modern World* (Baton Rouge: Louisiana State University Press, 1979). Genovese finds a "low incidence" of slave revolts in the United States during

the nineteenth century, a circumstance he related to the "living space" created by pater-nalism. But Genovese agrees with Herbert Aptheker on the point that the cause of slave revolts was slavery and asks the pertinent question: "if the slaves had not risen at Stono, in southern Louisiana, in Southampton County, if they had not come close to rising in Richmond and in Charleston, if they had not risen at all, would the sober, martial, ex-perienced political leader of the slaveholding class have risked a dangerous confrontation with the North, including their own traditional northern political allies, simply because they were hearing horror stories from other slave countries?" He concludes that slave revolts "and the fear they inspired drove the slaveholders into a fateful constitutional and political confrontation . . . that ended with the destruction of the slaveholders' regime." In this framework slave revolts in the United States can only be judged to have had enormous political significance (see pp. 116, 117).

1. The Imposition of White Rule

1. Report of Carl Schurz to President Johnson, in U.S. Congress, Senate, 39th Cong., 1st sess., Exec. Doc. no. 2, quoted in W. E. B. Du Bois, *The Gift of Black Folk* (reprint, Millwood, N.Y.: Kraus-Thomson, 1975), p. 201.

2. See Donald E. Reynolds, "The New Orleans Riot of 1866, Reconsidered," *Louisiana History*, Winter 1964, pp. 5, 14.

3. For the most comprehensive treatment of the New Orleans violence, see Gilles Vandal, "The New Orleans Riot: The Anatomy of a Tragedy" (Dissertation, College of William and Mary, 1978); also see Gilles Vandal, "The Origins of the New Orleans Riot of 1866, Revisited," *Louisiana History* 22, no. 2 (1981): 135–65, and Vandal's preliminary paper, "The New Orleans Riot" (manuscript). Vandal too easily dismisses circumstantial evidence pointing to the likelihood that the 1866 violence resulted from conspiracy, but his work illuminates several aspects of the incident—the role of the Civil Rights Act in infuriating the city's racists, the lawless conduct of the police, and the considerable in-volvement of "respectable" whites in the July 30 violence ("New Orleans Riot: Anatomy," pp. 187–89, 221, 253, 254). Vandal also cites evidence indicating that white supremacists feared that the convention might be able to put in place a new state constitution, and there is little question but that the key element of the new document would be enfranchisement of blacks ("New Orleans Riot: Anatomy," pp. 166, 268). In other work Vandal has illuminated the general climate of statewide racial violence prevailing in Reconstruction Louisiana. He finds reasonable General Sheridan's estimation that between 1866 and 1875 some 3,500 persons were either killed or wounded. See Gilles Vandal, "Violence in Re-constructed Louisiana: The Use of the U.S. Army as a Peacekeeping Force" (Paper delivered at the American Historical Association meeting, 1982), pp. 6, 10, 11. Also see John Carver Edwards, "Radical Reconstruction and the New Orleans Riot of 1866," *International Review of History and Political Science*, August 1973, pp. 48–64.

4. Regarding the New Orleans and Memphis violence see U.S. Congress, House, *New Orleans Riots*, 39th Cong., 2nd sess., H. Rept. 16; and *Memphis Riots and Massacres*, 39th Cong., 1st sess., H. Rept. 101. Concerning urban racial violence in the aftermath of the Civil War, Leon Litwack, writes: "If the postwar riots and violence were intended to teach the freedmen 'not to arouse the fury of the white man,' they taught him that and considerably more. Law enforcement agencies and officers, if not co-conspirators in vio-lating the rights of ex-slaves, might be expected to protect or ignore the violators. Neither the Union Army nor the Freedmen's Bureau could be trusted to afford them adequate protection; instead, Union troops in some localities alternated with native whites as the

principal aggressors. To seek a redress of grievances in the courts of law, as many freedmen quickly discovered, resulted invariably in futility if not personal danger." See Leon Litwack, *Been in the Storm So Long* (New York: Knopf, 1979), pp. 281, 282.

5. James Gilbert Ryan, "The Memphis Riots of 1866: Terror in a Black Community during Reconstruction," *Journal of Negro History,* July 1977, pp. 243–57; Melinda Meek Hennessey writes that the Memphis violence was mainly a conflict between poor people but fails to consider the involvement of leaders of the white community. Hennessey does observe that at the very least "Memphis's gentlemen of property and standing, embittered by disfranchisement and defeat, did little to help bring the violence to a close." See Melinda Meek Hennessey, "To Live and Die in Dixie: Reconstruction Race Riots in the South" (Doctoral dissertation, Kent State University, 1978), pp. 24, 25, 31.

6. Bobby L. Lovett, "Memphis Riots: White Reaction to Blacks in Memphis, May 1865–July 1866," *Tennessee Historical Quarterly,* Spring 1979, pp. 9–33.

7. Harold D. Woodman, "Sequel to Slavery: The New History Views the Postbellum South," *Journal of Southern History* 43 (1977): 523–54.

8. Jonathan M. Wiener, *Social Origins of the New South: Alabama, 1860–1865* (Baton Rouge: Louisiana State University Press, 1978), p. 221.

9. Ibid., pp. 58, 61, 62, 63, 69.

10. Roger L. Ransom and Richard Sutch, *One Kind of Freedom* (Cambridge: Cambridge University Press, 1977), pp. 27, 30, 31.

11. Ibid., pp. 87, 177.

12. See Allen W. Trelease, *White Terror* (New York: Harper & Row, 1971); Herbert Shapiro, "The Ku Klux Klan during Reconstruction: The South Carolina Episode," *Journal of Negro History* 49 (1964): 34–55; Otto H. Olsen, "The Ku Klux Klan: A Study in Reconstruction Politics and Propaganda," *North Carolina Historical Review* 39 (1962): 340–62; Herbert Shapiro, "Afro-American Responses to Race Violence during Reconstruction," *Science and Society,* Summer 1972, pp. 158–70.

13. B. Lt. Col. C. D. Emory to Meade, November 23, 1868; Williams to B. Brig. Gen. R. Drum, January 1, 1869, General George C. Meade Papers, Historical Society of Pennsylvania, Philadelphia.

14. Vernon Lane Wharton, *The Negro in Mississippi, 1865–1890* (New York: Harper Torchbooks, 1965), pp. 181–98; Trelease, *White Terror,* pp. 241, 242.

15. Joel Williamson, *After Slavery* (Chapel Hill: University of North Carolina Press, 1965), pp. 266–73. See testimony of black militia captain regarding Hamburg in U.S. Congress, Senate, *South Carolina in 1876,* 44th Cong., 2nd sess., Misc. Doc. no. 48, pp. 34–45, 47.

16. See Melinda Meek Hennessey, "Racial Violence during Reconstruction: The 1876 Riots in Charleston and Cainhoy" (Paper, Southern Historical Association, 1983); "Reconstruction Politics and the Military: The Eufaula Riot of 1874," *Alabama Historical Quarterly,* Summer 1976, pp. 112–25; "Race and Violence in Reconstruction New Orleans: The 1868 Riot," *Louisiana History* 20, no. 1 (1979): 77–91; "Political Terrorism in the Black Belt: The Eutaw Riot," *Alabama Review,* January 1980, pp. 35–48; also see Harry P. Owens, "The Eufaula Riot of 1874," *Alabama Review,* July 1963, pp. 224–37. Owens writes: "The people of Eufaula, who had dreaded the thought of a slave uprising and who had considered the Negro as less than a human being, could not, in less than a decade, accept political dominance by the Negro. . . . the Democrats applied economic coercion and intimidation in an effort to force the Negro to abandon the Republican party. They were prepared to resort to any means, if necessary" (pp. 236, 237).

17. Hennessey, "To Live and Die in Dixie," pp. 356, 403–6.

18. See W. McKee Evans, "The Ku Klux Klan and the Conservative Triumph" (Paper delivered at the Pacific Coast Branch meeting of the American Historical Association, 1971), p. 14.

19. Ibid., pp. 10, 11.

20. See Everett Swinney, "Suppressing the Ku Klux Klan" (Dissertation, University of Texas, 1967), p. 235.

21. Evans, "Ku Klux Klan," p. 17.

22. Rembert W. Patrick, *The Reconstruction of the Nation* (New York: Oxford University Press, 1967), p. 157.

23. Swinney, "Suppressing the Klan," pp. 236, 238.

24. Trelease, *White Terror*, p. 412.

25. Swinney, "Suppressing the Klan," p. 292.

26. William Gillette, *Retreat from Reconstruction, 1869–1879* (Baton Rouge: Louisiana State University Press, 1979), pp. 42–45, 55.

27. See W. E. B. Du Bois, *The Philadelphia Negro* (reprint, New York: Blom, 1967), pp. 39–42; also *Philadelphia Public Ledger*, October 11, 1871. Harry C. Silcox, who has most carefully studied the 1871 violence, finds that William McMullen, the fourth-ward Democratic boss, "unquestionably" was behind much of what occurred. See Harry C. Silcox, "Politics from the Bottom Up: The Life of Ward Boss William McMullen, 1824–1901" (manuscript, 1985).

28. *Philadelphia Inquirer*, October 11, 1871; *Philadelphia Public Ledger*, October 12, 1871; Du Bois, *Philadelphia Negro*, p. 41.

29. *Philadelphia Inquirer*, editorial, October 14, 1871; Roger Lane, *Roots of Violence in Black Philadelphia, 1860–1900* (Cambridge: Harvard University Press, 1986), pp. 10, 18.

30. *Philadelphia Inquirer*, October 14, 1871; *Philadelphia Public Ledger*, October 14, 1871.

31. See Harry C. Silcox, "Nineteenth Century Philadelphia Black Militant: Octavius V. Catto (1839–1871)," *Pennsylvania History*, January 1977, pp. 53–76; Octavius V. Catto, *"Our Alma Mater": An Address Delivered at Concert Hall on the Occasion of the Twelfth Annual Commencement of the Institute for Colored Youth* (Philadelphia: Sherman, 1864); *Harper's Weekly*, October 28, 1871, p. 1005; *Philadelphia Public Ledger*, October 16, 1871.

32. *Philadelphia Inquirer*, October 17, 1871.

33. U.S. Congress, *The Joint Select Committee to Inquire into the Condition of Affairs in the Late Insurrectionary States*, 42nd Cong., 2nd sess. (Washington, D.C.: Government Printing Office, 1872).

34. Williamson, *After Slavery*, p. 271; Hennessey, "To Live and Die in Dixie," pp. 339, 340.

35. U.S. Congress *Joint Select Committee* testimony, 7: 1037. Henry M. Turner, later bishop of the African Methodist Episcopal Church, told the committee that in Macon there resided "a great number of very high-toned and dignified citizens," men of wealth, "who are really apprehensive that were they to start any violence there the thing would recoil on them." Turner stated that previously threats had been made against himself and another Republican, a Mr. Long, but the black community took effective action. "Word was brought to the authorities of the city that the negroes were armed and guarding the houses of Long and Turner. That caused a meeting to be held in the city hall, a kind of harmonial meeting, I will call it, at which several speeches were made by white and colored men. Resolutions were passed denouncing any disorder, and guaranteeing to colored people that protection

should be given to them, and that if any injury was done to them they could make the matter known to the city authorities, and go home and go to sleep quietly. I may say, however, that the colored people told them to their faces that if one colored man was killed they would burn their town down. I judge that may have had some effect in producing this public meeting of reconciliation."

36. Quoted in Lerone Bennett, *Black Power, USA* (Baltimore: Penguin Books, 1967), p. 129.

37. W. McKee Evans, *Ballots and Fence Rails* (Chapel Hill: University of North Carolina Press, 1969), pp. 101, 102; Williamson, *After Slavery*, pp. 265, 266.

38. U.S. Congress, *Joint Select Committee* testimony, 7: 1040.

39. Ibid., 3: 46, 47; 5: 1410–12.

40. Speech of Job E. Stevenson of Ohio, May 30, 1872, in U.S. Congress, *Congressional Globe*, 42nd Cong., 2nd sess., p. 4028.

41. George B. Tindall, *South Carolina Negroes, 1877–1900* (Columbia: University of South Carolina Press, 1952), p. 161; also see Tindall, "The Liberian Exodus of 1878," *South Carolina Historical Magazine*, July 1952, pp. 133–45.

42. For a comprehensive account of the 1879 "Exodus," see Nell Painter, *Exodusters: Black Migration to Kansas after Reconstruction* (New York: Knopf, 1977). Also useful is Robert G. Athearn, *In Search of Canaan: Black Migration to Kansas, 1879–80* (Lawrence: Regents Press of Kansas, 1978).

43. See, "The North Aroused," *Topeka Colored Citizen*, editorial, May 31, 1879, quoted in Leslie H. Fishel, Jr., and Benjamin Quarles, eds., *The Black American: A Documentary History* (Glenview, Ill.: Scott, Foresman, 1970), pp. 290, 291; also see "The Proceedings of a Mississippi Migration Convention in 1879," *Journal of Negro History* 4 (1919): 51–54.

44. U.S. Congress, Senate, *Report and Testimony of the Select Committee of the United States Senate to Investigate the Causes of the Removal of the Negroes from the Southern States to the Northern States*, 3 vols., 46th Cong., 2nd sess., S. Rept. 693 (Washington, D.C., 1880).

45. This discussion of the Danville violence is based on the evidence found in Charmion Higgenbotham, "The Danville Riot of 1883" (Master's thesis, Virginia State College, 1955), and John T. Melzer, "The Danville Riot, November 3, 1883" (Master's thesis, University of Virginia, 1963); also see Charles E. Wynes, *Race Relations in Virginia, 1870–1902* (Charlottesville: University of Virginia Press, 1961), pp. 29–34.

46. For text of the "Danville Circular," see La Wanda Cox and John H. Cox, eds., *Reconstruction, the Negro, and the New South* (Columbia: University of South Carolina Press, 1973), pp. 258–63. One observer, University of Virginia student Cornelius H. Fauntleroy, bluntly characterized the circular: "The Danville Circular and Riot won the day in Virginia. The former was the greatest fraud ever published to a confiding public. Some unessential particulars were true, but the main statements were either out and out lies, or the grossest exaggerations. There is almost indubitable grounds for the belief that the circular was concocted many days or months *before* the time it was issued in Danville, with a view to springing it on the people just before the election and too late for its falsehood to be exposed." See Wynes, *Race Relations*, p. 29. Whatever the time sequence, it is clear the document was carefully framed to appeal to race prejudice.

47. See William Ivy Hair, *Carnival of Fury: Robert Charles and the New Orleans Race Riot of 1900* (Baton Rouge: Louisiana State University Press, 1976), pp. 15, 26, 28, 31.

48. See U.S. Congress, Senate, *Report of the Special Committee to Inquire into the*

Mississippi Election of 1883, 48th Cong., 1st sess. S. Rept. 512. Twenty-seven black persons were among those testifying in this inquiry.

49. Hair, *Carnival of Fury*, pp. 34, 35.

50. See Philip S. Foner and Ronald L. Lewis, eds., *The Black Worker during the Era of the Knights of Labor*, vol. 3 in *The Black Worker: A Documentary History from Colonial Times to the Present* (Philadelphia: Temple University Press, 1978), pp. 153, 154.

51. Ibid., pp. 159, 179–82, 191–207, 208–9 (for account of December 2 protest meeting in New Orleans attended by 300 blacks), 209, 210.

52. The *New Orleans Mascot* on November 5, 1887, commented on the violence against the sugar laborers, noting that the governor was "usually very sluggish and tardy in his movements, but in dispatching his minions armed with gatling guns and improved rifles to terrorize and bulldoze unarmed laborers of the country he has shown an activity and an energy that proves he is fully alive to the danger that besets his continued rule." The paper further observed that the black laborers on the sugar plantations were "treated more like slaves than their fathers were in the days of slavery." And the *Mascot* saw the violence aimed at blacks as threatening white workers: "If Governor McEnery is justified in sending armed janissaries against the colored Knights of Labor in St. Mary and other interior parishes, should he not be justified in sending them against white Knights of Labor in Orleans parish? There is no more reason why a strike of cane-cutters in the country is to be put down by gatling guns than is a strike of shoemakers, bricklayers or cotton handlers in the city" (quoted in the *New Orleans Pelican*, November 12, 1987). The *Pelican*, November 12, 1887, published a protest by the Knights of Labor, New Orleans District Assembly no. 102, against the official violence against the strikers. Regarding the 1887 violence, also see Philip S. Foner, *Organized Labor and the Black Worker, 1619–1973* (New York: Praeger, 1974), pp. 60, 61. Foner stresses that Knights national leader Terence Powderly failed to rally the organization against the terror in Louisiana. Earlier, in 1880, black sugar workers had organized and struck for higher wages. At that time the conflict was not marked by violence although the state militia was sent to the affected areas and strike leaders were arrested, tried, and imprisoned for trespass. See La Wanda Cox, "The American Agricultural Wage Earner, 1865–1900," *Agricultural History*, 22 (1948): 95–114.

53. See C. Vann Woodward, *Tom Watson, Agrarian Rebel* (New York: Macmillan, 1938).

54. See Lawrence Goodwyn, "Populist Dreams and Negro Rights: East Texas as a Case Study," *American Historical Review*, December 1971, pp. 1435–56.

55. See John C. Marr, "History of Matagorda County" (Dissertation, University of Texas, 1928), pp. 166–69. Accounts of the episode in the *Galveston Daily News* indicate fears of a plantation uprising. The *News'* first item on the Matagorda conflict reported that "all the laborers on the plantations of Dr. Chinn, Wells Thompson and White, Williams and Croom are under arms and commanded by resolute leaders." The next day the *News* reported that Sheriff Wadsworth of Matagorda County was notified "of the impending danger of an outbreak of blacks that might result as disasterously as a slave uprising." The paper also reported that because blacks in the neighborhood of plantations along Caney Creek greatly outnumbered whites an uprising "would mean the extermination of all the white families" (September 27, 28, 1887). Marr gives the name of the black constable as Jerry Matthews whereas the name is reported as "Massena" in the *Galveston Daily News*.

56. Goodwyn, "Populist Dreams," pp. 1439–42.

2. Lynching and Black Perspectives

1. Richard Hofstadter wrote regarding lynching: "there is no great history of the subject that assesses its place in the political culture of the South." More than a decade after Hofstadter wrote, this history still remains to be written. See Hofstadter, "Reflections on Violence," p. 4; Edward L. Ayers, *Vengeance and Justice: Crime and Punishment in the 19th-Century American South* (New York: Oxford University Press, 1984), p. 250.

2. Reliable statistics concerning punishment of lynchers exist for the first three decades of the twentieth century. Between 1900 and 1930 there were twelve instances of conviction with sixty-seven individuals involved. None of these individuals was sentenced to execution. See James Harmon Chadbourne, *Lynching and the Law* (Chapel Hill: University of North Carolina Press, 1933), p. 14.

3. See Anne Braden, *The Wall Between* (New York: Monthly Review Press, 1958), pp. 20, 21, 24, 25. Braden recalls the comment of a southern gentleman, "A leader in his church and in the community," who stated in the heat of argument: "We have to have a good lynching every once in a while to keep the nigger in his place."

4. Monroe N. Work, ed., *Negro Year Book, 1931–1932* (Tuskegee, Ala.: Tuskegee Institute Press, 1931), p. 293.

5. James Elbert Cutler, *Lynch-Law* (New York: Longmans, Green, 1905), p. 172.

6. Ray Stannard Baker, *Following the Color Line* (New York: Harper Torchbooks, 1964), pp. 176, 177. In a study published in 1914 W. E. B. Du Bois and Augustus F. Dill found that of 2,855 lynch-law murders between 1885 and 1913 "the accusation of assault on women was made in only 706 or 24.4 percent, less than a fourth of those cases." See W. E. B. Du Bois and A. Dill, *Morals and Manners among Negro Americans* (Atlanta: Atlanta University Press, 1914), p. 44.

7. Philip S. Foner, ed., *Life and Writings of Frederick Douglass* (New York: International Publishers, 1955), 4: 324–42.

8. Ibid., pp. 430–42; see *New York Times*, May 18, 1886, for account of Philadelphia public meeting protesting the Carrollton murders; outrage at the Carrollton violence was also expressed in the black press. The *Cleveland Gazette* reported that a party of fifty white men on horseback had surrounded Carrollton court house and killed blacks present at a trial following the shooting of a white man. North Carolina black congressman James E. O'Hara proposed that the House of Representatives conduct an investigation of this violence, but this resolution was not adopted. The *Gazette* commented: "It seems strange that the United States Congress takes official cognizance of the killing and maltreatment of alien Asiatics, and refuses to listen to the appeal by a Representative for an investigation of the massacres of seventeen citizens of the United States by a mob which has the power to persuade or overawe the State and local authorities of Mississippi." The *Gazette* observed the contradiction that although the House, upon President Cleveland's recommendation, considered compensation in the case of Chinese immigrant laborers murdered at Rock Spring, Wyoming, it ignored the Mississippi events. See *Cleveland Gazette*, March 27, April 3, 1886; Vernon Lane Wharton stresses that several influential Mississippi newspapers deplored the Carrollton violence, but still no action was taken to punish the killers. See Vernon Lane Wharton, *Negro in Mississippi*, pp. 223, 224.

9. Foner, *Life of Douglass*, 4: 491–523.

10. See Emma Lou Thornbrough, *T. Thomas Fortune: Militant Journalist* (Chicago: University of Chicago Press, 1972), pp. 14–17.

11. Timothy Thomas Fortune, *Black and White: Land, Labor, and Politics in the South*

(reprint, New York: Arno Press, 1968), pp. 81, 117, 118, 126–30, 136–38, 142, 143. Fortune was farsighted in understanding the national dimension of the American racial question, writing in 1891 that "fifty years hence, it will be to this government all that the Irish question is to-day to the government of Great Britain, and perhaps more." Fortune was unusual in combining the roles of editor of the black press and staff member on the white *New York Evening Sun*. See I. Garland Penn, *The Afro-American Press and Its Editors* (Springfield, Ill.: Willey, 1891), pp. 137, 480.

In 1890 Fortune was instrumental in the organizing of the Afro-American League, whose purpose, according to Penn, was "to prevent mob violence and intimidation." At the 1890 founding convention Fortune defended agitation and stated that blacks must "fight fire with fire.... It is time to face the enemy and fight inch by inch for every right he denies us." The league's constitution outlined a program of protest aimed at such manifestations of racial oppression as brutal prison conditions and lynchings; migration from "terror-ridden" sections was encouraged. See Penn, *Afro-American Press*, p. 138, and August Meier, *Negro Thought in America, 1880–1915* (Ann Arbor: University of Michigan Press, 1963), p. 129.

Fortune's response to growing racial terrorization was framed in the context of his awareness of the extent of racial violence that marked Reconstruction and of the prevailing indifference of much of American society to such violence. Fortune wrote: "As I stand before the thirteen bulky volumes, comprising the 'Ku Klux Conspiracy,' being the report of the 'Joint Select Committee to inquire into the condition of affairs in the late Insurrectionary States,' on the part of the Senate and House of Representatives of the United States, reported February 19, 1872, my blood runs cold at the merciless chronicle of murder and outrage, of defiance, inhumanity and barbarity on the one hand, and usurpation and tyranny on the other." Fortune saw Reconstruction violence not only as an indictment of southern racism but also as a rebuke to the ruling Republican party, writing: "I arraign the dominant party of the time for base ingratitude, subterfuge and hypocrisy to its black partisan allies" (Fortune, *Black and White*, pp. 99, 100).

12. Peter Gilbert, ed., *The Selected Writings of John Edward Bruce: Militant Black Journalist* (New York: Arno Press, 1971), pp. 24, 29, 31, 32, 38, 39, 47, 48, 68, 71, 75, 83, 84.

13. Litwack, *Been in the Storm*, pp. 279, 450, 451.

14. See Edwin S. Redkey, ed., *The Writings and Speeches of Henry McNeal Turner* (reprint, New York: Arno Press, 1971), p. 26.

15. Ibid., p. 38.

16. Ibid., p. 42.

17. Ibid., pp. 54–57.

18. See text of original convention call, Turner's opening address, and subsequent *Voice of Missions* editorial comment in ibid., pp. 145–60.

19. Edwin S. Redkey, *Black Exodus* (New Haven: Yale University Press, 1969), p. 191.

20. *Cincinnati Enquirer*, November 30, 1893.

21. *Cincinnati Commercial Gazette*, December 2, 1893.

22. *Ibid.*, November 30, 1893; in 1891 Tourgee was instrumental in forming an inter-racial civil rights organization, the National Citizens Rights Association, that on a mass-membership basis would work against racial injustice. Bishop Turner wished Tourgee success in this endeavor but saw "no future in this country for the Negro" and desired federal aid in getting "manly, and self-reliant black men" out of the United States. See Otto H. Olsen, *Carpetbagger's Crusade: The Life of Albion Winegar Tourgee* (Baltimore: Johns Hopkins University Press, 1965), pp. 312–19.

23. *Cincinnati Commercial Gazette,* December 1, 1893.
24. Diary of Ida B. Wells, March 18, September 4, 1886, Regenstein Library, University of Chicago.
25. Ida Wells-Barnett, *On Lynchings* (reprint, New York: Arno Press, 1969), pp. 4, 5, 18, 19; Bettina Aptheker, "The Suppression of the *Free Speech:* Ida B. Wells and the Memphis Lynching, 1892," *San Jose Studies* 3, no. 3 (1977): 34–40; Alfreda M. Duster, ed., *Crusade for Justice: The Autobiography of Ida B. Wells* (Chicago: University of Chicago Press, 1970), pp. 47–62; David M. Tucker, "Miss Ida B. Wells and Memphis Lynching," *Phylon* 32, no. 2 (1971): 112–22; David M. Tucker, "Ida Wells-Barnett and the Memphis Lynchings" (Paper delivered at the Southern Historical Association meeting, 1982).

Following the lynching, *Free Speech* editorialized: "The city of Memphis has demonstrated that neither character nor standing avails the Negro if he dares to protect himself against the white man or become his rival. There is nothing we can do about the lynching now, as we are outnumbered and without arms. The white mob could help itself to ammunition without pay, but the order was rigidly enforced against the selling of guns to Negroes. There is therefore only one thing left that we can do; save our money and leave a town which will neither protect our lives and property, nor give us a fair trial in the courts, but takes us out and murders us in cold blood when accused by white persons." According to Wells, the aftermath of the lynching left Memphis business "practically at a standstill." See Duster, *Crusade,* pp. 52, 53. *Free Speech* also called for punishment of the lynchers, demanding that "the murderers of Calvin McDowell, Will Stewart and Tom Moss be brought to justice." The newspaper said, "In the name of God and in the name of the law we have always obeyed and upheld and intend to uphold and obey in the future." See Aptheker, "Suppression," p. 37. It is noteworthy that in defending the 1892 violence the *Memphis Evening Scimitar* revealed its racist recollection of the 1866 violence in the city: "The bloody riot of 1866, in which so many Negroes perished," the *Evening Scimitar* said on June 4, "was brought on principally by the outrageous conduct of the blacks towards the whites on the streets." See Wells-Barnett, *On Lynchings,* p. 17.

The Memphis lynchings profoundly affected Mary Church Terrell, notable leader of Afro-American women, who had been a childhood friend of victim Tom Moss. In her autobiography she recalled that Moss and the others were murdered "because they were succeeding too well." Noting that normal people are shocked at lynchings, Terrell added that when one has known the victim and known him to be beyond reproach "the horror and anguish which rend her heart are indescribable." The lynchings had profound psychological significance in her life, having occurred while she awaited the birth of a baby. For a long time, she wrote, she could not think of anything else but the mob's murder of Tom Moss. The baby had died a few days following birth, and Mrs. Terrell was greatly grieved. But while mourning it occurred to her "that under the circumstances it might be blessed dispensation of Providence that his precious life was not spared. The horror and resentment felt by the mother, coupled with the bitterness which filled her soul, might have seriously affected the unborn child... the more I thought how my depression which was caused by the lynching of Tom Moss and the horror of this awful crime might have injuriously affected my unborn child, if he had lived, the more I became reconciled to what at first seems a cruel fate." In Terrell's recollection there is evident that special pain felt by one who knows of a lynching not in terms of a terrible news story but as the barbarism inflicted on someone who has been a part of one's life. There is the pain of the woman and mother who gives birth to life but sees the life of another, close to her, taken away for no reason but racial identity. See Mary Church Terrell, *A Colored Woman in a White World* (Washington, D.C.: Ransdell, 1940), pp. 105, 106, 108.

26. Frederick Douglass, Introduction to *Southern Horrors*, in Wells-Barnett, *On Lynchings*.

27. During her visits to England Ida Wells-Barnett made extensive reference to her experiences in Memphis; Memphis business leaders, particularly concerned with the cotton trade, took note and were finally impelled to speak out against lynching. See Tucker, "Miss Wells and Memphis Lynching," p. 121.

28. Wells-Barnett, *Southern Horrors*, pp. 11, 12.

29. Wells-Barnett, *A Red Record*, in Wells-Barnett, *On Lynchings*.

30. See chapter 8, "Miss Willard's Attitude," in Wells-Barnett, *Red Record*, pp. 80–90; Ruth Bordin, *Francis Willard: A Biography* (Chapel Hill: University of North Carolina Press, 1986), p. 216.

31. Wells-Barnett, *Red Record*, pp. 97–99; also see Thomas C. Holt, "The Lonely Warrior: Ida B. Wells-Barnett and the Struggle for Black Leadership," in John Hope Franklin and August Meier, eds., *Black Leaders of the Twentieth Century* (Urbana: University of Illinois Press, 1982), pp. 45, 46. Holt points out that Wells-Barnett understood the need for economic pressure against southern whites while she stressed moral appeal to northern interests that could produce that pressure.

32. Bettina Aptheker points out that Ida Wells-Barnett defended "the racial integrity of Black manhood" and "simultaneously affirmed the virtue of Black womanhood and the independence of white womanhood." From this point of view, she emphasizes, "the antilynching movement of Black women may also be understood as a movement against rape." See Bettina Aptheker, *Woman's Legacy: Essays on Race, Sex, and Class in American History* (Amherst: University of Massachusetts Press, 1982), pp. 62, 63.

33. W. E. B. Du Bois, *The Souls of Black Folk* (Millwood, N.Y.: Kraus-Thomson, 1973), p. 226.

34. Alexander Crummell, *Africa and America: Addresses and Discourses* (reprint, New York: Negro Universities Press, 1969), pp. 49, 51, 53, 54, 64, 66, 69, 71, 81, 124, 125, 395–404.

35. The Zeke High episode is detailed in U.S. Congress, *Joint Select Committee* testimony, 9: 1356–60, 10: 1565–83.

36. Herbert Aptheker, "Mississippi Reconstruction and the Negro Leader Charles Caldwell," *Science and Society* 9 (1947): 340–71.

37. The clergyman, referred to by the *Galveston Daily News* as "preacher Norwood," was also reported to have said "the majority of the colored people wanted homes where they could dwell in peace, educate their children and worship God according to their creed. There were bad and good colored and white men in all countries, and he hoped that in the future the good of both colors would have the controlling power." The *News* reporter added: "The whites of this place seem to have great confidence in Norwood's honesty and straightforward manner of conducting himself." The *News* had its own explanation of the conflict: "The negroes are generally in large numbers on the plantations. When their work is done they gather in large parties at some given point, where liquor is circulated and the influential fire-brand harangues them on their rights and the wrongs that are constantly heaped upon by the whites. If a negro is killed or beaten the theme becomes rich, and the listening negroes, under the influence of whisky [sic] and the weird oratory of the speakers, are soon ready for any scheme that may be set on foot by leaders" (September 30, 1887).

38. See Ida Wells-Barnett, *Mob Rule in New Orleans*, in Wells-Barnett, *On Lynchings*.

39. Hair, *Carnival of Fury*, p. 171.

40. The autopsy report on Charles listed thirty-four bullet holes in the torso and noted that the skull was "almost beaten to a pulp" (ibid., p. 180).

41. Some weeks after the 1900 New Orleans events racist editor Henry J. Hearsey

expressed the concern that "some Yankee scoundrel will write [Charles's] life and depict him as the negro Coeur de Lion." Actually, it was to be a black woman of the South, Ida Wells-Barnett, who pioneered in publicly hailing Charles's courage. More recently, historian Sig Synnestvedt described Charles as "one of the proudest black martyrs in American history." William Ivy Hair writes that "Charles' primary conviction was that his own life should continue as long as possible, consistent with dignity," too quickly concluding this is inconsistent with martyrdom. See Hair, *Carnival of Fury,* pp. xiii, 2; Sig Synnestvedt, *The White Response to Black Emancipation* (New York: Macmillan, 1972), p. 57.

42. Hair, *Carnival of Fury,* pp. 107, 108; W. E. B. Du Bois, *Dusk of Dawn* (New York: Shocken Books, 1968), p. 67. A further perspective on Du Bois's response to the Hose incident emerges from what, years later, he told an interviewer. Du Bois initially hoped to utilize the Sam Hose incident as a prod to develop a reaction against lynching. The point was that the emptiness of the allegations made against Hose was clear. Du Bois remembered: "What had happened was that a black plantation laborer wasn't paid at the—it might have been at the end of the year, but at any rate his plantation owner didn't settle with him, and Sam Hose made a fuss about it, and they got into a fight, and the plantation owner was killed. They started then to find Sam Hose and they couldn't find him. And then, suddenly, there was the accusation that Sam Hose had raped the wife. Now, everybody that read the facts of the case knew perfectly well what had happened. The man wouldn't pay him, so they got into a fight, and the man got killed—and then, in order to arouse the neighborhood to find this man, they brought in the charge of rape. Even from the newspapers you could see there was no foundation to it." But the reality was that the white-supremacist South was not interested in the facts of the case. W. E. B. Du Bois interview, 1960 (Oral History Project, Columbia University), pp. 147, 148.

3. In the Context of Empire

1. *Washington Post,* September 29, October 6, 13, 14, 24, 25, November 19, 1898; also, for accounts of Madisonville, Ohio, incident, see *Cincinnati Enquirer,* November 18, 19, 22, 1898. On November 18 the *Enquirer* reported: "The searchers were in a furious mood and threats of lynching are freely indulged in."

2. See Helen G. Edmonds, *The Negro and Fusion Politics in North Carolina, 1894–1901* (Chapel Hill: University of North Carolina Press, 1951), pp. 158–77, for account of Wilmington violence. Edmonds points out that photos of the Wilmington mob reveal "white men and boys...dressed in collars, hats, ties, and fashionable garments of the period, armed with shot guns and sticks." In short, "the mob was not composed of white hoodlums." The violence was based on a public political program that urged replacing many black employees with whites and that demanded, in the spirit of the mob that years earlier murdered the abolitionist editor Elijah Lovejoy, that the local Republican newspaper cease publication and the editor depart the city within twenty-four hours (pp. 166, 168). The violence carried through a political coup d'état in which the local Fusion government was forced from office (p. 171). For a view of Wilmington as a manifestation of the racist Radical view that blacks ultimately had no place in the South, see Joel Williamson, *The Crucible of Race: Black White Relations in the American South since Emancipation* (New York: Oxford University Press, 1984), pp. 195–201; also see H. Leon Prather, Sr., *We Have Taken a City: Wilmington Racial Massacre and Coup of 1898* (Rutherford, N.J.: Fairleigh Dickinson University Press, 1984). Also see Henry Litchfield West, "The Race War in North Carolina," *Forum,* January 1899, pp. 578–91. West was essentially sympathetic with the North Carolina white-supremacy movement and accepted as valid a variety

of racist stereotypes, but he candidly described the class nature of Wilmington racism, noting that "the white supremacy movement had its inspiration and encouragement almost entirely in the desire of the business and taxpayer interests" to be rid of what he called "bad" government. He reported that at meetings held in pursuance of the slogan "the whites must rule" those attending included ministers, lawyers, doctors, merchants, railroad officials, cotton exporters, and other substantial white Wilmingtonians (pp. 579, 587, 590).

3. Thomas R. Cripps, Introduction to Jack Thorne, *Hanover* (reprint, New York: Arno Press 1969), p. i.

4. *Washington Post,* October 24, 1898.

5. Ibid., October 29, 1898.

6. Ibid., October 30, 1898; the *Post's* correspondent was, no doubt, Henry Litchfield West, author of the January 1899 article in the *Forum* outlining the North Carolina events. West later, 1902–10, served as a District of Columbia commissioner.

7. *Washington Post,* November 1, 1898.

8. Ibid., November 2, 1898.

9. Ibid., November 5, 1898.

10. Ibid., November 6, 1898.

11. Ibid., November 7, 1898.

12. *St. Louis Post-Dispatch,* November 1, 3, 1898.

13. Telegram, Carr to McKinley, November 9, 1898, William McKinley Papers, series 1, microfilm reel 5, Library of Congress, Washington, D.C.

14. *Washington Post,* November 9, 1898.

15. Ibid., November 10, 1898.

16. See Hayumi Higuchi, "White Supremacy on the Cape Fear: The Wilmington Affair of 1898" (Master's thesis, University of North Carolina at Chapel Hill, 1980), pp. 69, 148.

17. *Washington Post,* November 11, 1898.

18. Ibid., November 12, 1898.

19. Ibid., November 13, 15, 1898.

20. John C. Dancy, *Sand against the Wind: The Memoirs of John C. Dancy* (Detroit: Wayne State University Press, 1966), pp. 68, 69.

21. See National Archives, RG60, Department of Justice file 17743–1898.

22. W. E. B. Du Bois, *The Black North in 1901: A Social Study* (New York: Arno Press, 1969), p. 44; Jerome Anthony McDuffie, "Politics in Wilmington and New Hanover County, 1865–1900: The Genesis of a Race Riot" (Doctoral dissertation, Kent State University, 1979), pp. 737, 791; U.S. Bureau of the Census, Eleventh Census of the United States, microfilm reel 1; Twelfth Census, microfilm reel 1.

23. See Jane Cronly, "Account of the Race Riot in Wilmington, N.C.," Cronly Family Papers, William R. Perkins Library, Duke University.

24. Bassett to Adams, November 14, 1898, Herbert Baxter Adams Papers, William R. Perkins Library, Duke University.

25. Tourgee to McKinley, November 23, 1898, McKinley Papers, series 1, reel 5.

26. See Higuchi, "White Supremacy," pp. 43, 44, 49, 50.

27. Quoted in McDuffie, "Politics in Wilmington," p. 654.

28. Higuchi, "White Supremacy," pp. 18, 19, 142, 143.

29. See Tom Henderson Wells, "The Phoenix Election Riot," *Phylon,* Spring 1970, pp. 58–69.

30. See James A. Hoyt, *The Phoenix Riot* (Greenwood, 1938).

31. Benjamin E. Mays, *Born to Rebel* (New York: Scribner, 1971), pp. 1, 17.

32. *Washington Post,* November 12, 13, 15, 1898.

33. Ibid., November 14, 1898; the *Washington Post* on November 18 also reported a protest meeting held in New York City on November 17 at Cooper Union; the *New York Times*, November 18, reported a crowd of 6,000 as attending this meeting, at which one speaker, Elizabeth B. Grannis, was cheered for stating that before venturing abroad America must learn how to treat its own citizens.

34. *Washington Post*, November 21, 1898.

35. Ibid., November 22, 23, 1898.

36. See *New York Evening Post*, editorial, November 18, 1898, quoting Washington, in Louis R. Harlan, ed., *The Booker T. Washington Papers* (Urbana: University of Illinois Press, 1975), 4: 524.

37. *Washington Bee*, November 5, 19, 1898; *Cleveland Gazette*, November 19, 1898.

38. John Campbell Dancy, the black United States collector of customs at Wilmington, shortly after the Wilmington violence privately described Manly's response to Rebecca Felton as "indiscreet and inflammable utterance." Manly had also refused to suspend publication and so, Dancy hoped, quiet the excited atmosphere. Dancy stated his harsh evaluation of what Manly had done: "The whole race this day in the state of North Carolina feels the fearful effect of that great blunder." It should be noted, however, that Manly had opposed Dancy's candidacy for the collector of customs post. See Higuchi, "White Supremacy", p. 108. See Dancy to J. E. Bruce, January 30, 1899, Edward Bruce Papers, box 2, folder 10, Schomburg Center for Research in Black Culture, New York Public Library. See Thorne, *Hanover*, pp. 6, 9, 10, 47, 68–70, 116, 117, 123. Following the Wilmington violence Felton declared that if it required lynching "to protect woman's dearest possession from ravening, drunken human beasts, then, I say, lynch a thousand Negroes a week, if it is necessary." Regarding Manly she asserted that "the slanderer should be made to fear a lyncher's rope rather than occupy a place in New York newspapers." See clipping in National Archives, RG60, Department of Justice file 17743–1898.

39. Chesnutt to Green, December 1, 1900, John P. Green Papers, Western Reserve Historical Society Library, Cleveland.

40. See *Cleveland World*, October 20, 1901.

41. Charles W. Chesnutt, *The Marrow of Tradition* (reprint, Ann Arbor: University of Michigan Press, 1969), pp. xv, xvii, 110–14, 179, 182, 192, 231, 232, 275–77, 282–84; William L. Andrews, *The Literary Career of Charles W. Chesnutt* (Baton Rouge: Louisiana State University Press, 1980), p. 199; the theme of lynching that Chesnutt considered in *The Marrow of Tradition* is also present in one of his short stories, "The Sheriff's Children." In this story the sheriff shields a black prisoner from the lynch mob and in the course of the encounter learns that the man is actually his own unacknowledged son whom years earlier he had sold to a slave trader. In this tale, as is consistently the case in his writing, Chesnutt focuses upon the distortions in human values produced by racism. See Charles W. Chesnutt, "The Sheriff's Children," in *The Wife of His Youth and Other Stories of the Color Line* (reprint, Ridgewood, N.J.: Gregg Press, 1967), pp. 60–93.

42. *Washington Post*, December 30, 1898.

43. Morris speech and Williams comment in folder, "Editorials of Charles H. Williams," State Historical Society of Wisconsin. Dr. Charles Satchell Morris (1865–1931), prominent black Baptist clergyman, served as pastor at the Myrtle Church, West Newton, Mass., and at New York's Abyssinian Baptist Church. Trained for the law as well as the ministry, Morris had served Frederick Douglass as secretary. See obituary in *Chicago Defender*, August 1, 1931.

44. See Herbert Aptheker, ed., *A Documentary History of the Negro People in the United States* (New York: Citadel Press, 1951), p. 789.

45. See Theodore Roosevelt, "The Rough Riders," *Scribner's*, April 1899, pp. 420–40; in a letter he wrote but apparently did not send to a white army officer, Roosevelt again expressed some racist perceptions of blacks. He observed that "colored regular troops usually fight excellently" but added that "taking the average colored regular as compared to the average white regular, there were differences against the former which would have to be carefully considered in using them on an extended scale." Stating that black soldiers "under most conditions do admirably" if directed by white officers whom they trusted, Roosevelt also reported an incident of "extraordinary panic" by some black troops and gave a racist explanation for the phenomenon. "I attributed the trouble to the superstition and fear of the darkey, natural in those but one generation removed from slavery and but a few generations removed from the wildest savagery." See Roosevelt to Robert J. Fleming, May 21, 1900, in Elting E. Morison, ed., *The Letters of Theodore Roosevelt* (Cambridge: Harvard University Press, 1951), 2: 1304–6. Later, during the 1900 election campaign, Roosevelt dropped derogatory references from his public comments about black troopers. See Willard B. Gatewood, Jr., *Black Americans and the White Man's Burden, 1898–1903* (Urbana: University of Illinois Press, 1975), p. 244.

46. Gatewood, *Black Americans*, p. 230. Willard B. Gatewood, Jr., *"Smoked Yankees" and the Struggle for Empire* (Urbana: University of Illinois Press, 1971), pp. 32, 35, 36, 65, 74, 75, 84, 126, 153, 154, 157, 159, 160, 162, 164, 245, 259, 268, 280, 281.

47. Gatewood, *Black Americans*, pp. 32, 33, 110.

48. Ibid., p. 198.

49. Ibid., pp. 221, 321; also, for black response to imperialism, see George P. Marks, III, ed., *The Black Press Views American Imperialism* (New York: Arno Press, 1971).

4. The Violence of the Progressive Era

1. Frank Moss, comp., *Story of the Riot* (reprint, New York: Arno Press, 1969), p. 2; see account of incident in Gilbert Osofsky, "Race Riot, 1900: A Study of Ethnic Violence," *Journal of Negro Education*, Winter 1963, pp. 16–24.

2. Moss, *Story of the Riot*, pp. 3–5.

3. Something of the prejudice shaping white New York opinion is reflected in the comment of a *New York Times* columnist, quoted by Osofsky, that regarding "the citizen of African descent.... His crude melodies and childlike antics are more than tolerated in the music halls of the best class." See Gilbert Osofsky, *Harlem: The Making of a Ghetto* (New York: Harper & Row, 1963), pp. 46–52. It is ironic that New York newspapers had only recently criticized the violence erupting in the Robert Charles episode in New Orleans; also see *New York Times*, September 13, 1900, for account of Carnegie Hall meeting. Several themes were struck in the speeches made at this meeting. The Reverend W. H. Brooks of Saint Mark's Church, who presided, said: "We mean to fight for our rights but let me caution you that while this tension is on we must do nothing which will cost us the sympathy of the best people. We must show that we can rise higher than the men who attacked us a few nights ago." The Reverend N. D. Cook of Bethel AME Church declared that the meeting was called to protest "against mob violence, in any and every form whether it be instigated by the worthless negro, the degraded white man, the corrupt Tammanyite, or the brutal police officer." Cook observed that southern race haters must be gloating, but he advised that southerners "hold their peace until they shall have atoned for the thousands of murders, burnings and lynchings which lie at their door." The *Times* reported that the speech of the Reverend Robert S. MacArthur of Calvary Baptist Church made a sensation. MacArthur's main point was the culpability of Tammany Hall, and he

asked the audience: "Does not imperialism flourish in New York? Have we not a Czar?" Most to the point among the speeches, however, was that delivered by Miss M. R. Lyons of Brooklyn. Lyons had a definite course of action to propose: "Words are worthless. We must have action. We cannot afford to be silent lest we be misunderstood. The question is, What are you going to do about it?.... The trouble with the negroes is that they have never been united on a single question. Are you united now?.... Let every negro get a permit to carry a revolver. You are not supposed to be a walking arsenal, but don't you get caught again. Have your houses made ready to afford protection from the fury of the mob, and remembering that your home is your castle and that no police officer has a right to enter it, unless he complies with the usages of the law, see that he does not."

4. Charles Crowe, "Racial Violence and Social Reform: Origins of the Atlanta Riot of 1906," *Journal of Negro History,* July 1968, p. 253.

5. See John Dittmer, *Black Georgia in the Progressive Era, 1900–1920* (Urbana: University of Illinois Press, 1977), pp. 130, 131.

6. Ibid., pp. 131–40.

7. See *Southern Workman,* editorial, November 1906, pp. 579–80, quoting Nicholas Worth [pseud.], "The Autobiography of a Southerner since the Civil War," *Atlantic Monthly,* October 1906, pp. 474–88.

8. Baker, *Following the Color Line,* p. 9.

9. *Atlanta Constitution,* September 23, 1906.

10. Baker, *Following the Color Line,* p. 11.

11. Ibid., pp. 12, 13. John Dittmer, in his study of black Georgia during the Progressive period, notes that although blacks "were unable to offer effective resistance when trapped downtown or caught in white sections of the city, they did fight back successfully when the mobs invaded their neighborhoods." It is also Dittmer's view that white authorities were likely to have underestimated the extent of white casualties. See Dittmer, *Black Georgia,* pp. 129, 130.

12. Baker, *Following the Color Line,* pp. 13, 14.

13. Ibid., pp. 16, 17.

14. Walter White, *A Man Called White* (reprint, New York: Arno Press, 1969), pp. 10–12; Herbert Aptheker, *Afro-American History: The Modern Era* (New York: Citadel Press, 1971), p. 73.

15. Reverdy C. Ransom, *The Spirit of Freedom and Justice* (Nashville: Sunday School Union, 1926), pp. 117–21.

16. William English Walling, "The Race War in the North," *Independent,* September 3, 1908, p. 529; see James L. Crouthamel, "The Springfield Race Riot of 1908," *Journal of Negro History,* July 1960, pp. 164–81.

17. Walling, "Race War," pp. 530, 531.

18. See text of Ida B. Wells-Barnett's speech in Philip S. Foner, ed., *The Voice of Black America* (New York: Capricorn Books, 1975), 2: 72, 73.

19. Walling, "Race War," p. 534.

20. Ibid., pp. 531, 532.

21. For accounts of Brownsville episode, see Jack D. Foner, *Blacks and the Military in American History* (New York: Praeger, 1974), pp. 95–103; Anne J. Lane, *The Brownsville Affair: National Crisis and Black Reaction* (Port Washington, N.Y.: Kennikat Press, 1971); John D. Weaver, *The Brownsville Raid* (New York: Norton, 1970).

22. See *New York Times,* December 27, 1972. Willis told the reporter: "None of us said anything, 'cause we didn't have anything to say. It was a frame-up straight through."

23. See W. E. B. Du Bois's 1948 essay, "From McKinley to Wallace," in Julius Lester, ed., *The Seventh Son: The Thought and Writings of W. E. B. Du Bois* (New York: Vintage Books, 1971), 2: 589; earlier, in 1912, Du Bois had referred to Roosevelt as "the perpetrator of the Brownsville outrage." See *Crisis* 5 (1912): 29.

24. Foner, *Blacks and the Military*, p. 99; in private correspondence Washington termed Roosevelt's action "a great blunder . . . all the more regrettable because of his waiting until just the day after election before putting the order into effect." Roosevelt acted without acceding to Washington's request that the action be delayed until Washington could present relevant information to him. See Louis R. Harlan and Raymond W. Smock, eds., *The Booker T. Washington Papers* (Urbana: University of Illinois Press, 1980), 9: 113, 118.

25. Foner, *Voice of Black America*, 2: 41, 42.

26. Ibid., p. 43.

27. *Messages and Papers of the Presidents* (New York: Bureau of National Literature, 1917), 16: 7029–33. Roosevelt urged the merits of education as a means of eliminating criminality, but for blacks it was education of a particular type, for "the best type of education for the colored man, taken as a whole, is such education as is conferred in schools like Hampton and Tuskegee." Roosevelt patronizingly added, regarding graduates of these schools, that they "turn out well in the great majority of cases, and hardly any of them become criminals" (p. 7032).

28. Robert V. Haynes, *A Night of Violence: The Houston Riot of 1917* (Baton Rouge: Louisiana State University Press, 1976), pp. 29, 30, 58.

29. Ibid., pp. 74, 75,

30. See Edgar A. Schuler, "The Houston Race Riot, 1917," *Journal of Negro History*, July 1944, p. 302.

31. Ibid., p. 303, quoting *Houston Post*, August 19, 1917; Haynes, *Night of Violence*, p. 79.

32. Haynes, *Night of Violence*, p. 23.

33. Ibid., pp. 119–20, 126, 140.

34. Schuler, "Houston Race Riot," p. 336; Haynes, *Night of Violence*, pp. 196, 199, 203–5.

35. El Paso newspaper clipping, n.d.

36. Associated Press dispatch, November 5, 1917.

37. *Houston Post*, November 6, 13, 15, 1917.

38. Haynes, *Night of Violence*, p. 4.

39. Foner, *Voice of Black America*, 2: 104, 105.

40. Haynes, *Night of Violence*, p. 274, quoting Du Bois.

41. See "The Waco Horror," supplement to *Crisis*, July 1916. Also see account, "An American Holiday," *Masses*, September 1916, in William L. O'Neill, ed., *Echoes of Revolt: The Masses, 1911–1917* (Chicago: Quadrangle Books, 1966), pp. 239–42.

42. *Dallas Times Herald*, March 3, 1910; *Dallas Morning News*, March 4, 1910.

43. *Dallas Times Herald*, March 3, 4, 5, 1910.

44. George C. Edwards, *Pioneer at Law* (New York: Norton, 1974), pp. 25, 26, 34, 35.

45. See account in letter of anonymous witness published in the *Crisis* in Fishel, and Quarles, *Black American*, pp. 374–76.

46. Oscar Leonard, "The East St. Louis Pogrom," *Survey*, July 14, 1917, p. 331.

47. Ibid., p. 333.

48. "Report on the Special Committee Authorized by Congress to Investigate the East St. Louis Riots," in Anthony Platt, ed., *The Politics of Riot Commissions, 1917–1970*

(New York: Macmillan, 1971), p. 68. The report was marred by blatant manifestations of racism, with racial conflict described as "natural racial aversion" and the actions of black migrants crudely stereotyped. The report asserted: "White women were afraid to walk the streets at night; negroes sit in their laps on streetcars; black women crowded them from their seats; they were openly insulted by drunken negroes.... Corrupt politicians found the negro vote fitted to their foul purpose, and not only bought them on election day, but in the interval protected them in their dens of vice, their low saloons and barrel houses" (p. 62). The congressmen viewed blacks as both victims and provokers of violence.

49. Ibid., p. 70.

50. Ibid., pp. 78, 79.

51. Elliott Rudwick notes that local corporate executives "took no action to restore calmness and avert racial violence" during the critical weeks of May 1917 and adds that the businessmen's conduct "actually aggravated a dangerous situation." See Elliott Rudwick, *Race Riot at East St. Louis* (Cleveland: Meridian Books, 1966), p. 152. The House committee had stated that "railroads and the manufacturing establishments" shared the responsibility for the violence. See Platt, *Politics of Riot Commissions*, p. 61. At a New York meeting called to welcome the new ambassador of the Russian provisional government Theodore Roosevelt and Samuel Gompers exchanged heated recriminations concerning the episode. Gompers stressed the role of labor recruiters, and Roosevelt accused the labor leader of apologizing for murder. The argument provoked "wild and prolonged" disorder in the Carnegie Hall audience. The incident could only serve to widen the gulf between Afro-Americans and organized labor. See *New York Times*, July 7, 1917.

52. See W. S. Reese, Jr., to U.S. Attorney General, June 15, 1903, RG 60; Pete Daniel, *The Shadow of Slavery* (New York: Oxford University Press, 1973), pp. 59, 60; for a description of the late-nineteenth-century convict lease system that often veiled peonage, see Ayers, *Vengeance and Justice*, pp. 185–222.

5. The Focusing of Debate

1. See "The Life Story of a Negro Peon," in Hamilton Holt, ed., *The Life Stories of Undistinguished Americans* (New York: Pott, 1906), pp. 185, 191, 194.

2. Text of Wells-Barnett speech in Foner, *Voice of Black America*, 2: 71–75.

3. See Ida B. Wells-Barnett, "How Enfranchisement Stops Lynching," *Original Rights Magazine*, June 1910, pp. 42–53.

4. See Harold F. Gosnell, *Negro Politicians* (Chicago: University of Chicago Press, 1967), p. 26.

5. Mary Church Terrell, "Lynching from a Negro's Point of View," *North American Review*, June 1904, pp. 854, 855, 858, 860, 861, 865; Terrell's article was written in response to a piece by Thomas Nelson Page in the January 1904 *North American Review* that defended lynching. See Terrell, *Colored Woman*, p. 225. As noted by Trudier Harris, the *Vicksburg Evening Post* account provides the basis for a fictionalized version in Sutton E. Griggs's 1905 novel *The Hindered Hand*. See Sutton E. Griggs, *The Hindered Hand* (New York: AMS Press, 1969), pp. 133–35. Trudier Harris, *Exorcising Blackness* (Bloomington: Indiana University Press, 1984), pp. 1, 2. The Springfield 1904 violence involved the lynching on March 7 of a black man, Richard Dixon, who allegedly had shot and killed a Springfield policeman. Dixon was hung from a telephone pole in the city's center and following this a mob rampaged through the black neighborhood known as the "Levee." See "Guide to Springfield and Clark County" in WPA files, Ohio Historical Society, Columbus. The statement of the International Socialist Bureau was a ringing attack on racism.

Signed by representatives of seventeen of the parties affiliated with the bureau, the manifesto declared: "The interest of the working class demands the unity of all workers without distinction of race, and it demands the energetic protest of Socialist Democracy against the abominable acts committed daily in the United States against the Negro." See Philip S. Foner, *American Socialism and Black Americans* (Westport, Conn.: Greenwood Press, 1977), pp. 126, 127.

6. Du Bois, *Dusk of Dawn*, p. 67. According to Mary Church Terrell, Hose had killed his employer, Alfred Cranford, in a dispute over wages. The local newspaper offered a reward for Hose's capture and predicted lynching and further announced a public consensus that Hose should be tortured and burned at the stake. Terrell added that in Atlanta special trains were made up to take "the Christian people" of the city to the site of the burning. Terrell, "Lynching," p. 859.

7. Du Bois, *Souls of Black Folk*, in *Three Negro Classics* (New York: Avon Books, 1965), pp. 217, 282, 283, 285, 313, 329–31, 336.

8. Du Bois, *Philadelphia Negro*, pp. 235, 241, 249, 259, 283, 284.

9. Du Bois, 1960 interview, Oral History Project, p. 133.

10. Du Bois, *Black North in 1901*, pp. 13, 15, 24, 26, 42, 43, 46.

11. Du Bois, *Souls of Black Folk*, in *Three Negro Classics*, pp. 297, 347, 373, 375–77.

12. Aptheker, *Documentary History*, pp. 898, 899.

13. Ibid., p. 903.

14. Du Bois, *Souls of Black Folk*, p. 313. Du Bois went on to connect this rural dimension of terror to the formation of the Black Belt, a connection largely ignored by subsequent scholarship. The Black Belt, he wrote, "was primarily a huddling for self-protection,—a massing of the black population for mutual defense in order to secure the peace and tranquillity necessary to economic advance."

15. Aptheker, *Documentary History*, p. 909. The response of the progressive *Outlook* magazine to the Harpers Ferry address was an affirmation of support for segregation and a declaration that the Niagara movement would be more useful "if it demanded more of the Negro race and put less emphasis on its demands for the Negro race" (September 1, 1906, pp. 3, 4).

16. Lester, *The Seventh Son*, 1: 422–26. Following publication of "A Litany of Atlanta," the economist E. R. A. Seligman wrote Du Bois that although the Atlanta events had "amazed and disgusted" him he had not realized "the horror of it all" until he read Du Bois's poem. See Herbert Aptheker, ed., *The Correspondence of W. E. B. Du Bois* (Amherst: University of Massachusetts Press, 1973), 1: 123.

Booker T. Washington and his adjutant, Emmett J. Scott, falsely stated that Du Bois had cowered at Calhoun School in Alabama during the course of the riot. Scott wrote an anonymous article to that effect, and in 1911 Washington wrote T. Thomas Fortune: "Du Bois did run away from Atlanta. All the time that the riot was going on, Du Bois was hiding at the Calhoun School in Alabama. . . . He remained there until the riot was over and then came out and wrote a piece of poetry bearing upon those who were killed in the riot." Louis Harlan described this account as a "distortion" and notes that "Du Bois returned home to Atlanta University and his beleaguered family as soon as possible." See Louis R. Harlan, *Booker T. Washington, the Wizard of Tuskegee: 1901–1915* (New York: Oxford University Press, 1983), pp. 300, 376.

17. W. E. B. Du Bois, "From the Point of View of the Negroes," *World Today* 11 (1906): 1173–75.

18. William M. Tuttle, Jr., Introduction to "W. E. B. Du Bois' Confrontation with White

Liberalism during the Progressive Era: A Phylon Document," *Phylon*, September 1974, pp. 241–58.

19. Lester, *The Seventh Son*, pp. 13, 14.

20. W. E. B. Du Bois and Martha Gruening, "The Massacre of East St. Louis," *Crisis*, September 1917, pp. 219–38. Du Bois also discussed the East St. Louis violence in his autobiographical volume *Darkwater*. Again his focus was upon the relation of labor competition to race hatred, and he vividly, fiercely portrayed what had taken place: "So Hell flamed in East St. Louis! The white men drove even black union men out of their unions and when the black men, beaten by night and assaulted, flew to arms and shot back at the marauders, five thousand rioters arose and surged like a crested storm-wave, from noonday until midnight; they killed and beat and murdered; they dashed out the brains of children and stripped off the clothes of women; they drove victims into the flames and hanged the helpless to the lighting poles. Fathers were killed before the faces of mothers; children were burned; heads were cut off with axes; pregnant women crawled and spawned in dark, wet fields." Du Bois wrote that the blacks fought "like beasts at bay," but they were caught between the factories and their homes. See W. E. B. Du Bois, *Darkwater* (New York: Schocken Books, 1969), pp. 94, 95.

21. Booker T. Washington, *Up from Slavery*, in *Three Negro Classics*, pp. 70, 71.

22. Du Bois, *Souls of Black Folk*, in *Three Negro Classics*, p. 251.

23. See Louis R. Harlan, ed., *The Booker T. Washington Papers* (Urbana: University of Illinois Press, 1972), 1: 149–54.

24. Foner, *Voice of Black America*, 1: 646; Washington's statement was also quoted in the *Birmingham Age-Herald*, April 26, 1899, and in this version Washington was quoted to the effect that he felt "constrained to keep silent and not engage in any controversy that might react on the work to which I am now lending my efforts." See text in Louis R. Harlan and Raymond W. Smock, eds., *The Booker T. Washington Papers* (Urbana: University of Illinois Press, 1976), 5: 90, 91. According to Harlan, however, Washington was moved to more public pronouncement concerning lynching as a result of public outcry over the Georgia killings. See Louis R. Harlan, *Booker T. Washington* (New York: Oxford University Press, 1972), pp. 262, 263.

25. See Louis R. Harlan, ed., *The Booker T. Washington Papers* (Urbana: University of Illinois Press, 1974), 3: 362–64.

26. See *Tuskegee News* account of Harris incident in Harlan, *Washington Papers*, 3: 558–60; also see Louis R. Harlan and Pete Daniel, "A Dark and Stormy Night in the Life of Booker T. Washington," *Negro History Bulletin* 33 (1970): 159–61.

27. Harlan, *Booker T. Washington*, pp. 173, 175.

28. See Harlan and Smock, *Washington Papers*, 9: 62–67, 69, 70, 74, 75, 77, 84, 86, 87, 92–94, 112, 116, 117, 158–61, 172.

29. Harlan, *Washington, Wizard of Tuskegee*, p. 308.

30. Text of Washington speech, in Foner, *Voice of Black America*, 2: 36–38.

31. Harlan, *Washington, Wizard of Tuskegee*, p. 308, 322.

32. Ibid., pp. 379–404; also see Willard B. Gatewood, "Booker T. Washington and the Ulrich Affair," *Phylon* 30 (1969): 286–302.

33. See Louis R. Harlan and Raymond W. Smock, eds., *The Booker T. Washington Papers* (Urbana: University of Illinois Press, 1981), 11: 19, 20, 47, 52, 71, 356, 358, 366, 386.

34. Minutes of NAACP board meeting, May 2, 1911, NAACP Papers, Library of Congress, Washington, D.C. At this same meeting Chairman Villard suggested that the Civil

Rights Committee should prepare a list of 500 to 1,000 people who could be called upon to send letters or telegrams of protest when a particular incident occurred.

35. See Herbert Aptheker, ed., *A Documentary History of the Negro People in the United States, 1910–1932* (Secaucus, N.J.: Citadel Press, 1973), pp. 37, 38.

6. Confrontation

1. John H. Bracey, Jr., August Meier, and Elliott Rudwick, eds., *The Afro-Americans: Selected Documents* (Boston: Allyn & Bacon, 1972), pp. 397–402. Wilson's statement against lynching came approximately a year after the silent protest march of 10,000 persons along New York's Fifth Avenue on July 28, 1917, and Kelly Miller's stirring public appeal to Wilson of August 4, 1917. Moved especially by the East St. Louis violence, Miller called upon the president, "speaking for the people of the United States to put an end to lawlessness wherever it raises its hideous head." He urged Wilson to ask Congress for the power to prevent lynching and to "quicken the conscience of the nation by a stirring message to Congress calling attention to this growing evil which is gnawing at the vitals of the nation." Wilson did considerably less than Miller asked. See Kelly Miller, "Disgrace of Democracy," in *The Everlasting Stain* (Washington, D.C.: Associated Publishers, 1924), pp. 140, 156.

2. Stephen Graham, *Children of the Slaves* (London: Macmillan, 1920), pp. 205–7.

3. Ibid., pp. 202, 203; Ocmulgee and Pope City lynchings reported also in NAACP board minutes, September 1919, NAACP Papers.

4. *Atlanta Constitution*, July 25, 1919; Graham, *Children of the Slaves*, pp. 204, 205.

5. *Charleston News and Courier*, May 12, 1919; Department Commander Henry E. Sharpe to U.S. Army Adjutant General, May 22, 1919, National Archives, RG 60.

6. See Richard C. Cortner, *A Mob Intent on Death: The NAACP and the Arkansas Riot Cases* (Middletown Conn.: Wesleyan University Press, 1987); see also the account of the incident in Arthur I. Waskow, *From Race Riot to Sit-in* (New York: Anchor Books, 1967), pp. 121–42. Waskow finds an "occupational" rather than a class or racial appeal in the words of a Progressive Union song, but the class emphasis is clear in the text of a union circular: "This union wants to know why it is that the laborers cannot control their just earnings" (p. 122). Walter F. White, "Massacring Whites' in Arkansas," *Nation*, December 6, 1919, pp. 715, 716; Walter F. White, "The Race Conflict in Arkansas," *Survey*, December 13, 1919, pp. 233, 234. In a pamphlet issued by the American Civil Liberties Union William Pickens summed up the roots of the Phillips County violence: "The cause of all this was the attempt of the Negro tenants and share croppers to sell their cotton in the open market for a price between 30 and 40 cents a pound, instead of selling it to their respective landlords for prices ranging around 15 cents." Pickens pamphlet, "Lynching and Debt-Slavery," quoted in Aptheker, *Documentary History, 1910–1932*, p. 320.

7. *Moore v. Dempsey*, Supreme Court of the United States, 261 U.S. 86 (1923), quoted in Albert P. Blaustein and Robert L. Zangrando, eds., *Civil Rights and the American Negro* (New York: Trident Press, 1968), pp. 341, 342. Ida B. Wells-Barnett recalls in her autobiography that the prisoners told her of having been beaten, given electric shock, "and in every possible way terrorized" while held at the Helena jail before removal to Little Rock. Duster, *Crusade for Justice*, p. 402.

8. Claude McKay, "If We Must Die," in Stephen Henderson, *Understanding the New Black Poetry* (New York: Morrow, 1972), p. 117.

9. Chicago Commission on Race Relations, *The Negro in Chicago* (Chicago: University

of Chicago Press, 1922); Waskow, *Race Riot to Sit-in* pp. 38–104; William M. Tuttle, Jr., *Race Riot: Chicago in the Red Summer* (New York: Atheneum, 1972); Carl Sandburg, *The Chicago Race Riots, July 1919* (New York: Harcourt Brace & World, 1969). In his introduction to the Sandburg book Walter Lippmann sets the race question in a broader context, but his analysis lacked any sense of the special urgency of challenging racism. "Until we have learned to house everybody," he wrote, "employ everybody at decent wages in a self-respecting status, guarantee his civil liberties, and bring education and play to him, the bulk of our talk about the 'race problem' will remain a sinister mythology. In a dirty civilization the relation between black men and white will be a dirty one" (p. xix). Sandburg in his account noted that in the course of the violence thousands of white and black workers "stood together" and rejected violence. According to Sandburg this was the first time "that a large body of mixed nationalities and races" proclaimed opposition to violence that would divide workers (pp. 5–6).

In his autobiography longtime black revolutionary Harry Haywood recalled preparations for self-defense made by a group of veterans. The men set up a Browning automatic weapon in an apartment on Fifty-first Street near State, waiting to ambush likely attackers. See Harry Haywood, *Black Bolshevik* (Chicago: Liberator Press, 1978), p. 82.

10. See "A Report on the Chicago Riot by an Eye-Witness," *Messenger*, September 1919, pp. 11–13.

11. See William M. Tuttle, Jr., "Views of a Negro during 'The Red Summer' of 1919," *Journal of Negro History*, July 1966, pp. 209–18.

12. Waskow, *Race Riot to Sit-in*, pp. 110–19.

13. Ibid., pp. 21–37.

14. Aptheker, *Documentary History, 1910–1932*, pp. 259–60.

15. *New York World*, November 28, 1919.

16. W. E. B. Du Bois, in *Crisis*, May 1919, quoted in Theodore G. Vincent, ed., *Voices of a Black Nation* (San Francisco: Ramparts Press, 1973), pp. 80–82.

7. Garvey and Randolph

1. See Robert A. Hill, ed., *The Marcus Garvey and Universal Negro Improvement Association Papers* (Berkeley: University of California Press, 1983), 1: 189.

2. See John Hope Franklin, Foreword to E. David Cronon, *Black Moses: The Story of Marcus Garvey* (Madison: University of Wisconsin Press, 1969), p. xix.

3. W. E. B. Du Bois article, "Back to Africa," in John Henrik Clarke, ed., *Marcus Garvey and the Vision of Africa* (New York: Vintage Books, 1974), p. 116. Upon Garvey's death in 1940, Du Bois said that Garvey had been "an astonishing popular leader" (quoted in Cronon, *Black Moses*, p. 204).

4. E. David Cronon writes that by 1920 Garvey "had attracted a large active following and that he had aroused the attention of most American Negroes and masses of blacks elsewhere in the world" *Black Moses*, (p. 207).

5. Roi Ottley, *New World A-coming* (reprint, New York: Arno Press, 1969), p. 81.

6. Robert A. Hill, Introduction to Hill, *Marcus Garvey Papers*, 1: lxvii, lxviii.

7. Ibid., pp. 209, 210. James Weldon Johnson recalled Garvey's role at the meeting: "The man spoke, and his magnetic personality, torrential eloquence and intuitive knowledge of crowd psychology were all brought into play. He swept the audience along with him." James Weldon Johnson, *Black Manhattan* (reprint, New York: Atheneum, 1968), p. 253.

8. Hill, *Marcus Garvey Papers*, 1: 212–20.

9. Ibid., p. 374.

10. Ibid., 2: 41, 42, 120.

11. Ibid., p. 456.

12. Ibid., 1: 397; 2: 42.

13. Ibid., 1: 502.

14. Ibid., 2: 438.

15. Ibid., pp. 115, 116.

16. Ibid., pp. 128–31.

17. Ibid., 1: 288, 308, 378–80.

18. Ibid., 2: 571–75.

19. Ibid., 1:401–3; 2:72.

20. Ibid., 1: lxxviii–lxxxi.

21. Quoted in Theodore G. Vincent, *Black Power and the Garvey Movement* (Berkeley, Calif.: Ramparts Press, n.d.), p. 19.

22. Ibid., pp. 190, 191; among black newspapers that sharply criticized Garvey for his contact with the Klan was the *California Eagle:* "Mr. Garvey here is your hat and please be on your way.... We want you to distinctly understand that the Ku Klux Klan is strictly un-American and the Negro who stands for this dastardly institution stands as a traitor to his race. Move on 'Mark Us,' move on" (September 9, 1922), quoted in Emory J. Tolbert, *The UNIA and Black Los Angeles* (Los Angeles: Center for Afro-American Studies, UCLA, 1980), p. 78.

23. Vincent, *Black Power,* pp. 205, 206.

24. Tony Martin, *Race First: The Ideological and Organizational Struggles of Marcus Garvey and the Universal Negro Improvement Association* (Westport, Conn.: Greenwood Press, 1976), pp. 276, 277; Vincent, *Black Power,* pp. 197, 198.

25. Hill, *Marcus Garrey Papers* 1:lxxxi; Cronon, *Black Moses,* pp. 194–95.

26. Amy Jacques Garvey, ed., *The Philosophy and Opinions of Marcus Garvey* (reprint, New York: Atheneum, 1969), 2: 3, 4.

27. Martin, *Race First,* p. 60.

28. A. Philip Randolph, "Lynching: Capitalism Its Cause, Socialism Its Cure," *Messenger,* March 1919, pp. 9–12, quoted in August Meier, Elliott Rudwick, and Francis L. Broderick, eds., *Black Protest Thought in the Twentieth Century,* 2d ed. (Indianapolis: Bobbs-Merrill, 1971), pp. 85–91.

29. "How to Stop Lynching," *Messenger,* editorial, August 1919, pp. 8–10.

30. "Lynching a Domestic Question," *Messenger,* editorial, July 1919, pp. 7, 8.

31. "How to Stop Lynching," pp. 9–10.

32. "The Cause of and Remedy for Race Riots," *Messenger,* editorial, September 1919, pp. 20, 21.

33. W. A. Domingo, "Did Bolshevism Stop Race Riots in Russia?" *Messenger,* September 1919, pp. 26, 27.

8. Struggle on a Higher Level

1. Chicago Commission, *Negro in Chicago,* pp. 131–33.

2. Ibid., pp. 59–64, 481; Grover Cleveland Redding, an adherent of the Abyssinians, was convicted of murder in connection with the two deaths and was hanged on June 24, 1921. It should be noted that an agent for U.S. and British intelligence services and likely agent-provocateur, one R. D. Jonas, had for some time attached himself to Redding and the Abyssinians. See Hill, *Marcus Garvey Papers,* 1:531, 532; also see Vincent, *Black Power,* pp. 85–87, for account of Redding, Jonas, and the Abyssinian movement. Vincent

characterizes the group as "probably the most extreme expression of post–World War I black radicalism" (p. 86).

3. Chicago Commission, *Negro in Chicago*, pp. 481–84.

4. See account of Lowry lynching in William Pickens, "The American Congo: Burning of Henry Lowry," in Nancy Cunard, ed., *Negro: An Anthology* (New York: Ungar, 1970), pp. 21–23; Pickens's article appeared initially in the *Nation*, March 23, 1921.

5. Scott Nearing, *Black America* (New York: Schocken Books, 1969), pp. 198–201; Walter White, *Rope and Faggot* (New York: Knopf, 1929), pp. 23–25.

6. See *Memphis News Scimitar*, January 26, 1921.

7. *New York Times*, April 30, May 1, 1929; W. E. B. Du Bois, "Opinion," *Crisis*, June 1923, p. 55. An echo of the response of the University of Missouri students is seen in 1931 in the approval expressed by the *Daily Illini*, student newspaper at the University of Illinois, of a lynching at Maryville, Mo. See *Pittsburgh Courier*, January 31, 1931.

8. See Hugh M. Dorsey, *A Statement from Governor Hugh M. Dorsey as to the Negro in Georgia* (1921).

9. Judith Stein, *The World of Marcus Garvey: Race and Class in Modern Society* (Baton Rouge: Louisiana State University Press, 1986), p. 156.

10. Scott Ellsworth, *Death in a Promised Land: The Tulsa Race Riot of 1921* (Baton Rouge: Louisiana State University Press, 1982), pp. 8–11.

11. Ibid., pp. 20–22, 107.

12. Ibid., pp. 25–32

13. Ibid., pp. 33–38.

14. Ibid., pp. 38–44.

15. Ibid., p. 7.

16. Ibid., p. 51; see Walter White, "The Eruption of Tulsa," The *Nation*, June 29, 1921, in Aptheker, *Documentary History, 1910–1932*, pp. 327–32.

17. Resolution and Walter White report on Tulsa in NAACP board minutes, June 13, 1921, NAACP Papers, Library of Congress, Washington, D.C.; Ellsworth, *Death in a Promised Land*, p. 88.

18. Chandler Owen, "Tulsa," *Messenger*, July 1921, pp. 218–20.

19. See John Hope Franklin, Foreword to Ellsworth, *Death in a Promised Land*, pp. xv–xvii.

20. Bill of particulars, quoted in Walter White, "The Sweet Trial," *Crisis*, January 1926, p. 127.

21. David E. Lilienthal, "Has the Negro the Right of Self-Defense?" *Nation*, December 23, 1925, p. 724.

22. White, "The Sweet Trial," p. 126.

23. David A. Levine, *Internal Combustion* (Westport, Conn.: Greenwood Press, 1976), pp. 153–58; *Argument of Clarence Darrow in the Case of Henry Sweet* (New York: NAACP, 1927), p. 30, quoting *Detroit Free Press*.

24. *Argument of Clarence Darrow*, p. 31; Levine, *Internal Combustion*, pp. 165, 166.

25. See Sidney Fine, *Frank Murphy: The Detroit Years* (Ann Arbor: University of Michigan Press, 1975), p. 152.

26. *Amsterdam News*, November 18, 1925; *Baltimore Herald*, November 2, 1925, clipping in NAACP Papers, D–87, Library of Congress.

27. Telegram, Johnson to W. H. McKinney, September 12, 1925, NAACP Papers, D–85; White to Johnson, September 16, 1925, NAACP Papers, D–85; Sweet, Davis, Morse, and Washington to McKinney, September 29, 1925, NAACP Papers, D–85; Johnson to H. S. Huntington, September 29, 1925, NAACP Papers, D–85; Johnson to *New York*

World, October 30, 1925, in NAACP Papers, D–87; White, "The Sweet Trial," p. 126. White wrote here that the case was "the dramatic high point" of the antisegregation struggle. He added that the NAACP was moved by the consideration that "a completely fair trial" would show blacks that their situation in the United States was not as hopeless as sometimes seemed to be the case.

28. White to W. K. McGill, October 6, 1925, NAACP Papers, D–86; telegram, Johnson to Darrow, October 7, 1925, NAACP Papers, D–86; Du Bois to Darrow, October 7, 1925, NAACP Papers, D–86; Kenneth G. Weinberg, *A Man's Home, a Man's Castle* (New York: McCall, 1971), p. 64, quoting Du Bois; regarding Darrow's early NAACP affiliation, see Aptheker, *Correspondence of Du Bois,* 1: 169.

29. NAACP statement announcing Darrow appointment, October 16, 1925, NAACP Papers, D–86.

30. White to Darrow, October 20, 1925, NAACP Papers, D–86.

31. Fine, *Frank Murphy,* pp. 146, 151, 156; Murphy was a long-term consistent opponent of racism, as evidenced in his dissent in the 1944 Supreme Court *Korematsu* decision regarding the wartime internment of Japanese-Americans. Justice Murphy vigorously attacked what he termed "this legalization of racism" and went on to add: "Racial discrimination in any form and in any degree has no justifiable part whatever in our democratic way of life." See *Korematsu v. United States,* 323 U.S. 214 (1944); also see Peter Irons, *Justice at War: The Story of the Japanese American Internment Cases* (New York: Oxford University Press, 1983), pp. 335, 336.

32. Arthur Garfield Hays, *Let Freedom Ring* (New York: Liveright, 1937), p. 231.

33. Arthur Garfield Hays, opening speech, November 16, 1925, NAACP Papers, D–86.

34. *Detroit Free Press,* November 19, 1925.

35. Ibid.

36. White, "The Sweet Trial," p. 128.

37. *Detroit Free Press,* November 25, 26, 1925; Levine, *Internal Combustion,* pp. 181, 182; Hays, *Let Freedom Ring,* p. 230, quoting Countee Cullen poem. Hays wrote regarding the prosecutor's view of waiving rights that "there are some rights which one cannot waive and remain free, such as the right to live, and the right to refuse to be intimidated, whatever the cost (p. 201).

38. See Aptheker, *Documentary History, 1910–1932,* p. 519, quoting Johnson.

39. *Argument of Clarence Darrow.*

40. Lilienthal, "Right of Self-defense," p. 725.

41. Announcement of January 4, 1925, meeting, NAACP Papers, D–44.

42. Telegram, Johnson to Darrow October 7, 1925, NAACP Papers, D–86; NAACP memo, NAACP Papers, D–86; Johnson to *Philadelphia Ledger,* November 16, 1925, NAACP Papers, D–87.

43. See Clement E. Vose, *Caucasians Only: The Supreme Court, the NAACP, and the Restrictive Covenant Cases* (Berkeley: University of California Press, 1967), pp. 52–54.

44. Weinberg, *A Man's Home,* pp. 62, 63, quoting Du Bois.

45. Richard Bardolph, ed., *The Civil Rights Record: Black Americans and the Law* (New York: Crowell, 1970), p. 202, citing decision *Corrigan v. Buckley,* 271 U.S. 323 (1926).

46. See NAACP monthly column, *Crisis,* November 1921, p. 21; along with Johnson, the delegation included such figures as Washington chapter president Archibald Grimke, Tuskegee Institute principal R. R. Moton, Emmett J. Scott, Kelly Miller of Howard University, John Hope, Mary Church Terrell, and NAACP counsel James A. Cobb; Haynes, *Night of Violence,* pp. 309–14. The delegation, in the course of its visit with Harding,

referred to the danger posed by the Ku Klux Klan. Harding responded: "I do not believe the Ku Klux Klan is aimed at your people." For an account of this encounter by one of the participants, see Gloria T. Hull, ed., *Give Us Each Day: The Diary of Alice Dunbar-Nelson* (New York: Norton, 1984), pp. 81–86.

47. Robert Minor, "After Garvey—What?" *Workers Monthly,* June 1926, quoted in Clarke, *Marcus Garvey,* pp. 165, 166.

48. White, *Rope and Faggot,* pp. 179–89, 195, 226.

49. Walter F. White, *The Fire in the Flint* (reprint, New York: Negro Universities Press, 1969).

50. White, *Rope and Faggot,* pp. 29–33; *Daily Worker,* January 11, 1927; I. A. Newby, *Black Carolinians: A History of Blacks in South Carolina from 1895 to 1968* (Columbia: University of South Carolina Press, 1973), pp. 242–45; Walter White, "The Shambles of South Carolina," *Crisis,* December 1926, pp. 72–75; NAACP column, *Crisis,* January 1927, pp. 141–42.

51. See Pete Daniel, *The Shadow of Slavery: Peonage in the South* (Urbana: University of Illinois Press, 1972), pp. 149–69; Pete Daniel, *Deep'n as It Come: The 1927 Mississippi River Flood* (New York: Oxford University Press, 1977), pp. 138–41. See accounts in *Daily Worker,* May 28, June 6, 20, July 13, 18, 1927; also Walter White, "The Negro and the Flood," *The Nation,* June 22, 1927, pp. 688, 689. White reports that in "hundreds of cases" blacks were forced at the point of a gun to work on the levees even after it was clear they would not hold. The *Daily Worker,* May 28, quotes White as stating that numerous blacks were swept to their deaths when the break came. A recent study of Hoover's racial policies finds that Hoover and the Red Cross "accomplished a great deal" for blacks caught in the flood but notes that commitment to voluntarism blocked implementation of a land resettlement program and that months after the flood many blacks "knew only that reforms had been few and fleeting." See Donald J. Lisio, *Hoover, Blacks, and Lily-Whites: A Study of Southern Strategies* (Chapel Hill: University of North Carolina Press, 1985), pp. 3–20.

9. Turning Left

1. Charles V. Willie recollection of Chivers, in "Walter R. Chivers—an Advocate of Situation Sociology," *Phylon,* September 1982, pp. 242–48.

2. Arthur F. Raper, *The Tragedy of Lynching* (Chapel Hill: University of North Carolina Press, 1933), pp. 1, 4, 6, 7, 11, 19, 20; Gunnar Myrdal, *An American Dilemma* (New York: McGraw-Hill, 1964), 2: 564.

3. Raper, *Tragedy of Lynching,* p. 19.

4. See Aptheker, *Documentary History, 1910–1932,* p. 721.

5. Workers [Communist] party statement, quoted in Amy Jacques Garvey, ed., *Garvey and Garveyism* (New York: Collier Books, 1970), pp. 171, 172.

6. Cyril V. Briggs, "Declaration of War on the Ku Klux Klan," *Crusader,* January 1921, quoted in Vincent, *Voices of a Black Nation,* p. 129.

7. William Z. Foster, *The Negro People in the United States* (New York: International Publishers, 1970), p. 460. In Herbert Aptheker's view the ANLC's membership was not numerous but "its contacts were wide and its impact considerable." Aptheker, *Documentary History, 1910–1932,* p. 656. A rather disparaging view of the ANLC's impact is presented in Haywood, *Black Bolshevik,* pp. 143–47. According to Work, *Negro Year Book, 1931–1932,* during April 1926 "100 colored men and women" representing the congress sought to join an American Federation of Labor march but were turned away by the Central Labor

Union. As the marchers reached Faneuil Hall, however, they found the ANLC contingent in the front rows where they continued to sit (pp. 152, 153). In November 1930 A. Philip Randolph testified at a session of a special congressional investigating committee regarding Communist influences among blacks. Regarding the ANLC, he stated that its membership was "very small" but added, "the group is much stronger and much more extensive than the membership implies." Asked to explain the appeal of this movement Randolph replied: "as a general thing, there is discontent and unrest among the Negroes as a whole throughout the country, and that unrest and discontent arises as a result of the existence, I believe, of a recrudescence in lynchings at the present time. Then you have, also, the existence of widespread peonage in the South." See U.S. Congress, *Hearings before a Special Committee to Investigate Communist Activities in the United States*, 71st Cong. 2nd sess., 6, 1: 345.

    8. See ANLC, "A Call to Action," in Aptheker, *Documentary History, 1910–1932*, pp. 488–93.

    9. Ibid., pp. 656–71.

    10. The league proposed a "Bill of Civil Rights for the Negro," which called for enactment of a law providing the death penalty for participation in lynching or other acts of violence against persons because of race, color, or nationality. The league's proposal was endorsed by the International Labor Defense and the National Scottsboro Action Committee and was presented to Congress and the president by the Free the Scottsboro Boys marchers. See International Labor Defense statement, "Thirteen Lynchings in First Six Months of 1933," in "Lynching" folder, Schomburg Collection, New York Public Library.

    11. *New York Times*, April 26, 1931.

    12. Vincent, *Voices of a Black Nation*, p. 177, quoting Ford article in *Negro Worker*, June 1931.

    13. See "A Statement by the N.A.A.C.P. on the Scottsboro Cases," and Clarence Darrow, "Scottsboro," in *Crisis*, March 1932, pp. 81, 82.

    14. *Daily Worker*, April 24, 1931. Later, however, Pickens sharply attacked tactics of mass agitation and protest. For an account of Pickens's shifting position, as presented at a Chattanooga church meeting, see Angelo Herndon, *Let Me Live* (reprint, New York: Arno Press, 1969), p. 124.

    15. Henry Lee Moon, *Balance of Power* (Garden City, N.Y.: Doubleday, 1949), pp. 123, 124.

    16. Du Bois, *Dusk of Dawn*, pp. 298, 299. Du Bois also noted that one of the effects of the controversy was to strengthen the tendency of other NAACP leaders to avoid formulating a program of economic reform.

    17. Nell Irvin Painter, *The Narrative of Hosea Hudson* (Cambridge: Harvard University Press, 1979), p. 83.

    18. Herndon, *Let Me Live*, pp. 93, 94.

    19. George Robbins, "Chicago Demonstration," *New Masses*, September 1931, p. 17; Ralph Ellison, *Invisible Man* (New York: Signet, 1964), pp. 232–45; also see account of Chicago episode in Mauritz Hallgren, *Seeds of Revolt* (New York: Knopf, 1933), pp. 178, 179.

    20. St. Clair Drake and Horace R. Cayton, *Black Metropolis* (New York: Harper Torchbooks, 1962), 1: 86.

    21. Robbins, "Chicago Demonstration."

    22. *Chicago Tribune*, August 4, 5, 6, 7, 9, 1931.

    23. *Chicago Defender*, August 8, 15, 1931.

    24. James W. Ford, *The Right to Revolution for the Negro People* (New York: Harlem Section, Communist Party, n.d.), quoted in Foner, *Voice of Black America*, 2: 184–91.

25. See *The Mob Still Rides: A Review of the Lynching Record, 1931–1935* (Atlanta: Commission on Interracial Cooperation, 1935).

26. Maya Angelou, *I Know Why the Caged Bird Sings* (New York: Random House, 1969), pp. 16–18, 36.

27. Charles S. Johnson, *Growing Up in the Black Belt* (New York: Schocken Books, 1967), pp. 4–6.

28. Hortense Powdermaker, *After Freedom* (New York: Viking Press, 1939), pp. 32, 33, 53, 54, 173, 174, 332, 335, 351. In her autobiography Powdermaker recalls that her compassionate view of Indianola whites was "severely jolted" when one afternoon while driving along a country road she encountered some twenty-five "rough-looking white men" who were hunting a black man who allegedly had raped a white woman. Powdermaker recalls of these whites: "Their faces, now transformed with brutality and hate, were frightening." See Hortense Powdermaker, *Stranger and Friend: The Way of an Anthropologist* (New York: Norton, 1966), pp. 188, 189. As late as 1986 a *Washington Post* reporter found that Indianola was dominated by a propertied white elite "that runs this Mississippi Delta town like an antebellum plantation, ceding power only gradually to the black majority in a manner and at a pace of its own choosing" (April 21, 1986).

29. Allison Davis and John Dollard, *Children of Bondage* (New York: Harper Torchbooks, 1964), pp. 201–3, 240, 247–49.

30. Allison Davis, *Leadership, Love, and Aggression* (New York: Harcourt Brace Jovanovich, 1983), pp. 159–62.

31. Carl Carmer, *Stars Fell on Alabama* (New York: Literary Guild, 1934), pp. 15, 17, 30; *New York Times*, August 2, 14, 1933; Clarence Cason, *90° in the Shade* (Chapel Hill: University of North Carolina Press, 1935), pp. 114–19; Dan T. Carter, *Scottsboro* (New York: Oxford University Press, 1971), pp. 277, 278; Anthony J. Blasi, *Segregationist Violence and Civil Rights Movements in Tuscaloosa* (Washington, D.C.: University Press of America, 1980), pp. 22–26.

32. Carter, *Scottsboro*, p. 123.

33. See Elmer A. Carter, *Opportunity*, editorial, August 1931, pp. 234, 235; a letter sent by a sharecropper to Communist party headquarters in Birmingham expressed the urgent concern animating unionization: "The farmers of the South are in need. I ask you all please to help me. I have got 20 head in my family. I want you all to help get me to get some work or a mule and a plow and something to eat." See letter quoted in John Beecher, "The Share Croppers' Union in Alabama," *Social Forces* 13 (1934): 124–32. According to longtime Alabama activist Virginia Foster Durr, the sharecroppers' movement was aided by a Marxist study group in Montgomery. Today some of the members of that group "are among the richest people in Montgomery." See Hollinger F. Barnard, ed., *Outside the Magic Circle: The Autobiography of Virginia Foster Durr* (University: University of Alabama Press, 1985), p. 81.

34. Theodore Rosengarten, *All God's Dangers: The Life of Nate Shaw* (New York: Knopf, 1974), pp. 297, 304. Nate Shaw was the pseudonym Rosengarten used for the actual Ned Cobb.

35. Dale Rosen and Theodore Rosengarten, "The Narrative of Jess Hull, Alabama Tenant Farmer," *Radical America*, November–December 1972, pp. 67–68; also see Rosengarten, "Stepping over Cockleburrs: Conversations with Ned Cobb," in Marc Pachter, ed., *Telling Lives* (Washington, D.C.: New Republic Books, 1979), p. 122.

36. Henry Fuller, "Sunday at Camp Hill," *New Republic*, December 16, 1931, pp. 132–34.

37. Ibid., p. 133.

38. See account in Carter, *Scottsboro*, pp. 124–27; Fuller, "Sunday at Camp Hill," p. 133.

39. Carter, *Scottsboro*, p. 126; *Birmingham Age-Herald*, quoted in Beecher, "Share Croppers' Union," p. 126.

40. Harry Haywood, quoted in Aptheker, ed., *A Documentary History of the Negro People in the United States, 1933–1945* (Secaucus, N.J.: Citadel Press, 1974), p. 35.

41. Elmer Carter, *Opportunity*, editorial, August 1931.

42. *Chicago Defender*, July 25, 1931.

43. *Pittsburgh Courier*, July 25, August 1, 1931.

44. Beecher, "Share Croppers' Union," pp. 127–32.

45. Ibid., pp. 127–31; Rosengarten, *All God's Dangers*, pp. 307, 308, 309, 311, 312, 314.

46. Carter, *Scottsboro*, p. 178; Rosengarten, *All God's Dangers*, p. 339.

47. *Birmingham Post*, December 22, 1932, *Birmingham News*, December 20, 1932, quoted in Beecher, "*Share Croppers' Union*," pp. 130, 131.

48. Beecher, "Share Croppers' Union," p. 132; Elaine Ellis, "Woman of the Cotton Fields," *Crisis*, October 1938, quoted in Aptheker, *Documentary History, 1933–1945*, p. 335.

49. Albert Jackson, "Alabama's Blood-Smeared Cotton," *New Masses*, September 24, 1935, p. 13; the Labor Research Association estimated that in early 1936 the union had 12,000 members, mainly in Alabama, Mississippi, Louisiana, and North Carolina. See *Labor Fact Book No. 3* (New York: International Publishers, 1936), p. 145.

50. See Albert Jackson letter, "The Murder of Joe Spinner," *New Masses*, September 3, 1935, pp. 21, 22.

51. Painter, *Narrative of Hosea Hudson*, pp. 83, 84, 146, 152, 153, 154; also see similar account in Hosea Hudson, *Black Worker in the Deep South* (New York: International Publishers, 1972), pp. 60–64.

52. See text of Norman Thomas radio speech, "The Sharecroppers and the A.A.A.," in Southern Tenant Farmers' Union Papers, microfilm reel 1, Southern Historical Collection, University of North Carolina Library.

53. See "Reminiscences of H. L. Mitchell," 1957 (Oral History Project, Columbia University), p. 1.

54. Howard Kester, *Revolt among the Sharecroppers* (reprint, New York: Arno Press, 1969), p. 56. In 1935 an observer of the STFU in Arkansas reported in the *New Masses:* "in 1919 at Elaine, Arkansas, the misled white croppers were mobilized against the Negroes. Today the Share Croppers Union and now the Southern Tenant Farmers Union, asserts the need for complete unity of the southern working class. White workers and black workers join hands to build the future, while the planters quake in their high, mud-proof boots." Harold Preece, " 'Anarchy' in Arkansas," *New Masses*, February 12, 1935, p. 15.

55. See STFU constitution and bylaws, in Southern Tenant Farmers' Union Papers, microfilm reel 1.

56. Kester, *Revolt among the Sharecroppers*, pp. 62, 63; H. L. Mitchell, *Mean Things Happening in This Land* (Montclair, N.J.: Allenheld, Osman, 1979), p. 79.

57. Naomi Mitchison, "White House and Marked Tree," *New Statesman and Nation*, April 27, 1935, pp. 585, 586; Kester, *Revolt among the Sharecroppers*, p. 51.

58. See Josephine Johnson, "The Arkansas Terror," *New Masses*, June 30, 1936, pp. 12–14. Harold Preece in the *New Masses* explained the impact of the New Deal agricultural program upon the Arkansas croppers: "now the land, owned by an hereditary caste, is beginning to disgorge him. As acreage has decreased, so has the number of tenants. The

evicted families have simply exchanged the misery of plantation shacks for the misery of shacks in the slums of Little Rock and Hot Springs. . . . the remaining sharecroppers have been forced to give the product to landlords as part payment on fantastically large debts." Preece, " 'Anarchy' in Arkansas," p. 15.

59. W. J. Cash, *The Mind of the South* (reprint, New York: Vintage Books, n.d.), pp. 406, 407.

60. Mitchell, *Mean Things Happening*, p. 82.

61. David Eugene Conrad, *The Forgotten Farmers* (Urbana: University of Illinois Press, 1965), p. 173; Louis Cantor, *A Prologue to the Protest Movement: The Missouri Sharecropper Roadside Demonstration of 1939* (Durham: Duke University Press, 1969), p. 23; Mitchell, *Mean Things Happening*, p. 93.

62. Donald H. Grubbs, *Cry from the Cotton* (Chapel Hill: University of North Carolina Press, 1971), p. 68; Mitchell, *Mean Things Happening*, p. 171; Cantor, *Prologue*, p. 65; Jonathan Daniels, *A Southerner Discovers the South* (New York: Macmillan, 1938), p. 133.

63. Grubbs, *Cry from the Cotton*, p. 68; Kester, *Revolt among the Sharecroppers*, p. 73, 52; Mitchison, "White House and Marked Tree," p. 586.

64. Anthony P. Dunbar, *Against the Grain* (Charlottesville: University Press of Virginia, 1981), p. 107.

65. Jerold S. Auerbach, "Southern Tenant Farmers: Socialist Critics of the New Deal," *Labor History*, Winter 1966, p. 17; Cantor, *Prologue*, p. 109; Grubbs, *Cry from the Cotton*, pp. 66, 68.

66. Kester, *Revolt among the Sharecroppers*, pp. 75, 81; Johnson, "Arkansas Terror," p. 11.

67. Conrad, *Forgotten Farmers*, pp. 156, 157; an STFU report noted that Rodgers was tried by a jury composed of eleven planters and one businessman and sentenced to six months in jail and a $500 fine. See "Acts of Tyranny and Terror," in Southern Tenant Farmers' Union Papers, microfilm reel 1.

68. Mitchell, *Mean Things Happening*, pp. 62, 63.

69. In his biography of the Marxist Christian Claude Williams, Cedric Belfrage writes: "The landlords, themselves harassed from above by banks and mortgage companies . . . saw no way of maintaining their privileges in face of this movement save by violence. . . . When they found out that a tenant or day-laborer had joined the union, they, as deputy-sheriffs representing law and order, would as soon shoot him down as they would a suck-egg dog that came in their hen house." See Cedric Belfrage, *A Faith to Free the People* (New York: Dryden Press, 1944), p. 194.

70. H. L. Mitchell recalls that "for some reason" racists did not fire into the homes of white union leaders. See "Reminiscences of H. L. Mitchell," Oral History Project, p. 40.

71. Cash, *Mind of the South*, p. 125.

72. Grubbs, *Cry from the Cotton*, p. 100.

73. See "Acts of Tyranny and Terror," STFU Papers.

74. Grubbs, *Cry from the Cotton*, pp. 90, 91, 105, 106, 109, 110, 113.

75. Conrad, *Forgotten Farmers*, p. 161.

76. See Eleanor Ryan, "Toward a National Negro Congress," *New Masses*, June 4, 1935, p. 14.

77. Conrad, *Forgotten Farmers*, p. 92; Myra Page, "The Croppers Prepare," *New Masses*, January 11, 1936, p. 17.

78. Detailed coverage of the sharecroppers' protest was given by the *Daily Record*, Chicago Communist newspaper. See *Daily Record*, January 11, 12, 13, 14, 16, 17, 19, 20,

21, 23, 1939. The articles from January 14 on, written by Carl Hirsch, were particularly effective in conveying the flavor of what was happening; also see planter Thad Snow's account of the problems in cotton agriculture that led to the strike in *St. Louis Post-Dispatch*, January 22, 1939. Useful scholarly appraisals are found in papers by Lorenzo Greene and Arvarh Strickland at a session of the 1986 meeting of the Association for the Study of Afro-American Life and History (tape recording, Boddie Record, Cleveland).

79. Cantor, *Prologue*, p. 63; also see description of the protest in Thad Snow, *From Missouri* (Boston: Houghton Mifflin, 1954), pp. 240–85.

80. Irvin G. Wyllie, "Race and Class Conflict on Missouri's Cotton Frontier," *Journal of Southern History* May 1954, pp. 183–96.

81. Cantor, *Prologue*, pp. 85, 129, 138; Carl Hirsch letter, January 1939, from Sikeston, Missouri, furnished to author by James Klein, Dayton, Ohio.

82. Diary of Charles M. Barnes, in Charles Merlin Barnes Papers, Western Historical Manuscript Collection, University of Missouri–Columbia Library.

83. For account of FBI report, see *St. Louis Post-Dispatch*, March 13, 1939.

84. Thad Snow, handwritten draft of 1940 manuscript, in Thad Snow Papers, Western Historical Manuscript Collection, University of Missouri, St. Louis.

85. Grubbs, *Cry from the Cotton*, p. 97.

86. Thomas Cripps, *Slow Fade to Black: The Negro in American Film, 1900–1942* (New York: Oxford University Press, 1977), pp. 281, 282; also see Robert E. Burns, *I Am a Fugitive from a Georgia Chain Gang* (New York: Grosset & Dunlap, 1932).

87. See Jesse Crawford, "Cheating the Georgia Chain Gang," *Crisis*, June 1938, in Aptheker, *Documentary History, 1933–1945*, pp. 318–24. For an account of the origins of the chain-gang system, see Peter Wallenstein, "Conscripts and Convicts: From Road Duty to Chain Gang" (Paper delivered at 1986 Organization of American Historians meeting). According to Wallenstein, chain-gang members "were routinely whipped to maintain discipline and productivity" (p. 12).

88. See John L. Spivak, *A Man in His Time* (New York: Horizon Press, 1967), pp. 168, 169.

89. See prisoners' letters in John L. Spivak, "Flashes from Georgia Chain Gangs," in Cunard, *Negro*, pp. 127, 128.

90. Hilton Butler, "Murder for the Job," *Nation*, July 12, 1933, p. 44.

91. See letter by Ira De A. Reid in the *Nation*, September 6, 1933, p. 273; See T. Arnold Hill, "Railway Employees Rally to Save Their Jobs," *Opportunity*, November 1934, p. 346.

10. In the Midst of the New Deal

1. See *Pittsburgh Courier*, February 23, 1924; *Daily Worker*, February 8, 11, 12, 13, 18, 1924; *Opportunity*, editorial, April 1924, p. 98; W. E. B. Du Bois, "Opinion," *Crisis*, May 1924, p. 7. Du Bois described the Sanhedrin as "an interesting social occasion with no new ideas and no program."

2. See Aptheker, *Documentary History, 1933–1945*, p. 212. For overviews of congress history, see Lawrence S. Wittner, "The National Negro Congress: A Reassessment," *American Quarterly*, Winter 1970, pp. 883–901, and also John Streater, "The National Negro Congress: Race, Class, and the Left" (manuscript). A rather one-dimensional treatment, interpreting congress history as a process of Communist domination, is to be found in Wilson Record, *The Negro and the Communist Party* reprint, (New York: Atheneum, 1971), pp. 153–61. For an appraisal that locates the origins of the congress in Communist

popular front strategy while noting the organization's wide appeal, see Mark Naison, *Communists in Harlem during the Depression* (Urbana: University of Illinois Press, 1983), pp. 169–92.

3. Richard Wright, "Two Million Black Voices," *New Masses*, February 25, 1936.

4. Jervis Anderson, *A. Philip Randolph: A Biographical Portrait* (New York: Harcourt Brace Jovanovich, 1972), p. 231.

5. A. Philip Randolph, text of 1936 keynote address, in Aptheker, *Documentary History, 1933–1945*, pp. 212–20.

6. Wright, "Two Million Black Voices."

7. Memorandum, Wilkins to Board of Directors, March 9, 1936, NAACP Papers; also supplementary memorandum of March 10, 1936.

8. Text of Randolph 1937 speech in Aptheker, *Documentary History, 1933–1945*, pp. 262–64, 266–68.

9. Myrdal, *American Dilemma*, 2: 818. Myrdal was particularly impressed by Randolph, describing him as "one of the wisest statesmen in the present generation" (p. 817).

10. Wittner, "National Negro Congress," pp. 888–90. The petitions, jointly issued by the NNC and the Interdenominational Ministers' Alliance, were addressed to President Franklin D. Roosevelt. The petition stated: "On numerous instances the representatives of the people of Washington have pled with the Superintendent of the Police, Major Ernest W. Brown, and the Commissions of the District of Columbia to take effective action to curb these illegal invasions of the lives and liberties of American citizens by the police. These pleas have been to no avail. Police brutality has continued. . . . We have been forced to conclude that the responsible officials of the District of Columbia will not or cannot act to protect the lives and liberties of American citizens living under their jurisdiction. Our lives, our homes, our liberties each day are made less secure because of unrestrained and unpunished police brutality." Three bound volumes of signed petitions are in the possession of Mrs. John P. Davis, New York City.

11. Myrdal, *American Dilemma*, 2: 568. It appears Myrdal underestimated the significance of the Harlem incident for he stated that "the future looks fairly peaceful in the North" while predicting the probability of severe riots in the South.

12. *The Complete Report of Mayor LaGuardia's Commission on the Harlem Riot of March 19, 1935* (reprint, New York: Arno Press, 1969).

13. Ibid., pp. 113, 114, 116.

14. Ibid., pp. 116–19.

15. Ibid., pp. 119, 120.

16. Ibid., pp. 120, 121.

17. Ibid., p. 122.

18. Ibid., pp. 128, 129, 133, 134.

19. *New York Times*, March 21, 1935.

20. Ibid., March 22, 1935.

21. Ibid., March 21, 1935.

22. Ibid., March 21, 22, 1935.

23. Ibid., March 21, 1935.

24. See James W. Ford, *Hunger and Terror in Harlem* (New York: Harlem Section, Communist Party, 1935).

25. Alain Locke, "Harlem: Dark Weather-Vane," *Survey Graphic*, August 1936, pp. 457–62, 493–95; Alain Locke, ed., *The New Negro* reprint, (New York: Atheneum, 1968), pp. 3–16; text of Locke's 1925 *Survey Graphic* article.

26. See Victor Weybright to La Guardia, July 1, 1936, regarding prior submission of

Locke article, La Guardia Papers, New York Municipal Archives; Platt, *Politics of Riot Commissions*, p. 162.

11. The NAACP and Radical Voices

1. Aptheker, *Correspondence of Du Bois*, 1: 474, 479, 480.
2. W. E. B. Du Bois, "Marxism and the Negro Problem," *Crisis*, May 1933, pp. 103–15, 118.
3. W. E. B. Du Bois, "The Negro College," *Crisis*, August 1933, pp. 175–77.
4. W. E. B. Du Bois, "Postscript," *Crisis*, May 1934, pp. 147, 148.
5. Raymond Wolters, *Negroes and the Great Depression* (Westport, Conn.: Greenwood Press, 1970), pp. 285–92.
6. Ibid., pp. 303, 319.
7. Ibid., pp. 310, 313, 314, 315, 330.
8. Robert L. Zangrando, *The NAACP Crusade against Lynching, 1909–1950* (Philadelphia: Temple University Press, 1980), pp. 99–101, 130.
9. See James R. McGovern, *Anatomy of a Lynching* (Baton Rouge: Louisiana State University Press, 1982); National Association for the Advancement of Colored People, *The Lynching of Claude Neal* (New York: National Association for the Advancement of Colored People, 1934).
10. Zangrando, *NAACP Crusade*, p. 148, reporting 1937 Gallup poll.
11. Ibid., p. 150.
12. Julius Wayne Dudley, "A History of the Association of Southern Women for the Prevention of Lynching, 1933–1942," (Dissertation, University of Cincinnati, 1979), p. 254; Zangrando, *NAACP Crusade*, pp. 126, 127.
13. Dudley, "History," p. 149; Jacquelyn Dowd Hall, *Revolt against Chivalry* (New York: Columbia University Press, 1979), pp. 224, 225.
14. Dudley, "History," pp. 134, 288.
15. Ibid., p. 348.
16. Hall, *Revolt against Chivalry*, pp. 197, 240, 250.
17. Zangrando, *NAACP Crusade*, p. 153.
18. Wolters, *Negroes and Depression*, p. 352.
19. Myrdal, *American Dilemma*, 2: 830.
20. Loren Miller, "How 'Left' Is the N.A.A.C.P.?" *New Masses*, July 16, 1935, pp. 12, 13.
21. See joint ILD and NAACP letter in *New Masses*, July 9, 1935. Appeals in this case failed and Montjoy was executed December 17, 1937.
22. Langston Hughes, "Too Much of Race," *Crisis*, September 1937, p. 272.
23. William Pickens, "What I Saw in Spain," *Crisis*, October 1938, pp. 319–21, 330.
24. Louise Thompson, "Southern Terror," *Crisis*, November 1934, pp. 327, 328.
25. Roy Wilkins, "Two against 5,000," *Crisis*, June 1936, pp. 169, 170.
26. See Ralph J. Bunche, "A Critical Analysis of the Tactics and Programs of Minority Groups," *Journal of Negro Education* 4, no. 3 (1935): 308–20.
27. Davis, *Leadership, Love, Aggression*, pp. 155, 165, 166, 179.
28. Richard Wright, *Black Boy: A Record of Childhood and Youth* (New York: Harper & Row, 1945), p. 45.
29. Ibid., pp. 63, 64, 83, 84, 200, 201, 211, 255, 276, 281.
30. Richard Wright, *Uncle Tom's Children* (New York: Signet, 1949).
31. In *Black Boy* Wright recalls he had heard a story of a black woman who concealed

a gun in a burial sheet she took to the side of her lynched husband and then fired, killing four of the lynchers (p. 83).

32. Addison Gayle, *Richard Wright: Ordeal of a Native Son* (Garden City, N.Y.: Doubleday, 1980), p. 113.

33. Richard Wright, "How 'Bigger' Was Born," in Robert Hemenway, ed., *The Black Novelist* (Columbus: Merrill, 1970), p. 184.

34. Richard Wright, *Native Son* (New York: Signet, 1950).

35. See review by Benjamin J. Davis, J., in *New York Sunday Worker*, April 14, 1940; review by Samuel Sillen, in *New Masses*, March 5, 1940, pp. 24, 25; review by Mike Gold, in *New York Sunday Worker*, March 31, 1940.

12. Wartime Violence

1. National Negro Congress 1940 resolution, quoted by NNC president Max Yergan in speech, "Democracy and the Negro People Today," in Aptheker, *Documentary History, 1933–1945*, p. 393.

2. Ibid., pp. 390, 391; White, *A Man Called White*, pp. 186–88.

3. *Crisis*, November 1940, cover; Herbert Garfinkel, *When Negroes March* (Glencoe, Ill.: Free Press, 1959), pp. 34, 35.

4. See A. Philip Randolph, "The World Crisis and the Negro People Today," manuscript of 1940 speech, pp. 18, 25, in Schomburg Collection, New York Public Library; *New York Times*, April 28, 1940.

5. Ralph Bunche account of Randolph's remarks at 1940 Congress, quoted in Anderson, *A. Philip Randolph*, p. 237.

6. Ibid., p. 239; see reference to "Soviets of workers" in text of Randolph 1937 speech, quoted in Aptheker, *Documentary History, 1933–1945*, p. 264; A. Philip Randolph, "Why I Would Not Stand for Re-election as President of the National Negro Congress," *American Federationist*, July 1940, pp. 24, 25.

7. Among those expressing approval of Randolph's position at the 1940 congress was the labor secretary of the Socialist party. Randolph, acknowledging the support, endorsed working with the NAACP, "which is an organization which has no political entangling alliances." But Randolph himself was quite entangled in commitment to President Roosevelt. At the close of his congress remarks Randolph had said: "We hail Franklin Delano Roosevelt, President of the United States, as the greatest living champion of peace, democracy and good-will." See Randolph to Arthur G. McDowell, May 10, 1940, Socialist Party Collection, Duke University; Randolph, 1940 manuscript, Schomburg Collection, p. 33.

8. Garfinkel, *When Negroes March*, pp. 98–101, 68, 69. One of those serving on the youth contingent's executive committee was the attorney Conrad Lynn, by that time quite critical of the Communist party. Lynn writes that it was at his initiative that the committee was convened to condemn Randolph's cancelation of the march. Lynn writes: "Randolph's technique was a ploy typical of a Socialist; the thing a Socialist wanted to do was discredit a Democratic president....The deceit in this maneuver was that the march had been organized as unconditional. Many of us backed the preparations because we felt it would provide the opportunity for a revolutionary confrontation with the government. This, of course, was the last thing the Socialists had in mind." Conrad Lynn, *There Is a Fountain: The Autobiography of a Civil Rights Lawyer* (Westport, Conn.: Hill, 1979), p. 87.

9. Garfinkel, *When Negroes March*, p. 137; Richard Dalfiume notes that Roosevelt's Executive Order 8802 was accompanied by refusal to integrate the armed services. Dalfiume

writes: "The leaders of the MOWM had to accept this situation or risk possible embarrassment by having their bluff called. Once the executive order establishing the FEPC was issued, it was trumpeted as a great victory for Negroes, which served to distract attention away from what had been demanded but not conceded. The perpetuation of the story that American Negroes had forced the President to make a big concession also served Roosevelt by soothing the feelings of Southern Democrats: He had been *forced* to establish the FEPC. Interpreted in this way, the postponing of the March on Washington was a definite victory for Roosevelt." See Richard Dalfiume, *Desegregation of the U.S. Armed Forces* (Columbia: University of Missouri Press, 1969), p. 121.

10. The MOWM lost strength, Maurice Isserman writes in his study of the Communist party during World War II, "because of internal difficulties and its reluctance to undertake its long-promised civil disobedience campaign." See Maurice Isserman, *Which Side Were You On?* (Middletown, Conn.: Wesleyan University Press, 1982), p. 167. Regarding Randolph's movement and its promised civil disobedience campaign, Adam Clayton Powell, Jr., wrote: "An organization with a name that it does not live up to, an announced program that it does not stick to, and a philosophy contrary to the mood of the times cannot live. The March-on-Washington headquarters in New York is now a bookstore." See Adam Clayton Powell, Jr., *Marching Blacks* (New York: Dial Press, 1945), p. 159.

11. Ottley, *New World A-coming*, p. 311.

12. Ibid., p. 312.

13. Ibid., pp. 312–14.

14. See Williams letter in *Christian Century*, September 13, 1944, p. 1060.

15. See Florence Murray, ed., *The Negro Handbook, 1946–1947* (New York: Wyn, 1947), pp. 347–56, quoted in Aptheker, *Documentary History, 1933–1945*, pp. 525–40.

16. See *Crisis*, July 1943, p. 211.

17. S. I. Rosenman, comp., *The Public Papers and Addresses of Franklin D. Roosevelt, 1944–1945* (New York: Harper, 1950), 13: 66–70.

18. Walter White, Preface to Walter White and Thurgood Marshall, *What Caused the Detroit Riot? An Analysis* (New York: National Association for the Advancement of Colored People, 1943).

19. *Michigan Chronicle*, March 27, 1943.

20. Murray to Roosevelt, June 18, 1943, and Marcantonio to Roosevelt, June 16, 1943, OF 93c, Franklin D. Roosevelt Papers, Franklin D. Roosevelt Library, Hyde Park, N.Y.

21. See *Life*, August 17, 1942. The magazine stated that Detroit had perhaps the worst morale situation in the United States and added that the city could "either blow up Hitler or it can blow up the U.S." But the report's assessment of the situation put much of the blame on Detroit's workers and in portraying the city as polarized indiscriminately joined together as demagogues the Communists, Ku Klux Klan, Gerald L. K. Smith, and local Nazis. Under a photo of "Paradise Valley" in the black community the caption asserted that Detroit blacks had more grievances than others and also less interest in the war. The article warned about dissension but may itself have contributed to it; see B. J. Widick, *Detroit: City of Race and Class Violence* (Chicago: Quadrangle Books, 1972), pp. 100, 103. Also see report on Detroit situation of Police Lieutenant George R. Branton to Chief of Detectives, Detroit Police Department, July 2, 1943, Donald S. Leonard MSS, Michigan Historical Collection, Bentley Library, University of Michigan.

22. See Office of Facts and Figures, "Special Report on Negro Housing Situation in Detroit," March 5, 1942, in Rensis Likert MSS, box 9, folder 2, Michigan Historical Collection, pp. 1, 10–13, 15, 18.

23. Bureau of Agricultural Economics, Division of Program Surveys, Report to Office

of War Information, "The Social Dynamics of Detroit," pp. 34, 36, 39, 40, National Archives, RG 44, box 1814.

24. See U.S. Congress, House, *Congressional Record*, February 27, 1942, pp. 1763–70.

25. Ibid., April 21, 1942, pp. 3619–25.

26. *Michigan Chronicle*, March 14, May 2, 1942.

27. *Final Report of Governor's Committee to Investigate Riot Occurring in Detroit, June 21, 1943*, in Platt, *Politics of Riot Commissions*, pp. 200–21. The basis for the attack on the black press had already been established in hostile comments published by a variety of columnists and periodicals. Among those blaming the black press for incidents of racial violence was Richmond liberal editor Virginius Dabney. For a summary of this criticism, see Lee Finkle, *Forum for Protest: The Black Press during World War II* (Rutherford, N.J.: Fairleigh Dickinson University Press, 1975), pp. 62–77.

28. *Michigan Chronicle*, August 21, 1943.

29. See Adam Clayton Powell, Jr., "Michigan Fact Finding Committee Closes Eyes to Facts," *People's Voice*, August 21, 1943.

30. White and Marshall, *What Caused the Detroit Riot?* sec. 1, pp. 12–14; White, *A Man Called White*, pp. 226, 227.

31. Thurgood Marshall, "Activities of Police during the Riots June 21 and 22, 1943," in White and Marshall, *What Caused the Detroit Riot?* pp. 29–37. In the Sojourner Truth violence, a contributing factor was vacillation by federal officials, who twice switched positions regarding black occupancy of the project. When finally it was announced that blacks would move in on February 28 the Ku Klux Klan intervened, and the night before the move whites burned a cross near the site. The following day a mob attacked entering tenants, but police began arresting the black tenants. More than 200 blacks were apprehended along with a few whites. According to police inspector Chester E. Cox, 106 blacks were booked on specific charges. This confrontation highlighted the issue of police brutality and the refusal of city officials to act against racism, but it also brought closer together the black community and the labor movement. See August Meier and Elliot Rudwick, *Black Detroit and the Rise of the UAW* (New York: Oxford University Press, 1979), pp. 175–83; Robert Shogan and Tom Craig, *The Detroit Race Riot: A Study in Violence* (Philadelphia: Chilton Books, 1964), p. 87, quoting report by Gen. William E. Gunther; *New York Times*, June 27, 1943; Dominic J. Capeci, Jr., *Race Relations in Wartime Detroit: The Sojourner Truth Housing Controversy of 1942* (Philadelphia: Temple University Press, 1984).

32. Walter White memorandum, in White and Marshall, *What Caused the Detroit Riot?* pp. 20–23.

33. White, in White and Marshall, *What Caused the Detroit Riot?*, see pp. 9, 10.

34. Earl Brown, *Why Race Riots: Lessons from Detroit* (Public Affairs pamphlet), quoted in Aptheker, *Documentary History, 1933–1945*, pp. 443–53; *New York PM* August 12, 1943, for text of Biddle letter to Roosevelt. The *Michigan Chronicle* asserted that if Biddle really thought that stopping black migration to the cities would avoid racial friction "he should be rushed to a mental hospital without further delay" (August 21, 1943).

35. Alfred McClung Lee and Norman D. Humphrey, *Race Riot* (New York: Octagon Books, 1968), pp. 51, 55, 56.

36. Ibid., pp. 56, 63, 65, 66.

37. William J. Norton, "The Detroit Riots—and After," *Survey Graphic*, August 1943, pp. 317, 318.

38. "Crisis on the Home Front," *New Masses*, editorial, June 29, 1943, p. 3; in a leaflet

the Communist party of Michigan referred to "fifth column conspiracy" and stated that the smashing of such conspiracy was "primarily the responsibility of the white workers, the mighty unions and progressive organizations in closest cooperation with their Negro fellow citizens." Calling for a grand jury inquiry, the Communists described the Detroit violence as "an Axis inspired effort, organized for the purpose of wrecking the unity of the American people and helping fascism." Leaflet reproduced in Harvard Sitkoff, "The Detroit Race Riot of 1943," *Michigan History,* Fall 1969, p. 201.

39. Joseph North, "It Will Happen to You, Unless....," *New Masses,* July 6, 1943, pp. 2, 3; also see pp. 4–6 for report by Detroit editor Louis E. Martin.

40. See Harvard Sitkoff, "Racial Militancy and Interracial Violence in the Second World War," *Journal of American History,* December 1971, pp. 678–81.

41. North, "It Will Happen to You," p. 3.

42. Sitkoff, "Racial Militancy," pp. 670, 676. Black disappointment with FDR in 1943 was poignantly etched by Pauli Murray's poem, "Mr. Roosevelt Regrets":

> What'd you get, black boy,
> When they knocked you down in the gutter,
> And they kicked your teeth out,
> And they broke your skull with clubs
> And they bashed your stomach in?
> What'd you get when the police shot you in the back,
> And they chained you to the beds
> While they wiped the blood off ?
> What'd you get when you cried out to the Top Man?
> When you called the man next to God, so you thought,
> And you asked him to speak out to save you?
> What'd the Top Man say, black boy?
> Mr. Roosevelt regrets.....

See *Crisis,* August 1943, p. 252. Following the poem, *Crisis* quoted the newspaper *PM's* account of Roosevelt's comment on recent racial violence: "I share your feeling that the recent outbreaks of violence in widely spread parts of the country endanger our unity and comfort our enemies. I am sure that every true American regrets this."

43. White, *A Man Called White,* pp. 231, 232. The script of the CBS show, written by William N. Robson, vividly portrayed the issues of racism highlighted by the Detroit events. Reference was made to the spreading of false rumors within both the white and the black communities, and the broadcast told of blacks along Hastings Street smashing store windows and overturning the cars of white motorists and also of "a hundred thousand white men armed with lengths of pipe and beer bottles" who beat up blacks along Woodward Avenue "until their arms ached." The rioters were termed "insurrectionists," and the point was made that in one day of violence one million man hours of labor had been wasted. Detroit was ranked with Bataan and Corregidor as defeats in the war effort. The human consequences were itemized—1,800 persons arrested, 600 injured, 35 dead—and Robson did not omit the detail that of twenty-nine blacks killed, seventeen had been shot by the police. Regarding a white mob that threatened the black students attending graduation ceremonies at Northeastern High School, those in the mob were identified as "Kluxers, cowards and crackpots." The broadcast stressed the world context of the violence, quoting from Axis radio broadcasts that sought to exploit the situation. Tokyo Radio was quoted

as asking: "How can America hope to bring an order of liberty and equality among the more complicated, vastly more difficult family of races in the world, when it can't manage its own race problem?" The Detroit violence was linked to the tradition of fascism. Robson wrote: "Remember, these street riots are not new. They have their pattern—a pattern cut in the streets of Leipzig and Berlin and Munich nearly a generation ago when gangs of German youth armed with beer bottles and lead pipe asserted their right to mob rule with the same brawling methods we have seen at work on our Main Streets. The pattern is the same, the victim similar. The minority which is most easily recognized. Adolf Hitler, who invented the technique, predicted long ago how well it would work here in America." Closing the broadcast was a brief speech by Wendell Willkie in which the 1940 Republican candidate forthrightly listed rights to which black citizens were entitled—the right to protection under the law, a right to equal educational opportunity, and the right to the elimination of all arbitrary restrictions on voting. Willkie also spoke of the right to equal economic opportunity and the urgency of meeting the human need for adequate housing. In Willkie's view, if private enterprise could not solve the housing need then the government had to step in, "preferably local but, if necessary, federal." Willkie, as well as Robson the scriptwriter, saw the link with the question of fascism. Willkie closed his remarks with the comment: "The desire to deprive some of our citizens of their rights—economic, civic, or political—has the same basic motivation as actuates the fascist mind when it seeks to dominate whole peoples and nations." See William N. Robson, "Open Letter on Race Hatred," in Eric Barnouw, ed., *Radio Drama in Action: Twenty-Five Plays of a Changing World* (New York: Farrar & Rinehart, 1945), pp. 62–77.

44. Louis Martin, "Prelude to Disaster: Detroit," *Common Ground*, Autumn 1943, pp. 21–26.

45. Elmer A. Carter, July 10 column, and P. L. Prattis column, quoted in "The Negro Press on the Riots," *Common Ground*, Autumn 1943, pp. 101–3.

46. James Wechsler report from Detroit, *New York PM*, August 1, 1943.

47. "Negro Discrimination and the Need for Federal Action," *Lawyers Guild Review* 2, no. 6 (1942): 21.

48. See "Public Statement Offering the Service of the National Lawyers Guild, Detroit Chapter, to Indigent Worthy Defendants Involved in the Recent Race Rioting," June 25, 1943, National Lawyers Guild Papers, Meiklejohn Civil Liberties Institute, Berkeley, Calif.

49. See "Statement Unanimously Adopted by the Executive Board, Detroit Chapter, National Lawyers Guild on the Recent Disorders in Detroit," National Lawyers Guild Papers.

50. See "Analysis of Reports of Governor's Fact Finding Committee, Adopted by Detroit, National Lawyers Guild, September 9, 1943," National Lawyers Guild Papers.

51. Dominic Joseph Capeci, Jr., "The Harlem Riot of 1943" (Dissertation, University of California, Irvine), 1970, pp. 190, 191; Ben Richardson, "Can It Happen in Harlem Again?" *New Masses*, August 17, 1943, pp. 14–16; Sitkoff, "Racial Militancy," p. 675.

52. Claude Brown, *Manchild in the Promised Land* (New York: Macmillan, 1965), pp. 12–14.

53. Sidney Poitier, *This Life* (New York: Knopf, 1980), pp. 63, 64. Another vivid recollection is found in James Baldwin's "Me and My House…," *Harper's Magazine*, November 1955, pp. 54, 60, 61.

54. *New York PM*, August 3, 1943.

55. White, *A Man Called White*, p. 233.

56. Capeci, "Harlem Riot," pp. 194–96; White, *A Man Called White*, p. 236.

57. Capeci, "Harlem Riot," p. 131; regarding New York's private colleges and uni-

versities, even shortly after World War II, Dr. Dan Dodson, head of the Mayor's Committee on Unity, informed the United Parents Association that no black person held a professorship at any of these institutions. See *Daily Worker*, February 21, 1946.

58. Capeci, "Harlem Riot," p. 177.

59. See footnote reference to June 30, 1954, interview with Newbold Morris in Charles Garrett, *The La Guardia Years; Machine and Reform Policies in New York City* (New Brunswick, N.J.: Rutgers University Press, 1961), p. 386.

60. Capeci, "Harlem Riot," pp. 58, 312, 313.

61. See *People's Voice*, August 21, 1943.

62. Walter White, "Behind the Harlem Riot," *New Republic*, August 16, 1943, pp. 221, 222. White asked anyone who would criticize the Harlemites "to put himself in the place of the looters."

63. See Albert Deutsch articles, *New York PM*, August 3, 4, 1943.

64. See *People's Voice*, August 7, 14, 1943.

65. Capeci, "Harlem Riot," pp. 349–52.

66. Powell, *Marching Blacks*, pp. 171, 172.

67. *Monthly Summary of Events and Trends in Race Relations* 1 (1944): 2. The figure of 242, covering the period between March 1 and December 31, was provided in the "Review of the Month," initialed by Charles S. Johnson.

68. See "Editorials," *Crisis*, July 1943, p. 199.

69. See Merl E. Reed, "The FEPC, the Black Worker, and the Southern Shipyards," *South Atlantic Quarterly*, Autumn 1975, pp. 446–67; Louis Ruchames, *Race, Jobs, and Politics: The Story of the FEPC* (New York: Columbia University Press, 1953), pp. 58, 59.

70. See Office of War Information, "Negroes and the War: A Study in Baltimore and Cincinnati" (1942), p. 13 ("Notes on Baltimore") and pp. i–iii, vi ("Quotation from Interviews"), in Likert Collection.

71. Langston Hughes, "Beaumont to Detroit, 1943," *Common Ground*, Fall 1943, p. 104; also see Hughes's poem "Good Morning, Stalingrad" in Thomas Yoseloff, ed., *Seven Poets in Search of an Answer* (New York: Ackerman, 1944), pp. 44–46.

72. *New York Times*, January 26, 27, 1942; in 1948 Robert E. Cushman, Cornell University professor and member of President Truman's Committee on Civil Rights, noted that within forty-eight hours of a January 1942 Missouri lynching—almost certainly a reference to the Sikeston incident—German and Japanese radio began broadcasting the news, and this propaganda helped break down resistance in the Dutch East Indies. See Robert E. Cushman, "Our Civil Rights Become a World Issue," *New York Times Magazine*, January 11, 1948. Also see Dominic J. Capeci, Jr., "The Lynching of Cleo Wright: Federal Protection of Constitutional Rights during World War II," *Journal of American History*, March 1986, pp. 859–87. Capeci stresses that the murder spurred Justice Department efforts to elaborate a basis for federal intervention against lynchings.

73. William L. Patterson, *Sikeston: Hitlerite Crime against America* (St. Louis: Communist Party of Missouri, 1942).

74. Drake and Cayton, *Black Metropolis*, 2: 740. Maurice Isserman also takes issue with the view that the party abandoned the black struggle during the World War II period. He writes that the Communists were most outspoken in pushing the CIO to fight for equal employment rights for blacks. Isserman contends that the Communist position forced the black struggle within narrow channels but writes: "The Communists did not abandon the struggle for black rights during the war." Isserman observes that black people did not appear to have perceived a policy of abandonment, as shown in the fact that "the Com-

munists reached the high-water mark of their political influence in Harlem during the very years when, if the conventional account was true, they logically ought to have been losing strength." Isserman, *Which Side Were You On?*, pp. 141, 169. An additional comment of interest is that made by Adam Clayton Powell, Jr., in 1945: "Today there is no group in America including the Christian church that practices racial brotherhood one tenth as much as the Communist Party." See Powell, *Marching Blacks*, p. 69.

75. Horace R. Cayton, "The Negro's Challenge," *Nation*, July 3, 1943, pp. 10–12.

76. *Michigan Chronicle*, July 3, 1943.

77. Bayard Rustin, "The Negro and Non-Violence," in Rustin, *Down the Line: The Collected Writings of Bayard Rustin* (Chicago: Quadrangle Books, 1971), pp. 8–12. See account of Rome, Georgia, incident of police brutality directed against Roland Hayes and Mrs. Hayes in Charles S. Johnson, *To Stem This Tide* (Boston: Pilgrim Press, 1943), pp. 77, 78. Johnson writes: "This case is important not so much because it was Roland Hayes, a world famed artist who was maltreated, but because the treatment was justified by the Governor of the state and the local officials, and because the 'good citizens' of the community were afraid to condemn the practice either publicly or privately" (p. 77).

78. See August Meier and Elliot Rudwick, *CORE: A Study in the Civil Rights Movement, 1942–1968* (New York: Oxford University Press, 1973), p. 20. For a recollection of the early days of CORE by one of the organization's founders, see James Farmer, *Lay Bare the Heart: An Autobiography of the Civil Rights Movement* (New York: Arbor House, 1985), pp. 83–116, 355–360. Farmer, somewhat at variance with Meier and Rudwick, argues that CORE had a "dual parentage," himself and the Chicago Fellowship of Reconciliation group led by Houser.

79. Meier and Rudwick, *CORE*, p. 21.

80. See Meier, Rudwick, and Broderick, *Black Protest Thought*, pp. 239–43.

81. In *Morgan v. Virginia*, 328 U.S. 373 (1945), the Supreme Court found that "seating arrangements for the different races in interstate motor travel require a single, uniform rule to promote and protect national travel." See Bardolph, *Civil Rights Record*, pp. 285, 286.

82. Meier and Rudwick, *CORE*, pp. 33–39; James Peck, *Freedom Ride* (New York: Simon & Schuster, 1962), pp. 14–27; also see accounts in Lynn, *There Is a Fountain*, pp. 108–13. According to Lynn, the riders escaped serious violence at Chapel Hill due largely to the efforts of "virtually suicidal young Communists" who, armed with rifles, stationed themselves on the roof of the minister's home where the activists had gathered (p. 112).

13. Victory without Peace

1. See *A Petition to the United Nations on Behalf of 13 Million Oppressed Negro Citizens of the United States of America* (New York: National Negro Congress, 1946). W. E. B. Du Bois noted of this petition that "it is well done but it is too short and not sufficiently documented." Aptheker, *Correspondence of Du Bois*, 3: 163.

2. Herbert Aptheker to author, June 1984.

3. See *An Appeal to the World: A Statement on the Denial of Human Rights to Minorities in the Case of Citizens of Negro Descent in the United States of America and an Appeal to the United Nations for Redress* (New York: NAACP, 1947). A Soviet proposal to have the petition considered by the UN Human Rights Commission was rejected on December 3, 1947, by vote of eleven to one. According to Du Bois, Eleanor Roosevelt, representing the United States delegation, informed him of the State Department view that it would be unwise to put the petition before the forthcoming 1948 General Assembly

session. Aptheker, *Correspondence of Du Bois,* 3: 186–89. In a letter read to the NAACP board Mrs. Roosevelt explained that at Geneva United States opposition to receiving the petition was based on Soviet refusal to accept complaints directed against the USSR. Noting she took the same position as Jonathan Daniels, who also voted to reject the association appeal, Mrs. Roosevelt added: "we must accept all or none as we could not let the Soviets get away with attacking the United States and not recognize their own shortcomings." Clearly, the U.S. position reflected a concern with jockeying for advantage in the United Nations and failed to give much weight to the value of a great power's setting an example by opening its domestic shortcomings to world scrutiny. See NAACP board minutes, February 9, 1948, NAACP Papers, Library of Congress.

4. See *New York PM,* March 3, 1946; *Daily Worker,* February 7, 9, 12, 19, 20, 22, 28, March 8, 9, 1946; *Daily Worker* pamphlet, *Dixie Comes to New York* (1946); see editorial, "Murder," in *Crisis,* March 1946, p. 72.

5. Charles Mole, "Willie Earle Incident" (Paper, 1972, University of Cincinnati); see *People's Voice,* editorial, May 31, 1947, for condemnation of verdict in the case. The newspaper called for death sentences and urged blacks to "raise all manner of hell" until government leaders acted. For British comment that the South Carolina trial represented "a reawakening of judicial conscience," see *New Statesman and Nation,* May 31, 1947, pp. 388, 389.

6. Richard Kluger, *Simple Justice* (New York: Vintage Books, 1977), pp. 4, 6, 8.

7. Ibid., pp. 3, 14–17, 525; *Pittsburgh Courier,* December 22, 1951.

8. J. Wayne Dudley, "The Rosa Lee Ingram Case and Its Social Implications" (Paper, University of Cincinnati, 1970); Gerda Lerner, ed., *Black Women in White America: A Documentary History* (New York: Vintage Books, 1971), pp. 190–93. In the appeal to the UN Du Bois wrote: "This crucifixion of Mrs. Rosa Lee Ingram is of one piece with Georgia's treatment of Colored women. . . . It is clear that the part of this nation which boasts its reverence for womanhood is the part where the women of Africa were slaves and concubines of white Americans for two and a half centuries; where their daughters in states like Virginia became human brood mares to raise domestic slaves when the African trade stopped; and where their granddaughters became mothers of millions of mulattoes. Today those colored women and their children bear the chief burden of the share-cropping system where Southern slavery still lingers. . . . It may seem a very little thing for 59 nations of the world to take note of the injustice done a poor colored woman in Georgia . . . yet after all, is it in the end so small a thing to 'do justly, to love mercy and walk humbly' in setting 'this mad world aright'?" See W. E. B. Du Bois, *Against Racism: Unpublished Essays, Papers, Addresses, 1887–1961,* ed. Herbert Aptheker (Amherst: University of Massachusetts Press, 1985), pp. 261–65. Also see W. E. B. Du Bois Papers, microfilm reel 64, University of Massachusetts Library, Amherst.

9. See William L. Patterson, ed., *We Charge Genocide: The Crime of Government against the Negro People* (New York: International Publishers, 1970), p. 62. Detailed coverage of the Columbia episode was provided by the *Daily Worker* via reports by correspondents Carl Hirsch, Robert Minor, and Harry Raymond. See *Daily Worker,* esp. February 27, 28, March 1, 2, 4, 5, 6, 7, 9, 11–14, 16, 19, April 1, 9, 10, May 31, June 2, 3, 5, 7, 9, 17, 19, 20, 26, July 3, 11, August 15, 16, 20, September 19, 23, 24, 28, October 2, 4, 5, 11, November 16, 20; also see report by NAACP attorneys Maurice Weaver and Z. Alexander Looby, "What Happened at Columbia?" *Crisis,* April 1946, pp. 110, 111, 125. The report details the damage inflicted on black business establishments in the course of the mob assault.

10. *People's Voice,* March 9, 1946; *Crisis,* editorial, April, 1946, p. 105.

11. Zangrando, *NAACP Crusade*, pp. 172–74; William C. Berman, *The Politics of Civil Rights in the Truman Administration* (Columbus: Ohio State University Press, 1970), p. 45; White, *A Man Called White*, pp. 309–21. See Harry Raymond's vivid account of incident involving Thurgood Marshall, *Daily Worker*, November 20, 1946. In his autobiography Roy Wilkins confirms Raymond's account of the threat to Marshall, but there is no mention of Raymond as the third person in the car that followed the police vehicle carrying Marshall away. See Roy Wilkins, with Tom Matthews, *Standing Fast: The Autobiography of Roy Wilkins* (New York: Viking Press, 1980), pp. 188, 189.

12. *Daily Worker*, June 28, July 1, 2, 1946. Also see account of convention in *Crisis*, August 1946, pp. 249, 250. See text of Marshall speech in NAACP Collection, IIA 34, Manuscript Division, Library of Congress.

13. *To Secure These Rights: The Report of the President's Committee on Civil Rights* (New York: Simon & Schuster, 1947).

14. For a further account of this multiple Georgia lynching, see *Pittsburgh Courier*, August 3, 1946.

15. Donald R. McCoy and Richard T. Ruetten, *Quest and Response* (Lawrence: University Press of Kansas, 1973), pp. 92–94.

16. Truman's notation on Walter White is found in White to Truman, November 23, 1945, file 413; telegram, Washington branch, NAACP, to Truman, January 1947, OF 93–B; memorandum, Niles to Matt Connelly, February 19, 1947, enclosing memo from Robert K. Carr to Niles, February 18, 1947, OF 596–A; all in Harry S. Truman Library, Independence, Mo. Truman's notation regarding Walter White was made in the midst of a dispute with the NAACP regarding Truman's overturning of an FEPC directive mandating fair employment practices by the government-seized Capitol Transit Company in Washington. On November 23, the same day that White wrote Truman, the NAACP telegraphed the president urging support of the proposed FEPC policy. See McCoy and Ruetten, *Quest and Response*, pp. 27, 28.

17. Wright to Truman, July 18, 1946, OF 93, Truman Library. Walter White of the NAACP termed the blinding of Isaac Woodward an incident of "sheer brutality and fascist terror," a story that was without parallel in his experience. See account of episode in *Daily Worker*, July 13, 1946.

18. McCoy and Ruetten, *Quest and Response*, pp. 45, 46.

19. Berman, *Civil Rights in Truman Administration*, pp. 51, 52.

20. Ibid., p. 52; McCoy and Ruetten, *Quest and Response*, p. 48; see newspaper accounts in Philip S. Foner, ed., *Paul Robeson Speaks: Writings, Speeches, Interviews, 1918–1974* (New York: Bruner, Mazel, 1978), pp. 173–78.

21. Berman, *Civil Rights in Truman Administration*, p. 77.

22. See J. Wayne Dudley, " 'Hate' Organizations of the 1940s: The Columbians, Inc.," *Phylon*, Fall 1981, pp. 262–74; *Daily Worker*, December 11, 31, 1946, January 2, 1947.

23. See Arnold R. Hirsch, *Making the Second Ghetto: Race and Housing in Chicago, 1940–1960* (Cambridge: Cambridge University Press, 1983), pp. xi, xii, 41, 42, 52–59, 90, 94, 97, 201, 246, 247.

14. Peekskill

1. Howard Fast, *Peekskill: USA, a Personal Experience* (New York: Civil Rights Congress, 1951), p. 11. In 1980 Fast still saw a relation of Peekskill to fascism. Fast to author, October 1, 1980. For police version of August 27 incident, see report to Troop "K"

Commander, New York State Police, Thomas E. Dewey MSS, University of Rochester Library.

2. *Peekskill Evening Star,* August 23, 1949, clipping in Police Reports folder, Dewey MSS.

3. Fast, *Peekskill,* pp. 24, 29, 34, 99.

4. State police report, August 28, 1949, Police Reports folder; Troop Commander D. F. Glasheen report to Commanding Officer, New York State Police, September 15, 1949, Police Reports folder; Algernon B. White to Dewey, August 27, 1949, Civil Rights Congress special folder; all in Dewey MSS.

5. Holmes, Hays, and Baldwin to Dewey, August 30, 1949; Holmes, Hays, and Baldwin to McGrath, August 30, 1949, both in Dewey MSS.

6. Leaflet copy in Dewey MSS.

7. Fast, *Peekskill,* pp. 62–67; New York state police investigator R. Davis quoted Benjamin J. Davis as stating at the Harlem rally: "We are not pacifists and we are going to stand up toe to toe and slug it out." Davis reportedly added that if authorities failed to give protection "we will be prepared to defend ourselves." R. Davis of Troop "K" to Troop Commander, August 31, 1949, Dewey MSS.

8. David King Dunaway, *How Can I Keep from Singing? Pete Seeger* (New York: McGraw-Hill, 1981), p. 13.

9. Ibid., p. 19.

10. Fast, *Peekskill,* p. 86.

11. Mario Cassetta, quoted in Dunaway, *How Can I?,* p. 21.

12. See ACLU news release, September 8, 1949, American Civil Liberties Union Records and Publications, 1917–1975, microfilm reel 12.

13. *Violence in Peekskill* (New York: American Civil Liberties Union Pamphlet, 1950). Howard Fast, in 1980, notes the difficulty with regard to Peekskill of separating anticommunism from racial animosity. Fast to author, October 1, 1980.

14. *Nation,* September 10, 1949, pp. 213, 214.

15. *Nation,* September 17, 1949, p. 263.

16. *Nation,* September 24, 1949, p. 291; *New York Times,* September 15, 1949; for Westchester County prosecutor George M. Fanelli's report praising police conduct, see *New York Times,* September 8, 1949.

17. *Pittsburgh Courier,* September 3, 1949.

18. Ibid., September 10, 1949.

19. Horace R. Cayton, "Fear and Guilt of White America," *Pittsburgh Courier,* September 10, 1949.

20. *Pittsburgh Courier,* editorial, September 10, 1949.

21. Dunaway, *How Can I?,* pp. 10, 11.

22. See text of Du Bois 1946 speech in Foner, *Voice of Black America,* 2: 221–26.

23. See Lester, *The Seventh Son,* 2: 596, 597.

24. See text of NAACP speech in Philip S. Foner, ed., *W. E. B. Du Bois Speaks: Speeches and Addresses, 1920–1963* (New York: Pathfinder Press, 1970), pp. 222–27.

25. Aptheker, *Correspondence of Du Bois,* 3: 244.

26. See Lester, *The Seventh Son,* 2: 601–8; also see W. E. B. Du Bois, "The Negro since 1900: A Progress Report," *New York Times Magazine,* November 21, 1948. In discussing aspects of progress in black status, Du Bois noted there had been "an abatement in mob violence" and that the "most barbarous expression of race hate, lynching has notably decreased." He also observed that there existed "a long record of effort on the part of

white Americans to help black folk." The article is remarkable for its balanced and far-sighted perspective on the racial situation, with no hint of bitterness over Du Bois's difficulties with the NAACP officialdom. He traced in detail the contributions made by the association in raising the position of blacks and though he referred to "a great revolution" following the two world wars he offered no set timetable. He wrote of the Negro: "He is long-suffering and patient. But whether it takes thirty years or a thousand, equality is his goal and he will never stop until he reaches it." Once again providing an agenda for the civil rights movement, Du Bois spelled out the components of equality: "abolition of separate schools, the disappearance of 'Jim Crow' travel; no segregation in public accommodations; the right to vote, the right to think and the right to speak, the right to work and to live in a decent home, and the right to marry any person who wishes to marry him."

15. Executions, Little Rock, Genocide

1. McGehee quoted in Charles H. Martin, "Black Protest, Anti-Communism, and the Cold War: The Willie McGee Case" (Paper delivered at 1980 meeting of the Association for Study of Afro-American Life and History), p. 8, account of delegation meeting with Gov. Fielding Wright, July 25, 1950; Aubrey Grossman of the Civil Rights Congress recalls that at the meeting Governor Wright, Judge McGehee, and Attorney General Coleman were present. Telephone interview with Grossman, July 24, 1981. In 1950 and 1951 both Willie McGee and his wife Mrs. Rosalee McGee signed affidavits stating that the alleged rape victim, Mrs. Willamette Hawkins, had initiated a sexual relationship with McGee. According to Mrs. McGee, the affair had started "at least" as early as 1942. Willie McGee outlined how the situation had developed: "I became well acquainted with Mrs. Troy Hawkins and one day after I worked there off and on for about a year I was waxing floors with her in the house and she showed a willingness to be familiar and let me have intercourse with her in the back room. After that she frequently sent for me to do work which gave opportunities for intercourse which she accepted, and on occasions after dark she took me in her automobile out to a place near the grave yard where we had intercourse." In the final appeal to the federal courts the McGee defense stated that "Mrs. Hawkins had been intimately acquainted with the plaintiff over a period of many years, and had sexual relations with him over a long period of time." See Rosalee McGee affidavit, July 25, 1950, Willie McGee affidavit, February 3, 1951, in Ernest Goodman McGee case file; also see defense petition to United States District Court, Southern District of Mississippi, May 5, 1951, in Goodman McGee case file, Goodman Law Office, Detroit, Michigan.

2. Martin, "Black Protest," p. 7; also see Aubrey Grossman, "Lawyers on Trial," *Masses and Mainstream*, August 1951, pp. 30, 31.

3. See *McGee v. State* 33 (So. 2nd 843); also see *McGee v. State* 40 (So. 2nd 843).

4. *Jackson Daily News*, May 9, 1951.

5. *Ibid.*, May 8, 1951. In this last court hearing on the case the attorneys worked under great pressure. They might have requested testimony from Willie McGee, but as attorney Ernest Goodman recalls, the time consumed would have foreclosed recourse to any other conceivable legal appeals. The only hope with a glimmer of reality was for a Supreme Court stay, and the judgment was that would not be affected by McGee's testimony. Goodman to author, May 5, 1981. It is also possible that testimony by McGee as to the voluntary nature of the sexual relationship might only have further inflamed the public mood of whites in Mississippi.

6. Interview with Ernest Goodman, Detroit, Mich., April 2, 1981.

7. John Herbers to author, November 10, 1980.

8. *Jackson Daily News*, May 8, 9, 1951.

9. *Ibid.*, quoted in Jessica Mitford, *A Fine Old Conflict* (London: Joseph, 1977), p. 155.

10. *Time*, May 14, 1951, p. 26.

11. *Life*, May 21, 1951, p. 44.

12. Max Lerner, "The Just and Unjust," *New York Post*, May 8, 1951; Mary Mostert, "Death for Association," *Nation*, May 5, 1951. Mostert accepted at face value a white newspaperman's comment that "Communist support has just about sent McGee to the chair" and also operated within cold war logic in implying that a relevant issue in the case was whether the lack of a fair trial stopped or promoted communism (p. 421); John Cogley, "Willie McGee," *Commonweal*, May 25, 1951, p. 158. Cogley stated that "no decent American shared the crocodile tears and phony indignations" of Communists, but he also deplored the lack of a full-scale public reaction to the case.

13. See John Henry Faulk, *Fear on Trial* (Austin: University of Texas Press, 1983), p. 141.

14. Mitford, *Fine Old Conflict*, p. 148.

15. Martin, "Black Protest," p. 9; Grossman recalls that his assailants included two Jackson policemen and two Laurel officers. He also recalls that on the day of his arrival in Jackson the local newspaper editorialized that the United States was spending money to kill Communists in Korea whereas money could be saved by killing them here. Telephone interview with Grossman, July 24, 1981. Carl Rowan quotes the *Jackson Daily News* as declaring: "Why the hell go to Korea to shoot Communists when the hunting is good on home grounds?" See Carl Rowan, *South of Freedom* (New York: Knopf, 1952), p. 177.

16. Mitford, *Fine Old Conflict*, pp. 149–54; Martin, "Black Protest," p. 12.

17. James Baldwin, *Going to Meet the Man* (New York: Dial Press, 1965), pp. 242, 245.

18. Mitford, *Fine Old Conflict*, p. 154; Grossman observes that the reason for executing McGee at the Laurel courthouse in a portable electric chair brought to town for that purpose was to simulate as closely as possible the setting of a lynching.

19. *Jackson Daily News*, May 8, 1951.

20. Mitford, *Fine Old Conflict*, p. 157.

21. *Jackson Daily News*, May 8, 1951.

22. Herbers to author, November 10, 1980.

23. Rowan, *South of Freedom*, pp. 176, 185, 186.

24. *Pittsburgh Courier*, January 23, 1954.

25. Robert W. Burns, "I Who Am About to Die," *Pittsburgh Courier*, January 23, 1954.

26. *Pittsburgh Courier*, January 30, 1954.

27. *Ibid.*, February 6, 1954. Marshall and Carter were quoted as stating: "From the very beginning of this case, we have held a fundamental conviction of the innocence of these men."

28. *Ibid.*, February 6, 13, 20, 1954. The place where the trials were held was identified by the *Guam News* as the Parker Manor Service Club, described as spacious with a panoramic view of the sea and cliffs (May 10, 1949). The variation in names given the club may have reflected a difference in common usage.

29. See Herbert Aptheker, "Two Hangings on Guam," in Aptheker, *Afro-American History*, pp. 218–44.

30. See White, *A Man Called White*, pp. 278–85.

31. Brownell to Eisenhower, "In the Matter of the Commutation of Sentence of Robert

W. Burns and Herman P. Dennis, Jr.," p. 5; Finding of the Department of the Air Force Judicial Council, July 18, 1950, regarding case of Herman P. Dennis, Jr.; Finding of United States Air Force Board of Review, November 29, 1949, pp. 12, 13; all in Dwight D. Eisenhower Library, Abilene, Kansas. A statement by Calvin Dennis repudiating his confession was already contained in the Burns–Dennis case file during 1951, when the Truman administration considered the case. See Calvin Dennis to Mrs. Lee, August 28, 1949, in Truman Papers, OF.

32. See United States Supreme Court Reports, *Burns* v. *Wilson*, 346 U.S. 137.

33. See United States Court of Appeals, District of Columbia Circuit, 91 App. DC 208.

34. Vann to President of the United States, January 10, 1954; Vann to *Courier* readers, January 19, 1954; Schuyler letter addressed "To All My Friends," January 20, 1954; Shanley to Vann, January 26, 1954; Nunn to Shanley, January 29, 1954; Shanley to Nunn, February 3, 1954; Nunn to Shanley, February 22, 1954; Shanley to Nunn, February 26, 1954, all in Eisenhower Library.

35. "Southern Manifesto," in Anthony Lewis, *Portrait of a Decade* (New York: Random House, 1964), p. 44.

36. Eisenhower, quoted in Kluger, *Simple Justice*, p. 753. Also see Earl Warren, *The Memoirs of Earl Warren* (Garden City, N.Y.: Doubleday, 1977), pp. 289–92, regarding Eisenhower's refusal to support the *Brown* decision. Warren wrote: "With his popularity, if Eisenhower had said that black children were still being discriminated against long after the adoption of the Thirteenth, Fourteenth, and Fifteenth Amendments, that the Supreme Court of the land had now declared it unconstitutional to continue such cruel practices, and that it should be the duty of every good citizen to help rectify more than eighty years of wrong-doing by honoring that decision, if he had said something to this effect, we would have been relieved, in my opinion, of many of the racial problems which have continued to plague us." Warren recalled that prior to the *Brown* decision Eisenhower had said of southern opponents of desegregation: "All they are concerned about is to see that their sweet little girls are not required to sit in school alongside some big overgrown Negroes" (p. 291). William O. Douglas shared Warren's critical view of Eisenhower's approach to the desegregation decision, noting that Eisenhower encouraged foot dragging in the process of enforcing the *Brown* decision. Douglas wrote: "Ike's ominous silence on our 1954 decision gave courage to the racists who decided to resist the decision ward by ward, precinct by precinct, town by town, and county by county." See William O. Douglas, *The Court Years, 1939–1975* (New York: Random House, 1980), p. 120.

37. See account in William M. Chace and Peter Collier, eds., *Justice Denied* (New York: Harcourt Brace, 1970), pp. 315–19; also account in William Bradford Huie, *Three Lives for Mississippi* (New York: WCC Books, 1965), pp. 18–34. The *New York Times* reported that Mabry was one of four persons arrested for inciting to riot in the aftermath of the attack on Nat ("King") Cole. The Birmingham police apparently had been alerted to watch for trouble and were stationed in the wings, but still the attackers were able to climb the stage and knock Cole to the floor. See *New York Times*, April 11, 1956.

38. See NAACP, *M is for Mississippi and Murder* (1956), in NAACP pamphlet file, NAACP Records, Manuscript Division, Library of Congress, Washington, D.C.

39. Daisy Bates, *The Long Shadow of Little Rock* (New York: McKay, 1962), pp. 34–36, 40–43, 62, 66–68. The lynching Mrs. Eckford recalled was indeed an act of savagery. The *New York Times* reported that the body of the victim, John Carter, aged twenty-two "was dragged behind an automobile through the main street of the city and then saturated with gasoline and burned at one of the principal business corners in the Negro section while thousands of persons looked on . . . the mob dragged the body to the corner and made

a bonfire of it." The police, the *Times* reported, directed congested traffic around the scene. See *New York Times,* May 5, 1927; in the 1946 case, against which Bates protested, the three pickets, Roy Cole, Louis Jones, and Jesse Bear, strikers at the Southern Cotton Oil Co., had been convicted of criminal responsibility for violence occurring in the course of a strike. The violence was the fatal stabbing of union organizer Walter Campbell as the result of a clash with Otha Williams, scab. See account in *Daily Worker,* March 26, 1946. For an account of the 1957 crisis that outlines the legal and political maneuvering from which came the violence at Central High School, see Tony Freyer, *The Little Rock Crisis: A Constitutional Interpretation* (Westport, Conn.: Greenwood Press, 1984).

40. Bates, *Long Shadow,* pp. 70, 71. Tony Freyer writes that Grace Lorch and her husband Lee, mathematics professor at Philander Smith College, "rendered invaluable and dedicated service to the cause of racial justice in the capital city." Freyer adds that the "known communist affiliations" of the couple led the NAACP to sever any connection, and indeed by 1958 the Lorches had moved to Canada. See Freyer, *Little Rock Crisis,* p. 131. It should be noted that this separation occurred after Grace Lorch was summoned by Senator Eastland's Internal Security Subcommittee.

41. Bates, *Long Shadow,* p. 75.

42. Ibid., pp. 92, 93.

43. Ibid., pp. 93, 94.

44. Wilkins to Powell, September 19, 1957, quoted in Wilkins, *Standing Fast,* p. 251.

45. Bates, *Long Shadow,* p. 99.

46. Ibid., pp. 162, 163, 169.

47. Franklin speech quoted in Foner, *Voice of Black America,* 2: 291–300.

48. Eisenhower speech of September 24, 1957, quoted in Blaustein and Zangrando, *Civil Rights,* pp. 457, 458.

49. Patterson, *We Charge Genocide.*

50. Before going ahead with drafting the petition, Patterson consulted with William Z. Foster, Communist party national chairman; and also with J. Finley Wilson, grand exalted ruler of the Elks; Roscoe Dunjee, publisher of the Oklahoma *Black Dispatch;* the Reverend Charles A. Hill of Detroit; Bishop W. J. Walls of Chicago; and Bishop R. R. Wright of Philadelphia. See William L. Patterson, *The Man Who Cried Genocide* (New York: International Publishers, 1971), p. 176.

51. In submitting the petition Patterson urged Secretary General Lie, on the basis that authority to investigate violations of human rights was conferred by the general provisions of the UN Charter, to place the matter before the UN Commission on Human Rights. Patterson, *Man Who Cried Genocide,* p. 187.

52. *Pittsburgh Courier,* November 24, December 1, 8, 1951.

53. Ibid., July 21, September 29, October 6, 1951.

54. Ibid., November 24, December 15, 1951.

55. See U.S. Congress, Senate, Hearings before a Subcommittee of the Committee on Foreign Relations, *The Genocide Convention,* 81st Cong., 2nd sess. pp. 158, 162, 164, 181, 199, 201, 229.

56. Ibid., pp. 13, 21, 35, 48, 53.

57. Ibid., pp. 84, 125, 126, 137.

58. Ibid., pp. 217, 220.

59. Ibid., pp. 479, 483.

60. Ibid., pp. 131, 132.

61. Patterson, *We Charge Genocide,* p. 44.

62. Ibid., p. 49.

63. Ibid., pp. 49, 50.

64. Ibid., pp. 58–77,

65. As a countermeasure against any possible impact *We Charge Genocide* might have on world opinion, the United States Information Agency in 1951 published a brochure, *The Negro in American Life.* This publication stressed three themes: (1) Only a brief interval had passed since the abolition of slavery; (2) blacks had made remarkable progress in the United States; and (3) the United States government had supported steps to improve the position of blacks in American society. The assertion was made that "any honest and informed observer" knew that "over the past fifty years the average Negro has made progress on every front—social, economic, educational—at a tremendous pace." Although there were some overt distortions in the text of the brochure, as in the comment that the pattern of black economic life was "much the same as that of the white population," the most serious distortion was the failure to portray candidly the extent of racism still present in American society. The foreign reader of *The Negro in American Life* would need to turn elsewhere to discover that police brutality was yet a matter of concern, that de jure segregation still governed public education in a number of American states, and that many thousands of black citizens were still disfranchised. This reader would be told of President Roosevelt's having established the FEPC but was not told that Congress had refused to authorize a permanent FEPC. See *The Negro in American Life,* available from the International Communications Agency, under provisions of the Freedom of Information Act.

66. U.S. Congress, Senate, Hearings before a Subcommittee of the Committee on Foreign Relations, *Genocide Convention,* 92nd Cong., 1st sess., pp. 18, 19.

67. Ibid., p. 57.

68. In a speech to the United Nations General Assembly, March 17, 1977, President Jimmy Carter assured the world organization he would work closely with the U.S. Congress in seeking ratification of the Genocide Convention, along with other international agreements. The Genocide Convention, however, continued to languish in the Senate. See text of Carter speech in *New York Times,* March 18, 1977. Also see Carter letter to Senate urging ratification, May 23, 1977, in U.S. Congress, Senate, Committee on Foreign Relations, *Genocide Convention,* 95th Cong., 1st sess., p. 54. Ratification, however, was opposed by Senator Jesse Helms of North Carolina who argued that the convention would "internationalize the domestic criminal law of the nations which are parties to it" (p. 106). It is not clear from Helms's statement what if any crime he would consider international in nature.

In hearings held during November 1979 concerning four international human rights treaties, the Senate Foreign Relations Committee excluded the Genocide Convention from direct consideration, but at several points reference was made to the issue. Deputy Secretary of State Warren Christopher in his testimony noted that the convention "is a pervasive force that stands in the world, unratified by the United States." Senator Pell responded that, for "domestic political reasons, we seem unable to move ahead with it." Christopher expressed hope that before the end of the 96th Congress the convention could be considered again. A representative of the American Jewish Committee noted the Senate's "melancholy record" with respect to the Genocide Convention and urged the committee to expedite consideration. See U.S. Congress, Senate, Hearings before the Committee on Foreign Relations, *International Human Rights Treaties,* 96th Cong., 1st sess., pp. 18, 402.

In December 1981 the Senate Foreign Relations Committee again held hearings on the Genocide Convention. By this time the American Bar Association had reversed positions on the issue and taken a position favoring ratification. The organization most prominently identified with opposition to the convention was now the ultraright Liberty Lobby. Among those appearing to support ratification was Senator William Proxmire, the most consistent and outspoken Senate voice for favorable action, and former senator Jacob Javits. Also urging ratification were Richard N. Gardner, Columbia University law professor, representing the Ad Hoc Committee on the Human Rights and Genocide Treaties, and two representatives of the American Bar Association, Dean Thomas Burgenthal and law professor John Norton Moore. Gardner, Burgenthal, Moore, and Proxmire, in varying degrees, all viewed the Genocide Convention as an instrument of effective cold war policy. Gardner stressed that refusal to ratify contributed to American political isolation. "One way we can defend our national security in the non-military field," he observed, "is by waging the diplomacy of ideas, because what is going on in Italy, in Europe and around the world is a struggle, an ideological struggle, between ourselves and the Soviet Union and those who believe in their philosophy." Burgenthal argued that ratification was one of those acts "which demonstrate that this country shares mankind's aspirations for freedom and human dignity which communism so brutally suppresses." Moore quoted approvingly an earlier Burgenthal comment to the effect that the Soviet Union had to be confronted on the ideological level and that a sound human rights policy "provides the U.S. with an ideology that distinguishes us most clearly from the Soviet Union and seriously undercuts the ideological appeal of Communism." Senator Proxmire urged that the Communist nations should not be permitted "to take the high moral ground" in international exchanges regarding human rights. With regard to the racial implications of the Genocide Convention, Professor Gardner placed on the record an article coauthored by Arthur Goldberg and himself. In terms of the definition of genocide, Gardner and Goldberg argued that the treatment of the black community in the United States, "which admittedly has suffered widespread discrimination for many years...does not fall within the definition." This hearing did not lead to full Senate consideration of the issue, as the Reagan administration at least until September 1984 took no position for or against ratification. On September 6, 1984, the New York Times reported that the administration would now favor ratification. See New York Times, September 6, 1984; Congress, Senate, Hearings before the Committee on Foreign Relations, The Genocide Convention, 97th Cong., 1st sess., pp. 19, 69, 75, 113, 119. Regarding the vote for ratification, see New York Times, February 20, 1986.

16. The Emergence of Dr. King

1. Martin Luther King, Sr., with Clayton Riley, Daddy King: An Autobiography (New York: Morrow, 1980), pp. 24, 28–33, 85.

2. See Aptheker, Afro-American History, p. 267.

3. David L. Lewis, King: A Critical Biography (Baltimore: Penguin Books, 1970), pp. 44, 45; in a second edition of the biography Professor Lewis again writes that King was not an original philosopher, but the reference to derivative intelligence is absent. See David L. Lewis, King: A Biography (Urbana: University of Illinois Press, 1978), pp. 44, 45.

4. Lewis, King: A Critical Biography, p. 45; Lerone Bennett, Jr., "When the Man and the Hour Are Met," in C. Eric Lincoln, ed., Martin Luther King, Jr.: A Profile (New York: Hill & Wang, 1970), pp. 13, 14.

5. Meier, Rudwick, and Broderick, Black Protest Thought, p. 291.

6. Martin Luther King, Jr., 1956 pamphlet, quoted in ibid., pp. 291–302; in his "Letter to the North," William Faulkner took the classic position that segregation was a regional matter to be dealt with by the white South, and there was even a note of threat in his response to the demand for implementation of desegregation. Noting that he was opposed to compulsory segregation, the novelist also stated: "I am just as strongly against com-

pulsory integration." Faulkner went on to explain that if compelled to vacate the middle ground "where we could have worked to help the Negro improve his condition" moderates like himself would need to make a new choice. That choice would be one of alignment with the new underdog, "the white embattled minority who are our blood and kin." Faulkner was unable to view self-critically the role of the white moderates of the South or to come to grips with the racial question as involving matters of constitutional rights. See *Life*, March 5, 1956; Martin Luther King, Jr., "Walk for Freedom," *Fellowship* 12 (1956): 5–7. The magazine reported that the King article resulted from a trip to Montgomery by Fellowship of Reconciliation secretary Glenn E. Smiley. Describing King as "a quiet-spoken, nattily dressed young Negro minister," *Fellowship* declared he had revealed himself "as a pillar of nonviolent strength, carved on the Gandhian model."

7. See Louis E. Lomax, *The Negro Revolt* (New York: Signet Books, 1963), p. 92.

8. Bennett, "Man and Hour Are Met," p. 10; in *Song of Solomon*, novelist Toni Morrison presents a sharply etched fictional portrait of black response to the Till lynching. Regarding the basic facts Morrison wrote: "A young Negro boy had been found stomped to death in Sunflower County, Mississippi. There were no questions about who stomped him—his murderers had boasted freely—and there were no questions about the motive. The boy had whistled at some white woman, refused to deny he had slept with others, and was a Northerner visiting the South." When one of the characters in the novel states that the lynchers would be caught he receives a pointed answer: "They'll catch 'em, all right, and give 'em a big party and a medal." To the charge that Till had a knife, another character responds: "He could have had a wad of bubble gum, they'd swear it was a hand grenade." See Toni Morrison, *Song of Solomon* (New York: Knopf, 1977), pp. 80–82.

9. See Wilkins, *Standing Fast*, pp. 225–27; also Stephen B. Oates, *Let the Trumpet Sound: The Life of Martin Luther King, Jr.* (New York: Harper & Row, 1982), pp. 64, 65.

10. Bennett, "Man and Hour Are Met," pp. 16, 17; in this speech Dr. King also took the ground that the Montgomery movement would be guided "by the highest principles of law and order." Martin Luther King, Jr., *Stride toward Freedom* (New York: Ballantine Books, 1960), p. 51; Oates, *Let the Trumpet Sound*, pp. 70, 71, quoting King's Holt Street Church speech.

11. See Vincent Harding, "Religion and Resistance among Antebellum Negroes," in August Meier and Elliot Rudwick, eds., *The Making of Black America* (New York: Atheneum, 1968), 2: 179–97. See James Melvin Washington, ed., *A Testament of Hope: The Essential Writings of Martin Luther King, Jr.* (San Francisco: Harper & Row, 1986), p. xvii.

12. Coretta Scott King, *My Life with Martin Luther King, Jr.* (New York: Holt, Rinehart & Winston, 1969), pp. 129, 130.

13. King, *Stride toward Freedom*, pp. 41, 42.

14. See Tom Johnson, "The Rev. King Is Boycott Boss," *Montgomery Advertiser*, January 19, 1956.

15. *Montgomery Advertiser*, December 12, 1955.

16. Reinhold Niebuhr, *Moral Man and Immoral Society*, quoted in Kenneth L. Smith and Ira G. Zepp, Jr., *Search for the Beloved Community* (Valley Forge, Penn.: Judson Press, 1974), p. 94. Niebuhr looked to American blacks to undertake a campaign, fashioned in the spirit of Gandhi, that would fuse the "aggressiveness of the new and young Negro with the patience and forbearance of the old Negro, to rob the former of its vindictiveness and the latter of its lethargy." Prescient in his call for a campaign of mass black non-cooperation with racist institutions, Niebuhr essentially saw racial change in terms of how

a minority was to obtain its rights from the majority without specifically analyzing the roots of racial oppression. See Reinhold Niebuhr, *Moral Man and Immoral Society* (New York: Scribner, 1932), p. 254.

17. Niebuhr to Ira G. Zepp, Jr., September 22, 1969, quoted in Smith and Zepp, *Search*, p. 97.

18. King, *Stride toward Freedom*, p. 67.

19. Bennett, "Man and Hour Are Met," p. 32, 13.

20. King, *Stride toward Freedom*, p. 42; Coretta King, *Life with King*, p. 115; King, *Stride toward Freedom*, p. 42; Bennett, "Man and Hour Are Met," p. 15.

21. King, *Stride toward Freedom*, pp. 43, 44.

22. King, *Daddy King*, p. 154.

23. King, *Stride toward Freedom*, pp. 47–53.

24. Coretta King, *Life with King*, p. 121; King, *Stride toward Freedom*, p. 68.

25. See "Youthful Minister's Humility Gives Boycotters New Spirit," *Jet*, April 12, 1956, p. 25.

26. See "Bombing, Harassment Don't Stop Foot-Weary Negro Boycotters," *Jet*, February 16, 1956, pp. 11, 12.

27. Ibid., p. 12.

28. King, *Stride toward Freedom*, p. 69.

29. Ibid., pp. 120, 121; Lewis, *King: A Critical Biography*, pp. 74, 75; at Dr. King's trial the prosecution called several black witnesses who said they had been threatened to compel their support of the boycott. Defense attorney Fred Gray told the court that one of these witnesses, Ernest Smith, worked as janitor in the county courthouse and another, Beatrice Smith, was employed by the mother-in-law of Montgomery mayor Gayle. At the trial it was disclosed that Gayle was a member of the Montgomery Citizens Council. See *Montgomery Advertiser*, March 22, 1956, for account of defense testimony.

30. See *New York Times*, December 29, 1956, January 11, 1957; King, *Stride toward Freedom*, pp. 140–44. Following the January 28 violence King delivered a sermon at Dexter Avenue Baptist Church. The *Advertiser* quoted King as declaring: "Tell Montgomery they can keep shooting and I'm going to stand up to them; tell Montgomery they can keep bombing and I'm going to stand up to them. If I had to die tomorrow morning I would die happy because I've been to the mountain top and I've seen the promised land and it's going to be here in Montgomery. The old Montgomery is passing away and segregation is dying." See *Montgomery Advertiser*, January 28, 1957.

31. King, *Stride toward Freedom*, p. 142.

32. The *Montgomery Advertiser* editorial entitled "Shall Montgomery Surrender?" asked: "Is Montgomery to be a city in which bullets fly between sundown and sunup?" The paper called for a firm response to the threat of violence, urging the assignment of as many police as needed to insure peaceful operation of the buses. The issue as seen by the *Advertiser* had passed beyond the question of segregation and was now "whether it is safe to live in Montgomery, Alabama." Expressing concern about the prospect of retaliatory violence, the paper also indicated that further violence was counterproductive from the segregationist standpoint. "Those," it said, "who are at this moment seeking enactment of unbearable civil rights legislation welcome such events, for they serve their cause." The same issue of the *Advertiser* carried the advertisement signed by the chairman's council of the Men of Montgomery. It began: "The problem facing us today is not a question of segregation or integration—it is violence!" Stating that the "responsible citizens" of the community looked to public officials to find and prosecute the guilty, the statement added: "Violence, by white or colored, cannot be tolerated. We call upon you who are causing

this violence to realize you are accomplishing nothing but hatred, you are rapidly destroying our city" (January 11, 1957).

33. King, *Stride toward Freedom*, p. 175.

34. Ibid., p. 90.

35. Appeal to Eisenhower, quoted in William Robert Miller, "The Broadening Horizons: Montgomery, America, the World," in Lincoln, *Martin Luther King, Jr.*, p. 44.

36. See *New York Amsterdam News*, February 23, March 2, 9, April 6, May 11, 1957.

37. For text of King speech, see Foner, *Voice of Black America*, 2: 303–8.

38. *New York Amsterdam News*, June 1, 1957.

39. See text of Du Bois article, "Watchword for Negroes: Register and Vote," in Lester, *The Seventh Son*, 2: 652, 653; earlier, during the course of the Montgomery struggle, Dr. and Mrs. Du Bois had written Dr. King, expressing their support of the Montgomery movement. See reply by King in Aptheker, *Correspondence of Du Bois*, 3: 399, 400.

40. See transcript of June 4, 1957, New York television interview in Lester, *The Seventh Son*, 2: 702, 703.

41. W. E. B. Du Bois, "Gandhi and the American Negroes," *Gandhi Marg* 1, no. 3 (1957): 175–77.

42. W. E. B. Du Bois, "Crusader without Violence," *National Guardian*, November 9, 1959.

43. See Martin Luther King, Jr., "Who Speaks for the South?" *Liberation*, March 1958, pp. 13, 14. King sought to place the civil rights struggle within the mainstream of American democratic tradition, stressing the continuity of the battle to enlarge the franchise from the era of the founding fathers to the adoption of the Nineteenth Amendment. With regard to those who fought for the extension of voting rights to women, King stated: "From these women we have learned how social changes take place through struggle." He specifically identified two southern politicians that he believed did not speak for the region, Georgia's segregationist governor Marvin Griffin and Senator James Eastland. "They speak only for a wilful but vocal minority," King declared. As to who truly represented the South, he listed Harry Ashmore and Lillian Smith as symbolizing the sentiments of "millions of Southerners, whose voices are yet unheard, whose course is yet unclear and whose courageous acts are yet unseen." He appealed to these millions to speak out.

44. Coretta King, *Life with King*, pp. 162–65, 341–43; Lewis, *King: A Critical Biography*, pp. 96, 97.

45. Miller, "Broadening Horizons," p. 55.

46. Ibid., p. 66.

47. Lillian Smith in the *Saturday Review* wrote that King in this book faced problems of form, focus, and narrative that he did not solve successfully and the book had a slow start. But she also predicted the book would become a "classic story" and said further: "This is the most interesting book that has come out of the current racial situation in the South; important as documentary, full of accurate facts that historians will value; exciting as one dramatic scene after another unfolds; wise and compassionate in its point of view." See Smith, "And Suddenly Something Happened," *Saturday Review*, September 20, 1958, p. 21; Abel Plenn in the *New York Times* found that the book showed King "to be an original thinker as well as a man of generous spirit." Plenn saw in the book an adventure, that undertaken by an individual and also by "a whole, oppressed people." See Plenn, "The Cradle Was Rocked," *New York Times Book Review*, October 12, 1958, p. 24; Harold R. Isaacs in the *New Republic* was more cautious. He wrote that King had thrown down "a rigorous challenge to American white society and to Negroes." But Isaacs was not certain of the response King would elicit from whites or blacks. He wrote: "Among Negroes

the process of re-assertion is still one of great inner conflict, uncertainty, division and impulses to strike back." See Isaacs, "Civil Disobedience in Montgomery," *New Republic,* October 6, 1958, p. 19.
    48. See James E. Jackson, "The Rev. King's Outlook," *Political Affairs,* December 1958, pp. 57–59.
    49. Louis E. Burnham, "Rev. King's Own Story of Montgomery," *National Guardian,* October 20, 1958.

17. Robert F. Williams and the Black Muslims

    1. King, *Stride toward Freedom,* pp. 69, 70.
    2. James Forman, *The Making of Black Revolutionaries* (New York: Macmillan, 1972), pp. 84, 85.
    3. Julian Mayfield, "Challenge to Negro Leadership: The Case of Robert Williams," *Commentary,* April 1961, p. 302.
    4. Williams brought a variety of experiences to his new position as local NAACP leader. He had lived in North Carolina, Michigan, California, New York, and West Virginia. A veteran of both the United States Army and the Marine Corps, he had worked in Detroit automobile plants and had also studied at West Virginia State College, North Carolina College, and Johnson C. Smith College. Williams was in Detroit during the 1943 racial eruption, and according to his biographer he was convinced that the auto magnates could have prevented the violence. While in Detroit Williams had some contact with the Communist movement, read the *Daily Worker,* and wrote a story, "Some Day I Am Going Back South," that was published in the newspaper. Williams saw the Communists as opponents of racism and was impressed that the party had a number of blacks among its leadership. See Robert Carl Cohen, *Black Crusader: A Biography of Robert Franklin Williams* (Secaucus, N.J.: Stuart, 1972).
    5. Forman, *Making of Black Revolutionaries,* p. 164; Robert F. Williams, *Negroes with Guns* (New York: Marzani & Munsell, 1962), p. 51.
    6. The petition described Williams and Perry as officeholders in "the Communist in-spired NAACP" and demanded that city and county officials order the two activists to leave. The petition further asserted that if the two men were removed from the scene "the White and Negro could live in this City and County without any trouble or ill will." Much of this text was taken up with listing the number of "Communist-front citations" held by such NAACP officers and supporters as W. E. B. Du Bois, Herbert Lehman, Roy Wilkins, Thurgood Marshall, Eleanor Roosevelt, Benjamin E. Mays, and A. Philip Randolph. The petition did not openly proclaim its Klan origins, but it clearly represented the spirit of personal intimidation that characterized the Klan. The November 11, 1957, *Monroe En-quirer* stated that on the previous Saturday between 1,000 and 1,500 persons had signed the petition. See text of petition and *Enquirer* clipping in NAACP Papers, Manuscript Division, Library of Congress.
    7. Forman, *Making of Black Revolutionaries,* p. 166; Williams, *Negroes with Guns,* pp. 53–57.
    8. See interview with Robert F. Williams, *Black Scholar,* May 1970, p. 3. According to Carl Cohen, the self-defense arsenal eventually came to over 600 guns, including rifles, various makes of pistols, automatic carbines, and machine guns. See Cohen, *Black Crusader,* p. 99.
    9. Julian Mayfield, quoted in Forman, *Making of Black Revolutionaries,* p. 167.

10. Martin Luther King, Jr., "The Social Organization of Non-Violence," quoted in Williams, *Negroes with Guns*, p. 14.

11. Regarding Robert F. Williams's appeal to President Eisenhower, White House aide E. Frederick Morrow informed the North Carolina activist that the case lay outside federal jurisdiction. Morrow noted in his diary that "North Carolina law permitted, in instances of this kind, the committing of children to institutional homes until the state social agency had determined that they were ready to be returned to their own homes." See E. Frederick Morrow, *Black Man in the White House* (New York: Coward-McCann, 1963), p. 274.

12. See Mayfield account in Forman, *Making of Black Revolutionaries*, pp. 172–74. After sentencing the boys to an indefinite term at the Morrison Training School for Negro Delinquent Boys, Judge Price told Ted Poston of the *New York Post:* "Everybody is satisfied about how it came out. The mothers are satisfied and so is everybody else. Somebody must be trying to stir up race trouble by telling you about it." See *New York Post*, November 10, 1958; also see account in Lynn, *There Is a Fountain*, pp. 141–57. Lynn recalls the view editor Harry Golden took of the case, a view that stressed the irrational fears aroused by the emergence of parallel aspirations for a better future on the part of blacks and women. Golden stated that southern white men "have decided there must be some reason why their women are getting restless at the same time as the Negroes. They have drawn the conclusion that a sexual relationship is involved." According to Lynn, Eleanor Roosevelt was moved by the facts in this case to call President Eisenhower and appeal for action to end this injustice. Eisenhower, in turn, called Governor Hodges, and the boys were quickly released.

13. Forman, *Making of Black Revolutionaries*, pp. 175, 176; Mayfield, "Challenge to Negro Leadership," p. 298. Williams himself writes that several brothers of the rape victim had wanted to kill her white attacker before the trial but that he had persuaded them not to do anything. See Williams, *Negroes with Guns*, p. 62.

14. See Williams interview as quoted in Williams, *Negroes with Guns*, p. 63. The full report of the interview, however, notes that Williams continued: "But it is apparent that there is no Fourteenth Amendment nor court protection of Negroes' rights here, and Negroes have to defend themselves on the spot whenever they are attacked by whites" (xerox of *Carolina Times* interview, n.d.).

15. Wilkins's May 6 statement, quoted in Mayfield, "Challenge to Negro Leadership," p. 299; for account of Mack Charles Parker lynching, see Edward Howard Smead, Jr., "The Lynching of Mack Charles Parker in Poplarville, Mississippi, April 25, 1959" (Doctoral dissertation, University of Maryland 1979).

16. Williams's attorney, Conrad Lynn, quoted in Forman, *Making of Black Revolutionaries*, p. 177. Lynn was pleased that Williams did not disavow what he had said but rather held to his position regarding self-defense. See Lynn, *There Is a Fountain*, p. 160.

17. Forman, *Making of Black Revolutionaries*, p. 177; Mayfield, "Challenge to Negro Leadership," p. 300.

18. NAACP resolution, quoted in Williams, *Negroes with Guns*, p. 67. For full text of NAACP resolutions on this matter, see Gloster B. Current, "Fiftieth Annual Convention," *Crisis*, August–September 1959, pp. 400–10. In the preamble to the Resolutions Committee report, the convention noted that the association had consistently supported the right of self-defense "by defending those who have exercised the right of self defense, particularly in the Arkansas Riot Case, the Sweet case in Detroit, the Columbia, Tenn., Riot cases and the Ingram case in Georgia." Regarding the Williams case, the Resolutions Committee report contended that Williams had "suggested violence as a means of redress of wrongs and not in self-defense of rights of person or property." Among those who argued the national position in the floor debate was Daisy Bates, the leader of the Little Rock deseg-

regation struggle, who argued that Williams's statement provided material to the racists. Williams gave an impassioned defense of his position, asking delegates "not to come crawling to these whites on your hands and knees and make me a sacrificial lamb." The *Crisis* report declared that, under a unit rule, the vote was 781 to 0, although noting that press accounts stated seventeen persons had cast negative votes.

19. Martin Luther King, Jr., quoted in Williams, *Negroes with Guns*, pp. 12–15.

20. Williams, *Negroes with Guns*, pp. 40, 63.

21. Ibid., p. 41.

22. See E. U. Essien-Udom, *Black Nationalism* (New York: Dell, 1965), pp. 84, 85.

23. See C. Eric Lincoln, *The Black Muslims in America* (Boston: Beacon Press, 1961), p. 134.

24. Alex Haley, "Mr. Muhammed Speaks," *Reader's Digest*, March 1960, p. 101.

25. See introduction by Benjamin Goodman to Goodman, ed., *The End of White World Supremacy: Four Speeches by Malcolm X* (New York: Merlin House, 1971), pp. 2–6; *The Autobiography of Malcolm X* (New York: Grove Press, 1964), pp. 236, 237; *New York Amsterdam News*, May 4, 18, 1957; regarding the Harlem protest against police brutality, the *Pittsburgh Courier* reported that police had commented that the hundreds at the police station and the hospital were "the most orderly crowd" they had ever seen (May 4, 1957).

26. Elijah Muhammed, quoted in Lincoln, *Black Muslims*, p. 205.

27. Ibid.; Essien-Udom, *Black Nationalism*, pp. 314, 316.

28. Essien-Udom, *Black Nationalism*, pp. 128, 171, 310, 312, 313.

29. Lincoln, *Black Muslims*, pp. 147, 148, 153.

30. Ibid., pp. 148–50, 153.

31. Charles Silberman, *Crisis in Black and White* (New York: Random House, 1964), pp. 152, 153; James Baldwin, *Notes of a Native Son* (New York: Bantam Books, 1968), p. 30. In a television interview with Kenneth Clark on May 24, 1963, Baldwin gave this appraisal of the Muslims: "It is the only movement in the country that you can call grass roots. I hate to say that, but it's true. Because it is the only—when Malcolm talks or the Muslim ministers talk, they articulate for all the Negro people who hear them, who listen to them." Interview quoted in Fishel and Quarles, *Black American*, p. 527; James Baldwin, *The Fire Next Time* (New York: Dial Press, 1963), pp. 82, 83.

32. See transcript of "The Hate that Hate Produced" (July 23, 1959, telecast), furnished courtesy of CBS News.

BIBLIOGRAPHY

Manuscript Collections

Adams, Herbert Baxter, Papers. William R. Perkins Library, Duke University.

Barnes, Charles Merlin, Papers. Western Historical Manuscript Collection, University of Missouri–Columbia Library.

Bruce, Edward, Papers. Schomburg Center for Research in Black Culture, New York.

Cronly Family Papers. William R. Perkins Library, Duke University.

Dewey, Thomas E., Papers. University of Rochester Library.

Goodman, Ernest, Papers. Willie McGee case file.

Green, John P., Papers, Western Reserve Historical Society Library, Cleveland.

La Guardia, Fiorello, Papers. New York City Municipal Archives.

Leonard, Donald S., Papers. Michigan Historical Collection, Bentley Historical Library, University of Michigan.

Likert Rensis, Papers. Michigan Historical Collection, Bentley Historical Library, University of Michigan.

McKinley, William, Papers. Library of Congress.

Meade, General George C., Papers. Historical Society of Pennsylvania. Philadelphia. Manuscript Division.

NAACP Papers. Library of Congress.

National Lawyers Guild Papers. Meiklejohn Civil Liberties Institute. Berkeley, California.

Roosevelt, Franklin D., Papers. Franklin D. Roosevelt Library, Hyde Park, New York.

Snow, Thad, Papers. Western Historical Manuscript Collection, University of Missouri, St. Louis.

Southern Tenant Farmers' Union Papers. Microfilm edition. Southern Historical Collection, University of North Carolina Library.

Truman, Harry S. Papers. Official Files, 93, 93–B, 413, 596–A, Harry S. Truman Library Independence, Missouri.

Wells, Ida B., Papers. Regenstein Library, University of Chicago.

Books and Pamphlets

Abcarian, Richard, ed. *Richard Wright's Native Son: A Critical Handbook.* Belmont, Calif.: Wadsworth Publishing, 1970.

Anderson, Jervis. *A. Philip Randolph: A Biographical Portrait.* New York: Harcourt Brace Jovanovich, 1972.

Angelou, Maya. *I Know Why the Caged Bird Sings.* New York: Random House, 1969.

Andrews, William L. *The Literary Career of Charles W. Chesnutt.* Baton Rouge: Louisiana State University Press, 1980.

525

An Appeal to the World: A Statement on the Denial of Human Rights to Minorities in the Case of Citizens of Negro Descent in the United States of America and An Appeal to the United Nations for Redress. New York: NAACP, 1947.

Aptheker, Bettina. *Woman's Legacy: Essays on Race, Sex, and Class in American History.* Amherst: University of Massachusetts Press, 1982.

Aptheker, Herbert. *Afro-American History: The Modern Era.* New York: Citadel Press, 1971.

————. *American Negro Slave Revolts.* New York: Columbia University Press, 1943.

————, ed. *The Correspondence of W. E. B. DuBois.* 3 vols. Amherst: University of Massachusetts Press, 1973–78.

————, ed. *A Documentary History of the Negro People in the United States.* New York: Citadel Press, 1951.

————, ed. *A Documentary History of the Negro People in the United States, 1910–1932.* Secaucus, N.J.: Citadel Press, 1973.

————, ed. *A Documentary History of the Negro People in the United States, 1933–1945.* Secaucus, N.J.: Citadel Press, 1974.

Athearn, Robert G. *In Search of Canaan: Black Migration to Kansas, 1879–80.* Lawrence: Regents Press of Kansas, 1978.

Ayers, Edward L. *Vengeance and Justice: Crime and Punishment in the 19th-Century American South.* New York: Oxford University Press, 1984.

Baker, Ray Stannard. *Following the Color Line.* New York: Harper Torchbooks, 1964.

Baldwin, James. *The Fire Next Time.* New York: Dial Press, 1963.

————. *Going to Meet the Man.* New York: Dial Press, 1965.

————. *Notes of a Native Son.* New York: Bantam, 1968.

Bardolph, Richard, ed. *The Civil Rights Record.* New York: Crowell, 1970.

Barnard, Hollinger F., ed. *Outside the Magic Circle: The Autobiography of Virginia Foster Durr.* University: University of Alabama Press, 1985.

Barnouw, Eric, ed. *Radio Drama in Action: Twenty-Five Plays of a Changing World.* New York: Farrar and Rinehart, 1945.

Bates, Daisy. *The Long Shadow of Little Rock: A Memoir.* New York: David McKay Company, 1962.

Belfrage, Cedric. *A Faith to Free the People.* New York: Dryden Press, 1944.

Bennett, Lerone. *Black Power, USA.* Baltimore: Penguin Books, 1967.

Berman, William C. *The Politics of Civil Rights in the Truman Administration.* Columbus: Ohio State University Press, 1970.

Berry, Mary Frances. *Black Resistance / White Law: A History of Constitutional Racism in America.* New York: Appleton-Century-Crofts, 1971.

Blaustein, Albert P., and Zangrando, Robert L., eds. *Civil Rights and the American Negro.* New York: Trident Press, 1968.

Bordin, Ruth. *Frances Willard: A Biography.* Chapel Hill and London: The University of North Carolina Press, 1986.

Bracey, John H., Jr., Meier, August, and Rudwick, Elliott, eds. *The Afro-Americans: Selected Documents.* Boston: Allyn and Bacon, 1972.

Braden, Anne. *The Wall Between.* New York: Monthly Review Press, 1958.

Brown, Claude. *Manchild in the Promised Land.* New York: Macmillan, 1965.

Burk, Robert Fredrick. *The Eisenhower Administration and Black Civil Rights.* Knoxville: University of Tennessee Press, 1984.

Burns, Robert E. *I Am a Fugitive from a Georgia Chain Gang.* New York: Grosset and Dunlap, 1932.

Cantor, Louis. *A Prologue to the Protest Movement: The Missouri Sharecropper Roadside Demonstration of 1939.* Durham, N.C.: Duke University Press, 1969.

Capeci, Dominic J., Jr. *Race Relations in Wartime Detroit: The Sojourner Truth Housing Controversy of 1942.* Philadelphia: Temple University Press, 1984.

Carmer, Carl. *Stars Fell on Alabama.* New York: Literary Guild, 1934.

Carter, Dan T. *Scottsboro: A Tragedy of the American South.* London: Oxford University Press, 1971.

Cash, W. J. *The Mind of the South.* New York: Alfred A. Knopf, 1941.

Cason, Clarence. *90° in the Shade.* Chapel Hill: University of North Carolina Press, 1935.

Catto, Octavius V. *"Our Alma Mater": An Address Delivered at Concert Hall on the Occasion of the Twelfth Annual Commencement of the Institute for Colored Youth.* Philadelphia: C. Sherman, Son and Co., 1864.

Chace, William M., and Collier, Peter, eds. *Justice Denied.* New York: Harcourt, Brace, 1970.

Chadbourne, James Harmon. *Lynching and the Law.* Chapel Hill: University of North Carolina Press, 1933.

Chesnutt, Charles W. *The Marrow of Tradition.* Reprint. Ann Arbor: University of Michigan Press, 1969.

————. *The Wife of His Youth and Other Stories of the Color Line.* Reprint. Ridgewood, N.J.: Gregg Press, 1967.

Citizens' Protective League. *Story of the Riot.* Reprint. New York: Arno Press, 1969.

Clarke, John Henrik, ed. *Marcus Garvey and the Vision of Africa.* New York: Vintage Books, 1974.

Cohen, Robert Carl. *Black Crusader: A Biography of Robert Franklin Williams.* Secaucus, N.J.: Lyle Stuart, 1972.

Conrad, David Eugene. *The Forgotten Farmers.* Urbana: University of Illinois Press, 1965.

Cox, La Wanda, and Cox, John H., eds. *Reconstruction, the Negro, and the New South.* Columbia: University of South Carolina Press, 1973.

Cripps, Thomas. *Slow Fade to Black: The Negro in American Film, 1900–1942.* New York: Oxford University Press, 1977.

Cronon, E. David. *Black Moses: The Story of Marcus Garvey and the Universal Negro Improvement Association.* 2d ed. Madison: University of Wisconsin Press, 1981.

Crummell, Alexander. *Africa and America: Addresses and Discourses.* Reprint. New York: Negro Universities Press, 1969.

Cutler, James Elbert. *Lynch-Law.* New York: Longmans, Green, 1905.

Dalfiume, Richard M. *Desegregation of the U.S. Armed Forces.* Columbia: University of Missouri Press, 1969.

Dancy, John C. *Sand Against the Wind: The Memoirs of John C. Dancy.* Detroit: Wayne State University Press, 1966.

Daniel, Pete. *Deep'n As It Come: The 1927 Mississippi River Flood.* New York: Oxford University Press, 1977.

————. *The Shadow of Slavery: Peonage in the South.* Urbana: University of Illinois Press, 1972.

Daniels, Jonathan. *A Southerner Discovers the South.* New York: Macmillan, 1939.

Darrow, Clarence. *Argument of Clarence Darrow in the Case of Henry Sweet.* New York: NAACP, 1927.

Davis, Allison. *Leadership, Love and Aggression.* New York: Harcourt Brace Jovanovich, 1983.

528 BIBLIOGRAPHY

Davis, Allison, and Dollard, John. *Children of Bondage*. New York: Harper Torchbooks, 1964.

Davis, Allison, Gardner, Burleigh B., and Gardner, Mary R. *Deep South: A Social Anthropological Study of Caste and Class*. Chicago: University of Chicago Press, 1941.

DeCanio, Stephen J. *Agriculture in the Postbellum South: The Economics of Production and Supply*. Cambridge: MIT Press, 1974.

Dittmer, John. *Black Georgia in the Progressive Era: 1900–1920*. Urbana: University of Illinois Press, 1977.

Dixie Comes to New York. New York: *Daily Worker* pamphlet, 1946.

Dixon, Thomas, Jr. *The Leopard's Spots: A Romance of the White Man's Burden—1865–1900*. New York: A. Wessels Company, 1906.

Douglas, William O. *The Court Years, 1939–1975*. New York: Random House, 1980.

Drake, St. Clair, and Cayton, Horace R. *Black Metropolis*. 2 vols. New York: Harper Torchbooks, 1962.

Du Bois, W. E. B. *Against Racism: Unpublished Essays, Papers, Addresses, 1887–1961*. Edited by Herbert Aptheker. Amherst: University of Massachusetts Press, 1985.

————. *The Black North In 1901: A Social Study*. Reprint. New York: Arno Press, 1969.

————. *Darkwater: Voices from within the Veil*. New York: Schocken Books, 1969.

————. *Dusk of Dawn: An Essay Toward an Autobiography of a Race Concept*. New York: Schocken Books, 1968.

————. *The Gift of Black Folk*. Reprint. Millwood, N.Y.: Kraus-Thomson, 1975.

————. *The Philadelphia Negro: A Social Study*. Reprint. New York: Benjamin Blom, 1967.

————. *The Souls of Black Folk*. Millwood, N.Y.: Kraus-Thomson, 1973.

————. *The Souls of Black Folk* in *Three Negro Classics*. New York: Avon Books, 1965.

Du Bois, W. E. B., and Dill, A. *Morals and Manners among Negro Americans*. Atlanta: Atlanta University Press, 1914.

Dunaway, David King. *How Can I Keep from Singing: Pete Seeger*. New York: McGraw-Hill, 1981.

Dunbar, Anthony P. *Against the Grain*. Charlottesville: University Press of Virginia, 1981.

Duster, Alfreda M. *Crusade for Justice: The Autobiography of Ida B. Wells*. Chicago: University of Chicago Press, 1970.

Edmonds, Helen G. *The Negro and Fusion Politics in North Carolina, 1894–1901*. Chapel Hill: University of North Carolina Press, 1951.

Edwards, George C. *Pioneer at Law*. New York: Norton, 1974.

Ellsworth, Scott. *Death in a Promised Land: The Tulsa Race Riot of 1921*. Baton Rouge: Louisiana State University Press, 1982.

Essien-Udom, E. U. *Black Nationalism*. New York: Dell Books, 1965.

Evans, W. McKee. *Ballots and Fence Rails*. Chapel Hill: University of North Carolina Press, 1969.

Farmer, James. *Lay Bare the Heart: An Autobiography of the Civil Rights Movement*. New York: Arbor House, 1985.

Fast, Howard. *Peekskill: USA, a Personal Experience*. New York: Civil Rights Congress, 1951.

Faulk, John Henry. *Fear on Trial*. Austin: University of Texas Press, 1983.

Fine, Sidney. *Frank Murphy: The Detroit Years*. Ann Arbor: University of Michigan Press, 1975.

Finkle, Lee. *Forum for Protest: The Black Press during World War II*. Rutherford, N.Y.: Fairleigh Dickinson University Press, 1975.

Fishel, Leslie, Jr., and Quarles, Benjamin, eds. *The Black American: A Documentary History.* Glenview, Ill.: Scott, Foresman, 1970.

Foner, Jack D. *Blacks and the Military in American History.* New York: Praeger Publishers, 1974.

Foner, Philip S. *American Socialism and Black Americans: From the Age of Jackson to World War II.* Westport, Conn.: Greenwood Press, 1977.

———. *Organized Labor and the Black Worker, 1619–1973.* New York: Praeger Publishers, 1974.

———, ed. *The Life and Writings of Frederick Douglass, IV.* New York: International Publishers, 1955.

———, ed. *Paul Robeson Speaks: Writings, Speeches, Interviews, 1919–1974.* New York: Bruner, Mazel, 1978.

———, ed. *The Voice of Black America: Major Speeches by Blacks in The United States, 1797–1973.* 2 Vols. New York: Capricorn Books, 1975.

———, ed. *W. E. B. Du Bois Speaks; Speeches and Addresses, 1920–1963.* New York: Pathfinder Press, 1970.

Foner, Philip S., and Lewis, Ronald L. *The Black Worker: A Documentary History from Colonial Times to the Present, III.* Philadelphia: Temple University Press, 1978.

Ford, James W. *Hunger and Terror in Harlem.* New York: Harlem Section, Communist Party, 1935.

Forman, James. *The Making of Black Revolutionaries.* New York: Macmillan, 1972.

Fortune, Timothy Thomas. *Black and White: Land, Labor and Politics in the South.* Reprint. New York: Arno Press, 1968.

Foster, William Z. *The Negro People in the United States.* New York: International Publishers, 1970.

Freyer, Tony. *The Little Rock Crisis: A Constitutional Interpretation.* Westport, Conn.: Greenwood Press, 1984.

Garfinkel, Herbert. *When Negroes March: The March on Washington Movement in the Organizational Politics for FEPC.* Glencoe, Ill.: Free Press, 1959.

Garrett, Charles. *The La Guardia Years: Machine and Reform Politics in New York City.* New Brunswick, N.J.: Rutgers University Press, 1961.

Garvey, Amy Jacques, ed. *Philosophy and Opinions of Marcus Garvey.* New York: Arno Press, 1969.

Gatewood, Willard B., Jr. *Black Americans and the White Man's Burden, 1898–1903.* Urbana: University of Illinois Press, 1975.

———. *"Smoked Yankees" and the Struggle for Empire: Letters From Negro Soldiers, 1898–1902.* Urbana: University of Illinois Press, 1971.

Gayle, Addison. *Richard Wright: Ordeal of a Native Son.* Garden City, N.Y.: Doubleday, 1980.

Genovese, Eugene D. *From Rebellion to Revolution: Afro-American Slave Revolts in the Making of the Modern World.* Baton Rouge: Louisiana State University Press, 1979.

Gilbert, Peter, ed. *The Selected Writings of John Edward Bruce, Militant Black Journalist.* New York: Arno Press, 1971.

Gillette, William. *Retreat from Reconstruction: 1869–1879.* Baton Rouge: Louisiana State University Press, 1979.

Goodman, Benjamin, ed. *The End of White World Supremacy: Four Speeches by Malcolm X.* New York: Merlin House, 1971.

Gosnell, Harold F. *Negro Politicians.* Chicago: University of Chicago Press, 1967.

Graham, Stephen. *Children of the Slaves.* London: Macmillan, 1920.

Griggs, Sutton E. *The Hindered Hand*. New York: AMS Press, 1969.
Grubbs, Donald H. *Cry from the Cotton: The Southern Tenant Farmers' Union and the New Deal*. Chapel Hill: University of North Carolina Press, 1971.
Hair, William Ivy. *Carnival of Fury: Robert Charles and the New Orleans Race Riot of 1900*. Baton Rouge: Louisiana State University Press, 1976.
Hall, Jacquelyn Dowd. *Jessie Daniel Ames and the Women's Campaign against Lynching*. New York: Columbia University Press, 1979.
Hallgren, Mauritz. *Seeds of Revolt: A Study of American Life and the Temper of the American People during the Depression*. New York: Alfred A. Knopf, 1933.
Harding, Vincent. "Religion and Resistance among Antebellum Negroes." In *The Making of Black America 1*, edited by August Meier and Elliott Rudwick, pp. 179–97. New York: Atheneum, 1968.
Harlan, Louis R. *Booker T. Washington: The Making of a Black Leader, 1856–1901*. New York: Oxford University Press, 1972.
———. *Booker T. Washington: The Wizard of Tuskegee, 1901–1915*. New York: Oxford University Press, 1983.
———, ed. *The Booker T. Washington Papers, III*. Urbana: University of Illinois Press, 1974.
———, ed. *The Booker T. Washington Papers, IV*. Urbana: University of Illinois Press, 1975.
———, ed. *The Booker T. Washington Papers, V*. Urbana: University of Illinois Press, 1976.
Harlan, Louis R., and Smock, Raymond W., eds. *The Booker T. Washington Papers, IX*. Urbana: University of Illinois Press, 1980.
———, eds. *The Booker T. Washington Papers, XI*. Urbana: University of Illinois Press, 1981.
———, eds. *The Booker T. Washington Papers, XII*. Urbana: University of Illinois Press, 1982.
Harris, Trudier. *Exorcising Blackness: Historical and Literary Lynching and Burning Rituals*. Bloomington: Indiana University Press, 1984.
Haynes, Robert V. *A Night of Violence: The Houston Riot of 1917*. Baton Rouge: Louisiana State University Press, 1976.
Hays, Arthur Garfield. *Let Freedom Ring*. New York: Liveright, 1937.
Haywood, Harry. *Black Bolshevik*. Chicago: Liberator Press, 1978.
Hemenway, Robert, ed. *The Black Novelist*. Columbus: Charles E. Merrill, 1970.
Herndon, Angelo. *Let Me Live*. Reprint. New York: Arno Press, 1969.
Hill, Robert A., ed. *The Marcus Garvey and Universal Negro Improvement Association Papers, Vols. 1 and 2*. Berkeley: University of California Press, 1983.
Hirsch, Arnold R. *Making the Second Ghetto: Race and Housing in Chicago, 1940–1960*. Cambridge: Cambridge University Press, 1983.
Hofstadter, Richard, and Wallace, Michael, eds. *American Violence: A Documentary History*. New York: Vintage Books, 1971.
Holt, Hamilton, ed. *The Life Stories of Undistinguished Americans*. New York: James Pott and Co., 1906.
Holt, Thomas C. "The Lonely Warrior: Ida B. Wells-Barnett and the Struggle for Black Leadership." In *Black Leaders of the Twentieth Century*, edited by John Hope Franklin and August Meier, pp. 39–61. Urbana: University of Illinois Press, 1982.
Hoyt, James A. *The Phoenix Riot*. Greenwood, 1938.

Hudson, Hosea. *Black Worker in the Deep South*. New York: International Publishers, 1972.

Huie, William Bradford. *Three Lives for Mississippi*. New York: WCC Books, 1965.

Hull, Gloria T., ed. *Give Us Each Day: The Diary of Alice Dunbar-Nelson*. New York: W.W. Norton, 1984.

Irons, Peter. *Justice at War: The Story of the Japanese American Internment Cases*. New York: Oxford University Press, 1983.

Isserman, Maurice. *Which Side Were You On?* Middletown, Conn.: Wesleyan University Press, 1982.

Johnson, Charles S. *Growing Up in the Black Belt*. New York: Schocken Books, 1967.

———. *Shadow of the Plantation*. Chicago: University of Chicago Press, Phoenix Books, 1966.

———. *To Stem This Tide: A Survey Of Racial Tension Areas In the United States*. Boston: Pilgrim Press, 1943.

Johnson, James Weldon. *Black Manhattan*. Reprint. New York: Atheneum, 1968.

Jones, James H. *Bad Blood*. New York: Free Press, 1981.

Kerlin, Robert T. *The Voice of the Negro, 1919*. New York: E. P. Dutton, 1920.

Kester, Howard. *Revolt among the Sharecroppers*. Reprint. New York: Arno Press, 1969.

King, Coretta Scott. *My Life with Martin Luther King, Jr.* New York: Holt, Rinehart and Winston, 1969.

King, Martin Luther, Jr. *Stride toward Freedom*. New York: Ballantine Books, 1960.

King, Martin Luther, Sr., with Riley, Clayton. *Daddy King: An Autobiography*. New York: William Morrow, 1980.

Kluger, Richard. *Simple Justice: The History of Brown vs. Board of Education and Black America's Struggle for Equality*. New York: Vintage Books, 1977.

Labor Fact Book No. 3. New York: International Publishers, 1936.

Lane, Anne J. *The Brownsville Affair: National Crisis and Black Reaction*. Port Washington, N.Y.: Kennikat Press, 1971.

Lane, Roger. *Roots of Violence in Black Philadelphia: 1860–1900*. Cambridge: Harvard University Press, 1986.

Lee, Alfred McClung, and Humphrey, Norman D. *Race Riot*. New York: Octagon Books, 1968.

Lerner, Gerda, ed. *Black Women in White America: A Documentary History*. New York: Vintage Books, 1971.

Lester, Julius, ed. *The Seventh Son: The Thought and Writings of W. E. B. Du Bois*. 2 vols. New York: Vintage Books, 1971.

Levine, David E. *Internal Combustion*. Westport, Conn.: Greenwood Publishers, 1976.

Lewis, Anthony. *Portrait of a Decade: The Second American Revolution*. New York: Random House, 1964.

Lewis, David L. *King: A Biography*. Urbana: University of Illinois Press, 1978.

———. *King: A Critical Biography*. Baltimore: Penguin Books, 1970.

Lincoln, C. Eric. *The Black Muslims in America*. Boston: Beacon Press, 1961.

———, ed. *Martin Luther King, Jr.: A Profile*. New York: Hill and Wang, 1970.

Lisio, Donald J. *Hoover, Blacks, and Lily-Whites: A Study of Southern Strategies*. Chapel Hill: University of North Carolina Press, 1985.

Litwack, Leon F. *Been in the Storm So Long: The Aftermath of Slavery*. New York: Alfred A. Knopf, 1979.

Locke, Alain, ed. *The New Negro*. Reprint. New York: Atheneum, 1968.

Lomax, Louis E. *The Negro Revolt*. New York: Signet Books, 1963.

Lumpkin, Katherine DuPre. *The South in Progress*. New York: International Publishers, 1940.

Lynn, Conrad. *There Is a Fountain: The Autobiography of a Civil Rights Lawyer*. Westport, N.Y.: Lawrence Hill and Co., 1979.

McCoy, Donald R., and Ruetten, Richard T. *Quest and Response*. Lawrence: University Press of Kansas, 1973.

McGovern, James R. *Anatomy of a Lynching: The Killing of Claude Neal*. Baton Rouge: Louisiana State University Press, 1982.

Malcom X. *The Autobiography of Malcolm X*. New York: Grove Press, 1964.

Marks, George P., III, ed. *The Black Press Views American Imperialism (1898–1900)*. New York: Arno Press, 1971.

Martin, Tony. *Race First: The Ideological and Organizational Struggles of Marcus Garvey and the Universal Negro Improvement Association*. Westport, Conn.: Greenwood Press, 1976.

Mays, Benjamin E. *Born to Rebel: An Autobiography*. New York: Charles Scribner's Sons, 1971.

Meier, August. *Negro Thought in America, 1880–1915*. Ann Arbor: University of Michigan Press, 1963.

Meier, August, and Rudwick, Elliott. *Black Detroit and the Rise of the UAW*. New York: Oxford University Press, 1979.

———. *CORE, a Study in the Civil Rights Movement, 1942–1968*. New York: Oxford University Press, 1973.

Meier, August, Rudwick, Elliott, and Broderick, Francis L., eds. *Black Protest Thought in the Twentieth Century*. 2d. ed. Indianapolis: Bobbs-Merrill Company, 1971.

Messages and Papers of the Presidents XVI. New York: Bureau of National Literature, 1917.

Miller, Kelly. *Race Adjustment* and *The Everlasting Stain*. New York: Arno Press, 1968.

Mitchell, H. L. *Mean Things Happening in This Land*, Montclair, N.J.: Allenheld, Osman, 1979.

Mitford, Jessica. *A Fine Old Conflict*. London: Michael Joseph, 1977.

The Mob Still Rides: A Review of the Lynching Record, 1931–1935. Atlanta: Commission on Interracial Cooperation, 1935.

Moon, Henry Lee. *Balance of Power: The Negro Vote*. Garden City, N.Y.: Doubleday, 1949.

Morison, Elting E., ed. *The Letters of Theodore Roosevelt II*. Cambridge: Harvard University Press, 1951.

Morrison, Toni. *Song of Solomon*. New York: Alfred A. Knopf, 1977.

Morrow, E. Frederick. *Black Man in the White House*. New York: Coward-McCann, 1963.

Murray, Florence, ed. *The Negro Handbook, 1946–1947*. New York: A. A. Wyn, 1947.

Myrdal, Gunnar. *An American Dilemma, I*. New York: McGraw-Hill, 1964.

Naison, Mark. *Communists in Harlem during the Depression*. Urbana: University of Illinois Press, 1983.

National Association for the Advancement of Colored People. *The Lynching of Claude Neal*. New York: National Association for the Advancement of Colored People, 1934.

———. *M is for Mississippi and Murder*. NAACP pamphlet, 1956.

Nearing, Scott. *Black America*. New York: Schocken Books, 1969.

Newby, I. A. *Black Carolinians: A History of Blacks in South Carolina from 1895 to 1968*. Columbia: University of South Carolina Press, 1973.

Niebuhr, Reinhold. *Moral Man and Immoral Society*. New York: Charles Scribner's, 1932.

Oates, Stephen B. *Let the Trumpet Sound: The Life of Martin Luther King, Jr*. New York: Harper and Row, 1982.

Olsen, Otto H. *Carpetbagger's Crusade: The Life of Albion Winegar Tourgee*. Baltimore: Johns Hopkins University Press, 1965.

O'Neill, William L., ed. *Echoes of Revolt: The Masses, 1911–1917*. Chicago: Quadrangle Books, 1966.

Osofsky, Gilbert. *Harlem: The Making of a Ghetto*. New York: Harper and Row, 1963.

Ottley, Roi. *'New World A-Coming': Inside Black America*. Reprint. New York: Arno Press, 1969.

Painter, Nell Irvin. *Exodusters: Black Migration to Kansas after Reconstruction*. New York: Alfred A. Knopf, 1977.

———. *The Narrative of Hosea Hudson: His Life as a Negro Communist in the South*. Cambridge: Harvard University Press, 1979.

Patrick, Rembert W. *The Reconstruction of the Nation*. New York: Oxford University Press, 1967.

Patterson, William L. *The Man Who Cried Genocide*. New York: International Publishers, 1971.

———. *Sikeston: Hitlerite Crime Against America*. St. Louis: Communist Party of Missouri pamphlet, 1942.

———, ed. *We Charge Genocide*. New York: International Publishers, 1970.

Peck, James. *Freedom Ride*. New York: Simon and Schuster, 1962.

Penn, I. Garland. *The Afro-American Press and its Editors*. Springfield, Ill.: Willey and Co., 1891.

A Petition to the United Nations on Behalf of 13 Million Oppressed Negro Citizens of the United States of America. New York: National Negro Congress pamphlet, 1946.

Pickens, William. "The American Congo: Burning of Henry Lowry." In *Negro: An Anthology*, edited by Nancy Cunard. New York: Frederick Ungar, 1970.

Platt, Anthony, ed. *The Politics of Riot Commissions: A Collection of Official Reports and Critical Essays*. New York: Macmillan, 1971.

Poitier, Sidney. *This Life*. New York: Alfred A. Knopf, 1980.

Powdermaker, Hortense. *After Freedom: A Cultural Study in the Deep South*. New York: Viking Press, 1939.

———. *Stranger and Friend: The Way of an Anthropoligist*. New York: W. W. Norton, 1966.

Powell, Adam Clayton, Jr. *Marching Blacks*. New York: Dial Press, 1945.

Prather, H. Leon, Sr. *We Have Taken a City: Wilmington Racial Massacre and Coup of 1898*. Rutherford, N.J.: Fairleigh Dickinson University Press, 1984.

Rable, George C. *But There Was No Peace: The Role of Violence in the Politics of Reconstruction*. Athens: University of Georgia Press, 1984.

Rampersad, Arnold. *The Art and Imagination of W. E. B. Du Bois*. Cambridge: Harvard University Press, 1976.

Ransom, Reverdy C. *The Spirit of Freedom and Justice*. Nashville: Sunday School Union, 1926.

Ransom, Roger L., and Sutch, Richard. *One Kind of Freedom*. Cambridge: Cambridge University Press, 1977.

Raper, Arthur F. *The Tragedy of Lynching*. Chapel Hill: University of North Carolina Press, 1933.

Record, Wilson. *The Negro and the Communist Party.* Reprint. New York: Atheneum, 1971.

Redkey, Edwin S. *Black Exodus: Black Nationalist and Back-to-Africa Movements, 1890–1910.* New Haven: Yale University Press, 1969.

——, ed. *Respect Black: The Writings and Speeches of Henry McNeal Turner.* New York: Arno Press, 1971.

Richardson, James F. *The New York Police, Colonial Times to 1901.* New York: Oxford University Press, 1970.

Rosengarten, Theodore. *All God's Dangers: The Life of Nate Shaw.* New York: Alfred A. Knopf, 1974.

——. "Stepping over Cockleburrs: Conversations with Neb Cobb." In *Telling Lives,* edited by Marc Pachter, pp. 105–31. Washington: New Republic Books, 1979.

Rosenman, S. I., comp. *The Public Papers and Addresses of Franklin D. Roosevelt, 1944–1945.* Vol. 13. New York: Harper Brothers, 1950.

Rowan, Carl. *South of Freedom.* New York: Alfred A. Knopf, 1952.

Ruchames, Louis. *Race, Jobs, and Politics: The Story of FEPC.* New York: Columbia University Press, 1953.

Rudwick, Elliott M. *Race Riot at East St. Louis, July 2, 1917.* Cleveland: Meridian Books, 1966.

Rustin, Bayard. *Down the Line: The Collected Writings of Bayard Rustin.* Chicago: Quadrangle Books, 1971.

Sandburg, Carl. *The Chicago Race Riots, July 1919.* New York: Harcourt, Brace and World, 1969.

Shogan, Robert, and Craig, Tom. *The Detroit Race Riot: A Study in Violence.* Philadelphia: Chilton Books, 1964.

Silberman, Charles. *Crisis in Black and White.* New York: Random House, 1964.

Smith, Kenneth L., and Zepp, Ira G. *Search for the Beloved Community.* Valley Forge: Judson Press, 1974.

Snow, Thad. *From Missouri.* Boston: Houghton-Mifflin 1954.

Spivak, John L. "Flashes From Georgia Chain Gangs." In *Negro: An Anthology,* edited by Nancy Cunard, pp. 127–28. New York: Frederick Ungar, 1970.

——. *Georgia Nigger.* Reprint. Montclair, N.J.: Patterson Smith 1969.

——. *A Man in His Time.* New York: Horizon Press, 1967.

Stein, Judith. *The World of Marcus Garvey: Race and Class in Modern Society.* Baton Rouge: Louisiana State University Press, 1986.

Synnestvedt, Sig. *The White Response to Black Emancipation.* New York: Macmillan, 1972.

Terrell, Mary Church. *A Colored Woman in a White World.* Washington: Ransdell Publishers, 1940.

Thornbrough, Emma Lou. *T. Thomas Fortune: Militant Journalist.* Chicago: University of Chicago Press, 1972.

Thorne, Jack. *Hanover.* Reprint. New York: Arno Press, 1969.

Tindall, George B. *South Carolina Negroes, 1877–1900.* Columbia: University of South Carolina Press, 1952.

Tolbert, Emory J. *The UNIA and Black Los Angeles.* Los Angeles: Center for Afro-American Studies, University of California, 1980.

Trelease, Allen W. *White Terror: The Ku Klux Klan Conspiracy and Southern Reconstruction.* New York: Harper and Row, 1971.

Tuttle, William M., Jr. *Race Riot: Chicago in the Red Summer of 1919.* New York: Atheneum, 1972.

Vincent, Theodore G. *Black Power and the Garvey Movement.* Berkeley, Calif: Ramparts Press, n.d.

———, ed. *Voices of a Black Nation.* San Francisco: Ramparts Press, 1973.

Violence in Peekskill. New York: American Civil Liberties Union pamphlet, 1950.

Vose, Clement E. *Caucasians Only: The Supreme Court, the NAACP and the Restrictive Covennant Cases.* Berkeley: University of California Press, 1967.

Warren, Earl. *The Memoirs of Earl Warren.* Garden City, N.Y.: Doubleday, 1977.

Washington, Booker T. *Up From Slavery* in *Three Negro Classics.* New York: Avon Books, 1965.

Washington, James Melvin, ed. *A Testament Of Hope: The Essential Writings of Martin Luther King, Jr.* San Francisco: Harper and Row, 1986.

Waskow, Arthur I. *From Race Riot to Sit-In, 1919 and the 1960s: A Study in the Connections between Conflict and Violence.* Garden City, N.Y.: Anchor Books, 1967.

Weaver, John D. *The Brownsville Raid.* New York: W. W. Norton, 1970.

Weinberg, Kenneth G. *A Man's Home, a Man's Castle.* New York: McCall Publishing, 1971.

Wells-Barnett, Ida. *On Lynchings.* Reprint. New York: Arno Press, 1969.

Wharton, Vernon E. *The Negro in Mississippi, 1865–1890.* New York: Harper Torchbooks, 1965.

White, Walter F. *The Fire in the Flint.* Reprint. New York: Negro Universities Press, 1969.

———. *A Man Called White.* New York: Arno Press, 1969.

———. *Rope and Faggot.* New York: Alfred Knopf, 1929.

White, Walter, and Marshall, Thurgood. *What Caused the Detroit Riot? An Analysis.* New York: National Association for the Advancement of Colored People, 1943.

Widick, B. J. *Detroit: City of Race and Class Violence.* Chicago: Quadrangle Books, 1972.

Wiener, Jonathan M. *Social Origins of the New South: Alabama, 1860–1865.* Baton Rouge: Louisiana State University Press, 1978.

Wilkins, Roy, with Mathews, Tom. *Standing Fast: The Autobiography of Roy Wilkins.* New York: Viking Press, 1982.

Williams, Robert F. *Negroes with Guns.* New York: Marzani and Munsell, 1962.

Williamson, Joel. *After Slavery: The Negro In South Carolina During Reconstruction, 1861–1877.* Chapel Hill: University of North Carolina Press, 1965.

———. *The Crucible of Race: Black-White Relations in the American South since Emancipation.* New York: Oxford University Press, 1984.

Wolters, Raymond. *Negroes and the Great Depression: The Problem of Economic Recovery.* Westport, Conn.: Greenwood, 1970.

Wood, Norman B. *The White Side of a Black Subject: A Vindication of the Afro-American Race.* Reprint. New York: Negro Universities Press, 1969.

Woodward, C. Vann. *Tom Watson, Agrarian Rebel.* New York: Macmillan, 1938.

Wright, Richard. *Black Boy: A Record of Childhood and Youth.* New York: Harper and Row, 1945.

———. *Native Son.* New York: Signet Books, 1950.

———. *Uncle Tom's Children.* New York: Signet Books, 1947.

Wynes, Charles E. *The Negro in the South since 1865: Selected Essays in American Negro History.* New York: Harper Colophon, 1968.

———. *Race Relations in Virginia, 1870–1902.* Charlottesville: University of Virginia Press, 1961.

Yoseloff, Thomas, ed. *Seven Poets in Search of an Answer*. New York: Bernard Ackerman, 1944.

Zangrando, Robert L. *The NAACP Crusade against Lynching, 1909–1950*. Philadelphia: Temple University Press, 1980.

Government Documents

Burns, Robert W., and Dennis, Herman P., Jr., File. Dwight D. Eisenhower Library, Abilene, Kansas.

———. Harry S. Truman Library, Independence, Missouri.

Chicago Commission on Race Relations. *The Negro in Chicago*. Chicago: University of Chicago Press, 1922.

Georgia. *A Statement from Governor Hugh M. Dorsey as to the Negro in Georgia*. 1921.

Hurley, Roger L. *Poverty and Mental Retardation*. Trenton: New Jersey Department of Institutions and Agencies, 1968.

National Commission on the Causes and Prevention of Violence. *To Establish Justice, to Insure Domestic Tranquility*. Final Report. Washington: GPO, 1969.

New York City. *The Complete Report of Mayor LaGuardia's Commission on the Harlem Riot of March 19, 1935*. Reprint. New York: Arno Press, 1969.

Ohio. "Guide to Springfield and Clark County." Works Progress Administration files. Ohio Historical Society, Columbus.

President's Committee on Civil Rights. *To Secure These Rights: The Report of the President's Committee*. New York: Simon and Schuster, 1947.

U.S. Bureau of Agricultural Economics. Division of Program Surveys, Report to Office of War Information. "The Social Dynamics of Detroit." Box 1814, RG 44, National Archives.

U.S. Congress. *Congressional Globe*. Speech of Job E. Stevenson. 42nd Congress, 2nd sess. May 30, 1872.

U.S. Congress. Hearings before the Committee on Foreign Relations. *International Human Rights Treaties*. 96th Congress, 1st sess.

U.S. Congress. Hearing before the Committee on Foreign Relations. *The Genocide Convention*. 97th Congress, 1st sess.

U.S. Congress. Hearings before a Special Committee to Investigate Communist Activities in the United States. Part 6, vol. 1. 71st Congress, 2nd sess.

U.S. Congress. *Joint Select Committee to Inquire into the Condition of Affairs in the Late Insurrectionary States*. 13 vols. 42nd Congress, 2nd sess. Washington: GPO, 1872.

U.S. Congress. House. *Memphis Riots and Massacres*. 39th Congress, 1st sess. House Report 101.

U.S. Congress. House. *New Orleans Riots*. 39th Congress, 2nd sess. House Report 16.

U.S. Congress. Senate. Committee on Foreign Relations. *Genocide Convention*. 95th Congress, 1st sess.

U.S. Congress. Senate. Hearing before a Subcommittee of the Committee on Foreign Relations. *The Genocide Convention*. 92nd Congress, 1st sess.

U.S. Congress. Senate. Hearings before a Subcommittee of the Committee on Foreign Relations. *The Genocide Convention*. 81st Congress, 2nd sess.

U.S. Congress. Senate. *Report and Testimony of the Select Committee to Investigate the Causes of the Removal of the Negroes from the Southern States to the Northern States*. 3 vols. 46th Congress, 2nd sess. Washington, 1880. Senate Report 693.

U.S. Congress. Senate. *Report of the Special Committee to Inquire into the Mississippi Election of 1882.* 48th Congress, 1st sess. Senate Report 512.
U.S. Congress. Senate. *South Carolina in 1876.* 44th Congress, 2nd sess. Senate Miscellaneous Document 48.
U.S. Court of Appeals. District of Columbia Circuit. 91 App. DC 208.
U.S. Department of Justice. National Archives, RG 60, File 17743–1898.
U.S. Information Agency. *The Negro in American Life.* Pamphlet, 1951.
U.S. Supreme Court Reports. Burns *vs.* Wilson. 346 US. 137.

Articles

Auerbach, Jerold S. "Southern Tenant Farmers: Socialist Critics of the New Deal." *Labor History,* Winter 1966, pp. 3–18.
Aptheker, Bettina. "The Suppression of the *Free Speech.* Ida B. Wells and the Memphis Lynching, 1892." *San Jose Studies* 3, no. 3 (1977): 34–40.
Bauer, Raymond A., and Bauer, Alice H. "Day to Day Resistance to Slavery." *Journal of Negro History,* October 1942, pp. 388–419.
Baldwin, James. "Me and My House...." *Harper's Magazine,* November 1955, pp. 54–61.
Beecher, John. "The Share Croppers' Union in Alabama." *Social Forces* 13 (1934): 124–32.
Bunche, Ralph J. "A Critical Analysis of the Tactics and Programs of Minority Groups." *Journal of Negro Education* 4, no. 3 (1935): 308–20.
Butler, Hilton. "Murder for the Job." *Nation,* July 12, 1933, p. 44.
Capeci, Dominic J., Jr. "The Lynching of Cleo Wright: Federal Protection of Constitutional Rights during World War II." *Journal of American History,* March 1986, pp. 859–87.
Carter, Elmer A. *Opportunity.* Editorial. August 1931, pp. 234, 235.
Cayton, Horace R. "The Negro's Challenge." *Nation,* July 3, 1943, pp. 10–12.
Cogley, John. "Willie McGee." *Commonweal,* May 25, 1951, p. 158.
Cox, La Wanda. "The American Agricultural Wage Earner, 1865–1900." *Agricultural History* 22 (April 1948): 95–114.
"Crisis on the Home Front." *New Masses.* Editorial. June 29, 1943, p. 3.
Crouthamel, James L. "The Springfield Race Riot of 1908." *Journal of Negro History,* July 1960, pp. 164–81.
Crowe, Charles. "Racial Violence and Social Reform: Origins of the Atlanta Riot of 1906." *Journal of Negro History,* July 1968, pp. 234–56.
Current, Gloster B. "Fiftieth Annual Convention." *Crisis,* August–September 1959, pp. 400–410.
Darrow, Clarence. "Scottsboro." *Crisis,* March 1932, p. 82.
Domingo, W. A. "Did Bolshevism Stop Race Riots in Russia?" *Messenger,* September 1919, pp. 26, 27.
Du Bois, W. E. B. "Crusader Without Violence." *National Guardian,* November 9, 1959.
———. "From the Point of View of the Negroes." *World Today* 11 (1906): 1173–75.
———. "Gandhi and the American Negroes." *Gandhi Marg.* 1, no. 3 (1957): 175–77.
———. "Marxism and the Negro Problem." *Crisis,* May 1933, pp. 103–15, 118.
———. "The Negro College." *Crisis,* August 1933, pp. 175–77.
———. "Opinion." *Crisis,* May 1924, p. 7.
———. "Postscript." *Crisis,* May 1934, pp. 147, 148.

Du Bois, W. E. B., and Gruening, Martha. "The Massacre of East St. Louis." *Crisis*, September 1917, pp. 219–38.

Dudley, J. Wayne. " 'Hate' Organizations of the 1940s: The Columbians, Inc.," *Phylon* (Fall 1981), 262–74.

Edwards, John Carver. "Radical Reconstruction and the New Orleans Riot of 1866." *International Review of History and Political Science*, August 1973, pp. 48–64.

Fuller, Henry. "Sunday at Camp Hill." *New Republic*, December 16, 1931, pp. 132–34.

Gatewood, Willard B. "Booker T. Washington and the Ulrich Affair." *Phylon* 30 (Fall 1969): 286–302.

Goodwyn, Lawrence. "Populist Dreams and Negro Rights: East Texas as a Case Study." *American Historical Review*, December 1971, pp. 1435–56.

Grossman, Aubrey. "Lawyers on Trial." *Masses and Mainstream*, August 1951, pp. 25–31.

Harlan, Louis R., and Daniel, Pete. "A Dark and Stormy Night in the Life of Booker T. Washington." *Negro History Bulletin* 33 (November 1970): 159–61.

Haley, Alex. "Mr. Muhammed Speaks." *Reader's Digest*, March 1960, pp. 100–104.

Hennessey, Melinda Meek. "Political Terrorism in the Black Belt: The Eutaw Riot." *Alabama Review*, January 1980, pp. 35–48.

———. "Race and Violence in Reconstruction New Orleans: The 1868 Riot." *Louisiana History* 20, no. 1 (1979): 77–91.

———. "Reconstruction Politics and the Military: The Eufaula Riot of 1874." *Alabama Historical Quarterly*, Summer 1976, pp. 112–25.

Hill, T. Arnold. "Railway Employees Rally to Save Their Jobs." *Opportunity*, November 1934, pp. 346, 350.

"How to Stop Lynching." *Messenger*. Editorial. August 1919, pp. 8–10.

Hughes, Langston. "Beaumont to Detroit, 1943." *Common Ground*, Fall 1943, p. 104.

———. "Too Much of Race." *Crisis*, September 1937, p. 272.

Jackson, Albert. "Alabama's Blood-Smeared Cotton." *New Masses*, September 24, 1935, p. 13.

Jackson, James E. "The Rev. King's Outlook." *Political Affairs*, December 1958, pp. 57–59.

Johnson, Charles S. "Review of the Month." *Monthly Summary of Events and Trends in Race Relations* 1 (January 1944): 2.

Johnson, Josephine. "The Arkansas Terror." *New Masses*, June 30, 1936, pp. 12–14.

King, Martin Luther, Jr. "Walk for Freedom." *Fellowship* 12 (May 1956): 5–7.

———. "Who Speaks for the South?" *Liberation*, March 1958, pp. 13–14.

Leonard, Oscar. "The East St. Louis Pogrom." *Survey*, July 14, 1917, pp. 331–35.

Lilienthal, David E. "Has the Negro the Right of Self-Defense?" *Nation*, December 23, 1925, pp. 724–25.

Locke, Alain. "Harlem: Dark Weather-Vane." *Survey Graphic*, August 1936, pp. 457–62.

Lovett, Bobby L. "Memphis Riots: White Reaction to Blacks in Memphis, May 1865–July 1866." *Tennessee Historical Quarterly*, Spring 1979, pp. 9–33.

"Lynching: A Domestic Question." *Messenger*. Editorial. July 1919, pp. 7, 8.

Martin, Louis. "Prelude to Disaster: Detroit." *Common Ground*, Autumn 1943, pp. 21–26.

Mayfield, Julian. "Challenge to Negro Leadership: The Case of Robert Williams." *Commentary*, April 1961, pp. 297–305.

Miller, Loren. "How 'Left' is the N.A.A.C.P." *New Masses*, July 16, 1935, pp. 12, 13.

Mitchison, Naomi. "White House and Marked Tree." *New Statesman and Nation*, April 27, 1935, pp. 585, 586.
Mostert, Mary. "Death for Association." *Nation*, May 5, 1951, p. 421.
"Murder." *Crisis*. Editorial. March 1946, p. 72.
"Negro Discrimination and the Need for Federal Action." *Lawyers Guild Review* 2, no. 6 (1942): 21–23.
"The Negro Press on the Riots." *Common Ground*, Autumn 1943, 101–3.
North, Joseph. "It Will Happen to You, Unless...," *New Masses*, July 6, 1943, pp. 2, 3.
Norton, William J. "The Detroit Riots—and After." *Survey Graphic*, August 1943, pp. 317, 318.
Olsen, Otto H. "The Ku Klux Klan: A Study in Reconstruction Politics and Propaganda." *North Carolina Historical Review* 39 (Summer 1962): 340–62.
Osofsky, Gilbert. "Race Riot, 1900: A Study of Ethnic Violence." *Journal of Negro Education*, Winter 1963, pp. 16–24.
Owen, Chandler. "Tulsa." *Messenger*, July 1921, pp. 218–20.
Owens, Harry P. "The Eufaula Riot of 1874." *Alabama Review*, July 1963, pp. 224–37.
Page, Myra. "The Croppers Prepare." *New Masses*, January 11, 1936, pp. 17, 18.
Pickens, William. "What I Saw in Spain." *Crisis*, October 1938, pp. 319–21, 330.
Preece, Harold. " 'Anarchy' in Arkansas." *New Masses*, February 12, 1935, pp. 14, 15.
"The Proceedings of a Mississippi Migration Convention in 1879." *Journal of Negro History* 4 (January 1919): 51–54.
Randolph, A. Philip. "Why I Would Not Stand for Re-election as President of the National Negro Congress." *American Federationist*, July 1940, pp. 24, 25.
Reed, Merl E. "The FEPC, the Black Worker, and the Southern Shipyards." *South Atlantic Quarterly*, Autumn 1975, pp. 446–67.
"A Report on the Chicago Riot by an Eye-Witness." *Messenger*, September 1919, pp. 11–13.
Reynolds, Donald E. "The New Orleans Riot of 1866, Reconsidered." *Louisiana History*, Winter 1964, pp. 5–27.
Richardson, Ben. "Can It Happen in Harlem Again?" *New Masses*, August 17, 1943, pp. 14–16.
Robbins, George. "Chicago Demonstration." *New Masses*, September 1931, p. 17.
Roosevelt, Theodore. "The Rough Riders." *Scribner's*, April 1899, pp. 420–40.
Rosen, Dale, and Rosengarten, Theodore. "The Narrative of Jess Hull, Alabama Tenant Farmer." *Radical America*, November–December 1972, pp. 65–84.
Ryan, Eleanor. "Toward a National Negro Congress." *New Masses*, June 4, 1935, pp. 14, 15.
Ryan, James Gilbert. "The Memphis Riots of 1866: Terror in a Black Community during Reconstruction." *Journal of Negro History*, July 1977, pp. 243–57.
Schuler, Edgar A. "The Houston Race Riot, 1917." *Journal of Negro History*, July 1944, pp. 300–38.
Shapiro, Herbert. "The Ku Klux Klan during Reconstruction: The South Carolina Episode." *Journal of Negro History* 49 (January 1964): 34–55.
Sitkoff, Harvard. "Racial Militancy and Interracial Violence in the Second World War." *Journal of American History*, December 1971, pp. 661–81.
"A Statement by the N.A.A.C.P. on the Scottsboro Cases." *Crisis*, March 1932, p. 81.
Terrell, Mary Church. "Lynching From a Negro's Point of View." *North American Review*, June 1904, pp. 853–68.
Thompson, Louise. "Southern Terror." *Crisis*, November 1934, pp. 327, 328.

Tindall, George B. "The Liberian Exodus of 1878." *South Carolina Historical Magazine*, July 1952, pp. 133–45.

Tucker, David M. "Miss Ida B. Wells and Memphis Lynching." *Phylon* 32, no. 2 (1971): 112–22.

Tuttle, William M., Jr. "Views of a Negro During 'The Red Summer' of 1919." *Journal of Negro History*, July 1966, pp. 209–18.

————, intro. "W. E. B. Du Bois' Confrontation with White Liberalism During the Progressive Era: A Phylon Document." *Phylon*, September 1974, pp. 241–58.

Vandal, Gilles. "The Origins of the New Orleans Riot of 1866, Revisited." *Louisiana History* 22, no.2 (1981): 135–65.

"The Waco Horror." Supplement to *Crisis*, July 1916.

Walling, William English. "The Race War in the North." *Independent* September 3, 1908, pp. 529–34.

Weaver, Maurice, and Looby, Z. Alexander. "What Happened at Columbia." *Crisis*, April 1946, pp. 110, 111, 125.

Wells, Tom Henderson. "The Phoenix Election Riot." *Phylon*, Spring 1970, pp. 58–69.

Wells-Barnett, Ida B. "How Enfranchisement Stops Lynching." *Original Rights Magazine*, June 1910, pp. 42–53.

West, Henry Litchfield. "The Race War in North Carolina." *Forum* January 1899, pp. 578–91.

White, Walter. "Behind the Harlem Riot." *New Republic*, August 16, 1943, pp. 220–22.

————. " 'Massacring Whites' in Arkansas." *Nation*, December 6, 1919, pp. 715, 716.

————. "The Race Conflict in Arkansas." *Survey*, December 13, 1919, pp. 233, 234.

————. "The Shambles of South Carolina." *Crisis*, December 1926, pp. 72–75.

————. "The Sweet Trial." *Crisis*, January 1926, pp. 125–29.

Wilkins, Roy. "Two Against 5,000." *Crisis*, June 1936, pp. 169, 170.

Willie, Charles V. "Walter R. Chivers—an Advocate of Situation Sociology." *Phylon*, September 1982, pp. 242–48.

Wittner, Lawrence S. "The National Negro Congress: A Reassessment." *American Quarterly*, Winter 1970, pp. 883–901.

Woodman, Harold D. "Sequel to Slavery: The New History Views the Postbellum South." *Journal of Southern History* 43 (November 1977): 523–54.

Wright, Richard. "Two Million Black Voices." *New Masses*, February 25, 1936.

Wyllie, Irvin G. "Race and Class Conflict on Missouri's Cotton Frontier." *Journal of Southern History*, May 1954, pp. 183–96.

Dissertations and Theses

Capeci, Dominic Joseph, Jr. "The Harlem Riot of 1943." Ph.D. diss., University of California, Irvine, 1970.

Dudley, Julius Wayne. "A History of the Association of Southern Women for the Prevention of Lynching, 1933–1942." Ph.D. diss., University of Cincinnati, 1979.

Hennessey, Melinda Meek. "To Live and Die in Dixie: Reconstruction Race Riots in the South." Ph.D. diss., Kent State University, 1978.

Higgenbotham, Charmion. "The Danville Riot of 1883." M.A. thesis, Virginia State College, 1955.

Higuchi, Hayumi. "White Supremacy on the Cape Fear: The Wilmington Affair of 1898." M.A. Thesis, University of North Carolina, 1980.

McDuffie, Jerome Anthony. "Politics in Wilmington and New Hanover County, 1865–1900: The Genesis of a Race Riot." Ph.D. diss., Kent State University, 1979.

Marr, John C. "History of Matagorda County." Ph.D. diss., University of Texas, 1928.

Melzer, John T. "The Danville Riot, November 3, 1883." M.A. thesis, University of Virginia, 1963.

Smead, Edward Howard, Jr. "The Lynching of Mack Charles Parker in Poplarville, Mississippi, April 25, 1959." Ph.D. diss., University of Maryland, 1979.

Streater, John Baxter, Jr. "The National Negro Congress: 1936–1947." Ph.D. diss., University of Cincinnati, 1981.

Swinney, Everett. "Suppressing the Ku Klux Klan." Ph.D. diss., University of Texas, 1967.

Vandal, Gilles. "The New Orleans Riot: The Anatomy of a Tragedy." Ph.D. diss., College of William and Mary, 1978.

Unpublished Papers

Dudley, J. Wayne. "The Rosa Lee Ingram Case and Its Social Implications." University of Cincinnati, 1970.

Evans, W. McKee. "The Ku Klux Klan and the Conservative Triumph." Pacific Coast Branch meeting, American Historical Association, 1971.

Hennessey, Melinda Meek. "Racial Violence during Reconstruction: The 1876 Riots in Charleston and Cainhoy." Southern Historical Association, 1983.

Martin, Charles H. "Black Protest, Anti-Communism and the Cold War: The Willie McGee Case." Association for Study of Afro-American Life and History, 1980.

Mole, Charles. "Willie Earle Incident." University of Cincinnati, 1972.

Silcox, Harry C. "Politics From the Bottom Up: The Life of Ward Boss William McMullen, 1824–1901." 1985.

Streater, John. "The National Negro Congress: Race, Class and the Left." University of Cincinnati, 1974.

Tucker, David M. "Ida Wells-Barnett and the Memphis Lynchings." Southern Historical Association meeting, 1982.

Vandal, Gilles. "The New Orleans Riot." 1977.

———. "Violence in Reconstructed Louisiana: The Use of the U.S. Army as a Peacekeeping Force." American Historical Association meeting, 1982.

Wallenstein, Peter. "Conscripts and Convicts: From Road Duty to Chain Gang." Organization of American Historians meeting, 1986.

Newspapers

Amsterdam News
Atlanta Constitution
Charleston News and Courier
Chicago Defender
Chicago Tribune
Cincinnati Commercial Gazette
Cincinnati Enquirer
Cleveland Gazette
Daily Record
Daily Worker
Dallas Morning News

Dallas Times Herald
Detroit Free Press
Galveston Daily News
Guam News
Houston Post
Jackson Daily News
Memphis News Scimitar
Michigan Chronicle
Montgomery Advertiser
New Orleans Pelican
New York PM

New York Times   Pittsburgh Courier
New York World   St. Louis Post Dispatch
People's Voice   Washington Bee
Philadelphia Inquirer   Washington Post
Philadelphia Public Ledger

INDEX